NW

RENAISSANCE MUSIC

The Norton Introduction to Music History

RENAISSANCE MUSIC

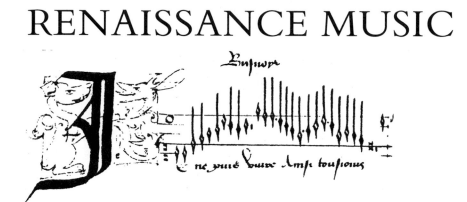

Music in Western Europe, 1400–1600

ALLAN W. ATLAS

Brooklyn College and the Graduate School, The City University of New York

W·W·NORTON & COMPANY

New York · London

The text of this book is composed in Bembo
Composition by University Graphics
Manufacturing by Maple-Vail
Cover illustration: Pieter Brueghel, *Peasant Dance,* courtesy of the
   Kunsthistorisches Museum, Vienna

Library of Congress Cataloging-in-Publication Data
Atlas, Allan W.
   Renaissance music: music in Western Europe, 1400–1600 /
Allan W. Atlas.
      p.   cm.—(The Norton Introduction to Music History)
   Includes bibliographical references and index.
   ISBN 0-393-97169-4
   1. Music—15th century—history and criticism.   2. Music—16th
century—history and criticism.   I. Title.   II. Series.
ML172.A84   1998
780'.9'02—dc21   97-19816
                                                                       MN

W. W. Norton & Company, Inc., 500 Fifth Avenue, New York, N.Y. 10110
                     http://www.wwnorton.com

W. W. Norton & Company Ltd., 10 Coptic Street, London WC1A 1PU
      1 2 3 4 5 6 7 8 9 0

FOR THONE AND ERIK

CONTENTS

PART ONE. THE 1380s TO THE 1420s

INCLUDED: BRASSART • CICONIA • B. CORDIER • DU FAY • DUNSTABLE • GRENON • POWER • SOLAGE • ZACHARIAS DE TERAMO

PART TWO. THE 1420s TO THE 1460s

INCLUDED: BINCHOIS • DU FAY • FERAGUT • FRANCHOIS • A. DE LANTINS • H. DE LANTINS • POWER

PART THREE. THE 1450s TO THE 1480s

INCLUDED: BEDYNGHAM • BUSNOYS • CARON • CORNAGO • DOMARTO •
FAUGUES • FRYE • GUGLIELMO EBREO • HAYNE VAN GHIZEGHEM • MARTINI
• MORTON • OCKEGHEM • PAUMANN • RAMOS DE PAREJA • REGIS • SER-
AFINO DALL'AQUILA • TINCTORIS • TOURONT • VINCENET

PART FOUR. THE 1470s TO THE 1520s

INCLUDED: AGRICOLA • BRUMEL • CARA • COMPÈRE • COPPINI • DALZA •
ENCINA • ESCOBAR • FÉVIN • FINCK • GHISELIN • HOFHAIMER • ISAAC •
JOSQUIN • LA RUE • MOUTON • NINOT LE PETIT • OBRECHT • PETRUCCI •
PISANO • RICHAFORT • SCHLICK • SPINACINO • TROMBONCINO • WEERBEKE

PART FIVE. THE 1520s TO THE 1550s

INCLUDED: ARCADELT • ATTAINGNANT • BERCHEM • BROWNE • BUUS •
CABEZÓN • G. CAVAZZONI • CLAUDIN DE SERMISY • CLEMENS NON PAPA •
CORNYSH • CRECQUILLON • FAYRFAX • FESTA • FRANCESCO DA MILANO •
A. GABRIELI • GERO • GERVAISE • GOMBERT • GOUDIMEL • JACQUET OF
MANTUA • JANEQUIN • JULIO SEGNI • LUDFORD • MERULO • MILÁN •
MORALES • NARVÁEZ • NOLA • PASSEREAU • PELLEGRINI • REDFORD • SACHS
• SENFL • TAVERNER • TYE • VERDELOT • WALTER • WILLAERT

PART SIX. THE 1550s TO c. 1600

INCLUDED: BULL • BYRD • CASULANA • DOWLAND • FARNABY • FERRA-
BOSCO • G. GABRIELI • GALILEI • GASTOLDI • GESUALDO • GLAREAN •
KERLE • LASSUS • LE JEUNE • LUZZASCHI • MARENZIO • MONTEVERDI •
MORLEY • MUNDY • PALESTRINA • RORE • RUFFO • TALLIS • VECCHI •
VICENTINO • VICTORIA • WEELKES • WERT • WILBYE • ZARLINO

List of Illustrations

Abbreviations

AcM	*Acta musicologica*
AnMc	*Analecta musicologica*
AnnM	*Annales musicologiques*
BJfhM	*Basler Jahrbuch für historische Musikpraxis*
BMB	*Biblioteca musica bononiensis*
CEKM	*Corpus of Early Keyboard Music*
CMM	*Corpus mensurabilis musicae*
DR	*Dance Research*
DTB	*Denkmäler der Tonkunst in Bayern*
DTÖ	*Denkmäler der Tonkunst in Österreich*
EDM	*Das Erbe deutscher Musik*
EECM	*Early English Church Music*
EM	*Early Music*
EMH	*Early Music History*
GSJ	*Galpin Society Journal*
HBSJ	*Historic Brass Society Journal*
Ima	*Instituta e monumenta*
ISM	*Israeli Studies in Musicology*
JAMIS	*Journal of the American Musical Instrument Society*
JAMS	*Journal of the American Musicological Society*
JHI	*Journal of the History of Ideas*
JLSA	*Journal of the Lute Society of America*
JM	*Journal of Musicology*
JMT	*Journal of Music Theory*
JRBM	*Journal of Renaissance and Baroque Music*
JRMA	*Journal of the Royal Musical Association*
JVGSA	*Journal of the Viola da Gamba Society of America*
LSJ	*Lute Society Journal*
MB	*Musica Britannica*
MD	*Musica disciplina*
MF	*Music Forum*
Mf	*Die Musikforschung*
ML	*Music & Letters*
MMA	*Miscellanea musicologica*
MME	*Monumentos de la música española*
MMR	*Masters and Monuments of the Renaissance*
MMRF	*Les Maîtres musiciens de la Renaissance française*
MPLSER	*Monumenta polyphoniae liturgicae Sanctae Ecclesiae Romanae*

MQ	Musical Quarterly
MR	Music Review
MRM	Monuments of Renaissance Music
MS	Musica e storia
MSD	Musicological Studies and Documents
MusAn	Music Analysis
NAWM	Norton Anthology of Western Music
PäMw	Publikationen älterer praktischer und theoretischer Musikwerke
PEMI	Publications of the Early Music Institute
PMFC	Polyphonic Music of the Fourteenth Century
PMLA	Publications of the Modern Language Association
PMM	Plainsong and Medieval Music
PMMM	Publications of Mediaeval Music Manuscripts
PPR	Performance Practice Review
PRMA	Proceedings of the Royal Musical Association
RBM	Revue belge de musicologie
RCM	Renaissance Church Music
RdM	Revue de musicologie
RIM	Rivista italiana di musicologia
RMF	Renaissance Music in Facsimile
RQ	Renaissance Quarterly
RRMAER	Recent Researches in the Music of the Middle Ages and Early Renaissance
RRMR	Recent Researches in the Music of the Renaissance
SMd	Schweizerische Musikdenkmäler
StudiM	Studi musicali
TCM	Tudor Church Music
TVNM	Tijdschrift van de Vereniging voor Nederlandse Muziekgeschiedenis
VfMw	Vierteljahrsschrift für Musikwissenschaft

Frequently cited books:

The Liber Usualis, with Introduction and Rubrics in English, ed. Benedictines of Solesmes (Tournai and New York: Desclee, 1961).

The New Grove Dictionary of Music and Musicians, 6th ed., ed. Stanley Sadie, 20 vols. (London: Macmillan, 1980).

Gustave Reese, Music in the Renaissance, rev. ed. (New York: Norton, 1959).

Oliver Strunk, ed., Source Readings in Music History, rev. ed., ed. Leo Treitler, vol. 3: The Renaissance, ed. Gary Tomlinson (New York: Norton, 1997).

Piero Weiss and Richard Taruskin, eds., Music in the Western World: A History in Documents (New York: Schirmer, 1984).

Forthcoming books of general interest:

The New Oxford History of Music, rev. ed., vol. 3 (1400–1520): ed. Reinhard Strohm; vol. 4 (1520–1640): ed. James Haar (Oxford University Press).

Leeman L. Perkins, *Music in the Age of the Renaissance* (Norton, in press).

The staff below shows the system of pitch identification used throughout this book.

Photo Credits

page 4: Ms Fr. 12476, cliché Bibliothèque Nationale, Paris; p. 7 By permission of the British Library, Add. 57950, fol. 121v.; p. 46: Dijon 517, fols. 21v–22r, cliché Bibliothèque Nationale, Paris; p. 47: Mellon Chansonnier, fols. 55r–56r, by permission of the Beinecke Library, Yale University; p. 70: Biblioteca Estense Universitaria di Modena; p. 73: Reproduced by courtesy of the Trustees, The National Gallery, London; p. 81: Alinari / Art Resource, NY: p. 82: Scala / Art Resource, NY; pp. 83 (top and bottom), 84 (left): Giraudon / Art Resource, NY; p. 84 (right): Scala / Art Resource, NY; p. 103: Musée des Beaux-Arts, Lille; p. 109: Courtesy of Archives departementales du Nord / Photo Desmarez; p. 133 (top): Spencer Collection. The New York Public Library. Astor, Lenox and Tilden Foundations: p. 133 (bottom): cliché Bibliothèque Nationale Paris; p. 154: Biblioteca Apostolica Vaticana; pp. 155, 193: cliché Bibliothèque Nationale, Paris; p. 194: Courtesy of the Biblioteca Nazionale Centrale, Firenze; p. 206: Musée Calvet, Avignon; p. 209: Copyright Board of Trustees, National Gallery of Art, Washington. Samuel H. Kress Collection; p. 211 (top): Scale / Art Resource, NY; p. 211 (bottom): Alinari / Art Resource, NY; p. 216: cliché Bibliothèque Nationale, Paris; p. 217 (top): Louvre Departement des Arts Graphiques, inv. 20676. Photo R. M. N. ©; p. 217 (bottom): © The Cleveland Museum of Art, 1997, Delia E. Holden Fund, 1960.73; p. 223: Courtesy of Bärenreiter Music Publishers; p. 227: Erich Lessing / Art Resource, NY; p. 231: Royal College of Physicians; pp. 259 (top and bottom), 260: By permission of the British Library; p. 261: Reproduced by arrangement with Broude Brothers Limited; p. 264: Alinari / Art Resource, NY; p. 276: © American Musicological Society; pp. 317, 319: By permission of the British Library; p. 326 (top left): Giraudon / Art Resource, NY; pp. 326 (top right and bottom), 328: Alinari / Art Resource, NY; p. 332: Scala / Art Resource, NY; pp. 333, 334: Giraudon / Art Resource, NY; p. 345: Paris BN 9346, cliché Bibliothèque Nationale Paris; p. 372: Liceo Musicale, Bologna; p. 397: By permission of the British Library; p. 433: Alinari / Art Resource, NY; p. 445: Courtesy of the Germanisches Nationalmuseum, Nurnberg; pp. 451, 452, 453: Alinari / Art Resource, NY; p. 461: The Boston Athanaeum; p. 462: cliché Bibliothèque Nationale, Paris; p. 463: Courtesy of the Biblioteca Nazionale Centrale, Firenze; p. 488: By permission of Musée Jacquemart-André, Paris; p. 507: Courtesy of Corbis-Bettmann; p. 511: Courtesy of Bärenreiter Music Publishers; p. 521: Art Resource, NY; p. 547: By courtesy of the Dean and Chapter of Westminster; p. 562: By permission of the British Library; p. 566: Courtesy of the Civico Museo Bibliografico Musicale, Bologna; p. 574: Photo by John Vincent; p. 575: Photo by Phyllis Dearborn Massar; pp. 577, 578: Alinari / Art Resource, NY; p. 589: Staatsbibliothek zu Berlin, Preussischer Kulturbesitz, Musikabteilung; p. 606: Courtesy of the Mansell Collection / TIME, Inc.; p. 612: The Metropolitan Museum of Art, Bequest of Mrs. H. O. Havemeyer, 1929. The H. O. Havemeyer Collection. [29.100.6]; pp. 625, 647: By permission of the British Library; p. 662: By courtesy of the National Portrait Gallery, London; p. 668: Courtesy of the Royal College of Music, London; p. 676: By permission of the British Library; p. 687: By courtesy of the National Portrait Gallery, London; p. 695: Courtesy of the Fitzwilliam Museum, University of Cambridge.

Preface

A preface is a confession of sorts: it permits the author to explain what should be clear in the first place, acknowledge debts, and, if textbook decorum otherwise prohibits it, write in the first person. I will do all three.

This book is addressed to three audiences: undergraduate music majors coming to music of the fifteenth and sixteenth centuries for the first time; graduate students who wish to have a compact overview of a period in which they do not necessarily intend to specialize (and if it entices a few of them to dig further into the music of an Ockeghem or a Victoria, so much the better); and finally, the vast group of early-music lovers, without whom the spectacular proliferation of virtuoso ensembles, concerts in incense-filled churches, and recordings would be largely for naught.

With the exception of Richard Hoppin's *Medieval Music*, our book (readers' and author's) covers a longer time span—from the late fourteenth century to the early seventeenth—than any other in the Norton Introduction to Music History series. But if the Middle Ages claims more centuries, the Renaissance (a term that virtually disappears from these pages until the Epilogue) preserves far more in the way of musical artifacts, in both number and kind. Our picture, then, is drawn with a very broad brush.

There are as many ways to organize a book on music of the fifteenth and sixteenth centuries as there are authors who would write one. At the highest level, we play it safe and follow a one-time-through, roughly chronological approach. Within that framework, the most crucial issue was, who or what should take center stage and keep the plot going—the composers or the music? I have opted for the music, so that individual composers play second fiddle to their works and often get disposed across a number of chapters.

Having placed the music in the forefront, I approached it in whatever manner the music itself seemed to dictate. Thus Part One draws stylistic distinctions for the period 1380s–1420s according to geography (a chapter each on England and the Continent, with the channel crossed more than once). Parts Two, Three, and Four follow three generations of composers over the course of a century (1420s–1520s), the chapters within each part covering Mass, motet, secular song, and instrumental music. Part Three also has a chapter on the patronage of music in the fifteenth century. With Parts Five and Six, which run from the 1520s to roughly 1600, we change gears once again. Though some chapters are still devoted to specific genres, most are now organized around broader themes: religion, music and words, music theory, the printing industry, and geography once again, as two chapters return to and focus on England.

One hundred and two of the pieces and movements that are discussed in some detail appear in the *Anthology of Renaissance Music*, which is issued in conjunction with this volume. Composers and pieces that are neither included in the anthology nor represented by a music example in the text generally go unmentioned (no name dropping here), though I am not ashamed to admit that an occasional piece in the *Anthology* or excerpt in the text appears there simply because I find it beautiful: music is more than something to be dissected—it may simply haunt us.

I have not hesitated to pose questions and leave them unanswered. I took it as a compliment when an undergraduate student, asked to compare an early draft with another textbook on Renaissance music, expressed a preference for the other book because that one "told it like it is." Obviously, I too have tried to write nonfiction, but knowledge includes recognizing what we do not or cannot know.

There is probably nothing more wrongheaded than a music history textbook that tries to turn its readers into music historians. Yet as I have learned from many semesters of teaching the music of this period, there is no more exciting way to approach fifteenth- and sixteenth-century music than through its own multifaceted voices. I have therefore built two projects in to the book that allow readers to gain some experience in confronting texts of the period. "Learning from Documents" gives students an idea of the equipment a scholar must bring to interpreting certain fifteenth-century archival documents. "Editing a Chanson" guides students through what I hope is a challenging but gratifying semester-long task of producing an edition of a song by Antoine Busnoys. As students will quickly learn, it is not work for the indecisive.

Our book differs from the others in the Norton Introduction series in two respects. First, it replaces the typical opening chapter on historical and cultural background with ten *intermedi* scattered through the book; each of these freezes a span of a few years and highlights matters that range from who was ruling where and the state of the economy to religious upheavals and landmarks in the visual and literary arts to a recipe for "friars' fritters" and how long it took to deliver the mail. Second, the historiographical discussion of "the Renaissance" appears in an epilogue, by which time readers have some two hundred years of music buzzing in their ears.

ACKNOWLEDGMENTS

There is not a single chapter in which I did not incur many scholarly debts, and it is with a deep sense of gratitude that I say thank you in public to those who helped me along the way.

Even before the first chapter was written, Paula Higgins, Jessie Ann Owens, and William Prizer read through a long and detailed outline and provided additional help at later stages; each of them influenced its final shape. I had also had the privilege to read in draft manuscript Leeman Perkins's forthcoming *Music in the Age of the Renaissance*. From the time I started writing, I bombarded Dennis Slavin with questions and ideas; his steady devil's advocacy bordered on the heroic. As the chapters rolled out and help was needed, a number of friends and colleagues were never more than a phone call or an office away: Jane Bernstein, Lawrence Bernstein, Stanley Boorman, Beth Bullard, David Cannata, Ruth De Ford, Rita Fleischer, Barbara Hanning, Herbert Kellman, Joel Lester, Robert Marshall, Honey Meconi, Floyd Moreland, Martin Picker, Joseph Ponte, Fred Purnell, Honora Raphael, William Sherzer, H. Colin Slim, Pamela Starr, Joseph Straus, Jennifer Thomas, Andrew Tomasello, Gary Tomlinson, Leo Treitler, Rob Wegman, and Richard Wexler. They saved both errors and hours.

Some people were kind enough to read, and improve, various chapters: Jane Bernstein, Lawrence Bernstein, Ruth De Ford, Julian Grimshaw, Barbara Hanning, Robin Leaver, Anne Stone, Richard Wexler, Peter Wright, and Laura Youens. Two went beyond the call of duty in this respect. Honey Meconi and Pamela Starr not only read and commented on the entire book while it was in manuscript, but tested it out in the classroom and shared their students' reactions with me. Somehow, "thank you" seems terribly insufficient.

A number of present and past students in the Ph.D. Program in Music at the Graduate School of The City University of New York gathered, sorted, checked, double-checked, and helped with translations: Carolina Carey, Mark Anson-Cartwright, Alessandra Ciucci, Joseph Darby, Kristine Day, Deborah Dimasi, J. Graeme Fullerton, Susan Jackson, Anne Johnson, Mark Pottinger, Ian Quinn, Michael Sumbera, Elizabeth Wollman, Sevin Yaraman, and the staff at RILM; at Queens College, Anna Bottazzi. Two library staffs made my work easier: that at the CUNY Graduate School and that at the Hewlett-Woodmere Public Library, where Millicent Vollono often worked miracles. The team at W. W. Norton was stupendous: thanks to Suzanne La Plante for not taking no as an answer; Michael Ochs, for constant encouragement, steady reason, and a healthy dose of common sense; Martha Graedel, whose organizational skills never failed to amaze; and Susan Gaustad, who edited the manuscript with unmatched skill and sensitivity and whose hundreds of suggested revisions and "yellow-flag" queries have made this a better book. I am grateful to Kenneth Yarmey for an expert job in setting the music examples. Other thank you's: to Geoffrey Marshall, Marc Sicklick, Peg Rivers, Leanna Florence, and Barry and Claire (all of whom know why); and most, *most*, **most** of all, to Thone and Erik, who endured my hermit-like existence for twenty months.

PART ONE

THE 1380s TO THE 1420s

INCLUDED: BRASSART • CICONIA • B. CORDIER •
DU FAY • DUNSTABLE • GRENON • POWER • SOLAGE •
ZACHARIAS DE TERAMO

CHAPTER 1

The "English Sound"

> For they have a new way
> Of making pleasant consonance
> In high and low music
> In *ficta*, in rests, and in mutation;
> And they have taken the guise
> Of the English, and follow Dunstable.[1]

With these lines from his epic poem *Le champion des dames*, Martin le Franc described the stylistic innovations of Guillaume Du Fay and Gilles Binchois as he understood them from his vantage point at the court of Savoy in the early 1440s. Some thirty years later, Johannes Tinctoris, the most historical-minded music theorist of the fifteenth century, had this to say in the preface to his *Proportionale musices*: "At this time . . . the possibilities of our music have been so marvelously increased that there appears to be a new art, if I may so call it, whose fount and origin is held to be among the English, of whom Dunstable stood forth as chief."[2] Finally, to backtrack to the earliest witness of all, Ulrich von Richental, chronicler of events at the Council of Constance (in modern-day Germany, 1414–18), wrote that what impressed him most about a 1416 service performed by English singers at the Cathedral of Constance was the "sweet English song." The broad implications of this testimony seem clear enough: English music in the opening decades of the fifteenth century differed from music on the European Continent, and the English—with John Dunstable at the fore—influenced the likes of Du Fay and Binchois (Fig. 1-1) as well as other Continental composers of their generation. It is also clear that Continental musicians and audiences perceived that English music had a distinct sound of its own. What *was* this "English sound"?

THE ENGLISH SOUND

The chief characteristic of the English sound was its sonorous, chordal writing. We will approach it from a number of angles.

Dunstable's *Quam pulchra es*

There is no better example—we might even call it exaggerated—of the English sound than *Quam pulchra es*, by John Dunstable (c. 1390–1453; *An-*

---

1. Quoted after Fallows, "The Contenance Angloise," 196.
2. Strunk, *Source Readings*, 14–15.

Figure 1-1. Du Fay and Binchois, miniature in a copy of Martin Le Franc's *Le Champion des dames*, c. 1451 (Bibliothèque Nationale, Paris).

thology 1). What is there about the piece that would have struck the early-fifteenth-century Continental ear? No doubt it was (to use modern terminology) the largely triadic, C-major-like quality of the piece, or (in terms familiar to the fifteenth-century musician) the preponderance of imperfect consonances (thirds and sixths) and strictly controlled dissonance. Indeed, there is not a single unprepared dissonance between any two voices on a structurally important beat, a feature that has led modern scholars to apply the term "pan-consonant" to this piece and others like it. Nor are there any instances of parallel perfect consonances (fourths, fifths, and octaves), which contemporary Continental composers were still willing to tolerate.

Listeners on the Continent might also have noted the suppleness and expansiveness of the largely text-generated rhythm, which contrasted with the generally stiffer, harder-driving, and more complex rhythms of their own music. Finally, Continental audiences might have gasped at the "sensuousness" of measures 12–15, an effect produced by nothing more than a series of parallel first-inversion triads (in modern terms). To judge solely and thus perhaps unfairly from written sources, the English had a virtual monopoly on this device before the 1420s.

We should not, however, get the wrong idea. Not all English music of the period is marked by the apparent simplicity of *Quam pulchra es*; we will see that the English, and Dunstable in particular, were perfectly capable of handling the rhythmic complications of Continental music. Nor were the most distinctive stylistic features of *Quam pulchra es*—triads, supple rhythm, and careful declamation of the text—unknown to musicians on the Continent. Rather, it is a matter of degree. Triads and even parallel first-inversion triads appear in Continental music of the time, but not with the same consistency or the same self-conscious national identity. A piece such as Dunstable's wears those techniques on its sleeve, and it was surely the sonorous quality of pieces like it that Le Franc dubbed the "contenance angloise" and that Richental characterized as "sweet English song."

English Discant Style

While Dunstable was the greatest of the fifteenth-century English composers, he was neither the inventor nor the sole proponent of the style. A piece such as *Quam pulchra es* owes its triadic ring to a number of improvisatory practices that English musicians had probably cultivated for generations. (The fondness of the English for imperfect consonances even in written compositions stretches back at least to the thirteenth century.) These practices, which we generally lump together under the umbrella-like term "English discant," allowed singers to extemporize a three-part polyphonic fabric from a single plainchant melody. As so often happens, "improvisation" permeated "composition" (the line between them can be fine), and we can observe the resulting style operating in two works: Leonel Power's setting of the Marian chant *Ave regina caelorum* and an earlier, anonymous work, *Maria laude genitrix* (Ex. 1-1).

EXAMPLE 1-1. (a) Power, *Ave regina caelorum*, mm. 1–14, with the notes of the plainsong melody marked by asterisks; (b) Anonymous, *Maria laude genitrix*, mm. 1–8.

(a)

Power (d. 1445), who was probably slightly older than Dunstable, draws on the Sarum version (the version of the Catholic rite used at the Cathedral of Salisbury) of the *Ave regina* melody and places it in the middle voice. Around it, Power weaves a simple contrapuntal fabric, which features the contrary motion between voices that was advocated by the theorists but results nevertheless in a full-bodied, triadic sound. Indeed, the chordal sound of the music is further emphasized by the predominantly note-against-note writing.

The setting of *Maria laude genitrix* offers much the same, even though, like Dunstable's *Quam pulchra es*, the entire piece is freely composed. Unlike Power, though, the anonymous composer was less concerned with contrary motion between voices, and over the course of the work the two upper voices move in parallel fourths about two-thirds of the time. This practice combined with the frequent tendency of the lowest voice to move in parallel thirds with the middle voice results once again in a generous number of parallel first-inversion triads. Before pursuing this point, however, we should take note of the manuscript in which the two pieces appear.

The Old Hall Manuscript

The Old Hall manuscript (Fig. 1-2), so called because it was long housed at the College of St. Edmund, Old Hall (near Ware, England), is the most important English music manuscript of the early fifteenth century.[3] Containing 147 sacred pieces composed between 1370 and 1420, the manuscript constitutes a veritable anthology of English compositional styles of the time. Most striking, this important source is the first to transmit a sizable corpus of pieces with attributions to specific composers. And with his 21 (possibly more) works, Leonel Power is represented by three times as many pieces as any other com-

Figure 1-2. The Old Hall manuscript, fol. 121ᵛ, beginning of a Gloria by Roy Henry (King Henry V).

3. Now in the British Library, Ms Additional 57950; see *Census-Catalogue*.

poser. Two attributions that catch the eye are those to "Roy Henry," who is now assumed to be King Henry V, and who would not be the last English monarch to dabble in composition. Equally noteworthy is the "attribution" that fails to appear: Dunstable goes completely unrepresented in the original layer (or section) of the manuscript.

Though the provenance of the Old Hall manuscript—that is, where, when, and for whom it was compiled—cannot be established with certainty, at least the original layer was probably prepared during the 1410s for the private chapel of Thomas, Duke of Clarence (d. 1421), younger brother of Henry V. Power served in the duke's household as instructor of the choristers, which may account for his preeminence in the manuscript. Additions made to this original layer in the 1420s consist mainly of pieces by composers associated with the royal chapel of Henry VI, suggesting that the manuscript might eventually have come to reside at the royal household. While its exclusively sacred repertory, general lack of music by Continental composers (there are only two such pieces), and virtual exclusion of Dunstable provide a rather one-sided picture of the music at both of the chapels with which it was associated, the Old Hall manuscript nevertheless stands as the primary source of English music of the late fourteenth and early fifteenth centuries.

Faburden

One of the hallmarks of early-fifteenth-century English style is the use of parallel first-inversion triads, which appear in all three pieces discussed so far. Like the English sound in general, their use in art music probably derives from an improvisational practice that was known as *faburden*, which is described in an anonymous treatise, *The Sight of Faburden*, copied by one John Wylde in the 1430s or later:

> For the least process of Sights, natural and most in use, [it] is expedient to declare the Sight of Faburden. The which hath but two Sights: a third above the plainsong in Sight, the which is a sixth from the Treble in voice: and an even with the plainsong in Sight, the which is an octave from the Treble in Voice. These two accords the Faburdener must rule by the Mean of the plainsong. For when he shall begin his Faburden, he must attend to the plainsong, and set his Sight even with the plainsong and his Voice in a fifth beneath the plainsong. And after that, whether the plainsong ascend or descend, [he ought] to set his Sight always, both in rule and space, above the plainsong in a third. . . . And as often as he will, [he ought] to touch the plainsong—and void therefrom—except twice together, for that may not be, inasmuch as the plainsong Sight is an octave to the Treble and a fifth to the Mean, and so to every degree he is a perfect chord; and two perfect accords of one nature may not be sung together in no degree of Discant.[4]

From this description, we can determine how English singers of the period "improvised" three-part polyphony from a plainchant. Clearly, they put the preexistent chant in the middle voice. The lowest voice belonged to the *fa-*

---

4. Quoted after Trowell, "Faburden and Fauxbourdon," 47–48.

burdener, the only singer with a real choice of what note to sing. The faburdener had to "sight" (that is, visually imagine) a note that was either in unison with or a third above the plainsong and then, whichever note was sighted, sing a pitch that sounded a fifth lower. Moreover, the faburdener would begin the piece by sighting a unison—thus singing a fifth below the plainchant note—and, to the extent possible, begin and end each word on a sighted unison. In between, the faburdener was free to sight thirds above, thus producing a note that was (after transposing it down a fifth) a third below the plainsong. Meanwhile, the *treble*, or highest voice, sang a fourth above the chant, thus paralleling the faburdener at either a sixth or an octave above.

Following the anonymous theorist's prescriptions to the letter, a group of English singers could start with the Sarum version of the chant *Vos qui secuti* and end up with a polyphonic fabric such as the following:

EXAMPLE 1-2. A reconstruction of faburden on *Vos qui secuti*; the *mene* (middle, with plainchant) and treble on the upper staff, the faburdener on the lower staff (smaller notes are the sighted, or imagined, notes).[5]

To be sure, the result is hardly "high" art music. But works such as Dunstable's *Quam pulchra es* and Power's *Ave regina* took this fairly simple, even unsophisticated improvisational practice as their starting point, perhaps unconsciously, and absorbed it into art music of the highest quality, and so contributed significantly to the changing sound of early-fifteenth-century music.

As for the term "faburden," there was a long tradition in England—witnessed by Chaucer, among others—in which the word "burden" (probably derived from the French *bourdon*, a low drone) referred to the lowest part of a multivoice piece. The prefix "fa" probably was added as a result of the tendency of the faburden voice, when singing a fifth below the F of a plainsong, to sing B-flats and, consequently, E-flats (to keep fourths and fifths perfect), both of which would have been sung to the syllable *fa* (see Chapter 3). "Faburden," then, accurately described both the placement and the "tonal" orientation of the one voice part that truly improvised, and the term came to be used to describe the process as a whole.

5. After *New Grove*, 6: 352.

Fauxbourdon

By 1425–30 at the latest, Continental composers had developed their own counterpart to English faburden. Continental *fauxbourdon* can be seen clearly in the second parts of both the verse and the "Gloria Patri" of the three-part introit *Sapienciam sanctorum*, by Johannes Brassart (fl. 1420–45), who served in the imperial chapel of the Holy Roman Emperors during the 1430s and 1440s (*Anthology* 2).

The overall sound of this piece, while resembling that of faburden, was arrived at in a very different manner. Brassart first placed the plainchant melody in the top voice, here the *superius* (or *cantus*), transposing it up an octave and ornamenting it lightly (in *Anthology* 2, the notes of the plainsong are marked with an asterisk). He next *composed* the lowest voice, the *tenor*, which moves mostly note against note with the superius, mainly in sixths punctuated by the octave. Finally, rather than writing out the middle voice, he merely jotted down the instruction "a fauxbourdon." From this instruction, or *canon* (rule), the singer would know to double the chant-bearing superius at a fourth below. Thus fauxbourdon reaches us as a written practice in which the composer determined all three voices, in contrast to the English faburden technique, in which the lowest voice was improvised.

But fauxbourdon was not always quite so simple. Indeed, the earliest datable example of the technique (from 1427), the communion *Vos qui secuti* from Du Fay's *Missa Sancti Jacobi*, is far more artistic (Ex. 1-3):

EXAMPLE 1-3. Du Fay, the communion *Vos qui secuti* from the *Missa Sancti Jacobi*, mm. 1–11.

As he generally did in his fauxbourdon settings, Du Fay managed to maintain the emphasis on parallel $^6_3$ triads while giving the tenor at least some sense of independence.

Even with Du Fay's ingenuity, however, fauxbourdon wears quickly. There is simply not enough contrast. Composers soon recognized this lack of variety and assigned the technique to certain specific musical functions: short chant settings from the Proper of the Mass (as in Du Fay), short verse sections within longer settings (as in Brassart), and other small-scale pieces such as hymns and the Magnificat. The real importance of fauxbourdon, like that of English faburden, lay not in any aesthetic pretense of its own (though short bursts can be beautiful), but in the influence it had on compositions of a more ambitious kind. Just as the influence of faburden infuses a composition like Dunstable's *Quam pulchra es* with a distinctive sound, so the homophonic, triadic sonority of fauxbourdon lurks within a work like Du Fay's enticing setting of *Ave regina caelorum*, probably written before 1430 (*Anthology* 3). With no plainsong and with no more than an occasional nod toward parallel $^6_3$ chords, mainly at cadences, the piece is a thoroughly chordal, rhythmically simple work marked by crystal-clear declamation. We could even say that it represents a fauxbourdon-influenced style.

With both faburden and fauxbourdon, then, we see a process that is repeated many times in the history of Western music: a style of improvisation—call it an "unwritten tradition"—gives rise to a fairly limited, highly stylized written approximation that in turn becomes the basis for more ambitious, freely composed compositions. And in the opening decades of the fifteenth century, this process resulted in the emergence of what we now call the triad—a concept unknown to Dunstable, Du Fay, and their contemporaries, who would have "analyzed" their works and taught others how to write them in terms of intervals, first between superius and tenor and then between each of those two voices and any others. The triad soon became the underlying basis of composition, and transformed the sound of music.

ANGLO-CONTINENTAL CONTACTS

The idea that the English sent their "sounds" across the channel and that it transformed Continental styles overnight is obviously simplistic. Yet it is certain that the early 1400s saw ample contact between musicians from England and musicians of the Franco-Flemish tradition on the Continent. Whether we understand such contacts as instances of one tradition influencing the other, or merely contributing new elements to a common, ever-growing stylistic pool, or just rubbing elbows with an already established style seems immaterial. Here we will simply consider a few of the contacts, remembering that no one of them by itself played a decisive role.

English musicians were present at the Council of Constance, among them the Earl of Warwick's minstrels and the singers of the bishops of Norwich and Lichfield, who arrived after having performed in Cologne (in Germany). Contacts of a different sort came about through the protracted English occupation of northern France, beginning in 1417. Thus Binchois served an English nobleman and used a Sarum chant in one of his psalm settings. He even saw his best-known song, *De plus en plus* (see Ex. 5-7), quoted in Leonel Power's *Anima mea liquefacta est.*

As for Dunstable: not only did he serve John, Duke of Bedford, when the duke was Regent of France, but he actually owned land in English-occupied France. Eventually, in 1438, he joined the retinue of Humphrey, Duke of Gloucester, who opened channels of communication between England and the early Italian humanist movement. Perhaps it was through Gloucester's connections that a large number of works by Dunstable and other English composers found their way to Italy and came to be included in a manuscript copied at the Ferrarese court of Leonello d'Este in the late 1440s. Indeed, Dunstable is far better represented in Continental manuscripts than he is in English sources. Finally, the urban centers of the Low Countries (modern-day Belgium and the Netherlands), where a new tradition was just then taking root, stood at the very hub of Anglo-Continental trade, and a city such as Bruges was teeming with English merchants and diplomats who fostered their native musical tradition. In such ways, over two or three decades, Continental composers did indeed assimilate the English sound.

OTHER ENGLISH FEATURES

English music contributed more than its rich sonority, although that was certainly its most conspicuous feature. Another innovation was the idea of imbuing the five movements of the Ordinary of the Mass with a sense of musical unity by basing each of them on the same *cantus firmus*—a preexistent melody that formed the basis of a new polyphonic piece (a full discussion of this epoch-making idea appears in Chapter 9). We now look at three other features of English music that would eventually find their way to the Continent.

Paraphrase Technique

A favorite technique of the English was to place the cantus firmus (in this period, usually a chant melody) in the superius and paraphrase it—that is, embellish it—at times so lavishly that the identity of the original plainsong melody was nearly lost. A fine example of the practice occurs in the two-voice section of Dunstable's *Ave regina caelorum* (Ex. 1-4):

EXAMPLE 1-4. Dunstable, *Ave regina caelorum*, mm. 44–61, with the notes of the cantus firmus marked with asterisks.

Here Dunstable has taken the Sarum version of the plainsong melody, transposed it up a fifth (a customary ploy when placing it in the superius), and decorated it to the point where it is sometimes unrecognizable, as it is in the last phrase. The passage also highlights another typically English characteristic, the full-measure rest between the phrases on "Ave gloriosa" and "super omnes." We find the same one-measure rest just before the words "Veni, dilecte mi" in *Quam pulchra es* (*Anthology* 1, m. 30), where, however, it serves the rhetorical intent of setting off and thus emphasizing the words that follow. Indeed, the *coronas* (fermatas) over the notes on "Veni" might even have been a signal for melodic embellishment.

Migrant Cantus Firmus

While composers both in England and on the Continent customarily placed the cantus firmus in one voice and kept it there, the English sometimes permitted it to wend its way through the polyphonic fabric. An example of this technique appears in one of Power's triad-rich settings of *Salve regina*, which, rather mysteriously, is based on the chant melody *Alma redemptoris mater* (Ex. 1-5). The movement of the cantus firmus from superius to *contratenor* (middle voice) and back at measures 18–27 can be accounted for easily enough by Power's wish to keep the plainsong melody going while letting the superius drop out. At measures 68–79, on the other hand, his strategy differs: after placing the cantus firmus in the contratenor at measure 71, he keeps it there even when the superius reenters at measure 75.

EXAMPLE 1-5. Power, *Salve regina*, mm. 18–27 and 68–79.

THE MARIAN ANTIPHONS   Texts addressed to the Virgin Mary have figured prominently in the music discussed so far. There were, in fact, four famous Marian antiphons[6]—*Ave regina caelorum, Salve regina, Alma redemptoris mater,* and *Regina caeli letare*—that were sung throughout Europe at special votive (devotional) services dedicated to Mary. These were often sung in what was called the Lady Chapel, following the Office of Compline, the final prayer service of the day in the Roman liturgy. And in the early fifteenth century, English composers in particular produced numerous polyphonic settings of the antiphons.

Because there is no reason to assume that these texts held more aesthetic attraction for English composers than they did for anyone else, the abundance of English settings raises a question about their purpose. In fact, the English set the antiphons to meet the requirements of various institutions, including those outside the church itself, whose statutes often called for the Marian antiphons to be sung polyphonically and who put aside special compensations for the

6. Antiphons illustrate the difficulty in defining genres in medieval and Renaissance music. Usually, antiphons are short, predominantly syllabic chants that are sung in conjunction with psalms. The Marian antiphons, however, display none of these characteristics; they are so called because of their inclusion in a type of chant book known as an *antiphoner.*

singers who performed them. The statutes of Eton College, for example, dating from about 1453, called for the choristers of the college to participate in a votive service at the Lady altar each evening and to sing, "in the best manner they know," the *Salve regina* during Lent and the other Marian antiphons during the other seasons. Thus we see a kind of corporate patronage of music at work, which, though it did not go out and "chase" this or that specific composer, brought about the composition of polyphonic music in a particular genre. We will return to the subject of patronage from time to time throughout the book.

"Sweet" Thirds and Tuning Systems

Unfortunately, Ulrich von Richental was rather vague about the "sweet English song" that he heard at the Council of Constance. At first, we might assume that he was referring to the music itself, but it is equally possible that he was describing the manner of performance. And, though we can only speculate, it may be that what struck his ear was the English singers' manner of tuning.[7]

Vocal polyphony was performed according to Pythagorean tuning: that is, in accordance with the ideas of Pythagoras, who understood music as part of the mathematical sciences and whose teachings were passed down by generations of music theorists. Briefly (and at the risk of gross oversimplification), octaves and fifths were tuned purely—with the number of vibrations per second in perfect ratios of 2:1 and 3:2. Tuning this way, however, came at the expense of pure major and minor thirds, which to our ears would have sounded somewhat harsh and ragged with their respective ratios of 81:64 and 32:27. Yet for most medieval polyphony, with its emphasis on the perfect consonances, the pure tuning would have worked well enough.

The English, though, liked thirds and triads, and indeed made them a central feature of their style; but Pythagorean tuning would have left these sounding anything but "sweet." What English singers might have done, then, is flatten the fifths (eventually the successive fifths would have reached the point of sounding out of tune) in order to achieve pure thirds of 5:4 (major) and 6:5 (minor). In other words, they might have used a tuning system that approached what is known as mean-tone tuning (which would soon become the norm on keyboard instruments), and they would have done this in response to the triadic sonorities of the English sound. Thus, as they usually do, changes in musical style and in performance practice may well have gone hand in hand.

A DUNSTABLE WORK IN DETAIL

The two pieces by Dunstable that we considered earlier were English to the core and intimately small-scale. Yet Dunstable's most impressive compositions are his large-scale, isorhythmic motets, pieces in which we see the analytical

7. This paragraph and the next two are based on Covey-Crump, "Pythagoras at the Forge," 319–21.

mind of Dunstable the mathematician and astronomer (which he was) at work. Among his dozen works in this genre (about one-quarter of his entire output), which he cultivated with far greater frequency and virtuosity than any of his English contemporaries, one of the most impressive is the four-voice setting of *Veni sancte spiritus/Veni creator* (*Anthology* 4).

Before we look at Dunstable's motet in some detail, we must first understand how *isorhythm* (a modern term) works. There are two important elements: a recurring melody, called a *color*, and a recurring rhythmic pattern, called a *talea*. What makes isorhythm interesting is that, unlike a simple ostinato, the repetitions of melody and rhythmic pattern are not necessarily synchronized. Example 1-6 is a homemade illustration of the technique:

EXAMPLE 1-6. The elements of isorhythm: (a) a six-note color; (b) a ten-component (notes and rests) talea; (c) the two combined to form an isorhythmic voice part.

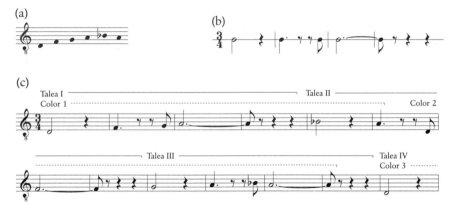

Here, the melody is clothed in a different rhythmic garb at each of its appearances, while the rhythmic pattern returns each time with a different melody.

Now to Dunstable's motet: for his cantus firmus, which lies in the lowest voice (tenor), Dunstable drew on the hymn *Veni creator spiritus*, sung on the feast of Pentecost (also called Whitsunday), though he quotes only notes 11–32 of the melody (Ex. 1-7):

EXAMPLE 1-7. The hymn *Veni creator spiritus*, stanza 1, with notes 11–32 numbered.

Example 1-8 shows the six paired taleae as they extend over three statements of the color:

EXAMPLE 1-8. The six taleae and three colores of the tenor in *Veni sancte spiritus / Veni creator.*

In this motet, Dunstable both simplifies and complicates the isorhythm. On the one hand, he makes each statement of the color coincide with exactly two statements of the talea, so that the second and third statements of the melody return with their original rhythmic pattern intact. This produces a clearer, more audible exposition of both melody and rhythmic pattern than does the non-synchronized combination of our homemade example. On the other hand, Dunstable employs a procedure that had already been widely used in the four-teenth century: each pair of taleae are presented in progressive *diminution* (notes of shorter duration), in the ratio 3:2:1: that is (in terms of modern notation), the dotted whole note tied to a dotted half note in taleae I and II ($3 \times \frac{3}{4}$—one measure in the tenor is equal to three measures in $\frac{3}{4}$ time in the upper voices) shrinks to a dotted whole note in taleae III and IV ($3 \times \frac{2}{4}$), and is further reduced to a dotted half note in taleae V and VI ($1 \times \frac{3}{4}$).

Dunstable also applies isorhythm to the upper voices, a device known today as *pan-isorhythm* (isorhythm in all voices). Here, though, he proceeds differently: the rhythm of each upper voice is the same in taleae I and II (with minor differences); with taleae III and IV, the upper voices unfold in a completely new rhythm; while taleae V and VI introduce a third configuration. Thus against the single isorhythmic pattern in the tenor, the upper voices present three different isorhythmic patterns, each comprising two taleae.

There are also touches of *isomelism* (another modern term): that is, at cor-responding points in each pair of taleae, the melody, or at least the melodic contour, in the upper voices is either identical or similar. Table 1-1 shows the points of melodic correspondence as they appear in the top voice:

Table 1-1.   Isomelic elements in the top voice of *Veni sancte spiritus/*
             Veni creator.

Talea pair	Odd-numbered taleae		Even-numbered taleae
I and II	mm. 22–24	=	mm. 67–69
	mm. 30–44	=	mm. 75–89
II and IV	m. 96	=	m. 111
	mm. 100–104	=	mm. 115–119
V and VI	mm. 129–130	=	mm. 144–145

Though it is the isorhythmic tenor that does the most to articulate the formal structure of the motet both rhythmically (the six taleae) and melodically (the three colores), the superius also plays an important role. Each of the tenor's six taleae begins with three measures of rest, in the next-to-lowest voice as well as the tenor (their real-time length grows shorter with the successive stages of diminution). During these rests, the superius, while singing the words of the liturgical sequence *Veni sancte spiritus* (from the Mass for Pentecost), quotes the melody of the *Veni creator* hymn (Ex. 1-7), presenting it phrase by phrase in each successive talea-opening duet (Table 1-2):

Table 1-2.   The *Veni creator* melody in the superius.

Talea	Portion of melody quoted
I	Veni creator spiritus
II	mentes tuorum visita
III	Imple superna gratia
IV	quae tu creasti pectora
V	Veni creator spiritus
VI	mentes tuorum visita

Thus the superius acts as a kind of melodic trope (a commentary on the tenor), as it presents the *Veni creator* melody in its entirety while the tenor has only notes 11–32. Another commentary is carried out by the next-to-highest voice, which begins like the superius, with the words "Veni sancte spiritus," but then continues independently with sentiments that echo those of the *Veni sancte spiritus* sequence.

Finally, Dunstable imbues the motet with a subtle play of number symbolism. Each talea of the tenor quotes precisely eleven notes of the *Veni creator* melody, alternately notes 11–21 and 22–32 in the successive odd- and even-numbered taleae. Indeed, it adheres to its eleven-note snippets so rigorously as to end each talea, including the final one, in the middle of a word. (Was the tenor performed on an instrument, sung without words?) Likewise, the superius presents the first eleven notes of the melody in the duet that opens talea I.

There is good reason for this insistence on the number eleven: the motet was intended for the feast of Pentecost, which, coming fifty days after Easter, celebrates the eleven apostles who remained to receive the gift of the Holy Spirit. Number symbolism of various kinds was one way in which composers of the period imbued their works with extra-musical meaning. And whether audible or not, the gesture would have been appreciated on a purely intellectual level by those who were aware of it.

As a coda to the discussion of Dunstable, it is worth noting that neither he nor Power was much disposed to write secular music. Power wrote no secular pieces at all, while Dunstable may have written only a single French chanson.

THE CAROL

There is no single precise definition of the carol. Its text could be in English or in Latin, or in a mixture of the two. Its subject could be religious or secular (religious carols often dealt with the birth of Christ—hence our Christmas carols). It could be heard both in church and at home; and its style could be either courtly or popular. Although the functions and social contexts of the carol were diverse, its musical-structural underpinning was fairly standard: a *burden* (refrain) presumably sung by a chorus alternated with successive verses taken by soloists.

One of the most attractive of the early-fifteenth-century carols is *Deo gracias, Anglia*, also known as the "Agincourt Carol" (*Anthology* 5) because it celebrates Henry V's victory over the French at the Battle of Agincourt (October 1415), a prelude to the lengthy British occupation of northern France that would begin two years later. Here, though, there is a wrinkle in the structure, for instead of a single burden, there are two, one for two voices, the other for three. Did one burden open the piece, with the other then coming between the verses? Or was one sung by soloists (*a 2*) and the other by a chorus (*a 3*)? In any event, *Deo Gracias* is a lively and fitting piece with which to end this chapter.

BIBLIOGRAPHICAL NOTE

Editions of the Music

The music itself can be studied in four important editions: *The Old Hall Manuscript, CMM* 46, ed. Andrew Hughes and Margaret Bent (American Institute of Musicology, 1969–73); John Dunstable, *Complete Works*, 2nd rev. ed., *MB* 8, ed. Manfred F. Bukofzer, rev. Margaret Bent, Ian Bent, and Brian Trowell (London: Stainer & Bell, 1970); Leonel Power, *Complete Works, CMM* 50, ed. Charles Hamm (American Institute of Musicology, 1969); and *Medieval Carols*, 2nd ed., *MB* 4, ed. John Stevens (London: Stainer & Bell, 1958).

General Studies

Two major works on English music of the period are the now-classic Frank Ll. Harrison, *Music in Medieval Britain*, 4th ed. (Buren: Knuf, 1980; originally published 1958), and John Caldwell, *The Oxford History of English Music*, vol. 1: *From the Beginnings to c. 1715* (Oxford: Clarendon Press, 1991), with an especially extensive bibliography. On church patronage of music, see Roger Bowers, "Obligation, Agency, and *Laissez-faire*: The Promotion of Polyphonic Composition for the Church in Fifteenth-Century England," in *Music in Medieval and Early Modern Europe: Patronage, Sources, and Text*, ed. Iain Fenlon (Cambridge: Cambridge University Press, 1981), 1–19. See also David Fallows's "Contenance Angloise: English

Influence on Continental Composers of the Fifteenth Century," *Renaissance Studies* 1 (1987): 189–208, which questions the traditional view about English influence on Continental music.

Dunstable

The best introduction to the life and works of Dunstable remains Margaret Bent, *Dunstaple* (London: Oxford University Press, 1981); new biographical information appears in Andrew Wathey, "Dunstable in France," *ML* 67 (1986): 1–36; Brian Trowell's "Proportion in the Music of Dunstable," *PRMA* 50 (1978–79): 100–41, is a detailed study of the structure of Dunstable's works, with an emphasis on number symbolism; still worth consulting for its insights is Manfred Bukofzer "John Dunstable: A Quincentenary Report," *MQ* 40 (1954): 29–49.

Power

A starting point is Roger Bowers, "Some Observations on the Life and Career of Lionel Power," *PRMA* 102 (1975–76): 103–27.

Faburden and Fauxbourdon

The literature is large and argumentive. Two clear-headed studies by Brian Trowell are "Faburden and Fauxbourdon," *MD* 13 (1959): 43–78, and "Faburden—New Sources, New Evidence: A Preliminary Survey," in *Modern Musical Scholarship*, ed. Edward Olleson (Stocksfield: Oriel Press, 1978), 28–78; see also Ernest Trumble, *Fauxbourdon: An Historical Survey*, Musicological Studies 3 (Brooklyn: Institute of Mediaeval Music, 1959); and, for a rather different point of view, Willem Elders, "Guillaume Dufay's Concept of Faux-Bourdon," *RBM* 43 (1989): 173–95; Andrew Kirkman, "Some Early Fifteenth-Century Fauxbourdons by Dufay and His Contemporaries: A Study in Liturgically Motivated Musical Style," *TVNM* 40 (1990): 13–35.

Also Cited

Census-Catalogue of Manuscript Sources of Polyphonic Music, 1400–1550, 5 vols., Renaissance Manuscript Studies 1 (American Institute of Musicology, 1979–88); Rogers Covey-Crump, "Pythagoras at the Forge: Tuning in Early Music," in *Companion to Medieval and Renaissance Music*, ed. Tess Knighton and David Fallows (New York: Schirmer Books, 1992), 317–26.

CHAPTER 2

Intermedio: 1414–1418

THE MAP OF WESTERN EUROPE

The map of western and central Europe in the second decade of the fifteenth century (Fig. 2-1) looked very different from that of today. Of the eight modern-day nations that made important contributions to fifteenth-century music—Austria, Belgium, England, France, Germany, Italy, the Netherlands, and Spain—only England and France were sovereign states. The other areas were either incorporated into political units that cut across modern boundaries, such as the Holy Roman Empire and the duchy of Burgundy, or splintered into city-states, principalities, and duchies or, as in Spain, into smaller kingdoms. Nor was the picture very different at the end of the century, by which time only Spain, unified at least in name under Ferdinand and Isabella in 1492, joined England and France as a sovereign state.

Figure 2-1. Map of western and central Europe, c. 1420 (B = Burgundian possessions, Byz = Byzantine possessions, E = emirate, K = kingdom, P = principality, Pap = papal).

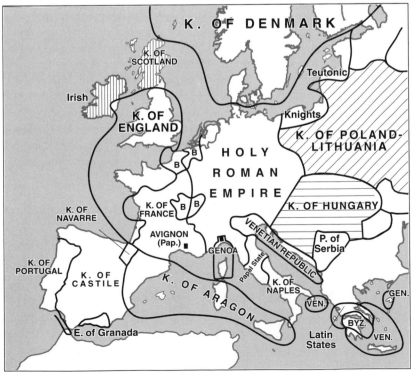

At the same time, some of the political power brokers of the period—the Valois dukes of Burgundy, for example, and the Trastemare kings of Aragón—headed states whose independence would not survive the fifteenth century. Yet while these states and rulers thrived, they not only played major political-economic roles, but often stood in the vanguard of artistic matters. Thus the dukes of Burgundy headed the wealthiest and most culturally ostentatious dynasty in Europe before the last duke died in 1477, while tiny Florence, a city-state that did outlast the century, was truly the artistic and intellectual "cradle of the Renaissance." We will follow the fortunes of both as the century progressed.

THE HUNDRED YEARS' WAR

War was endemic to the fifteenth and sixteenth centuries; there was hardly a decade in which national or local armies were not pitted against each other, whether for reasons of national pride, religious differences, or clanlike feuds that got out of hand. For some, war spelled disaster, as it ravaged the countryside and its inhabitants, especially when unpaid troops went marauding, as they often did. For others, though—monarchs, the nobility loyal to them, and a new class of professional soldiers of fortune—it was the very reason for which to live.

No conflict of the period had deeper underlying roots than the on-again, off-again war fought by England and France from 1337 to 1453. Its causes were many: territorial disputes over parts of southwestern France; claims by Edward III of England (1312–1377) to the French throne on the grounds that his mother came from the French royal family; the English view of France as a menace to England's lucrative textile trade with Flanders; and squabbles over fishing rights in the English Channel.

The war was fought on French soil, with most of the victories going to England. Indeed, two years after the English victory at Agincourt in 1415 (celebrated, as we have seen, in the carol *Deo gracias, Anglia, Anthology* 5), Henry V invaded and successfully occupied northern France with the support of the Duke of Burgundy, while the next English king, Henry VI, was even crowned King of France in 1431. The tide began to turn, though, when the French, led by Joan of Arc, broke the siege of Orléans in 1429. Six years later, Burgundy adopted a position of neutrality, and by 1453 the English withdrew from all but the port of Calais, which they would continue to hold for more than a century.

Though it is fair to say that the English won the battles while the French won the war, in the end both sides lost. England soon fell victim to internal factions and its own War of the Roses (1450–85), while France took decades to recover completely from the devastation wrought to both land and economy.

THE COUNCIL OF CONSTANCE

The fourteenth century was a disastrous one for the Catholic Church, which became something of a pawn in the tug-of-war of national ambitions. In 1305, Clement V was elected pope. A Frenchman, he chose to avoid the feuds raging among the Italian cardinals and nobility and, instead of heading for Rome, settled at Avignon, a papal fiefdom in southeastern France. Things went from bad to worse in 1378, as the papacy itself fell victim to national interests. The faction-ridden College of Cardinals elected two popes: Urban VI, who resided in Rome (supported by England and the Holy Roman Empire), and Clement VII, who remained at Avignon (backed by France, the Spanish kingdoms, and the Italian city-states). The church thus entered into a period known as the Great Schism.

In an effort to end the schism, Emperor Sigismund and the Holy Roman "conciliar" Pope John XXIII convened the Council of Constance, which ran from 1414 to 1418. The Council was attended by virtually everyone of political note in Europe, both ecclesiastical and secular, and succeeded in its most pressing objective: it ended the schism in 1417 by electing a single pope, Martin V (of the Roman Colonna family). A theological and political reactionary, Martin succeeded in restoring the authority of the papacy and its temporal power over the papal states in Italy. Moreover, he set the tone for the style of papal behavior for centuries to come: involvement in temporal affairs, waging of wars, and unbridled nepotism.

In other respects, the gathering at Constance fell short of conciliar goals, such as making the church a more representative, even democratic, institution and reforming what many saw as grave abuses of ecclesiastical powers. Simply put, neither Martin nor his successors were ready to share power with representative general councils. Indeed, the church failed to heed the calls for doctrinal reforms urged by both the Englishman John Wycliffe (c. 1320–1384), the first to translate the Bible into English, and the Bohemian Jan Hus (c. 1370–1415), whom the council invited to Constance only to burn him at the stake as a heretic. Even the bloody revolts carried on by the followers of these dissenters won no concessions from the popes. And Rome would pay dearly for its deafness a century later, when the seeds of discontent sown in the late fourteenth and early fifteenth centuries blossomed into Luther's Protestant Reformation.

HUMANISM

Humanism had many faces. Narrowly defined, humanism (a term coined—as was the very word "Renaissance"—in the nineteenth century) was a love affair with antiquity, especially with its literary texts, and therefore its grammar, rhetoric, poetry, history, and moral philosophy.

Humanism was born and developed in Italy. The Italians, after all, could see the remains of antiquity all about them, and there were even Greek-speaking colonies in the southern part of the boot. Slowly but surely, though, the humanist agenda was exported, and by the end of the fifteenth century its precepts were making serious inroads in other parts of Europe. In the sixteenth century, no one could escape them.

To be sure, knowledge about ancient literature was not new to the fifteenth century: Virgil, Ovid, Seneca, and others were well-known to the Middle Ages, and in the fourteenth century their works were studied closely by Petrarch, who brought to them a new and ultimately influential sensitivity. But what had only simmered, virtually bubbled over in the fifteenth century, as one text after another was not just rediscovered but was carefully edited and restored according to the new "science" of textual criticism. And since the texts dealt with everything from philosophy to politics, history, natural science, architecture, and rhetoric, the fifteenth-century humanists were able to form a picture of antiquity that was far more comprehensive than anything known to their predecessors.

But humanists were not content merely to read and study; they wished to imitate the ideas of antiquity. They modeled their own literary style (in Latin) after the works of the ancients, as they did their villas and palaces, freestanding nude statues, and even musical instruments and presumed styles of performance. Just as important to the humanist agenda was what might be called "civic humanism." It was Cicero, after all, who had encouraged participation in the affairs of government, and Florentines, for example, reveled in their republicanism, which they proudly compared with the despotism of archenemy Milan. Humanism was also a system of education, one that concentrated on the liberal arts, and the term *umanista* was applied to those who taught the *studiae humanitatis* (we will return to this subject in Chapter 6).

Though the humanist agenda made its most telling impact on music in the sixteenth century, traces of it are already apparent in the first half of the fifteenth. In a letter of 1429 to the Venetian statesman and poet Leonardo Giustinian, Ambrogio Traversari writes, in low-key fashion and with none of the polemics that would mark later humanist discussion: "I have known for a long time that your agile and certainly golden mind has succeeded also in those matters that, contrary to ancient [that is, more recent] custom, are better known to common people than to scholars, such as the ability to sing very sweet arias, [accompanying them] with sound."[1]

Here Traversari turns on its head one of the most commonplace assumptions about music in medieval culture—that the speculative knowledge of the *musicus* was of a higher order than the performing ability of the *cantor*. What Traversari appreciates about Giustinian is just the opposite: his instinctive gift for song and its expression in a tradition that is understood not just by the scholar, but by the "common people." For Traversari, then, music is no longer part of the *quadrivium* (together with mathematics, geometry, and astronomy), but a rhetorical, expressive art that can move the emotions. And this is exactly what the humanists would argue so vehemently throughout the fifteenth and sixteenth centuries.

MANUEL CHRYSOLORAS AND SOME HUMANIST FOLLOWERS

Born in Byzantium in 1350, Manuel Chrysoloras first visited the West in 1394 as an emissary of the Byzantine emperor and returned a few years later to hold a professorship of Greek at Florence in 1397–1400. (He died in 1415.)

1. Quoted after Pirrotta, *Music and Culture in Italy*, 145.

Perhaps more than anyone else, Chrysoloras introduced to the West the love of classical literature, philosophy, and art that would play so important a role in the humanist movement.

Bruni and Vergerio

Two of Chrysoloras's students were Leonardo Bruni and Pier Paolo Vergerio. Bruni (1370–1444), of humble origins, was the leading Greek scholar of his time. He completed new translations (into Latin) of Aristotle's *Ethics* and *Politics* and with his translations of some of Plato's works made that philosopher accessible in Latin for the first time. His *History of the Florentine People* stands out for two reasons: with its imitation of the graceful literary style of classical historians—as opposed, say, to the more chronicle-like approach of the recent past—the work set the tone for historical writing as a literary genre for the remainder of the period; and it emphasized the relationship between Florence and republican (rather than imperial) Rome, an important aspect of the Florentine political self-image and ideology. No ivory-tower scholar, Bruni played an active role in Florentine civic life. In all, he must be considered the central figure in Florentine humanism of the first half of the fifteenth century.

Pier Paolo Vergerio (1370–1444) was the first important theorist of humanist education. A tutor at the court of Padua, where he probably knew the composer Johannes Ciconia, his *Conduct Becoming Free Men* of around 1402 outlined the elements of a liberal education: grammar and logic at the outset, with history, moral philosophy, and eloquence to follow. After attending the Council of Constance, he entered the service of the King of Hungary and died in relative obscurity.

Poggio Bracciolini

Though not a student of Chrysoloras, Poggio (1380–1459) formed his outlook first in the same Florentine humanist circle and then as a *scriptor* (secretary) at the papal court, where he developed his passion for the authors of ancient Rome. Like Vergerio, he attended the Council of Constance, which he used as a jumping-off point to visit the libraries of such abbeys as St. Gall in Switzerland. There, in 1416, he made his famous discovery of a complete version of Quintilian's *On the Institution of Oratory*, which, with its thesis that excellence in oratory is tied to knowledge and virtue, soon played a major role in the humanist agenda.

BIBLIOGRAPHICAL NOTE

The Hundred Years' War
   Though slightly dated, Edouard Perroy's *Hundred Years War*, 2nd ed., trans. W. B. Wells (London: Capricorn, 1965), is a very readable account.

Council of Constance
   Two fine studies are John H. Mundy and Kennerly Woody, eds., *The Council of Constance: The Unification of the Church*, trans. Louise Ropes Loomis (New York: Columbia University Press, 1961); and Hubert Jedin, *Ecumenical Councils of the Catholic Church* (New York: Herder

& Herder, 1960). There is a concise biography of Jan Hus in Theodore K. Rabb, *Renaissance Lives: Portraits of an Age* (New York: Pantheon, 1993). For those who can handle the German, Manfred Schuler's "Die Musik in Konstanz während des Konzils 1414–1418," *AcM* 38 (1966): 150–68, is still the starting point on music at the council.

Humanism

Four classics on the subject are Paul Oskar Kristeller, *Renaissance Thought* and *Renaissance Thought II* (New York: Harper & Row, 1961, 1965); Hans Baron, *The Crises of the Early Italian Renaissance: Civic Humanism and Republican Liberty in an Age of Classicism and Tyranny* (Princeton: Princeton University Press, 1955); and Eugenio Garin, *Italian Humanism: Philosophy and Civic Life in the Renaissance* (New York: Harper & Row, 1965).

Also Cited

Nino Pirrotta, *Music and Culture in Italy from the Middle Ages to the Baroque* (Cambridge: Harvard University Press, 1984).

CHAPTER 3

The Low Countries

To say that Continental audiences found English music of the early fifteenth century fresh and distinctive leads us to ask, what was their own music like? To answer that question, we must back up to the mid-fourteenth century.

THE FRENCH *ARS NOVA*

If, around 1350, one style could rightfully claim to represent a "central" polyphonic tradition, it was that of the French *Ars nova*. With a legacy that reached back to the Parisian organa of Leonin and Perotin in the late twelfth century, and with the infusion of both the motet and the notational principles of Franco of Cologne in the thirteenth, French music of the mid-fourteenth century stood at the vanguard of new developments in the art of polyphony.

And new developments there were. With Philippe de Vitry and Guillaume de Machaut at their head, the French continued to break new stylistic ground and develop new polyphonic genres. There was, for instance, the isorhythmic motet, which stands as a kind of signature tune of the *Ars nova*—or at least of the rationalist side of the French approach to structure. At the other end of the spectrum, we find the widespread cultivation of secular polyphony. Composers, starting with Adam de la Halle (c. 1245–1285 or later) and Jean de l'Escurel (d. 1304) and continuing with Guillaume de Machaut (d. 1377), were attracted to the lyricism and effusions of courtly love as expressed in the musical-poetic forms known as the *formes fixes*: the *rondeau*, *virelai*, and *ballade*. These three structural schemes would dominate French poetry and music until the end of the fifteenth century. As for liturgical music, French composers of the four-teenth century became seriously interested in setting the sections of the Ordi-nary of the Mass—Kyrie, Gloria, Credo, Sanctus, and Agnus Dei—with Machaut even trying his hand at a unified cycle (an idea that would not really catch on for almost a century).

Finally, there were new notational principles, developed especially in the treatises of Johannes de Muris (*Ars novae musicae*) and Philippe de Vitry (*Ars nova*), that formed the basis of the notation of polyphonic music for some 250 years. In all, while there were important lateral traditions in both England and Italy, it was France that held the center.

The *Ars subtilior*

One of the features that pervaded French music through much of the four-teenth century was a penchant for complexity. This is particularly evident in the isorhythmic motet, with its often nonsynchronized taleae and colores and its use of proportional diminution in successive taleae.

During the last quarter of the century, this fondness for complication turned into something of an obsession. A group of composers active at such cultural centers as the courts of the schismatic antipope Clement VII at Avignon, Gaston Fébus of Foix in southwestern France, and Joan I of Aragón just across the Pyrenees came to revel (some would say exhaust themselves) in complexity. Once dubbed "mannerist," their style is now usually referred to as the *Ars subtilior* (subtle art).

We can see the salient features of the style in a ballade by the French composer Solage (fl. 1370–90). Example 3-1 shows the opening and closing measures of his *S'aincy estoit*. The work, which reaches us in a collection known as the Chantilly manuscript,[1] one of the major sources of the *Ars subtilior* repertory, praises Jean, Duke of Berry, a renowned bibliophile and patron of the arts around 1400:

EXAMPLE 3-1. Solage, *S'aincy estoit*, mm. 1–25 and 66–75.

1. Chantilly, Bibliothèque du Musée Condé, MS 564 (formerly 1047).

What strikes the ear (and the eye) immediately is the piece's rhythmic complexity, which operates on two distinct levels: voice against voice, with different
mensurations—which resemble but are not identical to our modern time sig-
natures-meters (see Chapter 4)—juxtaposed against one another; and within
the individual voice parts, with syncopation (the displacement of units of six
across our modern bar line) that runs rampant. Nor is it the rhythm alone that
is striking; unlike the pan-consonant style that we saw in Dunstable's *Quam
pulchra es*, the contrapuntal fabric here bristles with unprepared dissonances,

while the "tonal" logic sometimes leaves us shaking our heads (see mm. 8–9, for example).

While many *Ars subtilior* pieces are truly expressive, the aesthetics of subtlety also had room for displays of wit, not only in the music but on occasion in the poetry as well. Consider the poem of another Solage composition:

Fumeux fume par fumée,	Smoky smolders smokily,
Fumeuse speculacion.	In smoky speculation.
Qu'antre fummet sa pensée.	Thus he steeps his thoughts in smoke.
Fumeux fume par fumée.	Smoky smolders smokily.
Quar fumer molt li agrée,	For it suits him well to smoke,
Tant qu'il ait son entencion.	Until he gets his way.
Fumeux fume par fumée,	Smoky smolders smokily,
Fumeuse speculacion.	In smoky speculation.[2]

With a tonal language that is no less hazy than the poem it sets, the piece was no doubt appreciated by the literary-minded members of the Ordre des Fumeux (Order of Smokers).

If a sense of witty play was in fact part of the *Ars subtilior* aesthetic, the composers may in the end have outwitted themselves, for pieces such as *S'aincy estoit* leave little room for further rhythmic development. Solage has pushed the capabilities of the fourteenth-century notational system to its limits; and even if the notation could have expressed the mathematics of further complication, we must wonder if fourteenth-century performers could have managed it.

In the end, a reaction was bound to set in: a movement toward simplification and clarity. And when it did, around the turn of the fifteenth century, it emerged in the form of a new central tradition in the Low Countries, much of which fell within the domains of the dukes of Burgundy.

THE NEW CENTRAL TRADITION

It was not by accident that this new tradition was spawned in and around the duchy of Burgundy rather than in royal France. Patronage of the arts simply followed political power and commercial wealth. So when France fell on hard times around the turn of the fifteenth century, the void was filled by the independent duchy of Burgundy, which had been created by the French crown itself just a few decades earlier and had quickly grown into the most powerful and wealthy dynasty in Europe. How this came about is a multifaceted tale involving historical accident, intrigue, conflict, assassination, and war.

The decline of France: When Charles V died in 1380, he was succeeded by his son Charles VI. After Charles VI went insane in 1392, his uncle Philip the Bold, Duke of Burgundy, seized control of the realm. Though Philip took the challenges of Charles's younger brother Louis in stride, his own son and suc-

2. The translation, by Sylvia Huot, appears in Lefferts, "*Subtilitas*," 182.

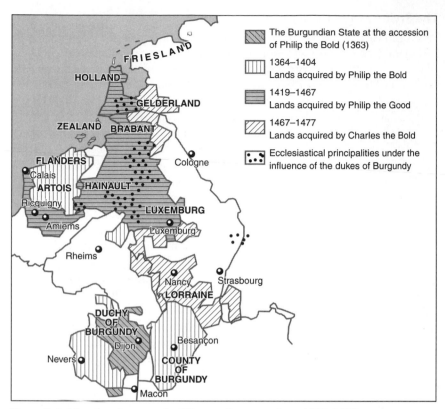

Figure 3-1. Map showing growth of Burgundian possessions, 1363–1477.

cessor, John the Fearless (succeeded in 1404), brought things to a head: he had cousin Louis assassinated on November 23, 1407, an act that set off civil war between royalists and supporters of Burgundy. Matters grew worse when the Hundred Years' War erupted again, as the English, with their Burgundian allies, ravaged France.

The ascent of Burgundy: In 1364, Charles V relinquished control of the area of eastern France known as Burgundy, and invested his younger brother Philip the Bold as duke. In 1369, Philip married Margaret of Flanders, and in 1389 he inherited her family's domains in the Low Countries, where he established his court. After Philip's son John the Fearless consolidated the patrimony, the next duke, Philip the Good (succeeded in 1419), added the territories of Holland, Brabant, and Hainaut (see Fig. 3-1). Thus the duchy of Burgundy incorporated such thriving urban-commercial centers as Bruges, Ghent, Antwerp, and Brussels, which, with their highly skilled craftsmen, banking and credit facilities, and internationally minded merchants, stood at the vanguard of the newly developing capitalism. And fed by Philip the Good's own love of ostentatious display, the Low Countries provided the means for lavish patronage of the arts.

The Style

We can hear the style of the new central tradition, or at least a few of its important features, in a chanson by Nicolas Grenon, whose career, with its often changing venues, typifies the peregrinations of many musicians during this period. Born around 1380, Grenon began his career at Paris and then served as master of the choirboys at the Cathedral of Laon. He later spent time in the Burgundian ducal chapel, served as master of the choirboys in the papal chapel of Martin V, and put in three separate stints at the Cathedral of Cambrai, where he must certainly have known Du Fay (he may even have been his teacher around 1410) and where he died in 1456.

What immediately sets Grenon's rondeau *La plus jolie et la plus belle (Anthology* 6) apart from the *Ars subtilior* style is its extreme simplicity, even intimacy. Gone are the complicated rhythms, both between voices and within them. Gone also is that sense of tonal meandering: the piece is built squarely on G, with all but one of the cadences coming on the tonic or dominant (again, in modern terminology). The clear sense of tonal coherence and the simplicity of the rhythm lend an almost popular, dance-like lilt to the piece. Indeed, we can see a "popularizing" trend at work in a good deal of the music written in the new style.

Yet not all pieces in the new central tradition were this straightforward and simple. In Baude Cordier's *Se cuer d'amant (Anthology* 7), the linear pull between voices is far more evident than it is in the homophonic piece by Grenon. Moreover, the cadences are less clear-cut, as not even once do all the voices come to a dead stop. Three other features of the piece are typical of the Franco-Flemish chanson in the opening decades of the fifteenth century: (1) the introductory melisma in the top voice, which may have anticipated the first syllable; (2) the changing function of the contratenor from one cadential spot to another (it takes the "leading tone" at mm. 4–5, functions as a bass voice with V–I motion at m. 5, and assumes its normal position in the middle at mm. 7–8); and (3) the vii^6–I cadence at mm. 13–14 (here with a full triad on I instead of the customary twofold leading-tone cadence, as the top voice descends from c″ to b′ rather than moving from c♯″ to d″). Finally, since the piece may predate 1400, it provides early evidence for the cultivation of the new, forward-looking Franco-Flemish style.

Though the chansons by Grenon and Baude Cordier are small-scale miniatures, the new central tradition of the Low Countries did not turn its back on the larger forms. What it did leave behind, however, was the extreme rhythmic complexity and lack of tonal focus that had marked the *Ars subtilior*. Clarity was one of its watchwords.

We should return to one interesting feature of Grenon's *La plus jolie et la plus belle*: its use of conflicting "key" signatures—one for the top voice and another for the two lower voices. While this phenomenon appears from the thirteenth century to the sixteenth, it is particularly prevalent in the fifteenth century, and always involves flats (sharps were generally not used in signatures), typically in one of the following combinations: ♮ ♮ ♭ ♮ ♭ ♭; ♭ ♭ ♭♭; and ♭ ♭♭ ♭♭. In other words, the lowest voice or voices tend to have one flat more than the higher. A number of explanations have been offered for the use of conflicting signatures: (1) they represent a transposition of the modes (see Chapter 7); (2) they accommodate the need for the upper voice to approach cadences with a raised leading tone; (3) they indicate a transposition of the hexachord system (see below); (4) they prevent the prohibited interval of the diminished fifth. In truth, these explanations are not mutually exclusive, though in terms of Grenon's piece, explanations 3 and 4 seem most relevant.

MUSICAL TRAINING

Although the active patronage of music often goes hand in hand with material wealth (no shortage of that in the Low Countries, whether courtly, civic-corporate, or ecclesiastical), the combination of the two suffices only to assure the consumption of music. To produce high-level art music, there must be a solid foundation of musical training that identifies talent early on and then proceeds to nurture the requisite craftsmanship. This the Low Countries provided through the *maîtrisse*, or choir school, attached to the great cathedrals and collegiate churches in the area (a collegiate church was presided over by canons, the governing body of the church, rather than a bishop), such as the Cathedral of Notre Dame (Du Fay's alma mater) and the church of St. Géry, both at Cambrai, St. Donatian at Bruges, and the Church of Our Lady at Antwerp.

We can get a good idea of the training at these schools from what the theorist Adrian Petit Coclico claims to have studied with Josquin Desprez. Though Coclico describes a curriculum that he followed in the sixteenth century, it is unlikely that the training had changed much, if at all:

> [A choirboy] will . . . apply himself to learn . . . the musical hand or scale . . . and soon he will recognize the individual clef symbols; immediately thereafter, he will begin to practice solmization in plainsong or Gregorian chant, and to pronounce musical syllables and their combinations in their order. To these he will add the knowledge of the eight modes. . . . Then he will recognize their signs, quantity, and values, soon after, the shapes of notes, ligatures, points, pauses; afterwards, the prolations, major and minor, augmentation, diminution, imperfection, alteration, syncopation, at the same time as the beats and certain proportions of utility. . . . He will then begin to sing, not only as [the music] is written but also with embellishments, and to pronounce skillfully, smoothly, and meaningfully, to intone correctly and to place any syllable in its proper place under the right notes. . . . when anyone has learned well those things I have indicated above, he can have also learned counterpoint and composition.[3]

For now, we will consider only the basic rudiments with which Coclico begins: the "hand or scale," *solmization* (our *solfeggio*), and the six-note hexachord system.

The Gamut

At the very base of the system was the *gamut*, or scale, which from the thirteenth century on extended from our low G (called "gamma ut"—hence the contraction "gamut") to *e''* (Ex. 3-2):

3. *Compendium musices* (1552); excerpted after Berger, *Musica Ficta*, 2.

EXAMPLE 3-2. The gamut (or scale).

What the gamut did was define the diatonic scale and, with the aid of the solmization system, locate the relative placement of whole steps and half steps along the way. All notes that fell within the gamut were said to be *musica recta* (right, or real) notes, while those outside belonged to the realm of *musica ficta* ("fictitious" music).

Solmization and Hexachords

In his *Epistola de ignoto cantu* (c. 1028–29), the theorist Guido d'Arezzo (c. 991–after 1033) noted that young singers learned melodies more quickly with a series of six syllables that helped them locate the relative position of the pitches. The syllables—*ut, re, mi, fa, sol,* and *la*—were derived from the initial syllables of the first six lines of the hymn *Ut queant laxis* and corresponded to the pitches *c, d, e, f, g,* and *a* (Ex. 3-3):

EXAMPLE 3-3. *Ut queant laxis.* [4]

UT que-ant la - xis   RE-so-na-re fi-bris   MI   -   ra ge-sto - rum   FA-mu-li tu-o - rum,

SOL   -   ve— pol-lu-ti   LA-bi-i re - a-tum,   San - cte— Jo-an-nes.

Four centuries later, what the typical choirboy learned was this: the gamut was made up of a series of seven interlocking *hexachords,* each consisting of a six-note ascending scale that was solmized with the "Guidonian" syllables (Ex. 3-4):

EXAMPLE 3-4. Gamut, hexachords, and solmization syllables.

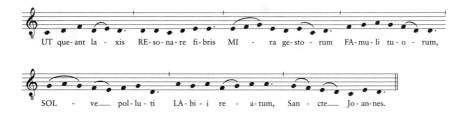

1. hard -	*ut*	*re*	*mi*	*fa*	*sol*	*la*				
2. natural - - - - -	*ut*	*re*	*mi*	*fa*	*sol*	*la*			
3. soft - - - - - - - - - - -	*ut*	*re*	*mi*	*fa*	*sol*	*la*		
4. hard - - - - - - - - - - - - -	*ut*	*re*	*mi fa*	*sol*	*la*		
5. natural - - - - - - - - - - - - - - - - - -	*ut*	*re mi*	*fa*	*sol*	*la*	
6. soft -	*ut*	*re mi*	*fa*	*sol*	*la*
7. hard -	*ut*	*re*	*mi fa*	*sol la*

Hexachords, then, could be built on G, c, f, g, c', f', and g'. Those on G were called *durum* (hard), after their natural (♮, the ancestor of our natural and sharp signs); hexachords on F were called *moll* (soft), after their "soft" B-flat (♭); and those on C were said to be *naturalis* (natural). The solmization syllables remained the same from one hexachord to another. Their main purpose was to locate the relative position of the whole steps and half step; the half step in each hexachord always came between the syllables *mi* and *fa*.

As a mnemonic device, the entire interrelated system of gamut, hexachords, and solmization syllables was often depicted on a diagram of a hand (see Fig. 3-2). We can imagine the following virtuoso demonstration: the choirmaster starts on low G by pointing to the tip of the thumb, then goes up the scale by spiraling down the thumb, across the top of the palm, up the little finger, across the finger tips, two joints down on the index finger, across again, up one joint on the ring finger, and over to the same joint on the middle finger; then, turning the hand around and pointing to the nail on the middle finger, the choirmaster elicits a clear *e" (la)* from the singers. Bravo!

One problem inherent in Guido's solmization system was its six-step limit. What happened if a melody exceeded the six notes of any *ut*-through-*la* hexachord? In that case, the singer had to "mutate," that is, switch from one hexachord to another. A simple illustration of the way this was done appears

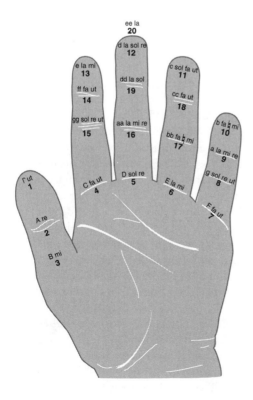

Figure 3-2. Guidonian hand, numbers added.

in Georg Rhau's *Enchiridion*, a manual for choirboys published in 1518 (Ex. 3-5):

EXAMPLE 3-5. Georg Rhau, *Enchiridion*, an example of mutation.

According to Rhau's instructions, the singer begins in the natural hexachord, mutates through the hard and soft hexachords, and then returns to the natural, with "pivot" syllables being used at the points of mutation.

Three final points: first, the solmization system was purely pedagogical. As Franchinus Gafurius put it in his *Practica musicae* of 1496, solmization syllables were "almost mandatory for the instruction of youth"; they were, however, to be abandoned as soon as the singers could proceed without them. Second, when a piece called for notes that were not accounted for on the hand, the singer either "transposed" the hexachords flatward, thus extending the range of *musica recta*, or entered into the realm of *musica ficta*. And third, instructors taught mainly, if not entirely, by oral presentation; the choirboys learned by rote, repeating things *ad infinitum* and committing what they had learned to memory. The process by which writing and books supplanted oral transmission during our two-hundred-year period was a slow one.

JOHANNES CICONIA

If, in the first decade of the fifteenth century, a knowledgeable musician had been asked to name the most talented composer alive, the answer would probably have been Magister Johannes Ciconia de Leodio. Until recently, Ciconia was thought to have been born in Liège around 1335. We now know better, as his biography has been fundamentally revised, demonstrating in a spectacular way how the study of Renaissance music is a dynamic and exciting process.

Two documents have played a crucial role in the revision of Ciconia's biography. The first is a notice from the church of Saint-Jean l'Evangeliste at Liège in 1385 that refers to both a choirboy and a canon (and thus an adult) with the name "Johannes Ciconia." The second, dated 1405 at Padua, refers to the composer Johannes Ciconia as the "son of the deceased Johannes of Liège." From these documents, we learn that there must have been two people named Johannes Ciconia, father and son. And it must be the choirboy of 1385 who was the composer and who could therefore hardly have been born before the 1370s; all earlier notices about Johannes Ciconia refer to the father, himself a well-placed ecclesiastic.

Just when Ciconia left Liège is not known, but he was in Rome and Milan in the 1390s. Shortly after the turn of the fifteenth century, Ciconia moved to Padua, where he became a cantor at the cathedral and developed a close association with Francesco Zabarella, a leading jurist of the period and a major force behind the Council of Constance. That Ciconia spent his mature years in Italy is significant, as his sojourn marks the beginning of a migratory wave of leading composers of the Low Countries to Italy that went on for nearly two centuries. Ciconia died in Padua in 1412.

French and Italian Secular Music

Just as Ciconia's biography has been revised, so too has the traditional assessment of his music, which held that Ciconia single-handedly developed a new style by blending together elements of fourteenth-century French and Italian music. To be sure, Ciconia could write in both styles. His virelai *Sus une fontayne*, for example, shows all the rhythmic complexities of the *Ars subtilior* (Ex. 3-6). At the same time, Ciconia had full command of the lyrical, often virtuoso-like Italian trecento (fourteenth-century) style, as his madrigal *Una panthera* (the panther was the heraldic beast and mythical founder of Lucca) demonstrates (Ex. 3-7).

More than any other composer of the time, Ciconia possessed full mastery of both national styles of secular music.

EXAMPLE 3-6. Ciconia, *Sus une fontayne*, mm. 1–7.

EXAMPLE 3-7. Ciconia, *Una panthera*, mm. 1–16.

An Isorhythmic Motet

Ciconia's most impressive compositions are his large-scale motets. One of the finest is *Ut te per omnes/Ingens alumnus Padue*, the texts of which praise Francesco Zabarella (Ciconia's patron) and St. Francis (Zabarella's patron saint), the play on names being no accident (*Anthology* 8).

The motet is pan-isorhythmic; that is, it is isorhythmic in all voices, like Dunstable's *Veni sancte spiritus/Veni creator*. But how different Ciconia's conception of isorhythm is from Dunstable's: here the rhythm of measures 57–110 simply repeats that of measures 1–54. Nowhere is there any play of nonsynchronized talea and color or progressive diminution in successive taleae. Moreover, the motet is freely composed from top to bottom; there is no preexistent cantus firmus in the tenor (lowest voice), as there was in Dunstable's work. And Ciconia's upper voices constitute a real duet between equal partners that share the same range and employ imitation and outright echo effects. The echoes are particularly effective at measures 20–26, with their statements of the various declensions of the name "Francis."

The old assessment of Ciconia credited him with blending together the French and Italian styles in a work such as this one: the genre (motet) and isorhythm were supposedly French, while the tunefulness, melodic and harmonic expansiveness, tonal logic, bouncy rhythms, and echo-like imitation were Italian. But there was a tradition of motet composition in northern Italy itself. And with its duet-like upper voices over a freely composed tenor, almost simplistic use of isorhythm, and other style characteristics mentioned above, Ciconia's motet fits squarely into this north Italian tradition.

It was not, then, so much that Ciconia blended together the styles from the two sides of the Alps as that the composer himself became Italianized. To put it somewhat broadly, we see here a phenomenon that would be repeated frequently during the fifteenth and sixteenth centuries: the meeting of Franco-Flemish contrapuntal technique with the humanist spirit of Italy. What Ciconia's personal genius contributed was a sense of real musical drama, something that no other composer of the period could match until the young Du Fay, also working in Italy, came along in the 1420s.

Music Against the Schism

Though it may be an unfair ploy, we can gain an appreciation of Ciconia's fertile imagination by comparing a small but telling touch in one of his Gloria settings with one by a native Italian contemporary, Antonius *dictus* Zacharias de Teramo. With their play on the word "pax" (peace) in the opening "Et in terra pax," both settings have been associated with pleas for reconciliation in connection with the papal schism (Ex. 3-8):

EXAMPLE 3-8. (a) Ciconia, Gloria No. 1, mm. 1–7; (b) Antonius *dictus* Zacharias de Teramo, Gloria "Anglicana," mm. 1–7.

Ciconia dramatizes the plea for peace by shooting "pax" through all three voices twice in an arpeggiated sequence; Antonius, on the other hand, while employing the same echo effect, flattens the whole thing out by reiterating the same *f* three times in the same register.

The two pieces also call attention to the propagandistic role that music might have played in helping to end the papal schism. We may well ask, who heard these musical pleas to end the schism, and what effect did the pleas have? No doubt Francesco Zabarella heard Ciconia's. But Zabarella belonged to the cultural elite and was already committed to the cause of reconciliation. Was Ciconia merely preaching to the converted? Or could this music have seeped down more deeply through the social strata? Further, were there any "popular" songs that carried the reconciliation message to a wider audience? Apparently there were, for in 1395 the Parisian police issued the following edict: "It is forbidden to all singing minstrels and song-makers to compose, say, or sing, whether here or elsewhere, any musical ditties that make mention of the pope, the king, or the lords of France, with reference to the fact of the unity of the Church."[5] Indeed, the late fourteenth and early fifteenth centuries may well have had their own "We shall overcome"!

O rosa bella: Ciconia and Dunstable/Bedyngham

No discussion of Ciconia can skip over what may be his most astonishing work, his setting of a modest little poem, *O rosa bella (Anthology* 9). The poem, a *ballata* that is often attributed to the Venetian statesman and poet Leonardo Giustinian (1387/88–1446), reads as follows:

	Poetry	Music
O rosa bella, o dolçe anima mia, non mi lassar morire, in cortesia.	*ripresa*	**A**
Ay, lassa me dolente! deço finire per ben servire e lealmente amare.	*piedi*	**b**
Socorimi ormay del mio languire, cor del cor mio, non mi lassar penare.		**b**
Oy, idio d'amore, che pena è questa amare! Vide che io mor' tuto hora per questa iudea.	*volta*	**a**
O rosa bella, o dolçe anima mia, non mi lassar morire, in cortesia.	*ripresa*	**A**

(O beautiful rose, o my sweet soul,
don't let me die, for the sake of kindness.

Alas, must I end sorrowfully
because I served well and loved loyally?

Help me now in my pining,
heart of my heart, don't let me suffer.

O god of love, how painful is this love!
See that I die every hour because of this thought.

O beautiful rose, o my sweet soul,
don't let me die, for the sake of kindness.)

5. Quoted after Strohm, *The Rise of European Music*, 20.

(Capital letters in the "Music" column indicate that both music and text are repeated; lower-case letters represent a return of the music, but with new verses.) The musical-poetic form of the ballata is **A b b a A**; that is, (1) the *ripresa* (refrain) is sung to the **A** section, which ends with a strong sense of tonal closure; (2) the *piedi* (feet), which introduce new rhymes, are then sung to **b b**, where there may or may not be first and second endings, as there are in Ciconia's setting; (3) the *volta* (turn), so called because its final rhyme "turns" back to one in the *ripresa* (though here, "iudea" stretches things a bit), is sung to the same music as the *ripresa* (**a**); and (4) the *ripresa* text is repeated with its original music and brings the piece to an end.

What is remarkable about Ciconia's setting is the pure passion of the rhetorical declamation. This is particularly evident at the words "non mi lassar morire" (don't let me die) / "Vide che io mor' tuto hora" (See that I die every hour; mm. 19–24) in the *ripresa* and *volta*, respectively, and at "Ay, lassa me" (Alas, must I end) / "Socorimi" (Help me; mm. 44–49) in the *piedi*. Ciconia's sense of drama is most apparent at the latter spot, as the insistent lover (represented by the cantus, or top voice) can seemingly control himself no longer and keeps closing the time interval of the cantus-tenor imitation (eventually abolishing it altogether) while slowly building to the high, climactic c''. In fact, *O rosa bella* anticipates not only the humanist aesthetic of the late-sixteenth-century madrigal—that music must above all else express the meaning and emotion of the text—but when performed by a solo voice and instrument, the even more word-oriented outlook of the monodists and early Baroque opera.

Ciconia was not the only composer to set *O rosa bella*. Indeed, the most well-known treatment of the poem—during the fifteenth century as well as today—has conflicting attributions to both Dunstable and John Bedyngham (*Anthology* 10). This setting served as the basis for numerous arrangements, instrumental as well as vocal, sacred as well as secular, by composers both great and barely known. It was one of the great hits of the fifteenth century. The stylistic differences between this setting and Ciconia's are obvious. Whereas Ciconia uses imitation between cantus and tenor as an expressive device, the Dunstable/Bedyngham setting uses it structurally, thus betraying its later date and pointing to Bedyngham as the more likely composer. Most striking, though, the composer either misunderstood or purposely circumvented the structure of the ballata: the opening section, which sets the *ripresa* and the *volta* and with which the piece should end, cadences on the "dominant." To perform the piece as a ballata, then—at least to perform it as written—leaves us hanging in midair tonally, and we must probably settle for a rendition that follows either an **a a b b** scheme or a strophic **a b a b**.

THE SIGNIFICANCE OF THE LOW COUNTRIES

When the new central tradition developed in the Low Countries around 1400, it rooted itself firmly. Until the 1520s, it defined the international-cosmopolitan style of polyphonic art music; nearly all composers of importance hailed from its spawning grounds, with both composers and compositions quickly fanning out in all directions.

Even in the decades that followed, when other styles and aesthetic points of view also came to the fore, the contrapuntal style of the Low Countries was still thought of as the "classical" style, and with some modifications, still formed the basis of Palestrina's style in the later 1500s. In the end, the polyphonic art music of the fifteenth and sixteenth centuries—whether sacred or secular or in between—must be regarded as very much a northern art, best designated by the term "Franco-Flemish."

BIBLIOGRAPHICAL NOTE

Editions of the Music

Five large-scale editions present the relevant repertories: Willi Apel, *French Secular Compositions of the Fourteenth Century*, 3 vols., *CMM* 53 (1970–72); Gilbert Reaney, *Early Fifteenth-Century Music*, 7 vols., *CMM* 11 (1955–83); Gordon K. Greene, *French Secular Music*, 5 vols., *PMFC* 18–22 (1981–89); Kurt von Fischer and F. Alberto Gallo, *Italian Sacred Music*, *PMFC* 12 (1976) and *Italian Sacred and Ceremonial Music*, *PMFC* 13 (1987). Ciconia's music is edited in *The Works of Johannes Ciconia*, *PMFC* 24, ed. Margaret Bent and Anne Hallmark (Monaco: L'Oiseau-lyre, 1985).

General Studies

At present, the best survey of music in France and the Low Countries from the 1380s to the 1420s appears in the relevant chapters in the brilliant study by Reinhard Strohm, *The Rise of European Music, 1380–1500* (Cambridge: Cambridge University Press, 1993). See also Richard Hoppin, *Medieval Music* (New York: Norton, 1978), 470–501.

Burgundy

Craig Wright's *Music at the Court of Burgundy, 1364–1419: A Documentary History*, Musicological Studies 28 (Henryville, Penn.: Institute of Mediaeval Music, 1979), a fine survey of music at the courts of Philip the Bold and John the Fearless, the first two dukes of Burgundy, is particularly rich in historical-political background.

Johannes Ciconia

The starting point is the complete edition by Bent and Hallmark, *The Works of Johannes Ciconia*, which contains a summary of most of the recent developments in Ciconia biography. The following should be added to the studies cited there: Giuliano Di Bacco and John Nádas, "Verso uno 'stile internazionale' della musica nelle cappelle papali cardinalizie durante il Grande Schisma (1378–1417): Il caso di Johannes Ciconia da Liège," in *Collectanea*, vol 1: *Capellae apostolicae sixtinaeque collectanea acta monumenta* 3 (Rome: Biblioteca Apostolica Vaticana, 1994), 7–74. The biographical revision was begun by David Fallows in "Ciconia padre e figlio," *RIM* 11 (1976): 172–77. See also Hallmark, "Some Evidence for French Influence in Northern Italy, c. 1400," in *Studies in the Performance of Late Mediaeval Music*, ed. Stanley Boorman (Cambridge: Cambridge University Press, 1983), 193–225. Ciconia was also active as a theorist; his two treatises are edited and translated in Oliver B. Ellsworth, *Johannes Ciconia: Nova musica and De proportionibus*, Greek and Latin Music Theory 9 (Lincoln: University of Nebraska Press, 1993).

Gamut, Hexachord, Solmization

There is a concise introduction to the subject in Sarah Mead, "Aspects of Renaissance Theory," in *A Performer's Guide to Renaissance Music*, Performer's Guides to Early Music 2, ed. Jeffery T. Kite-Powell (New York: Schirmer, 1994), 289–96. For a more extended discussion, see Karol Berger, *Musica Ficta: Theories of Accidental Inflections in Vocal Polyphony from Marchetto da Padova to Gioseffo Zarlino* (Cambridge: Cambridge University Press, 1987). See also Carl Parrish, "A Renaissance Music Manual for Choirboys," in *Aspects of Medieval and Renaissance Music: A Birthday Offering to Gustave Reese*, ed. Jan LaRue (New York: Norton, 1966), 649–64.

Also Cited

Peter Lefferts, "*Subtilitas* in the Tonal Language of 'Fumeux fume,'" *EM* 16 (1988): 176–83.

CHAPTER 4

Editing a Chanson: The Notation

There is no better way to study the music of the fifteenth and sixteenth centuries than to approach it the way musicians who created and performed it did: through its own notation. And so that our study of notation does not become an abstract exercise, we will use it as the starting point of a larger project: an edition of a rondeau by Antoine Busnoys, *A vous sans autre*. Our work will be split up into four parts: we begin by learning to read and transcribe white *mensural* notation (white because the larger note values are void, mensural be-cause the notation is "measured") in the form it took from about the 1430s on; after transcribing the piece, we wrestle with some troublesome issues of *musica ficta*; then we tackle the equally knotty problem of *text underlay*, fitting together the words and the music; and after transcribing the piece as it appears in one individual manuscript, we collate this version with those in other sources, evaluate any variants, and draw up a "Critical Report."

Mid–fifteenth-century chansons were, as a rule, written for three voices, each with its own range: cantus (or superius), tenor, and contratenor. In this respect, *A vous sans autre* is somewhat unusual, in that all three of its voices lie in the same high range. Yet it is a good piece on which to cut our editorial teeth: not only is the notation relatively unproblematical, but the song appears in only two easy-to-read manuscripts, which transmit the piece with rather similar readings. The poem is likewise unproblematical; it also contains an interesting acrostic, and stands as a wonderful expression of a woman's voice. And finally, the chanson is beautiful and fairly easy to perform.

As we look at the manuscripts, it will be helpful to know something about the foliation system. *Foliation*, as opposed to pagination, means that only the *folios* (or leaves, each comprising both front and back) are numbered. Thus the first page of a manuscript, which is always a right-hand page, is the *recto*, right side, of folio 1, usually designated fol. 1^r (occasionally just 1). On the back of folio 1^r is its *verso*, or back, designated fol. 1^v. The following right-hand page is fol. 2^r, and so on. Folios usually come in pairs, on a single sheet folded in the center to make up a *bifolium* (containing a total of four pages). Two or more *bifolia* folded up as a single group make up a *gathering*. A manuscript consists of many gatherings sewn together.

DIJON 517 AND THE MELLON CHANSONNIER

A vous sans autre reaches us in two manuscripts: Dijon 517, fols. xviii^v–xix^r (in modern foliation, 21^v–22^r), probably compiled in the Loire Valley during the 1460s, and the so-called Mellon Chansonnier, fols. 55^v–56,^{r} written at the

Aragonese court of Naples no later than the mid-1470s.[1] Figures 4–1 and 4–2 reproduce the folios of the Dijon and Mellon manuscripts on which the piece appears. There are a number of features to note about these manuscripts before turning to details of the notation itself.

Choirbook Format

The first thing to catch our eye is the layout of the music. The three voice parts are arrayed separately across the "opening" (two facing folios), in what is called choirbook format. In Dijon 517, the superius, the highest voice, stands alone on fol. 21^v, with the first part of the poem written between the staves, directly beneath the music with which it goes, while the remainder of the poem appears on empty staves at the bottom of the folio. The tenor and contratenor, meanwhile, appear one above the other (the tenor on top) on the facing fol. 22^r, each voice supplied only with a text *incipit* (beginning). There is, then, no full score. And indeed, the sixteenth century would see still another format gain popularity, one even further removed from the idea of a score: partbooks, in which the voice parts no longer even appear on facing folios but are written (or printed) in completely separate volumes.

The Attribution

We can see that Dijon 517 attributes the piece to Busnoys, as the composer's name appears in the usual position: above the superius. Mellon, on the other hand, transmits the work without an attribution. Thus were Mellon the only extant source for the work, *A vous sans autre* would be one of countless anonymous compositions. At best, a sharp-eared Busnoys expert might assign the work to him on stylistic grounds, though that is always risky business.

Why did Mellon fail to include Busnoys's name? Was it an oversight on the part of the scribe, or was the name already missing on the exemplar from which the scribe was copying? Certainly, Mellon contains other pieces that it ascribes to Busnoys, and one would think that Johannes Tinctoris, one of the most knowledgeable musicians of the period and under whose supervision the manuscript was written, would have known that the chanson was by Busnoys. It is a question fraught with difficulties, with no simple answer.

Artwork

Just as striking as anything having to do with the music is the artwork in both manuscripts. In Dijon 517, the capital initials "A" and the humorously grotesque faces that grow out of them are of the black-and-white, pen-and-ink variety. The initials and tendrils in Mellon, on the other hand, dazzle the

---

1. The full designations for these manuscripts are Dijon, Bibliothèque Publique, MS 517, and New Haven, Yale University, Beinicke Library for Rare Books, MS 91. The sobriquet "Mellon Chansonnier" honors Paul Mellon, who donated the manuscript to the Yale University Library. The poem alone (without music) appears in two printed poetry anthologies from the early sixteenth century: *Le Jardin de plaisance et fleur de rethorique* (Paris: Antoine Vérard, c. 1501) and *S'ensuyt le Jardin de plaisance & fleur de rethoricque . . .* (Lyons: Olivier Arnollet, c. 1525).

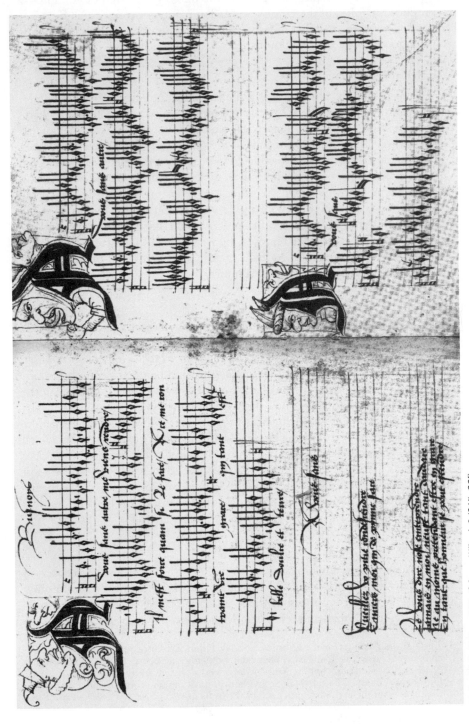

Figure 4-1. Dijon 517, fols. xviii^v–xix^r (21^v–22^r).

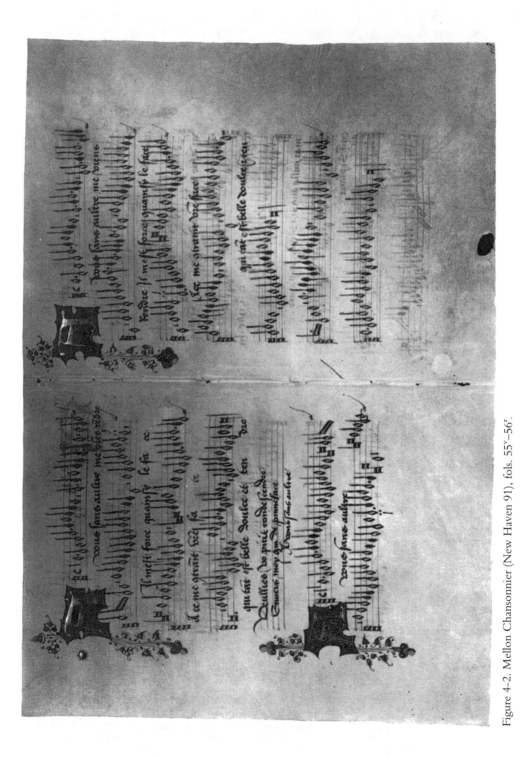

Figure 4–2. Mellon Chansonnier (New Haven 91), fols. 55ᵛ–56ʳ.

eye with their brilliant reds, blues, and golds. Indeed, this artwork was executed at the workshops of Christoforo Majorana and Matteo Felice, two of the busiest manuscript illuminators in late-fifteenth-century Naples.[2] It is easy to see why many music manuscripts of the period are as enticing to art historians as they are to musicologists.

Materials and Size

The folios of both manuscripts are made of high-quality parchment obtained from lamb skins and measure 17.3 × 12.6 centimeters (Dijon 517) and 13.5 × 19.2 centimeters (Mellon)—not much larger than a postcard. And considering their size, the lavish care with which they were produced, the cost that was no doubt incurred, and the scribal errors in the music that were never corrected, it is unlikely that they were actually used for performances. Rather, they served as a collector's repository of a song repertory that was highly appreciated, or a kind of fifteenth-century coffee-table book.

THE NOTATION OF THE MUSIC

We can now proceed to look at the notation in some detail.

Notes and Rests: Modern Equivalents

Table 4-1 shows the range of note shapes and rests that we encounter in the notation of the fifteenth century (*A vous sans autre* contains neither the first nor the last of these):

Table 4-1.   Note shapes and rests.

Quality	Notes	Rests
maxima		
longa		
breve		
semibreve		
minim		
semiminim		
fusa		
semifusa		

2. The opening folios of the manuscript are reproduced in color as the frontispiece in Perkins and Garey, *The Mellon Chansonnier*, vol. 1. The artworks in manuscripts of the period are

What modern values should we assign to fifteenth-century notes and rests? Most present-day editors use either 2:1 or 4:1 reductions depending on the tempo they wish the modern transcription to imply. Table 4-2, which omits the maxima and semifusa, illustrates the choices:

Table 4-2. Fifteenth-century notes and their modern equivalents in (a) 2:1 and (b) 4:1 reductions (rests follow suit).

Original note shape	2:1	4:1
𝆶	𝅝 ⌐ 𝅝	𝅝
𝆵	𝅝	𝅗𝅥
◇	𝅗𝅥	𝅘𝅥
𝅘	𝅘𝅥	𝅘𝅥𝅮
𝅘	𝅘𝅥𝅮	𝅘𝅥𝅯
𝅘	𝅘𝅥𝅯	𝅘𝅥𝅰

Since the contratenor of *A vous sans autre* calls for fusae in the original notation (see the contratenor's middle staff in Dijon 517), which will translate into sixteenth notes in a 2:1 reduction and thirty-seconds in 4:1, we are probably better off with the 2:1 reduction, lest we give the impression of too fast a tempo. Moreover, the 2:1 reduction will give us the rather comfortable relationship of one fifteenth-century breve as the equivalent of one modern measure.

Mensuration Signs: Tempus and Prolation

The most profound difference between fifteenth-century notation and our own is this: in modern notation, each note—unless dotted or otherwise modified, as with a group of three notes under a triplet sign—stands in a 2:1 relationship with the next larger and smaller notes. Thus there are two half notes to a whole note, while the half note is itself equal to two quarter notes. In fifteenth-century notation, the relationships are more complicated. There were four mensuration signs, with the sign for a given piece usually appearing at the head of each voice part (notice the small C at the beginning of each part of *A vous sans autre*). Each mensuration sign informed the singer about two things: the *tempus* and the *prolation* of a piece. The tempus defined the durational relationship between breve and semibreve, either perfect (triple) or imperfect (duple); while the prolation governed the relationship between semibreve and

---

usually referred to as "illuminations" or "miniatures" (the latter term comes from the Latin *minium*, which refers to the red lead with which that color was produced).

minim, either major (triple) or minor (duple). Table 4-3 shows how the system worked:

Table 4-3.   The four mensuration signs and their breve-semibreve and semibreve-minim relationships.

Imperfect tempus/minor prolation

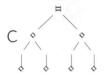

Perfect tempus/minor prolation

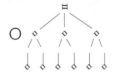

Imperfect tempus/major prolation

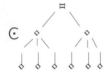

Perfect tempus/major prolation

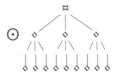

As we can see, the four mensuration signs and the relationships they imply are somewhat similar to—but not precisely the same as—our modern time signatures and meters. Using a reduction in which the fifteenth-century semibreve equals our half note or dotted half note, we may express the approximate relationships between the fifteenth-century mensurations and our time signatures as follows: $C = \frac{4}{4}$, $O = \frac{3}{2}$, $\mathbb{C} = \frac{6}{4}$, $\odot = \frac{9}{4}$.

We should, at the risk of complicating things for a moment (it will not affect our work on *A vous sans autre*), look at one more important concept of mensural notation. Though Table 4-3 shows that in perfect tempus (O or ⊙) the breve was worth three semibreves, not all breves were in fact three times longer than the semibreve. One of the features of the notation was the idea of "imperfection": under certain circumstances, most often if the breve was followed by a single semibreve in a pattern such as ⊟ ◇ ⊟ ◇ ⊟ ◇, the breve was imperfected and lost one-third of its value, that one-third being picked up by the semibreve that followed it. Thus, when performing music in which the tempus was perfect or the prolation major, the singer had always to ask if any given breve or semibreve was perfect (worth three of the next smaller value) or was being imperfected (worth only two of the next value). Though it may sound complicated, the notation has numerous visual signposts built in to it, and with some practice even a piece in perfect tempus/major prolation—where both the breve and the semibreve can be imperfected by notes before and after it—becomes rather routine.

As for the relationships between longa and breve, minim and semiminim, and semiminim and fusa: these are, for our purposes, always duple.

Fortunately, for the novice editor, the mensuration sign at the head of each voice part of *A vous sans autre* is that of imperfect tempus/minor prolation (C), so that all notes stand in a 2:1 relationship to one another, just as they do in our own system of notation.

Ligatures

In addition to the notes that are written separately, shown in Table 4-1, there is a category of note types called *ligatures*, in which two or more notes are written as a single unit. Though ligatures come in a variety of shapes, each with its own mensural value, *A vous sans autre* has but two— and —both of which are ligatures "with opposite propriety": each note of the ligature is the equivalent of the lozenge-shaped semibreve. The presence of ligatures in the original notation is usually indicated in modern transcriptions by placing a bracket above the notes that make up the ligature:

Minor Color

As Table 4-1 shows, breves, semibreves, and minims are void, unfilled notes. Sometimes, though, scribes used a device called *coloration*, which blackens notes that are normally void and generally reduces their value by one-third. When applied to semibreves and minims in imperfect tempus/minor prolation, the coloration results in triplets; when applied to breves in perfect tempus, it causes a two-measure *hemiola* pattern.

In *A vous sans autre*, however, there is a type of coloration called *minor color*, in which a semibreve and the minim that follows it are both blackened (so that the blackened minim looks like the normal semiminim). When this happens (see, for example, in Dijon 517, the last two notes of the first staff of the tenor or the first two notes of the second staff of the contratenor), both semibreve and minim lose some of their value and become the equivalent of a dotted minim followed by a semiminim. And though the blackened minim is now indistinguishable in appearance from the semiminim, the visual context—the blackened minim always follows a blackened semibreve—signals the presence of minor color. Finally, as we can see in the superius near the beginning of the third staff, minor color can also be applied to the second semibreve on a ligature with opposite propriety and the minim that follows it. In the transcription, instances of the minor color are usually shown by placing a broken bracket above the two notes involved:

Dotted Notes

In imperfect tempus / minor prolation, a dotted note has the same meaning that it does in our system of notation: the dot increases the value of the note by one-half. Thus the first note of the superius—a dotted semibreve—would, assuming that we use a 2:1 reduction, be transcribed as a dotted half note. Dotted notes present no problems in *A vous sans autre*.

Clefs

All three voices are notated with a "C" clef on the second line of the staff (our mezzo-soprano clef). Our middle C thus falls on this second line. Indeed, treble clefs were rare before well into the sixteenth century; bass clefs, on the other hand, were rather common.

The *signum congruentiae*

Counting back thirteen characters from the end of the second staff of the superius (include the two notes on the ligature as a single character and count the semibreve rest), we come to a semibreve *e'*, above which there are three dots and a squiggle; in Mellon, there is a similar sign, not only in the superius, but at the analogous places in the other voices as well. This is the *signum congruentiae* (sign of congruence), and it served two purposes: (1) since *A vous sans autre* is a rondeau, it marked the so-called *medial cadence*, the point in both the short strophe and the short refrain from which the singer returned to the beginning of the piece (see Chapter 5); and (2) if, as in Mellon, the *signum* appeared in all voices, it told the performers that all the notes so marked had to be sung at the same time. When we begin to transcribe the music, simply enter the *signum* above its proper note; we will make use of its road-map-like qualities when we begin to underlay the text in Chapter 21.

The "Cut" C

Not far from the end of each voice part in Dijon 517, there is a C with a stroke through it (in the superius, at the very end of the penultimate staff; in the tenor, about halfway through the final staff; in the contratenor, after the second note of the final staff). If we compare the analogous spots in Mellon, we notice that the "cut" C is not present. Advice to beginners: in transcribing *A vous sans autre* after Dijon 517, indicate in the transcription where the sign appears; then *ignore it* until we reach Chapter 30.

TRANSCRIBING THE BUSNOYS CHANSON

We are ready to start transcribing, and we begin with the somewhat arbitrary decision to transcribe *A vous sans autre* after Dijon 517. Let's begin with the superius, taking it no farther than the first semibreve rest on the first staff. This is a natural place to stop, as it coincides with the end of the first line of the poem. More important, though, if we proceed to transcribe the superius from beginning to end, we may either run into an error in the manuscript and not recognize it or commit our own error without being aware of it, in both instances because we have no contrapuntal-harmonic control against which to check our transcription. Even experienced hands will generally transcribe a short section of a voice part (usually the one that appears to have the least complications), make an x at the point at which they stopped, bring the other voices up to about the same point (making more x's), check the contrapuntal-harmonic sense of the passage, and then repeat the procedure until the transcription is done.

Example 4-1 shows the superius up to the point at which we stopped:

EXAMPLE 4-1. Superius, mm. 1–9.

We can now bring the tenor up to the same point, while we might let the contratenor continue past the other voices until it reaches its first rest (Ex. 4-2):

EXAMPLE 4-2. All three voices: superius, mm. 1–9; tenor, mm. 1–8; contratenor, mm. 1–14.

Two final points remain to be made before we continue with the remainder of the piece. First, we will probably feel most comfortable transcribing *A vous sans autre* with modern, regularly recurring bar lines that mark off measures of $\frac{4}{4}$ (the equivalent of a breve), although some editors would disagree. Second, we should use pencil and have plenty of erasers on hand.

Good luck!

BIBLIOGRAPHICAL NOTE

Notation Manuals

Though sadly out-of-date in many respects, and with facsimiles that leave much to be desired, the standard textbook on the notation of the period is still Willi Apel, *The Notation of Polyphonic Music, 900–1600*, 5th ed. (Cambridge: Mediaeval Academy of America, 1953); there is a far better collection of facsimiles on which to practice in Heinrich Besseler and Peter Gülke, *Schriftbild der mehrstimmigen Musik*, Musikgeschichte in Bildern III/5 (Leipzig: VEB Deutscher Verlag, 1973).

Dijon 517 and Mellon

The Dijon manuscript is available in a facsimile edition entitled *Dijon, Bibliothèque Publique, Manuscrit 517*, Publications of Mediaeval Musical Manuscripts 12, ed. Dragan Plamenac (Brooklyn: Institute of Mediaeval Music, n.d.); for Mellon, see Leeman L. Perkins and Howard Garey, *The Mellon Chansonnier*, 2 vols. (New Haven: Yale University Press, 1979), which contains facsimile and modern editions on facing pages in one volume and a detailed study in the other.

PART TWO
THE 1420s TO THE 1460s

INCLUDED: BINCHOIS • DU FAY • FERAGUT • FRANCHOIS •
A. DE LANTINS • H. DE LANTINS • POWER

CHAPTER 5

French Secular Song

When Guillaume Du Fay, Gilles Binchois, and their contemporaries began composing around 1420, they inherited—both from the newly formed central tradition of the Low Countries and from the older *Ars nova*—a rich mix of compositional conventions and audience expectations. And none of these weighed more heavily on them throughout their careers than those associated with French secular, polyphonic song (chanson).

We can see this clearly in the works of Du Fay. For instance, a comparison of Du Fay's early and late motets shows not only the kind of changes in surface style—melody, rhythm, harmony, texture—that we would expect from any composer whose career spanned half a century, but a fundamental redefinition of the genre itself. Simply put, motets of the 1460s were very different kinds of compositions from those of the 1420s. French secular song, in comparison, seemingly stood still. Though the style of Du Fay's chansons certainly changed as the decades rolled by, both the underlying structures and the aesthetic framework of the genre remained basically the same. In large part, this was a result of the tenacity with which the so-called *formes fixes*—rondeau, virelai (and later the *bergerette*), and ballade—maintained their grip on the imagination of both poets and composers. Indeed, for the two centuries from around 1300 to 1500, the three *formes fixes* defined the very shape of French secular song.

THE *FORMES FIXES* I

Over the course of his career, Du Fay cultivated all three forms. Here we will look at his treatment of the ballade and the rondeau (reserving the virelai/bergerette for Chapter 14 and the next generation of composers).

The Ballade: *Resvellies vous*

The most spectacular of Du Fay's ballades, all of which date from relatively early in his career, is *Resvellies vous et faites chiere lye* (*Anthology* 11), which reaches us as an *unicum* (a piece that is unique to a single source) in the important manuscript Oxford 213, compiled in or around Venice during the 1420s–1430s and especially valuable both for the dates that it assigns to pieces and for certain

insights into the relationship between music and text.[1] This chanson was written together with a five-movement Mass for the July 1423 wedding of Carlo
Malatesta and Vittoria Colonna, niece of Pope Martin V, with both bride and
groom being mentioned in the poem. We can best understand the structure of
the ballade and the brilliant way in which Du Fay toys with our expectations
by laying out the poem in its entirety (translations are in *Anthology*):

	Rhyme	*Music*
Resvellies vous et faites chiere lye	a	**a**
Tout amoureux qui gentilesse amés,	b	
Esbates vous, fuyes merancolye,	a	**a′**
De bien servir point ne soyes hodés.	b	
Car au jour d'ui sera li espousés,	b	**b**
Par grant honneur et noble seignourie;	a	
Ce vous convient ung chascum faire feste,	c	
Pour bien grignier la belle compagnye;	a	
Charle gentil, c'on dit de Maleteste.	c	**(C)**
Il a dame belle et bonne choysie,	a	**a**
Dont il sera grandement honnourés;	b	
Car elle vient de tres noble lignie	a	**a′**
Et de barons qui sont mult renommés	b	
Son propre nom est Victoire clamés;	b	**b**
De la colonne vient sa progenie.	a	
C'est bien rayson qu'a vascule requeste	c	
De cette dame mainne bonne vie	a	
Charle gentile, c'on dit de Maleteste.	c	**(C)**

Though the ballade had more than one stanza, Du Fay and other composers
of the time wrote music only for the first, with that music then repeated for
all subsequent stanzas in strophic fashion. All stanzas therefore had the same
number of lines, number of syllables in each line, and rhyme scheme. Within
each stanza, Du Fay's setting proceeds as follows:

a: the opening section, which consists of a couplet with the rhyme scheme
a b, is sung to the point marked with the *signum congruentiae* (.S., m. 15), which,
with its lack of harmonic closure, sets up

a′: a repeat of the opening section, now with the second couplet (which
retains the a b rhyme scheme) and now sung right through to the double bar,
with the codetta-like section after the *signum* serving as a second ending with
closure on the tonic;

b: this section, which may vary in number of lines from one ballade to
another, presents new music and, after the customary start with the b rhyme,
introduces new rhymes along the way;

(C): this final line also appears at the end of the second stanza and so functions
as a refrain.

We can thus hear each stanza of the ballade as a two-part structure—**a a′** | | **b**
(the two **a** sections constituting a single part with repeat)—with a recurring
refrain (**C**) tucked in at the end of the **b** section.

1. Oxford, Bodleian Library, MS Canonici 213.

Du Fay's music both reinforces and, at one point, intentionally undermines the poetic structure. Music and poetry work together at measure 23, where the articulation between the **a** and **b** sections, already marked by a clear-cut cadence, is underscored by a change of mensuration, from imperfect tempus/ major prolation ($^6_8$) to perfect tempus/minor prolation ($^3_4$). Much less clear, on the other hand, is the precise point at which the refrain begins. In the poem, it begins with the words "Charle gentil" (m. 50). But the four measures that set those words—and they are set with such rhetorical flourish that the bridegroom could not possibly have missed the compliment—do not sound like the firm-footed beginning of anything. Rather, with their lack of rhythmic pulse, homophonic texture, and movement to the dominant, the four chords seem to float in a transition-like trance meant only to set us up for what follows. And when the combination of resolution to the tonic, strong driving rhythm, and motivic recollection of the ballade's opening virtually explodes at measure 54 (with the head-spinning *g'*-sharp of m. 3 now straightened out as a *g'*-natural), the effect is not unlike that of a recapitulation in sonata-allegro form, and we hear measure 54 as the beginning of a concluding section. Where, then, does the refrain really begin? We cannot say. The song is a masterstroke of structural ambiguity.

Two other points might be made about the structure of *Resvellies vous*. First, as he customarily did in his ballades, Du Fay closes the refrain with an extended "melodic rhyme"; that is, measures 60–67 quote measures 15–22 and thus confirm the recapitulation-like function of measure 54. Second, lurking beneath the rocket-like, virtuoso roulades and occasional screeching harmonic twists, there is a silent underpinning of a type of number symbolism known as *gematria*. Applied to the Latin alphabet, gematria works as follows: a = 1, b = 2, c = 3, and so on (i and j both equal 9 and u and v 20). Now, *Resvellies vous* runs on for a total of seventy-three breves. Significantly, 73 is the sum of the letters needed to spell out "Colonne"; and it is therefore the gematrical value of the name itself that establishes the durational framework for the piece as a whole. In all, *Resvellies vous* stands as one of the great virtuoso showpieces of Du Fay's early career.

The Rondeau: *Adieu m'amour*

Far more popular than the ballade, which fell out of favor by about 1440, was the rondeau, which accounts for some 80 percent of the total fifteenth-century chanson repertory. As an example of a rondeau, we turn to one of Du Fay's mature works, *Adieu m'amour, adieu ma joye* (*Anthology* 12), and begin once again as the composer would have begun, by reading the poem:

	Poetic section	Rhyme	Music
Adieu m'amour, adieu ma joye,	refrain	a	**A**
Adieu le solas que j'avoye,		a	
Adieu ma leale mastresse.		b	
Le dire adieu tant fort me blesse,		b	**B**
Qu'il me semble que morir doye.		a	

	Poetic section	Rhyme	Music
De desplaisir forment lermoye.	short strophe	a	**a**
Il n'est reconfort que je voye,		a	
Quant vous esloigne, ma princesse.		b	
Adieu m'amour, adieu ma joye,	short refrain	a	**A**
Adieu le solas que j'avoye,		a	
Adieu ma leale mastresse.		b	
Je prie a dieu qu'il me convoye,	long strophe	a	**a**
Et doint que briefment vous revoye,		a	
Mon bien, m'amour et ma deesse.		b	
Car adquis m'est, de ce que laisse,		b	**b**
Qu'apres ma paine joye aroye.		a	
Adieu m'amour, adieu ma joye,	refrain	a	**A**
Adieu le solas que j'avoye,		a	
Adieu ma leale mastresse.		b	
Le dire adieu tant fort me blesse,		b	**B**
Qu'il me semble que morir doye.		a	

Here the pattern of the recurring refrain is more complicated than that of the ballade. (In the "Music" column, **A** and **B** represent the two distinct sections of music; capitals indicate a return of the music with the original text, and lowercase letters a return with new text.) First, Du Fay followed custom and composed only enough music to set the five lines of the initial refrain, splitting it into two distinct sections of three plus two lines (**A** and **B**), with the most definitive internal cadence—called the medial cadence—coming at the end of line three, marked with a *signum congruentiae*. A performance of the complete rondeau would follow this five-step sequence:

A–B: the singers perform the refrain from beginning to end;

a: after completing the refrain, they go back to the beginning and sing the three lines of the short strophe, stopping at the *signum congruentiae*;

A: from the *signum*, they then make another return to the beginning, sing the three lines of the short refrain, and pull up at the *signum*;

a–b: back to the beginning, this time for the long strophe, which is now sung to the music of the refrain in its entirety;

A–B: back to the beginning for one final rendition of the entire refrain.

Thus the form of the rondeau as a whole may be represented as **A B a A a b A B**. Now, *Adieu m'amour* is a rondeau *cinquain*; that is, its refrain is five lines long, with its internal division of three plus two lines defining the scheme of both the short refrain and the strophes. Even more popular, though, was the rondeau *quatrain*, with a refrain of four lines. A typical example is Du Fay's *Par le regard*, the refrain of which reads as follows:

Par le regard de voz beaulx yeulx	By the glance of your beautiful eyes
Et de vo maintieng bel et gent	And [the sight] of your fair and noble demeanor,
A vous, belle, viens humblement	To you, beauty, I come humbly
Moy presenter, vostre amoureux.	To present myself, your suitor.[2]

2. From Perkins and Garey, *The Mellon Chansonnier*, 2:402.

Here the medial cadence divides the refrain into two plus two lines, and both short strophe and short refrain are also two lines each. Similarly, the rhyme scheme is reduced from the a a b b a of the *cinquain* to a b b a. Otherwise the overall form remains the same.

We have looked at *Resvellies vous* and *Adieu m'amour* from one point of view only: musical-poetic structure. But there are other important features of the poetry and music of the French chanson.

ASPECTS OF THE POETRY

Here we consider three aspects of the poems: themes, rhetorical techniques, and voice.

Themes and Sentiments

Though Du Fay and his contemporaries wrote their share of May Day songs and set poems that welcomed in the New Year, the predominant theme in fifteenth-century French secular song was courtly love. Typically, the poet might invoke the pain of unrequited love, separation from the beloved, a plea for the favor of love, promises of faithful love, oaths of undying service to the beloved, and praise for the beloved's beauty and character. Recall the words of *Adieu m'amour*: goodbye to love, joy, and consolation, all of which, as we learn in line 3, are embodied in the loyal mistress, who is both princess and goddess; to part wounds so deeply that it seems to cause death; and only the sight of the beloved again will bring joy. Here, at least, there is a note of optimism at the end. As often as not, however, the melancholy and grief are unrelieved. Indeed, the ideas of grief and pain, supplication, and promises of fidelity are never-ending leitmotifs, and *deuil, douleur, grief, larmes, peine, plourer, mercy, secours, supplier, serviteur, servant*, and *léauté* are catchwords that appear in numbers beyond count.

Rhetorical Techniques

If the subject matter of the poems is somewhat limited, the technical facility with which such poets as Charles d'Orléans, Alain Chartier, and Christine de Pisan expressed their ideas is extremely varied. In *Adieu m'amour*, for example, the lover utters the word "adieu" nine times in lines 1–11, always with the meaning of goodbye. But line 12 then introduces a deft play on the word, for to whom does he now pray for comfort: "a dieu"! Still more subtle is the ambiguity built in to the word "regard" in the opening line of *Par le regard*. Here "le regard," a noun that governs both "beaulx yeulx" (line 1) and "vo maintieng" (line 2), travels in two different directions: in line 1, it is the "glance" that travels from the woman's eyes to the speaker, while in line 2 it is the "sight" that goes from the speaker to the woman. This ambiguity is a conceit thoroughly worthy of the poets known as the *grands rhétoriqueurs*.

Voice

"Voice" refers to the speaker of the poem, the fictive identity behind the first-person "je." And in nearly every instance, it is a man who is speaking, who suffers unrequited love, who must unwillingly separate from the beloved, and who promises undying service to the woman if she will bestow on him the favor of her love.

There is more than a little irony here, for in a period that often treated women as little more than fodder for the convent, the poetry turns social reality—as most knew it—on its head. As the fourteenth-century moralist Fra Paolino of Certaldo put it (addressing men, naturally):

> Woman is a vain and frivolous thing. . . . If you have women in your house, keep an eye on them. Survey the premises often, and while going about your business keep them in a state of apprehension and fear. . . . Women should emulate the Virgin Mary, who did not leave her house to go drinking all over town, ogle handsome men, or listen to a lot of idle talk. No, she stayed home, behind closed doors, in the privacy of her own home, as was only proper.[3]

Yet the female voice does break through; and unlike the male voice, which customarily addresses the beloved directly, the female more often speaks *about* the beloved. We will look at a magnificent example, Binchois's setting of Christine de Pisan's *Dueil angoisseus*, later in the chapter.

DU FAY'S MUSICAL STYLE

We now take up three features of Du Fay's chansons: mensuration and rhythm, texture and cadences, and words and music. But first we would do well to consider at least the opening portion of a third Du Fay song: the autobiographical rondeau *Adieu ces bons vins de Lannoys* (Ex. 5-1), which can stand for the style that bridges the chronological gap between *Resvellies vous* and *Adieu m'amour*.

EXAMPLE 5-1. Du Fay, *Adieu ces bons vins de Lannoys*, mm. 1–18.

3. Quoted after La Roncière, "Tuscan Notables," 285.

Mensuration and Rhythm

For present purposes, we may divide Du Fay's (c. 1398–1474) output into three periods: the conventional early, middle, and late. *Resvellies vous*, which dates from the summer of 1423, is in imperfect tempus/major prolation, and its rhythm may be characterized as hard-driving, with accents that fall on and confirm the strong beats of the measures and without any over-the-bar-line syncopation. This was the mensural-rhythmic style that Du Fay and his contemporaries inherited from their predecessors, and would not last beyond about the mid-1430s.

Though the manuscript Oxford 213 dates *Adieu ces bons vins de Lannoys* from 1426, so that it too is a relatively early work, its mensuration and rhythmic style are harbingers of things to come. The mensuration is now perfect tempus/ minor prolation, and the rhythm has broadened out and "softened" considerably. It is, however, still tied to the bar line, and it too lacks over-the-bar-line syncopation. Finally, *Adieu m'amour*, a work from Du Fay's maturity (from the 1450s?), is in imperfect tempus/minor prolation (with diminution). Here the rhythm has taken on a very different character: it seems to flow with a suppleness and unpredictability that almost makes the bar line irrelevant (as at mm. 16–17, where "Le dire adieu" is, for all intents and purposes, in triple meter).

We can thus see the direction of a broad trend: from the hard-driving, almost motorlike $\frac{6}{8}$ inherited from the fourteenth century, Du Fay moved on to a more gentle $\frac{3}{4}$ and finally, starting probably in the 1440s, to a duple meter in which the surface rhythm is just as apt to conflict with the metrical framework as to conform with it. Moreover, this trend reflects the changes in the mensuration and rhythm of fifteenth-century music as a whole.

Texture and Cadences

To our ears, the texture of *Resvellies vous* is very much treble-dominated. Despite occasional snippets of imitation (mm. 7–8 and 15–18), the melodic action is clearly in the superius, and the two lower voices seem to blend together to form a subsidiary accompaniment.

We may begin to hear a different interrelationship between the voices of *Adieu ces bons vins de Lannoys*. Now superius and tenor seem to form a duet, (granted, most of us would still prefer to hum the superius than the tenor), with the contratenor often taking on the role of "filler": leaping octaves, keeping the motion going when the other voices cadence, and even climbing above the superius in order to complete a triad at measure 11. The superius-tenor duet is even more pronounced in *Adieu m'amour*. Here, all phrases but the first begin with imitation between those two voices, while the **B** section (m. 16) begins with imitation in all three voices. Thus imitation, which seemed almost incidental in *Resvellies vous*, is now being used to articulate the very structure of the work. Another trend that appears undeniable: we seem to hear a progression from a melody-and-accompaniment-like, treble-dominated texture to one in which superius and tenor form a duet of almost equally lyrical partners, to one in which imitation begins to bring about a sense of equality among the voices.

Du Fay and his contemporaries, however, would have considered all three pieces to be governed by the same basic principle: a cantus-tenor duet formed the structural-contrapuntal backbone of the chanson and could stand as a self-sufficient unit without the aid of the contratenor. The permissible intervals between cantus and tenor were the third, fifth, sixth, and octave; the fourth, theoretically a perfect consonance, was treated as a dissonance, as were seconds and sevenths.

Just how deeply ingrained the cantus-tenor duet was in the minds of fifteenth-century composers can be seen from the instructions that the Italian theorist Nicolaus Burtius provides in his *Musices opusculum* (1487) for how to compose a chanson: "Compose first the *cantus*, or soprano, as they say, with due care, then the tenor, amended and checked for any correction, and finally the contrabass [contratenor], composed without making any dissonances with the other two."[4] Moreover, cantus and tenor were completely self-sufficient with respect to the all-important function of forming cadences, which articulate the structure of a work. Example 5-2 illustrates the possible cadential formulas in three-part writing:

EXAMPLE 5-2. Three-part cadential formulas, 1400–50.

---

4. Translated after Miller, *Nicolaus Burtius*, 84–85.

Significantly, it was the contrapuntal movement of cantus and tenor from sixth to octave—not the apparent V–I harmonic motion of the contratenor— that was understood to form the backbone of the cadence. In fact, the V–I movement of the contratenor came about almost by accident. According to fifteenth-century rules of consonance-dissonance and voice leading, the possibilities for the contratenor were limited: in the penultimate sonority, the contratenor could sing a note a third above the tenor (producing a vii⁶ chord, in our terminology) or a fifth below it. And if it opted for the latter, V–I motion was the result.

Du Fay's earliest compositions, many of them written in Italy during the 1420s, make fairly liberal use of imitation, one of the stylistic trademarks of Italian music. There is no finer example than his powerful setting of *Vergene bella*, the first stanza from the prayer to the Virgin Mary that concludes Petrarch's *Canzoniere* (Ex. 5-3):

EXAMPLE 5-3. Du Fay, *Vergene bella*, mm. 1–4, 45–50, 69–74.

Subsequently, imitation plays less of a role in his secular output until it makes a comeback in the late chansons. Even here, though, it is never used in quite the systematic and pervading fashion that we will find in the chansons of Busnoys or the still later composers of the Josquin generation.

One contemporary of Du Fay, however, may be singled out for the lavish use of imitation in his secular music of the 1420s–1430s: Hugo de Lantins of Liège, who, like Du Fay, was active in Italy. Example 5-4 illustrates the beginning of each line of text in Hugo's rondeau *A ma damme*. Perhaps no other Franco-Flemish composer of the time rivaled Hugo in his use of imitation.

EXAMPLE 5-4. Hugo de Lantins, *A ma damme*, mm. 1–11, 14–24.

Music-Word Relationships

It is almost three-quarters of a century since Knud Jeppesen published his extremely influential study-edition of the Franco-Flemish chanson, *Der Kopen-hagener Chansonnier*, and concluded that composers of the Du Fay generation did little in their secular songs to express or illustrate the meaning of the text. Opinion has generally had it that the chanson was a formalistic art, tied to the dictates of the *formes fixes*, and that not until the Josquin generation did composers begin to express the meaning of the text in a manner that was easy for all to hear. This view has only recently begun to break down; scholars have come to recognize that overt madrigalian word painting, which plays so large a role in the sixteenth century and which we cannot easily find in the chansons of Du Fay and his contemporaries, was not the only means of expressing a text. Rather, we must try to approach the poetry in the manner of fifteenth-century composers—to read the poem as they might have read it.

There are, to be sure, some easy-to-hear instances of text expression in Du Fay's chansons. No one can possibly miss the superius's affective leap of a diminished fourth and the subsequent (horizontal) clash of *f*-sharp and *f*-natural at the beginning of the virelai *Helas mon dueil* (Ex. 5-5):

EXAMPLE 5-5. Du Fay, *Helas mon dueil*, mm. 1–4.

And what else do the four sustained chords that scream out "Charle gentil" in *Resvellies vous* (mm. 50–53) do other than express the text? Had Carlo failed to realize what the piece was about until then, those four measures would certainly have clued him in. Yet such moments are few and far between. To understand Du Fay's more subtle means of expression, we will return to *Adieu m'amour* and take the setting of the refrain line by line:

Line 1—Just as there are two parallel poetic phrases ("Adieu m'amour" and "adieu ma joye"), so there are two parallel musical phrases in the superius, the second of which can be understood as an embellishment of the first; further, we should remember that the highest note in the two phrases is *a'*.

Line 2—As the speaker becomes more reflective, recalling the "solace" he has known, the beginning of the musical phrase is less extroverted, largely syllabic: seven successive syllables get seven separate notes. Moreover, this line introduces the first person ("j'avoye"), which Du Fay underscores with a new high note, *b'*-flat.

Line 3—The musical phrase broadens out; a new high note is introduced, *c"*, and the range of the phrase covers an entire octave. All of this intensifies the music as we reach the "leale mastresse," the loyal mistress, the whole point of the first two lines.

Line 4—The poem now speaks about talking ("Le dire adieu"), and the three musical voices literally conduct a dialogue with one another, as Du Fay introduces the first instance of imitation that involves all three parts; further, the line ends with the briefest, least conclusive cadence so far, as if the wound ("blesse") caused by saying farewell were too painful to linger over.

Line 5—The final line echoes line 2 by once again introducing the active first person, and the music follows suit by recalling the syllabic style of that line and even peaking, at least initially, on the same b'-flat.

Now, there are at least three possible objections to this analysis. (1) We may well be analyzing not Du Fay's music-word relationship but the text underlay devised by the editor of the Du Fay edition. Yet we probably *are* analyzing Du Fay, since even if we believe that the composer left the nitty-gritty of which syllable went with which note up to the singer, there were certainly parameters within which any fifteenth-century singer would have stayed, and it is unlikely that any singer would have come up with something radically different from what appears in the Du Fay edition. (2) The analysis accounts for the refrain of the poem only. That, however, is the heart of the poem, and the refrain is in effect a through-composed composition in its own right. (3) Did Dufay really read and react to the poem that way, and is it fair to apply to fifteenth-century music and poetry critical techniques that might not have been practiced in the fifteenth century? The answer to the first part must be that we do not and cannot know. As for the second, while it is always instructive to approach music (or literature or art) of the past from the points of view of the composer (or writer or artist), there is no reason to stop there, to throw overboard the experiences and insights that have accrued over the centuries; to do so merely impoverishes us.

PERFORMANCE PRACTICE

Historians often take their most dogmatic and axe-grinding stands over questions for which there are no simple answers. To a certain extent, this is the situation that faces us when we try to establish how French secular song was performed. Until recently, there was an almost unquestioned assumption that the chansons of Du Fay, Binchois, and their contemporaries (as well as those of the surrounding generations) were examples of "accompanied song"; that is, the top line was sung by a solo voice, while the lower lines were played on instruments. The late 1970s and early 1980s witnessed a fundamental reassessment of this assumption, as a few scholars argued that chansons were customarily sung *a cappella*, one singer to a part, with the voices that had no text in the manuscripts themselves singing the superius's text or "la, la, la"–like vocalizations. This view did not go unchallenged: indeed, it was quickly dubbed the "new secular *a cappella* heresy." What we will do here is look at the evidence we have for performance practices, not to settle the matter one way or another, but to gain an appreciation of the difficulty of interpreting the evidence. There are three main types of evidence: literary descriptions in chronicles and poems; iconographic depictions in paintings, manuscript miniatures, and tapestries; and the music manuscripts themselves.

Literary Descriptions

There are many references to performances in the fifteenth-century romance *Cleriadus et Meliadice*. Two of them read as follows:

Les menestrers . . . commencerent a corner. . . . La feste dura langue piece. Et quant il eubrent assez dansé les menestrers cesserent et se prinrent a chanter.	The minstrels began to play loud wind instruments. . . . The entertainment lasted a long time. And when they [the courtiers] had danced their fill, the minstrels ceased and they [the courtiers] began to sing.
Cleriadus . . . si appella ung de ses escuiers pour tenir tenor a luy et a l'enfant.	Cleriadus . . . called one of his squires to hold the tenor for himself and the child.[5]

From these excerpts, the *a cappella* proponents might argue that (1) the first passage contains a clear distinction between instrumental music and singing; not until the professional minstrels ceased playing their instruments did the courtiers begin to sing; and (2) in the second passage, the reference to the squire who "holds" the tenor should be interpreted to mean that he is singing; moreover, since he joins Cleriadus and the child, the trio is performing a polyphonic song, in which instruments are nowhere mentioned. In both instances, then, a song is rendered in an all-vocal performance.

On the other hand, there are literary descriptions that might point in the other direction. Here are two brief excerpts from the chronicle that describes Philip the Good's Feast of the Pheasant of 1454:

Fut joué . . . d'un leux aveuc deux bonnes voix.	There was played . . . by a lute with two good voices.
Juèrrent les deux menestrelz aveugles . . . de vielles, et aveuc eulx ung leu bien accordé; et chantoit aveuc eulx une damoiselle . . . nommée Pacquette.	The two blind minstrels played . . . with vielles, and with them, a well-tuned lute; and a young lady named Pacquette sang with them.[6]

But while the context makes it clear that we are dealing with secular music, and the singers and instrumentalists are performing together, some proponents of the *a cappella* tradition would take issue: there is no evidence that the songs are polyphonic. And that, in fact, is a major problem: many of the references to combinations of voices and instruments are simply not precise enough about the kind of music being performed. For all we know, Pacquette could have been singing a monophonic "folk" tune, with the instrumentalists simply doubling the singer.

5. Page, "The Performance of Songs," 442–43, 448.

6. Quoted after Marix, *Histoire*, 39–40.

Figure 5-1. *Fountain of Youth*, miniature from a manuscript at the Biblioteca Estense, Modena.

Iconographic Depictions

One of the best-known pieces of iconographic evidence in support of the *a cappella* tradition is the depiction of the *Fountain of Youth* that appears in a northern Italian manuscript of around 1470 (Fig 5-1). There are four different performances, taking place at different times. Slightly to the right and just behind the fountain is a group of three shawm (a double-reed wind instrument) players and a slide trumpeter, members of the so-called *alta cappella* (see Chapter 16); next to them is a minstrel who plays on a three-holed fife, accompanying himself on a tabor (drum); at the bottom of the fountain is a lutenist, whose hand position seems to indicate that he is playing with a plectrum (pick). And finally, behind and to the left of the fountain is a group of three singers, a rolled-out sheet of music in their hands. Moreover, we know what they are singing: the three-part chanson *Mon seul plaisir*, attributed to both Du Fay and

John Bedyngham. And though the music manuscripts of the period usually
transmit the piece with text in the upper voice only, the poem can easily be
sung by all three parts (Ex. 5-6):

EXAMPLE 5-6. Du Fay/Bedyngham, *Mon seul plaisir*, mm. 1–6, with text
underlayed in all three parts.

Somewhat more difficult to interpret is a tapestry of around 1420 from Arras
(Fig. 5-2). For one thing, the large-scale "program" the artist is illustrating in
the set of five tapestries to which this one belongs remains unknown. Moreover,
no one is actually singing in the tapestry (all mouths are closed). Yet the presence of the woman playing her harp and the explicit reference on the music
scroll to another real chanson—*De ce que fol pensé*, by the fourteenth-century
composer Pierre des Molins—may well imply that French secular songs were
sometimes performed with instruments.

Figure 5-2. Tapestry from Arras, c. 1420 (Musée des Arts Decoratifs,
Paris).

The Music Manuscripts

Contrary to what we may think, the actual manuscripts that transmit fifteenth-century French secular songs often raise more questions than they answer. Du Fay's *Adieu m'amour*, for example, reaches us in only two manuscripts,
both of Italian provenance: a Ferrarese manuscript from the middle of the
century and a Neapolitan from around 1480.[7] In the first, the scribe has entered
the poem beneath both superius and tenor, leaving the contratenor with only
an incipit (this is the way the piece is presented in *Anthology* 12); in the later
manuscript, only the superius has the text, though the tenor has an occasional
cue word, which might be taken as an indication that it too was sung (the
contratenor once again has only an incipit).

But can we say, therefore, that in a "correct" performance of *Adieu m'amour*
the superius and tenor were sung, while the contratenor was played on an
instrument or sung without text? Had Du Fay's chanson been included in any
French chansonnier of the 1460s and had the scribe followed the customary
practice, the text would have been in the superius only; could we then decide
that it was the superius only that was sung, while both lower voices were either
left to instruments or relegated to voices without words? One final point: many
Italian manuscripts of the late fifteenth century include no texts at all, while
some French manuscripts from around 1500 include text for each of the voices.

What can we conclude from all this? If we believe that the manuscripts closely
reflect local performance traditions and compositional styles, then it would seem
that *Adieu m'amour* could have been performed differently at different times
and places. If, on the other hand, we believe that these manuscripts were rarely
used for performance, perhaps they fail to reflect performance traditions at all.
In the end, the best approach is one that avoids dogmatic claims in any direction, rids itself of the modern (nineteenth-century) notion that there is one
version and one version only of a piece of music, and gives credit to the creative
resources of fifteenth-century musicians.

On the Use of the Harp

Assuming that instruments did sometimes participate in the performance of
French secular song, which instruments took part? Fifteenth-century court culture distinguished between instruments *haut* (loud) and *bas* (soft), and there can
be little doubt that it was the soft instruments that took part in the intimate
fifteenth-century art song, with the lute and harp being the most popular. Since
the lute will be dealt with in Chapter 25, we will look briefly here at the harp.

In his *Musica instrumentalis deudsch* of 1529, Martin Agricola describes a harp
with a single row of twenty-six gut strings, tuned diatonically from F to c''',
but with the possibility of tuning the B strings as naturals or flats. The harp was

---

7. Porto, Biblioteca Pública Municipal, MS 714; and Montecassino, Biblioteca dell'Abbazia,
   MS 871, respectively.

a "high-class" instrument, often played by the most literate of musicians: composers. We have already seen it in the hands of Binchois (Fig. 1-1); it was responsible for Baude Fresnel's nickname (Chapter 3); and it was the instrument of such composers as Richard de Loqueville (possibly one of Du Fay's teachers) and, later in the century, Hayne van Ghizeghem. The harp was also the instrument of, among others, Carlo Malatesta of Rimini (uncle of the Carlo in Du Fay's *Resvellies vous* and a leading figure at the Council of Constance) and Charles the Bold of Burgundy. In all, the harp was a favorite instrument in performances of French secular song in the early fifteenth century, a position it held until it was gradually supplanted by the lute later in the century.

GILLES DE BINS (*DIT* BINCHOIS)

No discussion of French secular music in the first half of the fifteenth century would be complete without reference to Gilles Binchois (c. 1400–1460; Fig. 5-3). Though he is often mentioned in the same breath with Du Fay, the music of two composers is quite different.

One of the most notable differences between the chansons of Binchois and Du Fay involves their sense of long-range tonal coherence. It is usually possible to predict the final cadence of a Du Fay song based on nothing more than the opening measures; for example, after listening to the first few measures of *Adieu*

Figure 5-3. Jan van Eyck, *Portrait of a Young Man* (Binchois?), 1432 (National Gallery, London).

ces bons vins de Lannoys (Ex. 5-1), we could guess that the song ends on D. We cannot do that quite as confidently with Binchois's chansons. His best-known song, *De plus en plus*, shows why (Ex. 5-7):

EXAMPLE 5-7. Binchois, *De plus en plus*, superius, with tenor and contratenor at cadences.

After cadences on C or G at measures 2, 4, and 8 lead us to think that C will be the eventual goal of the piece, we naturally hear the medial cadence on D as an open-ended one (m. 12); yet it is that same D on which the piece ends. *De plus en plus* is also typical of Binchois's rhythmic style: we always know where the bar line is.

One of the most beautiful of Binchois's chansons is *Dueil angoisseus*, a setting of a ballade by Christine de Pisan (*Anthology* 13). The piece, for which there are three different versions (two for three voices, but with different contratenors, and one for four voices), presents us with a problem we often face when we try to bridge the aesthetic gap of half a millennium. The poem is a powerful lament, written on the death of Christine's husband. Yet despite the tension of the opening hemiola in the superius and the sweep of an ascending tenth in the tenor, the music settles into what might strike us as a too-tame F major (Lydian mode in fifteenth-century terms; see Chapter 7).

Where is the musical rage to match that of the poem? For some of us, it just isn't there. But there is hardly a greater disservice we can do the music of the period (and ourselves) than expect it to drown us in a Mahler-like bath of emotionalism. Philip the Good may have sobbed uncontrollably when he heard the song. In any event, *Dueil angoisseus* has survived five centuries to reach us. We should try to meet it on its own aesthetic terms.

BIBLIOGRAPHICAL NOTE

Editions of the Music

Du Fay's songs appear in the *Opera omnia*, vol. 6, ed. Heinrich Besseler, *CMM* 1 (American Institute of Musicology, 1964), now revised by David Fallows (1994); Binchois's songs appear in *Die Chansons von Gilles Binchois (1400–1460)*, ed. Wolfgang Rehm, Musikalische Denkmäler 2 (Mainz: B. Schott, 1957); a new edition of Binchois's chansons by Dennis Slavin is in preparation. For a selection of chansons by contemporaries of Du Fay and Binchois who hailed from Liège, including Hugo de Lantins, see Charles van den Borren, *Pièces polyphoniques profanes de provenance liègoise (XVᵉ siècle)*, Flores musicales belgicae 1 (Brussels: Editions de la librarie encyclopedique, 1950).

Du Fay's Chansons

The best introduction to Du Fay's chansons, and to his music in general, is David Fallows, *Dufay* (London: J. M. Dent, 1982); see also Fallows's *Songs of Guillaume Dufay*, *MSD* 47 (American Institute of Musicology, 1994), which constitutes the commentary to his revision of vol. 6 of the *Opera omnia*; concerned entirely with matters of chronology, Charles Hamm, *A Chronology of the Works of Guillaume Dufay Based on a Study of Mensural Practice* (Princeton: Princeton University Press, 1964), is a musicological classic. For a detailed study of tonal coherence in the chansons, see Leo Treitler, "Tone System in the Secular Works of Dufay," *JAMS* 18 (1965): 131–69; on music-word relationships (and the analysis of *Adieu m'amour* presented here), there are the pathbreaking essays by Don Randel, "Dufay the Reader," *Studies in the History of Music*, vol. 1: *Music and Language* (New York: Broude Bros., 1983), 38–78, and "Music and Poetry, History and Criticism: Reading the Fifteenth-Century Chanson," in *Essays in Musicology: A Tribute to Alvin Johnson*, ed. Lewis Lockwood and Edward Roesner (Philadelphia: American Musicological Society, 1990), 52–74.

Binchois's Chansons

Walter H. Kemp's *Burgundian Court Song in the Time of Binchois: The Anonymous Chansons of El Escorial, MS V.III.24* (Oxford: Clarendon Press, 1990) is the most comprehensive stylistic discussion of Binchois's secular works; on the balance between poetry and music in the songs, see Dennis Slavin, "Some Distinctive Features of Songs by Binchois: Cadential Voice Leading and the Articulation of Form," *JM* 10 (1992): 342–61; one should keep an eye out for the *Proceedings of the First International Binchois Conference*, ed. Slavin and Andrew Kirkman, which will be published by Oxford University Press and include the papers presented at a conference held at The City University of New York, October 30–November 1, 1995.

The Poetry of French Secular Song

Leeman L. Perkins and Howard Garey's *Mellon Chansonnier* (New Haven: Yale University Press, 1979), vol. 2, contains an excellent survey of the themes, metrics, language, spelling, pronunciation, and structure of the *formes fixes*; see also chapter ix in Howard Mayer Brown, *A Florentine Chansonnier from the Time of Lorenzo the Magnificent: Florence, Biblioteca Nazionale Centrale, MS Banco Rari 229, MRM* 7 (Chicago: University of Chicago Press, 1983). On the woman's voice in particular, see Paula Higgins, "Parisian Nobles, a Scottish Princess, and the Woman's Voice in Late Medieval Song," *EMH* 10 (1991): 145–200, and "The 'Other Minervas': Creative Women at the Court of Margaret of Scotland," in *Rediscovering the Muses: Women's Musical Traditions*, ed. Kimberly Marshall (Boston: Northeastern University Press, 1993), 169–85; see also Brown, "Women Singers and Women's Songs in Fifteenth-Century Italy," in *Women Making Music: The Western Art Tradition, 1150–1950*, ed. Jane Bowers and Judith Tick (Urbana: University of Illinois Press, 1986). For those who can handle the French: Paul Zumthor, *Le masque et la lumière: La poétique des grands rhétoriqueurs* (Paris: Editions du Seuil, 1978). On the social world behind the poetry, see the classic study by Johan Huizinga, *The Waning of the Middle Ages* (New York: Doubleday, 1954; originally published 1919).

Performance Practice

The literature is always stimulating and at times wonderfully argumentative; perhaps the most balanced introduction to the problem is Fallows, "Secular Polyphony in the Fifteenth Century," in *Performance Practice: Music Before 1600*, ed. Howard Mayer Brown and Stanley Sadie (New York: Norton, 1989), 201–21. For arguments in favor of *a cappella* performance: Christopher Page, "Machaut's 'Pupil' Deschamps on the Performance of Music: Voices or Instruments in the 14th-Century Chanson," *EM* 5 (1977): 484–91, "The Performance of Songs in Late Medieval France," *EM* 10 (1982): 441–50, and "The English *a cappella* Heresy," in *Companion to Medieval and Renaissance Music*, ed. Tess Knighton and David Fallows (New York: Schirmer, 1992), 23–29; Slavin, "In Support of 'Heresy': Evidence for the *a cappella* Performance of Early Fifteenth-Century Songs," *EM* 19 (1990): 178–90. For the anti–*a cappella* argument: Brown, review of the 1985 CD entitled *Courtly Songs of the Later Fifteenth Century*, directed by Christopher Page (Hyperion A66194), which appeared in *EM* 15 (1987): 277–79, and, as though he were anticipating the outbreak of the controversy, "Instruments and Voices in the Fifteenth Century Chanson," in *Current Thought in Musicology*, ed. J. W. Grubb (Austin: University of Texas Press, 1978), 89–137. See also Louise Litterick, "Performing Franco-Netherlandish Secular Music," *EM* 8 (1980): 474–85; Craig Wright, "Voices and Instruments in the Art Music of Northern France during the 15th Century: A Conspectus," in *Report of the Twelfth Congress, Berkeley 1977. International Musicological Society*, ed. Daniel Heartz and Bonnie Wade (Kassel: Bärenreiter, 1980), 643–49.

Also Cited

Charles de la Roncière, "Tuscan Notables on the Eve of the Renaissance," in *A History of Private Life*, vol. 2: *Revelations of the Medieval World*, ed. Georges Duby, trans. Arthur Goldhammer (Cambridge, Mass.: Belknap Press, 1988); Jeanne Marix, *Histoire de la musique et des musiciens de la cour de Bourgogne sous la règne de Philippe le Bon (1420–1467)*, Sammlung Musikwissenschaftlicher Abhandlungen 28 (Strasbourg: Heitz, 1939); Clement Miller, trans. and ed., *Nicolaus Burtius: Musices opusculum*, MSD 37 (American Institute of Musicology, 1983).

CHAPTER 6

Intermedio: 1424–1428

THE FIRST HUMANIST SCHOOL

Among the students of Pier Paolo Vergerio at Padua around the turn of the fourteenth century was a young man of more humble origins than most university students of the time: Vittorino da Feltre (1378–1448). Though Vittorino himself never became one of the major humanist scholars of the period, he absorbed Vergerio's innovative ideas about humanist education. As his contemporary biographer, Bartolomeo Platina, put it: "He affirmed an education which rendered a man able, according to the time and the needs, to treat of nature, of morals, of the movements of the stars, of geometry, of harmony and music, of numbering and measuring."[1]

In 1423, Vittorino accepted an invitation from Gianfrancesco Gonzaga, Marquis of Mantua, to serve as tutor to the children of both the marquis and his principal courtiers. Opened the following year, Vittorino's Mantuan school was in effect Europe's first boarding school. Vittorino welcomed the children of other nobles, both Italian and non-Italian, and those from outside court circles altogether, a number of whom lacked the means to pay for their education and were thus recipients of "financial aid." Only one group was excluded from the school, which eventually grew to about seventy students: young women.

As one would expect from a school with a humanist orientation, the core of the curriculum consisted of Latin and Greek grammar and literature, rhetoric and dialectic. But it was broad enough to include mathematics, philosophy, language instruction, and even a rigorous dose of "physical education." Nor was religious practice neglected, for the humanists sought not to negate the precepts of Christianity, but to reconcile them with the study of antiquity.

The curriculum also included music, the study of which was recorded by, among others, the theorist Johannes Legrense de Namur (called Gallicus, c. 1415–1473). Born in France, Gallicus moved to Italy, studied under Vittorino at Mantua, and became one of the teachers there. Gallicus tells us that the starting point for the study of music was Boethius (c. 480–c. 524), the writer most responsible for transmitting the music theory of antiquity to the Middle Ages and beyond. Yet Vittorino held views about music that ran counter to those of such medieval theorists as Guido of Arezzo and Marchettus of Padua, and it is clear that his Mantuan academy was doing anything but blindly con-

---

1. Quoted after Palisca, *Humanism in Italian Renaissance Musical Thought*, 7.

tinuing the traditions of medieval learning; rather, it was considering antiquity from fresh points of view.

Vittorino was himself an amateur musician, and the curriculum seems also to have included practical music making. Platina tells us that he "took on teachers who gave lessons in singing and the lyra to those who showed promise, imitating in this, as in other things, the Greeks. He said that in these ways too, with singing and harmony, their souls were led toward the praiseworthy beauty of virtue."[2] As we will see in later chapters, Vittorino's idea that "modern" music should imitate that of antiquity would have profound implications for the music of the sixteenth century.

LIFE IN FLORENCE

We can catch a glimpse of two aspects of everyday life in the commune of Florence by considering two means of raising money for the commune that were newly established in the 1420s: the Dowry Fund and the *catasto*.

The Dowry Fund

In 1425, Florence was short of funds needed to sustain a war it was fighting with Milan. In order to raise money quickly, the commune established the Monte delle Doti (Dowry Fund), which worked as follows: upon the birth of a daughter, a family would buy "stock" in the daughter's name; this matured at the end of fifteen years (the customary age of marriage) and earned between 4 and 8 percent interest, depending on the economy. With "dowry inflation" running rampant throughout Italy—the Neapolitan nobility, for example, saw the average dowry of 1,200 ducats in the mid-fifteenth century (four times the salary of a university professor) almost double by the beginning of the sixteenth—this was a good, even necessary, investment. But the commune also benefited. First, it was the recipient of the initial investment, a kind of financial quick fix. Even more advantageous, however, was this: if the daughter died before marriage (and death between infancy and the mid-teens was common), entered a convent, or for any other reason did not marry, the commune kept the money. Further, when times were hard, the commune did not always pay the dowry as promised. In the late 1470s, for example, its payments fell approximately a year and a half in arrears, and it sometimes paid only about a quarter of the sum due.

Why was the dowry so important? We can let Alessandra Macinghi Strozzi tell us, as we read a letter she wrote to her son in 1447:

> We have placed our Caterina with the son of Parente di Pier Parenti, who is an upstanding young man, virtuous and a bachelor, rich and 25 years old, with a silk workshop. . . . I am going to give her a dowry of 1,000 florins; that is 500 that she will have from the Fund in May next year, and the other 500 I have to give her in cash . . . when she joins her husband. . . . If I had not taken this step she would not have been married this twelfth-month, for he who takes a wife wants cash. . . . This step has been taken for the best, for

2. Quoted after Prizer, "Musical Learning in Quattrocento Mantua" (forthcoming).

she is 16 and there was no time to be lost marrying her off. We did have the chance of putting her in a better position and with more gentility, but with 1,400 or 1,500 florins.[3]

LIFE IN THE CONVENT   It was indeed to the convent that many a young girl went, often because her family could not afford the dowry needed for a proper marriage. In fifteenth-century Florence, about 12 percent of the female population were nuns, the majority coming from down-and-out branches of aristocratic families.

Life in the convent varied from one place to another. In 1400, Christine de Pisan offered this almost idyllic description of a visit to her daughter at the priory of Saint-Louis de Poissy.

Ainsi partout traçasmes maint pas	We walked everywhere, many steps,
Et par gran cours	through great, broad courts,
Larges, longues plus d'un chenal le cours	longer than a river's course,
Ou grans chantiers de busche furent sours,	where great wooden structures were going up,
Bien pavées et belles a tous tours.	handsomely paved and beautiful from every angle.[4]

For women from the upper socioeconomic classes, life in a well-endowed convent could be luxurious.

For the poor, on the other hand, convent life could be unbearable. As a rebellious, recently liberated ex-nun tells us in a mid-century, southern Italian song, the convent was a prison that even knew outright physical and sexual abuse.

Ora may, que ffora·n ço,	Now that I'm outta there
non vol'essere piu monequa;	I don't wanna be a nun anymore;
que arça li sia la tonequa	let 'em burn the tunic,
a qui se la vesta piu.	those who still wanna wear it.
Soro mia: tu ay cagione;	Sister, you're right;
m'a' ben digcho la vertate:	they told me the truth:
que no·nx' a pejo presone	there's no worse prison
que perder la libertate;	than to lose your freedom;
an porder da quuyli frate	to be with those friars,
si ·nxe stava piu, ero morte;	if I stayed there longer, I'd've died;
veniano tocar la porta;	they come knockin' on the door;
"Abra-me, que frate Petro so."	"Open up, it's Brother Peter."[5]

The Catasto of 1427

In 1427, still short of public revenues for their ongoing war with Milan, the Florentines levied a comprehensive income and real-estate tax: the *catasto*. The

---

3. Quoted after Gage, *Life in Italy at the Time of the Medici*, 29.

4. After Contamine, "Peasant Hearth to Papal Palace," 436.

5. Quoted after Atlas, *Music at the Aragonese Court of Naples*, 220–21.

tax returns (preserved at the Archivio di Stato, Florence) present a detailed demographic record of Florence and its environs. They account for a population of 246,210 people distributed among 59,770 "hearths" (tax units, or households), with the number of people per household averaging 3.91 in the city and 4.74 in the countryside. (Population in the early fifteenth century was actually lower than in the fourteenth, as recovery from the Black Plague of the mid-1300s, which carried off about a third of the population, was slow. Not until the sixteenth century did the population begin to boom again, but then to the point where it threatened levels of subsistence.) More specifically, the households broke down roughly as follows: 54 percent were single conjugal families, 18 percent multiple families, 13 percent people living alone, 10 percent extended conjugal families, and 2 percent unrelated individuals.

Income was taxed at a rate of 7 percent, property at .5 percent of its estimated value; to this was added a poll tax for males between the ages of eighteen and sixty. By the 1480s, a graduated income tax was in place, with the wealthiest citizens paying a little less than one-quarter of their income in taxes. And just how crippling these taxes were becomes evident when we realize that they were assessed two or three times each year and that people had to pay the full tax each time.

TWO ARTISTS

Though it may sometimes seem to us that Italy had a lock on the visual arts in the fifteenth century—and one could argue that no nation ever produced a greater uninterrupted series of artists than did Italy from Giotto through Michelangelo—the north was not without geniuses of its own. The following two artists, one Italian and the other Flemish, represent shining examples.

Masaccio (1401–c. 1428)

When in 1481 the humanist Cristoforo Landini attempted to describe the style of the artists of his century, he had this to say about Tommaso di Ser Giovanni di Mone Cassai, called Masaccio: "Masaccio was a very good imitator of nature, with great and comprehensive *rilievo*. . . . He was certainly as good and skilled in perspective as anyone else at that time."[6] We can see these characteristics of Masaccio's style in two great masterpieces: *The Trinity with the Virgin, St. John, and Donors*, at the Florentine church of Santa Maria Novella (1425), and *The Tribute Money*, from the great cycle of frescoes in the Brancacci Chapel of Santa Maria del Carmine, also in Florence (c. 1427).

Perspective is the illusion of portraying three-dimensional space on a two-dimensional surface. To achieve the illusion—the mathematics of which were being worked out by the architect Brunelleschi (see Chapter 7)—painters often prepared a grid-like schema with parallel vertical and horizontal lines, in which

6. Quoted after Baxandall, *Painting and Experience in Fifteenth-Century Italy*, 118.

Figure 6-1. Masaccio, *The Trinity with the Virgin and St. John, and Donors*, fresco, 1425 (S. Maria Novella, Florence).

all lines that recede from the picture plane converge at a single point, the "vanishing point." In *The Trinity* (Fig. 6-1), in which Masaccio's scratched grid lines are still visible, the progressive narrowing of the rectangles of the coffered ceiling provides the illusion of the vault extending the space in front of the viewer, who sees the fresco from an exceptionally low viewpoint (the vanishing point coincides with Christ's feet).

Figure 6-2. Masaccio, *The Tribute Money*, fresco, c. 1427 (Brancacci Chapel, S. Maria del Carmine, Florence).

In *The Tribute Money* (Fig. 6-2), Masaccio's mastery of *rilievo* (relief) is evident in his use of light, tone, and color (as opposed to the earlier emphasis on sharp outline) to give his figures a sense of massive, solid, sculpture-like weight. Moreover, there is a naturalistic—indeed, almost peasant-like—simplicity about the figures, while the position of the vanishing point behind Christ's head lends the work a sense of formal coherence in which figures and landscape are united as one.

Jan van Eyck (c. 1380–1441)

Foremost among northern artists in the first half of the fifteenth century was Jan van Eyck of Flanders, court painter to Philip the Good. Van Eyck's most stupendous work is undoubtedly his *Ghent Altarpiece* for the church of Saint Bavo, begun by his brother Hubert in 1426 and completed by Jan in 1432 (Fig. 6-3). Standing twelve feet high and eight or sixteen feet wide (with its wings closed or open, respectively), the twenty panels, painted with glazed oils on wood, narrate two different events: *The Annunciation* on the outer panels (seen when the wings are closed), *The Adoration of the Lamb* on the inner panels (seen with the wings open).

One of the most striking effects of van Eyck's work is the alternation between the factual, photo-like realism on the one hand, as in the depiction of the angel playing the organ—which, despite its apparent verisimilitude, could never have existed in the real world—and the visionary on the other, as in the portrayals of Adam and Eve (Fig. 6-4). Indeed, if we compare van Eyck's treatment of Adam and Eve in *The Ghent Altarpiece* with Masaccio's version in another Brancacci fresco, *The Expulsion from Paradise* (Fig. 6-5), we see that whereas van Eyck represents Adam and Eve as symbols of sin, Masaccio speaks to us of real human tragedy. Van Eyck the northerner, Masaccio the Italian: in the late 1420s

Figure 6-3. Jan van Eyck, *The Ghent Altarpiece*, with wings closed (above) and opened (below), 1426–32 (St. Bavo, Ghent).

Figure 6-4. *Ghent Altarpiece*, panels showing Adam and Eve.

Figure 6-5. Masaccio, detail from *The Expulsion from Paradise*, fresco, c. 1427 (Brancacci Chapel, S. Maria del Carmine, Florence).

and early 1430s, the world could look somewhat different from different sides of the Alps.

Yet for all their differences, both Masaccio and van Eyck were observing and representing the world in new ways. A sense of naturalism, enhanced by the development of perspective, was in the air. Viewers could see themselves— that is, their own reality—on the wall or the panel. No longer did God—or the proverbial angels on a pinhead—stand at the center of things: people did.

BIBLIOGRAPHICAL NOTE

Vittorino Da Feltre and Humanist Education

The great work on the impact of humanist thought on music in Italy is Claude V. Palisca, *Humanism in Italian Renaissance Musical Thought* (New Haven: Yale University Press, 1986). On Vergerio and music in particular, see William F. Prizer, "Musical Learning in Quattrocento Mantua," a chapter in his forthcoming *Music in Renaissance Mantua* (Oxford University Press).

Everyday Life

Two studies that treat various aspects of everyday life during this period brilliantly are Philippe Ariès and Georges Duby, eds., *A History of Private Life*, vol. 2: *Revelations of the Medieval World*, trans. Arthur Goldhammer (Cambridge, Mass.: Belknap Press, 1988); and Fernand Braudel, *Civilization and Capitalism, 15th–18th Century*, vol. 1: *The Structures of Everyday Life: The Limits of the Possible*, trans. Sian Reynolds (Berkeley and Los Angeles: University of California Press, 1992; originally published 1979). See also Timothy B. Husband and Jane Hayward, eds., *The Secular Spirit: Life and Art at the End of the Middle Ages* (New York: Dutton, 1975). In the same vein but limited only to Italy: John Gage, *Life in Italy at the Time of the Medici* (New York: Capricorn, 1970); the 1427 Florentine tax records are analyzed in David Herlihy and Christiane Klapisch-Zuber, *The Tuscans and Their Families: A Study of the Florentine Catasto of 1427* (New Haven: Yale University Press, 1985).

Music in Convents

On women making music in convents, see Anne Bagnall Yardley, "'Ful weel she soong the service dyvyne': The Cloistered Musician in the Middle Ages," in *Women Making Music: The Western Art Tradition, 1150–1950*, ed. Jane Bowers and Judith Tick (Urbana: University of Illinois Press, 1986), 15–38; and Craig A. Monson, *Disembodied Voices: Music and Culture in an Early Modern Italian Convent* (Berkeley and Los Angeles: University of California Press, 1995), as well as the essays—particularly those by H. Colin Slim, Patrick Macey, Robert Kendrick, and Monson—in Monson, ed., *The Crannied Wall: Woman, Religion, and the Arts in Early Modern Europe* (Ann Arbor: University of Michigan Press, 1992).

Masaccio

There is a comprehensive discussion in Luciano Berti, *Masaccio* (University Park: Pennsylvania State University Press, 1967); on the Brancacci Chapel, see Mario Salmi, *Masaccio: Cappella Brancacci—Chiesa di S. Maria del Carmine in Firenze* (Milan: Amilcare Pizzi, n.d.), and Andrew Ladis, *The Brancacci Chapel* (New York: Braziller, 1993). Michael Baxandall's *Painting and Experience in Fifteenth-Century Italy: A Primer in the Social History of Pictorial Style*, 2nd ed. (Oxford: Oxford University Press, 1988), is a brilliant study on how to look at fifteenth-century art through fifteenth-century eyes.

Van Eyck

On the Ghent altarpiece, see Valentin Denis's *Jan van Eyck: The Adoration of the Mystic Lamb* (Milan: Arti grafiche Ricordi and Belgian National Commission for UNESCO, 1964), which has wonderful reproductions, including a foldout that simulates the closed and open wings of the altarpiece.

Also Cited

Philippe Contamine, "Peasant Hearth to Papal Palace: The Fourteenth and Fifteenth Centuries," in *A History of Private Life*, vol. 2: *Revelations of the Medieval World*, ed. Georges Duby, trans. Arthur Goldhammer (Cambridge, Mass.: Belknap Press, 1988), 425–505; Allan W. Atlas, *Music at the Aragonese Court of Naples* (Cambridge: Cambridge University Press, 1985).

CHAPTER 7

The Old Motet and the New

DEFINITIONS

Asked to define the term "motet" in a concise and pithy sentence or two, Du Fay and his contemporaries might have been hard-pressed to comply. Even Tinctoris was rather vague in his *Terminorum musicae diffinitorium*, published in 1495 and the most famous of early music dictionaries: "A motet is a composition of moderate length, to which words of any kind are set, but more often those of a sacred nature."[1] We will not be able to do much better; but this difficulty reflects the looseness with which the term was used. The first half of the fifteenth century in particular was a period of transition for the motet, as the relatively clear-cut characteristics that had defined the genre in the fourteenth century gave way to pieces in a number of styles.

Briefly, and acknowledging that the edges will grow ever rougher as we move on chronologically, we may think of the motet as a setting of a Latin text that does not itself have a fixed place in the liturgy (Mass or Office). Thus for most of the fifteenth century, settings of such strictly liturgical texts as hymns and the Magnificat (both part of the Vespers service) as well as introits and sequences (both part of the Mass) may be said to stand outside the motet repertory, as such texts were generally set in a less elaborate style.

We may also distinguish between three stylistic types and two primary social functions. First, there was the legacy from the *Ars nova*: the large-scale isorhythmic motet with its preexistent cantus firmus in the tenor and polytextual verbal fabric. Works of this kind were generally intended for grand ceremonial occasions such as royal weddings, dedications of cathedrals, papal coronations, and signings of peace treaties. And while these motets provide us with some of the most impressive music of the early fifteenth century, they would enjoy their last gasp by the 1440s, after which many of their characteristics were adopted in the even grander cyclic cantus-firmus Masses (see Chapter 9).

A second stylistic type was the so-called cantilena-style motet (the terminology is modern), examples of which we have seen in the *Ave regina caelorum* settings by Power and Du Fay (in Chapter 1). Here the entire scale is smaller and more intimate, a preexistent cantus firmus may or may not be present, and a single text suffices for all voices. In general, there is a sense of lyricism and expressiveness that is lacking in the more formal isorhythmic works. These motets were intended for religious-devotional purposes, and were often sung in services devoted to the Virgin Mary.

Finally, a third type of motet clearly adopted the prevailing treble-dominated,

1. *Dictionary of Musical Terms*, 42–43.

chanson style of the period. Thus a work such as *Francorum nobilitati* (Ex. 7-1) by the French composer Beltrame Feragut (c. 1385–c. 1450) is not very different from Du Fay's *Resvellies vous* in terms of its general stylistic features:

EXAMPLE 7-1. Feragut, *Francorum nobilitati*, mm. 1–11 and 72–82.

Such motets could be sung on both ceremonial and religious-devotional occasions.

Francorum nobilitati raises an interesting question, one that tests our ability to draw conclusions from evidence that is completely circumstantial. Is it possible, even though the text of the motet fails either to mention any names other than the composer's (mm. 78–80) or to provide any explicit extra-musical reference, to determine the occasion for which it was written? When combined with the knowledge that the motet appears in two northern Italian manuscripts and was probably composed there around that time, the text does provide clues. Here is the first part of the motet:

Francorum nobilitati te tua bonitas associavit, princeps, cissuras malorum muniens, scelera puniendo et preveniendo deinceps; custos vere ovilis, cadentisque populi tua industria vigil destruendo malitiam et diabolica confundens, optime pugil.	Prince, your excellence united you to the nobility of the French, guarding against the thrusts of evil, punishing and overcoming the wicked; true guardian of the flock, by your diligence preventing the fall of your people, destroying the wicked and confounding the diabolical, noblest of warriors.[2]

The remainder deals with "divine secrets" that "shine forth like the sun," and the text ends with the composer's hope for the prince's longevity and the wish to enter the prince's service.

Clearly, the VIP to whom the motet is addressed enjoyed a close relationship with the French and, since the composer seeks employment with him, must have maintained an entourage of musicians. And among the northern Italian dynasties, none harped on its French connections with greater enthusiasm than the Este dynasty of Ferrara. In fact, in January 1431, Charles VII of France gave Niccolò d'Este, then the Marquis of Ferrara, the right to quarter the emblem of Ferrara (an eagle) with that of France (three gold lilies on a field of blue). Moreover, the allusion to the sun recalls the sun symbol that is prominently displayed in an illuminated Bible written for Niccolò in the 1430s. Finally, Feragut served off and on at the court of Ferrara from the 1420s to 1438.

Can we therefore conclude that Feragut composed *Francorum nobilitati* for Niccolò d'Este? There is nothing that speaks against such a connection. Could the piece have been written for someone else? Of course. One old hypothesis has it that the motet honors a French churchman who was raised to the nobility. And we must allow for the possibility that Feragut wrote the piece in honor of one person and then reused it for another. It would not have been the only instance of someone being honored with a second-hand motet.

AN ISORHYTHMIC MOTET: DU FAY'S *NUPER ROSARUM FLORES*

Dateline Florence, Feast of the Annunciation, March 25, 1436 (also New Year's Day; see Chapter 8). Attended by his entourage, including the papal

2. After Lockwood, *Music in Renaissance Ferrara*, 34–35.

Figure 7-1. Florence, S. Maria del Fiore (the Duomo).

singers (Du Fay among them), Pope Eugene IV reconsecrated the old Cathedral of Florence, Santa Reperata, and renamed it Santa Maria del Fiore. The occasion marked the culmination of a rebuilding project that had begun almost a century and a half earlier, in the 1290s, and the near completion of Filippo Brunelleschi's (c. 1377–1446) magnificent octagonal dome, one of the landmarks of Western architecture (Fig. 7-1). It was for this occasion that Du Fay composed the grand isorhythmic motet *Nuper rosarum flores (Anthology* 14), certainly one of the most written-about compositions of the fifteenth century.

The Preexistent Cantus Firmus

Du Fay chose an appropriate plainchant as his cantus firmus: *Terribilis est locus iste*, the introit sung at the opening of a Mass celebrating the dedication of a church (Ex. 7-2). The cantus firmus thus serves an obvious emblematic function, one that would certainly have been recognized in 1436.

EXAMPLE 7-2. The opening of the introit *Terribilis est locus iste.*[3]

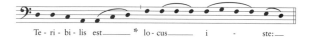

Te - ri - bi - lis est_____ * lo - cus_____ i - ste:__

3. After *Liber usualis*, 1250.

Du Fay's treatment of the cantus firmus in *Nuper rosarum flores* seems to be unique in the motet repertory of the period. Drawing on only the first phrase of the plainchant, Du Fay places the melody in tenor I and tenor II simultaneously—at its original pitch in tenor II (the higher voice), at the fifth below in tenor I. In addition, the two voices present the melody in a free canon: these statements differ rhythmically, and they seem, given their fragmentary, stop-and-start movement, almost to take take turns playing the roles of *dux* (leading voice) and *comes* (imitating voice).

Isorhythmic Structure

Both tenors are isorhythmic, and each presents the cantus firmus four times. Since each statement of the cantus firmus equals one synchronized statement of the talea and color, the motet consists of four taleae (plus a short tag on the word "Amen"). Each of the taleae—they begin at measures 1, 57, 113, and 141—gets under way with twenty-eight breves (fourteen measures) of rest in the tenors, during which the upper voices (here called triplum and motetus) spin out a rhythmically free duet (there is no pan-isorhythm). That over, the tenors present the cantus firmus over the course of another twenty-eight breves (dotted whole notes). Each talea is therefore fifty-six breves long, and each is marked by a sense of inner timbral contrast, as duos alternate with the full four-voice texture.

To this point, there has been nothing exceptional about the isorhythm. What gives the piece its special character, however, is the proportional relationship of one talea to the next. For while the customary practice was to have each successive talea exhibit progressive diminution—as, for instance, we saw in Dunstable's *Veni sancte spiritus/Veni creator* (Chapter 1), where the three pairs of taleae formed a ratio of 3:2:1—the four mensuration signs in *Nuper rosarum flores* produce the proportions 6:4:2:3; that is, $O = 6$, $C = 4$, $\mathbb{C} = 2$, $\oplus = 3$. Example 7-3 lays out the rhythm of the proportional relationships as these occur in tenor II:

EXAMPLE 7-3. The proportional relationships of the taleae in *Nuper rosarum flores*, tenor II, mm. 29–56, 85–112, 127–140, 155–168.

Why did Du Fay turn "backward" in the final talea (which, however, still sounds as though it is moving along faster than any of the others)? The answer lies in the symbolism of the 6:4:2:3 relationship, a point to which we will turn presently.

Isomelic Structure

Although the upper voices are rhythmically unrelated from one talea to the next, they do share some audible melodic relationships. Indeed, the isomelism in *Nuper rosarum flores* surpasses that in any other of Du Fay's works, in terms of both density and sophistication. The melodic interrelationships are most notable at the point in each talea (except the third) at which the two tenors enter; there the strong turn to a G-minor-like feeling, made all the more emphatic by the B-flat–F-sharp diminished fourths and the full triads produced by the "divisi" writing in the motetus, can hardly be missed (Ex. 7-4):

EXAMPLE 7-4. Isomelism in the upper voices of *Nuper rosarum flores*: (a) talea I, mm. 29–33; (b) talea II, mm. 85–89; (c) talea IV, mm. 155–157. The tenors are shown nonrhythmically.

The divisi writing in the motetus is noteworthy. Until the beginning of the fifteenth century, polyphony was primarily a vehicle for solo voices, one singer to a part. Only in the fifteenth century, as the northern choir schools began to

turn out an ever-increasing number of singers who were well versed in the
intricacies of mensural notation and as choirs began to expand in size, did the
idea of polyphony with more than one singer on a part become firmly established. And with its divisi notation in the motetus, we can be sure that Du Fay
intended *Nuper rosarum flores* for a choir of more than one to a part, perhaps,
given the ten singers in the papal chapel at the time, for some combination of
two or three to a part. (Were the tenor parts for voices only, voices with
instrumental doubling, or for instruments alone?)

Just as prominent as the isomelic passages shown in Example 7-4 are the "variations" with which the top voice brings each talea to its conclusion (Ex. 7-5):

EXAMPLE 7-5. Isomelism in the top voice at the conclusion of each talea of
Nuper rosarum flores: (a) talea I, mm. 49–56; (b) talea II, mm. 105–112;
(c) talea III, mm. 137–140; (d) talea IV, mm. 165–68.

And though it may not be apparent to the ear, it is hard to miss the visual
analogy between the contraction-expansion of the variations and the conver-
gence and separation of the ribs that articulate the octagonal form of the dome.
Needless to say, these variations on a theme also add to the tonal coherence of
the work.

Symbolism

If *Nuper rosarum flores* has captured the imagination of scholars and fascinated
audiences, the cause is as much its spectacular display of symbolism as its intrinsic
beauty.

In 1973, the symbolism was interpreted to mean that the isorhythmic proportions 6:4:2:3 realized in sound the proportions of Santa Maria del Fiore
itself: specifically, the proportions of nave (6) to transept (4) to apse (2) to

elevation of the dome (3). Du Fay would, according to this hypothesis, have learned about these proportions from Brunelleschi himself, as they were both in Florence at the time.

We now know that the proportions of the cathedral do not add up to precisely 6:4:2:3, and that the symbolism lies elsewhere. Du Fay, who was well-versed in matters of theology, derived the proportions from a biblical tradition according to which the ratio 6:4:2:3 described the proportions of the Temple of Solomon: the overall length was 60 cubits (a cubit is about 18 inches), the "nave" 40 cubits, the sanctum sanctorum 20 cubits, and the height 30 cubits. Moreover, both temple and its proportions stood as a symbol of every consecrated church in Christendom (in this instance, Santa Maria del Fiore).

But Du Fay's symbolism goes beyond the proportional relationship of 6:4:2:3. For example, we might interpret the composer's use of the canonic cantus firmus, tenor II above tenor I, as a reflection of Brunelleschi's having superimposed his exterior dome over a smaller interior dome, or as a musical-structural allusion to the relationship between Santa Maria del Fiore and the "mother church" of all Marian foundations, Santa Maria Maggiore in Rome. Further, we might understand Du Fay's frequent play on the number seven as a reference to church and Virgin, or as a musical analogue of the thickness (measured in *braccia*, or arm lengths) of the eight ribs that articulate the octagonal dome. Du Fay makes one piece of symbolism absolutely explicit: the reference to Eugene IV as the successor to Christ and Peter (mm. 44–47). Here the word "successor" is set imitatively, so that one voice "succeeds" the other, while the name "Eugenius" is announced with crystal-clear homophony.

This discussion of symbolism has hedged a bit: "might understand," "might interpret," and so on. Apologies are not necessary, though. For in dealing with symbolism of the period, we should not ask, "What does it mean?" but rather, "What can it mean?"[4] In all, *Nuper rosarum flores* is a celebration in sound of the events that took place in Florence on March 25, 1436.

An "Earwitness" Account

What did those who were present that day think of Du Fay's *Nuper rosarum flores* and the rest of the music for the ceremony? Giannozzo Manetti, a well-educated Florentine humanist, gave this account:

> First there was a great line of trumpeters, lutenists, and flutists, each carrying his instrument . . . in his hands, and dressed in red clothing. Meanwhile, everywhere there was singing with so many and such various voices, such harmonies exalted even to the heaven, that truly it was to the listener like angelic and divine melodies; the voices filled the listeners' ears with such a wondrous sweetness that they seemed to become stupefied, almost as men were fabled to become upon hearing the singing of the sirens. . . . And then, when they made their customary pauses in singing, so joyous and sweet was the reverberation that mental stupor, now calmed by the cessation of those sweet symphonies, seemed as if to regather strength from the wonderful sounds.

4. Peck, "Public Dreams and Private Myths," 466.

But at the Elevation of the Most Sacred Host, the whole space of the church was filled with such choruses of harmony and such a concord of divers instruments that it seemed . . . as though the symphonies and songs of the angels and of divine Paradise had been sent forth from the heavens to whisper in our ears an unbelievable celestial sweetness. Wherefore at that moment I was so possessed by ecstasy that I seemed to enjoy the life of the Blessed here on earth; whether it happened so to others present I know not, but concerning myself I can bear witness.[5]

Manetti's account is both fascinating and frustrating. Although he thought the music at the ceremony beautiful and was deeply moved by it, he lacked the technical vocabulary—or chose to avoid it (the former is more likely)—to give us a true musician-like account of what he heard. Yet buried in the hyperbole is a potentially valuable nugget of information: if we hazard that the choruses and instruments that he heard at the Elevation of the Host were those of *Nuper rosarum flores*, Manetti has identified the precise moment in the ceremony at which the motet was performed. Yet even if the music at the Elevation was not Du Fay's motet, Manetti's reference to the combination of choruses and "divers instruments" at that point in the Mass tells us, as we will see, something about contemporary performance practice.

It is worthwhile to compare the account given by Manetti with a wonderful anecdote from late-sixteenth-century Munich. There, the story goes, when the "common people" heard motets of Orlande de Lassus performed in the streets during the annual Corpus Christi procession, the combination of melodies in polyphony made them think that the devil himself had taken possession of the ducal court singers. As Manetti felt obliged to tell us, he was speaking only for himself!

MODE AND POLYPHONY

To this point, we have been free with our use of such modern terminology as "tonal," "tonic," "first-inversion triad," and even "G-minor-like," all of which would have been meaningless to musicians of the fifteenth and sixteenth centuries. But a sense of tonal coherence their music did have (especially Du Fay's), and if asked what governed it, some of them might have explained the phenomenon in terms of the system of church modes.

By the early fifteenth century, Western modal theory was some seven centuries old. Developed as a system for classifying and categorizing the corpus of Gregorian chants according to their melodic characteristics, modal theory was first extended to the analysis of polyphonic music only in the late fifteenth century. Table 7-1 shows the essential features (for our purposes) of the eight church modes.

A few words of explanation: (1) There are four finals—*d, e, f,* and *g*—pitches on which the melody can end. (2) Each final has two modes assigned to it: the *authentic* mode ranges from the final to the octave above; the *plagal* mode ranges from the fourth below the final to the fifth above. (3) The ambitus given for

5. Quoted after Weiss and Taruskin, *Music in the Western World*, 81–82.

Table 7-1. The eight church modes.

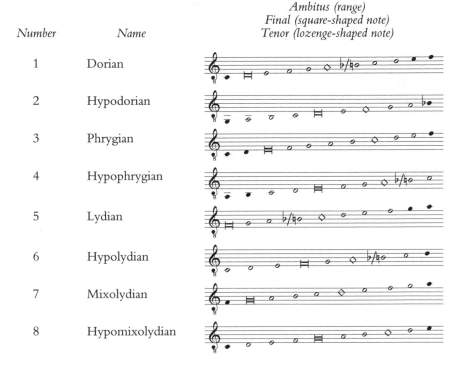

		Ambitus (range)
Number	Name	Final (square-shaped note)
		Tenor (lozenge-shaped note)

1	Dorian
2	Hypodorian
3	Phrygian
4	Hypophrygian
5	Lydian
6	Hypolydian
7	Mixolydian
8	Hypomixolydian

each mode varies in different theoretical accounts; the table gives the widest possible ambitus, with notes that lie outside the modal octave shown as black. And (4) the tenor of each mode is derived from the tenor of the *psalm tone* (a fixed melody to which Psalm verses were sung) for that mode.

To the information in Table 7-1 we must add a few more concepts, beginning with the so-called *species of fifth and fourth*. The species are the conjunct *pentachords* (five pitches) and *tetrachords* (four pitches) that constitute each modal octave. In the authentic modes, the tetrachord is above the pentachord; in plagal modes, it is below. Thus mode 1 consists of the pentachord *d–a* and the tetrachord *a–d'*, while mode 2 is made up of the tetrachord *A–d* and the pentachord *d–a*.

From the way in which a melody fits the species of fifth and fourth that constitute the mode to which it belongs, theorists derived five classes of melodies: (1) "perfect"—a melody that fills its modal octave (combined species of fifth and fourth) exactly; (2) "imperfect"—a melody whose range is narrower than that of its modal octave; (3) "more than perfect"—a melody that goes beyond its modal octave; (4) "mixed"—an authentic melody that descends into the plagal tetrachord below the final, or a plagal melody that extends into the upper tetrachord of the authentic ambitus; and (5) "co-mixed"—a melody that emphasizes a species of fifth or fourth that does not belong to its mode. Finally, melodies that conform to a transposed version of a mode were said to be "irregular."

With the basic theoretical terminology now at hand, we can take up the question of mode as it was applied to polyphony by turning to Tinctoris's *Liber de natura et proprietate tonorum* (1476), the first treatise to address the matter:

> When some Mass or chanson or whatever other composition . . . is made from different parts carried through in different tones [modes], if anyone asks of what tone such a composition may be, he [who is] interrogated ought to reply, for the whole, according to the quality of the tenor [voice], because that is the chief part and the foundation of the whole relationship. And if one be asked in particular, about some part, of what tone it may be in a composition of this sort, he will reply, this [tone] or that. For, if anyone were to say to me, "Tinctoris, I ask you, of what tone is the song "Le Serviteur" [by Du Fay?], I would reply "in general, of an irregular first tone [Dorian on *c*], because the tenor, the principal part of the song, is of such a tone." If however he were to ask in particular, of what tone the superius or contratenor might be, I would reply in particular, [that] the one and the other were of the second tone, also irregular [Hypodorian on *c*].[6]

Example 7-6 shows the beginning and end of *Le serviteur*.

EXAMPLE 7-6. Dufay (?), *Le serviteur*, mm. 1–11 and 27–33.

Now, notwithstanding Tinctoris's mistake in assigning the contratenor to the second mode (its ambitus places it squarely in an authentic mode), his methodology and conclusion are clear enough: the mode of a polyphonic piece as a whole is determined by the mode of the tenor voice, the "principal part of the song," and *Le serviteur* is therefore in the Dorian mode (mode 1) transposed to C, hence irregular.

But Tinctoris's method may not work so neatly with a piece such as *Nuper rosarum flores*, which turns out to be difficult to assign to a mode because the two tenors are in two different modes. Theoretically, a transposed (to G) Hypodorian probably holds sway.

But is that what we hear? Despite the flat in the signature of the motetus, the duet that opens each talea has a distinctly "major" (Mixolydian) quality. In fact, the piece as a whole seems to shift back and forth between Mixolydian (major third) and Dorian (minor third) sonorities on G. Thus to say that *Nuper rosarum flores* is in mode 2 is a bit misleading, and we are faced with the problem of just how relevant the system of church modes is as an analytical tool and how meaningful it was to composers when they sat down to write a piece. There is no simple answer. While the eight-mode system and Tinctoris's methodology seem almost irrelevant to *Nuper rosarum flores*, they are the only way to understand the modally ordered cycles by such sixteenth-century composers as Cipriano de Rore and Palestrina. Likewise, to say that Du Fay's *Adieu m'amour* and Binchois's *Dueil angoisseus* (Chapter 5) are in mode 6 (Hypolydian) provides a perfectly meaningful description of certain tonal aspects of those pieces. We will return to the problem of mode and polyphony in considerably greater detail in Chapter 35.

A "TENOR" MOTET: DU FAY'S *AVE REGINA CAELORUM* (III)

The isorhythmic motet gave its last gasp in the 1440s; around the middle of the century, a new style of motet—sometimes called (today) a "tenor" motet—began to take shape. And while it was no less grand in conception than the isorhythmic motet, it turned away from the formal rigidity of the *Ars nova* toward a greater sense of expressivity.

We hear the new style in Du Fay's third and final setting of the antiphon *Ave regina caelorum* (*Anthology* 15). Copied at the Cathedral of Cambrai in 1464–65 (which thus provides a *terminus ante quem*, "date prior to which," for its composition), this was the motet that Du Fay asked in his will to have sung at his deathbed. As it happened, time did not permit his wish to be carried out, and the motet was sung together with a Requiem Mass on the following day, November 28, 1474. Both the text and the melody of the antiphon are treated with a great deal of freedom: Du Fay inserts personalized *tropes* (added text) to the antiphon and lavishly decorates the melody, which is stated in the tenor.

Ave regina caelorum could cause trouble on a listening exam, as a number of its stylistic characteristics tend to be associated with music written later in the century. First, there is the rhythmic integration of the tenor with the other voices, which, together with the occasional use of imitation—including "anticipatory imitation" (to risk an oxymoron), in which one voice anticipates the tenor's presentation of the cantus firmus—brings us close to the kind of equality among the voices that is characteristic of succeeding generations. Second, the piece contains paired imitation (mm. 45–48), one of the trademarks of the Josquin style. And third, unlike the isorhythmic motet, with its preplanned, mathematically precise edges, *Ave regina caelorum* seems to unfold "naturally": clear-cut cadences, changes in texture and vocal orchestration, and contrasts between complexity/simplicity and tension/relaxation (always carefully geared to the sense of the text and the phrases of the antiphon melody) all work together to articulate the sections of the piece in a way that we comprehend immediately. More than any large-scale work considered thus far, *Ave regina caelorum* is a masterpiece of musical pacing.

Two of the textual tropes and Du Fay's setting of them deserve special mention. Though the music of the fifteenth century, like that of any other period, ranges from the ravishingly beautiful to the painfully boring, we do not generally think of fifteenth-century music as "spine-tingling." Yet it would be difficult to find a more appropriate description for Du Fay's turn to C minor when he asks for mercy with the tropes "Miserere tui labentis Dufay" (Have mercy on your dying Du Fay—mm. 21–29) and, especially, "Miserere, miserere supplicanti Dufay" (Have mercy on your supplicant Du Fay—mm. 86–96). No wonder the composer quoted the second of the tropes in the Agnus Dei of his *Missa Ave regina caelorum*.

From where did this new style of motet writing come? Probably from the very genre, ironically, that replaced the isorhythmic motet around the middle of the century as the composition of choice for grand ceremonial occasions: the big, four-voice, cyclic cantus-firmus Mass. Thus there is a neat stylistic circle, with the isorhythmic motet giving way to but at the same time influencing the cyclic cantus-firmus Mass, which in turn developed alongside and influenced the late-fifteenth-century tenor motet.

Finally, Du Fay's setting of the *Ave regina caelorum* melody calls attention to a common problem. The version that Du Fay used as the cantus firmus must certainly have differed from that in the *Liber usualis* (the most frequently used modern-day chant book—see Chapter 9). This is not unusual. Not only did chant melodies vary from one locale to another, but there could even be differences in the very chants that were associated with a specific feast: thus a singer moving from, say, Antwerp to Cambrai (both of which fell within the diocese of Cambrai) might well have had to learn a whole new set of chants for a given feast. Even some of the feasts themselves might have been unfamiliar, since a saint who was highly venerated in one locale might have been relatively unimportant in another. In all, the study of local liturgies can go a long way in helping us not only to determine the geographical-chronological provenance of polyphonic compositions, but also, as a consequence, to fill in the often sketchy biographies of composers.

DU FAY'S LIFE

Du Fay was the greatest, most prolific, most universal (in terms of the styles and genres he cultivated), and most famous composer of his time. We should therefore consider his life and career, which can be sketched in greater detail than that of any other fifteenth-century composer.

Early Years

Du Fay was born Willem Du Fayt,[7] near Brussels, possibly on August 5, 1397, the illegitimate son of an unknown father and Marie Du Fayt. He received his early education at the Cathedral of Notre Dame de Cambrai, where he was admitted as a choirboy in August 1409. To judge from the highly unusual gift of a *Doctrinale* (a book on grammar, rhetoric, and the *ars versificatoria*) that was presented to him around 1411–12, he must have demonstrated tremendous musical and intellectual potential even in his early teens. The finishing touches on his musical education were probably provided by the composer Richard Locqueville, who came to Cambrai as master of the boys in 1413.

It is likely that Du Fay attended the Council of Constance, as the Cathedral of Cambrai sent a sizable delegation to the council, and Du Fay was absent from the cathedral for a period of time beginning in November 1414. There, if not before, he would have had ample opportunity to hear the new currents in English music. By November 1417, Du Fay was back in Cambrai, at the church of St. Géry, where he is listed as a subdeacon through the Lenten season of 1420.

1420–39

By the summer of 1420, Du Fay seems to have begun serving as a kind of court composer to the Malatesta family, who governed (officially as papal vicars, practically as longtime strongmen) the towns along Italy's Adriatic coast from Rimini through Pesaro to Fano. And it was during his "Malatesta period" of the early 1420s that Du Fay established himself as a composer of international repute. In 1424, Du Fay returned home and took up residence at Laon, a half-day's journey from Cambrai. Though the family crisis involving the welfare of his mother that seems to have precipitated his return came to naught, he remained there until the beginning of 1426, when he once again bid farewell to the area, this time with the autobiographical rondeau *Adieu ces bons vins de Lannoys*.

---

7. He most likely dropped the final "t" when he went to Italy, where it would, mistakenly, have been pronounced.

In the spring of 1427, Du Fay was back in Italy, now at Bologna, in the retinue of the papal legate Cardinal Louis Aleman. And it was probably here, at age thirty, that he was ordained a priest. In October 1428, he became a singer in Martin V's papal chapel, where he remained into the reign of Eugene IV, who succeeded Martin in 1431. The position was both prestigious and potentially lucrative, as papal singers had the opportunity to hold a number of absentee benefices (ecclesiastical offices that brought in revenues; see Chapter 13). In fact, the pursuit of benefices would occupy Du Fay for years, sometimes miring him in extended lawsuits and other legal problems.

Du Fay left the papal chapel in August 1433; six months later, he was appointed choirmaster at the wealthy and powerful court of Savoy, first under Duke Amadeus VIII and then under his son Louis. There, after the seemingly unproductive years at Rome, his creativity once again spilled forth, and he produced his great cycle of hymn settings and his first late-style secular songs. It was also at Savoy that Du Fay, Binchois, and Martin le Franc came together, a meeting that would later be recalled in Le Franc's poem *Le champion des dames*.

By June 1435, Du Fay had begun a second term with the papal chapel, where he remained through May 1437. It was during this stint that he composed *Nuper rosarum flores* and received his much-sought-after benefice at the Cathedral of Cambrai. But with the political climate around Eugene IV becoming ever more unfavorable, Du Fay left the papal chapel and once again found work at Savoy, this time for about two years. What is fascinating about this shuttling from pope to Savoy to pope and back to Savoy is that Du Fay kept moving between two patrons who stood on opposite sides of the political fence. In fact, at the Council of Basle (convened by Eugene IV in 1431 at the behest of those who hoped that the earlier Council of Constance would be followed by periodic General Councils that would reform the church), Du Fay, who attended as part of the delegation from the Cathedral of Cambrai, found himself caught in a three-way political tug-of-war between the deposed Eugene IV, the former Amadeus VIII, now Pope Felix V and part of the anti-Eugene faction, and Philip the Good of Burgundy, who supported Eugene and under whose influence the Cambrai delegation certainly fell.

It was during the 1430s that Du Fay had contacts with the Ferrarese court of Niccolò d'Este, which helps to explain the wealth of music by Du Fay that appears in Ferrarese manuscripts from the middle of the century, and also received his *baccalaureate in decretis*, or bachelor of canon law degree.

Final Decades at Cambrai

By December 1439, Du Fay was back at the Cathedral of Cambrai, where, except for a few months in Italy in 1450 and a period from April 1452 to the end of 1458 (part of which was spent back at Savoy, part perhaps in France), he spent the rest of his life as a canon. He was kept busy with administrative tasks that ranged from representing the cathedral in a legal dispute at the court of Burgundy (1446)—where, though never on the payroll, he seems to have enjoyed some kind of unofficial association—to undertaking an inventory of the cathedral's property to masterminding a tree-cutting expedition (both in 1461). On the musical side, he not only continued to compose, but also supervised the long-term project of recopying the cathedral's music books.

Du Fay died on November 27, 1474, a relatively wealthy man. We are fortunate in having not only his last will and testament, but also the executor's account of how his assets were distributed. The total value of his property was over 1,822 *livre*, more than twice that left by Binchois, who had died in 1460 after spending almost all of his adult life in the employ of Philip the Good. The estate included cash, silver, jewelry, furniture, and books, among these Guido d'Arezzo's *Micrologus*, poetry by Virgil, works by Martin le Franc, and a book of "old songs." The only thing Binchois owned that Du Fay did not was a horse.

Reputation and Personality

Du Fay was clearly held in high esteem in his later years. For example, the text of a well-known motet, *Omnium bonorum plena*, by the young Loyset Compère, probably written in the late 1460s or early 1470s, asks the Virgin Mary to intercede on behalf of fourteen well-known musicians of the day, including Busnoys, Ockeghem, Tinctoris, and a certain Des Prez (either the famous Josquin or, perhaps, the Burgundian singer Pasquier Despres). Du Fay, the only composer of his generation who is cited, stands at the very head of the roll and is described as "luna totius musicae atque cantorum lumine" (moon of all music and light of singers—see Ex. 7-7):

EXAMPLE 7-7. Compère, *Omnium bonorum plena*, mm. 146–158.

A very different form of tribute comes in a letter the Florentine organist Antonio Squarcialupi wrote to Du Fay on May 1, 1461, calling him "the greatest ornament of our age," and informing him that Lorenzo de' Medici "delights exceedingly in the greater refinement of your music, and for that reason admires your art and respects you as a father."[8] The same letter carried a request that Du Fay set to music a poem Lorenzo had recently completed. (If Du Fay complied, the music has been lost.)

But Du Fay's fame proved fleeting. By around 1500, just a quarter century after his death, Du Fay's music was largely forgotten. Certainly, it was no longer being copied into music manuscripts with any frequency. Moreover, the newly born business of music printing—always a barometer of current tastes—excluded him almost completely. If his music was remembered at all, it was mainly in the works of theorists who continued to cite certain passages as examples of rhythmic and metrical intricacy.

Trying to learn what kind of person a fifteenth- or sixteenth-century composer was can be an exercise in frustration. For no matter how voluminous and detailed the documentation, the result is somewhat like a child's coloring book: the outlines—the whats, wheres, and whens—are drawn sharply enough, but the colors and shadings, the composer's individuality, are invariably missing. As often as not, we are dealing with faceless names. (We may actually know what Du Fay looked like, from the depiction on his funeral monument [Fig. 7-2; note the form, in both bottom corners, in which his name appears: the syllable "Du," the note *fa* in the shape of a longa, and the letter "y," which confirms the three-syllable pronunciation of his name].)

Yet perhaps something of Du Fay's personality does come through. His dogged pursuit of benefices and the attendant legal problems seem, at the very least, to speak for someone with a business sense. Further, the constant comings and goings between the papal chapel and Savoy in the 1430s suggest that Du Fay was a keen observer of the shifting political winds. Perhaps his retreat to Cambrai tells us that they were blowing a bit too strongly for his own comfort. And finally, this well-educated, highly cosmopolitan genius who had hobnobbed with Europe's leading political power brokers in the 1420s and 1430s

8. Quoted after Fallows, *Dufay*, 76.

Figure 7-2. Du Fay's funeral monument.

was content to spend the last half of his life tending to the affairs of a cathedral—albeit one of the great ones of northern Europe. Evidently he knew his own worth and was content with it.

BIBLIOGRAPHICAL NOTE

Editions of the Music

Du Fay's motets appear in volume 1 of the *Opera omnia* (1966) edited by Heinrich Besseler; these also appear in volume 2 of the earlier (discontinued) edition (1947–49) that was begun under the editorship of Guillaume de Van and is worth consulting. There is a good selection of motets by Du Fay's contemporaries in Charles van den Borren, *Polyphonia sacra: A Continental Miscellany of the Fifteenth Century* (London: Plainsong & Medieval Society, 1962).

Du Fay's Biography

The most comprehensive account is David Fallows's *Dufay* (London: Dent, 1982). This and all other post-1975 studies lean heavily on the seminal study by Craig Wright, "Dufay at Cambrai: Discoveries and Revisions," *JAMS* 28 (1975): 175–229. Both Fallows and Wright are supplemented by two articles of Alejandro Enrique Planchart, "Guillaume Du Fay's Benefices and His Relationship to the Court of Burgundy," *EMH* 8 (1988): 117–72, and "The Early Career of Guillaume Du Fay," *JAMS* 46 (1993): 341–68. On Du Fay's association with the court of Ferrara, see Lewis Lockwood, "Dufay and Ferrara," in *Papers Read at the Dufay Quincentenary Conference, Brooklyn College, December 6–7, 1974*, ed. Allan W. Atlas (Brooklyn: Brooklyn College, 1976), 1–25, and *Music in Renaissance Ferrara, 1400–*

1505 (Cambridge: Harvard University Press, 1985). Finally, one must acknowledge the stupendous contribution that Heinrich Besseler made to Du Fay studies during the 1950s and 1960s (see the bibliography in Fallows, *Dufay*).

Du Fay's Motets

One begins with Fallows, *Dufay*. On *Nuper rosarum flores* in particular (and the symbolism discussed above), see Wright's "Dufay's *Nuper rosarum flores*, King Solomon's Temple, and the Veneration of the Virgin," *JAMS* 47 (1994): 395–439, which now supersedes Charles W. Warren, "Brunelleschi's Dome and Dufay's Motet," *MQ* 59 (1973): 92–105; see also Patricia Carpenter, "Tonal Coherence in a Motet of Dufay," *JMT* 17 (1973): 2–65. Among other items of interest on individual motets are Ernest Trumble, "Autobiographical Implications in Dufay's Song-Motet 'Juvenis qui puellam,'" *RBM* 42 (1988): 31–82; Margaret V. Sandresky, "The Golden Section in Three Byzantine Motets of Dufay," *JMT* 25 (1981): 291–306; Willem Elders, "Humanism and Early-Renaissance Music: A Study of the Ceremonial Music by Ciconia and Dufay," *TVNM* 27 (1977): 65–101; and Samuel E. Brown Jr., "New Evidence of Isomelic Design in Dufay's Isorhythmic Motets," *JAMS* 10 (1957): 7–13.

Mode and Early Fifteenth-Century Polyphony

The starting points are Harold S. Powers, "Mode," in *New Grove*, 12: 376–404, and Bernhard Meier, *The Modes of Classical Vocal Polyphony*, trans. Ellen S. Beebe (New York: Broude Bros., 1988; originally published 1974); there is a concise discussion in Liane Curtis, "Mode," in *Companion to Medieval and Renaissance Music*, ed. Tess Knighton and David Fallows (New York: Schirmer, 1992), 255–64. For discussions of mode in relation to Du Fay, see Leo Treitler, "Tone System in the Secular Works of Dufay," *JAMS* 28 (1965): 131–69; William Peter Mahrt, "Guillaume Dufay's Chansons in the Phrygian Mode," *Studies in Music from the University of Western Ontario* 5 (1980): 81–98; and the article by Patricia Carpenter cited above.

Number Symbolism

Vincent F. Hopper's *Medieval Number Symbolism: Its Sources, Meaning, and Influence on Thought and Expression* (New York: Columbia University Press, 1938) is an often-cited classic in the field. See also Russell A. Peck, "Public Dreams and Private Myths: Perspectives in Middle English Literature," *PMLA* 90 (1975): 461–68. On number symbolism in music, see Willem Elders, *Symbolic Scores: Studies in the Music of the Renaissance*, Symbola et emblematica 5 (Leiden: Brill, 1994), and for those who can handle the German, his earlier *Studien zur Symbolik in der Musik der alten Niederländer* (Bilthoven: Creyghton, 1968).

Analytical Method

For a summary of opposing ideas about analyzing "old" music with "modern" analytical methods, see Peter Schubert, "Authentic Analysis," *JM* 12 (1994): 3–18.

Also Cited

Johannes Tinctoris, *Terminorum musical diffinitorium/Dictionary of Musical Terms*, trans. Carl Parrish (New York: Norton, 1963).

CHAPTER 8

Learning from Documents:
Payroll and Inventory Notices

How and where do we find the information needed to reconstruct the life of Du Fay or, for that matter, any other composer of the period? Occasionally, biographical tidbits can be ferreted out of the music itself. For instance, we assume that Du Fay was closely associated with the Malatesta family during the 1420s because he wrote a series of compositions that celebrate important events in the lives of three family members. In general, though, the music itself does not go very far in this respect.

It is therefore to the *archives* that we go, to the repositories of the centuries-old, everyday records of the institutions served by the composers and other musicians: princely courts, urban municipalities, churches large and small, and the body to which so many roads led, the greatest dispenser of all kinds of perquisites, the papal *curia* (governing body). In the archives we find payroll registers, correspondence, minutes of the chapter meetings of the great cathedrals and collegiate churches, supplications for benefices, dispensations from vows, and the multitude of documents that record the fabric of everyday life, from house rentals to legal disputes.

We will examine three different kinds of archival documents from the fifteenth century. Here, we look at two payroll notices and the inventory of Du Fay's library. Chapter 12 will test our ability to reconstruct a small slice of Johannes Tinctoris's life from two jargon-filled legal notices.

TWO PAYROLL NOTICES

These notices come from opposite ends of Italy and from different quarters of the century. We look first at the one that is easier to read.

Mid-Century Naples

Figure 8-1 shows a page from a payroll register drawn up in the treasury of the Aragonese court of Naples. The entry is written in Catalan—the language of the court's treasury under Alfonso I, who had ruled his kingdom of Aragón from Catalan-speaking Barcelona before becoming King of Naples in 1441—and records payments to five of the king's employees. It dates from December 13 (evident from the very first line: "Item / a xiij del dit *et present* mes de Dehembre) [1448]," the year having been identified on a previous folio.[1]

---

1. The document is preserved at the Archivio di Stato, Naples, *Tesoreria antica frammenti*, St. 227, vol. XIII, fol. 12^r. In the transcriptions of the documents, scribal abbreviations are resolved in italics.

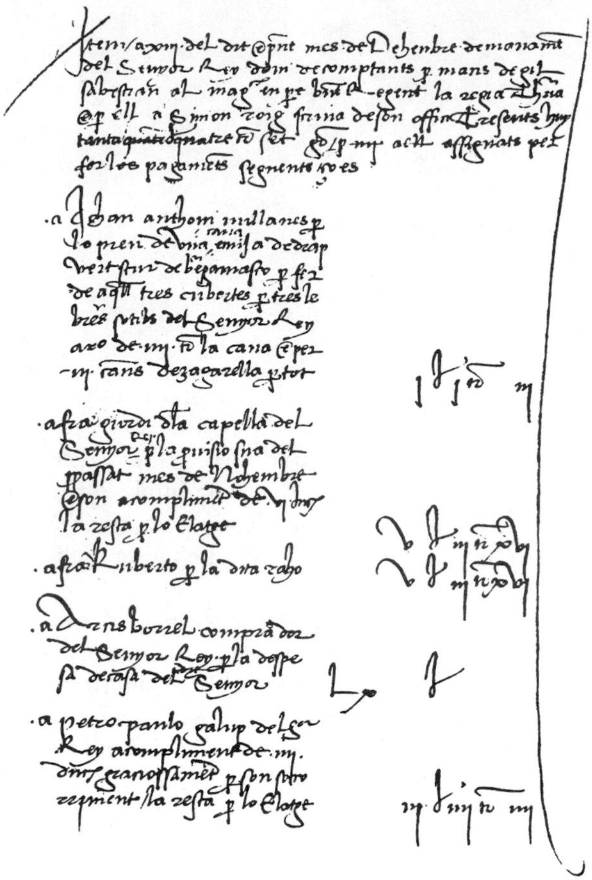

Figure 8-1. Page from payroll register, Aragonese court of Naples, 1448 (Archivio di Stato, Naples).

The record of the payments to the two chapel members begins in the middle of the page:

a fra giordi dela capella del Senyor Rey per la provisio sua del ppassat mes de Novembre et son acompliment de vj ducati la resta per lo elatge.

To Fra Giordi of the chapel of the king, for his salary of the past month of November, the sum of six ducats, the deduction for the payroll tax.

v ducati iij tarì xvi

5 ducats 3 tarì 16 [grani]

a fra Ruberto per la dita raho.

To Fra Ruberto for the same reason.

v ducati iij tarì xvi

5 ducats 3 tarì 16 [grani]

Before turning to the substance of the document, we should take note of the folio number (not shown in the reproduction above): ccccl. Obviously, this was a large register (more than 450 folios), probably containing an entire year's worth of entries. Yet owing to the ravages of time and such catastrophes as fires, earthquakes, and wars—not to mention the ever-present need for wrapping paper (between the time the document was no longer needed and the time that its historical value was recognized)—it has been reduced to a mere fragment. Unfortunately, this is an all-too-frequent situation, and losses are measured not only in terms of individual folios, but in whole volumes, series

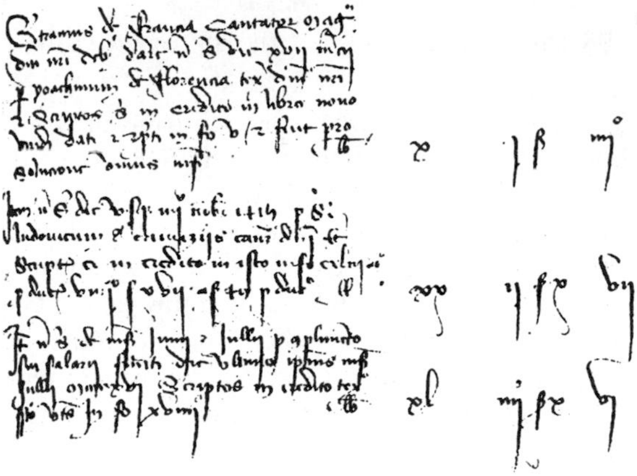

Figure 8-2. Page from payroll register, Brescian court of Pandolfo III Malatesta, 1416 (Sezione di Archivio di Stato, Fano).

of volumes, and entire collections. Thus archival research depends very much on chance, on what has and has not survived. And it is not uncommon to find gaps of a decade here or a quarter century there in the records of a given institution. For some institutions, nothing at all remains.

The payroll notice tells us that Giordi and Ruberto were clerics (from the designation "fra"), members of the king's chapel, present at the court in November 1448, and presumably still there when their salaries for that month were recorded in mid-December (payment was usually made only after services were rendered). Each received a monthly salary of six ducats, though a 4 percent payroll tax, the *elatge*, reduced the take-home pay to 5 ducats, 3 tarì, 16 grani. This three-tiered monetary system, only one among the many then current, worked as follows: 1 ducat = 5 tarì, 1 tareno = 20 grani, and 1 grana = ⅟₆₀₀ of an ounce of gold. Finally, though Giordi and Ruberto were members of the chapel, they were not necessarily singers or, more to the point, singers of polyphony. As we will see in Chapter 13, a princely chapel was not made up of singers only.

Early-Fifteenth-Century Brescia

Figure 8-2 presents a page from another payroll register, this one from the court that Pandolfo III of the Malatesta dynasty maintained in the northern Italian city of Brescia from 1404 through the middle of 1421:[2]

[MCCCCXVI]	[1416]
Beltramus de Francia cantator magnifici domini nostri debet dare numerati sibi die xvii martij per Yoachinum de Florencia texaurarius domini nostri et scriptos sibi in credito in libro novo viridi dati et scripti in fo V / et fuit pro solucione unius mensis	[To] Beltramus of France, singer of our magnificent lord, must be given his pay, 17th day of March, by Joachim of Florence, treasurer of our lord, and written by him in credit in the new green book, entered and written on folio 5 / and it was for one month's salary
libre xj solidi iiij	lire 11 shillings 4 [pence 0]

2. The document is preserved at the Sezione dell'Archivio di Stato di Fano, *Codici malatestiani*, vol. 58, fol. 114ᵛ.

Written in the somewhat cramped hand of Gioacchino of Florence, the court bookkeeper, and crawling with abbreviations,[3] this notice has a very different look from the first. Other differences catch our eye as well. The treasurer notes that this entry is derived from one on folio 5 of the "new green book," indicating that this must be some kind of secondary entry. In fact, volume 58 of the *Codici malatestiani*, from which this page is taken, is a master ledger of sorts that not only brings together multiple entries for a single person that were originally scattered through a number of registers, but then gathers together in a single list all the individuals of the same occupation. An archival researcher's dream!

There is also a different monetary system at work: lire-soldi-denari *imperiali*, in which 1 lira = 20 soldi and 1 soldo = 12 denari. This is the three-tier system that England, for example, only recently abandoned. Obviously, the difference in monetary systems could cause problems if we wished to compare the relative worth of Beltramus's salary at Brescia in 1416 with that of Giordi and Ruberto at Naples in 1448. For not only would we need to take into account thirty years' worth of possible inflation and possible differences in the cost of living at the two places, but we would have to determine the exchange rates between the Neapolitan ducat and the imperial lira. Yet here too the archives come to the rescue, since fifteenth-century bankers and merchants, faced with the same problem when conducting everyday business, left behind notes about exchange rates. Thus we know that at about mid-century, 1 ducat traded for about 3.2 lire. On paper, then, Giordi and Ruberto earned about one and a half times as much as Beltramus.

By itself, this entry does not provide much information about Beltramus, who can be identified as the composer-singer Beltramus Feragut, the composer of the motet *Francorum nobilitati* (discussed in Chapter 7). But it becomes meaningful when placed into context: the first entry for Beltramus at Brescia is noted on November 4, 1415, and credits him with 22 lire and 17 soldi, which, since his base monthly salary was 11 lire and 4 soldi, must be two months' salary; payments to him are then recorded again on March 17, 1416 (Fig. 8-2), April 16, June 20 (for May-June), and July 3; and since he had just been paid for June two weeks earlier, this last payment must be an advance for the month of July. Stringing these notices together and keeping in mind that payment was normally made after services were rendered (the advance on July 3 notwithstanding), we can conclude that Beltramus arrived at Brescia at the beginning of September 1415 and left at the end of July 1416. The lack of payments in December 1415 and January-February 1416 does not necessarily mean that Beltramus was absent for a while; we simply do not have records for those months.

In all, then, the four payment notices fill in eleven months of Beltramus's life. And when we gather further information from other archives, a picture of the basic whats, whens, and wheres of his career slowly begins to emerge.

---

3. Only the most experienced paleographers go to work without a copy of Cappelli's *Dizionario di abbreviature latine ed italiane* at their side.

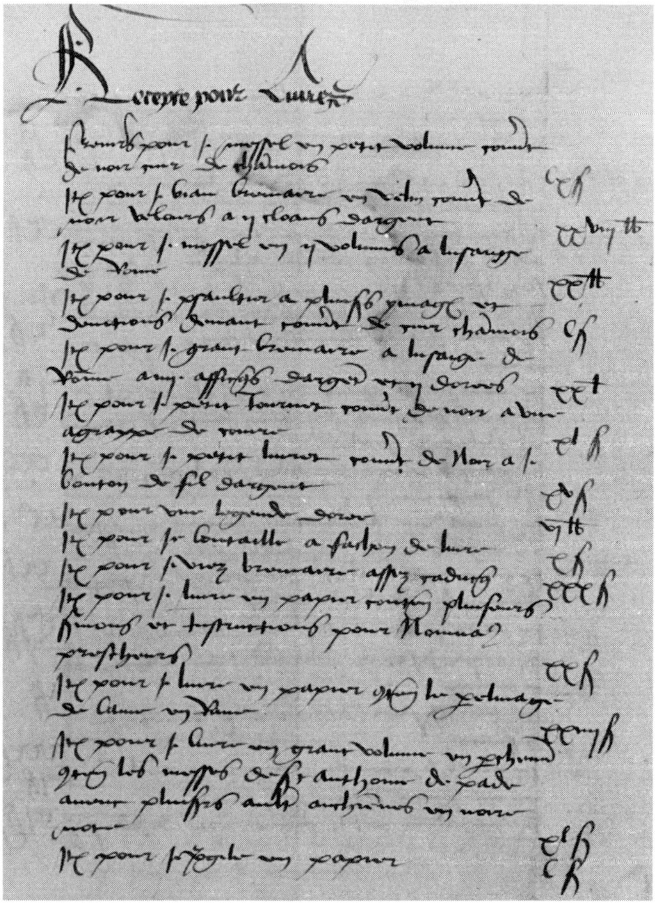

Figure 8-3. Page from inventory of Du Fay's library, 1474–76
(Archives départementales du Nord, Lille).

DU FAY'S LIBRARY

We now turn to the first page of the executor's inventory of Du Fay's library
(Fig. 8-3).[4] Here is a good chance to try transcribing a difficult-to-read French
hand. The following is a translation of the title and first two entries (which
might help some to work backward from the English):

RECEIPT FOR BOOKS

First for a small missal covered with black chamois skin leather	lx sous
Item, for a fine breviary in vellum covered with black velours with two silver clasps	xxviij livres

(Not everything in life is simple!)

4. Reproduced after Wright, "Dufay at Cambrai," 214. The inventory is preserved at Lille,
   Archives départementales du Nord, 4 G 1313, pp. 6–7, 66.

THE MORAL

There are several lessons to be learned from this mini-survey of archival documents. First, those who use archives in their work must have some facility with the languages involved and possess the ability to decipher handwriting that was often intended to be read by no one except the writer. Second, they must have time. Reading through thousands of payroll entries or hundreds of letters can't be done quickly; archival researchers generally measure their small-scale projects in terms of months, the larger ones in years. Third, archivists must possess patience! They sometimes sit for days without finding anything immediately relevant to their study.

Finally, archivists need luck. They are looking to discover material that is unknown, if not to everyone, at least to those in their field. (Musicologists generally pick up archival leads through studies of political, social, or economic history or a tip from a friendly local archivist.) And sometimes they simply don't find it, either because it doesn't exist, which becomes evident only after an unsuccessful search, or because no one has any idea where it might be hidden. For example, if the singers of a prince's chapel accompanied him on a military campaign, the payments to them might be recorded not in the chapel registers but among the "military expenses." In the end, archival research is somewhat like looking for the proverbial needle in the haystack, and successful archivists not only possess the instincts of a bloodhound, they learn as much as possible about the organization of their archives before they buy the plane ticket.

A POSTSCRIPT: NEW YEAR'S DAY

As we learned in Chapter 7, when the Florentines celebrated the consecration of Santa Maria del Fiore and the Feast of the Annunciation on March 25, 1436, they were also celebrating New Year's Day. Though in some localities the day on which the new year began was January 1 (which coincides with the Feast of the Circumcision and which became more and more the custom as the sixteenth century rolled along), that day was by no means universal during the fifteenth century: Venice celebrated on March 1, most French-speaking localities popped champagne on Easter Sunday, and perhaps the most popular New Year's Day coincided with Christmas, on December 25. To make matters more confusing, different establishments within the same city sometimes reckoned the new year from different days, with the guilds of notaries in particular often going against the established grain. Thus the archival researcher must be alert when, say, a letter from the papal chancery (which celebrated New Year's Day on December 25) to the King of France (who celebrated on Easter Sunday) is dated December 27, 1452, and the response is dated March 3, 1451, actually some nine and a half weeks later. The solution: the date of both letters must be converted to "modern style" (New Year's Day on January 1). Thus the papal letter really dates from December 27, 1451, while the royal response was written on March 3, 1452.

BIBLIOGRAPHICAL NOTE

About Archives

For a guide to the holdings and organization of one of the world's great archives, see Leonard E. Boyle, *A Survey of the Vatican Archives and Its Medieval Holdings* (Toronto: Toronto University Press, 1972); on doing archival research on music specifically in French archives, see François Lesure, "Archival Research: Necessity and Opportunity," in *Perspectives in Musicology*, ed. Barry S. Brook, Sherman Van Solkema, and Edward O. E. Downes (New York: Norton, 1972), 56–79.

Paleography

Of the many manuals that help students through the thickets of paleographical problems, one of the best is Bernhard Bischoff, *Latin Palaeography: Antiquity and the Middle Ages*, trans. Dáibhí ó Crónín and David Ganz (Cambridge: Cambridge University Press, 1989; originally published 1979); Adriano Cappelli's *Dizionario di abbreviature latine ed italiane*, 6th ed. (Milan: Hoepli, 1967), is the indispensable guide to the world of scribal abbreviations.

Dates and Money

For the many problems that arise in connection with dates and calendar systems, see Cappelli's *Cronologia, cronografia e calendario perpetuo*, 3rd ed. (Milan: Hoepli, 1969), which does not require much Italian. A helpful guide to calculating exchange rates between monetary systems is Peter Spufford, Sarah Tolley, and Wendy Wilkinson, *Handbook of Medieval Exchange*, Guides and Handbooks 13 (London: Royal Historical Society, 1986).

Archivists in Action

There is a convenient collection of articles based on archival research in Barbara Haggh et al., eds., *Musicology and Archival Research*, Archives et bibliothèques de Belgique 46 (Brussels: Archives gènèrales du Royaume, 1995).

Also Cited

Craig Wright, "Dufay at Cambrai: Discoveries and Revisions," *JAMS* 28 (1975): 175–229.

CHAPTER 9

The Cyclic Mass and Vespers

If the great stylistic innovation of the first half of the fifteenth century was the establishment of the triad as the underlying basis of polyphony, the great innovation in terms of genre must surely be the development of the cyclic, five-movement, tenor cantus-firmus Mass. Before tracing that development, though, we should be familiar with the basic structure of the Mass.

THE STRUCTURE OF THE MASS

As the commemoration of the Eucharist (the sacraments of the Last Supper), the Mass is the central service of the Christian liturgy. Table 9-1 outlines its parts.

Two basic distinctions must be made. First, some items of the Mass were sung as plainchant, while others were simply recited or intoned in a monotone-like fashion (with slight melodic inflexions): only the former served as the basis for polyphonic Masses. The other crucial distinction is between the Proper of the Mass and the Ordinary. While the texts and melodies of the Proper vary from day to day and feast to feast (each is therefore appropriate to a particular feast only), the texts of the Ordinary (though not necessarily their chant melodies) remain the same throughout the liturgical year. And though composers did not neglect the Proper of the Mass completely (both Heinrich Isaac and William Byrd wrote monumental Proper cycles), it was on the five movements of the Ordinary of the Mass—Kyrie, Gloria, Credo, Sanctus, and Agnus Dei—that they focused their attention from the fourteenth century on.

We should keep three things in mind. First, although modern-day concerts and recordings generally present the five movements of fifteenth- and sixteenth-century polyphonic cyclic Masses one after the other as though they were multimovement compositions akin to the symphony or string quartet, the Masses were conceived as part of the liturgy. Thus after the Gloria of, say, a Du Fay or Josquin or Palestrina Mass, the collect and epistle of the day were intoned, the gradual, alleluia, and sequence of the particular feast were sung, and the gospel of the day was read; only then did the choir sing the composer's polyphonic Credo.[1]

1. Among recent recordings that intersperse the appropriate Proper chants (or polyphonic settings of those chants) between the movements of the polyphonic Ordinary are Josquin's *Missa Pange lingua* (Ensemble Clément Janequin and the Ensemble Organum, Harmonia Mundi HMC 901239) and Nicholas Ludford's *Missa Benedicta et venerabilis* (The Cardinall's

Table 9-1.   The structure of the Mass.

Sung as plainchant		Spoken, or recited in monotone fashion	
Proper	Ordinary	Proper	Ordinary
1. Introit			
	2. Kyrie		
	3. Gloria		
		4. Collect	
		5. Epistle	
6. Gradual			
7. Alleluia (or, on certain occasions: Tract)			
8. Sequence (standard until the Council of Trent)			
		9. Gospel	
	10. Credo		
11. Offertory			
			12. Offertory prayers
		13. Secret	
		14. Preface	
	15. Sanctus		
			16. Canon
			17. Pater noster
	18. Agnus Dei		
19. Communion			
			20. Postcommunion
	21. Ite missa est (or Benedicamus Domino)		

Second, the plainchants for any given feast are musically unrelated to one another; we should not expect to find any melodic interrelationships among the Ordinary chants that are sung on any particular day. Indeed, it was only during the thirteenth and fourteenth centuries that certain chants for the Ordinary came to be associated with one another and were grouped together into the cycles that we find in modern liturgical books.

Third, though we customarily lavish our attention on the great polyphonic masterpieces, the day in, day out music for both Mass and Office during our period was plainchant, even at the greatest of cathedrals and wealthiest of courts. In fact, plainchants continued to be composed in the fifteenth century, with no less a figure than Du Fay among those who composed them. Grand polyphonic Mass compositions were generally intended for special occasions.

Musick, Academy Sound and Vision CD GAU 132). A third recording, of Machaut's *Messe de Nostre Dame*, includes portions of the Mass that are spoken (Taverner Consort, EMI CDC7 47949 2).

THE FOURTEENTH-CENTURY LEGACY

To appreciate just what composers of the first half of the fifteenth century accomplished, we should return to the *Ars nova* once more and briefly consider the state of Mass composition in the middle of the fourteenth century.

Machaut's Mass

Today, Guillaume de Machaut's *Messe de Nostre Dame* is without doubt the most famous piece from the mid-fourteenth century. Its fame rests on its being the first known instance of one individual setting the entire Ordinary (the Ite missa est included) with the express intent that all the movements form a single entity. Yet even if we assume that the Mass was composed in a single shot and that a recurring six-note melodic motive is more than just a stock formula, there is no strong sense of musical unity from one movement to another: though the Kyrie, Sanctus, Agnus Dei, and Ite missa est are all entirely iso-rhythmic, each is built on a different plainchant; the Gloria and the Credo are freely constructed, with no isorhythm or plainsong cantus firmus; and the first three movements cadence on D, the last three on F. Whatever sense of unity we may perceive through the course of the Mass, then, is probably more psychological and "mood-related" than anything else.

Machaut's idea of setting the Ordinary in its entirety was not fast to catch on. Most fourteenth- and early-fifteenth-century composers remained content to set just a single movement, which would then have been stored away in a manuscript that bound all the movements of a single type (all the Glorias, all the Credos, and so on) together. Presumably, a choirmaster who wished to have the Ordinary sung polyphonically from beginning to end would then pick and choose from among these settings.

"Composite" Cycles

A small group of polyphonic Masses are preserved as cycles even though they were probably not originally intended as such: these are the so-called Tournai (pre-Machaut), Toulouse, Barcelona, and Sorbonne Masses. But with the exception of the Sorbonne Mass, in which the Agnus Dei recalls sections from both the Kyrie and the Sanctus, there are no close musical connections between the movements. Rather, they reflect what must have been the standard practice of compilation by a choirmaster. They are Masses that got caught in the act of being compiled.

THE EARLY FIFTEENTH CENTURY

Though composers continued to write single movements in the opening decades of the fifteenth century, they also began to look beyond the individual movement. Initially, they thought in terms of paired movements: Gloria and Credo, Sanctus and Agnus Dei. They then widened their horizons to encompass the Ordinary as a whole. At the same time, the techniques through which composers began to impose a sense of unity on the now-joined-together movements became more audible. And it is to this evolving process that we now turn, keeping in mind that the road from simple to complex, from covert to overt was not necessarily straightforward. Indeed, the 1420s and 1430s saw all of the techniques being used, even by a single composer.

Individual Movements

There is hardly a better-known example of an independent Mass movement than Du Fay's rather atypical *Gloria ad modum tubae*, in which the lower voices imitate trumpet-like fanfares beneath the canonic upper voices (Ex. 9-1):

EXAMPLE 9-1. Du Fay, *Gloria ad modum tubae*, mm. 1–13, 91–110.

Just how tenaciously the idea of setting a single movement proved to be can be seen not only from the many such works by Du Fay and Binchois, but also from the continued practice of some manuscript compilers of grouping like movements together until well into the late 1430s.

Mass Pairs

There were two ways in which a composer might pair movements. One of these we might call the "suspect" technique (since to a certain extent we can do no more than suspect that two movements were intended to be a pair): although the two movements share no obvious motivic relationships, they agree with respect to such things as clefs (and thus range), signatures, mensuration schemes, number of voices and number of texted voices, and modal finals (both at the end of each movement and at major points of articulation along the way). Thus we suspect that the following Gloria and Credo by Johannes Franchois were intended to form a single paired entity (Table 9-2):

Table 9-2.   Johannes Franchois, paired Gloria-Credo.

	Clefs/Signatures	Mensuration	Voices	Finals
Gloria	C_1 C_3 C_3/$\flat\flat\flat$	₵	3^1	(G A) D
Credo	C_1 C_3 C_3/$\natural\flat\flat$	₵	3^1	(G C) D

Note: The subscript shows the line on which the C clef sits; the superscript indicates the number of voices with text; finals in parentheses are those at major internal divisions.

Moreover, one of the two manuscripts in which the movements appear places them directly after one another, while the other names Franchois as the composer of both of them.[2]

Yet the similarities between the two movements tell us little about the act of composition. Did Franchois write both movements at the same time, or did he add one to the other at some remove? Is the back-to-back transmission in one of the manuscripts simply the work of the person who compiled the manuscript? Can we be sure that the pairs are really the composer's and not ours? In the end, such pairs will almost always be suspect.

A second technique composers used to pair movements was to relate them motivically. Example 9-2 contains excerpts from an anonymous Gloria and Credo that appear back-to-back in a manuscript written at the French-influenced Lusignan court on Cyprus during the 1410s:[3]

EXAMPLE 9-2. Anonymous, (a) Gloria, mm. 1–6, 27–28; (b) Credo, mm. 1–5, 75–76.

2. The manuscripts are Bologna, Civico Museo Bibliografico Musicale, MS Q 15, copied in northern Italy in the second quarter of the century, and Oxford 213.

3. Turin, Biblioteca Nazionale, MS J.II.9.

There can be no doubt that the two movements were intended to be sung during the same Mass. Both open with head-motives that are not only almost identical, but are treated in the same dialogue-like fashion in the upper voices. Even more ear-catching is the relationship between the movements at measures 27–28 and 75–76: not only does the same change in mensuration occur, but the metrical gears shift on the same melodic motive and with the same dialogue-style banter. But even this pair also raises questions: (1) Why is it only the Gloria that has a presumably added fourth voice? (2) Were the movements written at the same time? (3) Since both movements are anonymous, how do we even know they were written by the same composer?

Besides the Gloria and Credo, the other customary pair of Mass movements consisted of the Sanctus and Agnus Dei. Both of these pairings reflected certain similarities in text and structure. The Gloria and Credo stand apart in two important respects: they both have extremely long texts, which usually caused them to be set in syllabic, declamatory fashion; and the opening words of each—"Gloria in excelsis Deo" and "Credo in unum Deum"—are intoned by the celebrant. The polyphony then gets under way with "Et in terra pax" and "Patrem omnipotentem," respectively. The Sanctus and Agnus Dei (and Kyrie, which was sometimes added to this pair) are related by their relative brevity and tripartite structure. In all, the pairing of Gloria-Credo and Sanctus–Agnus Dei was so pervasive that it is evident even in complete five-movement polyphonic Masses.

Five-Movement Spans

The technique of unifying movements by means of motive came to be extended to the Ordinary as a whole. Example 9-3 gives the opening measures of all five parts of Arnold de Lantins's *Missa Verbum incarnatum* (the title is from the textual trope in the Kyrie), the movements of which appear consecutively in all three manuscripts that transmit them:

EXAMPLE 9-3. Arnold de Lantins, *Missa Verbum incarnatum*, opening measures of each movement.

As we would expect, clefs and signatures agree throughout, as do the finals of each movement. In addition, the movements are related through a network of common (or at least similar) head-motives: the Sanctus and Agnus Dei are almost identical in all three voices; the Kyrie, Gloria, and Credo are closely related; and all five movements bear a family resemblance to one another. Here we can see that the idea of pairing lingers on: the motivic relationship, reinforced by identical mensuration schemes, is clearest between Gloria and Credo and between Sanctus and Agnus Dei.

THE CYCLIC CANTUS-FIRMUS MASS: THE ENGLISH CONTRIBUTION

As composers were groping for ways in which to unify the movements of the Ordinary, the English (working in France?) took the big leap and established the procedure that became the standard (though with variations) for the remainder of the fifteenth and sixteenth centuries: they based all five movements on the same preexistent melody, thus explicitly—and very audibly—binding them together to produce what we call the cyclic cantus-firmus Mass. Just who was the first to do this and when is not clear. But the chief candidates are John Dunstable, Leonel Power, and John Benet, to whom the earliest cycles are attributed (sometimes with conflicting attributions), and who probably came upon the idea during the 1420s or early 1430s.

Power's *Missa Alma redemptoris mater*

The clearest and most straightforward procedure appears in Power's Mass on the Marian antiphon *Alma redemptoris mater*, for which we have only four movements, Gloria through Agnus Dei (*Anthology* 16 provides the Gloria and Credo). Drawing on the first two phrases of the antiphon melody (Ex. 9-4), Power imposes a rhythmic pattern on them and quotes them literally—the rhythmic pattern always intact—in each of the movements.

EXAMPLE 9-4. The Marian antiphon *Alma redemptoris mater* as far as Power quotes it, transposed to F.[4]

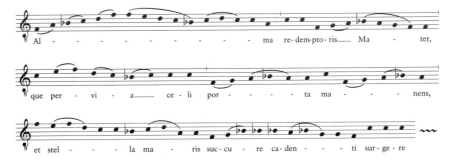

Several aspects of Power's treatment of the cantus firmus (in the tenor) call for comment. First, not only is the rhythmic value of each pitch retained from movement to movement, but so is the number of measures of rest between segments of the melody. Thus from the point in each movement at which it enters (at the beginning in the Gloria and Agnus Dei, at mm. 37 in the Credo and 10 in the Sanctus), the tenor behaves rather like the tenor of an isorhythmic motet. In fact, Power's Mass is like a giant isorhythmic motet in which each talea constitutes an entire movement. Second, Power's treatment of the antiphon seems almost odd: there is a four-measure rest between the sixteenth and seventeenth notes of Power's tenor (in the Gloria, mm. 17–20), even though in the original chant those notes set two syllables within a single word, the "pto-ris" of "redemptoris"; the single largest articulation point within each movement (marked by a change in mensuration and/or vocal "orchestration") tears still another of the chant's words apart—"porta" (in the Gloria, m. 59); and the strong F-major feeling of the chant melody is denied at the final cadence of each movement.

Yet chant melodies had long been subject to seemingly capricious segmentation and loss of modal identity when they were used as cantus firmi in po-

---

4. After Dunstable, *Complete Works,* 161.

lyphony—Dunstable, for example, sacrificed the phrase structure of the *Veni creator spiritus* melody for the sake of number symbolism in *Veni sancte spiritus/ Veni creator spiritus*. In other words, Power and his contemporaries were willing to sacrifice one or another aspect of the chant's melodic identity for the sake of gaining unity across the movements of the cyclic Mass. In effect, the chant became subservient to the aesthetic-structural aims of the polyphony.

Finally, we may note one seemingly peculiar feature of the Credo: beginning at measure 38, the upper voices sing different parts of the text simultaneously. This technique appears frequently in English Masses of the period. By shortening the overall length of the text, composers could set the Credo more melismatically than usual.

Though the idea of using the same cantus firmus in each movement seems to have caught on quickly, not all Masses of the period treat the preexistent melody quite as strictly as the *Missa Alma redemptoris mater* does. For example, while the cantus-firmus melody of a *Missa Rex seculorum* attributed to both Dunstable and Power remains the same in each movement, the rhythm varies from one movement to the next. In a *Missa Sine nomine* with ascriptions to Dunstable, Power, and Benet, the cantus-firmus melody is subjected to new ornamentation in each movement. Clearly, there were still compositional decisions to be made.

The *Caput* Mass

Among those who made such decisions, including some that would stick, was the anonymous English composer who wrote the *Caput* Mass in the early 1440s (see *Anthology* 17 for the Sanctus). Like Power, the composer stated the cantus firmus, drawn from the final melisma of the word "caput" from the Sarum antiphon *Venit ad Petrum*, in isorhythmic fashion from one movement to the next; a similar head-motive in the upper voices begins each movement, further adding to the overall sense of unity.

Even more important, though, were the decisions affecting the polyphonic texture: (1) four voices instead of the customary three; (2) the cantus firmus/ tenor as the next-to-lowest voice instead of the usual lowest; (3) the tenor conceived in conjunction with the voice below it, which, with its frequent leaps of fourths and fifths, begins to take on the character of a bass part; and (4) a contra altus (next-to-highest voice) that, while it fills out and enriches the harmony in the four-part sections, is not essential to the contrapuntal framework. In effect, the unknown English composer hit upon what would become the standard texture of the four-voice, cantus-firmus Mass for the remainder of the century and beyond.

DU FAY'S CANTUS-FIRMUS CYCLES

Du Fay's career as a composer spanned half a century, from the isorhythmic motet *Vasilissa ergo gaude* (his earliest datable work), which bid farewell to Cleofe Malatesta as she set off for Byzantium in August 1420, to the *Missa Ave regina caelorum,* possibly composed for the dedication of the Cathedral of Cambrai in 1472. During those five decades, his Mass settings covered the entire spectrum of formal and stylistic types: isolated movements with and without a preexistent chant melody, motive-related pairs and complete cycles unified only by means of a head-motive, cycles of the Proper of the Mass, and finally the great cyclic cantus-firmus Masses of his maturity, to which we now turn.

The *Missa Se la face ay pale*

Du Fay probably wrote the ballade *Se la face ay pale (Anthology* 18a) during the 1430s, when he was resident at the court of Savoy. It was on the tenor part of this chanson—which appears to be the only through-composed ballade of the century—that Du Fay composed his Mass *(Anthology* 18b), probably for an important Savoyard-related ceremony in the early 1450s, which would place it among the earliest Masses to be based on a secular cantus firmus.

Du Fay used a number of means to achieve a sense of audible cyclic unity. The most obvious involves the tenor cantus firmus. Du Fay drew the tenor of the Mass from the tenor of the chanson, quoting it note for note both melodically and rhythmically. Three of the movements—Kyrie, Sanctus, and Agnus Dei—present the chanson tenor one time each, dividing it into three well-defined segments that span the entire movement. The Gloria and Credo, on the other hand, each state the cantus firmus three times in its entirety in a 3:2:1 diminution pattern in which, on its final appearance, it is moving in *integer valor*—that is, after successive statements in triple and duple augmentation, it moves at the speed actually called for by the notation, and thus as quickly as it had in the chanson and as quickly as the voices that surround it in the Mass. Table 9-3 sums up the disposition of the cantus firmus throughout the Mass.

What strikes the eye—and, with repeated listenings, the ear as well—is the way in which the cantus firmus defines structural-proportional relationships both within and across movements. Most obvious is Du Fay's treatment of the Gloria and Credo: both are cast in the form of huge, proportionally identical isorhythmic motets. Here is clear evidence of the influence wielded on the cyclic cantus-firmus Mass by the isorhythmic motet and the Gloria-Credo-pairing tradition.

Further, just as the 3:2:1 ratio governs the statements of the cantus firmus in both the Gloria and the Credo, so it determines the length of the introductory duets over the course of the last three movements: 18:12:6 = 3:2:1. Given these identical sets of ratios, we can hear interrelationships between movements in different ways. For instance, we can perceive the Credo as (1) standing at the midpoint of the composition as a whole, (2) the second half of a pair with the Gloria, and (3) standing at the beginning of a 3:2:1 proportional chain (already set up in the Gloria) with the opening duets of the final three movements. Compelling as these relationships might appear, however, we must remember that except for the Kyrie and Gloria, the movements were widely separated from one another when performed in their liturgical context, and we

Table 9-3.   Disposition of the cantus firmus in the tenor of the
             Missa Se la face ay pale.

Movement	Cantus firmus	Speed
Kyrie		
Kyrie I	**A + B**	2× *integer valor*
Christe	no cantus firmus	
Kyrie II	**C**	2× *integer valor*
Gloria		
Et in terra pax	(18) **A + B + C**	3× *integer valor*
Qui tollis	(18) **A + B + C**	2× *integer valor*
Cum sancto spiritu	(18) **A + B + C**	*integer valor*
Credo		
Patrem omnipotentem	(18) **A + B + C**	3× *integer valor*
Et iterum	(18) **A + B + C**	2× *integer valor*
Confiteor	(18) **A + B + C**	*integer valor*
Sanctus		
Sanctus	(12) **A**	2× *integer valor*
Pleni sunt caeli	no cantus firmus	
Osanna I	**B**	2× *integer valor*
Benedictus	no cantus firmus	
Osanna II	**C**	2× *integer valor*
Agnus Dei		
Agnus I	(6) **A + B**	2× *integer valor*
Agnus II	no cantus firmus	
Agnus III	**C**	2× *integer valor*

Note: The letters **A, B,** and **C** refer to the segments of the chanson tenor as marked in the chanson (*Anthology* 18a). Numbers in parentheses refer to the length of the introductory duets (when present) as measured in units of the *tactus* (beat) of the original notation.

can only wonder if such relationships were meant to be perceived. In any case, they point to the important place that number and proportion occupied in the aesthetic vision of the period.

The chanson tenor is neither the only means of musical unification nor the only part of the chanson on which Du Fay drew. The unity of the Mass is further underscored by the head-motive with which each of the last four movements begins and to which the superius of the Kyrie certainly alludes. Moreover, each movement ends with a short tag in the contratenor voice; and while this little figure seems innocuous enough, it is reinforced by a similar figure at the end of most internal subsections and stays in our ear because it adds weight, sometimes with the help of a nearby B-flat, to the F side of the ambivalent F/C tonal ledger.

Finally, though the Mass's reference to the chanson is seemingly single-minded in its concentration on the tenor, there are at least a few allusions to the polyphonic fabric of the chanson as a whole. These occur near the end of each movement (beginning at measures 64, 192, 192, 122, and 79) where we find the fanfare-like C-major triad that the chanson tosses back and forth between its own superius and tenor shortly before its conclusion (m. 25). This borrowing, though a small one, provides still another means of musical unity and is, as we will see, a harbinger of things to come.

With the *Missa Se la face ay pale*, Du Fay arrived at the overall texture and relationship between voice parts that he would use in his remaining cantus-firmus cycles: the superius, which clearly displays the greatest amount of melodic interest, stands alone at the top; contratenor and tenor, which cross one another at will, lie about a fifth below; and a fifth below them lies the bassus, which, even more strongly than in the earlier English *Caput* Mass, takes on the function of directing the harmonic motion. In short, Du Fay has achieved a synthesis of sorts between the linear and the vertical, between counterpoint and harmony, between "additive" and "simultaneous" composition (see Chapter 18 for a discussion of these last two terms).

One of the things that must strike the listener about Du Fay's Mass is the almost "classical" clarity of form, from the clear-cut cadences, which clarify the phrase structure within each section, to the duos, which help to articulate the overall structure of each movement by providing textural and timbral contrast.

The duos are fascinating, for they do more than merely lighten the texture. Their fleeting rhythm contrasts with the more slowly moving surface rhythm of the four-part sections; except for the duos that open a movement solidly on C, they tend to push the tonal center more and more toward F as the movement progresses, thus preparing the final cadences on that pitch; and they provide virtually the only instances of imitative counterpoint (see, for example, the "Pleni sunt caeli," m. 50, the "Benedictus," m. 99, and Agnus II, m. 51). The duos themselves fall into two distinct groups: those that lead to a statement of the cantus firmus maintain a single two-voice texture from beginning to end and are introductory in character, cadencing in such a way as to set up the cantus firmus, while those that constitute quasi-independent sections without cantus firmus ("Christe," "Pleni sunt caeli," "Benedictus," and Agnus II) present different combinations of two-part writing and always end with a textural crescendo of three parts and a firm sense of tonal closure. Thus Du Fay clearly differentiates between the duos according to their different functions.

The *Missa L'homme armé*

Du Fay's next (?) cyclic cantus-firmus Mass was based on the famous *L'homme armé* melody (Ex. 9-5), about which we will learn more in Chapter 11.

EXAMPLE 9-5. The version of the *L'homme armé* melody used by Du Fay.

cun se vie - nge ar - mer, d'un hau - bre - gon de fer.

Du Fay's treatment of the cantus firmus in the *L'homme armé* Mass differs from earlier practice in two respects. First, all the cantus-firmus Masses discussed so far had the cantus firmus confined to the tenor from beginning to end. Here, the *L'homme armé* melody permeates other voices. This important innovation is particularly clear, for example, in the Gloria, at the words "Tu solus domi-nus," where the middle part of the melody is tossed back and forth between tenor and bassus (Ex. 9-6):

EXAMPLE 9-6. Du Fay, *Missa L'homme armé*, Gloria, mm. 142–158.

Even more adventurous is the presentation of the cantus firmus in the Agnus Dei (*Anthology* 19). In Agnus I, the bass anticipates the fanfare-like figure of the cantus firmus at measures 13–14 and may allude to the opening of the tune at measures 23–24; at measures 31–34, contra altus and tenor present the melody simultaneously at different speeds and different pitch levels. Agnus II, though tenorless, is saturated with the cantus-firmus melody from measure 57 on. Then at the beginning of Agnus III, a verbal canon (rule or instruction) reads, "Cancer eat plenus sed redeat medius," which can be translated as "The crab proceeds whole but returns half." Here the tenor first sings the cantus firmus in retrograde motion (backward, like a crab) in long notes and then (at m. 113) turns around and sings it from the beginning twice as quickly.

Because we cannot date the Mass with any certainty, we do not know if Du Fay was breaking new ground with all this manipulation of the cantus firmus or following the lead of a new generation of composers who were coming to maturity around the middle of the century. In any event, Du Fay's Mass is one of the most complex and musically rich works of the time.

The *Missa Ave regina caelorum*

No discussion of Du Fay's Ordinary cycles would be complete without paying tribute to an astounding passage in the Agnus Dei of his *Missa Ave regina caelorum* (Ex. 9-7):

EXAMPLE 9-7. Du Fay, *Missa Ave regina caelorum*, Agnus Dei, mm. 72–82.

On the words "Miserere, miserere, miserere nobis," Du Fay quotes the passage with which he had set the trope "Miserere, miserere supplicanti Du Fay" in his large-scale motet on the antiphon (see mm. 86–96 in *Anthology* 15 and Chapter 7). Though generally thought to have been written for the dedication of the Cathedral of Cambrai in July 1472, and thus a very public work, this Mass, with its allusion to the antiphon trope, is an equally personal plea for salvation. In the *Missa Ave regina caelorum*, Du Fay sums up everything he had accomplished in his earlier Mass cycles. It is probably the crowning masterpiece of his career, analogous in the context of his life's work to Bach's *Art of Fugue*, Beethoven's late quartets, and Verdi's *Otello* and *Falstaff*.

A FICTIVE COMPOSITION MANUAL

Though the fifteenth century has left us many treatises on counterpoint, there is nothing that might be called a composition manual, nothing that provides the young would-be composer with instructions on how to compose certain types of pieces. The following set of guidelines (using the *Caput* Mass and Du Fay's *Missa Se la face ay pale* as models) is intended for the young composer of around 1450 who might have been gearing up to write a cyclic cantus-firmus Mass, and is therefore pure make-believe.

(1) Choose a cantus-firmus melody that is neutral, that is, equally foreign to and thus equally applicable to each part of the Ordinary; do not choose a chant that is itself part of the Ordinary, for while the Kyrie plainchant is appropriate to the polyphony for that movement, it will clash liturgically with the other movements. You can draw on a chant from the Proper of the Mass or from the Office, or on the tenor part from a fashionable polyphonic chanson or on a monophonic "pop" tune (and don't worry if the words are a bit racy).

(2) Use the same cantus firmus in all five movements.

(3) Place the cantus firmus in the tenor voice, that is, the next-to-lowest part; this permits any note to be harmonized three ways (as opposed to two possibilities if it is placed in the lowest voice, since fourths are forbidden between the lowest voice and any other).

(4) In general, assign the cantus firmus larger, more slowly moving note values than those in the other voices, though you can subject it to diminution (or even further augmentation) at will.

(5) Except in the Kyrie, where you might wish to have all four voices enter at once, reserve the entry of the cantus firmus for a while, letting it enter together with the bassus after the upper voices have presented an introductory duet.

(6) Omit the cantus firmus altogether at certain places: "Christe," "Pleni sunt caeli," "Benedictus," and Agnus II; these sections should be filled with duets that combine the other three voices in various ways.

(7) Further unify the movements by beginning them all with a common head-motive.

WHY THE CYCLIC CANTUS-FIRMUS MASS?

What made composers want to impose a sense of musical unity on the five sections of the Ordinary in the first place? After all, only the Kyrie and Gloria are sung back-to-back, and the plainchants for the Ordinary are themselves musically unrelated.

Two different reasons have been suggested. One is purely musical: the idea of unity was an aesthetic one, and the process of unification illustrates the triumph of musical-aesthetic values over the practical aspects of the liturgy, which in no way call for such unity. The other explanation is that the cyclic Mass developed to meet the very requirements of the liturgy. For instance, since the words of the Ordinary remain the same throughout the liturgical year, to let a single cantus firmus—with its textual associations—run through each movement serves to tie the music to a specific occasion. The cantus firmus becomes an emblem of sorts, one that makes the polyphony appropriate for the specific celebration at hand. Thus what could have been more appropriate than for Leonel Power to base a Mass dedicated to the Virgin on the Marian antiphon *Alma redemptoris mater*, or for Du Fay to commemorate one Savoyard celebration with a Mass based on a cantus firmus drawn from a chanson he composed for an earlier one?

In the end, the two reasons seem to complement one another. For while the choice of cantus firmus would have been dictated by social-liturgical demands, the urge to unify in the first place probably had musical-aesthetic roots. Why else, after all, would the early practice of unifying cantus-firmus-*less* movements by means of a head-motive or other musical device have developed if unity itself had not been a compositional goal?

PROPER AND PLENARY CYCLES

Though it is the cyclic setting of the Ordinary of the Mass that usually commands our attention, fifteenth-century composers by no means neglected the Proper of the Mass, whose texts and music changed from day to day and feast to feast. In fact, a hefty percentage of the seven voluminous mid-century Trent manuscripts (see Chapter 11) is devoted to settings of the Proper, often arranged in cycles of introit, gradual, alleluia, offertory, and communion, eleven of which might be by Du Fay. As we saw in Chapter 1 (*Anthology* 2) in connection with Johannes Brassart's setting of the introit *Sapienciam sanctorum*, composers generally set the movements of the Proper in a small-scale fashion, with the plainchant melody paraphrased in the top voice.

One other type of Mass that deserves mention is the so-called plenary Mass, in which a composer set both the Ordinary and the Proper for a given feast. Though most of the extant plenary cycles seem to be after-the-fact compilations of movements that were not necessarily meant to go together, Du Fay wrote one complete cycle that was definitely intended as a single unit, the *Missa Sancti Jacobi*. Composed for the Bolognese church of San Giacomo Maggiore in 1427–28, the cycle consists of all five movements of the Ordinary and settings of four Proper chants for the Feast of St. James the Greater (see Ex. 1-3 for the communion).

MUSIC FOR THE VESPERS SERVICE

In addition to the Mass, the liturgy contained a daily round of services, eight each day, called the Office, or Divine Hours. These consisted of

(1) Matins—observed chiefly in monastic institutions, traditionally during the middle of the night;

(2) Lauds—observed at daybreak;

(3) Prime—at the first hour of the day;[5]

(4) Terce—at the third hour of the day, mid-morning;

(5) Sext—at noon;

(6) None—at the ninth hour of the day, mid-afternoon (Nos. 3–6 together constitute the "Little Hours");

(7) Vespers—at twilight, when indoor lamps were lit; and

(8) Compline—before retiring. As we have seen, the Marian antiphons were traditionally sung after Compline.

It was the Vespers service that came to be most heavily invested with polyphony. The order of the service was as follows:

- opening salutation and response;
- four or five psalms, each preceded and followed by an antiphon (monastic institutions sang four psalms; cathedrals, churches, and the great secular courts sang five);
- a few verses from the Scriptures;
- a hymn (in monasteries, preceded by a responsory);
- the Magnificat, preceded and followed by an antiphon;
- concluding prayers and the salutation *Benedicamus Domino*, with its response, *Deo gratias*.

A Binchois Magnificat

Fifteenth- and sixteenth-century composers lavished most of their attention on the hymn and Magnificat. In fact, after the Ordinary, the Magnificat was the most frequently set portion of the liturgy. As plainchant, the Magnificat, a biblical canticle (similar to a psalm, but not among the Psalms of David) whose text is drawn from Luke 1: 46–55, is sung to a declamatory melodic formula known as a *tone*. Example 9-8 shows the *solemn tone* (for major feasts) to which the Magnificat is chanted when sung to tone 3 (the formulas vary according to the tone, which must be compatible with the mode of the antiphons that surround it at a given feast).

This tone forms the basis of Binchois's *Magnificat tercii toni* (*Anthology* 20), no doubt intended for the Burgundian court chapel of Philip the Good. After setting the second half of the first verse ("Anima mea Dominum"), Binchois follows the customary *alternatim* (alternation) procedure—also used in setting

5. Not until the fourteenth century was the day divided into twenty-four equal units. Before then, daytime (sunrise to sunset) and nighttime (sunset to sunrise) were each divided into their own "hourly" segments, so the length of the hour would vary according to season and latitude. For example, since northern Germany had a shorter period of daylight during the winter than southern Italy, and since the hours of daylight in both areas had to be divided equally, northern Germany had shorter daytime hours.

EXAMPLE 9-8. The solemn Magnificat tone for tone 3, verses 1–2.[6]

1. Ma - gni - fi - cat*   a - ni - ma me - a—— Do - mi - num.——
2. Et ex - sul - ta - vit spi - ri - tus me - us*—— in De - o sa - lu - ta - ri— me - o.——

hymns, psalms, and sequences—of writing polyphony for the even–numbered verses only, leaving the others to be sung to plainchant (or perhaps played on an organ). Equally typical for the period is the fauxbourdon-like setting with an embellished version of the liturgical tone in the top voice.

The setting is instructive on at least two counts. First, it illustrates the rather functional character of polyphony for the Office as compared with the grand style of the cyclic Mass. And second, it reminds us that while he is best-known to us as a writer of songs, Binchois turned out a substantial amount of sacred music, most if not all of it for the Burgundian court, and little of it ever aspiring to the emotional heights achieved, among composers of his own generation, by Du Fay and Du Fay alone.

LITURGICAL BOOKS

Although we have already had recourse to the *Liber usualis* in earlier chapters, we should now put that very handy book into perspective. Table 9-4 shows the spectrum of liturgical books that would have been used during the fifteenth and sixteenth centuries:

Table 9-4.   A selection of liturgical books, arranged in order from the general to the specific.

Type of book	Function
Missale	Texts for the Mass, including those sung to plainsong, but without the music.
Graduale	Chants for the Mass.
Breviarium	Texts for the Office.
Antiphonale	Chants for the Office, but not including those for Matins.
Martirologium	"Lives" of the saints, used in conjunction with the Office.
Pontificale	Ceremonies presided over by a bishop, such as the consecration of a church or ordination of a priest.
Rituale	Ceremonies presided over by a priest, such as baptism and marriage.

As for the *Liber usualis* (a modern compilation issued by the Benedictine monks of Solesmes, pathbreaking chant scholars of the late nineteenth cen-

---

6. *Liber usualis*, 215. Contrary to what one might expect, the third and fourth Magnificat tones are on A. The asterisks indicate the points at which the cantor stops; the choir then takes over where the text begins again.

tury):[7] it is a compendium of the most important items for the most important feasts, all culled from the missal, gradual, breviary, and antiphonal. As a one-volume shortcut it is undeniably handy; it is also undeniably dangerous if we never look beyond it. At the very least, we need to have recourse to the modern versions of the gradual and antiphonal, for both the Roman and Sarum rites. And as we saw in Chapter 7 in connection with Du Fay's *Ave regina caelorum*, we must often seek out the chant books that were used within a specific diocese during a specific period; also, many chants that were in use during the fifteenth and sixteenth centuries were subsequently dropped from the liturgy and therefore do not appear in modern chant books at all.

THE LITURGICAL CALENDAR

The liturgical calendar consists of two cycles of feasts that run concurrently: the *temporale* (Proper of the Time) and the *sanctorale* (Proper of the Saints). In general, the *temporale* celebrates feasts that commemorate events in the life of Christ, and is anchored by the fixed date for Christmas (the Nativity, on December 25) and the movable feast of Easter (the Resurrection, on the first Sunday after the first full moon following the vernal equinox, therefore anywhere from March 22 to April 25). These feasts in turn determine the timing of Advent (the beginning of the liturgical year) and Lent, the seasons that lead up to Christmas and Easter, respectively, as well as such feasts as Circumcision (one week after Christmas, January 1), Pentecost (or Whitsunday, the seventh Sunday after Easter), Trinity Sunday (a week after Pentecost), and Corpus Christi (the Thursday after Trinity Sunday).

The *sanctorale* consists of feasts with fixed dates that commemorate specific saints; for instance, the Nativity of Saint John the Baptist on June 24. And since certain saints were more highly venerated at one place than at another, a piece that honors a particular saint may provide a clue to the provenance of the piece and therefore to the whereabouts of its composer at the time of composition. Thus a composition that celebrates Saint Januarius (in Italian, San Gennaro, September 19) could hardly have been written for a place other than Naples or its environs, he being the patron saint of that city. Should a movable feast of the *temporale* land on the same day as one that is fixed within the *sanctorale*, a system of ranks decides which feast takes precedence.

PERFORMANCE PRACTICE

To think that we can perform such works as Power's *Missa Alma redemptoris mater* or Du Fay's cantus-firmus Masses just as they were performed in the fifteenth century is wishful thinking; there is simply too much we do not—

---

7. Often shortened to *Liber*, the full title is *Liber usualis missae et officii pro dominicis et festis duplicibus cum canti gregoriano* (Book of Common Practice for Mass and Office for Sundays and Double Feasts with Gregorian Chants).

and probably cannot—know. Yet on some issues, a near-consensus among scholars has taken shape. Among these are polytextuality and the *a cappella* tradition.

Polytextuality

In the edition of the Gloria and Credo of Power's *Missa Alma redemptoris mater* that appears in *Anthology* 16, the tenor sings the words not of the Mass but of the original antiphon. In effect, the editor has given us a polytextual Mass. Was this a commonplace procedure? It is difficult to say, but fifteenth-century manuscripts provide some evidence for its having been used. Moreover, because the lower voices of cantus-firmus Masses generally move more slowly than the upper voices, they often do not have enough notes to accommodate the lengthy Gloria and Credo texts. In all, polytextuality, with the tenor and perhaps even the bassus singing a second text in trope-like fashion, seems perfectly feasible, provided that the text is in Latin and is liturgical in character.

The *a cappella* Tradition

If there is one conclusion with which there is widespread agreement, it is that under normal circumstances fifteenth-century polyphony for the liturgy was performed either by voices alone or, at most, with the accompaniment of an organ. The consensus is fed by two streams of evidence: iconographic and archival.

Figure 9-1. Papal choir at the canonization of Brigitta of Sweden at the Council of Constance, 1415, as depicted in a copy of Ulrich of Richental's *Chronicle* (New York Public Library).

Figure 9-2. Philip the Good at Mass with his chapel, manuscript miniature, c. 1460 (Bibliothèque Nationale, Paris).

The iconographic evidence consists mainly of manuscript illuminations that depict music being performed within a liturgical context. Invariably, the scenes show a group of singers without the participation of instruments. For example, Figure 9-1 depicts the papal chapel celebrating the canonization of Saint Brigitta at the Council of Constance in 1415, while Figure 9-2 shows Philip the Good observing Mass with his Burgundian court chapel. In both scenes, the singers are unaccompanied.

As for the archival evidence, not only did the Cathedral of Cambrai—for which Du Fay wrote at least his last two cantus-firmus Masses—and the Sistine Chapel explicitly forbid the use of instruments, but neither institution even possessed an organ. Other establishments, though, did have organs, and they could certainly have been used in alternation with the polyphonic verses of a piece such as Binchois's *Magnificat*. Perhaps they were even used on occasion to double—or play alone—the cantus-firmus part of the large-scale tenor Masses.

There were other exceptions to what seems to have been the *a cappella* rule. At the Council of Constance, the English singers performed with trumpets and organ, while instruments joined singers at the Masses celebrated in honor of the weddings of Maximilian I and Bianca Maria Sforza in 1473 and Constantine Sforza and Camilla of Aragón in 1475. Moreover, the court of Savoy consistently recorded a trumpeter among the members of the chapel in the early 1450s, about the time that Du Fay is presumed to have written the *Missa Se la face ay pale* for that court. And finally, we read in Giannozzo Manetti's description (Chapter 7) of the Mass for the consecration of the Cathedral of Florence in 1436 that the music consisted of choruses and "divers instruments."

To be sure, these instances of voices with instruments raise further questions: Did instrumentalists really play together with the singers, or did they play before, between, and after them? Did the instruments actually double the voice parts in polyphonic compositions? Did the mixture occur during the Mass itself, and what were the duties of the Savoyard trumpeter? On the other hand, how do we know that the unaccompanied singers depicted in Figures 9-1 and 9-2 are singing polyphony and not plainsong? And what constitutes "normal"? Were any of the grand, cyclic cantus-firmus Masses composed for normal liturgical occasions?

We should keep three things in mind, all of which have to do with the nature of historical research. First, the present consensus for the *a cappella* tradition, while certainly grounded on compelling evidence, represents a recent reaction to an earlier belief that fifteenth-century liturgical polyphony was performed with whatever forces happened to be at hand; and that notion was itself a reaction to a romanticized, late-nineteenth-century view that came close to equating its own *a cappella* ideal with the singing of angels. As often happens when the pendulum is newly set in motion, it swings far in the opposite direction before eventually settling down around the middle. Second, whenever we close the door on a question with too loud a bang, it is often we who get locked in. And third, sometimes the most difficult thing for historians to do is say, "We don't know."

BIBLIOGRAPHICAL NOTE

Editions of the Music

Du Fay's music for Mass and Office (including the nonauthentic *Caput* Mass) is scattered through the *Opera omnia, CMM* 1, ed. Heinrich Besseler (American Institute of Musicology, 1951–66), vols. 2–5; for the Proper cycles attributed to Du Fay, see Laurence Feininger, ed., *MPLSER*, ser. II, vol. 1 (Rome, 1947). Binchois's sacred music is edited in Philip Kaye, *The Sacred Music of Gilles Binchois* (Oxford: Oxford University Press, 1992); for a review of Kaye's edition, see Andrew Kirkman and Philip Weller, "Binchois's Texts," *ML* 77 (1996): 566–96. All the Masses with attributions to Dunstable appear in the *Complete Works*, ed. Manfred F. Bukofzer, *MB* 8, 2nd rev. ed., ed. Margaret Bent, Ian Bent, and Brian Trowell (London: Stainer & Bell, 1970). There is a convenient edition of Power's *Missa Alma Redemptoris Mater*, Antico Church Music, *RCM* 1, ed. Gareth Curtis (Newton Abbot: Antico Editions, 1982). A group of English Masses is edited in *Fifteenth-Century Liturgical Music II: Four Anonymous Masses, EECM* 22, ed. Margaret Bent (London: Stainer & Bell, 1979); and a selection of early Mass pairs and cycles is in Charles van den Borren, *Polyphonia sacra: A Continental Miscellany of the Fifteenth Century* (London: Plainsong & Medieval Music Society, 1962).

Early Pairs and Cycles

A good starting point is still Manfred F. Bukofzer's classic study, "*Caput*: A Liturgico-Musical Study," in *Studies in Medieval and Renaissance Music* (New York: Norton, 1950), 217–310; on techniques of pairing, see Charles Hamm, "The Reson Mass," *JAMS* 18 (1965): 5–21, and Philip Gossett, "Techniques of Unification in Early Cyclic Masses and Mass Pairs," *JAMS* 19 (1966): 205–31; on structural aspects of the early English cycles, see Gareth Curtis, "Musical Design and the Rise of the Cyclic Mass," in *Companion to Medieval and Renaissance Music*, ed. Tess Knighton and David Fallows (New York: Schirmer, 1992), 154–64; on the cantus firmus as emblem, see Geoffrey Chew, "The Early Cyclic Mass as an Expression of Royal and Papal Supremacy," *ML* 53 (1972): 254–69.

Du Fay's Masses

The most comprehensive survey is David Fallows, *Dufay* (London: Dent, 1982), chapters 13–15; there are important articles by Alejandro Enrique Planchart, "Guillaume Dufay's Masses: Notes and Revisions," *MQ* 58 (1972): 1–23, "Guillaume Dufay's Masses: A View of the Manuscript Tradition," in *Papers Read at the Dufay Quincentenary Conference*, ed. Allan W. Atlas (Brooklyn: Brooklyn College, 1976), 26–60, and "Fifteenth-Century Masses: Notes on Chronology and Performance," *StudiM* 10 (1981): 3–29. The *Missa Se la face ay pale* is discussed in Thomas Brothers, "Vestiges of the Isorhythmic Tradition in Mass and Motet, ca. 1450–1475," *JAMS* 44 (1991): 1–56; on the *L'homme armé* Mass, see Leo Treitler, "Dufay the Progressive," in *Dufay Quincentenary Conference*, 115–27; on the *Ave regina* Mass, see Rob C. Wegman, "*Miserere supplicanti Dufay*: The Creation and Transmission of Guillaume Dufay's *Missa Ave regina celorum*," and Planchart, "Notes on Guillaume Dufay's Last Works," both in *JM* 13 (1995): 18–54 and 55–72, respectively.

Performance Practice

A concise introduction to the problem as it concerns the fifteenth and sixteenth centuries is in Christopher A. Reynolds, "Sacred Polyphony," in *Performance Practice: Music Before 1600*, ed. Howard Mayer Brown and Stanley Sadie (New York: Norton, 1989), 185–200. On the iconographical evidence for the *a cappella* tradition, see two articles by James W. McKinnon, "Representation of the Mass in Medieval and Renaissance Art," *JAMS* 31 (1978): 21–52, and "Fifteenth-Century Northern Book Painting and the *a cappella* Question: An Essay in Iconographical Method," in *Studies in the Performance of Late Mediaeval Music*, ed. Stanley Boorman (Cambridge: Cambridge University Press, 1983), 1–17. The issue of polytextuality is discussed in Planchart, "Parts with Words and without Words: The Evidence for Multiple Texts in Fifteenth-Century Masses," in *Studies in the Performance of Late Mediaeval Music*, 227–51; Gareth Curtis, "Brussels, Bibliothèque Royal MS 5557, and the Texting of Dufay's *Ecce ancilla Domini* and *Ave regina celorum* Masses," *AcM* 51 (1979): 73–86. On Cambrai, see Craig Wright, "Performance Practices at the Cathedral of Cambrai," *MQ* 64 (1978): 295–328; see also the entries for performance practice in the Bibliographical Notes of Chapters 22 and 37.

CHAPTER 10

Intermedio: 1453–1454

THE STATE OF EUROPE AT MID-CENTURY

In 1454, the brilliant and ambitious churchman-humanist Enea Silvio Piccolomini of Siena (1405–1464), then papal legate in Germany and a few years away from becoming Pope Pius II (1458), wrote to a friend in Rome:

> I cannot persuade myself that there is anything good in prospect. . . . Christianity has no head whom all will obey. Neither the pope nor the emperor is accorded his rights. There is no reverence and no obedience; we look on pope and emperor as figureheads and empty titles. Every city-state has its king, and there are as many princes as there are households.[1]

It is a glum but accurate assessment of the political situation at mid-century: the Hundred Years' War between England and France was only now winding down, Germany was embroiled in disputes with Hungary and Bohemia, the Aragonese and Genoese waged war over shipping lanes in the western Mediterranean, and both England and the Iberian Peninsula were on the verge of anarchy owing to feudal coalitions and arguments about succession to the throne. Yet the most immediate cause of Enea Silvio's pessimism may well have been the emptiness of the European response to an event that had occurred fourteen months earlier, one that had shaken both the church and the humanist intellectuals to the core.

THE FALL OF CONSTANTINOPLE

On May 29, 1453, after a siege of about seven weeks, the Ottoman armies of Sultan Mehmet II (d. 1481) breached the walls of Constantinople, and so put an end to the Christian Byzantine Empire. For the short term, the immediacy of the Turkish threat was perhaps more symbolic than real, though the Muslim Turks had already occupied a large area of the Balkans for almost a century, and they would soon be at war with Venice (1463–79) and even occupy the southern Italian city of Otranto (1480–81). The Turkish conquest elicited different responses from different people.

Philip the Good's Response

Philip called for a crusade against the Turks, and to this end convened the Knights of the Order of the Golden Fleece (which he had founded in 1429) at

---

1. Quoted after Gilmore, *The World of Humanism*, 1.

Lille on February 17, 1454. There he threw what must have been one of the great parties of the fifteenth century: the Feast of the Pheasant. A court chronicler, Mathieu d'Escouchy, has left a description of the festivities, which included eighteen *entremetz*, or entertainments, between the courses of the meal, one of which consisted of the following:

> After the church musicians and the pastry musicians had played four times each in turn, there entered a stag, wondrously large and fine, and on it was mounted a boy of twelve. And on his entry this boy began to sing the treble part of a song, most loud and clear, and the stag sang the tenor, with no one else visible except the child and the artificial stag. And the song they sang was called "Je ne vis oncques la pareille." After this interlude with the white stag, the singers in the church took up a motet, and afterwards, from the pastry, a lutenist accompanied two good singers.[2]

The chanson mentioned is probably by Binchois (though a late-fifteenth-century manuscript attributes it to Du Fay). No doubt the knights enjoyed the party, but they ate and ran, and not toward Constantinople.

Pius II's Response

Having become pope, Pius too campaigned for a crusade to liberate Constantinople. He was no more successful in rallying support than Philip had been, and he died in the Italian port city of Ancona in 1461, waiting for allied warships that never came.

Du Fay's Response

Du Fay mourned the loss of the Byzantine capital by commemorating it in music. On February 22, 1454 or 1456 (the year is not specified), he wrote from Geneva to Piero and Giovanni de' Medici at Florence (it is his only known autograph letter):

> In this past year I wrote four Lamentations for Constantinople which are rather good: three of them are for four voices and the texts were sent to me from Naples. I do not know whether you have them there. If you do not have them, be so kind as to let me know and I shall send them to you.[3]

Unfortunately, only one of the settings has survived: the polytextual "chanson-motet" *O tres piteulx / Omnes amici ejus*, the tenor of which quotes the plainsong responsory sung at Matins on Good Friday during the recitation of the Lamentations of Jeremiah (Ex. 10-1). There is a touch of poignancy in Du Fay's having composed these lamentations on the fall of Constantinople, since they may have jogged memories of happier times, when he had written two Byzantium-related motets for members of the Malatesta family (in the 1420s).

---

2. Quoted after Weiss and Taruskin, *Music in the Western World*, 83.
3. Quoted after D'Accone, "The Singers of San Giovanni," 319.

EXAMPLE 10-1. Du Fay, *O tres piteulx/Omnes amici ejus*, mm. 13–21.

The Effect on the Florentine Slave Trade

A fascinating document from late-fourteenth-century Florence lists the names, ethnic origins, and physical characteristics of 357 slaves sold in Florence between July 4, 1366, and March 2, 1397: 274 Tartars, 30 Greeks, 13 Russians, 8 Turks, 4 Circassians, 5 Bosnians/Slavs, 1 Cretan, and 22 Arabs, or Saracens. No such ethnic mixture would have been possible in the second half of the fifteenth century. With the fall of Constantinople (and other slave-trading ports in Asia Minor), the Black Sea and Crimean slave markets were effectively closed to the Italians, and what slaves continued to be imported into Tuscany were almost exclusively Slavs and Greeks from the Dalmatian coast or Moors and Ethiopians from Africa. Needless to say, the laws of supply and demand drove up the price of slaves substantially.

GUTENBERG AND PRINTING

During the weeks in which Constantinople was besieged, the Mainz gold-smith Johann Gensfleisch zum Gutenberg (1394/99–1468) was at work on his famous forty-two-line Bible, so called because each column (two per page) had forty-two lines of type (Fig. 10-1). Probably begun in 1452, it was published in 1456.

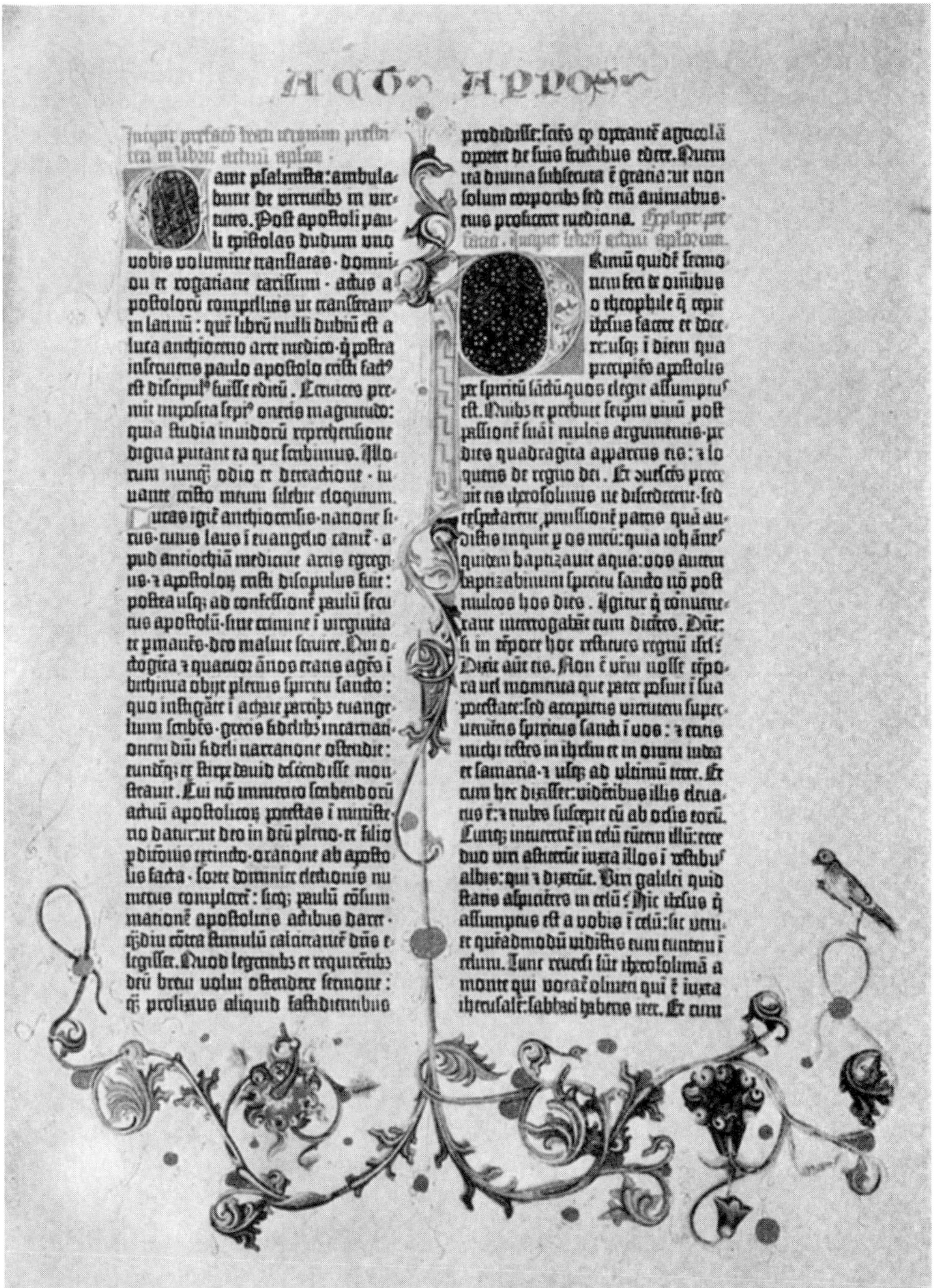

Figure 10-1. A page from the 42-line Gutenberg Bible.

Gutenberg neither invented printing nor introduced it to Europe. The first honor, in the form of printing from wooden blocks, belongs to the Chinese about a millennium earlier. And Europe already knew the technique of producing single-sheet woodcuts on a press by around 1420 and saw its first block books—collections of such sheets in book form—by about 1430. What Gutenberg did was to revolutionize the technology: he replaced wood with metal and the solid, one-piece block with a separate piece of type for each letter or character. These were held in place in a mold and could be arranged and rearranged at will. The process is called printing from movable type. In addition, Gutenberg worked out a system for casting multiple pieces of type, since even a single page might require any one letter a few hundred times; he developed a new kind of ink that would adhere to the metal type; and he used a modification of the common winepress to impress the letters of the metal type onto the waiting paper. Gutenberg's genius was such that his process saw no substantial improvement for more than three centuries.

Gutenberg's technology changed the world. It placed more knowledge and ideas into more hands and minds more quickly (his workshop could run off about three hundred pages a day) and more inexpensively than ever before. As long as he could learn to read, the ironsmith in Bohemia now had the same access to information as the Florentine patrician. And in the wars of social and religious ideas that would take center stage in the sixteenth century, books, pamphlets, and *broadsides* (single sheets printed on one side only) would become the prime ammunition (though bullets and cannonballs were never far behind). Without them, Martin Luther may well have ended up another Jan Hus.

THE PEACE OF LODI

If Enea Silvio Piccolomini had looked only at Italy instead of at Europe as a whole, he might have found a ray of hope. The Italian peninsula at mid-century was dominated by five major powers who were often at odds (if not at war) with one another: Milan, long under the rule of the Visconti family, but recently fallen under the control of the *condottiere* (hired-gun)-turned duke, Francesco Sforza; the Republic of Venice, governed by an oligarchy of about two hundred patrician families, with an elected *doge* at their head; Florence, also oligarchic, with the Medici calling the shots; the Kingdom of Naples, ruled by the Spanish House of Aragón; and the papacy, concerned with matters temporal as well as spiritual (see Fig. 10-2).

In April 1454, Venice and Milan, which had been constantly at odds over the land that separated them, signed a peace treaty in the small town of Lodi (near Milan); in August, Florence signed on; and early in 1455, Pope Nicholas V and a reluctant King Alfonso I of Naples joined the signatories. In effect, the Peace of Lodi was a five-way, mutual nonaggression pact, one that pretty much maintained the peace until 1494, when, in the face of the invading French armies, each member was quick to betray the others. As we will see in Chapter 23, the Italians would pay dearly for their falling-out, as the French invasion

Figure 10-2. Map of Italy after the Peace of Lodi, 1454.

paved the way for the so-called Wars of Italy, which continued until 1559 and which eventually led to centuries of foreign occupation by France, Spain, and the Habsburg emperors.

Finally, the Peace of Lodi was notable for another reason. Before the middle of the fifteenth century, the art of diplomacy consisted of sending diplomats on round-trip missions as needed. With the signing of the treaty in 1454, however, the signatories, still suspicious of one another, determined to keep ambassadors (who doubled as spies) at rival courts on a permanent basis. And it was not long before the practice spread beyond the Alps, and the modern system of diplomacy was born.

BIBLIOGRAPHICAL NOTE

The Fall of Constantinople

Steven Runciman's *Fall of Constantinople, 1453* (Cambridge: Cambridge University Press, 1965) is a classic account; see also chapter 1 of Myron P. Gilmore, *The World of Humanism, 1453–1517*, The Rise of Modern Europe 2 (New York: Harper & Row, 1962; originally published 1952). The effect on the slave market is discussed in Iris Origo, "The Domestic Enemy: The Eastern Slaves in Tuscany in the Fourteenth and Fifteenth Centuries," *Speculum* 30 (1955): 321–66.

Gutenberg and Printing

There is a concise introduction to the early development of printing in S. H. Steinberg, *Five Hundred Years of Printing*, rev. ed. (New Castle, Del.: Oak Knoll Press, 1996); see also the references in the Bibliographical Note to Chapter 29.

The Peace of Lodi/Diplomacy

The classic work on the origins of modern diplomacy is Garrett Mattingly, *Renaissance Diplomacy* (Boston: Houghton Mifflin, 1955).

Also Cited

Frank D'Accone, "The Singers of San Giovanni in Florence during the 15th Century," *JAMS* 14 (1961): 307–58.

PART THREE

THE 1450s TO THE 1480s

INCLUDED: BEDYNGHAM • BUSNOYS • CARON • CORNAGO •
DOMARTO • FAUGUES • FRYE • GUGLIELMO EBREO •
HAYNE VAN GHIZEGHEM • MARTINI • MORTON • OCKEGHEM •
PAUMANN • RAMOS DE PAREJA • REGIS • SERAFINO DALL'AQUILA •
TINCTORIS • TOURONT • VINCENET

CHAPTER 11

Toward Abstraction in Mass and Motet

By the mid-fifteenth century, two fundamental questions about how to set the Ordinary of the Mass had been resolved: composers now customarily set all five movements and imposed on them a sense of musical unity by basing each on the same preexistent material. And this practice would, with some innovations and exceptions, hold for the remainder of the fifteenth and sixteenth centuries.

The innovations must have begun immediately, as the 1450s saw a new generation of composers come into prominence, the two most famous of whom were Johannes Ockeghem and Antoine Busnoys, composers at the courts of France and Burgundy, respectively. The innovations were of two types. First, there was a new (or rekindled) spirit of artifice, a kind of abstract complexity, especially in the manipulation of the preexistent cantus firmus; composers seemingly vied with one another to individualize their works and demonstrate their mastery of the contrapuntal "art of the Netherlanders" (as it has often been called). And second, composers no longer limited their borrowing to a single-line cantus-firmus melody; rather, they turned increasingly to polyphonic chansons for their models and quoted the entire polyphonic fabric of the songs.

Before we look at these procedures in detail, some words of caution are necessary. (1) If during the first half of the fifteenth century the road from individual Mass movement to unified pairs to complete cyclic Masses was not always straight, what road there is in the third quarter of the century was downright circular, as the same composer could write a straightforward cantus-firmus Mass one day, do tricks with the cantus firmus the next, and then either incorporate the entire polyphonic fabric of a chanson or forgo preexistent material altogether on still another. (2) Although the composers who emerged in the 1450s were a generation younger than Du Fay, influence went in both directions; many of the younger composers' works preceded and quite possibly influenced some of Du Fay's late masterpieces. And (3) the task of dating compositions from 1450 to about 1480 is treacherous, and often we can only guess at the chronology of even so well-known a body of works as the Masses of Ockeghem; we cannot even be certain that Du Fay's *Missa Se la face ay pale*, the "classical" model of the cyclic cantus-firmus Mass, antedates the innovations seen in Petrus de Domarto's *Missa Spiritus almus*.

ARTIFICE AND COMPLEXITY I

In his *Missa Se la face ay pale*, Du Fay presented the cantus firmus at different levels of augmentation. What remained constant, however, was the original rhythm of the preexistent melody. In other words, any manipulation was purely proportional. This practice began to change around 1450.

Domarto's *Missa Spiritus almus*

Though we know that Petrus de Domarto was flourishing at mid-century, he is one of those shadowy figures whose biography cannot be pinned down with confidence. In any event, his *Missa Spiritus almus*, probably written just around 1450, points in new directions. Although the cantus firmus, drawn from the responsory *Stirps Jesse*,[1] is written out in identical fashion in each movement, it continually appears under different mensuration signs, which alter the rhythm of the melody. Example 11-1 shows the points at which the cantus firmus enters in Kyrie I (under the mensuration sign ○) and the "Christe" (under C):

EXAMPLE 11-1. Domarto, *Missa Spiritus almus*: (a) Kyrie I, mm. 4–9; (b) "Christe," mm. 4–11.

1. The chant appears in *Antiphonale sacrosanctae romanae ecclesiae* (Tournai: Desclée, 1949), 129. The Tree of Jesse, with its images of the Holy Ghost hovering above Mary as branch and Christ as flower, was a favorite Marian symbol.

Now, one could say that the rhythm of the cantus firmus in the *Missa Rex seculorum* by Dunstable or Power also changes from movement to movement (see Chapter 9). Yet how different both the effect and the aesthetic intent are in Domarto's Mass. Whereas the rhythmic changes in the early English Mass seem almost improvisatory in their apparent freedom, those in Domarto's work are strictly preplanned and serial-like in their construction. This treatment of the cantus firmus was widely adopted in the second half of the century.

Busnoys's *Missa L'homme armé*

Antoine Busnoys's Mass on the famous "armed man" melody is a seminal work. Whether or not it was the first of the *L'homme armé* Masses, it was clearly the direct model for Obrecht's Mass on the same melody, shares many similarities with Ockeghem's, and was quoted verbatim in Du Fay's (or was it the other way around?).

Busnoys is most adventurous in the Credo and Agnus Dei. If the Credo merely transposes the cantus firmus down a fourth, the Agnus Dei (*Anthology* 21) places it in the bassus in inversion (recall Du Fay's use of retrograde motion in his own Agnus Dei), first in the customary augmentation and then, given the exceptionally fast-moving surrounding voices, in what amounts to quadruple augmentation. These two movements also provide a glimpse into Busnoys's mind from another angle. Both transposition and inversion are signaled by means of enigmatic verbal canons: "Ne sonites cacephaton/Sume lichanos hypaton" (Don't sound a cacophony, take the D below) for the transposition down a fourth, and "Ubi thesis assint ceptra,/ibi arsis et e contra" (Where the scepters descend, there ascend and vice versa) for the inversion. Busnoys enjoyed such arcane Greek and Latin puzzles, and scattered them throughout his works.

Still another sign of the Mass's artifice concerns the segmentation of the cantus firmus. The *L'homme armé* melody (see Ex. 11-2, below) falls neatly into an **ABA** pattern. Whereas Du Fay always quoted the melody in segments that respected this ready-made division, Busnoys divides the melody at various points within the **B** section, thus imposing on it a somewhat unnatural formal design.

The Credo underscores one more aspect of Busnoys's penchant for artifice. The Mass as a whole is constructed in such a way that the durational proportions of the various movements and subsections express the Pythagorean harmonic ratios (for instance, 2:1, 3:2, 4:3). There is only one exception: the "Et incarnatus est" of the Credo, which stands at the center of the work and whose thirty-one breves will not fit into the Pythagorean scheme. Yet if (as one hypothesis has it) the tradition of *L'homme armé* Masses originated in connection with Philip the Good's Order of the Golden Fleece, the number thirty-one is highly symbolic: there were thirty-one knights in Philip's order.

In all, Busnoys's *Missa L'homme armé* represents the third quarter of the fifteenth century as well as any work of the time: it belongs to—and was influential in forming—what might be called the "age of *L'homme armé*"; it exemplifies that period's constructivistic, complex approach to treating the cantus firmus; it rolls out its somewhat angular melodies and rhythms with the never-ending variety that characterizes works of the time, and pushes them forward with a clear sense of harmonic motion; its duos revel in imitation, so much so that we must wonder if it was not in the duo sections of the great cantus-firmus Masses that the idea of pervading imitation, so typical of the following generation, was born; and it is smaller and more compact, and thus more typical of its time, than Du Fay's bigger and flashier Mass on the same cantus firmus. It is also just as beautiful.

THE *L'HOMME ARMÉ* TRADITION

No preexistent melody so captured the imagination of fifteenth- and six-teenth-century composers of Masses as did the *L'homme armé* tune (Ex. 11-2):

EXAMPLE 11-2. The *L'homme armé* tune.

Three words about the melody: In some Masses, the melody appears with a flat in its signature, in others without the flat; thus the tune circulated in both the Mixolydian and Dorian (transposed to G) modes. Notes within brackets might have originated in an early polyphonic setting. And some Masses call for *g*, others for *e*.

From around 1460 through the early Baroque period, there are (counting both fragmentary and lost works) about forty Masses based on the *L'homme armé* melody. Table 11-1 provides four roughly chronological groups of some of the composers who wrote them:

Table 11-1. Composers of *L'homme armé* Masses (the order within each group is alphabetical).

I. *1450s–1480s*

Philippe Basiron
Antoine Busnoys
(Philippe ?) Caron
Guillaume Du Fay
Guillaume Faugues

Johannes Ockeghem
Johannes Regis (1 or 2)
Johannes Tinctoris
Anonymous cycle of 6 (by Busnoys?)
    in MS Naples VI.E.40

II. *Roughly 1480s–1520s*

Juan de Anchieta
Antoine Brumel
Loyset Compère
Josquin Desprez (2)
Pierre de la Rue (2)
Jean Mouton
Jacob Obrecht
Marbriano de Orto
Matthaeus Pipelare
Bertrandus Vaqueras

III. *1520s–1600*

Robert Carver
Andreas De Silva
Cristóbal de Morales
Giovanni Pierluigi da Palestrina (2)
Juan de Peñalosa
Ludwig Senfl

IV. *Seventeenth century*

Giacomo Carissimi

In addition, a number of secular pieces incorporated the melody, the most significant of which for the development of the tradition is the mid-fifteenth-century setting ascribed to the English composer Robert Morton (see below).

Origins

Where, when, and with whom did the melody and the earliest Masses based on it originate? In his *Toscanello in musica* of 1523, the theorist Pietro Aaron had this to say:

Si esistima, che da Busnois fussi trovato quel canto chiamato lome armé notato con il segno puntato, & che da lui fussi tolto il tenore.

It is believed that by Busnoys was found that song called the "armed man," notated with the dotted sign, and that by him was taken the tenor.[2]

On the other hand, what may be the earliest polyphonic piece to incorporate the melody is a chanson that combines the *L'homme armé* tune with a humorous rondeau, *Il sera pour vous*, which urges the Burgundian court singer Symon le Breton to grab a celery stalk and do battle with the "dreaded Turk." This song survives in two versions: one for three voices and without ascription (*Anthology* 22), the other with an added fourth voice and an attribution to "Borton." Thus the chanson has usually been associated with the English composer Robert Morton ("Borton" being read as a corruption), a singer at the Burgundian courts of Philip the Good and Charles the Bold.

What can we make of all this? One provocative hypothesis suggests that (1) Busnoys wrote the chanson (the hypothesis gives greater weight to the "B" than to the "orton";[3] (2) the chanson served as a model for both Busnoys's and Ockeghem's Masses; (3) Busnoys's Mass is probably the earliest in the tradition (no other *L'homme armé* Mass has been shown to antedate it); and (4) perhaps Busnoys even composed the *L'homme armé* melody itself. Yet there is no evidence that Busnoys wrote the polyphonic chanson; Aaron, after all, does not say that he "composed" it, only that he "found" it (though just what does that mean?); and though Busnoys's Mass is certainly one of the earliest in the tra-

2. The very literal translation follows Strohm, *The Rise of European Music*, 470.

3. A more recent view holds that "Borton" is the little-known composer Pieter Bordon of Ghent.

dition, whether it is first, second, or third cannot be decided on the evidence currently available. In the end, we can do no more than note that the earliest *L'homme armé* Mass with a secure date is one by Johannes Regis, which was copied at Cambrai in 1462; and next in line is the Mass by (Philippe ?) Caron, copied at Rome in 1463.

For whom or for what were the early *L'homme armé* Masses destined? Two of the most enticing possibilities connect the Masses with Philip the Good's Order of the Golden Fleece, which Philip hoped would mount a crusade against the Turks, and with a special Christmas Mass at which the Holy Roman Emperor unsheathed a sword to symbolize the defense of Christianity against the Turks. Certainly, Masses on the "armed man" melody would have been emblematic of both occasions.

Finally, if Busnoys did not compose the melody, under what circumstances did it originate? Was it, as seems likely, a popular monophonic tune, or (less likely) was it conceived as a voice part in a polyphonic chanson? Were its origins courtly or urban? Was it written in response to the Turkish conquest of Constantinople, with Philip the Good or his son and successor, Charles the Bold, as the "armed man"? Perhaps one day we will know the answers.

ANTOINE DE BUSNE (*DIT* BUSNOYS)

Though Busnoys's date of birth remains unknown, his name tells us that he probably came from the hamlet of Busne, in the Pas-de-Calais of northern France. The earliest known document concerning Busnoys, a record of the Apostolic Penitentiary (Rome) placing him at the Cathedral of Tours sometime before February 1461, casts light on an apparent mean streak in his personality:

> Anthoine de Busnes, cleric and perpetual chaplain in the cathedral of Tours, beat a certain priest in the cloister of the same church, and arranged to have him beaten by others, and encouraged these beatings, at five separate times, such that blood was shed; on account of which he incurred the sentence of excommunication under which, unaware of the law, and not in contempt of the Keys [of St. Peter], he celebrated and took part in Mass and other divine Offices. The said priest having fully recovered, nor having been rendered unfit for service, [Busnoys] asks to be absolved [of the crime of bloodshed], and also asks dispensation for the irregularity [of having attended and celebrated Mass while excommunicated].[4]

His rowdiness notwithstanding (many church documents record what seems to have been widespread clerical violence), Busnoys remained at Tours, where he rose to the rank of sub-deacon at the church of St. Martin in April 1465. The implications of his tenure there may be significant, for the treasurer of the church since 1459 was none other than Ockeghem, and we can only wonder what musical exchanges may have taken place between them. Five months later, Busnoys turned up at the collegiate church of St. Hilaire-le-Grand at

4. Quoted after Starr, "Rome as the Centre of the Universe," 260.

Poitiers, where he was a candidate for the position of master of the choirboys; but though described as "maxime expertus in musica et poetria" (most expert in music and poetry), some of the canons preferred to retain the apparently inadequate in-house candidate.

From the text of the motet *In hydraulis* (see below), we know that Busnoys began an association with Charles the Bold shortly before Charles became Duke of Burgundy in June 1467. He became a full-fledged member of the Burgundian court chapel in 1471, remaining there off and on after Charles's death in 1477 until 1483. Busnoys's whereabouts during the final decade of his life are uncertain; we know only that he is mentioned as deceased in the November 6, 1492, chapter minutes of the Bruges church St. Sauveur.

Busnoys was highly esteemed during his lifetime. Tinctoris dedicated his *Liber de natura et proprietate tonorum* (1476) to Busnoys and Ockeghem, calling them "the most outstanding and most famous professors of the art of music," while the Spanish theorist Bartolomé Ramos de Pareja drew on a number of Busnoys pieces in his *Musica practica* (1482) in order to show how composers deployed clever verbal canons to signal the transposition, inversion, or retrograde treatment of a cantus firmus. And though Busnoys is best-known to us as a song composer (he wrote about seventy-five), he was also an important composer of sacred music. Indeed, if the cycle of six anonymous *L'homme armé* Masses and a few others that have recently been attributed to him are in fact his, Busnoys would figure as one of the major Mass composers of the second half of the fifteenth century.

ARTIFICE AND COMPLEXITY II

Composers of the period did not reserve their ingenuity only for pieces based on preexistent cantus-firmus melodies. At times they made up their own cantus firmus, and at times they did without that structural scaffold altogether.

Busnoys's *In hydraulis*

The motet *In hydraulis* (*Anthology* 23) holds a special place among Busnoys's works. First, it is the only one of his compositions that can be dated with even approximate accuracy. Since Busnoys refers to himself in the poem as "illustris comitis / De Charolois indignum musicum" (unworthy musician of the illustrious Count of Charolais), the work must date from between the time Busnoys first entered Charles's service—after September-October 1465—and June 15, 1467, when Charles succeeded his father, Philip the Good, as Duke of Burgundy and would therefore no longer have been referred to as the Count of Charolais.

Second, Busnoys addresses the *secunda pars* (second part) of the motet directly to Ockeghem and refers to himself as one of the latter's progeny ("propaginis"). Now, there are many claims from the fifteenth and sixteenth centuries about one composer having studied with another, and there is always the question of how literally we should take them. Yet in this instance, we should recall the two composers' St. Martin of Tours connection in the early 1460s, and there are references in Tinctoris linking the two. In any event, whether Busnoys studied formally with Ockeghem or not, he certainly thought of the slightly older(?) musician as a teacher.

In hydraulis is a fine example of a composition in which the composer has constructed a new cantus firmus, in this case a sixfold statement of a three-note figure (Ex. 11-3):

EXAMPLE 11-3. Busnoys, *In hydraulis*, opening statement of the tenor cantus firmus in original note values.

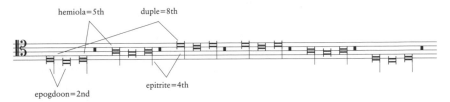

This arch-shaped "melody" reflects the Pythagorean ratios mentioned in the motet's text: "Epitrite and hemiola / epogdoon and duple produce / the concord of fourth and fifth / the tone and the octave." Moreover, since the arch in its entirety is stated four times altogether (starting at mm. 19 and 61 in the first part, and 36 and 76 in the second), each time under a different mensuration sign, the duration of the various sections of the motet are also governed by the Pythagorean proportions: 6:4:3:2.

In hydraulis may well have a companion piece, Ockeghem's motet *Ut heremita solus*: the opening reference to a "hermit" (beyond which there is no text) applies nicely to St. Anthony Abbot, the most famous of the Christian hermits and Busnoys's own patron saint; it is based on a "homemade" cantus firmus every bit as constructivist as that of *In hydraulis*; each statement of the cantus firmus in the *prima pars* (first part) runs on for 108 semibreves, this number being the gematrial equivalent of B (2) U (20) S (18) N (13) O (14) Y (23) S (18); and the head-motive is closely related to the motive with which the *secunda pars* of *In hydraulis* begins on the very words "Haec Ockeghem" (Ex. 11-4).

EXAMPLE 11-4. Opening motives of the superius in (a) Ockeghem, *Ut heremita solus*, and (b) Busnoys, *In hydraulis* (second part).

Though we do not know the date of Ockeghem's work and thus which piece has chronological priority, we can hardly doubt that the later of the two works returns the musical compliment contained in the earlier one.

Ockeghem's *Missa Prolationum*

In some respects, the most intellectually impressive examples of artifice and complexity are those works in which composers deprived themselves of the traditional building block of the cantus firmus and depended entirely on their own imagination. One example of this type, Johannes Ockeghem's *Missa Prolationum* (*Anthology* 24 for the Kyrie and Sanctus), has been called "perhaps the most extraordinary contrapuntal achievement of the fifteenth century."[5] The work is constructed mainly as a series of double canons, each for two voices. The interval between the voices of the successive canons grows steadily from the unison in Kyrie I through the octave at the "Osanna" of the Sanctus, after which it contracts to the fourth in the "Benedictus" and Agnus Dei I and finishes at the fifth in Agnus Dei II and III; as a cycle of canons at different intervals, then, the Mass is like Bach's *Goldberg Variations*. Moreover, in some of the canons, the two voices begin together, each voice in a different mensuration, so that each will hold certain notes longer than its partner; in effect, superius and contratenor sing one canon in $\frac{2}{2}$ and $\frac{3}{2}$ meters simultaneously, while tenor and bassus sing another canon in $\frac{6}{4}$ and $\frac{9}{4}$ simultaneously.

We can get a graphic view of how this works by looking at the original notation of Kyrie I and II as it appears in the so-called Chigi Codex (Fig. 11-1). The canons for the upper and lower voices of Kyrie I appear at the top of the facing folios. Only one voice is notated for each canon; the two mensuration signs in each voice part indicate that the two voices to be derived from the notation move along in different mensurations, while the single C clef indicates that the canon is at the interval of the unison. In Kyrie II, which starts on the next-to-last system of each folio, the paired mensuration signs are written a third apart, thus indicating that here the canons are at the interval of a third.

We might look at the canon for the upper voices of Kyrie I (on the verso of the opening) in greater detail. The melody begins with a series of breves; the voice in perfect tempus sings these as perfect breves (each one equal to three semibreves), while the voice in imperfect tempus sings them as imperfect breves (each one equal to two semibreves); thus the voice in imperfect tempus will move along more quickly and pull ahead of the voice in perfect tempus. This continues until both voices begin to hit the shorter notes—semibreves, minims, and semiminims, all of which are imperfect no matter what the tempus—at which point the distance between the two voices becomes fixed at whatever distance had been reached, and the canon becomes regular.

Not every section of the Mass is a double-mensuration canon. The "Christe," in fact, is not a canon at all. Rather, the lower voices of each pair sing

5. *New Grove* 13: 493.

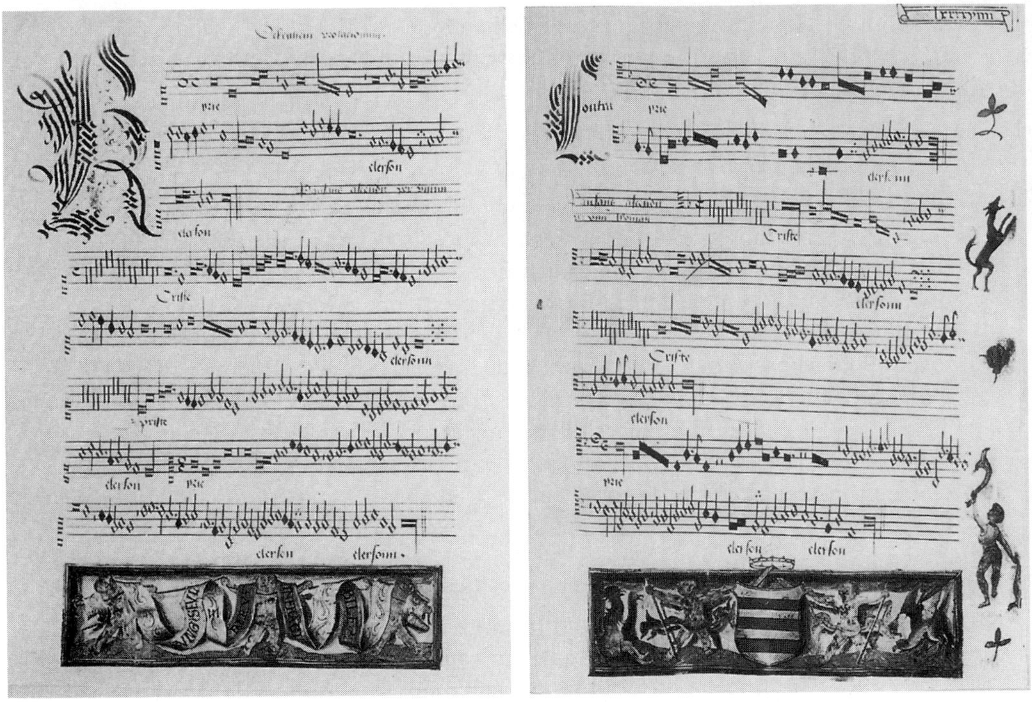

Figure 11-1. Opening from the Chigi Codex showing beginning of Ockeghem's *Missa Prolationum*.

two duets that are answered in dialogue-like fashion by the upper voices of each pair, but a major second higher each time.

In all, the *Missa Prolationum* is a technical tour de force. Yet Ockeghem paid a price for his contrapuntal genius, for writers on music from the sixteenth century to the nineteenth, some of whom probably never heard a note he wrote, came to see him as little more than a skilled contrapuntist, and a pedantic one at that.

JOHANNES OCKEGHEM

Ockeghem (more often spelled "Okeghem" in contemporary sources) was born in the village of Saint-Ghislain in the present-day Belgian province of Hainaut, then part of the duchy of Burgundy, between 1410 and 1425. Documents show that he was a singer, first at the Church of Our Lady at Antwerp in 1443–44 and then in the service of the Duke of Bourbon in 1446–48. In 1450 or 1451, he joined the French royal chapel (Fig. 11-2), where, until his death on February 6, 1497, he served Charles VII, Louis XI, and Charles VIII.

That three successive kings of France regarded Ockeghem highly is evident from the prestigious positions they bestowed on him: first, *premier chappelain*, then the lucrative post of treasurer of the Abbey of St. Martin at Tours (of which the kings of France were hereditary abbots), and in 1464, *maître de la chapelle de chant du roy*, all of which he held for the remainder of his life. Other highlights of his career were his meeting with Du Fay at Cambrai in 1464 and, for this apparently little-traveled musician, a trip to Spain in 1470.

Ockeghem also received praise from his contemporaries. Tinctoris listed him first among the composers of his generation, and noted that he had the finest bass voice of his day. The poet-musician Jean Molinet praised his "artful masses and harmonious motets." And upon his death, Ockeghem was eulogized in laments by Molinet (*Nymphes des bois*, set to music by Josquin), Guillaume Crétin, and Erasmus of Rotterdam. But perhaps the most remarkable praise appears in Cosimo Bartoli's *Ragionamenti accademici* of 1567: "[Ockeghem was] almost the first in these times to rediscover music, which was almost entirely dead, just as Donatello rediscovered sculpture."

Bartoli's assessment is exceptional in that it came at a time when Ockeghem was beginning to be viewed as a composer of three or four pieces notable for their contrapuntal tricks. Thus by the eighteenth century, Charles Burney in

Figure 11-2. Manuscript miniature showing French royal chapel(?); the tall figure in the foreground is presumed by some to be Ockeghem.

his *General History of Music* (1782) could find nothing better to say about him than that his works displayed "a determined spirit of patient perserverance." Only in the nineteenth century did a reassessment get under way, and then the pendulum swung hard in the opposite direction: Ockeghem was described as "romantic," "irrational," and "mystic." There is still hard work to be done on this difficult-to-characterize composer.

Ockeghem's career sheds light on a broader subject. As noted in Chapter 3, the years around 1400 witnessed a geographical shift in the central tradition from France to the Low Countries. By the middle of the century, though, France was back on its artistic feet, enough so to entice Ockeghem to pass virtually his entire career at the French royal court. Moreover, such establishments as St. Martin at Tours (Busnoys and Ockeghem), St. Chapelle at Bourges (Guillaume Faugues, Philippe Basiron, Colinet de Lannoy), and the Cathedral of Orléans (Tinctoris was the master of the boys there in the early 1460s), all in the heart of the Loire Valley, had thriving musical institutions. The central tradition was now truly *Franco*-Flemish.

SOME IMPORTANT MUSIC MANUSCRIPTS

A number of the works we have considered reach us in the manuscripts that make up the monumental collection known as the Trent Codices (Domarto's Mass and Busnoys's *In hydraulis*) or in the later Chigi Codex (Ockeghem's *Missa Prolationum* and Busnoys's *Missa L'homme armé*).

The Trent Codices

This collection consists of seven manuscripts housed at two different locations in the northern Italian (Tyrolean) city of Trent.[6] The manuscripts transmit more than 1,500 pieces by eighty-eight composers (from the famous to the otherwise unknown); the chronology of the repertory spans the better part of the years 1400–1480. Together, the seven manuscripts form the largest and most important collection from the fifteenth century. The two oldest codices are MSS 87 and 92, probably copied in the Tyrolean city of Bolzano during the 1430s–1440s. Trent 93 may have been copied at the start of the 1450s, while MSS 88–91 are mainly the work of one scribe, Johannes Wiser, who probably copied them out over the course of a decade starting in the mid-1450s (he became rector of the Cathedral of Trent in 1459); he left his signature on the final folio—465^v—of MS 90.

What purpose did the Trent Codices serve? They could hardly have been used for performance: at about twelve by nine inches, they are too small for a choir to have sung from, and they contain their share of scribal errors that were left uncorrected. Were they intended merely as repositories of music to satisfy Trent's humanist-oriented church dignitaries? Most likely they served as ex-

6. MSS 87–92 are kept at the Museo Provinciale d'Arte, located in the Castello del Buon Consiglio; MS 93, which was separated from the others, is now at the Biblioteca Capitolare.

emplars from which performance copies could be made as needed, in which case they bear witness to what must have been an extraordinarily rich musical life. Trent, after all, was a major stopping point and commercial center on the heavily traveled trade route that crossed the Alps through the Brenner Pass. Whatever their original purpose, the Trent Codices, which were "discovered" only a century ago, deserve their status as the most thoroughly studied manuscripts of the fifteenth century.

The Chigi Codex

In contrast to the utilitarian Trent Codices, the Chigi Codex (Fig. 11-1) is a magnificently decorated "presentation" manuscript; even the edges of its folios are gilded.[7] Its original layer was copied at the Habsburg-Burgundian court at Brussels, probably during the period 1498–1503, and certainly for the long-lived (1418–1515) Burgundian nobleman Philippe Bouton, whose coat of arms and motto—"Ung soeul Boutton"—appear toward the end of the codex. Although the manuscript contains a good deal of music by composers of the Josquin generation (some of it added later), the highlight of its repertory is a group of thirteen Masses by Ockeghem. In fact, the Chigi Codex almost contains a complete edition of Ockeghem's Masses (only one cycle and an isolated Credo are missing). Also well represented is the composer Johannes Regis, with six motets (half of those in the manuscript). The Chigi Codex is one of our most precious turn-of-the-century manuscripts and might even represent a kind of Ockeghem (and Regis?) memorial volume.

ARTIFICE AND COMPLEXITY III

Quite aside from the various kinds of complexity we have seen in the Masses discussed so far, the third quarter of the fifteenth century witnessed two important developments in Mass composition: Masses based on secular chansons came to outnumber those based on plainchant melodies; and composers frequently drew on not just a single voice part of the chanson (the tenor), but the entire polyphonic fabric. Two Masses will illustrate the point.

Ockeghem's *Missa Fors seulement*

There is hardly a more powerful, brooding work from this period than the five-voice Mass (only the Kyrie, Gloria, and Credo survive, or is that all Ockeghem wrote?) that Ockeghem based on his rondeau *Fors seulement l'actente que je meure* (*Anthology* 25a and b for chanson and Kyrie). The clearest and most direct reworking of the entire polyphonic texture of the song appears at the beginning of the Kyrie. Superius and contratenor spin out the opening phrase of the chanson's superius in close imitation, while bassus I presents the song's original contratenor transposed down a fifth, thus altering the modal orientation of the chanson. With the cadence at measure 11, it seems as if Ockeghem is

7. Rome, Biblioteca Vaticana, Chigiana, C. VIII. 234.

content to quote just the tenor of the chanson in the tenor of the Mass, with both bassus parts alluding to the chanson contratenor. But with the start of Kyrie II (m. 47), which corresponds to the beginning of the **B** section of the rondeau (m. 42), and with the chanson tenor first in the tenor and then the contratenor of the Mass, Ockeghem reworks the original polyphonic fabric in an almost fantasia-like manner, the original polyphony sometimes there, sometimes not.

The *Missa Fors seulement*, then, displays three different approaches to the preexistent material: it may simply quote the tenor of the chanson in cantus-firmus-like fashion, now in one voice, now in another, and always at the same rate of speed as the voices that surround it; it may draw on all the chanson voices in succession (as in the Gloria and Credo); and it may draw on all the voices simultaneously. In the end, however, it is the use of the chanson tenor as cantus firmus that clarifies the structure of each movement.

Vincenet's *Missa O gloriosa regina mundi*

Vincenet's Mass is based on the motet *O gloriosa regina mundi* by Johannes Touront, a composer who seems to have been popular in central Europe, but about whose life we have not a single document. Example 11-5 shows the opening measures of Touront's motet and each movement of Vincenet's Mass:

EXAMPLE 11-5. (a) Touront, *O gloriosa regina mundi*, mm. 1–8. Vincenet, *Missa O gloriosa regina mundi*: (b) Kyrie, mm. 1–8; (c) Gloria, mm. 1–7; (d) Credo, mm. 1–6; (e) Sanctus, mm. 1–7; (f) Agnus Dei, mm. 1–14.

(c)

(d)

(e)

(f)

Thus Vincenet treats the preexistent material differently at the beginning of each movement; he alludes to, reworks, even comments on his model, using it as a springboard for his own imagination. And in a way, the comments go in both directions, for the text of Touront's motet—"O glorious Queen of the world"—serves as an unheard trope on the text of the Mass and makes it specific to the Marian occasion for which it was no doubt written.

The Idea of *Imitatio*

Central to humanist ideas about artistic creativity was the concept of *imitatio*, the imitation of specific models—as relevant for the student, who learned by imitation, as for the master, who imitated in order to pay homage to, compete with, or comment on a model. Here is how Tinctoris expressed the idea: "Just as Virgil took Homer as his model in his divine work, the Aeneid, so by Hercules do I use these [composers] as models for my own small productions; particularly have I plainly imitated their admirable style of composition insofar as the arranging of concords is concerned."[8]

But is this, as some would have it, what drove composers to rework or quote polyphonic models in their Masses? Three points raise a caution flag. First, whereas in literature both the model and the imitation were in the same genre,

8. *The Art of Counterpoint*, 15.

composers usually crossed genres—that is, they based Masses on secular songs and motets. Moreover, the fifteenth-century Franco-Flemish composers who are said to have been influenced by humanist ideas of *imitatio* were products of the northern *maîtrises*, where they received anything but a thorough human-ist-classical education. Finally, the tradition of basing new polyphonic com-positions on preexistent material was already centuries old by the time *imitatio* became a hot intellectual topic in Italy. Yet such speculation has a point: to mull over the interesting is as valuable as considering the definite.

Terminology

Lacking any fifteenth-century terminology, what should we call a cantus-firmus Mass that also quotes its model's entire polyphonic fabric? Using the recently proposed term "imitation Mass" confronts us with the problem that the sixteenth century itself used the Latin form of that term—*Missa ad imita-tionem*—to describe Masses that, while based on the idea of reworking the entire polyphonic fabric of their model, used models built on successive points of imitation and thus lacked a structural tenor voice of their own; thus the six-teenth-century "imitation Mass" itself had no structural cantus firmus. Equally misleading is "parody Mass," a modern term for the sixteenth century's own "imitation Mass."

Whatever term we use, we must remember that although these fifteenth-century Masses draw on more than one voice of the polyphonic model, they usually retain the tenor of that model as their own structural voice; they are in effect still cantus-firmus Masses.

OCKEGHEM'S STYLE

We can consider the general style of Ockeghem, the most imposing figure of his generation, by comparing three stylistic elements—timbre, texture, and tonality—as they appear in his Masses and those of Du Fay.

Timbre

Du Fay's Masses on *Se la face ay pale*, *L'homme armé*, and *Ave regina caelorum* descend, respectively, to B, c, and A, and even those low notes are not reached very often. The largest total ambitus in any of the three works is that of the *Ave regina* Mass: nineteen notes.

We need not look beyond the low C's and D's at the entrance of bassus II in Ockeghem's *Missa Fors seulement* to realize that the soundscape has deepened considerably. Nor is this a fluke. Ockeghem's motet *Intemerata Dei mater* de-scends just as low, as does a Mass by Tinctoris. who seems almost self-conscious about its extremely low range, since he takes pains to describe the work as being "extra manum" (outside the hand, beyond the gamut; see Chapter 3). And while we must always consider the possibility of different tunings, lack of fixed pitch, and/or transposition, there can be no doubt that Ockeghem and his contemporaries enlarged the available musical space, most notably in their cultivation of the lower register. The difference in sound strikes our ears immediately: Du Fay tends to be high and brilliant; Ockeghem and his contemporaries are generally wider (the *Missa Prolationum* has an ambitus of twenty-two notes), lower, and darker.

Texture and Tonality

Du Fay basically retained the four-voice texture established by the anonymous *Caput* Mass: the tenor is the structural voice; the superius has the "melody"; the bass, with its frequent skips of fourths and fifths, guides the harmonic motion; and the altus is something of a filler. Each voice, then, has its specialized function.

We hear something different in the *Missa Fors seulement*. Aside from the added fifth voice, the textural relationship between the voices has changed. Since the tenor (or occasionally another voice) presents the cantus firmus in note values that blend in with those of the other voices, we tend not to hear it as a distinctive, scaffold-like part. As for the melody, where is it? There is now less specialization among the voices, as they all contribute more or less equally to the thick web of nonimitative counterpoint. This sense of blending and equality is reinforced by the melodies themselves and the phrase structure within which they roll out. Whereas Du Fay builds long melodic arches by the constant generation of sharply defined motives that reach clear-cut cadential points and then start again, Ockeghem writes melodies that seem to meander and cadence where they will. Perhaps we can sum up the difference in approaches as follows: were we to spend an evening listening to Du Fay and Ockeghem Masses, it is probably the Du Fay we would whistle in the shower that night (though the opening motive of *Fors seulement* might haunt us for days).

Because Ockeghem's bass parts sometimes sing as lyrically as any other voice, they tend not to direct the harmonic motion with quite the force of Du Fay's. And since Ockeghem tends to cadence less frequently and clearly, his music is generally less tonal-sounding than Du Fay's.

ARTIFICE AND COMPLEXITY IV

Some Masses either use or allude to more than one preexistent model.

Multiple Cantus-Firmus Melodies

In what was presumably his next-to-last cantus-firmus Mass, the *Missa Ecce ancilla domine/Beata es Maria*, Du Fay drew on two different antiphons, both associated with Marian celebrations. When Johannes Regis decided to write a Mass on the same *Ecce ancilla domine* antiphon, which is sung at the Feast of the Annunciation, March 25, not only did he combine it with one other antiphon from the same feast, but he worked in the melodies of five other Marian antiphons, for a total of seven cantus firmi in all. Somewhat more modest is Regis's *Missa Dum sacrum mysterium/L'homme armé*, in which that most famous of all cantus-firmus melodies is combined with a number of chants drawn from the Feast of St. Michael. And though composers never made a habit of combining multiple cantus-firmus/plainsong melodies, Jacob Obrecht would eventually work miracles with the idea.

One Cantus Firmus with a Sneaky Allusion to Another

In his *Missa Clemens et benigna*, a Mass clearly intended for a Marian celebration, (Philippe ?) Caron seems to work in motivic allusions to an anonymous Italian song, *Madonna par la torno*, an anonymous French chanson, *Hélas, mestresse, m'amie*, and Johannes Joye's chanson *Mercy mon dueil*, which pleads for mercy. The unsung texts of all three works, which were presumably recognized by the performers and listeners, complement the emotion of the plainsong cantus firmus. Caron's Mass thus stands as a wonderful example of the way in which the fifteenth century comfortably coordinated the sacred and secular worlds.

THE FIVE-VOICE TENOR MOTET

Although the five-voice tenor motet has its share of artifice and complexity, it is a distinctive enough sub-genre to be treated on its own.

Regis's *Clangat plebs flores*

The composer who most assiduously cultivated this genre was Johannes Regis (known also as Jean le Roy; c. 1425–1495/96). Though he has long been in the shadow of Ockeghem and Busnoys, lately Regis's stock has risen dramatically in the eyes of historians: as we have seen, his motets occupy a prominent position in the Chigi Codex; his *Missa L'homme armé*, copied at Cambrai in 1462, is the earliest Mass on that melody for which there is a precise *terminus ante quem*; he enjoyed the distinction of having served as an assistant to Du Fay at the Cathedral of Cambrai, probably in the 1440s; and he is often cited as a stylistic link between Du Fay and Josquin.

We can see the essential characteristics of the five-voice tenor motet in Regis's *Clangat plebs flores* (*Anthology* 26): (1) it is in two *partes*, the first in triple meter, the second in duple; (2) the cantus firmus is drawn from a plainsong melody—the antiphon *Sicut lilium inter spinas*—and assigned to the tenor; (3) the tenor is the last voice to enter, preceded by a series of trios and duets; and (4) the tenor begins in long notes (at least for the duration of the *prima pars*) and then becomes integrated into the prevailing rhythmic movement of the other voices.

Regis's motet was singled out by Tinctoris in Book III of his *Art of Counter-*

point as an illustration of the rule that "variety must be most accurately sought for in all counterpoint." And variety is certainly apparent in Regis's treatment of the cantus firmus, each statement of which is treated differently from the others. In statement I (mm. 16–60), the tenor sings the cantus firmus in long note values, with a rest between the first two fragments of the melody that is so long as to seem irrational. After cutting right through the articulation between the two *partes* as though it were not there (a piece of structural artifice if there ever was one), the tenor reacts to the new duple meter, shortens its note values, and falls into two-bar patterns in which it leads an alternation of five-voice tutti statements and tenorless duos. In statement II (mm. 85–109), the tenor embellishes the melody and integrates it into a series of duos (a texture that stood in contrast with the cantus firmus in the first statement). And in statement III (mm. 110–122), the tenor rattles off the cantus firmus as though it cannot wait to be finished with it. No work that we have considered up to this point treats its cantus firmus in a more varied manner.

TWO PROBLEMATIC BIOGRAPHIES

Two composers we have encountered in this chapter, Petrus de Domarto and Vincenet, provide good object lessons in the difficulty of reconstructing the biographies of fifteenth-century musicians.

Petrus de Domarto

All we know about the life of Petrus de Domarto is that he is listed as a newly arrived singer at the Church of Our Lady at Antwerp during the period June–December 1449, and that his name is not included in that church's records for 1450 (the records for subsequent years are lost).

Recently, Domarto has been tentatively identified with the singer Pierre de Maillart called Petrus (d. 1477), a member of the Burgundian chapel of Philip the Good from 1436 through 1451. Is the identification tenable? Perhaps we will never know, since a crucial piece of evidence is missing. Maillart was certainly at Philip's court in 1447, and he is recorded there again in 1450, which squares nicely with Domarto's not being listed at Antwerp in that year. Unfortunately, though, the Burgundian account books for 1449 (as well as for 1448) are missing, and without the control that the 1449 accounts would provide, the issue remains unresolved: were Maillart present at Burgundy, he and Domarto could not be the same, while his absence from Burgundy that year would make the identification plausible.

Vincenet

This problem ends happily. The Vincenet article in the *New Grove* (19: 781) tentatively identifies the composer of the *Missa O gloriosa regina mundi* as "Joh[annes] Vicenot" and claims that he was a member of the papal chapel in 1426–28. To this we may add that Vicenot remained with the papal chapel through June 1429, he was a priest, and he hailed from Toul (just west of Nancy, in Lorraine).

Yet it is evident that our composer, whose full name—Vincentius du Briquet—has only recently come to light, cannot be identified with the papal singer of the 1420s. We know from a document that has long been available that Vincenet left a widow, Vanella, who in 1479 was residing at Naples; Vincenet, then, was married and therefore not a priest. Also a 1469 payment record states unequivocally that Vincenet came from the province of Hainaut.

Obviously, there are two Vincenets, not one; and this little story teaches us two lessons. First, *New Grove* has conflated the lives of two people with the same name (and Vincenet/Vicenot is not the only such fifteenth-century pair to plague us). And second, what we do not know or can only speculate about today may become entirely clear tomorrow, as research continues to yield new archival documents, manuscript fragments, and so on. Sometimes we do get smarter!

BIBLIOGRAPHICAL NOTE

Editions of the Music

Busnoys: the Masses and motets appear in the *Collected Works*, Parts 2–3, *The Latin-Texted Works*, ed. Richard Taruskin, *MMR* 5/2–3 (New York: The Broude Trust, 1990). **Caron**: *P. Caron: Les Oeuvres complètes*, 2 vols., ed. James Thompson (Brooklyn: Institute of Mediaeval Music, 1971–76). **Ockeghem**: *Collected Works*, vols. 1–2 (Masses), 2nd ed., ed. Dragan Plamenac, vol. 3 (motets), ed. Richard Wexler (New York: American Musicological Society, 1966, 1992); a new edition of the Masses in 12 fascicles is in the course of publication, *Johannes Ockeghem—Masses and Mass Sections*, ed. Jaap van Benthem (Utrecht: Koninklijke Vereniging voor Nederlandse Muziekgeschiedenis, 1994–); for an edition of the *Missa Cuiusvis toni* that realizes it in all the modes, see George Houle, ed., *Ockeghem's "Missa cuiusvis toni" in Its Original Notation and Edited in All the Modes* (Bloomington: University of Indiana Press, 1992). **Regis**: *Opera omnia*, CMM 9, ed. Charles Lindenburg (American Institute of Musicology, 1956). **Tinctoris**: *Opera omnia*, CMM 18, ed. William Melin (American Institute of Musicology, 1976). **Vincenet**: *The Collected Works of Vincenet*, RRMMAER 9–10, ed. Bertran E. Davis (Madison: A-R Editions, 1978).

General Studies

Perhaps the best starting point is the exceptionally rich account of the period in Reinhard Strohm, *The Rise of European Music, 1380–1500* (Cambridge: Cambridge University Press, 1993), part IV, chapter 2; on cantus-firmus treatment, see Edgar H. Sparks, *Cantus Firmus in Mass and Motet, 1420–1520* (Berkeley and Los Angeles: University of California Press 1963); for the motet, those who can manage the German should consult Wolfgang Stephan's *Die burgundisch-niederländische Motette zur Zeit Ockeghems* (Kassel: Bärenreiter, 1937; reprint 1973), still one of the best general discussions of style for the music of 1450–80; see also Dolores Pesce, *Hearing the Motet: Essays on the Motet of the Middle Ages and Renaissance* (London: Oxford University Press, 1996). Three articles, all dealing with the Mass, are more specialized in their focus: J. Peter Burkholder's "Johannes Martini and the Imitation Mass of the Late Fifteenth Century," *JAMS* 38 (1985): 470–523, which must be followed up with the "Communications" of Leeman L. Perkins and Reinhard Strohm, as well as Burkholder's response, in *JAMS* 40 (1987): 130–39, 576–78; Christopher A. Reynolds's "Counterpoint of Allusion in Fifteenth-Century Masses," *JAMS* 45 (1992): 228–60, is an ear-opener; Rob C. Wegman, "Petrus de Domarto's *Missa Spiritus almus* and the Early History of the Four-Voice Mass in the Fifteenth Century," *EMH* 10 (1990): 235–303.

Ockeghem

There is no single comprehensive study on Ockeghem in any language; one can only hope that the *Proceedings of the Colloque Ockeghem* (Tours, February 3–8, 1997), ed. Philippe Vendrix, will begin to fill the gap. The bibliographical starting point is Martin Picker, *Johannes Ockeghem and Jacob Obrecht: A Guide to Research* (New York: Garland, 1988); on Ockeghem's style, see Manfred F. Bukofzer, "*Caput*: A Liturgico-Musical Study," in *Studies in Medieval and Renaissance Music* (New York: Norton, 1959), 217–310; the two most detailed studies of the Masses and motets are both in German: Marianne Henze, *Studien zu den Messenkompositionen Johannes Ockeghems*, Berliner Studien zur Musikwissenschaft 12 (Berlin: Merseburger, 1968), and Andrea Lindmayr's *Quellenstudien zu den Motetten von Johannes Ockeghem* (Laaber: Laaber Verlag, 1990), which deals mainly with problems of dissemination. There is an interesting essay on Ockeghem's setting of the words "qui tollis peccata mundi" by Clemens Goldberg, "Text, Music, and Liturgy in Johannes Ockeghem's Masses," *Musica disciplina* 44 (1990): 185–231; Ockeghem's relations with the French court are dealt with in Leeman L. Perkins, "Musical Patronage at the Royal Court of France under Charles VII and Louis XI (1422–83)," *JAMS* 37 (1984): 507–66. One should watch for Lawrence F. Bernstein's forthcoming study on the reception of Ockeghem's music.

Busnoys

One should start with the following items by Paula Higgins: *Antoine Busnoys: Methods, Meaning, and Context in Late Medieval Music* (Oxford: Clarendon Press, 1997), which grew out of a conference held at Notre Dame University in 1992 (Higgins is editor), "*In hydraulis* Revisited: New Light on the Career of Antoine Busnois," *JAMS* 39 (1986): 36–86, and the forthcoming *Parents and Preceptors: Authority, Lineage, and the Conception of the Composer in Early Modern Europe* (Oxford: Oxford University Press). There are stimulating discussions of the Masses and motets in the *Collected Works*, parts 2–3: *The Latin-Texted Works*; Sparks's "Motets of Antoine Busnois," *JAMS* 6 (1953): 216–26, is concise, if a little dated.

The L'homme armé *Tradition*

Among the important works are Judith Cohen's *Six Anonymous "L'homme armé" Masses in Naples, Biblioteca Nazionale, MS VI E 40*, MSD 21 (American Institute of Musicology, 1968), and her similarly titled edition of the Masses in *CMM* 85 (American Institute of Musicology, 1981); Lewis Lockwood, "Aspects of the *L'homme armé* Tradition," *PRMA* 100 (1973–74): 97–122; Leeman L. Perkins, "The *L'homme armé* Masses of Busnoys and Okeghem," *JM* 3 (1984): 363–96; Richard Taruskin's "Antoine Busnoys and the *L'homme armé* Tradition," *JAMS* 39 (1986): 255–93 (which probably overstates Busnoys's role), and the responses by Barbara Haggh, Don Giller, David Fallows, and Taruskin in *JAMS* 40 (1987): 139–53 (much of Taruskin's argument is repeated in the essay that appears in the *Complete Works* edition); Michael P. Long, "'*Arma virumque cano*': Echoes of a Golden Age," in *Antoine Busnoys* (see above); Don Giller, in "The Naples *L'Homme armé* Masses and Caron: A Study in Musical Relationships," *CMC* 32 (1981): 2–28, tries to attribute the anonymous Naples Masses to Caron (and fails).

The Idea of imitatio

For opposing views on the matter, see Howard Mayer Brown, "Emulation, Competition, and Homage: Imitation and Theories of Imitation in the Renaissance," *JAMS* 35 (1982): 1–48 (for), and Honey Meconi, "Does *Imitatio* Exist?" *JM* 12 (1994): 152–78 (against); see also Rob C. Wegman, "Another 'Imitation' of Busnoys's *Missa L'Homme armé*—and Some Observations on *Imitatio* in Renaissance Music," *JRMA* 114 (1989): 189–202. For a view from outside the world of music, see G. W. Pigman, "Versions of Imitation in the Renaissance," *RQ* 33 (1980): 1–32.

The Trent Codices and the Chigi Codex

There is a thematic index of Trent 87–92 in Guido Adler and Oswald Koller, *Sechs Trienter Codices*, *DTÖ* 14–15 (Vienna: Österreichischer Bundesverlag, 1900; reprint, 1959–70); this also includes an edition of selected pieces, as do the following volumes of *DTÖ*: 22 (1904), 38 (1912), 53 (1920), 61 (1924), 76 (1933). An extremely useful collection of essays (many in English) is Nino Pirrotta and Danilo Curti, eds., *I codici musicali trentini a cento anni dalla loro riscoperta* (Trent: Museo Provinciale d'Arte, 1986). For object lessons on how the study of paper and handwriting can shed light on the origins of manuscripts, see Peter Wright, "The Compilation of Trent 87_1 and 92_2," *EMH* 2 (1982): 237–71, "On the Origins of Trent 87_1, and 92_2," *EMH* 6 (1986): 245–70, and "Paper Evidence and the Dating of Trent 91," *M&L* 76 (1995): 487–508; the entire set of Trent Codices is published in a somewhat unreliable facsimile: *Codex Tridentinus 87–93* (Rome: Vivarelli & Gullà, 1970). The classic study of the Chigi manuscript is Herbert Kellman, "The Origins of the Chigi Codex: The Date, Provenance, and Ownership of Rome, Biblioteca Vaticana Chigiana, C VIII 234," *JAMS* 11 (1958): 6–19; the entire manuscript appears in a facsimile edition, *Vatican City, Biblioteca Apostolica Vaticana, MS Chigi C VIII 234*, with introduction by Kellman, *RMF* 22 (New York: Garland, 1987).

Also Cited

Pamela F. Starr, "Rome as the Centre of the Universe: Papal Grace and Music Patronage," *EMH* 11 (1992): 223–62; Alex Preminger, ed., *Princeton Encyclopedia of Poetry and Politics* (Princeton: Princeton University Press, 1965).

CHAPTER 12

Learning from Documents:
An Ecclesiastical Notice

The three archival documents that we looked at in Chapter 8 were rather straightforward. The two payroll notices provided testimony that a certain person was employed at a certain place at a given time and was paid an amount of money for services rendered. Likewise, the inventory of Du Fay's books, no matter how difficult to read and transcribe, required little if any interpretation.

Other documents, however, are more complicated, and we must sometimes dig a bit in order to recreate the events to which they refer. And if on top of the story that they seem half to tell and half to hide they are filled with such problems as fifteenth-century ecclesiastical-legal jargon, long-forgotten calendar systems, now-obscure Latin place names, and little-known people, we have our work cut out for us.

The notice that follows is a good example, and it provides us with an opportunity to test our mettle as historians. But first, the document should be placed in context: as it is only because historians knows the context that they recognize the importance of the document in the first place.

The notice comes from one of the collections of the Vatican archives—the *Libri annatarum*, or Books of Annates[1]—and concerns the theorist Johannes Tinctoris, whose name, however, appears as "Trutoris". The notice may answer a small but nagging question having to do with Tinctoris's association with the Aragonese court of Naples. Tinctoris is last heard from at Naples in an official capacity in October 1487, when he was instructed to go north in order to recruit new singers for the court. It is clear from the notice that he returned to Naples, but we want to know both if he was still at Naples as of the date(s) of the document and if he was there as an employee of the court. The document also unfolds a sequence of events concerning a benefice for Tinctoris, and we will want to unravel that little story.

The document:

Die 24ᵃ Nicolaus Rembert, canonicus Cameracensis, ut principalis et privata persona obligavit se Camere apostolica pro Iohanne Trutoris, clerico Cameracensis diocesis, pro annata

24th [September 1488] Nicolaus Rembert, canon of Cambrai, as principal and private person, obligated himself to the apostolic Camera for Johannes Trutoris, cleric of the diocese

---

1. Rome, Biblioteca Apostolica Vaticana, Fondo dell'Archivio di Stato, *Annatae*, Reg. 36, fol. 14ᵛ.

canonicatus et prebende collegiate S. Gertrudis Nivellensis, Leodiensis diocesis (50 lib. Turon. par.), per obitem Iohannis de Campis extra Curium defuncti vacan[tium]. Sub dato 5° idus decembris anno 4°. Et promisit solvere dictam annatam infra annum aut Cameram certificare infra mensem de possessione non habita.

of Cambrai, for the annate for the canonicate and prebend at the collegiate church of St. Gertrude of Nivelle, diocese of Liège (50 *livres tournois*), which became vacant through the death of Johannes de Campis outside the Curia. Dated 5 *ides* December, year 4 [of Innocent VIII's reign]. And he promises to pay the said annate within a year or else certify to the Camera within a month of not having taken possession.

To which the following was added in the margins:

Die 27ᵃ februarii 1490 prefatus Nicolaus, procurator ipsius Iohannis Trutoris, ut patet publico instrumento publicato manu Francisci Pappacode, notarii Neapolitensis in Neapoli, ubi ipse Iohannes moram habet, sub anno Domini 1488, indictione 7, die 18ᵃ mensis septembris predicto anno 5°, vigore dicti instrumenti obligavit ipsum Iohannem principalem pro dicta annata.

27th February 1490 [1491], the prementioned Nicolaus, procurator for the same Johannes Trutoris, as evident from the public instrument issued by the hand of Francesco Pappacoda, Neapolitan notary of Naples, where the same Johannes is accustomed to live, dated the year of our Lord 1488, indiction 7, 18th of the month of September, of the presaid year 5, by the authority of the said instrument, obligated the same Johannes as principal for the said annate.

To unravel the sequence of events from beginning to end and to understand who is doing what and why, we need to become familiar with some terminology: canon, apostolic Camera, annate, canonicate, prebend, curia, *ides*, procurator, indiction; we must also identify Nicolaus Rembert and Johannes de Campis, and learn something about the collegiate church of St. Gertrude at Nivelles. On matters of ecclesiastical terminology, there are any number of dictionaries and encyclopedias devoted to the history, development, and terminology of the Roman church. Rembert and Johannes de Campis will require burrowing into studies of papal music patronage. Calendar matters clear up nicely with the help of the Adriano Cappelli book cited in Chapter 8, not to mention the entry on "calendar" in the *Encyclopaedia Britannica*. If all else fails, the document is discussed at length in Ronald Woodley, "Iohannis Tinctoris: A Review of the Documentary Biographical Evidence," *JAMS* 34 (1981): 217–48.

CHAPTER 13

The Patronage of Music

With the third quarter of the fifteenth century, the most prestigious of music ensembles, the choirs of singers attached to the great courts and churches—the chapels—entered something of a golden age. As Tinctoris put it in the preface to his *Proportionale musices* of 1473–74:

> The most Christian princes . . . desiring to augment the divine service, founded chapels after the manner of David, in which at extraordinary expense they appointed singers to sing pleasant and comely praise to our God with diverse . . . voices. And since the singers of princes, if their masters are endowed with the liberality which makes men illustrious, are rewarded with honor, glory, and wealth, many are kindled with a most fervent zeal for this study.[1]

Though Tinctoris's flowery language was meant to feed the ego of his own employer, King Ferrante I of Naples, his testimony is on the mark. Chapels that had been flourishing throughout the century (those at the Cathedral of Cambrai and the court of Burgundy, for example) continued to do so; others, which had either fallen on hard times (the French royal chapel and the chapel at the Cathedral of Florence) or had been provincial or small-scale in character (those at Naples and Ferrara) were reorganized and quickly grew into major musical forces; still others (the choir founded by Pope Sixtus IV for his new Sistine Chapel and the chapel created at Milan by Duke Galeazzo Maria Sforza) were newly born. We now look at these chapels in more detail.

THE CHAPELS

In the fifteenth century, the term *cappella* (Italian; *capella* in Latin) could refer to a place of worship, whether a side chapel in a church or the private place of prayer within a princely palace; it could refer to the entire body of chaplain-clerics who looked after the spiritual needs of the great secular courts, with music as one of their tools; or it could refer specifically to the musicians who performed the music of Mass and Office, whether in a church (or monastery or convent) or in the private household of either a high-ranking prelate or a secular ruler. And especially when the term was used in connection with a princely court, the last two meanings were not always clearly separated, since the singers who performed the music were part of the larger religious apparatus of the court and often did double duty—musical and spiritual—themselves.

1. Strunk, *Source Readings*, 14.

Size

Overall, as the fifteenth century progressed, the important chapels in France, the Low Countries, and Italy grew in size. For example, chapel members at the court of Savoy numbered 10 in 1449 and 23 (including 2 organists) in 1461; Naples' forces grew from 14 in 1444 to 22 forty years later. There were exceptions, however, and occasionally the process of growth was temporarily halted by political, economic, or religious dislocations. Thus the temporary decline of the Medici after the death of Lorenzo the Magnificent in 1492 coupled with the rise of the religious reformer Fra Girolamo Savonarola caused the chapel at the Florentine Duomo and Baptistry to be disbanded altogether in March 1493, just a month or so after it had grown to 18 members, its largest contingent ever.

Two points about this growth: First, though Italian religious institutions followed the trend, even the grandest of them—the already large papal chapel excepted—began to catch up to their northern counterparts only at the end of the century. Indeed, when Josquin joined the chapel of the Cathedral of Milan in 1459, he increased its strength from six to seven adult voices. The Milanese must have been thrilled with such a force, since not too long before that they had been singing polyphony with just one singer to a part.

Second, with the exception of the Sistine Chapel choir, it appears that throughout the century the choirs of the princely courts were larger than those of even the most musically prestigious churches. But do the numbers tell the whole story? Did all the members of a princely chapel function as singers, or, more pointedly, did every one of them sing polyphony? More than a few chapel rosters distinguish between singer-chaplains on the one hand and chaplains on the other. As much to raise questions as to answer them, let us look at the organization of one court chapel in particular, that of Burgundy in 1469, as it is defined in both a payroll register and the newly drawn-up household ordinances of the court.

The Burgundian Chapel

Table 13-1 gives a payroll register from the Burgundian court of Charles the Bold. The roster tells us two things immediately: first, there was a four-rank hierarchy of first chaplain, other chaplains, *clercs*, and *sommeliers*, each rank with its own rate of pay; and second, a singer's rank was not based on whether or not he was a priest. In fact, the household ordinances make it clear that promotion from one rank to the next was dependent on the quality of the singer's voice and his good service, and could occur only when there was a vacancy.

What we cannot tell from the roster is whether all members of the chapel sang polyphony or even sang at all. Here, though, a passage from the household ordinances helps:

> For singing polyphony there shall be at least six high voices, three tenors, three contrabasses and two *moiens* [contratenor, or altus], excluding . . . four chaplains [who are priests and who officiate at] High Mass and the *sommeliers*

who, however, must sing with the above-mentioned if they are not occupied at the altar or in some other reasonable way.[2]

This seems to indicate that a minimum of fourteen singers were needed for polyphony, and that they were split up in such a way that there were six singers (certainly singing falsetto) on the top part, two on the altus, and three each on the tenor and bass; and that the *sommeliers* sang only if they had nothing else to do.

THE SOMMELIERS   Yet as we learn from other parts of the chapel ordinances, the *sommeliers* usually had any number of other things to do. Three of them attended to the duke in his oratory. Two others served at the altar and also looked after the altar jewels and cloths (as well as the other chapel furnishings), arranged for dining after the Mass, and made sure there was enough wood and candles. Further, the two most junior members of each group of *sommeliers* were charged with sleeping near the chapel in order to guard it. Clearly, the main function of the *sommeliers* was not musical.

THE FIRST CHAPLAIN   The 1469 ordinances devote ten paragraphs to the responsibilities of the first chaplain, who had to conduct all Masses and Offices in the absence of another officiating prelate, keep peace among the chaplains, give permission for a chaplain to be absent, choose the material for the chaplains' robes, take charge of the chapel payroll, make sure that the chaplains paid their debts, and exert authority over the duke's secular servants when they were in the chapel. To some extent, then, he was the chapel policeman.

What we wait for in vain is any reference to the first chaplain's musical duties. We cannot be sure if Philippe Siron was a skilled singer who could handle one of the voice parts of a complicated polyphonic Mass or motet, did his best just to manage plainsong, or was an unmusical but skilled and highly valued administrator who was to be treated with reverence. Whatever the case, it was certainly his administrative role that earned him twice the salary of anyone else.

Siron's role accords with that of his counterparts at other princely courts. Thus the household ordinances of Aragonese Naples tell us that the post of *cappellano maggiore* was, in accordance with the court's Spanish heritage, to go automatically to the abbot of the Cistercian monastery of the Holy Cross in Spain; and even after the Neapolitan court broke with that tradition, no one who was not a bishop seems ever to have held the position. Likewise, the *magister capellae* of the Sistine Chapel customarily held the rank of bishop, a tradition that was broken only when Pope Leo X awarded the position to the singer-composer Elzéar Genet (known as Carpentras) in 1514.

We cannot conclude, however, that all courtly chapels of the period were headed by nonmusicians. The organization of the chapel varied from court to court. At Ferrara, for instance, the top spot went to the composer Johannes Martini; and when, in the first decade of the sixteenth century, Duke Ercole I d'Este removed the title *maestro di cappella* from whoever was the master of the choirboys, it was bestowed on a succession of great composers: Josquin Desprez,

2. Quoted after Fallows, "Specific Information," 110.

Table 13-1.   A payroll register for January 1469 from the Burgundian court of Charles the Bold.

First chaplain (36 sous per day)[a]

   Philippe Siron*

Chaplains (18 sous per day)

Robert de le Pele*	Robert Oliver*
Anthoine Mauret*	Jehan Lambert de la Bassee
Constans Breuwe de Languebrouc	Mathias Coquel
Estienne de le Mote*	Pierre le Cannone*
Anthoine de Franceville*	Jehan Pintot dit Nicodemus
Gilles Brits*	Philippe de Passaige

Clercs (12 sous per day)

Claude le Petit*	Pasquier des Pres*
Robert Morton*	Johannes de Tricht

Sommeliers (stewards, 11 or 7 sous per day)

Jehan le Caron	Coppin Buckel
Wautre Maes*	Pierrequin du Wez
Gillet de Bousies	Pierrequin Basin

(In addition, the chapel had a *fourrier*, or quartermaster, who is not named.)
Source: After Fallows, "Specific Information," 113.
[a]The sou was a middle-denomination coin: there were sixteen sous to the French franc, florin, and *livre tournois* (that is, of Tours); the sou was worth twelve derniers.
*Indicates priest. Note that all members of the chapel were men; women were barred.

Jacob Obrecht, and Antoine Brumel. Nor should we forget that the *premier chapelain* at the royal court of France was Ockeghem. In fact, as the fifteenth century drew to a close, the courtly chapels came to be increasingly identified with their purely musical role, and their leaders were more often singers and composers.

OTHER POSITIONS   The Burgundian chapel included a number of positions other than those listed in the table. On the liturgical-ceremonial side, there were the duke's confessor, almoner (a person who distributed alms), and assistant almoner, as well as the chaplain to the *maistre d'ostel* (chief administrative officer); no doubt, these posts were filled by priests. Two roles for which the ordinances do not account were certainly known at other courts: master of the boys and a contingent of music scribes. Among well-known musicians who were paid for copying music at one time or another were Josquin at Milan and Vincenet at Naples, while Du Fay (as we saw in Chapter 7) supervised the copying of choirbooks at the Cathedral of Cambrai. Finally, the ranks of the Burgundian chapel were rounded out by the *fourrier*, a caretaker of sorts who arranged for the chapel's accommodations when it was on the move, and the *porteur d'orgues*, who is simply described as a "servant."

    Thus, the various positions in a fifteenth-century princely chapel are best understood as lying along a continuum. At one end were those whose main jobs were primarily liturgical, ceremonial, and administrative; at the other were the singers who were concerned primarily with making music, both polyphony (written and improvised) and plainsong; and in the middle were members of the chapel, who no doubt did both. And if the musical ability of some chapel members did not extend to reading mensural notation and singing polyphony, perhaps they raised their voices only in the many parts of the service that were sung in plainsong.

SCHEDULE OF "PERFORMANCES"   The Burgundian ordinances call for a High Mass—celebrated in accordance with the liturgy of the Cathedral of Paris, and with plainsong and polyphony ("a chant et deschant")—to be offered every day of the year. The chapel was also to celebrate Vespers and Compline each day, and on certain occasions, "first Vespers" for the eve of a feast. Some feasts—Christmas, Easter, Pentecost, and certain saints' days, to name just a few—were celebrated with both Matins and the Little Hours. And some members of the chapel probably took part in secular entertainments at the court. It seems, then, that the chapel gave Charles the Bold his money's worth.

THE SINGERS

What kind of people filled the ranks of the courtly chapels? The following gives us a glimpse of some of them, both as an aggregate and as individuals.

The French Royal Chapel

From 1451 (during the reign of Charles VII) through 1475 (Louis XI), the French royal chapel employed thirty-eight different members, some identified as singers, others as chaplains. Though we often think of this period as one in which singers were constantly on the move, most of the singers and chaplains of the French royal court stayed put. In fact, only six singers seem ever to have been employed at another court, and just two, the singer-composers Jehan Fresneau and Jehan Sohier, are known to have ventured as far as Italy.

Of the thirty-eight chapel members, three (possibly four) were definitely composers: Ockeghem, Jehan de Escatefer *dit* Cousin, Jehan Fresneau, and Jehan Sohier *dit* Fede (if that is the person lurking behind the entry for "Phede"). Fourteen were definitely singers and thus took part in polyphony (two of them are identified as *teneurs*), while fifteen—some singers, some chaplains—were definitely priests. So far as we know, none of the members of the chapel was married.

In short, we get a picture of a rather stable community of singers and chaplains, no doubt drawn to the royal chapel by generous salaries and the opportunity of collecting their share of lucrative benefices at wealthy French cathedrals and collegiate churches.

Some Family Men

Not all singers at the secular courts, or even at cathedrals, were priests or clerics. As the fifteenth century wore on and chapels became increasingly professionalized, we find singers who were married and had families to support. One of the first of the illustrious nonclerical singer-composers was Heinrich Isaac, who joined the Florentine chapel of the cathedral and baptistry in 1484 and married the daughter of a local butcher.

At times career and family could come into conflict. In 1555, Pope Pius IV dismissed Palestrina from the Sistine Chapel on the grounds that he was married, which violated the chapel's statutes. And it was precisely such a conflict that led to a touching letter from a singer of the period. In 1471, Philippe de Dortench, married to a Florentine woman and at the time a singer in the chapel at Naples, wrote to Lorenzo the Magnificent (addressing him as *Chompare*, which probably indicates that Lorenzo was godfather to one of his children):

> Since my wife is desirous of returning to her native city and nags me every hour of the day, I would for this reason be happy to return there. I would see to it that you would always have a good, superior chapel; with the condition that I would like you to provide me with a suitable house for the rest of my life and in addition 6 gold ducats a month. So, dear *Chompare*, see if you can recall me there since you know that you will always have a [faithful] servant; and answer me and give me your reply through the person who gives you this letter; and please keep it a secret and be cautious, for were this to be known here I should be undone.[3]

So far as we know, Lorenzo did not comply.

A Wanderer: Johannes Cordier

One of the most famous singers in the late fifteenth century was the tenor Johannes Cordier, who appears on the scene in July 1460, when he was appointed a singer-clerk at the church of St. Donatian in Bruges, his city of birth. Seven years later, he was engaged as leader of the chapel at the Florence Cathedral and Baptistry. In Florence, Cordier impressed the young Lorenzo the Magnificent with his improvised singing to the accompaniment of the *lira da braccio* (a forerunner of the violin). But things soon turned sour: one of the chapel singers was thrown in jail for two weeks, and during the summer of 1468, Cordier apparently instigated a rebellion whereby the entire body of singers simply quit. Cordier's stay at Florence was over.

After a stint of at least two and a half years in the papal chapel beginning in January 1469, he moved on to the Neapolitan court of Ferrante I, where once again he caused trouble, this time precipitating an international crisis. Events unfolded as follows: Cordier left Naples at some point; by July 1474, Duke Galeazzo Maria Sforza of Milan was referring to him as "our singer," and in October Cordier's name appeared in the Milanese payroll registers. The problem was that Cordier had left Naples without permission. In 1475, letters flew back and forth, as Ferrante demanded that Cordier be returned, while Duke Galeazzo Maria insisted that one of his own musicians be sent home from Naples. Finally, when Naples and Milan were on the verge of breaking diplomatic relations (even though the ruling families were related by marriage),

3. Quoted after D'Accone, "The Singers of San Giovanni," 325.

Charles the Bold of Burgundy stepped in as arbitrator and awarded Cordier to Milan.

The Milanese loved Cordier. Aside from a handsome salary, the duke procured lucrative benefices for him and gave him a house in Milan. A 1476 court register shows that 387 members of the duke's household were allowed to stable horses (at the duke's expense) when traveling with him. Cordier was given a more generous allowance than either Josquin or the chapel master. In January 1477, Duke Galeazzo Maria's widow—the duke had been assassinated two weeks earlier on the day after Christmas as he was going to church (one of the period's favorite venues for such acts)—decided to reduce the size of the chapel; she wrote to Rome: "[We] continue to be of the opinion not to release these singers completely, but to choose some of the best [and retain them], among whom will be Cordier."[4]

But Cordier was soon on the move again. By 1480, he had joined the Habsburg-Burgundian chapel of Maximilian. After two years there, and fifteen years on the road, he returned to St. Donatian's at Bruges, where he became a canon in 1482, directed an Easter play (in which he took the role of Christ) in 1485, and accepted a one-year appointment as *succentor* (assistant music director) in October 1497. During this final period at Bruges, during which he still maintained contacts with Milan, Cordier enjoyed a close association with Obrecht, for whose services at Bruges in 1485 and then at Ferrara in 1487 he helped pave the way. Cordier died in Bruges in 1501, having lived a life that fulfills Ercole d'Este's description of the singers in his own court chapel: "They are all people who live from day to day like the birds on the branches."[5]

Benefices

How exactly did the system of benefices work? As noted earlier, a benefice was, in effect, a gift that customarily took the form of a canonicate or chaplaincy in a cathedral or collegiate or parish church and provided its holder with an income, in return for whatever spiritual duties the office required.

Although the right of conferring the overwhelming majority of such benefices fell to the popes, the most powerful of the secular rulers were often able to influence the dispensation of benefices in their own territories and thus lure the best singers to their courts with the promise of such prizes. At the same time, local bishops and cathedral chapters often nominated their own candidate for a benefice. Thus the road from papal conferral to actual "collation" (presentation of the benefice to its appointee) was often strewn with litigation, as pope, bishop, and secular ruler might each back a separate candidate.

For the singers, benefices were "ducats (or florins or *livres tournois*) from heaven" that could double or even more than double a singer's income. For example, Josquin's salary at the ducal chapel in Milan in the early 1470s was a

4. Quoted after Prizer, "Music at the Court of the Sforza," 165.
5. Quoted after Fallows, "The Contenance Angloise," 189.

mere 5 ducats per month, or 60 per year. But when he joined the chapel, Duke
Galeazzo Maria procured a benefice for him at Gozzano, a day's journey away
by coach (about forty miles). Josquin's 60-ducat salary at Milan would have
been augmented by another 95 or so from the benefice: 155 ducats per year
held one very nicely.

That a singer did not have to reside where he held a benefice was particularly
helpful. The many Franco-Flemish singers who were active in Italy could pe-
tition Rome for a nonresidential benefice in their native north; and upon quit-
ting Italy and returning home, the benefice and its income were still there for
them, much like a retirement pension. Singers could also pile up benefices. In
all, it was a lucrative, if cynical, business.

Income

Some singers of the period parlayed their musical and ecclesiastical-administrative skills into personal wealth. As we saw in Chapter 7, Du Fay died a
relatively rich man, while Ockeghem, thanks mainly to his position as treasurer
of St. Martin, also did extremely well for himself. Another example is the
Spanish singer-composer-chaplain Joan Cornago, who earned a bachelor's degree in theology from the University of Paris in 1449 and took up a position
in the Neapolitan chapel of Alfonso "the Magnanimous" in 1453. He was still
there in the mid-1460s, now as chief almoner to Alfonso's son and successor,
Ferrante I. Cornago earned the astounding salary of 300 ducats per year. As a
Franciscan, Cornago was bound to a vow of poverty, which was conveniently
waived by Pope Nicholas V within two months of Cornago's arrival at Naples.
As Table 13-2 shows, Cornago's salary may well have been the highest earned
by any singer in Italy during the fifteenth and early sixteenth centuries.

Table 13-2. A sample of singers' salaries at Naples, Milan, Florence,
and Ferrara.

	Date	Singer	Annual salary in ducats
Naples			
	1441	Miguel Nadal	36
	1448	Fra Giordi	72
	1471	Philippe de Dortench	120
Milan			
	1474	Antonio Guinati (chapel master)	168
	1474	Gaspar van Weerbecke	144
	1474	Josquin Desprez	60
Florence			
	1490	Petrequin Bonnel	24
Ferrara			
	1476	Johannes Martini	48
	1503	Josquin Desprez	200
	1504	Jacob Obrecht	100

It was probably not for his musical abilities alone that Cornago was paid so well. As chief almoner to the king, he was near the top of the ecclesiastical hierarchy of the court, and there is some evidence to suggest that he might even have served as a royal ambassador to Rome.

We can also measure Cornago's annual salary in the 1450s against a few nonmusical salaries at the court of Naples during the same decade: a mill worker earned 14 ducats, a laborer 18, a head cattleman 24, a professor of theology 300, and court chamberlain 3,000. Thus Cornago earned more than ten times as much as the king's head cattleman, but only one-tenth as much as the *may-ordomo* of the court. (The estimated income of the king himself was more than 800,000 ducats in 1444.)

To help us understand the buying power of these salaries: food prices from Milan for 1459–60 show that 1 ducat would have bought approximately 130 pounds of bread, 30 pounds of veal, 10 chickens, or 25 pounds of cheese or butter. Thus even allowing for possible differences in the cost of living at Naples and Milan, it seems clear that Cornago could not have eaten in a month all that 5 ducats (20 percent of his monthly salary) could buy. Moreover, he may have been receiving free room and board.

Other Perks

Cornago's salary might have been only the tip of his financial iceberg. It is almost certain, for instance, that he was receiving a cut of the taxes generated by the state-run salt monopoly; even a small percentage could have made him extremely wealthy. Nor was Cornago the only musician of the period to reap such favors. In the 1470s, the Duke of Milan gave his own chapel master, the handsomely salaried Antonio Guinati (see Table 13-2), a three-year concession that permitted the singer to exploit the duchy's mineral deposits; fifty years later, Henry VIII granted his singer Philip van Wilder the concession to import woad (an herb from which blue dye was made) from Toulouse and wine from Gascony.

Obviously, perquisites of such magnitude were not everyday occurrences. More frequent were such gifts as farms and houses, moving expenses, horses, barrels of wine, bushels of grain, extra clothing, or, as in Ockeghem's case, a cash annuity "in addition to his wages" and equal to his regular salary. Sometimes the perks were very down-to-earth. In 1484, the singers of the Florentine Cathedral and Baptistry were hired to sing at another Florentine church; the contract reads as follows:

> The herewith inscribed singers and men of good faith, singers in San Giovanni of Florence, oblige themselves to sing the Mass of figural music in the Chapel of the Annunziata on Saturday morning, throughout the year, serving the ceremonies of the Chapel honestly. And the Convent obliges itself to give them . . . the herewith inscribed things:
> First, a bed with sheets, a mattress, a spring, a pillow, and a blanket.
> Item, the laundering of all their clothes.

Item, the barber who will shave them once a week, well and honorably, to their contentment and pleasure.
Item, eight pairs of shoes and four pairs of slippers, according to their need, from time to time.
Item at Easter, material for a vest.
Item for [the feast of] St. John, a beret for each of them.
Item in the month of September, good cloth for a pair of trousers.
Item for Christmas, ten lengths of good cloth for a jacket.[6]

In sum, the job of chapel singer was a respected one. And for the singer who could augment his musical skills with administrative ability and take advantage of the benefice system, it could be an extremely lucrative one as well.

THE PATRONS

From our vantage point, the most visible patrons of the fifteenth century were the rulers of the great princely courts (who were not so much patrons as they were employer-consumers). And between salaries and perks, the cost to them of maintaining a chapel was, as Tinctoris put it, an "extraordinary expense." The chapel, moreover, was only one of the ensembles that most courts maintained. Why, then, were the rulers of the day so eager to invest in them? There are three interrelated answers.

First, many of them—Charles the Bold of Burgundy, Galeazzo Maria Sforza of Milan, and Ercole I d'Este of Ferrara, for example—enjoyed music passionately. Charles even dabbled in composition himself, while Galeazzo Maria confessed that he "delight [ed] in music and song more than any other pleasure."[7] Second, they were, in accordance with their times, truly devout. To invest in the chapel, therefore, was to invest in the salvation of their own soul. And third, to borrow from Tinctoris, for a prince to support a chapel was a sign that he was "endowed with the liberality which makes men illustrious." To be deemed illustrious and to have that luster rub off on the activities of the court, which was an extension of the ruler himself, was highly desirable. The chapel, then, was a visible symbol of splendor and power.

Costs

We are fairly well informed about the costs involved in the patronage system and the strategies of recruitment. In 1474, Galeazzo Maria Sforza spent about 5,000 ducats on the salaries of his thirty-one singers, which seemed to Tinctoris like a great expense; yet the duke also spent about the same on his forty dog handlers. Likewise, the 3,250 *livres tournois* that Charles VII spent on the French royal chapel in 1453–54 were far less than what was spent to keep the ladies of the court well dressed; and the 1,500 ducats that Alfonso the Magnanimous needed to maintain his chapel in 1455 was almost pocket change, as he was accustomed to spending about 1,000 ducats *a day* to maintain the court as a

6. Quoted after D'Accone, "The Singers of San Giovanni," 334–35.
7. Prizer, "Music at the Court of the Sforza," 151.

whole. In short, splendor and personal salvation could be purchased relatively cheaply.

Recruitment

Especially in Italy, the competition for the highly prized Franco-Flemish singers was intense. We have already seen the absurd lengths to which the courts of Milan and Naples would go in their dispute over the services of Johannes Cordier.

Briefly, there were three means of pursuing singers: (1) by posting agents (or ambassadors) abroad, as when the head of the Bruges branch of the Medici bank recruited Johannes Cordier for the Medici-supported Florentine chapel; (2) by "mail order," as it were, as when Ercole I d'Este informed the Bishop of Constance in a letter of December 10, 1471, that he was creating a chapel and was "seeking most excellent musicians, whom we are looking for everywhere" (with this letter, Ercole seems to have secured the services of Johannes Martini, who went on to serve the Ferrarese chapel for twenty-five years);[8] and (3) by sending singers north on recruitment missions, as when, in October 1487, Ferrante I of Naples instructed Tinctoris:

> Having need in our chapel . . . of some singers of a certain type . . . and not finding them hereabouts, we want you to go across the mountains to France and to any other region, country, or place where you think you may find them . . . exert and trouble yourself to find some good singer . . . and, upon finding him . . . bring him with you [that he may enter] our service and that of our chapel.[9]

As enticements, the Italian courts offered base salaries, benefices for those who were clerics, and other perks. A letter written on February 5, 1473, by the Mantuan ambassador at the court of Milan and addressed to Ludovico Gonzaga, the Marquis of Mantua, sums up the whole patronage process:

> His most illustrious Lordship [Duke of Milan] thanks your Lordship greatly for the effort you made concerning the tenor [Andrea da Mantova, a singer at the Ferrarese court]. He wishes very much to have him and says that he pays tenors twelve ducats a month. . . . His Excellency has . . . made a fine beginning with these singers and is spending fabulously for them. He has given to one alone . . . the equivalent of four thousand ducats in a house, land, money, clothing, and so forth and has made him his personal chamberlain. He is a young man of twenty-four from Liège . . . a tenor and married. His Lordship had also given others houses in Milan worth seven or eight hundred ducats each and has written to Rome to request the pope to agree that every bishop of [the duke's] principal cities . . . can confer benefices up to the sum of three hundred ducats . . . specifically for singers in order to have in every city a *cappella* in the cathedral. . . . He has written most insistently to the [papal] court and says that he wants to sustain music in Italy. And then his Excellency will be able to choose from these *cappelle* the best singers and in this way will have the best chapel of all.[10]

8. Lockwood, *Music in Renaissance Ferrara*, 131–32.

9. Atlas, *Music at the Aragonese Court of Naples*, 73.

10. With a slight change, quoted after Prizer, "Music at the Court of the Sforza," 156–57.

Patrons and the Music

One vast unknown in our understanding of music patronage in the fifteenth century concerns the triangle made up of patron, composer, and musical composition and especially how the interaction between the first two influenced the third. Whereas art historians have access to innumerable contracts in which the patron spelled out to the artist in great detail just what should be included in the painting, music historians have no such documents. Art historians can study the relationship between patron and artist in creating a work of art, but music historians study the relationship between patron and performers in re-creating a work of art. And whereas an art historian can state, "A fifteenth-century painting is the deposit of a social relationship,"[11] and show how an artist tailored a painting to the taste of a patron, music historians can only wonder if the same is true for a piece of music.

We can take Ockeghem's *Missa Fors seulement*, as an example. We can probably assume that it was written during the reign of Louis XI (1461–83), that the composer wrote the Mass at the French court, and that Louis, his wife Charlotte of Savoy, and their courtiers knew Ockeghem's chanson on which the Mass was based. On the other hand, we cannot assume that the work resulted from a commission; that if it was commissioned, Louis or someone else at the court commissioned it, as opposed to a patron outside the court; or that if Louis did commission it, Ockeghem employed this or that stylistic device because he knew that Louis had a keen ear for it. Indeed, Louis's interest in the music he heard in his chapel might well have stopped at "Let there be music!"

In the end, our lack of insight into how the equation patron + composer = composition worked does not permit us to go beyond such generalities as "The 'deliberate simplicity' of the double-choir compositions written for Ercole I d'Este's court of Ferrara reflects 'specific and demonstrable qualities of expression imposed by, or at least well suited to, a patron of unusually strong religious proclivities.'"[12] But do complicated canons do anything less?

Civic, Religious, and Corporate Patrons

While the chapels at the princely courts were the most glamorous of their kind, we should remember that they served a very closed socioeconomic circle: the ruler, his family, his retinue, and his honored visitors. Yet many polyphonic masterpieces did touch a wider spectrum of society, especially in the commercially thriving urban areas, where music was the concern of both city government and the prosperous merchant class.

Nowhere was this more evident than in the Low Countries, where music came to thrive in cities and towns such as Antwerp, s'Hertogenbosch, and even tiny Bergen op Zoom, which, with its semiannual business fairs, was a major meeting place for merchants from all over northern Europe. Musical patronage at these places can best be described as a combination of church, civic, cor-

11. Baxandall, *Painting and Experience in Fifteenth-Century Italy*, 1.
12. Lockwood, "Strategies of Music Patronage," 243–44.

porate, and private support. The diverse strands usually came together through the numerous trade guilds and lay-religious confraternities (especially those devoted to Mary), with varying amounts of financial help and sideline cheerleading from the local ruling bodies. Indeed, the musical scene at the churches, which provided the focal point, was vibrant enough to attract such important composers as (to look ahead a generation) Jacob Obrecht, Pierre de la Rue, Johannes Ghiselin *alias* Verbonnet, Jacques Barbireau, and Matthaeus Pipelare. The activities of the Guild of Our Lady in Bergen op Zoom, the home base of which was the Chapel of the Holy Virgin in the collegiate church of St. Gertrude, provide a good model of this kind of patronage.

Founded around 1470 through the joint efforts of the city council and Lord John II of Glymes, the guild had a lay membership of 750–1,100 (a sizable percentage of the adult population) and derived its revenues from initiation fees, dues, cash gifts, and bequests of estates and property. Through these revenues, the guild provided money for a choirmaster, five other singers, and an unspecified number of boys to sing at a daily *Lof*, or *Salve* service, the paraliturgical service devoted to Mary and celebrated after Compline with polyphonic music (later in the decade, with the accompaniment of an organ) followed by the ringing of the church bells (the tab for the latter to be paid by the church).

In addition, funds were made available for the choir to sing at Mass on six Marian feasts during the course of the year. And when in 1474 Lord John doubled the guild's revenues by turning over to it the taxes he had traditionally collected at the city's business fairs, the guild sank its newfound wealth into more music at more Masses. By the late 1480s, then, Bergen op Zoom's Guild of Our Lady was sponsoring music at the daily *Salve* service and perhaps an additional seventy or so Masses each year. As growing revenues increased the quantity of music, they seem also to have enhanced the quality of the singers. By the early 1500s, the Guild of Our Lady was one of the most illustrious musical institutions in the Low Countries, having employed at least two major composers: Obrecht (a native of the town) and Ghiselin.

There is something quite fitting about the public patronage we find in the Low Countries: the area that produced the greatest number of first-class composers in the fifteenth century probably had the greatest number of listeners to appreciate them.

BIBLIOGRAPHICAL NOTE

Patronage in General

   Two fine collections of essays dealing with patronage in the visual arts, literature, and politics (but not music) are *Patronage, Art, and Society in Renaissance Italy*, ed. F. W. Kent and Patricia Simons (Oxford: Clarendon Press, 1987), and *Patronage in the Renaissance*, ed. Guy Fitch Lytle and Stephen Orgel (Princeton: Princeton University Press, 1981); in the field of the visual arts, there is no better discussion of the relationship between artist and patron and how it shaped the work of art than Michael Baxandall, *Painting and Experience in Fifteenth-Century Italy: A Primer in the Social History of Pictorial Art* (Oxford: Clarendon Press, 1972);

for a collection of contracts between artists and painters, see David Chambers, *Patrons and Artists in the Italian Renaissance* (Columbia: University of South Carolina Press, 1971). In music, two works that question traditional musicological (predominantly archival) approaches to the study of patronage are Allan W. Atlas, "Courtly Patronage in the Fifteenth Century: Some Questions," in *Atti del XIV Congresso della Società Internazionale di Musicologia*, ed. Angelo Pompilio et al. (Turin: EDT, 1990), 3: 123–30; and Howard Mayer Brown, "Recent Research in the Renaissance: Criticism and Patronage," *RQ* 40 (1987): 1–10.

Overviews of the Music

Two invaluable articles are Frank A. D'Accone, "The Performance of Sacred Music in Italy during Josquin's Time, ca. 1475–1525," in *Josquin des Prez: Proceedings of the International Josquin Festival-Conference, 21–25 June 1971*, ed. Edward E. Lowinsky and Bonnie J. Blackburn (London: Oxford University Press, 1976), 601–18; and David Fallows, "Performing Ensembles in Josquin's Sacred Music," *TVNM* 35 (1985): 32–66.

Music at the Secular Courts

Aragón (Spain): Maria Carmen Gómez Muntané, *La Música en la Casa Real Catalano-Aragonesa Durante los Años 1336–1442* (Barcelona: Bosch, 1977). **Burgundy**: Craig Wright, *Music at the Court of Burgundy, 1364–1419: A Documentary History*, Musicological Studies 28 (Henryville, Penn.: Institute of Mediaeval Music, 1979); Jeanne Marix, *Histoire de la musique et des musiciens de la cour de Bourgogne sous le règne de Philippe le Bon (1420–1467)* (Strasbourg: Heitz, 1939); David Fallows, "Specific Information on the Ensembles for Composed Polyphony, 1400–1474," in *Studies in the Performance of Late Medieval Music*, ed. Stanley Boorman (Cambridge: Cambridge University Press, 1983), 109–59; Martin Picker, "The Habsburg Courts in the Netherlands and Austria, 1477–1530," in *The Renaissance*, ed. Stanley Sadie and Iain Fenlon (London: Macmillan, 1989), 216–42. **Ferrara**: Lewis Lockwood, *Music in Renaissance Ferrara, 1400–1505* (Cambridge: Harvard University Press, 1984), and "Strategies of Music Patronage in the Fifteenth Century: The *Cappella* of Ercole I d'Este," in *Music in Medieval and Early Modern Europe: Patronage, Sources, and Texts*, ed. Iain Fenlon (Cambridge: Cambridge University Press, 1981), 227–48. **France**: Leeman L. Perkins, "Musical Patronage at the Royal Court of France under Charles VII and Louis XI (1422–83)," *JAMS* 37 (1984): 507–66. **Milan**: Evelyn S. Welch, "Sight, Sound, and Ceremony in the Chapel of Galeazzo Maria Sforza," *EMH* 12 (1993): 151–90; William F. Prizer, "Music at the Court of the Sforza: The Birth and Death of a Musical Center," *MD* 43 (1989): 141–93; Patrick Macey, "Galeazzo Maria Sforza and Musical Patronage in Milan: Compère, Weerbeke, and Josquin," *EMH* 15 (1996): 147–212; Paul A. Merkley, "Patronage and Clientage in Galleazzo's Court," *MS* 4 (1996): 121–54. **Naples**: Allan W. Atlas, *Music at the Aragonese Court of Naples* (Cambridge: Cambridge University Press, 1985). **Savoy**: Marie-Thérèse Bouquet, "La cappella musicale dei duchi di Savoia dal 1450 al 1500," *RIM* 3 (1968): 233–85.

Civic-Religious Patronage

Antwerp: Kristine K. Forney, "Music, Ritual, and Patronage at the Church of Our Lady, Antwerp," *EMH* 7 1987): 1–57 (deals mainly with the sixteenth century). **Bergen op Zoom**: Rob C. Wegman, "Music and Musicians at the Guild of Our Lady in Bergen op Zoom, *c.* 1470–1510," *EMH* 9 (1990): 175–249. **Bruges**: Reinhard Strohm, *Music in Late Medieval Bruges*, rev. ed. (Oxford: Clarendon Press, 1990). **England**: Roger Bowers, "Obligation, Agency, and *Laissez-faire*: The Promotion of Polyphonic Composition for the Church in Fifteenth-Century England," in *Music in Medieval and Early Modern Europe*, 1–19. **Florence**: Frank A. D'Accone, "The Singers of San Giovanni in Florence during the 15th Century," *JAMS* 14 (1961): 307–58, and "Some Neglected Composers in the Florentine Chapels, ca. 1475–1525," *Viator* 1 (1970): 263–88; Blake Wilson, *Music and Merchants: The*

Laudesi Companies of Republican Florence (Oxford: Oxford University Press, 1992). **Milan**: Claudio Sartori, "Josquin Des Prés cantore del Duomo di Milano (1459–1472)," *AnnM* 4 (1956): 55–83. **Paris**: Craig Wright, *Music and Ceremony at Notre Dame of Paris, 500–1500* (Cambridge: Cambridge University Press, 1989). **Rome and the Papal Court**: Christopher A. Reynolds, *Papal Patronage and the Music of St. Peter's, 1380–1513* (Berkeley and Los Angeles: University of California Press, 1995); still extremely important is F. X. Haberl, "Die römische 'Schola cantorum' und die päpstlichen Kapellsänger bis zur Mitte des 16. Jahrhunderts," *VfMw* 3 (1887): 189–296; in addition, see Barbara Haggh, "Itinerancy to Residency: Professional Careers and Performance Practices in 15th-Century Sacred Music," *EM* 17 (1989): 359–66.

The Benefice System

Pamela F. Starr, "Rome as the Centre of the Universe: Papal Grace and Music Patronage," *EMH* 11 (1992): 223–62; Reynolds, "Musical Careers, Ecclesiastical Benefices, and the Example of Johannes Brunet," *JAMS* 37 (1984): 49–97.

Also Cited

David Fallows, "The Contenance Angloise: English Influence on Continental Composers of the Fifteenth Century," *Renaissance Studies* 1 (1987): 189–208.

CHAPTER 14

More Secular Song

French secular song carried its formal conventions, both poetic and musical, into the third quarter of the century: the *formes fixes* persisted. Yet there were new developments, both in the songs themselves and in their transmission. It was also this period that saw the rise of polyphonic song repertories outside the French-language mainstream. We will survey each of these developments in turn.

THE *FORMES FIXES* II

As noted in Chapter 5, almost the entire repertory of French secular song from around 1300 to nearly 1500 was shaped by one or another of the *formes fixes*: rondeau, virelai, and ballade. Having considered the ballade and the rondeau, we now turn to the virelai, specifically the one-stanza version that was cultivated in the mid- and late fifteenth century: the *bergerette*.

A Bergerette by Busnoys

No composer of the period seems to have cultivated the bergerette, both as poet and as musician, with as much pleasure as Busnoys. And though the structure of his *Je ne puis vivre* (*Anthology* 27) displays some irregularities in its number of lines and syllables, and therefore its rhyme scheme, we will use the piece as our example of a bergerette because of its many points of interest.

Here is the poem as it appears in the Mellon Chansonnier:

	Poem	*Music*
Je ne puis vivre ainsy tousjours Au mains que j'aye en mes dolours Quelque confort Une seulle heure ou mains ou fort; Et tous les jours Léaument serviray Amours Jusqu'a la mort.	refrain	**A**
Noble femme de nom et d'armes, Escript vous ay ce dittier cy.	*ouvert*	**b**
Des ieux plourant a chauldes larmes Affin qu'ayés de moy merchy.	*clos*	**b**
Quant a moi, je me meurs bon cours, Vellant les nuytz, faisant cent tours, En criant fort: "Vengeance!" a Dieu, car a grant tort Je noye en plours	strophe	**a**

Lorsqu'au besoing me fault secours,
Et Pitié dort.

Je ne puis vivre ainsy tousjours   refrain   **A**
Au mains que j'aye en mes dolours
Quelque confort
Une seulle heure ou mains ou fort;
Et tous les jours
Léaument serviray Amours
Jusqu'a la mort.

A complete performance, then, consists of the following five steps:

A: the refrain is sung to the first section of music from beginning to end;

b: the two-line *ouvert* is sung to the second section of music; it always introduces new rhymes and may—though not here—conclude with its own first ending;

b: the structurally parallel *clos* is repeated to the same music (whether the *ouvert* and *clos* share the same ending, as here, or have different ones, the ending(s) will lack a sense of tonal closure);

a: the strophe replicates the structure of the refrain and is sung to the same music;

A: the refrain is sung in its entirety one more time.

Busnoys was undeniably the greatest song composer of his generation, and *Je ne puis vivre* fully displays his genius. Consider, for example, its texture and meter/rhythm. First, at a time when cantus and tenor normally occupied ranges of their own, *Je ne puis vivre* places those voices in the same range. Busnoys seems to have liked this registral setup; and since he uses it in a number of pieces (including *A vous sans autre*, the chanson we are editing), we might wonder whether he did so in order to accommodate a specific group of performers.

Especially ingenious is the way Busnoys uses imitation to toy with our sense of meter and rhythm. After the imitative entry of the contratenor at the distance of a perfect breve (one full triple-meter measure), the tenor waits another four and two-thirds breves before making its entrance; when it finally does come in, it does so "off the meter," so to speak, and leaves us wondering just where the downbeat is. Busnoys continues to play with this metrical ambiguity beginning at measure 13. First, there is a canon between tenor and cantus in which the distance between the two voices, a perfect breve, reinforces the basic triple-meter framework, while melody and harmonic rhythm seem to be uncertain about the matter. Then, starting with the upbeat to measure 20, a second canon throws in the towel altogether with respect to triple meter: this canon is at the interval of two semibreves, neither voice begins on the downbeat, and the melodic-harmonic organization spells duple meter all the way. Only with the cadence at measure 25 do we feel a return to triple meter, as things must settle down for the final cadence of the refrain. Finally, as he often did in his bergerettes, Busnoys sets the *ouvert-clos* in a contrasting duple meter, and the single canon that spins out beginning at measure 33 now confirms the new metrical framework. So over the course of the song, we have gone from an unambiguous triple meter to various stages of ambiguity, to an unambiguous duple meter, and, with the return of the **a** and **A** sections, back to where we started. Though the plan becomes clear with "aural hindsight," it leaves us guessing along the way.

BUSNOYS AS MELODIST   We need only sing through the superius of virtually any of Busnoys's chansons in order to appreciate his gift for melody. And while it may be unfair to compare the work of a master with that of a journeyman (in this case, a colleague at the court of Charles the Bold), it does serve to drive home the point. Example 14-1 shows the opening phrases of Busnoys's *Ung plus que tous* and Adrien Basin's *Madame, faites moy savoir.*

EXAMPLE 14-1. Superius parts of (a) Busnoys, *Ung plus que tous*, mm. 1–10; (b) Basin, *Madame, faites moy savoir*, mm. 1–13.

Both phrases have much in common: the G-Dorian quality, the cadence on the tonic, and the initial four-note descent. Aesthetically, however, they are worlds apart. Even with the break and leap of a seventh at measures 5–6 (which coincides with the expected caesura after the fourth syllable of a decasyllabic line), Busnoys's melody always pushes forward, in part because of the four instances of syncopation (mm. 3, 4, 7, 9). Basin's melody is another story: it simply dies in measures 5–7.

BUSNOYS AND JACQUELINE   The first letters of each line in the poem of *Je ne puis vivre* (printed in bold) form an acrostic that spells out JAQUELJNE D'AQVEVJLE (j = i, v = u). This is not an accident. Three other Busnoys songs, *A vous sans autre*, *A que ville est abhominable*, and *Ja que lui ne s'i actende*, also include plays on the name, while the letters of the opening line of an anonymous chanson (by Busnoys?), *Pour les biens qu'en vous je parçoy*, can be juggled to provide this signed salutation: "Ces vers pour [these verses for] Bunoys, Jaqueline." Who was this Jacqueline de Hacqueville, who seems to have inspired what are probably the four best-known of Busnoys's songs?

Until recently, she was thought to be a Parisian noblewoman, the wife of Jean Bouchart, with whom Busnoys might have had an affair in the early 1460s. Yet Busnoys was active not at Paris but at Tours during those years. In addition, there was another woman named Jacqueline de Hacqueville, a lady-in-waiting (so probably of noble birth herself) first to the Scottish princess Margaret Stuart (1424–1445), teenage wife of the future Louis XI, and then to Marie d'Anjou, wife of Charles VII. Not only were a number of the ladies-in-waiting in those circles poets, but both *Ja que lui ne s'i actende* and *Pour les biens* clearly express a woman's voice and were therefore probably written by a woman, perhaps by Jacqueline de Hacqueville. In the end, the "Jacqueline" songs may reflect an honored intellectual pastime of the period: that of cultivated men and women partaking in a musical-literary exchange.

THE COMBINATIVE CHANSON

During the third quarter of the fifteenth century, a new type of chanson came into vogue: the "combinative" chanson (a modern term), which usually combined two melodies and their texts, one original and courtly, the other "popular." Though Busnoys was its special champion, we will look at the type through Ockeghem's sole contribution: the four-voice (customary in the combinative chanson) *S'elle m'amera je ne sçay/Petite camusette* (*Anthology* 28).

It is the superius-tenor structural duo that first catches our attention, where Ockeghem combines an original rondeau cinquain in the superius with what must have been a popular tune of the day—a *chanson rustique*—in the tenor (the upper one in the edition, and, at mm. 20–23, the contratenor). The difference in melodic style between the two types, softened somewhat by references to the pop tune in the superius, is matched by a difference in the poetry: the courtly language of one lover (in the superius) contrasts with the other's invocation of the pastoral imagery of Robin and Marion as he chides his own "little snubnose." No doubt it was the witty juxtaposition of disparate, even antithetical, elements that audiences appreciated.

The combination of courtly and popular also creates structural tensions in Ockeghem's song: the five phrases of the rondeau cinquain (mm. 1, 8, 16, 27, 37) clash with the simple **a b a'** and four phrases of the pop tune (mm. 3, 16, 24, 35); and as a result of the difference in the number of phrases, the tune cuts right through the medial cadence of the rondeau, causing problems at the point where the **a** and **A** sections of the rondeau must come to a halt and set up a return to the beginning of the song. Finally, Ockeghem permits the **a b a'** form of the pop tune to influence the rondeau, as the **B** section of the rondeau breaks with custom (m. 35 to the end) and reworks music from the **A** section (from m. 3).

The *chanson rustique*

It is not easy to define just what constituted a "popular" song in the fifteenth century. No doubt, *Petite camusette* and songs like it were enjoyed by people from a wide range of socioeconomic circumstances, just as today's hit songs are. And though many of the songs may have originated in a middle-class, urban environment, that they permeated the uppermost echelons of society is clear from their incorporation into the courtly genres (the combinative chanson, for example) and from their appearance in beautifully decorated manuscript collections. Stylistically, they are worlds apart from the *formes fixes*. Example 14-2 gives one of the well-known tunes:

EXAMPLE 14-2. The popular song *Marchez là dureau*.

Like *Petite camusette, Marchez là dureau* is cast in a simple **a b a** form, which is then repeated for subsequent stanzas, the **a** section functioning as a refrain. Melody and rhythm have an easygoing squareness about them, and the music-word relationship is almost entirely syllabic. Also down to earth are the poems, which deal with such everyday matters as love, carousing, bad marriages, politics, students who don't study, in equally everyday language. Thus the conventions and conceits of the *rhétoriqueurs* are conspicuously absent, and lovers tend to frolic in the woods (*Petite camusette*) instead of bemoaning their sad plights.

Chansons rustiques could appear in a number of guises: sung as monophonic melodies, incorporated into polyphonic settings, performed as part of theatrical productions, and even used as dance melodies. They may well have served as the impetus for the stylistic and structural loosening-up that would sweep through French secular song near the end of the century.

THE "HIT PARADE"

A curious thing happened in the third quarter of the fifteenth century: about a dozen or so chansons were written that gained such "hit" status with other composers (and presumably with audiences) during their own and the next two generations that they generated about three hundred new compositions (keyboard and lute arrangements not included). While some of the derivative works were Mass settings, the overwhelming majority were secular. Thus whole families of songs grew up around the likes of Ockeghem's *Fors seulement*, Du Fay's (?) *Le serviteur*, and the setting of *O rosa bella* attributed to both Dunstable and Bedyngham.

Hayne's *De tous biens plaine*

By far the "busiest" of these chansons—it generated more than fifty new works—was *De tous biens plaine* (*Anthology* 29) by Hayne van Ghizeghem. Hayne's life poses an instructive problem in biography. We first hear about Hayne in 1456, when as a young boy he entered the household of Charles the Bold, where he came to serve as composer, singer, lutenist, and *valet de chambre*. Thus he could hardly have been born prior to the 1440s, which places him not in the generation of Ockeghem and Busnoys, but in Josquin's. He is last heard from on December 9, 1476, with Charles at the siege of Nancy. The subsequent silence has led some to conclude that he died there. But only two of Hayne's chansons—*De tous biens plaine* is one—appear in manuscripts that were copied during the 1460s and 1470s; and when it finally begins to rain Hayne songs in the 1480s (about twenty in all), some pieces are in a more forward-looking style, transmitted mainly in manuscripts that were compiled at the French royal court and that favor composers who were active there. Thus another hypothesis is that Hayne moved on to the French court. Which, then, do we believe: the archival-documentary silence or the circumstantial evidence of the music manuscripts? We know only one thing for certain: Hayne was dead by 1497, since he is among the musicians Guillaume Crétin calls on, in his *Déploration* on the death of Ockeghem, to greet the great composer in the afterlife.

Example 14-3 shows four different arrangements of measures 1–7 of Hayne's original song:

EXAMPLE 14-3. (a) Hayne, *De tous biens plaine*, mm. 1–7; (b) Anonymous, *Odhecation*, mm. 1–7; (c) Anonymous, MS Florence 229, mm. 1–7; (d) Agricola (fourth arrangement), mm. 1–7; (e) Japart, *Je cuide/De tous biens plaine*, mm. 1–10.

(c)

De   tous_____bien_____plai-ne est ma mais-tres -

(d)

(e)

De tous biens

Je cuide

The anonymous version in (b) takes over Hayne's three voices in their entirety and adds a *si placet* ("if it pleases," or optional) altus; this was a popular procedure toward the end of the fifteenth century, as four-part writing became the custom in secular song. Version (c) retains Hayne's superius and tenor, but replaces the original contratenor with a new one (arrangements that feature a single replacement part almost always involve the contratenor). In version (d), Alexander Agricola has taken over only the tenor, which he uses as a cantus-firmus-style scaffold around which to write two new quickly moving voice parts; that this arrangement was intended for instrumental ensemble can hardly be doubted. Finally, Johannes Japart (e) keeps Hayne's tenor, anticipates it imitatively in the altus, recalls Hayne's superius in the bassus, and combines these three voices with the superius of another chanson, *Je cuide* (by either Japart or Pierre Congiet), to form a combinative chanson.

Why did composers rework these hit-parade songs? There are two possibilities: to help supply repertory for instrumental ensembles, and to compete with or pay homage to a fellow composer, with the goal of impressing colleagues and audiences alike. Whatever the reasons, the practice continued until about 1520, by which time a new hit parade had been formed and borrowing based on cantus-firmus technique had become old hat.

THE CHANSONNIERS

When Busnoys and Ockeghem were reaching their maturity as composers in the 1450s–1460s, the printing of polyphonic music was still decades away. Thus the dissemination and preservation of songs depended on manuscripts. Fate has been kind both to us and to the composers of the period, for it is from the third quarter of the fifteenth century on that we begin to witness a dramatic increase in the number of manuscripts that have survived the ravages of centuries. This is particularly true for French secular song, for the period starting around 1460 has left us an especially rich legacy of multicomposer anthologies known as *chansonniers*—not only from French-speaking areas, but from Italy and Germany as well. At times no bigger than a postcard, they were often written on high-quality parchment and lavishly decorated with illuminations. Indeed, many were destined for the likes of princes and their courtiers or for wealthy merchants. It was no doubt their sheer beauty that caused many of them to be preserved.

The Loire Valley

If any chansonniers can be called the blue bloods of our period, it is the group of five manuscripts consisting of Copenhagen 291, Dijon 517, Paris 57, the Laborde Chansonnier, and Wolfenbüttel 287.[1] These manuscripts were

1. Copenhagen, Kongelige Bibliotek, Thott 291, 8°; Paris, Bibliothèque Nationale, Département de la musique, Rés Vmc 57; Washington, D.C., Library of Congress, M2. 1 L25 Case (Laborde, named after a previous owner); Wolfenbüttel, Herzog August - Bibliothek, Guelf. 287 Extravagantium.

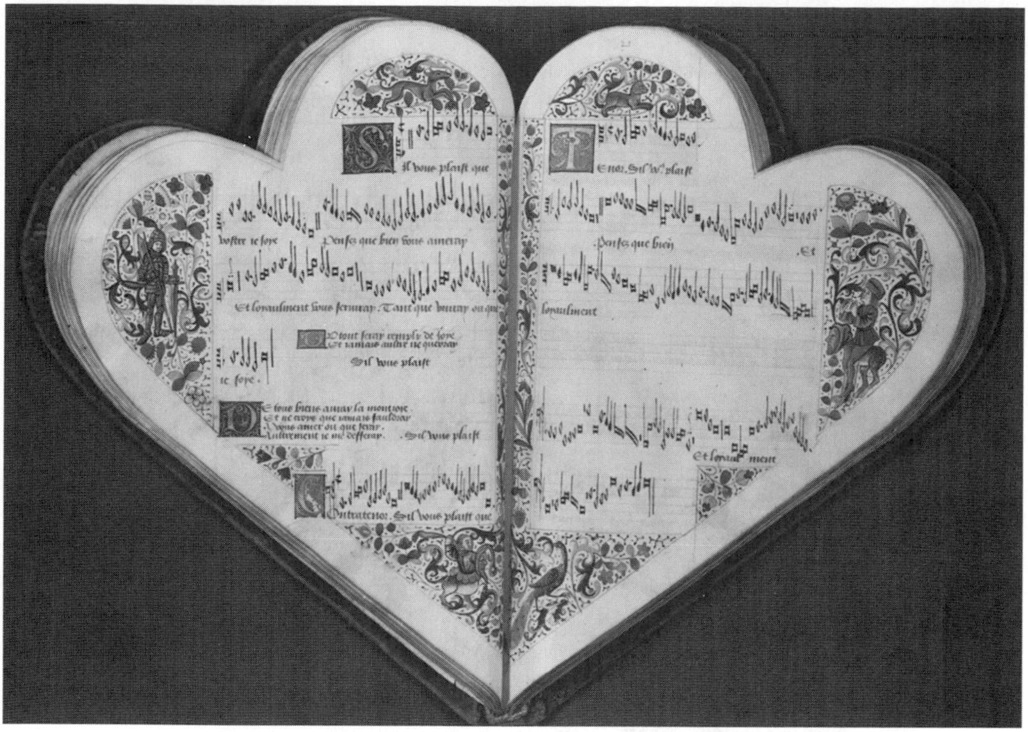

Figure 14-1. Opening from the Cordiforme Chansonnier showing Johannes Regis's *S'il vous plaist*.

long thought to have been compiled within the cultural sphere of the court of Burgundy, but recent studies have convincingly associated them with the Loire Valley area in France, with Paris 57 having been copied in the city of Bourges. Though Dijon 517 and Laborde contain later additions, the brunt of the compilation probably took place in the 1460s.

The manuscripts are important for several reasons: they preserve a total of 424 pieces (though with some duplication); they provide the fullest picture of French secular song as it developed within the cultural spheres of the French and Burgundian courts; and, as we might expect given their French-speaking provenance, they generally preserve the songs with their poems both intact and intelligible.

Savoy

One of the most exquisite manuscripts of the period is the Cordiforme Chansonnier, so called after its heart-shaped format (Fig. 14-1).[2] Written for Jean de Montchenu, a Savoyard priest, around 1470, the manuscript is notable for its mixed French- and Italian-language repertories, reflecting the position of Savoy as a crossroads between the two cultures.

2. Paris, Bibliothèque Nationale, Rothschild MS 2973.

Figure 14-2. Frontispiece to MS Banco rari 229 showing puzzle canon by Ramos de Pareja, painted in grisaille against blue background.

Italy

The gigantic collection Florence 229,[3] written at Florence around 1490, came into the possession of Alessandro Braccesi, a Florentine notary, humanist, and poet who, thanks to his Medici connections, became secretary of the republic's chancery and its ambassador to Siena. With its stunning decorations (see Fig. 14-2), 268 pieces, "compositional battle" between Heinrich Isaac and Johannes Martini (they alternate for the first nineteen pieces in the manuscript), inclusion of the Ockeghem-Busnoys generation as well as early Josquin and his contemporaries, and a generous number of pieces by composers who were active at Florence around 1490, Florence 229 must be accorded star billing among the late-fifteenth-century song collections of Italian provenance. In one area, though, it falls short: it often provides no more than the (sometimes mangled) incipit of its French poems, a trait it shares with most Italian collections of the period, suggesting that they were intended for use by instrumentalists.

3. Florence, Biblioteca Nazionale Centrale, Banco rari MS 229.

Germany

Although it is only a chansonnier in part (slightly more than half of its 292 works are sacred), the Glogauer Liederbuch, copied in northern Silesia (now part of Poland) around 1470, is instructive on a number of counts. (1) It appears to be the earliest extant set of partbooks; that is, each voice part—superius, tenor, and contratenor—is written in its own book, a format that would eventually become the norm beginning in the 1520s. (2) It is an important source of German polyphonic song. (3) Not only do many of its French chansons have no text at all, but others have had their original French verse replaced by Latin texts—*contrafacta*—a typical trait among manuscripts compiled in German-speaking areas when transmitting foreign music. And (4) it teaches us something about the vicissitudes of manuscripts: once part of the collection at the former Preussische Staatsbibliothek, the main library in Berlin before the East-West partition, the partbooks were reported missing after the end of World War II; they only recently resurfaced at the great Jagiellonian Library of Kraków, where librarians have been thoughtful enough to assign them their old call number.[4]

The Transmission of Music

As we can see even from this brief survey of a few important manuscripts, French secular song traveled far and wide, and did so fairly rapidly. But an Ockeghem or Busnoys song did not get from its point of origin to other locations via the large and often beautifully decorated manuscripts that reach us today; these did not circulate.

In general, the day-to-day circulation of music occurred by means of small, unbound fascicles (booklets), which might contain a single large-scale work (such as a Mass) or a number of short pieces. It was from such fascicles that the larger manuscripts were copied. There is a clear allusion to this fascicle-by-fascicle manner of circulation in a letter that the music scribe Jean Michel wrote to Sigismondo d'Este at Ferrara on July 5, 1516:

> I have received your letter together with a prayer motet. . . . Several times you have requested from me some new songs to have copied; it is true that . . . I lent my *registre* to Jacquet for copying. . . . I am sending you two motets for four voices . . . and one for six. . . . If these motets that I am sending you are good and pleasing to you, may it please you to have them copied and send me the copies. . . . Griveau [a singer] . . . sends you his books. . . . There are some good songs in them . . . have those that please you copied.[5]

Jean Michel's *registre* could have been a portfolio or volume of music, or an index of pieces that the scribe had available for making further copies should Sigismondo wish to order any.

With luck, a French chanson written, say, in the early 1460s by Busnoys or Ockeghem could have a life span of about four decades and be transmitted as

4. Kraków, Biblioteka Jagiellońska, MS 40098.
5. Lockwood, "Jean Mouton and Jean Michel," 224–27.

far afield as southern Italy and northern Silesia. And as it traveled, it was often subject to revision by music scribes, performers, or even other composers. Often these revisions found their way into the manuscripts we know today. Thus the version of a Busnoys chanson that appears in one manuscript will not necessarily be identical with its concordances in other manuscripts.

The changes could consist of little more than adding cadential ornamentation or filling in a third with a passing note, both of which may have reflected embellishments added by performers as a matter of course. On the other hand, as we saw in connection with Hayne's *De tous biens plaine* (Ex. 15-3c), a whole voice part could be replaced by a new one, in which case we must decide when a revision is so extensive that it constitutes a new composition.

At times the entire polyphonic fabric of a piece could be reworked. Busnoys's *Je ne puis vivre*, which we saw as it appears in the Mellon Chansonnier (*Anthology* 27), also appears in the manuscript Dijon 517; and while the two manuscripts transmit virtually identical versions for the first part of the bergerette, their readings for the **b** section could hardly be more different (Ex. 14-4):

EXAMPLE 14-4. Busnoys, *Je ne puis vivre*, mm. 28–32: (a) Mellon Chansonnier, (b) Dijon 517.

One version thus constitutes a wholesale revision of the other, raising some questions in the process: (1) Who was responsible for the revision, and when and where was it carried out? (2) Could Busnoys himself have decided to revise the work? (3) If not, and if Busnoys was even aware of the revision, did he approve of it, or could he not have cared less? (4) How do we decide which version is the original? Do we favor Dijon 517 because it was written in the Loire Valley at a time when Busnoys himself might have been looking over the scribe's shoulder? Or do we favor the Mellon Chansonnier on the grounds that that manuscript is later, and its version might therefore represent Busnoys's final intentions? Can we decide the issue on stylistic grounds? The questions mount. And to each, usually we can only answer: we don't know. In fact, the very notion of an *Urtext*—of an "original" or "definitive" version—does not exist for music of the fifteenth century, not in the sense that it does for a Beethoven symphony.

Compiling a Manuscript

How was a manuscript such as Dijon 517 or the Mellon Chansonnier put together? We can outline the successive stages: (1) parchment or paper was obtained from a local stationer, who scraped and smoothed it, cut it to the required size, organized it into fascicles, or gatherings, and perhaps even ruled the music staves; (2) the parchment or paper then went to the music copyist (and any court or church that strove to be an important center of music had its own scribes), who copied the music fascicle by fascicle (the unit of copying in which payment was normally recorded), leaving space for decorated initials and border illuminations; (3) the still-unbound fascicles were then sent to the illuminator's atelier, where the decorations were executed; (4) the loose fascicles next went back to the stationer's shop, where a final round of trimming might be carried out before the fascicles were sewn together and bound between leather- or cloth-covered boards (though only if so ordered, many manuscripts being left unbound); and finally, assuming a truly deluxe product, (5) the bound manuscript might be sent to a local metal worker for raised corner "bosses" (to protect the leather covers from being scuffed on table tops), possibly a row of inlayed jewels, and metal clasps to keep the manuscript tightly closed.

How long did the copying process take? In October 1502, a Mantuan scribe jotted down dates in a 123-folio-long manuscript: the first entry appears on folio 9ʳ and bears the date October 4, while the final folio has the inscription "finis laus deo 26 octubris 1502."[6] Thus 246 *pages* of music—with eight staves per page—took under a month. Suffice it to say that the scribe must have been working full time.

ENGLAND, GERMANY, AND SPAIN

Simply stated, the French chanson was the dominant tradition in fifteenth-century polyphonic song. There were, however, other traditions springing up around the middle of the century. Here we quickly review the various song types in England, Germany, and Spain, and ponder a bit the puzzle that was Italy.

England

As we saw in Chapter 1, Tinctoris lauded the generation of English composers headed by Dunstable as the "fount and origin" of the new (harmonic)

---

6. The manuscript is Paris, Bibliothèque Nationale, Département de la musique, Rés. Vm.[7] 676.

style. He was less gracious about the generation of post-Dunstable composers: "The French contrive music in the newest manner for the new times, while the English continue to use one and the same style of composition, which shows a wretched poverty of invention."[7] Harsh words, to be sure. But English song from 1450 was marked by some conservative traits.

JOHN BEDYNGHAM AND WALTER FRYE   We know little about Bedyngham's life: he died in 1459 or 1460 after having been a member of the London Guild of Parish Clerks from at least 1448–49 (the date of the earliest records) and a verger (attendant) in the chapel of St. Stephen, Westminster, a position that seems to have been reserved for an important composer. If all fifteen pieces attributed to him are really his, Bedyngham was a composer of some significance, with two pieces, *O rosa bella* (see *Anthology* 10 and Chapter 3) and *Mon seul plaisir* (also ascribed to Dunstable and Du Fay, respectively), on the late-fifteenth-century hit parade.

Frye might be the "Walter cantor" active at Ely Cathedral from the 1440s to the 1460s. Like Bedyngham, he was a member of the London Guild of Parish Clerks; the will of one Walter Frye was drawn up in London in August 1474 and proved at Canterbury on June 5, 1475. Frye also had a major hit, the song-motet *Ave regina celorum mater regis angelorum*, which, despite being transmitted with a Latin text in all sources, might originally have been a secular ballade.

Virtually the entire output of both composers is known only through Continental manuscripts, with the original English texts often giving way to the local language. One song attributed to both Bedyngham and Frye, *So ys emprentid in my remembrance* (*Anthology* 30), illustrates one of the most strikingly conservative traits of mid-century English song: it is in ballade form, the very *forme fixe* that Continental composers had abandoned a decade or two earlier.

CONFLICTING ATTRIBUTIONS   The conflicting attributions of *So ys emprentid*—the Mellon Chansonnier ascribes it to Frye, a contemporary Florentine manuscript to Bedyngham—points up a problem that plagues us continually as we try to figure out just who wrote what in the fifteenth and early sixteenth centuries. For instance, there are some 620 French chansons from about 1415 to 1480 that reach us with the names of their composers; of these, approximately 460 carry an attribution in only a single manuscript; the remaining songs carry ascriptions in two or more sources, and 48 of these are transmitted with conflicting attributions. Thus nearly 30 percent of the chansons that have ascriptions in two or more manuscripts involve conflicting attributions, while such chansons constitute about 7 percent of the total of attributed songs.

Traditionally, scholars have approached the problem with two firmly held assumptions: for any given conflict, one attribution must be right, the other wrong; and the conflicts came about accidentally, through scribal confusion

---

7. From the *Proportionale musices*; quoted after Strunk, *Source Readings*, 15.

and error. Likewise, there have been two methods for resolving the conflicts: stylistic analysis and source study. With the latter, scholars try to determine which manuscript, based on its own provenance and the whereabouts of the composer, is more likely to be telling the truth.

The problem with these assumptions is that the conflicts form a pattern that is anything but random or accidental; indeed, an overwhelming number of conflicting attributions involve composers who were active at the same place at the same time. And the methods for solving the conflicts are riddled with shortcomings. Often we do not know enough about the provenance of the manuscripts or the composers' lives, and even if we do, it could be that neither manuscript is a particularly good or bad witness for either composer. Moreover, style analysis can involve a dangerous dose of subjectivity; and it is particularly hard to invoke stylistic criteria for a repertory that is not marked by stark differences between composers or in which some composers left no more than a handful of pieces that can serve as a yardstick.

Is there a viable solution? One recent hypothesis holds out some promise: that the conflicts are not a matter of right and wrong, but may point to one composer's having revised the music of another composer, in which case both have a legitimate claim to the piece. Certainly, this might be true of the Frye/Bedyngham clash over *So ys emprentid*, as the Laborde Chansonnier transmits a version of the song that often differs from that in any of the other manuscripts.

Germany

At about the middle of the century, with the long-standing German tradition of monophonic song still very much alive, the German polyphonic *Tenorlied* (a modern term) came into prominence. Here a composer took a preexistent popular melody, used it as a cantus firmus, and spun two new voice parts around (sometimes below) it. One of the most attractive examples is the anonymous *Mein herz in steten trewen* in the Schedel manuscript (*Anthology* 31).[8] Typical of the genre is the song's *Barform*—**a a b** (further stanzas would repeat the pattern); text placed beneath the preexistent melody only (what does that say about performance practice?); and the rather free-flowing, almost meterless rhythm.

Spain

With Spain still splintered into a number of small kingdoms, it was Naples, ruled by the Spanish House of Aragón, that served as the mid-century cradle of Spanish polyphonic song. There the most important Spanish composer of the fifteenth century, Joan Cornago, was active and probably wrote most of his secular compositions. *¿Qu'es mi vida preguntays?* (*Anthology* 32), later revised by Ockeghem, is a good example. The poem is cast in the customary *canción* (song) form:

---

8. Munich, Bayerische Staatsbibliothek Germanicus monacensis 810 (formerly 3232).

	Rhyme	Section of poem	Music
¿Que'es mi vida, preguntays?	a	*estribillo*	**a**
Non vos la quiero negar,	b		
bien amar e lamentar	b		
es la vida que me days.	a		
¿Quien vos pudiera servir	c	*mudanza*	**b**
tambien como yo he servido?	d		
¿Mi trabaxado vivir	c		**b**
quien pudiera haver sofrido?	d		
¿Para que me, preguntays?	a	*vuelta*	**a**
La pena que he de passar,	b		
pues amar e lamentar	b		
es la vida que me days.	a		

Clearly, the canción is a close relative of the French virelai/bergerette and Italian ballata. The main difference lies in its not restating the opening four lines of verse, so that the *estribillo* does not function as a recurring refrain. Instead, there is a kind of internal mini-refrain, as the final line of the *vuelta* repeats that of the *estribillo*, while the penultimate lines of the two sections are similar.

ITALY

During the second half of the fourteenth century, two generations of Italian composers headed by Jacopo da Bologna (fl. 1350s–60s) and Francesco Landini (d. 1397) developed a truly original and glorious tradition of secular polyphony, echoes of which are still to be found in some of the music of the transplanted northerner Johannes Ciconia. To be sure, French influences crept in as the period wore on, and by the early 1400s Italian composers were for the most part writing in a northern, international style.

And then a strange thing happened: after the 1420s or so, Italian polyphonic art music—both secular and otherwise—seems to disappear, not to flourish again until the rise of the *frottola* repertory in the 1490s. What happened? Where did all the Italian composers go, and why?

Three Hypotheses

A number of explanations have been advanced: (1) continuing the process that had already begun in the late fourteenth century, Italian music (and even the poetry that served it in the case of secular song) simply caved in completely to French influences, a reflection of the same Francophilism that led the Este and the Medici to adopt the French lily for their coats of arms; (2) Italy lacked the great *maîtrises* (choir schools) of the Franco-Flemish cathedrals and churches, and thus lagged behind in training new generations of composers.

Neither of these explanations is entirely convincing. After all, there was no parallel drying up in painting, sculpture, or humanistic learning, in all of which, if anything, Italy took the lead. Nor did Italy lack training grounds for musicians: in the 1430s, Eugene IV established new cathedral schools in which music was part of the curriculum, and music played a role at Vittorino da Feltre's humanist school at Mantua. Moreover, by 1450–80, Italian poets were turning out "poetry for music"—*strambotti* and *barzellette*—by the bushel, and some, as we will see, was set polyphonically.

A third hypothesis, which has proved more influential, argues that Italy, under the influence of the humanist literati and their passion for classical antiquity, turned its back on both the complicated Franco-Flemish polyphony of the north and its own trecento tradition. Italians favored instead a simple, improvisatory style, in which Latin and Italian verses were sung "to the lyre" in imitation—or so they thought—of the ancients. But was this improvisatory style really valued more highly than the notated music of a Busnoys or an Ockeghem? And did the humanist disdain for polyphony, if indeed it was that, have any real influence? For if either of these was so, how do we explain the veritable explosion in the production of manuscripts in late-fifteenth-century Italy that contain mainly Franco-Flemish music, or the intensity with which the Italian courts vied with one another to secure the services of the best Franco-Flemish singers and composers? The puzzle of fifteenth-century Italy remains just that.

The "Unwritten Tradition"

Whatever the explanation for the disappearance of polyphonic music, improvisation, the basis of a so-called unwritten tradition, certainly existed, though the term "improvisation" should be used rather loosely. To what extent the improvisers performed in a truly extempore fashion and to what extent they carefully worked out their performances without writing them down are impossible to say. Moreover, it may be that some of their material was written but simply fails to survive, or that some of what does survive qualifies as written-down improvisation.

We should also recognize that there were sociological distinctions between the improvisers. At the bottom of the social scale were the street performers, called *cantarini* or *cantastorie* (story singers), with a wide range of styles and skills; the substance of their art is probably lost irretrievably. At the other end of the scale were performers who gained fame through their association with the princely courts, where they were especially well received and handsomely rewarded. Here we can draw a hazy line between poets who sang their verses to musical accompaniment and musicians who sang the poetry of others. Italy saw a long line of such performers, starting in the early fifteenth century and continuing without a break into the sixteenth, singing everything from Latin narrative verse to lyric poetry in the vernacular. To name just a few: the Venetian poet-statesman Leonardo Giustinian (d. 1446), whose name is associated with the verses of *O rosa bella*; the Florentine Antonio di Guido (d. 1486), a favorite of the Medici; Benedetto Gareth, who entertained the court of Naples with his recitations of Virgil; Pietrobono "dal chitarino" (1417–1497), resident at the court of Ferrara for more than half a century and praised for his singing and virtuoso lute playing; and perhaps the most famous of all, Serafino de' Ciminelli dall' Aquila (1466–1500), who sang his strambotti from one end of Italy to the other.

A STRAMBOTTO BY SERAFINO   One of the most popular musical-poetic genres of the late fifteenth century was the *strambotto*, which consisted of a single eight-line stanza rhyming either abababcc or abababab (the latter called the *strambotto Siciliano*). The Sicilian type appears in a poem by Serafino, *Sufferir son disposto*:

Sufferir son disposto omne tormento, tormento dove sia sine a reposo.	I am disposed to suffer every torment, torment where there is no repose.
Reposo me sarria esser contento, contento de l'Amor che porto ascuso.	Repose would make me content, content from the love hidden within me.
Ascuso focho nel mio petto sento, sento che me consuma el cor doglioso.	I feel a hidden fire in my breast, I feel that it consumes my sorrowful heart.
Doglioso vivo et del mio mal consento, consento de morir, o gloriuso.	I live in sorrow and with harsh consent, I consent to die, o glorious one.

Perhaps the polyphonic setting (*Anthology* 33) at least approximates the spirit of Serafino's style of improvisation: the superius delivers the poem in a style that amounts to heightened declamation; the counterpoint is simple, as the tenor does little more than follow the superius in parallel motion; and the final three couplets simply repeat the music of the first (with embellishments no doubt added in performance). The piece has all the earmarks of what we might call controlled improvisation.

Although the four manuscripts that transmit *Sufferir son disposto* write out all the parts as though the work were intended for an ensemble, Serafino's was primarily a soloist's art. Perhaps he accompanied himself with chords on the seven-string (two of them drones) *lira de braccio* (Fig. 14-3), which, with its associations with antiquity—it is often depicted in the hands of Orpheus, Apollo, and Pan—was the improvisers' favorite instrument. Sometimes, though, Serafino and other improvisers performed as part of a duo, accompanied by a *tenorista*, In this case, Serafino might have sung the melody and played the bottom line, while a companion took the tenor part on a lute, which in the late fifteenth century was making the transition from a single-line melody instrument to one capable of polyphony and chords.

Compared with the contrapuntal intricacy of a French chanson like Busnoys's *Je ne puis vivre*, Serafino's *Sufferir son disposto* might strike us as a trifle. Yet we must remember that one aspect of the work we can only wonder about is the style and manner of Serafino's performance, or, as his contemporaries would have called it, his *aria* (air). Perhaps we can conjure up Serafino in action through the description of another singer's *aria*. The scene is a banquet at the Roman palace of Paolo Orsini in 1489, the singer is Paolo's young son Fabio, and the writer is the Florentine humanist Angelo Poliziano:

Figure 14-3. Poet with *lira da braccio*, woodcut from *Epithome Plutarchi*, 1501.

He filled our ears, or rather our hearts, with a voice so sweet that . . . I was almost transported out of my senses. . . . His voice was not entirely that of someone reading, nor entirely that of someone singing: both could be heard, and yet neither separated one from the other; it was, in any case, even or modulated, and changed as required by the passage. Now it was varied, now sustained, now exalted and now restrained, now calm and now vehement, now slowing down and now quickening its pace, but always it was precise, always clear and always pleasant; and his gestures were not indifferent or sluggish, but not posturing or affected either.[9]

Serafino's "trifle" might well have been mesmerizing.

BIBLIOGRAPHICAL NOTE

Editions of the Music

Busnoys: the songs of Busnoys are being edited by Leeman L. Perkins for publication in the *Collected Works*, vol. 1, *MMR* 5/1 (New York: The Broude Trust). **Cornago**: *Complete Works*, *RRMMAER* 15, ed. Rebecca L. Gerber (Madison: A-R Editions, 1984). **Frye**: *Opera omnia*, *CMM* 19, ed. Sylvia Kenney (American Institute of Musicology, 1960). **Hayne van Ghizeghem**: *Opera Omnia*, *CMM* 74, ed. Barton Hudson (American Institute of Musicology, 1974). **Ockeghem**: the chansons appear in *Collected Works*, vol. 3, ed. Richard Wexler (New York: American Musicological Society, 1992). **Combinative chanson**: *The Combinative Chanson: An Anthology*, *RRMR* 77, ed. Maria Rika Maniates (Madison: A-R Editions,

9. Quoted after Pirrotta and Povoledo, *Music and Theatre from Poliziano to Monteverdi*, 36.

1989). **Monophonic songs**: Gaston Paris, *Chansons du XVe siècle* (Paris: Firmin-Didot, 1875; Johnson Reprint, 1965); Théodore Gerold, *Le Manuscrit de Bayeux* (Strasbourg: Palais de l'Université, 1921; reprint, Minkoff, 1971). **Families of songs**: Martin Picker, *Fors seulement: Thirty Compositions for Three to Five Voices or Instruments from the Fifteenth and Sixteenth Centuries*, RRMMAER 14 (Madison: A-R Editions, 1989); three editions by Richard Taruskin based on *Een vrolic wesen*, *J'ay pris amours*, and *D'ung aultre amer*, Ogni Sorte (Miami: Ogni Sorte Editions, 1979, 1982, 1983); Honey Meconi, *Fortuna desperata: Thirty-four Settings of an Italian Song*, RRMAER (Madison: A-R Editions, forthcoming). **Chansonniers**: for the Mellon Chansonnier and Florence 229, see the works by Perkins and Garey and Brown listed under "General Studies"; Knud Jeppesen, *Der Kopenhagener Chansonnier* (Copenhagen and Leipzig: Levin & Munksgaard and Breitkopf & Härtel, 1927; reprint, Broude Bros., 1965); the Laborde MS is being edited (modern and facsimile) by Richard Wexler for publication by the Library of Congress; Geneviève Thibault and David Fallows, *Chansonnier de Jean de Montchenu (Bibliothèque Nationale, Rothschild 2973 [I.5. 13])* (Paris: Société française de musicologie, 1991); *Das Glogauer Liederbuch*, ed. Heribert Ringmann, Joseph Klapper, and Christian Väterlein, EDMR 4, 8, 85–86 (Kassel: Bärenreiter, 1936, 1981). **Facsimile editions of chansonniers**: *Dijon, Bibliothèque Publique, Manuscrit 517*, ed. Dragan Plamenac, PMMM 12 (Brooklyn: Institute of Mediaeval Music, n.d.); *Chansonnier Nivelle de la Chaussée (Bibliothèque Nationale, Paris, Rés. Vmc. ms. 57, ca. 1460)*, ed. Paula Higgins (Geneva: Minkoff, 1984); for the Mellon Chansonnier, see below; *Kraków, Biblioteka Jagiellónska, Glogauer Liederbuch*, ed. Jessie Ann Owens, RMF 6 (New York: Garland, 1986).

General Studies

There are excellent surveys in Howard Mayer Brown, *A Florentine Chansonnier from the Time of Lorenzo the Magnificent: Florence, Biblioteca Nazionale Centrale, MS Banco Rari 229*, MRM 7 (Chicago: University of Chicago Press, 1983), which includes a complete edition of the manuscript, and Leeman L. Perkins and Howard Garey's *Mellon Chansonnier* (New Haven: Yale University Press, 1979), which presents the entire manuscript in both modern and facsimile editions. Busnoys and Ockeghem: there is a perceptive study of Busnoys's songs in George Perle, "The Chansons of Antoine Busnois," *MR* 11 (1950): 89–97; see also Catherine Brooks, "Antoine Busnois, Chanson Composer," *JAMS* 6 (1953): 111–35. Ockeghem's songs are discussed in the *Complete Works* (see above); see also David Fallows, "Johannes Ockeghem: The Changing Image, the Songs, and a New Source," *EM* 12 (1984): 218–30, and the Proceedings of the Busnoys and Ockeghem conferences cited in Chapter 11.

Chanson rustique and Combinative Chanson

On the *chanson rustique*, see Brown, "The *Chanson rustique*: Popular Elements in the 15th- and 16th-Century Chanson," *JAMS* 12 (1959): 16–26. The fundamental studies on the combinative chanson are by Maria Rika Maniates: "Mannerist Composition in Franco-Flemish Polyphony," *MQ* 52 (1966): 17–36, and "Combinative Chansons in the Dijon Chansonnier," *JAMS* 23 (1970): 228–81.

The "Hit Parade"

For a survey, begin with Honey Meconi, "Art-Song Reworkings: An Overview," *JRMA* 119 (1994): 1–42; two studies that deal with specific families are Irena Cholij, "Borrowed Music: 'Allez regrets' and the Use of Pre-existent Material," in *Companion to Medieval and Renaissance Music*, ed. Tess Knighton and David Fallows (New York: Schirmer, 1992), 165–76, and Helen Hewitt, "*Fors seulement* and the Cantus Firmus Technique of the Fifteenth Century," in *Essays in Musicology in Honor of Dragan Plamenac on his 70th Birthday*, ed. Gustave Reese and Robert J. Snow (Pittsburgh: University of Pittsburgh Press, 1969), 91–126.

England, Germany, Spain

England: David Fallows, "English Song Repertories of the Mid-Fifteenth Century," *PRMA* 103 (1976–77): 61–79, "Words and Music in Two English Songs of the Mid-Fifteenth Century: Charles d'Orléans and John Lydgate," *EM* 5 (1977): 38–43, and "Dunstable, Bedyngham, and *O rosa bella*," *JM* 12 (1994): 287–305; Sylvia Kenney, *Walter Frye and the Contenance Angloise* (New Haven: Yale University Press, 1964). **Germany**: Reinhard Strohm's *Rise of European Music, 1380–1500* (Cambridge: Cambridge University Press, 1993) is a good general survey; on the origins of the Tenorlied, see Martin Staehelin, "The Constitution of the Fifteenth-Century German Tenor Lied: Drafting the History of a Musical Genre," in *Music in the German Renaissance: Sources, Styles, and Contexts*, ed. John Kmetz (Cambridge: Cambridge University Press, 1994), 174–81. **Spain**: Robert Stevenson, *Spanish Music in the Age of Columbus* (The Hague: Nijhoff, 1960); Isabel Pope and Masakata Kanazawa, *The Musical Manuscript Montecassino 871: A Neapolitan Repertory of Sacred and Secular Music of the Late Fifteenth Century* (Oxford: Clarendon Press, 1978), which includes an edition of the manuscript; David Fallows, "A Glimpse of the Lost Years: Spanish Polyphonic Song, 1450–70," in *New Perspectives in Music: Essays in Honor of Eileen Southern*, ed. Josephine Wright and Samuel A. Floyd (Warren, Mich.: Harmonie Park Press, 1992), 19–36.

Italy and the "Unwritten Tradition"

One must begin with the work of Nino Pirrotta, especially "Music and Cultural Tendencies in 15th-Century Italy," *JAMS* 19 (1966): 127–61, which has been reprinted in *Music and Culture in Italy from the Middle Ages to the Baroque* (Cambridge: Harvard University Press, 1984); there is a particularly even-handed treatment in James Haar, *Essays on Italian Poetry and Music in the Renaissance, 1350–1600* (Berkeley and Los Angeles: University of California Press, 1986), especially chapters 2 and 4; see also William F. Prizer, "The Frottola and the Unwritten Tradition," *StudiM* 15 (1986): 3–37; Walter Rubsamen, "The Justiniane or Viniziane of the 15th Century," *ActaM* 29 (1957): 172–84.

Also Cited

Lewis Lockwood, "Jean Mouton and Jean Michel: New Evidence on French Music and Musicians in Italy, 1505–1520," *JAMS* 32 (1979): 191–246; Nino Pirrotta and Elena Povoledo, *Music and Theatre from Poliziano to Monteverdi*, trans. Karen Eales (Cambridge: Cambridge University Press, 1982).

CHAPTER 15

Intermedio: 1467–1469

Within two years of each other in the late 1460s, Charles the Bold and Lorenzo de' Medici (called "il Magnifico") took over the reigns of their respective families and the states they headed. And though both men were largely motivated by the same concerns—increasing and consolidating their power—it would be difficult to imagine two more different personalities, each of whom represented the end of a dynastic era.

CHARLES THE BOLD

Born in 1433, Charles (Fig. 15-1) became Duke of Burgundy upon the death of his father, Philip the Good, in June 1467. As we saw in Chapter 3, Burgundy had grown through marriage, purchase, and outright conquest from its original area around Dijon to include much of the Low Countries. It was Charles's desire to expand and glorify still further what was already the single most magnificent court in western Europe that set the tone for his brief but stormy eight-year reign.

Figure 15-1. Portrait of Charles the Bold by an unknown artist (Musée, Avignon).

Charles's Political Agenda

Charles had two main political objectives. First, he wished to build a corridor between the two parts of his duchy and thus link Burgundy proper (whose capital, Dijon, he visited only once during his entire reign) and its neighboring areas with the northern territories of the Low Countries. Second, he sought to upgrade his state to the level of a kingdom, which would extend east to the Rhine and from Switzerland to the North Sea and thus act as a buffer between France and the imperial territories of the Habsburgs.

The second of these objectives had been explored by Philip the Good as far back as the 1440s. It came to naught in 1473, as the Holy Roman Emperor Frederick III, the sole person with the authority to bestow a royal crown, chose not to grant one to Charles. Charles's policy of territorial expansion would embroil him in warfare for much of his reign and ultimately cost him his life. To build the corridor, Charles needed to acquire Alsace and Lorraine. But after purchasing Alsace, years of brutal campaigning for Lorraine ended in defeat and his death outside Nancy in January 1477.

Charles as Musician

By all accounts, Charles was never happier than when camped on the battlefield. Yet he was also, by all accounts, an accomplished musician, certainly one of the more talented of the music-loving nobility. That he lavished particular care on his chapel we saw in Chapter 13. In fact, he seems to have dragged his entire group of singers from one military encampment to another. Thus the Milanese ambassador reported in May 1475 during the ten-month siege of Neuss, "Even though [the duke] is in camp, every evening he has something new sung in his quarters; and sometimes his lordship sings, although he does not have a good voice; but he is skilled in music."[1]

As we might expect, Charles was most comfortable with secular music. Not only did he play the harp from the age of seven, he was also a composer: "he 'made' several chansons, well made and well notated," "he knew how to compose."[2] And at least one of Charles's chansons survives, if we can trust that an attribution to "Dux Burgensis" refers to him (Ex. 15-1):

EXAMPLE 15-1. Charles the Bold, *Madame, trop vous mesprenés*, mm. 1–15.

1. Giovanni Pietro Panigarola, quoted after Vaughan, *Charles the Bold*, 163.

2. The testimony comes from two court chroniclers, Olivier de la Marche and Philippe Wielant, respectively; quoted after Marix, *Histoire*, 19. The French equivalent of the verb "to make" was often used with reference to composing.

In all, Charles represents a type that was perfectly at home in the fifteenth century: the cultured soldier-prince, whose style of governing had its roots firmly in the feudalistic past.

Burgundy after Charles the Bold

Charles died without male heirs. With his death, the Valois dukes of Burgundy came to the end of their four-generations-old line, and their duchy underwent a change of political identity.

First, the original nucleus of the state, Burgundy proper, which had been ceded to Charles's great-grandfather, Philip the Bold, a century earlier, reverted to the French crown, which also annexed the county of Artois and the towns along the Somme. The possessions in the Low Countries, on the other hand, were absorbed into the Habsburg domains when, a few months after Charles's death, his daughter Mary of Burgundy married the future Holy Roman Emperor Maximilian I. They in turn passed the possessions on to their son Philip the Fair, who, as husband of Joanna, daughter of Ferdinand and Isabella, joined them to a united Spain. Finally, the sixteenth century saw the entire realm— much of Germany-Austria, the Low Countries, and all of Spain (with its possessions in the Americas)—united in the hands of Philip and Joanna's son (Charles the Bold's great-grandson), the Holy Roman Emperor Charles V, who thus ruled an empire the extent of which would not be matched until the time of Napoleon.

LORENZO DE' MEDICI ("IL MAGNIFICO")

Unlike the dukes of Burgundy, who ruled with absolute authority and by hereditary right, the Medici, beginning with Lorenzo's grandfather Cosimo in 1434, ruled Florence in the style of backroom political bosses. They had no choice: Florence was nominally a constitutional republic, its government and economy dominated by the *nobili popolani*, wealthy merchants of the seven principal guilds (wool merchants, cloth merchants, furriers, silk weavers, druggists, notaries, and—the one to which the Medici belonged—bankers).

In the fifteenth century, the Medici had neither titles nor official court; what they did have was money, gained from banking, mining, and other business interests. And with their generally sure sense of when to flaunt it, with their mastery of political patronage and mutual hand washing, with their talent for

Figure 15-2. Andrea del Verrocchio, terra-cotta bust of Lorenzo de' Medici, 1478 (National Gallery, Washington, D.C.).

linking their own well-being to that of Florence, and with their ability to maintain peace amid a faction-ridden oligarchy, the Medici managed to "rule" with the acquiescence of the populace at large, which mostly saw them as benefactors of the public good.

Lorenzo's Political Agenda

Born in 1449, Lorenzo (Fig. 15-2) took over the stewardship of Florence on the death of his father, Piero di Cosimo, in 1469. As he later wrote, perhaps disingenuously, in his memoires:

> The second day after [Piero's] death, although I was very young, being twenty years of age, the principal men of the city and of the State came to us in our house to condole with us on our loss and to encourage me to take charge of the city and of the State, as my grandfather and my father had done. This I did, though on account of my youth and the great responsibility and perils arising therefrom, with great reluctance, solely for the safety of our friends and of our possessions. For it is ill living in Florence for the rich unless they rule the State.[3]

Lorenzo's political agenda consisted mainly of balancing two sets of relationships: the Medici within Florence and Florence within Italy as a whole. It was the first of these that Lorenzo found most tricky, as he tried to walk the political tightrope strung by his predecessors. He showed little interest in everyday business affairs. And in 1480, with his revenues dwindling, Lorenzo and his backers

3. Quoted after Watkins, *Humanism and Liberty*, 160.

found it more convenient simply to "reform" the constitution, creating self-perpetuating layers of councils and committees that always got their way.

In the realm of foreign affairs, Lorenzo was something of a maverick: he envisioned the idea of a united Italy. Unfortunately for the Italians, his was an isolated voice. Faced with the invading French armies of Charles VIII in 1494, whose target was Naples, the various Italian states—including Florence, then ruled by Lorenzo's son Piero—looked no further than their own self-interest. The result was the beginning of the so-called Wars of Italy, which led to a period of foreign domination that did not end until the *risorgimento* (revival) and the unification of the country in the nineteenth century.

Lorenzo as Patron of the Arts

Florentine culture reached spectacular heights during Lorenzo's rule. Some of the artists who flourished then are Benozzo Gozzoli, whose *Procession of the Magi* (c. 1459) in the Medici palace is populated with members of the Medici family (Fig. 15-3); Domenico Ghirlandaio, whose most famous frescoes are in the private chapel of Francesco Sassetti (a banker in Lorenzo's circle) in the

Figure 15-3. Benozzo Gozzoli, detail from *The Procession of the Magi*, fresco, 1459; the two men to the left of center on brown mule and white horse, respectively, are Cosimo de' Medici and his son Piero (Lorenzo's grandfather and father); slightly behind them are the young Lorenzo (glancing sideways) and his younger brother Giuliano (two faces to the left); centered behind them, with a hat that bears his name, is the artist (Palazzo Medici-Ricardi, Florence).

Figure 15-4. Domenico del Ghirlandaio, detail from *St. Francis before Pope Onorio III*, fresco, c. 1485; Lorenzo is depicted as the tallest figure at the right (S. Trinita, Sassetti Chapel, Florence).

church of S. Trinità (Fig. 15-4), and in whose workshop the young Michelangelo learned his trade while living with Lorenzo's family; Sandro Botticelli, whose "mythologies"—including the famous *Primavera* (Fig. 15-5)—closely reflect Florentine intellectual currents of the time; and Lorenzo's own favorite sculptor, Andrea del Verrocchio (see Fig. 15-2), in whose workshop Leonardo

Figure 15-5. Sandro Botticelli, detail from *La primavera*, c. 1478 (Uffizi Gallery, Florence).

da Vinci worked. It is probably fair to say that no other city reached such glorious artistic heights within so circumscribed a time period until nineteenth-century Paris gave birth to the Impressionists.

Lorenzo himself commissioned little in the way of monumental art from these masters; rather, he set a tone and influenced those around him. His own tastes were of a more private sort: small paintings and bronze sculptures, antique coins and vases, cameos, jewels, and his most prized possession, the *Tazza Farnese* (Fig. 15-6), which a 1492 inventory of the Medici household valued at an astounding 10,000 florins. All of these lined the walls and hallways of his palace and country houses.

Lorenzo also played a central role in fostering the intellectual-literary climate of Florence, the symbolic centerpiece of which was the informal Platonic Academy. Included among the academicians were the leading Florentine literary figures of the day: Marsilio Ficino, Angelo Poliziano, Cristoforo Landino, Count Giovanni Pico della Mirandola, and Lorenzo himself. They would usually meet over a banquet at one of Lorenzo's houses in order to discuss such issues as platonic love, textual criticism, and the relative merits of the contemplative versus the active life and Latin versus the vernacular.

Lorenzo, author of some of the best Italian poetry of the period, was an avid amateur musician. He played the *lira da braccio* and, to judge from the many

Figure 15-6. The *Tazza Farnese* (Museo Archeologico, Naples).

that he owned, keyboard instruments as well. His patronage of music mirrored his own political position. Just as he had no official court, Lorenzo kept no private chapel; rather, as his father and grandfather had before him, he personally subsidized the choirs of the leading Florentine churches as well as the semiprofessional musical activities of the major guilds.

The Medici after Lorenzo

Lorenzo died on April 8, 1492. Two and a half years later, the Medici were expelled from Florence, a consequence of Lorenzo's eldest son and successor, Piero, having surrendered the city to Charles VIII's invading French armies. Not until 1512, when Lorenzo's second son, Giovanni, was heading the family, did the Medici return. Within a year, Giovanni, who had become a cardinal at age fourteen (thanks to Lorenzo's pulling strings), succeeded to the papacy as Leo X (1513–21). One of Leo's first acts was to appoint his cousin Giulio cardinal and Archbishop of Florence. The Medici were firmly in control again. (In 1527, Giulio followed his cousin to the papal throne as Clement VII.) Florence had one more respite from the Medici, during the so-called Last Republic of 1527–30. Again, though, the family bounced back. First Alessandro de' Medici took the helm, and then Cosimo I acquired the title Duke of Florence in 1537 and became Grand Duke of Tuscany in 1569. The Medici would rule as grand dukes for three more centuries with ever less distinction, though not without producing two queens of France along the way.

Lorenzo's Reputation

Was Lorenzo a tyrant or a hero? Surely, later generations of Florentines saw in him the beneficent patron who ruled Florence during one of its most peaceful and productive periods, the last ruler before the decline that began with the Italian Wars. This was the view taken up and romanticized by nineteenth-century historians, who saw Lorenzo as responsible for the great flowering of Florentine culture in the second half of the fifteenth century and who twisted "il magnifico," an everyday term of respect, into something akin to "the one and only magnificent one." Yet just how difficult it is to assess the man can be seen from a character sketch offered by the sixteenth-century Florentine historian Francesco Guicciardini: "We must conclude that under him the city was not free, even though it could not have had a better tyrant or a more pleasant one."[4]

BIBLIOGRAPHICAL NOTE

Charles the Bold

The standard study is Richard Vaughan, *Charles the Bold: The Last Valois Duke of Burgundy* (London: Longman, 1973). Incredibly, there is no comprehensive, easily available study of Charles's patronage of music; one must turn to an unpublished dissertation, David Fallows,

4. Guicciardini, *The History of Florence*, 76.

"Robert Morton's Songs: A Study of Styles in the Mid-Fifteenth Century," Ph.D. diss., University of California, Berkeley (1978), and his "Specific Information," cited in the Bibliographical Note to Chapter 13; see also the three items by Paula Higgins cited in the Bibliographical Note to Chapter 11 and the scattered references in Jeanne Marix, *Histoire de la musique et des musiciens de la cour de Bourgogne sous le règne de Philippe le Bon (1420–1467)* (Strasbourg: Heitz, 1939).

Lorenzo de' Medici

Fifteenth-century Florence has been studied more carefully than any other Italian center, so the literature on the Medici and Lorenzo is vast; an excellent starting point is chapter 2 of John R. Hale's *Florence and the Medici: The Pattern of Control* (London: Thames & Hudson, 1977); also good as an introduction is Ferdinand Schevill, *The Medici* (New York: Harper & Row, 1960; originally published 1949), as is Judith Hook's *Lorenzo de' Medici: An Historical Biography* (London: Hamish Hamilton, 1984), which is intended for the general reader. For a view of Lorenzo as patron of the arts, see Bernard Toscani, ed., *Lorenzo de' Medici: A New Perspective* (New York: Peter Lang, 1993); on Lorenzo's patronage of music, see Frank A. D'Accone, "The Singers of San Giovanni in Florence during the Fifteenth Century," *JAMS* 14 (1961): 307–58, and "Lorenzo the Magnificent and Music," in *Lorenzo il Magnifico e il suo mondo: Convegno internazionale di studi*, ed. Gian Carlo Garfagnini (Florence: Olschki 1994), 259–90. On the musical settings of Lorenzo's poems, see Walter Rubsamen, "The Music for 'Quant'è bella giovinezza' and Other Carnival Songs by Lorenzo de' Medici," in *Art, Science, and History in the Renaissance*, ed. Charles Singleton (Baltimore: Johns Hopkins University Press, 1968), 163–84.

Also Cited

Francesco Guicciardini, *The History of Florence*, trans. Mario Domandi (New York: Harper & Row, 1970); Renée N. Watkins, *Humanism and Liberty: Writings on Freedom from Fifteenth-Century Florence* (Columbia: University of South Carolina Press, 1978).

CHAPTER 16

Instrumental Music and Two Theorists

Our knowledge of instrumental music before 1450 is scanty at best. There must have been a great deal, and it certainly played an important role in court, civic, and religious life. Yet little of it has been preserved. The situation began to change during the three decades from around 1450 to 1480, and it was also during this period that theorists started paying attention to practical aspects of instrumental music, describing both the construction of instruments and the functions of various ensembles.

Here we will look at three different types of instrumental music: keyboard music, or more precisely, music for the organ; music for instrumental ensembles, what might be called the chamber music of the day; and music for that most popular activity, social dancing.

KEYBOARD MUSIC

Thanks to a treatise written around 1440 by the Netherlander Henri Arnaut de Zwolle (d. 1466), physician and astronomer at the courts of Burgundy and France, we have a fairly clear idea about the variety and design of fifteenth-century organs and stringed keyboard instruments, the latter both with plucking (harpsichord-like) and striking (clavichord-like) mechanisms Fig. 16-1).

Types of Organs

By the fifteenth century, large, stationary organs had become commonplace in churches throughout Europe. Generally situated in a rear gallery of the nave, they were fitted with multiple keyboards, stops, and ranks of pipes, as well as a row of pedals. Organists would improvise on chant melodies, play in alternation with the choir, and fill the gaps in the liturgy with preludes, interludes, and postludes.

There were also more modest-sized organs. The *portative,* small enough to be slung over the shoulder, had a single manual with a range of about two octaves starting around *c'*. Since the player had to operate the bellows with one hand, the portative was basically a melody instrument, or at least limited to whatever "polyphony" could be managed with a single hand (Fig. 16-2). The instrument was probably most often used within an ensemble.

Somewhat larger than the portative but still able to be transported was the *positive.* Often small enough to be placed on a table, it contained all the notes

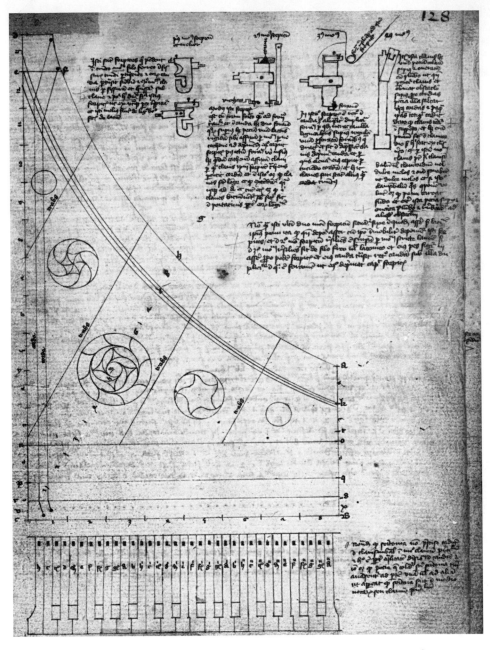

Figure 16-1. Henri Arnaut de Zwolle, drawing of harpsichord with description of different mechanisms, c. 1440 (Bibliothèque Nationale, Paris).

of the chromatic scale and had a two-to-three-octave range (beginning on *B*). Unlike the portative, it was played with both hands, its bellows pumped by a second person (Fig. 16-3; for a larger version, see Fig. 6-3). We can only wonder whether the air pressure supplied by the bellows of the smaller, tabletop models was sufficient to produce more than a whisper when the music called for three- or four-note chords.

Figure 16-2. *A Woman Playing the Portative Organ*, drawing by an unknown artist, c. 1440 (Louvre, Paris).

Figure 16-3. Israël van Meckenem, *An Organist and His Wife*, woodcut, c. 1490 (Cleveland Art Museum).

The Music

The richest extant body of organ music from the mid-fifteenth century comes to us from Germany and comprises four types of pieces: didactic (instructional) works; freely composed preambles, or preludes; settings of sacred and secular monophonic melodies; and arrangements of polyphonic works, especially French and German songs.

DIDACTIC WORKS   By far the most notable of the didactic works is the *Fundamentum organisandi* (1452), by Conrad Paumann, the leading figure in fifteenth-century German keyboard music. Born in Nuremberg around 1410, Paumann, who was blind from birth, became an organist, lutenist, and composer. After assuming the post of organist at the Nuremberg church of St. Sebald (by 1446 at the latest), Paumann broke his contract with the town officials and took an appointment in 1450 as organist at the Munich court of the dukes of Bavaria, a position he held—with time out for traveling—for the remainder of his life. In a way, his move from church to court was a sign of things to come, as courtly patronage was gaining ground on its ecclesiastical and civic counterparts throughout the Holy Roman Empire.

Paumann died in Munich on January 23, 1473. His tombstone in the Munich Frauenkirche contains a carved portrait of the musician holding a portative organ and surrounded by other instruments (including the lute, for which he may have developed the system of notation that became standard in Germany) and the following inscription: "Anno 1473, on the eve of the Conversion of St. Paul [January 24] died and was buried here the most artful master of all instruments and of Musica, Cunrad Pawman, knight, born blind in Nuremberg, whom God forgive."[1] Paumann's reputation remained alive in Germany through the eighteenth century.

A *fundamentum* was an exercise that taught the organist how to elaborate melodic figurations and formulas over a given cantus firmus in the tenor. In effect, *fundamenta* were solutions to contrapuntal problems intended for those who had to solve them at the keyboard. Paumann's *Fundamentum* constitutes a syllabus in keyboard counterpoint. It leads the organist through a series of short studies that show how to develop a florid counterpoint above cantus-firmus melodies that ascend and descend first by step and then by third, fourth, fifth, and sixth. Example 16-1 shows the first of Paumann's two solutions for handling a cantus firmus that moves in thirds:

EXAMPLE 16-1. Paumann, *Fundamentum organisandi*: (a) "ascensus per tercias," (b) "descensus per tercias."

(a)

1. Quoted after Strohm, *The Rise of European Music*, 489.

(b)

PREAMBLES/PRELUDES   If Paumann's exercises chug along in sewing-machine fashion, Adam Ileborgh's *praeludia,* copied at Stendal (northern Germany) in 1448,[2] stand at the other end of the rhythmic-metrical spectrum; their notation does not permit a more precise transcription of the rhythm than what appears in Example 16-2:

EXAMPLE 16-2. Ileborgh, *Praeambulum in c et potest variari in d f g a.*

As the title suggests, Ileborgh intended organists to transpose the preludes to other keys. Pieces such as these were used to fill gaps in the liturgy; perhaps the organist chose whatever final hooked up nicely with the chant that preceded or followed it. Still another prelude is introduced with the heading "Praeambulum bonum pedale seu manuale," which indicates that it was written for an organ with pedals.

Slim though their musical substance might be, Ileborgh's little *praeludia* are pathbreaking in three respects: they are apparently the earliest pieces to carry the title "prelude"; they are among the earliest compositions that seem to have grown out of the practice of "doodling" at the keyboard; and with their suggestion of transposition, they anticipate the late-sixteenth-century cycles of prelude-like compositions that explore the full range of modes (see Chapter 31).

ARRANGEMENTS OF MONOPHONIC MELODIES   One of the favorite techniques of organists was to take a monophonic melody—sacred or secular, quoted literally or embellished—and use it as a cantus-firmus-like scaffold on which to embroider virtuoso flights of fancy. Example 16-3 contains the opening measures of an anonymous arrangement of the basse danse tune known as *Collinetto* (the notes of the original melody are marked with an asterisk):

2. The manuscript is at the Curtis Institute of Music, Philadelphia.

EXAMPLE 16-3. (a) The dance tune *Collinetto*, notes 1–9; (b) Anonymous, *Collinit*, mm. 1–9.[3]

(a)

(b)

Such features as the upbeat in the shape of a turn, the hiccup-like effect in the middle voice at measures 3–4, and the trills, triplets, and nonstop motion are all typical of the style.

ARRANGEMENTS OF POLYPHONIC MODELS   Finally, organists often produced keyboard arrangements of polyphonic songs. *Anthology* 34 presents a well-known chanson, *Le souvenir*, by the English-born, Burgundian-employed composer Robert Morton, and an anonymous arrangement of it. The arranger

3. Buxheim *Orgelbuch*, No. 57.

quotes the tenor rather literally, subjects the superius to an avalanche of idiomatic keyboard embellishment, and freely alters the contratenor.

THE BUXHEIM ORGELBUCH AND ITS NOTATION   This arrangement of *Le souvenir* is one of two that appear in the Buxheim *Orgelbuch*, the most important keyboard source of the fifteenth century, copied around 1470 and named after the Bavarian monastery in which it was found.[4] With a repertory that may stem from Paumann's circle at Nuremberg and Munich, the collection contains pieces in all the types described above and can serve to illustrate the interesting system of notation, called *tablature*, with which German organists notated their music.

Figure 16-4 shows the folio that transmits the *Collinetto* arrangement of Example 16-3. After the heading "Sequitur ad huc semel Collinit 4^or notarum" (There follows another Collinit in measures of four), the music gets under way at the beginning of the fourth system. What is immediately familiar to us is the use of "score" and bar lines, both of which had already been present in the notation of keyboard music for at least a century. On the other hand, there is much that is different, for while the right hand is notated in mensural notation on a staff of seven lines [in order] (to avoid the use of ledger lines), the two voice parts of the left hand are written in two separate rows of alphabet notation. Within each hand, we may note the following characteristics:

Right hand: (1) there is no bar line after the four-note upbeat; (2) notes with descending stems ending in a loop signal a trill- or mordent-like embellishment (though there are none in the figure, notes with a descending stem only, without the loop, call for the note to be altered chromatically—lowered if attached to a B or E, raised if hanging from an F or C. Left hand: (1) pitches are indicated by means of an alphabet notation, which, clumsy as it might seem, was an effective space saver;[5] (2) duration is shown by means of dots (one dot = one semibreve) and vertical stems, with or without tails (one stem = one minim); (3) a horizontal line above a note indicates that it lies in the octave starting with *c'*; (4) the letter "b" denotes B-flat, while "h" is B-natural (still the custom in German-speaking countries); and (5) chromatic alterations are signaled by means of a loop extending from the right side of the letter.[6]

If we need evidence that scribes were human, we find it in the first measure of the penultimate system. After writing seventeen noteheads, the scribe became aware of having made a mistake by beginning to copy music that was to appear in the right hand two measures later. Rather than rub out the error, the scribe simply wrote "vacat" (vacant).

---

4. Munich, Bayerische Staatsbibliothek, Cim 352b (formerly Mus. ms. 3725).

5. By the 1550s, German tablature would be entirely alphabetic, a practice that persisted even through the time of J. S. Bach; see the Bach autograph shown in Apel, *The Notation of Polyphonic Music*, facs. 13, where Bach switches to all-letter tablature upon running out of space on the staves.

6. E-flats are always notated as D-sharps; the loop appended to the "d" stands for "is" (from "diesis"), and the German practice of referring to pieces as being in, say, "Dis" major (instead of E-flat major) can still be seen in the eighteenth century.

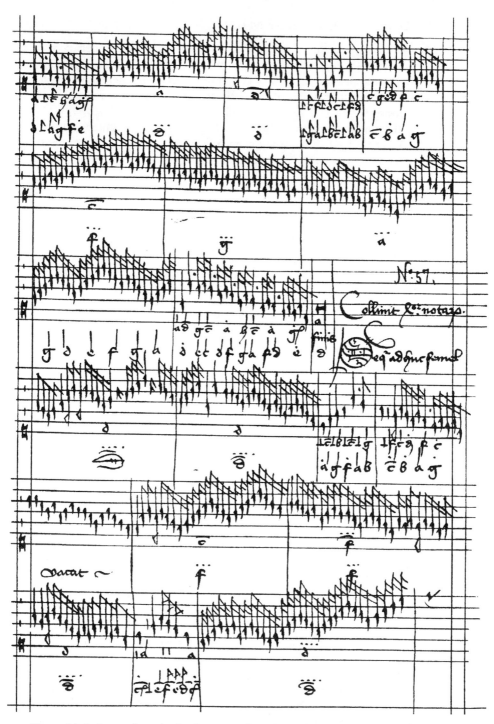

Figure 16–4. A page from the Buxheim *Orgelbuch* showing the end of No. 56 and the beginning of No. 57, *Collinit*.

INSTRUMENTAL ENSEMBLE MUSIC

Just as every court worthy of its name maintained a chapel of singers, it also retained a staff of instrumentalists. Likewise, towns both big and small customarily employed one or more groups of civic musicians. Instrumental ensemble music, then, was an integral part of fifteenth-century musical life and touched all levels of society.

In 1472, the Ferrarese court of Ercole I d'Este employed eighteen instrumentalists. As Table 16-1 shows, they were split into two groups according to function, a distinction strongly hinted at by their appearance in different places in the payroll registers:

Table 16-1.   Instrumentalists at the court of Ferrara, 1472.

Andrea trombeta	Andrea della Viola
Bazo d'Arezzo trombeta	Corrado d'Alemagna piffaro
Daniele trombeta	Francesco Malacise tenorista
Guasparo trombeta	Jacomo dell'arpa sonadore
Luzido trombeta	Piedro de Augustino trombone
Marco d'Arezzo trombeta	Pietrobono dal Chitarino
Raganello trombeta	Stefano da Savoia piffaro
Zilio trombeta	Zampaulo della Viola
	Zanino de Polo da Venezia piffaro
	Zoane d'Alemagna piffaro

Source: Lockwood, *Music in Renaissance Ferrara,* 318.

The Trumpeters

Despite the high salaries paid to the trumpeters (*trombeta*), their function was only marginally musical. With their pennant-draped field trumpets, they led processions, signaled the arrival of the duke or visiting potentates, announced government proclamations to the citizenry at large, and sounded military calls during the heat of battle.

Ercole's group of eight trumpeters was not even particularly large. The corps of imperial trumpeters numbered at least ten around the middle of the century, and the ever-ostentatious Sforza, dukes of Milan, had twenty in 1466. For special occasions, a court might combine its own corps of trumpeters with those employed both by the town and by neighboring or visiting nobles, who often traveled with their trumpeters in tow. Thus a chronicler describes the scene at the marriage of Alfonso d'Este to Anna Maria Sforza in 1491: "Having arrived at the basilica, and having acclaimed the bride, [the nobles] turn towards the city, shaking hands with the guests, while the trumpets rend the air with their shrill sounds—there are forty-six pairs of trumpeters."[7]

The fifteenth century made a rather gross distinction between two kinds of trumpets: the *trumpettes de guerre,* or "war trumpets," and the *trumpettes de ménestrels,* the "minstrel trumpets," capable of far greater versatility. The war trum-

7. Lockwood, *Music in Renaissance Ferrara,* 141.

pets came in three shapes: straight (four to eight feet in length), S-shaped, and "folded" (like the modern-day bugle). With neither valves nor slides, these trumpets were limited to the pitches of the overtone series.

Like the modern trombone, the *trumpette de ménestrel*—customarily an S-shaped or folded instrument—was outfitted with a slide mechanism: while players held the section of the trumpet with the mouthpiece firmly in place, they slid the longer portion of the instrument back and forth, thus changing the total length of the tubing. With a total of four positions, an instrument pitched in D would have been capable of the following notes (Ex. 16-4):

EXAMPLE 16-4. The notes of the slide trumpet in D; white notes are those of the overtone series, black notes preceding each white note are those played by lengthening the tube one position at a time, diamond-shaped notes are those obtained by "lipping."[8]

Thus the slide trumpet could hold its own on a voice part of a polyphonic composition.

Ercole's ten remaining instrumentalists would have been divided between the ensembles of *haut* and *bas*—loud and soft—instruments, a distinction that seems to have held until the end of the century. As Tinctoris tells us in his *De inventione et usu musicae*, the main function of these ensembles was to provide music for "feasts, dances, and public and private entertainments."

The Soft Ensembles

It is difficult to be specific about the makeup of the soft ensembles. What knowledge we have is based on visual depictions, literary references, and payroll rosters.

One more or less standard ensemble consisted of a large and a small lute (or a large lute and its smaller cousin, the cittern). Certainly such a duo was much in evidence at Ferrara, where the famed Pietrobono and his *tenorista* held forth (see Table 16-1 and Chapter 15). At a time when the lute was only beginning to be transformed from a melody-line-only instrument to one capable of polyphony, we may easily imagine three-part compositions being played in such a way that the lead lutenist (or cittern player) took the top voice, while the *tenorista* supplied the tenor and contratenor.

Other possibilities could have combined the larger lute, playing in the low register, with recorder, harp, portative organ, or a small, bowed string instrument above it. Or any of these could have joined with the larger positive organ or a larger bowed instrument, either one of which would have taken the lower voices. The tendency of musicians to double on some instruments added to the ensembles' flexibility.

8. After Polk, *German Instrumental Music*, 57.

The Loud Ensembles

Ensembles consisting of *haut* instruments appear to have been somewhat more standardized. By the 1450s, the standard group, called the *alta cappella* (or just *alta*), consisted of two or three shawms plus a brass player. Tinctoris describes the group this way: "For the lowest contratenor parts, and often for any contratenor part, to the shawm players one adds brass players who play very harmoniously upon the kind of horn which is called *trompone* in Italy, *sacque-boute* in France."[9]

The shawm, which would have been played by the instrumentalists listed as *piffari* (wind players) in Table 16-1, was a brilliant-sounding, double-reed instrument that came in two sizes: discant, with a range of about two octaves starting around *d'*, and tenor, also called a *bombard*, which went down to *g*. Endemic to the instrument was a wooden mouthpiece, the *pirouette*, which held the reed. The tenor shawm was customarily fitted with a key mechanism for its lowest hole, this being enclosed by a protective cover.

The Ferrarese wind players call for special comment. The contemporary Ferrarese chronicler Ugo Callefini related (perhaps with a bit of hometown pride) that on October 20, 1476, "there was danced a *ballo* at the court in Ferrara to the sound of the duke's wind band, which is considered to be the best in Italy, most especially his shawmist Corrado of Germany."[10] That Ugo should have singled out a German *pfeifer* for special praise was no accident, for German wind players were particularly prized in Italy. Indeed, there were family dynasties of such players, one of the most well-known being the Schubinger brothers of Augsburg: Michel, a bombard specialist who also played "viole" and lute; Augustein, a trombonist; and Ulrich, who played trombone, viol, and lute. All three enjoyed long and successful careers that played out in Italy, the Low Countries, and their native Germany.

The Repertory

What was composed specifically for instrumental ensembles, and what else, if anything, might they have played? The second question can be answered more easily than the first, while the answers to both lay to rest an old assumption about fifteenth-century instrumentalists.

Because depictions of instrumental ensembles, especially wind groups, invariably show the musicians playing without music (see, for example, Fig. 16-5), it was once fashionable to question their ability to read music and assume that they were always improvising. Two documents not only show that instrumentalists could handle the complexities of mensural notation, but shed light on what they played. In 1494, the Venetian trombonist Giovanni Alvise wrote to Francesco Gonzaga, Marquis of Mantua:

9. Quoted after Baines, "Fifteenth-Century Instruments," 20–21.

10. Quoted after Lockwood, "Pietrobono and the Instrumental Tradition at Ferrara," 119–20.

Figure 16-5. Lucas von Valckenborch, detail from *Spring Landscape*, 1587
(Kunsthistorisches Museum, Vienna).

> In these past days, we have made instrumental arrangements of certain mo-
> tets. . . . One of these is a work of Obrecht . . . for four voices. . . . And
> because we are six, I have added two bass parts to be played by trombones. . . .
> I am also sending you another motet, "Dimandase Gabrielem"; it is by Busnois
> and is for four voices. I have done another bass "contra" because we play it
> in five [parts].[11]

Thus instrumentalists felt free to adapt music that had originally been composed
for voices, as the Obrecht and Busnoys motets were.

Equally telling is the evidence provided by the Casanatense Chansonnier,[12]
a manuscript written at the court of Ferrara around 1480. Though its repertory
consists largely of three-part secular songs by the likes of Busnoys, Ockeghem,
and Hayne van Ghizeghem (together with early works by members of the
Josquin generation), it transmits the music with short text incipits only, and a
Ferrarese payment record describes the manuscript as "a book of polyphonic
music, written and notated by don Alessandro Signorello, *a la pifaresca*," that
is, for the Ferrarese wind band.[13] In fact, it seems to have been written shortly
after the arrival of the Augsburg bombardist Michel Schubinger.

11. Quoted after Polk, *German Instrumental Music*, 85.

12. Rome, Biblioteca Casanatense, MS 2856.

13. Lockwood, *Music in Renaissance Ferrara*, 225–26.

Instrumental ensembles thus freely appropriated music originally conceived for voices: they could play it note for note, transpose it to fit the range of their instruments, or fashion new arrangements altogether.

The problem of identifying works that were originally conceived for instrumental ensembles is more problematic. Pieces for such groups were not usually identified as such. Also, it is risky to use as a criterion modern-day notions of what is stylistically and idiomatically appropriate for instruments. Perhaps the most famous example of how this criterion can lead us astray occurs in connection with Heinrich Isaac's popular *Benedictus* (Ex. 16-5), which appears as a textless composition in about twenty sources devoted mainly to secular music:

EXAMPLE 16-5. Isaac, *Benedictus*, mm. 1–9 and 34–52.

With its tightly knit imitative sequences, rocket-like scales, and long, sustained notes, Isaac seems, as one scholar put it, to "have thrown off any restraint [he] might have felt when composing for voices, and show[s] very clearly that [he is] feeling his way toward an independent, instrumental style."[14] Yet the title should have served as a clue: the piece is actually the "Benedictus" section of Isaac's *Missa Quant j'ay au cor*, and was therefore conceived for voices. And even if we reverse the assumed order of events and argue that the piece was originally written for instruments and only later adopted for use in the Mass, the danger of using a style criterion is obvious: vocal and instrumental idioms were often interchangeable. Indeed, as late as the mid-sixteenth century, by which time music for instrumental ensembles had begun to take on a stylistic character of its own, music publishers were prone to advertise their wares as "buone da cantare et sonare" or "convenables tant à la voix comme aux instruments" (suitable for voices and instruments).

Nevertheless, certain works probably can be identified as having been written specifically for instrumental ensemble. The Glogauer Liederbuch transmits a series of textless compositions whose titles refer to such animals as a fox, peacock, rat, and cat. And it is hard to imagine that the *carmen*—a generic term used to designate an instrumental piece—*Der ratten schwantz* (The Rat's Tail) is anything but an instrumental work (Ex. 16-6):

EXAMPLE 16-6. Anonymous, *Der ratten schwantz*, mm. 50–70.

14. Hewitt, *Odhecaton*, 74.

At the risk of subjectivity: who would want to sing its angular lines?

Less obvious, because it is not so unvocal, is Johannes Martini's *La martinella* (*Anthology* 35), composed by the mid-1460s. The work displays none of the stylistic characteristics we often associate with instrumental pieces of the time: scale passages, nervous, often syncopated motives in one voice repeated against sustained tones in another, sequences, and so on. On first hearing, it might even pass for a somewhat longish rondeau. But while the phrase structure is rondeau-like, in the end it is all wrong. There are too many phrases, and they are too asymmetrical. If, for example, this were a five- or six-line rondeau, line 1 would cadence at measure 12; line 2 would end at measure 24, but where did it really begin—with the tenor-contra duet at measure 13, or with the point of imitation between superius and tenor at measure 17? Line 3 seemingly belongs to measures 32–40; so where, then, do measures 27–31 belong (with their two strong cadences on the tonic, no less)? And since when do rondeaux insert twelve-measure, triple-meter, dance-like digressions? No, this is an instrumental work, a "song without words" or an "instrumental chanson," to use two modern terms. To Martini must be assigned a significant role in the development of the freely composed, non-dance-related "instrumental fantasia."

DANCE MUSIC

One of the most visually stunning music manuscripts of this or any other period is Brussels 9085.[15] Written in gold and silver ink on black-dyed parchment for the Habsburg court of Burgundy, the manuscript is devoted not to any of the complex polyphonic genres but to simple, monophonic *basse danse* melodies, their choreographies, and a treatise that explains how the dance was done.

Dubbed the "queen" of dances by the Italian dancing master Domenico da Piacenza, the *basse danse* was a slow, stately, carefully choreographed couple dance, the favorite of courtly society from the mid-fifteenth century until well into the sixteenth. We can see how music and choreography worked by considering the most popular of all *basse danse* melodies, *La spagna*, for which there are at least 250 arrangements (everything from dance-like pieces for solo lute to polyphonic Masses) through the early seventeenth century.

Figure 16-6 shows the *La spagna* melody and its choreography as they appear in Michel Toulouse's *S'ensuit l'art et instruction de bien dancer*, published at Paris

---

15. Brussels, Bibliothèque Royale de Belgique, MS 9085. For a color reproduction, see Wangermée, *Flemish Music*, plates 57–58.

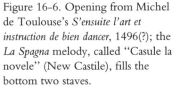

Figure 16-6. Opening from Michel de Toulouse's *S'ensuite l'art et instruction de bien dancer*, 1496(?); the *La Spagna* melody, called "Casule la novele" (New Castile), fills the bottom two staves.

in the 1480s or 1490s.[16] Though the Toulouse version of the melody contains a few errors, the tune and choreography can be reconstructed as they appear in Example 16-7:

EXAMPLE 16-7. The *La spagna* melody and its choreography (oblique slashes mark divisions between phrases of music and *mesures* in the choreography).[17]

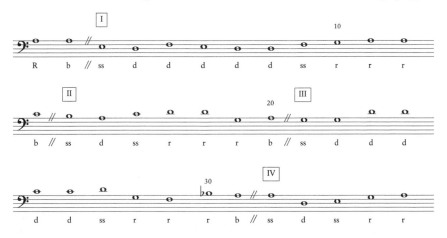

16. Only a single copy survives, at the Royal College of Physicians, London.

17. As reconstructed in Crane, *Materials for the Study of the Fifteenth-Century Basse Danse*, 46.

The letters stand for the steps of the choreography, explained in Table 16-2.

Table 16-2.   The choreography of the *basse danse.*

Steps	Execution
ss = *2 simples*	Left foot forward, raising body; right joins left; right forward, raising body; left joins right.
d = *double*	Left foot forward; right past left; left past right; right joins left (raising body with each step).
r = *reprise*	Left foot backward, raising body; right joins left.
b = *branle*	The directions are vague: step begins with the left foot, continues with the right, and is done with "wavering" motion.
R = *Reverence*	An introductory bow by the man.

Source: Heartz, "The Basse Dance," 289–91 (also Table 16-3).

Each of the four basic steps took the same amount of time to execute and coincided with one note of the melody. The steps were then organized into various sequences, or *mesures.* Table 16-3 shows three of them, together called *mesures très parfaites:*

Table 16-3.   The three *mesures très parfaites.*

grande:	ss d d d d d ss r r r b
moyenne:	ss d d d ss r r r b
petite	ss d ss r r r b

Finally, the *mesures* were strung together in various patterns to build the dance in its entirety. As Toulouse and Example 16-7 make clear, *La spagna* consists of five *mesures très parfaites,* alternating between *grande* and *petite,* which, however, do not necessarily coincide with the equally asymmetrical phrase structure. The *basse danse,* then, depended as much on the dancers' internal clock and memory as it did on their acrobatic ability.

The music was a less formal affair. The *La spagna* melody was probably played by the *alta cappella*'s trombonist and would have served as a cantus firmus, each of its notes receiving the same time value and each accompanying one step of the choreography. Above and around it, one or two shawms would have improvised or played counterpoints that had been more or less carefully worked out.

What did it all sound like? Most often we can only fill in the notes with our imagination. There is, however, one composition from the period (*Anthology* 36) that might approximate a real performance that came to be frozen in notation. The piece, descriptively titled *Falla con misuras* (False Measures), is for two voices and is attributed to another famous Italian dancing master, Guglielmo Ebreo of Pesaro (c. 1425–after 1480?).

What is fascinating about the florid upper voice is the layer of complexity that it adds to the dancers' already complicated task. For instance, while some of the steps—coinciding with a single dotted-whole note of the cantus firmus—are divided into four movements, all of the notes are divided into six beats. Thus the dancers often had to maintain a steady movement of four steps against six beats, a task made more difficult (or easier?) by the constant hemiola patterns. Indeed, at times it is impossible to say whether the music is in triple or compound-duple meter. Moreover, not only do the divisions between *mesures* not coincide with the phrase structure of the music, but only one of the strong cadences in the upper voice (m. 17) so coincides. Clearly, beneath the apparent elegance of the dance were asymmetry and tension at every level, between music and choreography as well as between the voice parts of the music itself (hence the title?).

POSTSCRIPT: TWO THEORISTS

As musical genres and styles underwent change in the fifteenth century, so too did the way music theorists thought and wrote about music. Indeed, theorists themselves were a changing breed. In earlier times, they tended to come from the ranks of university- or church-based mathematicians, theologians, and speculative philosophers. Raised in the tradition of Pythagoras and Boethius, they thought of music as number, belonging with arithmetic, geometry, and astronomy, though they spilled more than a little ink on such practical problems as mensural notation. In the fifteenth and sixteenth centuries, those who wrote about music came more and more from the world of practical musicians; and with the Greek theorist Aristoxenus as their guide, they relied on their personal judgment—on their ear!—to discriminate between good and bad. Ironically, this shift in emphasis was driven by two seemingly opposed trends: the increasing professionalization of music and the growing influence of humanism, for which music was not so much number as rhetoric and poetry.

Two of the most notable theorists of the late fifteenth century were Johannes Tinctoris and Bartolomeo Ramos de Pareja.

Johannes Tinctoris

The most encyclopedic theorist of his time, Tinctoris was born in the province of Brabant in the Low Countries around 1435. Nothing certain is known about his life until the 1460s, during which decade he sang at Cambrai under Du Fay's wing, received a master of arts degree in law at the University of Orléans (1462), and became master of the choirboys at the Cathedral of Chartres.

At some point in the early 1470s, Tinctoris assumed the post of chaplain at the Aragonese court of Naples, where he was the star of the musical establishment for almost twenty years, and where he apparently produced the whole of his theoretical output. In addition, he composed, recruited singers for the court chapel, probably oversaw the production of the Mellon Chansonnier, may have served as a legal adviser to the king, and certainly hobnobbed with the Neapolitan humanist circle.

With his departure from Naples in the early 1490s, information about Tinctoris becomes sparse: he likely spent some time in Rome and perhaps Buda (present-day Budapest) before returning home to Nivelles in Brabant. His benefice at the collegiate church of St. Gertrude was transferred to another cleric on October 12, 1511, so he must have died during the previous six months.

Between the early 1470s and early 1480s, Tinctoris wrote twelve treatises that cover virtually every aspect of music. Five are particularly noteworthy:

(1) *Terminorum musicae diffinitorium* (Dictionary of Musical Terms), probably dating from the early 1470s, is one of our earliest dictionaries of musical terms and the earliest ever to be printed (c. 1494).

(2) *Proportionale musices* (The Proportions of Music), written around 1473–74, takes up the complexities of mensural notation, especially the problems inherent in the use of proportion signs, which alter the durational values of the notes and determine tempo relationships between sections of a piece.

(3) *Liber de natura et proprietate tonorum* (On the Nature and Property of the Modes), dated November 6, 1476, and dedicated to Ockeghem and Busnoys, deals with the problem of mode and polyphony, and states clearly that the mode of the tenor determines the mode of the piece as a whole.

(4) *Liber de arte contrapuncti* (The Art of Counterpoint), from 1477, includes a detailed discussion of counterpoint and contains Tinctoris's most famous sentence: "There is no composition written over forty years ago that is thought by the learned as worthy of performance."[18] We will return to this provocative statement, with its implications for the historiography of music, in the Epilogue.

(5) *De inventione et usu musicae* (On the Invention and Uses of Music) is in some respects Tinctoris's most fascinating treatise. Although only a fragment survives, in the form of a printed edition from the early 1480s, the original manuscript is estimated to have been as long as the eleven other treatises combined; there is, then, the question of why Tinctoris had only a drastic abridgement printed. Here Tinctoris is at his most journalistic, referring to some of the great virtuoso performers of his day (Ockeghem is singled out as the finest bass, Pietrobono the greatest lutenist). It is also one of the first treatises to shed light on instruments and instrumental practices of the day.

Tinctoris must be regarded as the central music theorist of the fifteenth century. And though he still stands squarely in the tradition of those who preceded him, his empiricism, reliance on the ear, placement of the composer at the center of things, analyses of individual compositions, and openness to the world of secular music bring a previously unheard-of freshness to music theory. He was, in a quiet way, something of a revolutionary.

Bartolomé Ramos de Pareja

While Tinctoris was effecting change quietly over the course of a dozen treatises, Ramos (c. 1440–c. 1491), born in Baeza, near Madrid, did it with a

18. *The Art of Counterpoint*, 14.

bang in one. In his *Musica practica,* published at Bologna in 1482, he picked a fight with the two great authorities of medieval music theory: Boethius and Guido d'Arezzo.

His argument with Boethius was over tuning: "The regular monochord has been subtly divided by Boethius with numbers and measure. But although this division is useful and pleasant to theorists, to singers it is laborious and difficult to understand."[19] What Ramos objected to were such ratios as 81:64 for the major third and 32:27 for the minor third, used for the purpose of keeping all fifths and fourths pure. Rather, suggested Ramos, it was the thirds that should be made pure, tuned to 5:4 and 6:5, respectively, even at the expense of losing the purity of fifths and fourths. Ramos, then, was the first theorist to work out a complete tuning system using "just" intonation.

His scorn for Guido had to do with the six-step solmization system *ut, re, mi, fa, sol, la,* which he saw as being basically useless. In its place he proposed an eight-step sequence of syllables, one syllable for each of the eight diatonic notes of the octave, with the only mutation coming on the notes that were an octave apart. In effect, Ramos had devised the "fixed *do*" system.

Ramos's attacks on authority set off a storm among theorists and musicians that lasted almost forty years. Eventually his ideas won out, and by the mid-sixteenth century they had come to be accepted, though in somewhat modified guise.

BIBLIOGRAPHICAL NOTE

Editions of the Music

Keyboard music: three editions are indispensable: Willi Apel, *Keyboard Music of the Fourteenth & Fifteenth Centuries, CEKM* 1 (American Institute of Musicology, 1963); Bertha A. Wallner, *Das Buxheimer Orgelbuch,* 3 vols., *EDMR* 37–39 (Kassel: Bärenreiter, 1958–59); and the facsimile edition edited by Wallner, *Das Buxheimer Orgelbuch, Hs. mus. 3725 der Bayerischen Staatsbibliothek,* Documenta musicologica, ser. II, vol. 1 (Kassel: Bärenreiter, 1955). **Ensemble music**: the secular works of Martini, most of which are for instrumental ensembles, appear in Edward G. Evans Jr., ed., *Johannes Martini: Secular Pieces, RRMMAER* 1 (Madison: A-R Editions, 1975). **Dance music**: MS Brussels 9085 is edited in its entirety in James L. Jackman, *Fifteenth Century Basse Dances* (Wellesley: Wellesley College, 1964), while Ernest Closson's *Le Manuscrit dit des basses danses de la Bibliothèque de Bourgogne* (Brussels: Société des bibliophiles et iconophiles de Belgique, 1912) is a facsimile edition of the manuscript.

Keyboard Music

A good introduction to the organ in the fifteenth century is Peter Williams, *The European Organ, 1450–1850* (London: Batsford, 1966); the most extensive survey is Apel, *The History of Keyboard Music to 1700,* trans. and rev. Hans Tischler (Bloomington: Indiana University Press, 1972), especially chapter 5; see also the chapter by Alan Brown in Alexander Silbiger, *Keyboard Music before 1700* (New York: Schirmer, 1995). Eileen Southern's *Buxheim Organ Book* (Brooklyn: Institute of Mediaeval Music, 1963) is a thorough study of the manuscript; the best introduction to the notation of German tablatures appears in Apel, *The Notation of*

19. Quoted after Strunk, *Source Readings* (1965), 201.

Polyphonic Music, 900–1600, 5th ed. (Cambridge, Mass: Mediaeval Academy of America, 1953).

Instrumental Ensemble Music

There is a wonderful introduction to the instruments of the fifteenth and sixteenth centuries in David Munrow, *Instruments of the Middle Ages and Renaissance* (London: Oxford University Press, 1976); also helpful is Anthony Baines, "Fifteenth-Century Instruments in Tinctoris's *De inventione et usu musicae,*" *GSJ,* 3 (1950): 19–27; Keith Polk's *German Instrumental Music of the Late Middle Ages: Players, Patrons, and Performance Practice* (Cambridge: Cambridge University Press, 1992) is a gold mine of information on fifteenth-century instrumental ensembles. There is a fascinating quartet of articles dealing with the slide trumpet: Peter Downey, "The Renaissance Slide Trumpet: Fact or Fiction," *EM* 12 (1984): 26–33; and Herbert W. Myers, "Slide Trumpet Madness: Fact or Fiction," Polk, "The Trombone, the Slide Trumpet, and the Ensemble Tradition of the Early Renaissance," and Ross W. Duffin, "The *Trompette des menestrels* in the 15th-century *alta cappella,*" all in *EM* 17 (1989): 383–89, 389–97, 397–402. Nor can one overlook the tremendous contribution of Edmund Bowles, whose "Haut and bas: The Grouping of Musical Instruments in the Middle Ages," *MD* 8 (1954): 115–40, and "Iconography as a Tool for Examining the Loud Consort in the Fifteenth Century," *JAMIS* 3 (1977): 100–21, are basic. On the sackbut, see Keith McGowan, "The World of the Early Sackbut Player: Flat or Round," *EM* 22 (1994): 441–66. On the knotty matter of repertory, two essays are must reading: Warwick Edwards, "Songs Without Words by Josquin and His Contemporaries," and Louise Litterick, "On Italian Instrumental Ensemble Music in the Late Fifteenth Century," both in *Music in Medieval and Early Modern Europe: Patronage, Sources, and Texts,* ed. Iain Fenlon (Cambridge: Cambridge University Press, 1981), 79–92 and 117–30.

Dance Music

Fundamental for any study of the *basse danse* is Frederick Crane, *Materials for the Study of the Fifteenth-Century Basse Danse,* Musicological Studies 16 (Brooklyn: Institute of Mediaeval Music, 1968), with 106 presumed *basse danse* melodies; see also Daniel Heartz, "The Basse Dance: Its Evolution circa 1450 to 1550," *AnnM* 6 (1958–63): 288–340. On the *La spagna* setting, see Manfred F. Bukofzer, "A Polyphonic Basse Dance of the Renaissance," in *Studies in Medieval and Renaissance Music* (New York: Norton, 1950), 190–216. On Guglielmo Ebreo, see Otto Kinkeldey, "A Jewish Dancing Master of the Renaissance (Guglielmo Ebreo)," in *Studies in Jewish Bibliography and Related Subjects in Memory of Abraham Solomon Freidus (1867–1923)* (New York: Alexander Kohut Memorial Foundation, 1929), 329–72 (published separately by Dance Horizons in 1966); Guglielmo's treatise appears in translation in *De pratica seu arte tripuidii/On the Practice or Art of Dancing,* trans. and ed. Barbara Sparti (Oxford: Clarendon Press, 1993). For translations of other treatises, see *Fifteenth-Century Dance and Music: Twelve Transcribed Italian Treatises and Collections in the Tradition of Domenico da Piacenza,* 2 vols., ed. A. William Smith (Stuyvesant, N.Y.: Pendragon Press, 1995). On the social role of dance, see Sparti, "The Function and Status of Dance in the Fifteenth-Century Italian Courts," *DR* 14 (1996): 42–61.

Two Theorists

For a fine introduction to the changing winds of music theory in the late fifteenth century, see Edward E. Lowinsky, "Music of the Renaissance as Viewed by Renaissance Musicians," in *The Renaissance Image of Man and the World,* ed. Bernard O'Kelly (Columbus: Ohio State University Press, 1966), 129–77, reprinted with an added appendix in Lowinsky, *Music in the Culture of the Renaissance and Other Essays,* ed. Bonnie J. Blackburn (Chicago: Chicago University Press, 1989), 1:87–105.

Tinctoris: all but two of Tinctoris's treatises (the *Diffinitorium* and *De inventione et usu musicae*) appear in *Opera theoretica*, 2 vols., ed. Albert Seay, *CSM* 22 (American Institute of Musicology, 1975–78). A number of the treatises have been translated into English: *Dictionary of Musical Terms*, trans. and ed. Carl Parrish (London: Free Press, 1963; reprint, Da Capo, 1978); *The Art of Counterpoint (Liber de arte contrapuncti)*, trans. and ed. Albert Seay, *MSD* 5 (American Institute of Musicology, 1961); Albert Seay, "The *Proportionale Musices* of Johannes Tinctoris," *JMT* 1 (1957): 22–75; *Concerning the Nature and Property of Tones*, 2 vols., trans. and ed. Albert Seay, rev. ed. (Colorado Springs: Colorado College Music Press, 1976); there is a facsimile edition of the *Diffinitorium* in Documenta musicologica, ser. I, vol. 37, ed. Peter Gülke (Kassel: Bärenreiter, 1983). For a biography, see Ronald Woodley, "Iohannis Tinctoris: A Review of the Documentary Biographical Evidence," *JAMS* 34 (1981): 217–48; see also Christopher Page, "Reading and Reminiscence: Tinctoris on the Beauty of Music," *JAMS* 49 (1996): 1–31.

Ramos: for a translation of Ramos's treatise, see *Musica practica*, trans. and ed. Clement A. Miller, *MSD* 44 (American Institute of Musicology); a short excerpt concerning tuning is translated in Strunk, *Source Readings*, 133.

Also Cited

Reinhard Strohm, *The Rise of European Music, 1380–1500* (Cambridge: Cambridge University Press, 1993); Lewis Lockwood, "Pietrobono and the Instrumental Tradition at Ferrara in the Fifteenth Century," *RIM* 10 (1975): 115–33, and *Music in Renaissance Ferrara, 1400–1505* (Cambridge: Harvard University Press, 1984); Helen Hewitt, ed., *Harmonice Musices Odhecaton A* (Cambridge, Mass.: Mediaeval Academy of America, 1946); Robert Wangermée, *Flemish Music and Society in the Fifteenth and Sixteenth Centuries*, trans. R. E. Wolf (New York: Praeger, 1968).

CHAPTER 17

Editing a Chanson: Musica Ficta

The term *musica ficta* has acquired two separate but related meanings. In today's casual parlance, it refers to the application by editors and performers of accidentals (sharps, flats, naturals) that are not notated in the sources themselves. For musicians of the fifteenth and sixteenth centuries, the term referred specifically to those notes that fell outside the Guidonian hand and were therefore called "feigned" (*ficta* or *falsa*) notes, as opposed to the "true" or "correct" (*vera* or *recta*) notes within the hand (see Chapter 3). We will see how the two meanings come together.

Before we look at the "rules" of *musica ficta*, three preliminary remarks are necessary. First, that sources of the period failed to notate all required accidentals and that singers were expected to add them is undisputed. A long line of theorists make this perfectly clear, from the anonymous fourteenth-century author who wrote that "in general, it is not necessary to notate [accidentals],"[1] to Pietro Aaron, who wrote in the 1529 supplement to his *Toscanello in musica*:

> Doubts and disputations are circulating among some lovers of music about the signs of *b molle* [flat] and *diesis* [sharp], whether the composers are constrained by necessity to show them in their compositions, or whether the singer should be held to understand and recognize the hidden secret of all the places where these figures or signs are needed.[2]

Second, although the theorists supply certain rules and guidelines, the task of implementing them can be difficult. At times, adding an accidental in accordance with one rule will cause another rule to be broken. Occasionally, the singers seem to have had a choice of which rule to follow. And sometimes singers—like editors and performers today—disagreed with one another; thus the sixteenth-century papal singer Ghiselin Danckerts tells a story about a dispute that took place between a bass and a tenor in Rome around 1540 over whether or not the bass should flatten a series of low *B*'s at the opening of a work. We should not insist that every problem had one answer only; or if there was one, that we can know what it was.

Manuscripts of the period do include some notated accidentals (there are none in either of the sources for Busnoys's *A vous sans autre*), and we should be sure that we understand what they meant. They did not necessarily lower or raise a pitch by a half step, as is evident from the occasional flat before a C or F. Fifteenth-century composers did not think in enharmonic terms, and

---

1. From the so-called Berkeley manuscript; quoted after Berger, "Musica ficta," 107.

2. Quoted after the translation by Bergquist, *Toscanello in Music*, 3:12.

C-flat was not equivalent to B-natural. Rather, a flat sign before a note indicated that the singer should sing a note that could be sung with the syllable *fa*, while a natural or sharp sign called for *mi*. That the signs might also lower or raise a pitch by a half step was incidental. Fifteenth-century singers did not think in terms of the white and black keys of the piano; they thought in terms of the "places"—whole and half steps—in the Guidonian hand. Thus the singer confronted with a C preceded by a flat and then a B with no accidental at all reasoned as follows: (1) C = *fa*, (2) the B below it is therefore *mi*, so (3) I must sing a B that is a half step below C (since *mi* must always lie a half step below *fa*).

During the fifteenth and sixteenth centuries, at least seventy theorists had something to say about *musica ficta*. Their guidelines for the addition of accidentals were designed with three main purposes: to avoid certain harmonic discords, to avoid certain melodic intervals, and to produce certain progressions at cadences.

ACCIDENTALS TO AVOID HARMONIC DISCORDS

If there was one rule that was drummed into the head of every singer and composer, it was the prohibition of *mi contra fa*. This rule prevented one singer from singing a note that carried the solmization syllable *mi* while another sang a note called *fa*. Thus it prevented a diminished octave on B-natural (*mi*)–B-flat (*fa*) or an augmented fourth on F-natural (*fa*, in the natural hexachord on *c*)–B-natural (*mi*). In other words, it kept the perfect consonances perfect.

There were exceptions, however, and we might want to consider them in connection with *A vous sans autre*. For instance, *mi contra fa* might be tolerated if it involved nothing more than a short, nonstructural passing tone, or if a diminished fifth quickly resolved inward to a third: E-natural–B-flat resolving to F–A. In fact, there is evidence that what the theorists frowned upon was used with impunity by even the best composers. Tinctoris points out that he has found diminished fifths in the works of "many, many composers, even the most famous," and then gives examples from the works of Guillaume Faugues, Busnoys, and Philippe Caron (Ex. 17-1):[3]

EXAMPLE 17-1. Instances of diminished fifths (marked with an asterisk) in (a) Faugues, *Missa Le serviteur*; (b) Busnoys, *Je ne demande*; and (c) Caron, *Helas*.

(a)

3. *The Art of Counterpoint*, 130.

Even the wiliest of singers would have had trouble getting around these discords, for to flatten any of the offending bottom notes would result in equally offensive melodic tritones.

It appears that during the fifteenth and early sixteenth centuries, cross-relationships involving the above discords were used rather freely. Only around the mid-sixteenth century did the theorist Gioseffo Zarlino mount a real crusade against their use. In general, accidentals to prevent harmonic discords were the kind that were uppermost on the minds of fifteenth- and sixteenth-century musicians. They were added *causa necessitatis* (as the theorists put it), that is, by reason of necessity.

ACCIDENTALS TO AVOID PROHIBITED MELODIC INTERVALS

Singers were also taught to add accidentals in order to avoid such melodic intervals as the augmented fourth, diminished fifth, augmented octave, and *chromatic* semitone (that is, F to F-sharp, B-flat to B-natural, and so on).[4] These were prohibited whether going up or down, whether by skip or, if they marked the outer boundaries of a scale passage, by stepwise motion. In effect, they involved the same prohibition of *mi contra fa*.

---

4. Fifteenth- and sixteenth-century musicians distinguished between two kinds of semitones: the chromatic, in which the pitch class remained the same (as just described), and the diatonic (C-sharp to D, for example).

Again, there were exceptions. Singers could ascend from F-natural to B-natural as long as they continued on to C. Similarly, they could sing an ascending scale passage from E-natural to B-flat (a diminished fifth) if they quickly turned back down a half step to A (or if descending from B-flat to E-natural, they went up a half step to F).

Exceptions notwithstanding, singers sometimes ran into problems. For instance, Pietro Aaron gives the following example, drawn from the Agnus Dei III of Josquin's *Missa L'homme armé super voces musicales* (Ex. 17-2):[5]

EXAMPLE 17-2. Josquin, *Missa L'homme armé super voces musicales*, Agnus Dei III.

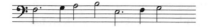

If the singer flattened the B in order to avoid the tritone it forms with the first note, F (which cannot be raised), that B-flat then produces a diminished fifth with the following note, E. Or did the singer start a chain reaction of sorts by first flatting the B and then going on to flatten the E? Aaron's solution: sing the F–B tritone in order to salvage the perfect fifth between B and E.

Another of the theorists' guidelines took the form of a little rhyme: *Una nota super la semper est canendum fa* (a note above *la* is always sung as *fa*). If, therefore, after an ascending scale from C to A in the natural hexachord (*ut, re, mi, fa, sol, la*, with *ut* = C) singers were faced with a B-natural that quickly returned to A, they would flatten the B in order that it could be called *fa* (instead of *mi*).

CADENCES

If accidentals added to correct discords were added *causa necessitatis*, those inserted at cadences were added *causa pulchritudinis* (by reason of beauty). One of the things about which all the theorists agreed concerns cadential formulas: when a cadence on a perfect consonance was approached by an imperfect consonance, one voice of the imperfect consonance was to reach its goal via a half step. Thus sixths resolving to octaves should be major sixths, thirds opening outward to fifths should be major thirds, and thirds closing in on a unison should be minor thirds. In effect, the outward resolution of sixth-to-octave and third-to-fifth produced what we call a leading tone.

Sixths resolving to octaves constituted the normal cadential motion of the superius and tenor in most pieces (see Ex. 17-3). Cadences in which superius and tenor ended on octave C's, E's, and F's had some half-step motion built in to them, since their approaching sixths were already major: D–B, F–D, and G–E, respectively. Cadences on D and G, on the other hand, were approached by the minor sixths E–C and A–F, respectively, and thus required the singer

5. Quoted after *New Grove*, 12: 808.

to supply the C-sharp and F-sharp. Singers would have thought of the C-sharp and F-sharp as carrying the solmization syllable *mi*, which they realized by constructing imaginary hexachords on A and D, respectively.

EXAMPLE 17-3. Cadences with sixths resolving to octaves.

As always, though, problems could crop up. For instance, at a cadence on A, the approaching sixth, B–G, could be made major either by raising the G or by lowering the B. Singers would let the modal context be the arbiter: raising the G would preserve the Dorian quality in which the second step (B) of the mode was a whole step from the final (A), while lowering the B would produce a Phrygian half step between those scale degrees.

Another problem arises because of the theorists' discussion of cadences in academic terms of two-part counterpoint. What did singers do when, as in Example 17-4, they were faced with the musical reality of three-part writing?

EXAMPLE 17-4. A three-part cadence on G.

Whoever sang the superius would have raised the F. But what did the contratenor do? Raise the C in order to produce a major third with the tenor, or leave it alone and thus produce a vertical tritone (C-natural against the raised F)? The first solution resulted in the so-called twofold (or double) leading-tone cadence (both modern terms), the signature cadence of the fourteenth and early fifteenth centuries. But was the C-natural still being raised in the 1450s and 1460s? At what point during the fifteenth century did that cadence become old-fashioned? As we will see in connection with *A vous sans autre*, it is a question with which we will have to struggle repeatedly.

A final problem concerns the medial cadence of a rondeau in which there was a full triad: did singers raise the third of the chord if it was not already major? Beginning in the 1510s, the answer was certainly yes. As for the period of Busnoys and his contemporaries, the evidence is not clear. The Mellon Chansonnier makes this problem razor sharp, since it explicitly raises a number of those thirds with notated sharp signs. From this, the editors of the Mellon Chansonnier conclude that the raised third at the medial cadence must already have been an established convention at the time. Yet one can argue precisely the opposite: that the notated sharps were necessary on the grounds that singers would not ordinarily have raised the third. The medial cadence in *A vous sans autre* will force us to come to terms with the problem.

OTHER FACTORS

Although the three categories discussed above are the ones on which the theorists spilled the most ink, we should be aware of other factors related to *musica ficta*.

Conflicting Signatures

As noted in Chapter 3, there are any number of pieces from the fifteenth century that have conflicting signatures. Most often, the upper voice has no flats, while the two below it have one flat each. One possible function of the signatures was to help singers avoid the prohibited harmonic discords. For example, signatures of ♮♭♭ (from top to bottom) protected singers against *mi contra fa* situations that involved diminished fifths between B-naturals in the lower voices and F's in the superius. The B-flats called for in the signatures of the lower voices provided ready-made perfect fifths. Since Dijon 517 and the Mellon Chansonnier both transmit *A vous sans autre* without any flats in the signature of any voice, this is a problem about which we need not worry.

Lute Intabulations

Lute arrangements, called *intabulations*, can often provide insight into the application of accidentals. Since lute tablatures direct the player's fingers to specific frets on the fingerboard (see Chapter 24), the notation is explicit regarding pitch, with no ambiguity about whether it should be B-flat or B-natural. But we have no lute arrangement of *A vous sans autre*, and even if we did, we would not necessarily be out of the woods. Sometimes lute arrangements of the same polyphonic piece will employ different accidentals. And since most lute arrangements of fifteenth-century polyphony date from the early sixteenth century, there is always a question of the chronological gap, as well as the difference in performance medium. In other words, can the accidentals in a lute arrangement from the 1510s serve as evidence of what took place some forty years earlier in a work conceived for voices?

Imitation

One problem with which we will have to deal in *A vous sans autre* is what to do when one voice imitates another within a changing harmonic or cadential context. Do we insist that the imitation be precise, that all intervals be kept the same size? Since the imitation in *A vous sans autre* is at the unison, the answer is probably yes, though seeking consistency raises an interesting problem in the very first phrase after the medial cadence.

We can now turn to the opening of *A vous sans autre* (Ex. 17-5):

EXAMPLE 17-5. Busnoys, *A vous sans autre*, mm. 1–12.

Note that in measures 3, 5, 6, 7, and 10, B and F (*mi contra fa*) momentarily clash one against one other. What accidentals, if any, should we add? At measure 11, there is a momentary B (contratenor) against E. This is fine, but what should we do with the B if at measure 10 we flatted the tenor's B when it sounded against the superius's F? And, with that decision in mind, how should we treat the cadence at measures 11–12: raise the G (in the tenor) raise the G and the D (superius), or leave both uninflected and lower the B (contratenor)? These are the kinds of decisions we are faced with as music editors.

BIBLIOGRAPHICAL NOTE

The literature on *musica ficta* is enormous and often contentious; the fundamental study is Karol Berger, *Musica ficta: Theories of Accidental Inflections in Vocal Polyphony from Marchetto da Padova to Gioseffo Zarlino* (Cambridge: Cambridge University Press, 1987). Three easier introductions to problems of *musica ficta* are Berger, "Musica ficta," in *Performance Practice: Music Before 1600*, ed. Howard Mayer Brown and Stanley Sadie (New York: Norton, 1989), 107–25 (a brilliantly concise statement on which much of the above is based); Rob C. Wegman, "Musica ficta," in *Companion to Medieval and Renaissance Music*, ed. Tess Knighton and David Fallows (New York: Schirmer, 1992), 265–74; and the fine article in *New Grove*, 12: 802–11, by Margaret Bent, Lewis Lockwood, Robert Donington, and Stanley Boorman.

One cannot pass over the problems of *musica ficta* without reference to the contributions of Edward E. Lowinsky; for the beginner, the best points of entry are his Foreword and Introduction, respectively, to *Monuments of Renaissance Music*, vols. 1 and 2 (Chicago: University of Chicago Press, 1964 and 1967), v–xxi and v–xvi. Nor should one pass over three fine contributions by Margaret Bent: "Musica Recta and Musica Ficta," *MD* 26 (1972): 73–

100, "Diatonic Ficta," *EMH* 4 (1984): 1–48, and "Accidentals, Counterpoint, and Notation in Aaron's *Aggiunta* to the *Toscanello in Musica*," *JM* 12 (1994): 306–44 (the conclusions in the first two of which are challenged by Berger).

Also Cited

Pietro Aaron, *Toscanello in musica*, trans. Peter Bergquist (Colorado Springs: Colorado College Music Press, 1970); Tinctoris, *The Art of Counterpoint*, trans. and ed. Albert Seay, *MSD* 5 (American Institute of Musicology, 1961).

PART FOUR
THE 1470s TO THE 1520s

INCLUDED: AGRICOLA • BRUMEL • CARA • COMPÈRE • COPPINI •
DALZA • ENCINA • ESCOBAR • FÉVIN • FINCK • GHISELIN •
HOFHAIMER • ISAAC • JOSQUIN • LA RUE • MOUTON •
NINOT LE PETIT • OBRECHT • PETRUCCI • PISANO • RICHAFORT •
SCHLICK • SPINACINO • TROMBONCINO • WEERBEKE

CHAPTER 18

Inventions in Style and Transmission

In his *Nymphes des bois*, a lament on the death of Ockeghem, the poet Jehan Molinet reeled off the names of four composers who should don mourning clothes and weep over the death of their figurative *bon père*: Josquin Desprez (c. 1440–1521), Pierre de la Rue (c. 1450/55–1518), Antoine Brumel (c. 1460–c. 1515), and Loyset Compère (c. 1445–1518). The roll call was set by Josquin (Ex. 18-1):

EXAMPLE 18-1. Josquin, *Nymphes des bois*, mm. 111–133.

Still another *déploration* on Ockeghem's death—this one by Guillaume Crétin—adds to the list of grieving composers: Alexander Agricola (?1446–1506),
Johannes Ghiselin (*alias* Verbonnet, dates unknown), Johannes Prioris (c. 1460–
c. 1514), and Gaspar van Weerbeke (c. 1445–after 1517). Finally, though neither poet accounts for them, Ockeghem's death must certainly have touched
the likes of Jacob Obrecht (1457/58–1505), Heinrich Isaac (c. 1450–1517),
and Jean Mouton (before 1459–1522), all giants of the time.

   This brief list of composers born during the years 1440–60 and active from
the 1470s through the 1520s, though incomplete, drives home a point. Never
before had a single generation produced so plentiful and brilliant a constellation
of composers: not only were they technical wizards, they could truly touch the
hearts of their listeners, both then and now.

   Just as the composers of this generation worked at virtually the dead center
of our two-hundred-year period, so their music occupies a central role. On the
one hand, they fully absorbed the style of the Du Fay and Busnoys-Ockeghem
generations. On the other, they modified that style to create a language so
spectacularly rich in its technical and expressive possibilities that it would eventually serve as the source of such stylistically diverse genres as the bouncy "Parisian" chanson, the hyperemotional madrigal of the *seconda prattica* (beginning
in the mid-sixteenth century), and the almost otherworldy sacred music of
Counter-Reformation Rome.

   In all, the generation of La Rue, Obrecht, Isaac, and Josquin occupies a
position around 1500 analogous to that held by Beethoven around 1800: they
respected the past, shaped the future, and made both their very own.

PERVADING IMITATION

   Although Josquin and his contemporaries were not the first to use imitation,
they were the first to make it the basic building block of their style. Whereas
in earlier chapters we took note of pieces in which imitation was used in a
systematic way, we now take note of pieces in which it is not. Moreover, while
imitation was earlier used in duet sections or superius-tenor duet of a three-

part texture, it now permeates all four (or more) voices. And where imitation previously behaved in a fairly predictable way, it now appears in countless permutations.

Josquin's *Ave Maria . . . virgo serena*

The new approach to imitation appears in Josquin's motet *Ave Maria . . . virgo serena* (*Anthology* 37), probably the piece most often cited to illustrate the stylistic innovations of Josquin and his generation, a work that was recorded on disc as early as 1937 and that one musicologist has dubbed the *Mona Lisa* of Renaissance music.[1] We will examine this brief masterpiece even before we look more closely at its composer. The text is pasted together from three different sources: the opening couplet ("Ave Maria, gratia plena,/Dominus tecum, virgo serena") is drawn from the corresponding plainchant sequence, sung at the Feast of the Annunciation; the independent five-stanza prayer that follows was well-known in the fifteenth century and appears in a number of Books of Hours (small, private collections of devotional prayers); and the concluding invocation ("O Mater Dei . . .") follows a common formula of the period. Of the twenty-seven lines or half lines that receive clear-cut motives of their own, no fewer than sixteen begin with a point of imitation. The effect, though, is anything but tedious, as the imitation is varied kaleidoscopically:

(1) In measures 1–31, the four half lines that open the piece are set with straightforward imitation running through all four voices at the unison and octave; yet the imitation is never mechanical, as voices may stop short after imitating the opening motive only (altus and bassus, mm. 18–25) or continue beyond that point, after which they go their independent ways (superius and tenor, mm. 17–24). Josquin also varies the order in which the voices enter and the time interval between them; thus the setting of "virgo serena" (mm. 23–28) has the altus leading for the first time, while the tenor seemingly jumps in a measure too soon.

(2) Measures 31–39 introduce paired imitation in which the two voices of each pair do not imitate one another; here there is an added twist, as the altus, which had just been paired with the superius, returns with the tenor and bassus, so that two voices are answered by three.

(3) Measures 54–65 present paired imitation in which the two voices of each pair are themselves imitative, and again there is a surprise: while all prior points of imitation had all voices enter on the same text, here the "Ave cujus nativitas" of superius and altus is answered by the "Nostra fuit solemnitas" of tenor and bassus.

(4) Measures 127–133 and 133–141 show paired imitation in which only one voice of each pair carries out the imitation precisely.

From time to time, Josquin relieves the predominantly imitative texture with

---

1. Jessie Ann Owens, "How Josquin Became Josquin," paper read at the conference "Making New Classics: Canon Formation in the Renaissance," held at Harvard University, April 4, 1992.

full, four-part chordal writing, most notably at measures 94–109 and 143–155, which set, respectively, the fourth quatrain and the concluding couplet with its added "Amen." But though both sections provide textural contrast, they serve different ends. The concluding chordal section (mm. 143ff.) truly grounds the tension of the motet as a whole, especially after the superius and tenor of the preceding section had rocked the rhythmic boat with their threes-against-twos (mm. 135–140). The homophony at "Ave vera virginitas" (m. 94), on the other hand, is ambivalent: while the simple repetition and symmetry provide a measure of repose, the shift from duple to triple meter (with a 3:1 "speeding up") and the "hidden" canon between superius and tenor, in which the two voices are at metrical cross-purposes, kick start the music with a jolt. Only at the next point of imitation can we relax; Josquin has thus turned the tables on the function of the two textures.

Our overall impression of *Ave Maria . . . virgo serena* is that it "breathes," exudes flexibility: there is imitation of all sorts, free contrapuntal writing, strict homophony, contrasts between high and low duets and between duets and four-part writing, shifting meters, terse motives that fit their words like gloves, meandering melismas (admittedly restrained), clear-cut cadences, and seamless overlapping phrases. And it all seems to happen effortlessly, without a trace of contrivance. In a way, what might be called Josquin's naturalism has supplanted Ockeghem's complexity and artifice. The years around 1500 were witnessing the dawn of a new world, and Josquin's motet, possibly composed at Milan—the birthplace of the new style?—as early as the 1470s, can stand for its musical realm.

NEW RELATIONSHIPS BETWEEN VOICES

With their insistence on pervading imitation, the composers of the Josquin generation altered the prevailing relationships between the voice parts. To re-view: the structural backbone of a late three-part chanson by Du Fay consisted of a tightly knit superius-tenor duet to which was "added" (a dangerous word) a third voice that was not essential to the contrapuntal-harmonic substance of the piece. Likewise, Du Fay's mature, four-part Masses contained the same superius-tenor duet texture (the tenor now a preexistent cantus firmus), a bass part that was guided by (and guided) the harmonic implications of the duet, and an altus that mainly filled things out. In other words, each voice played a defined role in a hierarchy.

With pervading imitation, those relationships changed. Clearly, imitation spells equality among the voices: each part is just as essential as any other. Leave one voice out and things will fall apart. Change is also evident in the two chordal passages of *Ave Maria . . . virgo serena*. The superius and bassus determine the motion in those sections, meaning that Josquin was hearing a succession of vertical sonorities—chords to us—and the tension-resolution they produce.

These changes have often been explained in terms of "successive" compo-sition giving way to "simultaneous" (or "harmonic") composition; that is, composers stopped writing one voice at a time (from beginning to end?) and began to conceive the entire polyphonic fabric as a whole. Ammunition for this view comes from the theorists. For instance, Pietro Aaron, in *Toscanello in musica* (1523), wrote that "many composers were of the opinion that the soprano should be composed first, then the tenor, and after the tenor the bass. . . . The modern composers had a better idea . . . because they take all the parts into consideration at once."[2]

Yet the question of successive versus simultaneous composition must surely rank among the great *non*-issues of music history. Should we really believe that Du Fay (or Busnoys or Ockeghem), even when using a preexistent cantus firmus as a springboard or composing a superius-tenor backbone, did not have the entire polyphonic fabric buzzing around in his ear? Composers of the Josquin generation continued to write cantus-firmus compositions; did they fail to "take all the parts into consideration at once" in those works? And for whom did theorists such as Aaron intend their prescriptions? Certainly they were not giving tips to masters. In short, to equate the earlier style, in which the voice parts adhere to a hierarchy of functions and the forward motion is determined more by the tension of counterpoint than by "chord progressions," with the idea of jigsaw-puzzle-like, successive composition seems questionable at best.

JOSQUIN DESPREZ

It is fair to say that Josquin Desprez (Fig. 18-1) has been the most heavily studied composer of our entire two-hundred-year period. Yet there are gaping holes in his biography, the chronology of his works is shaky, and there are serious questions about just what he did and did not compose. Confusing the issue further are a number of singers who were partial namesakes: Pasquier Desprez, Josse (Josquin) van Steelant, Johannes de Pratis (= des Prez), Josquin Doro. A Josquin who was active at Milan from 1459 to 1476 has generally been identified as the famous composer, but that identification has recently been questioned.

Figure 18-1. Petrus Opmeer, *Josquinus Pratensis*, woodcut from *Opus chronographicum orbis universi* (1611).

IOSQVINVS PRATENSIS.

2. Quoted after Blackburn, "On Compositional Process in the Fifteenth Century," 215.

Josquin was probably born around 1440, most likely in the Vermandois area of present-day Picardy. Though there is no documentation from his early years, there is testimony from the seventeenth century (thus extremely late) that he was a choirboy at the collegiate church at St. Quentin. As for contemporary statements that he studied with Ockeghem: not a shred of evidence points to that or any other teacher-student relationship.

1459–1476: Milan

The earliest secure reference to Josquin is a Milanese document of August 1459, which lists him as a *biscantor*—an adult singer of polyphony—at that city's cathedral and shows that he must have arrived there the month before. He remained at the cathedral through December 1472, earning the rather low salary of just over 1 ducat a month. Josquin next went crosstown and joined the *cantori di cappella* of Duke Galeazzo Maria Sforza, where he is recorded for the first time on January 18, 1473. There he received a benefice that brought his total income to 160 ducats per year, making him among the best-paid singers at the court. He no doubt remained with the chapel until it was partially disbanded following the duke's assassination on December 26, 1476.

Josquin's long stay in Milan must certainly have been a formative experience: his colleagues in the ducal chapel included Compère, Agricola, Weerbeke, and Martini, and what must have been a spirit of competition no doubt sharpened his compositional skills.[3]

1477–1489: On the Road?

In the decade following Galeazzo Maria's death, the gaps in our knowledge of Josquin's whereabouts become acute. There are only three documented "sightings" of the composer: as a singer at the court of René of Anjou at Aix-en-Provence (April 1477), in Milan one final time (April 1479), and at the collegiate church of Notre-Dame at Condé-sur-Escaut, in the province of Hainault (1483). Where was he the rest of the time? There is circumstantial evidence that from May 1479 until he entered the papal chapel in 1489, Josquin may have been in the retinue of the free-spending Ascanio Sforza, younger brother of the murdered Galeazzo Maria and a cardinal from 1484. If so, it may have been through Ascanio that Josquin made his first contacts with the court of Ferrara, where Ascanio was in exile in the early 1480s.

1489–1502: Rome, and On the Road Again?

Josquin entered the papal chapel during the reign of Innocent VIII, in June 1489, and remained there, with extended absences, into the reign of Alexander VI (1492–1503). His departure occurred sometime between February 1495 and 1500, a period for which the chapel's account books are missing. As we might

---

3. That the Milanese Josquin is the composer is the traditional assumption. For arguments pro and con, see the studies by Fallows, Macey, and Merkley cited in the Bibliographical Note.

expect of a savvy papal singer, Josquin acquired his share of benefices, all of them in his native north.

Josquin turns up again in 1501–2, this time in France, apparently enjoying a connection with the court of Louis XII. He also seems to have gone to Flanders around this time to recruit singers for the court of Ferrara. Two anecdotes from the Louis XII period, related in Glarean's *Dodecachordon* (1547), give us a peek at Josquin's wit. When Louis forgot about a promised benefice for Josquin, the composer wrote and had performed in the king's presence the motet *Memor esto verbi tui servo tuo* (Remember your word to your servant, since you have given me hope, Psalm 119). And on another occasion, when Louis, who had a poor voice, asked Josquin to write a chanson in which he could take part, Josquin complied with *Guillaume se va chaufer*, the tenor part of which, intended for the king, consists of a single note.

1503–1504: Ferrara

Josquin was chapel master—a post that was by now a primarily musical one, as opposed to ecclesiastical-administrative—at the Ferrarese court of Ercole I d'Este from mid-April 1503 to April 1504. The thought of recruiting Josquin had been in the Ferrarese air months earlier. On August 14, 1502, Ercole's agent Girolamo da Sestola wrote to the duke:

> My Lord, I believe that there is neither lord nor king who will now have a better chapel than yours if Your Lordship sends for Josquin. Don Alfonso [Ercole's son and heir] wishes to write this to Your Lordship and so does the entire chapel; and by having Josquin in our chapel, I want to place a crown upon this chapel of ours.

And just a few weeks later, another Ferrarese agent, Gian de Artiganova, wrote what is probably the most famous description of the composer:

> To me he [Isaac] seems well suited to serve Your Lordship, more so than Josquin, because he is more good-natured and companionable, and he will compose new works more often. It is true that Josquin composes better, but he composes when he wants to, and not when one wants him to, and he is asking 200 ducats in salary while Isaac will come for 120—but Your Lordship will decide.[4]

As we know, Ercole decided in favor of the temperamental Josquin, a decision that resulted in one of the most moving compositions of this or any other period: Josquin's setting of Psalm 50, *Miserere mei, Deus*. More problematic in terms of chronology is the *Missa Hercules dux ferrariae*, with its subject, or cantus firmus, on the vowels that make up the duke's name and title in Latin: H*e*rc*u*l*e*s d*u*x f*e*rr*a*r*i*ae = re, ut, re, ut, re, fa, mi, re (Ex. 18–2). Though Josquin may have written the Mass during his tenure at Ferrara, its style points to an earlier period, perhaps the early 1480s, when he might have been at Ferrara in the company of Ascanio Sforza.

---

4. Both letters are quoted after Lockwood, *Music in Renaissance Ferrara*, 203–4.

EXAMPLE 18-2. (a) Cantus firmus of the *Missa Hercules dux ferrariae*; (b) Kyrie, mm. 1–8.

1504–1521: Condé

Just as Du Fay retired to the relative tranquillity of the Cathedral of Cambrai after about twenty years on the international circuit, so Josquin, forty-five years after he arrived at Milan, went home, to Notre-Dame at Condé-sur-Escaut. There, on May 3, 1504 (just a few weeks after leaving Ferrara), he was admitted to the chapter as its provost. Whatever his ecclesiastical and administrative duties may have been, they did not interfere with his composing, since many of his masterpieces still lay before him.

Josquin died on August 27, 1521. Among the many contemporaries who sang his praises, one of the most effusive was Cosimo Bartoli, in his *Ragionamenti accademici* (1567). After crediting Ockeghem with having "rediscovered" music and comparing him with Donatello, Bartoli goes on to laud Josquin:

> Josquin . . . may be said to have been, in music, a prodigy of nature, as our Michelangelo Buonarroti has been in architecture, painting, and sculpture;

for, as there has not thus far been anybody who in his compositions approaches Josquin, so Michelangelo, among all those who have been active in these arts, is still alone and without a peer; both one and the other have opened the eyes of all those who delight in these arts or are to delight in them in the future.

Martin Luther (1483–1546) was more terse: "Josquin is master of the notes, which must express what he desires; on the other hand, other choral composers must do what the notes dictate."[5] Josquin was the first composer whose reputation reached truly mythic proportions and whose works were assigned the status of classics.

Problems of Chronology and Authenticity

To ponder the chronology of Josquin's output is to go around in circles. Unlike Du Fay, Josquin did not leave many works that can be dated securely on the basis of their references to specific events and then be used as stylistic yardsticks against which to measure other works. And even when we think we have such a piece, questions crop up. For example, *Plus nulz regretz* sets Jean Lemaire's poem in honor of the December 1507 peace treaty between England and the Holy Roman Empire. Though Lemaire probably wrote his poem within a week or two of the treaty's signing, Josquin may have waited three years to set it.

Two of Josquin's most famous works demonstrate the difficulties in even starker fashion. We have already seen that the *Missa Hercules dux ferrariae* has been assigned to both the early 1480s and 1503–4. Dates vary just as widely for *Ave Maria . . . virgo serena*: (1) the mid-1470s according to one dating of its earliest manuscript; (2) the late 1480s on the basis of style; and (3) September–October 1497 on the grounds of the conjectural connection with Cardinal Ascanio and a pilgrimage Ascanio made to the shrine of Loreto. Clearly, problems of chronology are inextricably intertwined with those of biography, and we will probably make little headway in one without advances in the other.

The difficulties with authenticity are no less great. The central problem in present-day Josquin research consists of sorting out which of the many attributions to Josquin are authentic and which are not. The *New Grove* catalogue of Josquin's works includes 315 compositions, 136 of which are classified as "doubtful and misattributed."[6] Further, more than 40 percent of the works attributed to Josquin appear only in manuscripts or prints that date from after his death, sometimes by as much as two or three decades; such posthumous attributions are at least suspect. A 1540 quip by the German music publisher Georg Forster is sobering: "A certain famous man said that Josquin produced more motets after his death than during his life."[7]

With some exaggeration, then, we may say that present-day Josquin scholarship holds few attributions sacred. Indeed, one of the compositions long re-

5. Both quotations are from Reese and Noble, "Josquin Desprez," 18–19.

6. Reese and Noble, "Josquin Desprez," 65–83.

7. Elders, "Who was Josquin?" in *International Josquin Symposium, Utrecht 1986*, 10–11.

garded as defining the very essence of Josquin's expressive style, the motet *Absalon, fili mi*, has recently been rerouted to the worklist of Pierre de la Rue.

Not many years ago, this section would have closed with a capsule summary of Josquin's significance. Now, however, such an effort seems premature, perhaps even foolhardy. To play it safe, we will circle back to our original point of departure and assess the significant achievements of Josquin and his contemporaries as a group, alluding both to features that we have considered here and to those still to come:

(1) they developed the technique of pervading imitation as the basic structural building block of their works, replacing what had been a hierarchical relationship between voices with a sense of greater homogeneity;

(2) they cultivated a sense of chordal sonority, and with it a greater feeling for tonal centers;

(3) they continued the shift away from Masses based on monophonic models to works that were based on polyphonic pieces; though they continued to use monophonic models, they developed new ways of treating them;

(4) they abandoned the two-hundred-year-old *formes fixes* in favor of freer, varying repetition schemes;

(5) they placed reins on freewheeling melismas and built their works on concise, sharply etched melodic motives whose rhythm was often generated by the words themselves; and

(6) they often expressed the sentiments of those words in a fashion that was easy to hear and that still sounds modern to our ears. All of these characteristics will become evident in the chapters that follow.

MUSIC AND THE PRINTING PRESS

The first example we have of music printed from movable type is a chant book from southern Germany dating from the early 1470s (Fig. 18-2). The unknown printer used the technique of multiple impressions: that is, staves, note heads (a type known as German gothic, or "horseshoe nail"), and text were printed in three separate operations, and the red decorative initials, rubrics, and line for the note *f* were later drawn in by hand. The final quarter of the fifteenth century also witnessed the development of fonts that could accommodate the various note shapes of mensural notation. An early example appears in Franciscus Niger's *Grammatica brevis*, printed at Venice in 1480 (Fig. 18-3). People who purchased this volume had to draw in the staff lines themselves. Finally, music was sometimes printed from engraved blocks of wood, especially music examples in treatises, as in Burtius's *Musices opusculum*, printed at Bologna in 1487 (Fig. 18-4).

Ottaviano dei Petrucci

On May 25, 1498, Ottaviano dei Petrucci of Fossombrone (1466–1539) received a "privilege" from the Republic of Venice, the major center of printing

Figure 18-2. The *Constance Gradual*, c. 1473 (British Library, London).

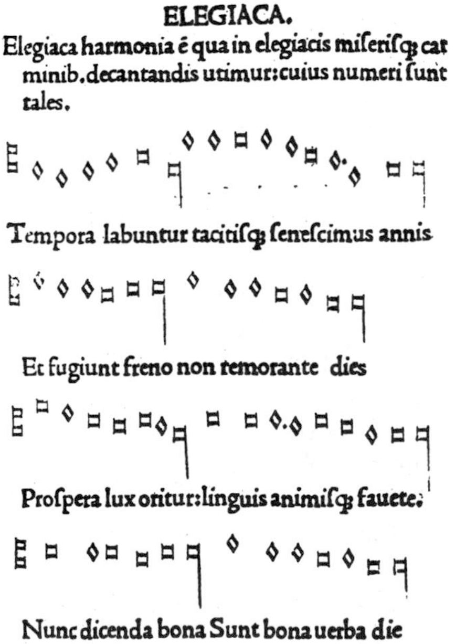

ELEGIACA.

Elegiaca harmonia ē qua in elegiacis miſeriſcӡ cat
minib. decantandis utimur: cuius numeri ſunt
tales.

Tempora labuntur tacitiſcӡ ſeneſcimus annis

Et fugiunt freno non remorante dies

Proſpera lux oritur: linguis animiſcӡ fauete:

Nunc dicenda bona Sunt bona uerba die

Figure 18-3. Franciscus Niger, *Grammatica*, 1480, earliest known print of mensural music.

tenor

contra

Figure 18-4. Nicolaus Burtius, *Musices opusculum*, 1487, music printed from woodblock.

Demõstrata mesurati cãt°fabricatõe:mõ oicẽdũ ãlŕ

and publishing in Italy, that granted him an exclusive twenty-year monopoly on the printing and selling of "canto figurado" (polyphony) and "intaboladure d'organo et de liuto" (organ and lute tablatures). Three years later, Petrucci turned out the first substantial collection of printed polyphony: the *Harmonice musices odhecaton A* of 1501, an anthology of ninety-six (though the Greek word "odhecaton" promises one hundred) French chansons and instrumental pieces by composers of both the Josquin and Busnoys-Ockeghem generations (Fig. 18-5). Printed only with short text incipits, and thus no doubt intended for instrumental ensembles, the *Odhecaton* must have been a commercial success, as Petrucci quickly followed it up with two similar collections: *Canti B* (1502) and *Canti C* (1503).

Sensitive to the demands of the marketplace, Petrucci expanded his printing venture to other repertories: eleven books of the popular northern Italian frottola, two multivolume series devoted to the motet, collections for lute alone and for lute and voice, and books of Masses devoted mainly to single composers, with three volumes of Josquin Masses heading the list. In all, Petrucci published sixty-one collections of music (the last in 1520), and with them attained a level of typographical elegance that has not been surpassed.

Petrucci's success quickly spawned imitators. Within just a few years, he was followed by the likes of Erhard Oeglin, Peter Schöffer, and Arnt von Aich in Germany and the brilliant engraver Andrea Antico in Italy. But the real explo-

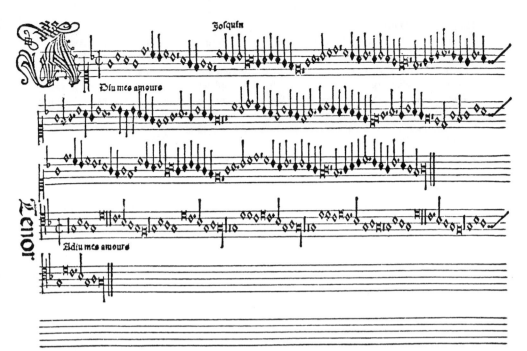

Figure 18-5. Ottaviano Petrucci, *Harmonice musices Odhecaton A*, 1501; fol. 16ᵛ, showing superius and tenor of Josquin's *Adieu mes amours*.

sion in music printing was still to come, and once it began—around 1530—it would not be stopped (see Chapter 29).

Music printing had a major effect on the transmission of music. Not only did printed copies of music reach a vastly wider audience than any single manuscript could, they did so far less expensively. For example, in 1481, the court of Ferrara paid ten ducats for a 116-folio parchment manuscript that displayed the duke's illuminated coat of arms and seventy-seven gold initials, but was seen by no one outside the twenty-nine singers of the ducal chapel; in 1513, Ferdinand Columbus, son of Christopher, was one of hundreds who purchased Petrucci's smaller *Motetti A* (1502) for little more than half a ducat. Moreover, printing made it possible for repertories to travel more widely and quickly than ever before and thus led to an almost overnight cross-fertilization of styles and genres. Petrucci's skill as a printer and daring as a businessman made the music of a Josquin or Isaac or Obrecht an almost popular household commodity, something polyphonic music had never quite been before.

BIBLIOGRAPHICAL NOTE

The literature on Josquin is voluminous; cited here are works that provide a wide overview or that deal with aspects of his life and career touched on in this chapter; further references appear in the Bibliographical Notes of Chapters 20–25.

Editions of the Music

The standard edition of Josquin's works is Albert Smijers, *Werken* (Amsterdam: Alsbach; Leipzig: Kistner & Siegel, 1921–56), with a partial revision and supplement by Myroslaw Antonowycz and Willem Elders, *Opera omnia: Editio altera* . . . (Amsterdam: Vereniging voor Nederlandse Muziekgeschiedenis, 1957–69). A completely new edition, the *New Josquin Edition*, under the general editorship of Elders and published by the Vereniging is now in progress; for a behind-the-scenes look at some of the problems involved, see Elders's "Reports" in *TVNM* 24 (1974): 20–82; 25 (1975): 54–64; 26 (1976): 17–40; 28 (1978): 31–37; 35 (1985): 3–8.

General Overviews

The best starting point for a succinct account of his life and works is Gustave Reese and Jeremy Noble's "Josquin Desprez," in *The New Grove High Renaissance Masters*, ed. Stanley Sadie (New York: Norton, 1984), 1–90, which contains the most authoritative worklist currently available; the most wide-ranging volume is *Josquin des Prez: Proceedings of the International Festival-Conference Held at The Juilliard School at Lincoln Center in New York City, 22–25 June 1971*, ed. Edward E. Lowinsky and Bonnie J. Blackburn (London: Oxford University Press, 1976). For those with a command of German, there is Helmuth Osthoff, *Josquin Desprez*, 2 vols. (Tutzing: Schneider, 1962–65). Finally, there is the forthcoming *Josquin Companion*, ed. Richard Sherr (Oxford University Press).

Biography

The following deal with specific aspects of Josquin's career. **Milan**: Claudio Sartori, "Josquin Des Prés cantore del Duomo di Milano (1459–1472)," *AnnM* 4 (1956): 55–83; Lora Matthews and Paul Merkley, "Josquin Desprez and His Milanese Patrons," *JM* 12 (1994): 434–63. David Fallows, in "Josquin and Milan," *PMM* 5 (1996): 69–90, argues that the Milanese Josquin is not our composer; Patrick Macey, in "Galeazzo Maria Sforza and Musical Patronage in Milan: Compère, Weerbeke and Josquin," *EMH* 15 (1996): 147–212, and Merkley, in "Patronage and Clientage in Galeazzo's Court," *SM* 4 (1996): 121–54, conclude that he is. **The court of René of Anjou**: Françoise Robin, "Josquin Des Prés au service de René d'Anjou," *RdM* 71 (1985): 180–81. **With Ascanio Sforza**: Edward E. Lowinsky, "Ascanio Sforza's Life: A Key to Josquin's Biography and an Aid to the Chronology of His Works," in *Proceedings*, 31–75. **The papal chapel**: Pamela Starr, "Josquin, Rome, and a Case of Mistaken Identity," *JM* 15 (1997): 43–65. **Ferrara**: Lewis Lockwood, "Josquin at Ferrara: New Documents and Letters," in *Proceedings*, 103–37, and *Music in Renaissance Ferrara, 1400–1505* (Cambridge: Harvard University Press, 1984). **Condé and the French and Habsburg-Burgundian connections**: Jeremy Noble, "New Light on Josquin's Benefices," in *Proceedings*, 76–102; Herbert Kellman, "Josquin and the Courts of the Netherlands and France: The Evidence of the Sources," in *Proceedings*, 181–216. On Josquin's myth-like status, see Jessie Ann Owens, "How Josquin Became Josquin: Reflections on Historiography and Reception," in *Music in Renaissance Cities and Courts: Studies in Honor of Lewis Lockwood*, ed. Owens and Anthony M. Cummings (Warren, Mich: Harmonie Park Press, 1997), 271–80, and Macey, "Josquin as Classic: *Qui habitat, Memor esto*, and Two Imitations Unmasked," *JRMA* 118 (1993): 1–43.

Authenticity

The place to start in order to appreciate the problems is Willem Elders and Frits De Haen, *Proceedings of the International Josquin Symposium, Utrecht 1986* (Amsterdam: Vereniging voor Nederlandse Muziekgeschiedenis, 1991).

Ave regina . . . virgo serena

There are interesting analyses of the piece in Cristle Collins Judd, "Some Problems of Pre-Baroque Analysis: An Examination of Josquin's *Ave Maria . . . virgo serena*," *MusAn* 4

(1985): 201–39; Irving Godt, "Motivic Integration in Josquin's Motets," *JMT* 21 (1977): 264–92.

Music Printing and Petrucci

Two good introductions to early music printing are Donald W. Krummel and Stanley Sadie, eds., *Music Printing and Publishing* (New York: Norton, 1990), and Alec Hyatt King, *Four Hundred Years of Music Printing* (London: British Museum, 1964). For a survey of Petrucci's career and output, see Stanley Boorman, "Petrucci," in *Music Printing and Publishing*, 365–69; the *Odhecaton* has been edited by Helen Hewitt and Isabel Pope, *Harmonice musices Odhecaton A* (Cambridge, Mass.: Mediaeval Academy of America, 1942); there is a facsimile edition published in the series *Monuments of Music and Music Literature in Facsimile* (New York: Broude Bros., 1973); on the complicated publication history of the collection, see Boorman, "The 'First' Edition of the *Odhecaton A*," *JAMS* 30 (1977); 183–207.

Also Cited

Bonnie J. Blackburn, "On Compositional Process in the Fifteenth Century," *JAMS* 40 (1987): 210–84.

CHAPTER 19

Intermedio: 1492

For those who call the Western Hemisphere home, no year has more instant name recognition than 1492. As much as any other, it was a watershed year, both realistically and symbolically, that marked the end of one epoch and the beginning of another.

TWO DEATHS

Lorenzo de' Medici

Lorenzo de' Medici, the "Magnificent," died on April 8. To commemorate his death, Angelo Poliziano and Heinrich Isaac—respectively the leading poet and composer in Medicean circles—collaborated on the splendid motet *Quis dabit capiti meo aquam?* (*Anthology* 38), which they infused with audible symbolism. The *secunda pars* (second part, mm. 65–101) begins with the words "Laurus impet[e] fulminis / illa iacet subito" (The laurel, struck down suddenly by a lightning bolt, lies there). The laurel clearly personifies Lorenzo, who even adopted the laurel wreath as one of his emblems. And here, Isaac has the tenor drop out (the instruction in the manuscripts reads: "Laurus to be silent"), while the bass, in ostinato fashion, intones the phrase "Et requiescamus in pace" (Let us rest in peace) on a snippet of chant drawn from the antiphon *Salva nos, Domine* (*Liber usualis*, 271–72).

When the tenor returns at the beginning of the *tertia pars* (third part, m. 102), it can manage nothing more than a single, sustained *a*, until, at the words "nunc muta omnia" (now all is silent), it picks up the bass's dirge-like motive of the previous part (which had been introduced as early as mm. 9–14). The overt symbolism could not have escaped those who heard the work in 1492. Finally, Isaac's descending ostinati, Phrygian/Aeolian mode, and fauxbourdon-like chains of $^6_3$ chords (mm. 9–11) would become the stock-in-trade of the musical lament; even today, they are immediately recognizable as musical signs of sadness.

Piero della Francesca

There is hardly a more striking illustration of 1492 as a symbol of both the passing of the old and the beginning of the new than the following coincidence: on the very day—Friday, October 12—that Christopher Columbus set foot on the island he called San Salvador (in the Bahamas), the great painter Piero

Figure 19-1. Piero della Francesca, *The Flagellation*, c. 1460 (Galleria Nazionale, Urbino).

della Francesca (b. 1420–22) was buried in his native town of Borgo San Sepolchro.

Oddly, Piero has been more warmly acclaimed in our century than he was in his own. Perhaps it is the intellectualism of his work that draws us to him: the underlying mathematics and emphasis on geometric forms (he wrote two mathematical treatises and another on perspective), the pale colors, the stillness, the general absence of razzle-dazzle, all of which are characteristic of *The Flagellation* (Fig. 19-1).

Puzzles abound in this painting: Are the individual pavement tiles rectangles, or are they squares well along in the course of their perspectival foreshortening? How many sources of light are there, from where do they emanate, and what do they signify? Why is Christ the smallest figure in the painting? Is the figure in the center of the forefront group an angel or an earthly mortal? And who are the two gentlemen on the left and right in the forefront, why are they the largest figures in the painting, and what relationship do they have to the scene in which Pontius Pilate looks on while Christ is tortured? Eight questions, no answers! Could Piero's contemporaries have done better? (No answers here either.) The painting is one of the most enigmatic of the period, worth every penny of a trip to the Galleria Nazionale at Urbino.

TWO BIRTHS

Had they wanted to, Ferdinand and Isabella could have spent much of 1492 sending out announcement cards.

The Unification of Spain

In 1469, Princess Isabella of Castile married Prince Ferdinand V of Aragón. And when in 1474 and 1479, respectively, the two heirs inherited their individual kingdoms, they united almost all of present-day Spain. The process of unification was then virtually completed in January 1492, when, after more than a decade of fighting, the armies of the "Catholic monarchs," as Ferdinand and Isabella were called, conquered the last stronghold of resistance: the Muslim kingdom of Granada.

The Spanish victory over the Muslims was celebrated throughout Christendom, especially in Rome and Naples, both of which—now that there was a Spanish pope, Alexander VI (Rodrigo Borja)—had close ties to Spain. And the celebrations had their musical fallout: the anonymous barzelletta *Viva el gran Re Don Fernando*, one of the earliest pieces of polyphony to appear in print, having been printed from a woodblock at Rome in March 1493, eight years before Petrucci issued his *Odhecaton*. Example 19-1 provides the *ripresa* and first stanza:

EXAMPLE 19-1. Anonymous, *Viva el gran Re Don Fernando*, *ripresa* and stanza 1.

The defeated Muslims, at least initially, were permitted to stay and openly practice their religion. It was another story for the Jews. In 1480, Ferdinand inaugurated the Spanish Inquisition (it would continue for some three centuries), the aim of which was to compel belief in Christian teachings. Many Jews converted—the Marranos—though some continued to practice their faith in secret. But with Spanish nationalism at a high point following the victory at Granada, Ferdinand clamped down. On March 31, 1492, he issued a proclamation: Jews were to accept baptism or face expulsion within three months (a similar decree went into effect against the Muslims in 1501). Upward of 165,000 Jews chose to leave Spain and spread out over Portugal, Italy, Greece, Turkey, and North Africa. The conquest of the Muslims and the expulsion of the Jews thus brought to an end a brilliant, centuries-long tradition of Christian-Muslim-Jewish multiculturalism that had left its mark on virtually every aspect of medieval Spanish culture.

The New World

Columbus's achievements were part of a growing tide. Already in the middle of the fifteenth century, Prince Henry of Portugal—called "the Navigator"—had established a kind of think tank that sought to reconcile geographical and astronomical theory with practical seafaring experience. By the time he died in 1460, Portuguese-sponsored expeditions were mapping the west coast of Africa. In 1488, Bartolomeo Diaz rounded the Cape of Good Hope, and a decade later Vasco da Gama continued up the east coast of Africa and then across the Indian Ocean to India itself.

As Portugal sailed to the east, Spain and England headed westward. Within a few years, Columbus was followed to the New World by John Cabot, a Genoese sailing for England (1497), and Amerigo Vespucci, a Florentine in the service of Spain (1499), while the next three decades saw the *conquistadores* claim large chunks of the New World for the growing Spanish empire. Balboa sighted the Pacific (1513), Cortés conquered Mexico (1519–20), Magellan's ships circumnavigated the globe (1519–22), and Pizarro overthrew the Incas of Peru (1527–33), with the help of a weapon even more potent than guns: smallpox, which ravaged the native Amerindian population.

How did the people of Christian Europe in particular come to dominate the seas and explore what was to them an unknown world? There were, after all, other cultures equally capable of doing so. For instance, during the period 1405–33, the Chinese, who already possessed the compass and were thus technologically more advanced than the Europeans, launched seven expeditions that went as far west as the east coast of Africa. And yet there were no far-reaching consequences. Likewise, the Islamic world, which fanned out from the Middle East to China and the south of Spain, had the most learned geographers of the time, enjoyed contacts with a greater number of cultures than anyone else, and could even claim Vasco da Gama's navigator as one of its own. Yet Islam too seemed to draw a line around itself and be content to remain within it.

The answer seems to lie not in technological or navigational skill and daring, but rather in the manner in which these different cultures financed their explorations. The Chinese expeditions, for instance, were supported and managed by the state, which, when it achieved its immediate goals, pulled in its sails. But though Ferdinand and Isabella risked some of their own wealth, Columbus himself had to raise about one-eighth of the necessary capital, while other funds came from private investors. Similarly, though Henry VII's charter to John

Cabot invested the explorer with the authority to claim for England any lands he might discover, it left the financing of the expedition up to Cabot and what merchants he could find to back him. Ultimately, the developing spirit of capitalism and individual entrepreneurship provided the driving force of European exploration, expansion, and, sad to say, exploitation.

While the Age of Exploration meant profits for its investors, it caused financial hardship for most working stiffs. Wealth from the New World poured into Europe and played havoc with the economy, as currencies were devalued and inflation ran high. In 1500, for example, a worker in the building trades in the German city of Augsburg earned a salary that enabled him to buy about one and a half times what was needed to maintain a family of five; a century later, a worker in the same trade was fortunate to earn three-quarters of what was needed for the same size household. In general, the sixteenth century was one of rising prices and stagnant incomes. And while the expansion into the New World was not the sole cause, it was certainly part of the problem.

BIBLIOGRAPHICAL NOTE

Piero della Francesca

Two good entry points to Piero's world are Ronald Lightbown, *Piero della Francesca* (New York: Abbeville Press, 1992), and Marilyn Aronberg Lavin, *Piero della Francesca* (New York: Abrams, 1992); those who can manage the Italian might look at the stupendous study by Eugenio Battisti, *Piero della Francesca*, 2 vols., rev. ed. (Milan: Electa, 1992); on the *Flagellation*, see Lavin, *Piero della Francesca: The Flagellation* (London: Penguin Press, 1972).

Spain

J. N. Hillgarth's *Spanish Kingdoms, 1250–1516*, 2 vols. (Oxford: Oxford University Press, 1976–78), is an excellent introduction to the history of Spain in this period.

The Age of Exploration

The literature on the exploration of the New World is voluminous; there are concise, clear-headed summaries in Myron P. Gilmore, *The World of Humanism, 1453–1517* (New York: Harper Torchbooks, 1962), and Fernand Braudel, *Civilization and Capitalism, 15th–18th Century*, vol. 1: *The Structures of Everyday Life: The Limits of the Possible* (Berkeley and Los Angeles: University of California Press, 1992); the classic study of Columbus is Samuel Eliot Morison, *Admiral of the Ocean Sea: A Life of Christopher Columbus*, 2 vols. (Cambridge: Cambridge University Press, 1942); see also Anthony Grafton, *New Worlds, Ancient Texts: The Power of Tradition and the Shock of Discovery* (Cambridge, Mass.: Belknap Press, 1992); for a fascinating account of how the Europeans altered the biological-ecological basis of the Western Hemisphere, see Alfred W. Crosby, *Germs, Seeds, and Animals: Studies in Ecological History* (Armonk, N.Y.: M.E. Sharpe, 1994).

CHAPTER 20

The Virtuoso Motet

It was in the motet that composers of the late fifteenth and early sixteenth centuries most daringly displayed their technical and expressive virtuosity. In fact, we can probably make a case that with the Josquin generation, Mass and motet exchanged places in a way: the motet now took on the cutting-edge quality that the cyclic Mass had displayed during the previous two generations, while the Mass began to show some signs of the conservatism that would characterize it as the sixteenth century wore on.

One way to measure the stock that composers of this generation placed in the motet is to consider the sheer quantity they turned out. Table 20-1 compares the production of Masses and motets by three representative composers from four generations:

Table 20-1. Mass and motet production across four generations.

Generation	Composer	Total number of works	Masses	Motets
Third quarter of 15th century	Busnoys	91	3	11 = 12%
	Ockeghem	13	22	11 = 17%
	Regis	13	3	8 = 61%
Late 15th/early 16th centuries	Josquin	315	41	155 = 49%
	La Rue	127	40	31 = 25%
	Mouton	163	18	116 = 71%
Mid-16th century	Clemens non Papa	512	17	231 = 45%
	Gombert	280	14	179 = 63%
	Willaert	412	9	183 = 44%
Late 16th century	Lassus	997	74	352 = 35%
	Palestrina	893	115	383 = 42%
	Victoria	200	22	106 = 53%

Sources: The numbers for Josquin, Lassus, Palestrina, and Victoria are drawn from the revised New Grove worklists that appear in Sadie, High Renaissance Masters; those for the other composers come from New Grove.

The trend is clear: the Josquin generation marks a turning point in motet production. Whereas only Regis, among composers of his generation, was something of a "motet specialist," eight of the nine composers from that point on devoted at least one-third of their output to the motet, while five of them approached or surpassed the 50 percent mark. In short, the motet became the representative sacred work of the sixteenth century.

There is another trend that screams out from the table, and that is the truly spectacular increase in productivity as a whole. Measured by the likes of Lassus or Palestrina, such mid-fifteenth-century giants as Busnoys and Ockeghem seem downright unproductive. The discrepancy can be explained in a couple of ways. First, although there is no telling how much music we have lost over the centuries, the losses are surely greater the further back we go, especially from the period before printing increased the chances of survival. Second, the very nature of what it meant to be a "composer" changed dramatically during the sixteenth century. Beginning around 1500, composers began to spend more time composing and less time with such matters as church affairs, administrative tasks, or obtaining degrees in canon law; the idea of composition as a profession became a reality. But it is also true that no matter how beautiful late-sixteenth-century music might be, there is—to risk exaggerating—less individuality from one motet to another among the almost four hundred by Palestrina than there is among the eleven that Ockeghem composed; as the sixteenth century moves along, a tinge of the formulaic becomes apparent.

We will look at the motet of the late fifteenth and early sixteenth centuries from the point of view of its virtuosity—in conveying the meaning and emotion of the text and in the use of canon and symbolism.

MUSIC AND TEXT

Measured in terms of such general style characteristics as cadential formulas, dissonance treatment, or manipulation of a cantus firmus, and with the lens held high enough to encompass our entire two-hundred-year period, the stylistic distance—that is, the difference in the sound of the music—between Josquin, La Rue, and Obrecht on the one hand and Busnoys and Ockeghem on the other is more a crevice than a chasm. The style of the younger composers evolved smoothly out of what preceded it. And once we are familiar with the music of late Du Fay, Busnoys, Regis, and Martini, we have no trouble adjusting to that of Compère, Isaac, Antoine Brumel, and Jean Mouton. Even the most characteristic feature of the younger composers—pervading imitation—had been forecast by the earlier generation.

There is one aspect of the younger composers' music, however, in which something quite new was going on: the relationship between music and text. This is not to say that there is only one way for music to express a text, or that composers before Josquin were at a loss how to go about it. We need only recall pieces such as Du Fay's *Adieu m'amour*, where the syntactical relationship between music and text is as tight, logical, and expressive as one could wish, or his *Ave regina caelorum*, with its plea for mercy expressed in a wrenching turn to C minor. Rather, the Josquin generation was the first to express the emotions of a text—especially sadness—in a way that sounds thoroughly modern and is immediately recognizable to our ears. Josquin and his contemporaries hit upon a new aesthetic of music-text relationship, one with which we, half a millennium later, are still very much in tune. And if we do not generally find quite the same pathos in the music of earlier composers, it may be because we fail to understand their aesthetic. Indeed, composers before Josquin were just as eager to "move the soul," and that listeners could respond feverishly is evident from the following passage from St. Augustine's *Confessions*:

> If I am not to turn a deaf ear to music, which is the setting for the words which give it life, I must allow it a position of some honor in my heart. . . . I realize that when they are sung, these sacred words stir my mind to greater religious fervour and kindle in me a more ardent flame of piety than they would if they were not sung. . . . But I ought not to allow my mind to be paralyzed by the gratification of my senses, which often lead it astray.[1]

We can hear the new expressivity in three motets from around 1500.

Josquin (?)/La Rue (?): *Absalon, fili mi*

There are few more puzzling pieces from this period than the famous *Absalon* lament (*Anthology* 39): who wrote it, when and for what occasion was it composed, why are there two different versions, and could either one really have been sung as notated? Though we will consider these issues presently, we should begin with what is known. The text is brief:

Absalon, fili mi,	Absalon, my son,
quis det ut moriar pro te,	would that I would die for thee,
fili mi Absalon.	my son Absalon.
Non vivam ultra,	Let me live no longer,
sed descendam in infernam plorans.	but descend into hell weeping.

Like many motet texts of the period, *Absalon* is something of a patchwork, drawing on 2 Samuel 19:4 ("and the king cried with a loud voice, 'Oh my son Absalom'"), Job 7:16 ("I would not live always: let me alone"), and Genesis 37:35 ("For I will go down into the grave unto my son mourning"), all passages in which fathers—David, Job, and Jacob, respectively—mourn the loss of sons. What is notable is that the compilation draws on the Hebrew Scriptures, which from the Josquin generation on became a rich mine for motet texts.

EXPRESSION AND RHETORIC   There is only one music source for *Absalon* that was compiled within striking distance of the two likely composers: London 8.G.VII, a manuscript copied in the busy Netherlands scriptorium of the Flemish scribe Pierre Alamire between 1516 and 1522 as a gift for Henry VIII and his wife Catherine of Aragon.[2] The manuscript transmits the motet with the following clefs, signatures, and vocal ranges (Ex. 20-1).

EXAMPLE 20-1. Clefs, signatures, and vocal ranges of *Absalon, fili mi*, as transmitted in MS London 8.G.VII.

---

1. Quoted after Treitler, *Music and the Historical Imagination*, 11.
2. British Library, MS Royal 8.G.VII.

The low range is astounding (as is the number of flats in the signature), clearly meant to convey an overall sense of mourning and bereavement. Even more to the point is the graphic setting of the last line: "but descend into hell weeping." Beginning at measure 60, the four voices present an imitative cascade of overlapping descending thirds, the same technique with which Josquin reeled off the names of the grieving composers in his *Nymphes des bois* (see Ex. 18-1) and which would become a sixteenth-century trademark device for representing grief. As they fall, the thirds outline arpeggios that descend through the circle of fifths from B-flat to G-flat. Then, after a deceptive cadence at measure 68 (and the tenor's plaintive ♭6–5 motion on "plorans" at that point seems to sum up the emotional anguish of the whole piece), the entire process of the cascading thirds and descent through the circle of fifths is repeated for rhetorical effect (mm. 69–85 = 52–68).

The composer, Josquin or La Rue, chose carefully when representing the descent into hell with arpeggios that go through the circle of fifths. The superius and tenor begin with a falling arpeggio on F–D–B-flat; altus and bassus continue with an interlocking B-flat–G–E-flat, answered by E-flat–C–A-flat, which then prompts the final A-flat–F–D-flat. What we have, then, is a repeated figure in which each successive statement interlocks with the one before it, forming a kind of chain link or ladder, known to students of rhetoric as a *climax*. Thus not only do we "hear" the visual image of descent, but we have the rhetorical rung-by-rung means of following it on its downward spiral.

We should not underestimate the importance of the union between music and rhetoric. Though this connection was not fully systematized until the so-called *Figurenlehre* in the works of such German theorists as Joachim Burmeister and Johannes Nucius in the early seventeenth century, the study of rhetoric was given tremendous impetus when Poggio Bracciolini made his famous Quintilian discovery in 1416 (see Chapter 2), and rhetoric became an important part of the humanist curriculum. While their application to music in the fifteenth century is not always easy to demonstrate, rhetorical figures came to play an important role in sixteenth-century music, with composers such as Josquin and Lassus gaining reputations as masters of musical "oration."

PROBLEMS OF PITCH   We can only wonder what early audiences made of *Absalon*. Indeed, the more they knew about music theory, the more confused they might have been. First, with its modulation around the circle of fifths to G-flat, *Absalon* stretches the fifteenth-century concepts of gamut and *musica ficta* to their limits. With one more step, the descent would have reached C-flat, lying in the realm of enharmonic relationships. Had it reached that point, *Absalon* might have become the centerpiece of the three-way debate by mail that the theorists Giovanni Spataro, Pietro Aaron, and Giovanni del Lago conducted during the 1520s–1530s, in part over the question of whether flats could be applied to C and F: could a flat (*fa*) be applied to notes that were already called *fa*? (See Chapter 26.)

Second, did Josquin or La Rue really expect anyone to sing a low B_1-flat?

To put that pitch into perspective: as we saw in Chapter 11, both Ockeghem and Tinctoris had hammered away at low D's and C's; centuries later, Mozart takes Osmin down to a D in *The Abduction from the Seraglio*, the Grand Inquisitor hits an E in Verdi's *Don Carlo*, and the dragon Fafner sings no lower than G-flat in Wagner's *Siegfried*. Was pitch fixed to the extent that a notated B_1-flat really signified a sound that vibrated at a predictable frequency, or was pitch relative, and could a note on any line or in any space be sung at whatever pitch was comfortable as long as the proper relationship of whole and half steps was maintained? In other words, did singers have the right to render clefs and signatures superfluous?

It is not an easy question to answer. And what might have held for one repertory—unaccompanied plainchant, for instance, where the idea of relative pitch and random transposition for the convenience of the choir is certainly feasible—might have been problematic in another. But in fact, polyphony probably did employ some kind of a fixed-pitch standard. As combined vocal and instrumental forces became more prominent from about 1500 on, limitations of the instruments would have lessened singers' possibilities for transposition. Also, some pieces (including *Absalon*) are transmitted at different pitch levels in different sources; why would anyone have bothered to write out transpositions if singers did not pay attention to notated pitch in the first place?

The problem of pitch in *Absalon* is compounded by the other version in which it was transmitted. Two mid-sixteenth-century German prints give the piece transposed up a ninth. And while this serves to lift the lowest voice up to a very comfortable c, it pushes the top voice, possibly sung by male falsettists, up to a virtually impossible b''-flat. Both versions thus seem to be unsingable by modern pitch standards. At what pitch level, then, was *Absalon* actually sung? There is what might be called an "average" range for Josquin's four-part music, and it is probably applicable to the other composers of his generation as well (Ex. 20-2):

EXAMPLE 20-2. The average range in Josquin's four-part music.[3]

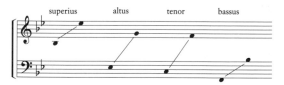

Thus Josquin's normal four-part writing occupies a middle ground between the two versions of *Absalon*, and though we still don't know why the sources transmit these extreme versions, perhaps that is where sixteenth-century choirs would have sung it.[4]

3. Based on Fallows, "The Performing Ensembles in Josquin's Sacred Music," 52–53.

4. In fact, the Hilliard Ensemble transposes the low version up an augmented fourth; the bass thus goes down to E, while the superius rises to a still-comfortable d'' (*Josquin Desprez: Motets et chansons*, EMI CDC 7 49209 2).

JOSQUIN OR LA RUE?   Who composed *Absalon, fili mi*? The problem and its nonresolution shape up as follows:

Contra Josquin: (1) not only does the most authoritative source for *Absalon*, London 8.G.VII, transmit the work without an attribution, but Josquin is not particularly well represented in the other manuscripts of the same Netherlandish scribal workshop; (2) it is precisely the posthumous, mid-sixteenth-century German attributions—all three of which might be dependent on one another—to Josquin about which Josquin scholars have grave doubts; and (3) a number of stylistic features in *Absalon* are not typical of Josquin's seemingly authentic music: for example, the low range, the leisurely pace with which the music rolls out, and the use of the proportion sign C2.

Pro La Rue: (1) not only was London 8.G.VII compiled on La Rue's home turf, but La Rue's works outnumber Josquin's in the Netherlands court manuscripts by more than two to one; (2) the work is sometimes associated with the death of Philip the Fair in 1506, in whose chapel La Rue had been singing for more than a decade; and (3) the very style characteristics, not least the low notated range, that speak against Josquin's authorship testify eloquently for La Rue's.

Given these circumstances, therefore, it is not surprising that recent Josquin scholarship stands on the verge of removing *Absalon* from the Josquin canon and reassigning it to Pierre de la Rue's. In any case, *Absalon* is a masterpiece no matter who wrote it.

PIERRE ALAMIRE   As noted above, the London 8.G.VII manuscript was copied by Pierre Alamire (c. 1470/75–after 1534), whose real name was Peter van den Hove. From 1509 until 1534, Alamire was "scribe and keeper of the books" at the Habsburg-Burgundian courts at Brussels and Malines. The fifty or so manuscripts he and his co-workers produced (including the Chigi Codex) contain a large portion of the contemporary Franco-Flemish repertory and almost the entire output of Pierre de la Rue. Besides preparing manuscripts for the ruling members of the Habsburg dynasty, the workshop filled orders for other leading patrons of the time: Pope Leo X; Frederick the Wise, Elector of Saxony; the Fuggers of Augsburg, perhaps the wealthiest family in Europe; and Henry VIII, for whom Alamire also supplied musical instruments and, during the years 1515–18, worked as an undercover agent against Richard de la Pole, exiled pretender to the English throne. He was the most sought-after music scribe of the early sixteenth century.

Josquin's *Miserere mei, Deus*

With *Miserere mei, Deus* (*Anthology* 40), which has been likened to Michelangelo's *Last Judgment* in the Sistine Chapel, Josquin "humanized" music, turned it into speech. The work dates from his Ferrarese sojourn of 1503–4 and was probably written—at the behest of Ercole d'Este—for Holy Week of 1504, since, as Psalm 50 (in the Catholic numbering system), *Miserere mei, Deus* is sung at Lauds on Holy (Maundy) Thursday, Good Friday, and Holy Saturday.

SPEECH   The speech-like quality of Josquin's prayer is evident from the outset, where the words "Miserere mei, Deus" are declaimed in a style that is little more than heightened speech. Josquin should not get all the credit for the idea. *Miserere mei, Deus* is a psalm, and when a psalm functions as part of the liturgy, it is sung to a *psalm tone:* a melodic formula that consists of a short intonation, a reciting tone that is reiterated as many times as there are syllables to be pronounced, a medial cadence, a return to the reiterated reciting tone, and a final cadence; this pattern is stated as many times as there are verses in the psalm. The overall effect is similar to a monotone-like recitative. Here is Psalm 50 as it is sung at Lauds on Maundy Thursday (Ex. 20-3):

EXAMPLE 20-3. Psalm tone for *Miserere mei, Deus*, verse 1, as sung at Lauds on Maundy Thursday.[5]

Mi - se - re - re me - i, De - us, se - cun - dum ma - gnam mi - se - ri - cor - di - am tu - am.

(intonation)   (reciting tone)   (medial   (reciting tone)   (final cadence)
                                 cadence)

Josquin did not use a real psalm tone; rather, he invented a psalm-tone-like motive and used it as the structural underpinning for the whole work.

The opening of the *secunda pars* (m. 170) also recollects human speech. Here Josquin plays with the opening word of verse 9 of the psalm, "auditui," twice breaking it off at the semantically self-sufficient "audi" and tossing it back and forth in a manner that verges on operatic dialogue. As in other works from this generation of composers, melismatic writing is at a premium. Instead, the rhythm is propelled—and even the melodic contours seem to be shaped—by the declamatory rhythm of the words themselves. It is little wonder that Josquin's sixteenth-century admirers considered him a musical orator.

STRUCTURE   When composers of the fifteenth century set psalms, they usually chose those that formed part of the Sunday Vespers service, paraphrased the psalm tone in the superius, and supported it in fauxbourdon fashion. The settings were functional at best. In the sixteenth century, polyphonic psalm settings gained musical weight. Josquin's *Miserere mei, Deus* stands near the beginning of this tradition: it is one of the earliest examples of a psalm text set from beginning to end (all twenty verses) in a thoroughly elaborate polyphonic style that abandons the preexistent psalm tone.

Yet Josquin, always concerned with articulating the large-scale structure of his works, tamed the three *partes* and 425 measures of *Miserere mei, Deus* with a logic that is both clear and audible. After setting forth the plaintive "Miserere" motive at the beginning of the work, Josquin repeats it—words and music— twenty-one times in ostinato fashion and always in tenor II (which sings nothing else). Thus the ostinato functions as a "ritornello" that marks the end of one verse and the beginning of another (and once, at m. 252, the midpoint of verse 14). Moreover, the ostinato does not stand still: in the first part, it begins

5. *Liber Usualis*, 652.

on *e′* and descends an octave, step by step, to *e*; in the second part, the process is reversed, and in part three, the descent begins again but this time only from *e′* to *a*. With its constantly changing pitch levels and alternation between whole and half steps (the latter on *E* and *B*), the ostinato keeps forcing cadences on different pitches and thus directs the tonal motion of the work. And since the ostinato generally draws the other four voices into its reiterated appeal for mercy, it serves as the focal point of the motet's timbral contrast.

JOSQUIN AND SAVONAROLA   Where did Josquin get the idea for this structural plan? Certainly not from the psalm itself, the twenty verses of which contain no hint of a recurring "Miserere." Rather, the answer probably lies in Girolamo Savonarola's *Meditation* on Psalm 50, written shortly before his death in 1498.

Savonarola was born in Ferrara in 1452. After joining the Dominican order at age twenty-two and convincing the populace that he heard the voice of God, he became the most famous preacher of his time. In 1490, he was invited to Florence by Lorenzo de' Medici, and when the Medici were exiled in 1494, he filled the political vacuum and imposed on the city a political-religious agenda that could be described as antifrivolous, complete with book, painting, and even lute burnings. Yet like many a demagogue, Savonarola went too far; and when his denunciations of papal corruption became too loud, Alexander VI excommunicated him. In April 1498, he was found guilty of heresy in a trial marked by torture; a month later, he was hanged and his body was burned at the stake.

Savonarola's *Meditation* was published for the first time at Ferrara in 1498, where Josquin surely came to know the work. The layout of the opening section is striking (Fig. 20-1): the words MISERERE MEI DEUS . . . keep recurring

Figure 20-1. A passage from Savonarola's *Meditation on Psalm 50*, 1498.

Reuerendi Piis .F. Hieronymi Sauonarolae de'Ferr. ordis praedicatoꝝexpositio in ꝑs . L . dũ erat i uiculis.

Nfoelix ego oĩm auxilio deſtitutus:Qui coelũ terrãꝗ offēdi: Quo iboꝗuo me uer-tã:ad quē confugiã꞉quis mei miſerebit꞉ Ad coelũ oculoſ leuare no audeo:qa ei grauiter peccaui .in terra refugiũ nõ iuenio:qa ei ſcandalũ fui.qd igiꝥ faciã꞉deſꝑaboꝛablit. miſericoꝛſ ē deus.pius ē ſalua tor meus.ſolus igiꝥ deus refugiũ meũ꞉iꝑe non deſpiciet opꝯ ſuũ:nõ ꞉epellet imagine ſui.Ad te igꝥ piiſſime deꝯ triſtis ac moeꝛēs uenio: qm̄ tu ſolus ſpes mea:tu ſolus refugium meũ. Quid aũt dicã tibi꞉cũ oculos eleuaꝛ nõ audeam꞉ Verba doloris effundã:Miſericordiã tuã mplo rabo:Dicam.

MISERERE MEI DEVS SECVN. MAG.MI.TV. Deus ꝗ luce habitas inacceſſibile꞉ Deus abſcõdit꞉ ꝗ ocu lis corporeis uideri nõ potes:nec itel lectu creato cõprehēdi: nec ligua ho minũ ꞉feu agelоꝝ explicari.Deꝯ meꝯ te incõprehēſibile quero ꞉te ieſſabile iuoco - Quicꝗd eſ꞉ꝗ ubiꝗꝯ es꞉Scio.n.te ſummã eſſe re꞉Si tũ es res꞉꞉ nõ potius omniũ reꝝ cauſã꞉ſi tũ ꞉ cauſa:nõ.n.inuenio no-mē:quomõ tuã ieſſabile maieſtate nomiare queã Deuſ ꞉quã ꝗ ea ꞉qcquid i te ē.tu ea.n. ipſa ſapiētia tua꞉bonitas tua꞉potētia tua꞉꞉ ſũma foelicitas tua. Cũ itaꝗꝰ ſis miſe ricoꝛ꞉qd es niſi ipſa miſericordia꞉qd autē ſum ego niſi ipſa miſeria꞉ecce ergo o miſericordia deus ecce miſeria coꝛã te꞉qd facies꞉꞉ miſericоꝛdia꞉꞉ceite opus tuã. Nũ qd a i

poteris recedere a natura tua:Et quod opuſ tuũ꞉miſeriá tollere:homies miſeros ſubleuare꞉ Ergo MISERERB ME.DEVS.Deꝯ iqui miſericordia tolle miſeriã mea꞉ Tolle peccata mea꞉ & eni ſũc ſũma miſeria mea.Suble ua me miſeꝛ꞉oſtēde i me opꝯ tuũ꞉Exerce i me uirtutem tuã.Abyſſuſ abyſſuꝝ iuocat꞉abyſſuſ miſeriae iuocat abyſ ſuꝝ miſericordiae꞉Abyſſus peccatoꝛ iuocat abyſſuꝝ gra tia꞉ꝥ Maior ē abyſſus miſericordiae ꝗ abyſſus miſeriae. Abſorbeat ergo abyſſus abyſſuꝝ꞉ Abſorbeat abyſſus mi ſericordiae abyſſuꝝ miſeriae. MISERERE.M.D.SE. M.MI.TVAM . Nõ ſecũdũ miſericordiã hominũ꞉quae parua ē꞉Sꝥ ſecũdũ tuã꞉ quae magna eſt꞉quae immēſa ē꞉ quae icõprehēſibilis ē꞉Quae oia peccata i ſmēluꝝ exce dit꞉Secũdũ illã magnã miſericordiã tuã꞉quae ſic dilexiſti mũdũ :ut filiũ tuũ unigenitũ dares꞉ Quae maior miſeri cordia eſſe pôꝥ꞉quae maior charitas꞉ Quis deſꝑare pôꝥ ꝗs nõ cõfidere꞉Deus fact꞉ ē hõ꞉ & p̓hominib꞉ crucifi-xus ē.Miſerere ergo deus ſecũdũ hãc miſericordiã tua꞉꞉ Qua filiũ tuũ ꝓ nobis tradidiſt꞉eqa ꝑ ipm̄ peccata mũ di abſtuliſti:qꝰ ꝑ cruce ei꞉ omŝ homieſ illumiaſti꞉qua ea ꝗ i coelis꞉& quae i terris ꝑ ipm̄ inſtauraſti꞉Laua me dõe in ſanguie eius꞉Illumia me i humilitate ei꞉꞉inſtau-ra me i reſurectiõe eius꞉ MISERERE.M.DEVS.Nõ ſecũdũ paruã miſericordiã tuã꞉ Parua.n.miſericordia tua eſt cũ hoies a corporalib꞉ miſeriis ſubleuas. Magna aũt qñ peccata dimittis꞉& hoies ꝑ gratiã tuã ſup altitudinē terrae ſubſtolis꞉Ita dõe miſerere mei ſecũdũ hãc magnã mi.tui꞉ut mead te cõuertas꞉ut peccata mea deleas: utꝓ gratiam tuã me iuſtifices꞉

ET. SECVNDVM.MVL.M. TV.D.INI.MEAM.

in bold capitals, like a visual ostinato. Here, without a doubt, is the source of Josquin's ritornello, the spark that inspired one of the most affective and deeply moving combinations of music and words in the history of Western music. Perhaps it was the unabashed emotion of this motet that, in 1538, led Johannes Ott, who had published the work in Germany a year earlier, to write: "What painter could render Christ's face in the agony of death as graphically as did Josquin in tones?"[6] Josquin's *Miserere* inspired a number of motets by composers of the next generation that were written as part of an anti-Medici political agenda and that made explicit the Josquin-Savonarola message.

Josquin's *Fama malum*

Fama malum, the text of which comes from Virgil's *Aeneid*, a popular source for sixteenth-century composers, contains a notable instance of word painting. The work opens with an expansive motive, each statement of which stretches out over three measures (Ex. 20-4a). The motive returns most prominently at measure 23 on the word "velocius" (swift), to which Josquin responds by doubling the motive's speed in the superius and tenor and chopping off the second half (the falling fifth) altogether in the altus (Ex. 20-4b). The speeding up is further highlighted by the reiteration of the motive off the beat, so that the effect is one of hurried syncopation.

EXAMPLE 20-4. Josquin, *Fama malum*: (a) mm. 1–7, (b) mm. 23–31.

6. In the preface to his *Secundus tomus novi operis musici*; quoted after Lowinsky, "Music in the Culture of the Renaissance," 524.

The setting of "velocius" is, to be sure, a small point. But it forecasts an idea that would take hold later in the century: expressing as literally and graphically as possible the meaning of individual words in the text. Combined with the Aristotelian concept that art should imitate nature, such word painting would become the aesthetic backbone of the late-sixteenth-century madrigal.

The Influence of Humanism

Who deserves the credit for this new attitude—and it was new—toward the relationship between music and text? The obvious answer is, humanism and the humanists. Motets like the three we have seen in this chapter result from the fallout of humanism's preoccupation with language, with the meaning and disposition of the word. But simply because Josquin and others turned to Virgil and neo-Latin verse does not mean that their motets are "humanist music." They are really hybrids of sorts: full-fledged products of Franco-Flemish poly-phony, but touched, even if indirectly, by the humanism that emanated from Italy. In fact, we might even argue that it was this very meeting of Franco-Flemish polyphony and the humanist desire for the expression of words and emotions that produced the greatest music of the sixteenth century.

CANONS

If there is anything that testifies to the distance between the Franco-Flemish composers of the Josquin era and the musical sensibilities of the humanists, it is the continued use of complicated polyphony. Though this now generally took the form of freewheeling points of imitation, there was also a conspicuous and virtuosic use of strict canon. We can see this canonic virtuosity in motets by two composers who sometimes get lost behind the bigger names: Jean Mouton and Antoine Brumel.

A Quadruple Canon by Mouton

Mouton spent the final two decades of his life, around 1502–22, as official composer of sorts at the French court, where he taught composition to a young law student named Adrian Willaert and thus played a major role in passing on the Franco-Flemish legacy to the next generation. He was particularly fond of

canon, especially as the controlling element of a piece, as in the eight-voice
Nesciens mater virgo virum (Ex. 20-5):

EXAMPLE 20-5. Mouton, *Nesciens mater virgo virum*, mm. 1–15.

Starting with an antiphon melody that he placed in tenor II, Mouton put together a quadruple canon, which runs along without interruption from the beginning to the end of the piece. The voices—only four of which are notated in the original until the canons break just before the final cadence—sing the four canons as follows: tenors II and I, basses II and I, altus II and superius II, and altus I and superius I.

A "Tight" Canon by Brumel

It is not only with the number of simultaneous canons that these composers dazzle us. Just as impressive are the various time intervals at which they spin the canons out, none more so than the tight interval of the minim in Antoine Brumel's *Laudate dominum in caelis.*

After stints at Chartres, Geneva, the court of Savoy, Laon, Notre Dame at Paris, and Savoy again, Brumel succeeded Josquin and Obrecht at Ferrara in 1506, by which time the duchy was ruled by Ercole's son Alfonso I. His lifetime contract called for an annual salary of a hundred ducats, an additional hundred ducats per year in benefices, a house in Ferrara, and travel expenses. He remained at Ferrara until the chapel was disbanded in 1510, after which time he drops out of sight.

Unlike Mouton's *Nesciens mater*, which is canonic from beginning to end, Brumel's *Laudate dominum in caelis* consists mainly of short bursts of canonic writing for two voices, alternating with noncanonic imitation and stark chordal writing. When the canons do appear, they are often at the head-spinning interval of a minim (transcribed here as an eighth note; Ex. 20-6):

EXAMPLE 20-6. Brumel, *Laudate dominum in caelis*: (a) mm. 19–25, (b) mm. 89–93.

The second of the two-part canons (mm. 23–25) begins at the interval of the semibreve (quarter note) and then tightens the distance to a minim by cutting in half the value of the fifth note of the *comes* (answer, in the bassus). Finally, we cannot help but wonder if these canons contain a bit of symbolism: could the two canons at measures 19–25 represent the sun/moon ("sol et luna") and stars/light ("stellae et lumen"), respectively; and could the added third voice in the canon at measures 89–93 be a result of the word "populo" (populace)?

What is so impressive about the canonic writing of the period is its feeling of effortlessness. Whereas Ockeghem's simultaneous mensuration canons in the *Missa Prolationum* almost call attention to themselves (they even give the Mass its name), Mouton's quadruple canon goes about its business without fanfare. It is probably the generation gap we are noticing: what strikes us as artifice and complexity in the 1450s and 1460s turns into sheer virtuosity by 1500.

SYMBOLISM

Symbolism in music, whether in the fifteenth and sixteenth centuries or any other, comes in many shapes and sizes. At times, it is perfectly obvious and audible, as we saw in Isaac's *Quis dabit capiti meo aquam*. At other times, when the symbolism is anything but clear, debates ensue as to whether the symbols are more the product of our imagination than the composer's.

In the music of the Josquin era, symbolism of the inaudible type appeared in various guises. Here we deal only with two: symbolism derived through the use of a *soggetto cavato dalle vocale* (a musical motive whose solmization syllables are drawn from the vowels of names or other words) and the more controversial number symbolism that depends on the application of gematria.

The *soggetto cavato dalle vocale*

As we saw in Chapter 18 in connection with Josquin's *Missa Hercules dux ferrariae*, a *soggetto cavato dalle vocale* yields a motive that itself becomes the symbol for that name. The *soggetto* symbolism is somewhat more subtle in another of Josquin's works, the motet *Illibata Dei virgo*, whose fame rests first and foremost on its presentation of the composer's name in the form of an acrostic in the *prima pars*:

Illibata Dei virgo nutrix,	**I**ncomparable Virgin, nurse of God,
Olympi tu regis o gentrix,	**O** thou Mother of the Olympian King,
Sola parens Verbi puerpera,	**S**ole parent and conceiver of the Word,
Quae fuisti Evae reparatrix,	**Q**uickening Redeemer thou wast of Eva's Fall,
Viri nefas tuta mediatrix,	**V**ouchsafing Mediator of man's sin,
Illud clara luce dat scriptura,	**I**n radiant light the Scriptures this reveal.

Nata nati alma genitura,

DES, ut laeta musorum
    factura

Praevaleat hymnus, et sit
    ave,

Roborando sonos, ut
    guttura

Efflagitent, laude teque
    pura

Zelotica arte clamet ave.

Nurturing womb—child of your
    Child—

DESign thou that the joyous
    melody, the Muses'

Paean, shall prevail and be an Ave,

Reverberating sounds wherewith
    our throats,

Entreat thee and, with pure praise
    and

Zealous art, proclaim thee our
    Ave.[7]

Quite aside from the acrostic, we see at a glance that the poem concerns the Virgin Mary. Josquin builds the motet on the following *soggetto*, which is disposed, as it so often was, in ostinato fashion in the tenor (Ex. 20-7):

EXAMPLE 20-7. Josquin, *Illibata Dei virgo*: the tenor's *soggetto* (*prima pars*).

Given the signature of one flat, the hexachords that would normally be built on C (natural), F (soft), and G (hard) move one step flatward to F, B-flat, and C, as the entire set of three hexachords is transposed down a fifth. Thus the motives $d'-a-d'$ and $g-d-g$ will have the solmization syllables *la-mi-la* in the natural (F) and soft (B-flat) hexachords, respectively. For whom is *la-mi-la* a symbol? For M*a-ri-a!* And should there be any doubt about the matter, it is put to rest by the eighth line of the *seconda pars*: "Consola 'la mi la' canentes in tua laude," which can be rendered as "Comfort those singing in thy praise, 'Maria.'" The *soggetto*, then, is very much a symbol for the subject of the piece.

Number Symbolism and Gematria

Hardly anything so irks symbolism skeptics as claims that the structure of a composition is determined by number symbolism, especially when the symbolism involves gematria. Yet the numbers are often there, and to insist that their presence is merely coincidence is to strain commonsensical notions of chance. For instance, not only does Josquin's name appear in the text of *Illibata Dei virgo* as an acrostic, it is embedded in his treatment of the tenor's *soggetto*. The three-note *la-mi-la* motive is stated twenty-nine times, after which the cantus firmus ends on a single note. There are therefore 88 notes in all, the number equivalent to the name "Desprez" (4 + 5 + 18 + 15 + 17 + 5 + 24). Josquin thus signs the piece both through the acrostic and through the number of notes in the tenor.

7. The translation, which ingeniously preserves the acrostic, is by William S. Heckscher and
    Virginia Callahan; it appears in Antonowytsch, "'Illibata Dei Virgo,'" 558–59.

THE FUNCTION OF THE MOTET

Unlike the Mass, the function of which liturgical propriety fixes precisely, the motet seems to float in space and time. Until recently, the thinking about the function of the motet went something like this: many motets from the period set a text that has its own prescribed place in the liturgy, whether in the Mass or in the Office; such motets also draw on the plainsong associated with the text, so that they must have been used as liturgical substitutes for the texts-plainsongs. Yet evidence indicates that the presumed one-to-one relationship between liturgical association (text and plainsong) and motet's function does not necessarily hold. Instead, as the sixteenth-century diaries of the Sistine Chapel make extremely clear, the motet, no matter what its text, was interpolated into the Mass as an *extra*-liturgical ornament, a filler of sorts, usually during the offertory, the Elevation of the Host, the communion, or at the very end of the Mass.

Even a motet that drew on a text and plainsong from the Office (Mouton's *Nesciens mater*, for instance) could be sung during the course of the Mass. The crossover applied to feasts as well; thus a motet that the Spanish composer Cristóbal de Morales based on an antiphon from the feast of Corpus Christi was sung at the Offertory of the Mass on Holy Thursday. The motet, then, could float in and out of various liturgical contexts, a quality that certainly led to the composition of many works based on either paraphrased or centonized (that is, a patchwork of) texts. Since the motet did not have a specific liturgical destination, it could set texts whose liturgical associations (or nonassociations) were just as free.

Finally, the motet was at home in a number of other contexts: (1) The seemingly endless supply of motets on Marian texts could be used at the devotional services that took place in Marian chapels after Compline. (2) At Milan in particular, a series of motets could be brought together to form a cycle called *motetti missales*, in which they served as substitutes for various parts of the Mass. (3) Motets were sung as dinner or after-dinner music; on one occasion in 1520, the music-loving Pope Leo X—who, had technology permitted, might have walked around with a Walkman—heard a Josquin *Salve regina* while sitting at the dinner table (thus combining two of his favorite pastimes, music and eating). And (4) as we saw in Chapter 17, motets could be played by instrumental ensembles.

The motet was at home virtually everywhere, and this flexibility no doubt helped it become the most popular sacred genre of the sixteenth century.

BIBLIOGRAPHICAL NOTE

Editions of the Music

All three composers (besides Josquin) whose works are discussed in the chapter have been—or are being—treated to complete works editions. **Antoine Brumel**: *Opera omnia*, *CMM* 5, 6 vols., ed. Barton Hudson (American Institute of Musicology, 1969–72). **Pierre de la Rue**: *Opera omnia*, *CMM* 97, ed. Nigel St. John Davison, J. Evan Kreider, and

T. Herman Keahey (American Institute of Musicology, 1989–). **Jean Mouton**: *Opera omnia*, *CMM* 43, ed. Andrew C. Minor (American Institute of Musicology, 1967–). In addition, there is an ambitious 30-volume project that will include hundreds of previously unpublished motets: *The Sixteenth-Century Motet*, ed. Richard Sherr (New York: Garland, 1991–).

General Studies

No single study surveys the entire motet repertory of the Josquin generation; one starting point is Edward E. Lowinsky's *Medici Codex of 1518: A Choirbook of Motets Dedicated to Lorenzo de' Medici, Duke of Urbino*, *MRM* 3–5 (Chicago: University of Chicago Press, 1968), which includes facsimile and modern editions of the manuscript Florence, Biblioteca Laurenziana, Doni 666, together with a discussion of the music (one must disregard Lowinsky's notions about the provenance of the manuscript).

Music and Words

A good discussion of the differences between the direct and indirect influences of humanism on the relationship between music and words is chapter 4, "The Impact of Humanism," in Don Harrán, *Word-Tone Relations in Musical Thought from Antiquity to the Seventeenth Century*, *MSD* 40 (American Institute of Musicology, 1986); on music and rhetoric, see George J. Buelow's article "Rhetoric and Music," in *New Grove*, 15: 793–803; see also Nigel Davison, "*Absalom, fili mi* Reconsidered," *TVNM* 46 (1996): 42–56.

Pitch

For an introduction to this knotty problem, see Kenneth Kreitner, "Renaissance Pitch," in *Companion to Medieval and Renaissance Music*, ed. Tess Knighton and David Fallows (New York: Schirmer, 1992), 275–83. See also Kreitner, "Very Low Ranges in the Sacred Music of Ockeghem and Tinctoris," *EM* 14 (1986): 477–79; Arthur Mendel, "Pitch in Western Music since 1500: A Re-examination," *AcM* 50 (1978): 1–93.

Symbolism

See the works by Willem Elders listed in the Bibliographical Note in Chapter 7.

The Function of the Motet

The required reading is Anthony M. Cummings, "Toward an Interpretation of the Sixteenth-Century Motet," *JAMS* 34 (1981): 43–59; see also Jeremy Noble, "The Function of Josquin's Motets," *TVNM* 35 (1985): 9–31.

Composition as Profession

See the important essay by Rob C. Wegman, "From Maker to Composer: Improvisation and Musical Authorship in the Low Countries, 1450–1500," *JAMS* 49 (1996): 409–79.

Also Cited

Stanley Sadie, ed., *The New Grove High Renaissance Masters* (New York: Norton, 1984); Edward E. Lowinsky, "Music in the Culture of the Renaissance," *JHI* 15 (1954): 509–53; Leo Treitler, *Music and the Historical Imagination* (Cambridge: Harvard University Press, 1989); David Fallows, "The Performing Ensembles in Josquin's Sacred Music," *TVNM* 35 (1985): 32–66; Myroslaw Antonowytsch, "'Illibata Dei Virgo': A Melodic Self-Portrait of Josquin des Prez," in *Josquin des Prez: Proceedings of the International Josquin Festival Conference,* ed. Edward Lowinsky and Bonnie J. Blackburn (London: Oxford University Press, 1976), 545–59.

CHAPTER 21

Editing a Chanson: Text Underlay

Now that we have considered the music-word relationship in three Josquin motets, it is time to do the same for our Busnoys chanson, but from a different point of view: How do music and words fit together in the first place? That we even have to ask the question might seem strange, for the relationship between syllables and notes is something we take for granted in the vocal music of composers from Monteverdi to Schubert to Stravinsky (or back to Gregorian chant, for that matter): the composer has made it clear.

Unfortunately, so everyday an assumption will not hold for most music of the fifteenth and early sixteenth centuries. Even a quick glance at *A vous sans autre* as it appears in either Dijon 517 or Mellon shows that the scribes made virtually no attempt to align notes and syllables with precision. And this is the rule rather than the exception. In fact, *A vous sans autre* presents more problems than most pieces, since it is not even clear which line of poetry goes with which phrase of music. It seems that matching words with music, like the addition of unnotated accidentals, was left up to the performers, so that we must wrestle with what is possibly the most frustrating task in preparing our edition of Busnoys's chanson: the problem of text underlay.

THE POEM

Any consideration of text underlay can only begin after we are fully acquainted with the poem. Here it is as it appears in the cramped script—called *lettre bâtard*—of Dijon 517:

1. **A** vous sans autre me viens rendre,   To you and no other do I come in surrender;
2. **Il** m'est force qu'ainsi le face;   So must I do perforce.
3. **A** ce me contraint *vostre* grace,   To this your grace constrains me,
4. **Qui** tant est belle, doulce et tendre.   [Your grace] so gentle, fair, and tender.

5. **Vueillez** vo pitié condescendre   Pray vouchsafe your pity
6. **Envers** moi qui de prime face   To me, who, at first sight,

7.   A vous sans autre me viens rendre,   [Comes] to you and no other in surrender;
8.   Il m'est force qu'ainsi le face.   So must I do perforce.

9. **Le** vous dire n'ose entreprendre,   I dare not tell you what I feel;
10. **Jamais** en moi n'eust tant d'audace;   Never could I be so bold

11.	**N**e au moins pretendant estre en grace					Except to ask the boon of being in your favor—		
12.	**E**n tant que honneur se [pout] estendre.					As far as honor will allow.		
13.	**A** vous sans autre me viens rendre,					To you and no other I come in surrender;		
14.	**I**l m'est force qu'ainsi le face;					So must I do perforce.		
15.	**A** ce me contraint vostre grace,					To this your grace constrains me,		
16.	**Q**ui tant est belle, doulce et tendre.					[Your grace] so gentle, fair, and tender.[1]		

(In Mellon, the final word of line 3 is "face," in line 12 and the penultimate word is "peult.")

The poem is a straightforward example of a rondeau quatrain, though one in which the short strophe (lines 5–6) links up with the short refrain (lines 7–8) in such a way that an abbreviated medial refrain of only one line might be in order. In addition, the first letter of each line forms an acrostic that produces "A IAQVELJNE"; thus *A vous sans autre* belongs among Busnoys's "Jacqueline" songs (see Chapter 14).

SYLLABIFICATION

Before aligning syllables and notes, we must split up each of the lines according to its proper syllabification. The refrain behaves as follows:

A	vous	sans	au	– tre	me		viens	ren	– dre,
Il	m'est	for	– ce	qu'ain	– si	le	fa		– ce;
A	ce	me	con	– traint	vos	– tre	gra		– ce,
Qui	tant	est	bel	– le	doul	– ce et	ten	– dre.	

In French poetry, all final syllables that end with the mute "e" are pronounced, but the final mute "e" syllable in the line is not included in the syllable count. Also, adjacent vowels ending one word and beginning the next are elided and counted as a single syllable (for instance, the words "doulce et" in line 4 constitute two syllables). Thus each line in the poem is octosyllabic. We may syllabify the remaining lines in similar fashion.

THE THEORISTS AND THEIR RULES

Though it may seem odd, there is not a single useful statement from the fifteenth century about how notes and syllables are to be aligned. The situation changes drastically in the sixteenth century. Beginning in the 1530s, theorists produced an avalanche of rules concerning text underlay. Four treatises in particular, none of which is devoted exclusively to the subject, form the core: Giovanni Maria Lanfranco, *Scintille di musica* (1533); Nicola Vicentino, *L'antica musica ridotta alla moderna prattica* (1555); Gioseffo Zarlino, *Le istitutioni harmo-*

1. The translation follows Perkins and Garey, *The Mellon Chansonnier*, 2: 364–65.

niche (1558); and Gaspar Stocker, *De musica verbali* (c. 1570). Stocker's discussion is particularly interesting. With an eye on history and style, he divides his rules into those that apply to contemporary composers (Willaert and after) and those that were used by the "antichi" (the Josquin generation); he then subdivides the two groups into rules that are obligatory and those that are not.

To read the rules is dizzying: some are addressed to singers, others to composers; at times the theorists contradict one another; even a single treatise will sometimes offer one rule that rubs against another; and there seem to be almost as many exceptions as there are rules. And looming over the entire matter: can anything these sixteenth-century theorists say be applied to a chanson by Busnoys that may date from the 1450s? The answer would seem to be a very cautious yes. Some of the rules are merely commonsensical, as when we are told to align the first syllable with the first note. Others seem to have origins that go back to the composition and performance of plainsong, such as the rule that a ligature—the equivalent, in a way, of a plainsong *neume*—can carry only one syllable. Moreover, Lanfranco, the earliest of the four theorists, does not seem to be spearheading an aesthetic-stylistic revolution, and the fact that there is far more agreement than disagreement among the theorists may indicate that a long-standing tradition was already in place. And finally, without them, we have nothing!

Following are seven of Lanfranco's rules, in the order in which he presents them:

(1) Semantic divisions of the text should coincide with the cadences of the musical phrases.

(2) Every separate note that is a minim (a quarter note in our transcription) or larger should receive a syllable of its own.

(3) A ligature should customarily receive no more than a single syllable.

(4) A semiminim (eighth note) that follows a dotted minim rarely gets a syllable of its own; nor does the note that follows it.

(5) In a series of semiminims, only the first gets a syllable, and this syllable is then sustained through the series and into the note that follows the semiminims.

(6) If there are more notes than syllables, it is usually the penultimate syllable that has the melisma, the last syllable being assigned to the last note.

(7) Words can be repeated if there are enough notes to accommodate them, though the repeated words should be semantically and syntactically self-sufficient.

BUSNOYS'S CHANSON

Text underlay is slow, painstaking work. The placement of virtually every syllable requires us to ask questions and make decisions, to try to ferret out both what Busnoys might have intended and what a fifteenth-century singer might have done. And as we do so, we must never lose sight of one thing: there is probably no single solution. It would be presumptuous of us to think we could find one. At best, there are parameters within which singers must have had a fair amount of leeway.

Example 21-1 shows four different ways in which the first five syllables of line 1, "A vous sans autre," might be underlaid beneath the first phrase of the superius:

EXAMPLE 21-1. *A vous sans autre*, superius, mm. 1–6.

Not a single solution manages to underlay the five syllables without violating one of Lanfranco's rules. Thus if we wish to follow rule 6 and assign the melisma to the penultimate syllable and reserve the final syllable for the final note of the phrase, we must violate the rule that prohibits placing a new syllable on the first note after a series (here a pair) of semiminims (rule 5). There is no way around the problem, as each solution places at least one new syllable after a semiminim (see rule 4). Indeed, the only way to avoid that would be to use up all five syllables on the first five notes, and that is simply unmusical.

Example 21-2 chooses one of the solutions for the first phrase and then takes the superius to the cadence in measure 8:

EXAMPLE 21-2. *A vous sans autre*, superius, mm. 1–8.

This solution is pretty straightforward; nothing else makes sense.

There are questions, though, when we reach the third phrase of music, beginning at measure 9; and in order to appreciate the problem at that point, we must consider the second line of the poem and look at the superius as it extends to the medial cadence (Ex. 21-3):

EXAMPLE 21-3. *A vous sans autre*, superius, mm. 1–19.

The first two lines of the poem consist of four semantically self-sufficient half lines, which, however, must be sung to five phrases of music. Do we introduce line 2 at measure 9, or do we extend line 1 through the third phrase, reserving line 2 for the phrase that begins on the final beat of measure 12? Introducing line 2 at measure 9 has the advantage of causing line 1 to end conclusively on the tonic *d′*, a characteristic of many fifteenth-century chansons, so that semantic and tonal closure coincide precisely.

On the other hand, reserving line 2 until measure 12 allows it to begin on a point of imitation between superius and tenor, as does each of the other three lines of the refrain. It is, after all, beneath the *a′* in measure 12 that the scribes of both Dijon 517 and the Mellon Chansonnier placed the first word of line 2; and though neither scribe took particular care in aligning notes with syllables, both seem to have paid attention to the more general coincidence of poetic lines and musical phrases.

In the end, the evidence that favors holding back line 2 until measure 12 is compelling. For the moment, then, we must make only one more decision: should phrase three simply be sung to a melisma on the syllable "dre," or should we, as Lanfranco and the other theorists say we can (rule 7), repeat the final portion of line 1, making sure that the repeated words can stand on their own semantically? Again, there is no right or wrong answer. Example 21-4 shows one possible solution to the underlay of lines 1 and 2 in their entirety:

EXAMPLE 21-4. *A vous sans autre*, superius, mm. 1–19.

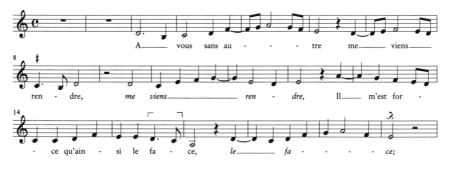

The next step is to complete the underlay of lines 3 and 4 of the refrain. Line 3 gets under way with the very next note of the superius (m. 20), while the final line begins on the *e′* of measure 32.

Having underlaid the refrain, we next proceed to the short (lines 5–6) and long (lines 9–12) strophes. One prevalent approach is to dispose the syllables of these lines so that they line up precisely with the same notes as the corresponding syllables of the refrain. Although this will usually work, and is generally the easiest way out, we will run into problems if we try it here. Unfortunately, *A vous sans autre* is one of those rondeaux in which the corresponding lines of the refrain, short strophe, and long strophe do not always have the *caesura*—the break that splits the line into semantically self-sufficient units—

after the same syllable. We can see this if we compare the first line of the refrain with its counterpart in the long strophe:

A	vous	sans		au	-	tre /	me	-	viens	ren	-	dre
Le	vous	di	-	re	n'o	-	se/en	-	tre	-	pren	-	dre

In line 1 of the refrain, the cadence after the fifth syllable preserves the semantic sense of the line. Having the cadence coincide with the same syllable of the first line of the long strophe, on the other hand, butchers the semantic sense of that line. Here, we must either squeeze six syllables beneath the first phrase—through "n'ose"—which precludes an elision with "entreprendre," or we fool Jacqueline for a moment, delay "n'ose," and give the first phrase only the four syllables "Le vous dire" and pack five syllables tightly into the second phrase. The first option seems preferable. In either event, the syllables of the two lines will not fall beneath the same notes.

As if underlaying the text to the superius alone were not enough trouble, we must decide if that is the only voice to which the text should be added. If not, we must then ask the same questions all over again for the other voices.

If there is any aspect of editing fifteenth-century secular song that will humble us, that will make us sweat, it is the text underlay. To be sure, some editors simply cop out: after all, does it really matter if a given syllable is one note to the west or two notes to the east? How can we know just how Busnoys wanted it or how a fifteenth-century singer performed it? There are, however, no excuses. A good edition is nothing less than a performance by the editor. And just as we would growl if we paid to hear a performance of Busnoys songs in which the performers merely hummed, we should not be satisfied with an edition that wished that the problem of text underlay would just go away.

BIBLIOGRAPHICAL NOTE

General

The fundamental study is Don Harrán's monumental *Word-Tone Relations in Musical Thought from Antiquity to the Seventeenth Century*, MSD 40 (American Institute of Musicology, 1986); for a succinct summary of the theorists' rules, see the valuable compilation in Gary Towne, "A Systematic Formulation of Sixteenth-Century Text Underlay Rules," MD 44 (1990): 255–87; 45 (1991): 143–68. Also useful: Graeme Boone, *Patterns in Play: A Model for Text-Setting Procedures in the Early Chansons of Guillaume Dufay*, AMS Monographs (Lincoln: University of Nebraska Press, 1998); Howard Mayer Brown, "Words and Music in Early Sixteenth-Century Chansons: Text Underlay in Florence, Biblioteca del Conservatorio, MS Basevi 2442," in *Formen und Probleme der Überlieferung mehrstimmiger Musik im Zeitalter Josquins Desprez*, Quellenstudien zur Musik der Renaissance 1, ed. Ludwig Finscher (Munich: Kraus, 1981), 97–141; Honey Meconi, "Is Underlay Necessary?" in *Companion to Medieval and Renaissance Music*, ed. Tess Knighton and David Fallows (New York: Schirmer, 1992), 284–91; Leeman L. Perkins, "Toward a Rational Approach to Text Placement in the Secular Music of Dufay's Time," in *Papers Read at the Dufay Quincentenary Conference*, ed. Allan W. Atlas (Brooklyn: Brooklyn College, 1976), 102–14;

The Four Core Theorists

Lanfranco: Don Harrán, "New Light on the Question of Text Underlay Prior to Zarlino," *AcM* 45 (1973): 24–56. **Vincentino**: Harrán, "Vincentino and His Rules of Text Underlay," *MQ* 59 (1973): 620–32. **Zarlino**: his discussion of text underlay is printed in *"On the Modes": Part Four of Le Istitutioni Harmoniche*, trans. Vered Cohen (New Haven: Yale University Press, 1983); and Strunk, *Source Readings*. **Stocker**: Edward E. Lowinsky, "A Treatise on Text Underlay by a German Disciple of Francisco de Salinas," in *Festschrift Heinrich Besseler zu Sechzigsten Geburtstag* (Leipzig: Deutscher Verlag für Musik, 1961), 231–51; Albert C. Rotola, *De musica verbali libri duo: Two Books on Verbal Music*, Greek and Latin Music Theory 5 (Lincoln: University of Nebraska Press, 1988).

Abbreviated Refrain

See Leeman L. Perkins and Howard Garey, eds., *The Mellon Chansonnier*, 2 vols. (New Haven: Yale University Press, 1979); Garey, "The Fifteenth-Century Rondeau as Aleatory Polytext," *Le Moyen français* 5 (1979): 193–236, and "Can a Rondeau with a One-Line Refrain Be Sung?" *Ars lyrica* 2 (1983): 9–21; Howard Mayer Brown, "A Rondeau with a One-Line Refrain Can Be Sung," *Ars lyrica* 3 (1986): 27–35; Allan W. Atlas, "Some Thoughts about One-Line Refrains in Ockeghem's Rondeaux," *Proceedings of the Colloque Ockeghem* (Tours, February 3–8, 1997).

Also Cited

Leeman L. Perkins and Howard Garey, eds., *The Mellon Chansonnier*, 2 vols. (New Haven: Yale University Press, 1979).

CHAPTER 22

Continuity and Transformation in the Mass

As we saw in Chapter 11, the third quarter of the fifteenth century witnessed an explosion in music for the Mass, as the genre expanded with both tremendous energy and a highly focused sense of direction. At the heart of all the activity was the cyclic setting of the Ordinary based on a structural cantus firmus. To review, the cantus firmus could appear in a number of guises: it could be quoted literally, in slowly moving note values; it could be manipulated rhythmically through diminution, augmentation, or mensural transformations; it could be transposed, turned upside down, or sung in retrograde motion; and its melody could be decorated through embellishment that ranged from light to lavish. In addition, a Mass that was based on a preexistent three-voice chanson might quote the entire polyphonic complex of the model, though eventually a single voice part invariably came to the fore and served as the structural scaffold.

Composers of the Josquin generation continued to cultivate this tradition. But they also wrote Masses based on two new principles: (1) Even when a preexistent melody (a plainsong, for example) served as the basis of a Mass, the new practice of pervading imitation stripped it of its role as a structural backbone in the tenor and sent it shooting—often with melodic embellishment—through all the voice parts; the result is often called a "paraphrase" Mass. (2) When basing a Mass on a preexistent polyphonic complex, composers began to turn to the contemporary motet literature and transform individual motives from the imitative, equal-voice, polyphonic fabric into the structural pillars of the Mass. The resulting "parody" or "imitation" Mass would come to be the favorite type of the sixteenth century. Thus pervading imitation, which must be regarded as the single most important stylistic innovation of the Josquin generation, had a profound impact on the Mass, influencing everything from its surface style to its structural foundations.

There were also developments that went beyond the choice and treatment of the model. Some Masses actually eschewed the idea of cyclic unity and used a different preexistent melody as the basis of each movement. And finally, a number of local Mass types took on new importance, especially in the German-speaking lands of central Europe.

Compared with the motets, the Masses of the Josquin generation may strike us as somewhat conservative and perhaps even colorless, lacking the motets' intense verbal component and the humanist-inspired emphasis on expressing the meaning and emotion of the text. But after all, we can excuse composers if they were not quite as moved by the formulaic "Glory to God on high, and on earth peace to men of good will" as they were, say, by "Let me live no longer, but descend into hell weeping." On the other hand, the Mass was no poor cousin in terms of compositional virtuosity: contrapuntal mastery, spectacular displays of ingenuity in treating a cantus firmus, whole movements cast as canons, tonal control of large-scale structures, and even feats of number symbolism abound.

We will approach the Mass differently than we did the motet. Rather than singling out specific characteristics, we will pull the lens back a bit and survey the numerous types of Masses that were cultivated. And if we lose some of the detail, we compensate by viewing the genre in all its variety.

THE HEART OF THE TRADITION

As noted above, Josquin and his contemporaries cultivated three clearly definable Mass types: cantus-firmus Mass, paraphrase Mass, and parody Mass, each of which grew out of techniques developed during the third quarter of the fifteenth century.

The Cantus-Firmus Mass and Obrecht

No composer seems to have been more content to continue the tradition of the scaffold-like cantus-firmus Mass than Jacob Obrecht. Obrecht was born on November 22 in 1457 or 1458; we can calculate the year from a recently discovered portrait of the composer (Fig. 22-1) that dates from 1496 and gives his age as thirty-eight. Furthermore, the text of one of his motets, *Mille quingentis*, written to commemorate the death of his father in 1488, tells us that he was the son of Willem Obrecht (a well-to-do civic trumpeter in the city of Ghent and a sometime employee of Philip the Good's court of Burgundy) and that he was born on St. Cecilia's Day (Cecilia is honored as the patron saint of music). We know nothing specific about Obrecht's life until August 1480, from which time until his death in July 1505 we can track him almost on a month-to-month basis.

Unlike the well-traveled Du Fay and Josquin or the court-connected Busnoys and Ockeghem, Obrecht led the relatively unglamorous, geographically circumscribed life of an everyday church musician. We might even say that he was stuck in a rut, as twice he completed a triangular circuit of positions at Bergen op Zoom, Bruges, and Antwerp, the three sides of which add up to a mere 140 miles. Only occasionally was this pattern broken: first by an appointment at the Cathedral of Cambrai and then by two trips to Ferrara, one in the 1480s, the other in the final year of his life, when he succeeded Josquin as Ercole I's chapel master (though at half Josquin's salary). Yet the Ferrarese sojourn ended on a sour note: Obrecht took up the post in September 1504;

Figure 22-1. Portrait of Jacob Obrecht by an unknown Flemish artist, 1496 (Kimbell Museum, Fort Worth).

in January 1505, Duke Ercole died, and two weeks later Ercole's son and successor, Alfonso I, summarily dismissed the composer. Obrecht died there in July, a victim of the plague.

We can only wonder why Obrecht (a priest and holder of a master's degree) never obtained a secure position at one of the great princely courts, something he no doubt craved. Certainly it was not for lack of talent (though there is circumstantial evidence that his voice was less than golden). More likely, the reason had to do with his apparently difficult personality. Obrecht's career is studded with broken contracts, overstayed leaves of absence, embezzlement of funds, and lack of care for the choirboys in his charge. This last problem is alluded to in a document of July 27, 1485, when Obrecht was choirmaster at the Cathedral of Cambrai: "[New] linen clothes are to be made for the little children of the choir, and the *magnus minister* is to tell their master [Obrecht] that he should look to their government and condition more carefully than he has done so far, for they have contracted scabies, which is not otherwise seen."[1]

Dereliction of duties and difficulties of personality aside, Obrecht enjoyed international repute as a composer. In some revisions of around 1480 to his *Complexus effectum musices*, Tinctoris reels off the names of the most distinguished musicians of the fifteenth century, mentioning Dunstable, Du Fay, Binchois, Ockeghem, Busnoys . . . and Obrecht, the only member of his gen-

1. Quoted after Wegman, *Born for the Muses*, 135.

eration to be so honored—and this when Obrecht was all of twenty-three! It was for his Masses in particular that Obrecht gained his fame.

MISSA FORTUNA DESPERATA   Composed around 1490, and thus one of Obrecht's mature masterpieces, the *Missa Fortuna desperata* is based primarily on the tenor of one of the great chanson hits of the late fifteenth century, *Fortuna desperata* (Ex. 22-1), sometimes attributed to Busnoys.

EXAMPLE 22-1. Busnoys (?), tenor of *Fortuna desperata*.

We can see Obrecht's mastery of cantus-firmus technique in the Gloria and Credo (*Anthology* 41), where he uses three of his favorite techniques: segmentation, though here the number of segments—just two—is very small; retrograde motion; and the use of the segmented cantus firmus to organize vast stretches of music (the two movements run on for almost 450 measures).

To appreciate Obrecht's ingenuity, we must look at the Gloria in some detail. Table 22-1 charts the comings and goings of the cantus firmus in the tenor, here the next-to-highest part:

Table 22-1.   Obrecht, *Missa Fortuna desperata*, Gloria; organization of
               sections with and without the cantus firmus.

Part I/Section 1 (measures 1–54)

	4 mm.	a2	no cantus firmus (CF; starts with tenor's *f'* "signal")
(m.5)	8 mm.	a3	no CF
(m.13)	30 mm.	a4	with CF, mm. 1–31 (of chanson tenor) retrograde
(m.43)	8 mm.	a3	no CF
(m.51)	4 mm.	a2	no CF

Part I/Section 2 (measures 55–109)

	12 mm.	a3	no CF (starts with tenor's *f'* signal)
(m.67)	30 mm.	a4	with CF, mm. 32–57 normal
(m.97)	12 mm.	a3	no CF

Part II/Section 1 (measures 110–163)

	6 mm.	a3	no CF (starts with tenor's *f'* signal)
(m.116)	6 mm.	a2	no CF
(m.122)	30 mm.	a4	with CF, mm. 1–31 retrograde
(m.152)	12 mm.	a3	no CF

Part II/Section 2 (measures 164–218)

	12 mm.	a3	no CF (starts with tenor's *f'* signal)
(m.176)	30 mm.	a4	CF, mm. 32–57 normal
(m.206)	12 mm.	a3	no CF (plus one extra measure at end for final long)

Source: Antonowytsch, "Renaissance-Tendenzen," 12f.

As we see in the table, there are two parts, each of which is divided into two sections; each section is fifty-four measures long (plus one final measure at the very end of the movement) and is announced by a signal-like *f'* in the tenor; each section begins and ends with a twelve-measure passage that lacks the cantus firmus, with this symmetry further reflected by the number of voices that take part; the middle of each section consists of a thirty-measure statement of the cantus firmus (within each of which there is a three-measure rest along the way); and the retrograde statement of the first half of the cantus firmus in section 1 of each part is answered by the normal statement of the second half of the cantus firmus in section 2, so that each section 2 is a mirror of the preceding section 1.

Had Obrecht stopped there, we would admire the rationalism of his ground plan; we will stand in awe of it by the time we reach the end of the Credo. That the Credo is up to something first becomes evident when we compare its length with that of the Gloria: both movements are 218 measures long. And like the Gloria, the Credo is divided into two parts of two sections each, with the cantus firmus sounding in thirty measures of each section. Table 22-2, which is concerned only with the thirty cantus-firmus measures of each section, shows how the movements are related:

Table 22-2.   Obrecht, *Missa Fortuna desperata*; relationship
between Gloria and Credo.

	Section of cantus firmus used	30-measure cantus-firmus period
GLORIA		
Part I/ Section 1	31 → 1	10 + 3r^a + 17
Part I/ Section 2	32 → 57	5 + 3r + 22
Part II/Section 1	31 → 1	10 + 3r + 17
Part II/Section 2	32 → 57	5 + 3r + 22
CREDO		
Part I/ Section 1	57 → 32	22 + 3r + 5
Part I/ Section 2	1 → 31	17 + 3r + 10
Part II/Section 1	57 → 32	22 + 3r + 5
Part II/Section 2	1 → 31	17 + 3r + 10

^{a}Three measures of rests.

Thus the Credo is a palindrome of the Gloria. The conception is intellectually stunning, even if it is probably not audible.

MISSA *DE TOUS BIENS PLAINE*   If Obrecht's segmentation of the cantus firmus in *Fortuna desperata* was used to articulate structure on the largest level, his use of the technique in the three-voice *Missa De tous biens plaine* approaches the spirit of a game. Example 22-2 gives the tenor of the Hayne van Ghizeghem chanson on which it is based:

EXAMPLE 22-2. Hayne van Ghizeghem, *De tous biens plaine*, tenor in original note values.

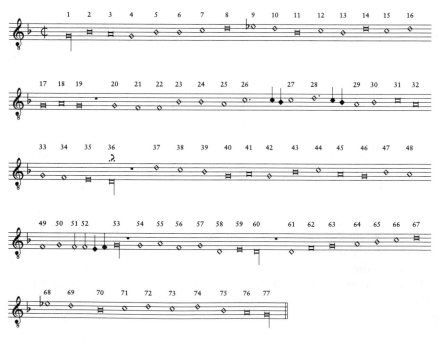

And example 22-3 shows two excerpts from the beginning of Obrecht's Credo:

EXAMPLE 22-3. Obrecht, *Missa De tous biens plaine*, Credo: (a) mm. 1–20, (b) mm. 38–50.

Obrecht first uses all the notes of Hayne's tenor that were notated as longs, then all the breves, and finally all the semibreves. Having used up all the notes by the end of the Credo's first section, Obrecht begins the plan again at the "Et incarnatus est," but now he plucks the notes—still ordered according to original note values—out of Hayne's melody in retrograde order.

In the Sanctus, Obrecht splits Hayne's tenor into eight segments and presents them in the following order: notes 1–4, 61–77, 54–60, 44–53, 37–43, 29–36, 20–28, and 5–19. In other words, the notes within each segment appear in their normal, recognizable order, but the segments themselves—after the first—are presented backward. For Obrecht, then, the cantus firmus became something of a plaything; and he often sacrificed its melodic identity to a conception of musical structure that verges on twentieth-century serialism.

ANOTHER SIDE OF OBRECHT   Obrecht was not interested only in highly rationalistic structures. He displays quite another side in the opening of the Kyrie of the *Missa Fortuna desperata* (Ex. 22-4):

EXAMPLE 22-4. Obrecht, *Missa Fortuna desperata*, Kyrie, mm. 1–31.

Here clarity and simplicity rule: cadences occur, for a while, every four measures; there is movement away from the tonic (m. 22) and back to it (mm. 29–31); and there are oft-repeated motives, pairs of voices running along in parallel tenths, and rhythmic regularity. The music can strike us as being countrybumpkinish, a view shared by Paolo Cortese in his *De cardinalatu* of 1510: "Iacobus Obrechius has been considered . . . in the whole style of composition somewhat rough." Glarean was kinder in his *Dodecachordon* (1547):

> All the works this man has left have a certain wondrous grandeur and an instrinsic quality of moderation. Indeed he was not such a lover of the unusual as was Josquin. He was one who displayed his talent, but without pretense, as if he preferred to await the judgment of the listener rather than to preen himself.[2]

The Paraphrase Mass

We enter a very different structural world with the paraphrase Mass, one in which fantasy perhaps gets the upper hand on rationalism. There is no better example of the paraphrase Mass than Josquin's *Missa Pange lingua*, possibly the latest of his Masses and certainly one of the most beautiful of the period. Josquin based the Mass on St. Thomas Aquinas's hymn *Pange lingua gloriosi corporis mysterium*, sung at Vespers on the Feast of Corpus Christi (Ex. 22-5):

EXAMPLE 22-5. The plainsong hymn *Pange lingua gloriosi*, first stanza, with phrases numbered 1–6.[3]

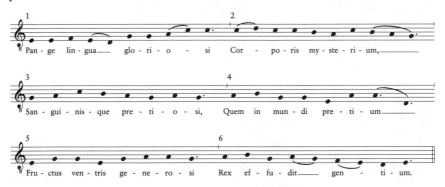

The Kyrie of the Mass (*Anthology* 42) provides a clear illustration of Josquin's paraphrase technique. To begin with, Josquin apportions the six phrases of the melody across the entire movement—two each in Kyrie I, "Christe," and Kyrie II—incorporating all but the final phrase into full-blown points of imitation. Table 22-3 shows the details (the numbers in parentheses are the measures at which the voices enter; italics indicate that the voice part carries the melody at its original pitch).

Nowhere in the Kyrie, then, does Josquin relegate the plainsong melody to any one voice in scaffold-like fashion (we must wait until the Agnus III for the

---

2. Both quotations are drawn from Wegman, *Born for the Muses*, 282–84. Glarean also tells us that among the choirboys who had once been in Obrecht's charge was the young Erasmus of Rotterdam, who would become the most famous northern humanist of his time (see Chapter 23).

3. *Liber usualis*, 957.

Table 22-3. Josquin's treatment of the *Pange lingua* melody.

Kyrie I:	Phrase 1	T	(1)	B	(2)	S	(5)	A (6)
	Phrase 2	B	(9)	T	(10)	S	(11)	
Christie:	Phrase 3	B	(17)	A	(19)	T	(25)	S (27)
	Phrase 4	A	(35)	B	(37)	S	(42)	T (44)
Kyrie II:	Phrase 5	S	(53)	A	(54)	T	(57)	B (58)
	Phrase 6	S	(60)					

entire melody to emerge in the superius). Rather, the hymn tune darts from voice to voice, permeating every corner of the polyphonic fabric. Nor do any of the voices quote the plainsong melody exactly. At times, in fact, Josquin isolates a single motive from the plainsong and develops it extensively, as in the final exclamation of "Kyrie eleison" (m. 60 to the end): the falling third *b′–g′*, drawn literally from the chant, first descends sequentially in the superius (mm. 61–63), the *a′* and *g′* themselves outlining the plainsong melody along the way; the falling third motive then sneaks in again at measure 64, inverts itself into the powerful rhythmic buildup at measures 65–66, and finally stretches out in the altus and bassus in a way that grounds the energy in the coda-like measures 68–69. Thus the plainsong melody is a constant source of melodic inspiration.

At times, though, it is not so easy to pinpoint the precise source of that inspiration. As a case in point, consider a short passage in the Gloria (Ex. 22-6):

EXAMPLE 22-6. Josquin, *Missa Pange lingua*, Gloria, mm. 73–82.

While the setting of "Qui sedes ad dexteram Patris" probably looks back to the *c'–g* fourth that characterizes both phrases 2 and 3 of the chant, the motive on "miserere nobis" seems little more than a cadential gesture that reminds us of the plainsong's Phrygian mode.

The paraphrase Mass may be characterized as follows: it is based on a single-line preexistent model, usually a plainsong melody; it typically wraps that model in a cloak of melodic embellishment; it rolls the model out phrase by phrase (or motive by motive) and scatters it through the polyphonic fabric by means of points of imitation; and it may include large stretches of material with barely a gesture toward the model. What it does not do is place the preexistent melody in a single voice and use it as the melodic-structural scaffold on which the Mass as a whole hangs. For the sixteenth-century composer who wished to write a Mass based on a plainsong, the paraphrase Mass became the route most frequently taken.

The Parody (or Imitation) Mass

As we saw in Chapter 11, composers were basing Masses on a polyphonic model and quoting all the voices of that model simultaneously in the third quarter of the fifteenth century. Yet these works were finally cantus-firmus Masses, since it was the tenor of the polyphonic model that ultimately served as the structural backbone of a Mass.

To some extent, this practice continued among the composers of the Josquin generation. We see it in Obrecht's *Missa Fortuna desperata*, at the opening of Kyrie II (Ex. 22-7):

EXAMPLE 22-7. (a) Busnoys (?), *Fortuna desperata*, mm. 1–9; (b) Obrecht, *Missa Fortuna desperata*, Kyrie II, mm. 1–9.

But this was not the future. That lay in looking to a new type of polyphonic model: the contemporary motet, which was already thoroughly imitative, had sharply etched motives that could be shaped into new points of imitation and carried no structural cantus firmus of its own. This Mass type, which remained the favorite throughout the sixteenth century, is generally called a parody or imitation Mass.

MOUTON'S *MISSA QUEM DICUNT HOMINES* Jean Mouton based his Mass, which he may have written to celebrate the meeting of Francis I and Pope Leo X in 1516, on a similarly named motet by his younger contemporary Jean Richafort (c. 1480–c. 1547), which served as the basis of several other parody Masses. We can see the relationship between Mass and motet in Example 22-8, which shows the openings of Richafort's motet and Mouton's Gloria:

EXAMPLE 22-8. (a) Richafort, *Quem dicunt homines*, mm. 1–23; (b) Mouton, *Missa Quem dicunt homines*, Gloria, mm. 1–19.

(a)

(b)

Having followed Richafort's motet rather closely for nineteen measures, Mouton continues with freely composed music until he approaches the end of the first section of the Gloria; there he draws on the closing material of Richafort's *prima pars* (Ex. 22-9).

What the two examples make clear is this: (1) the art of parody technique lies not in literal quotation but in thoroughly reworking and transforming the material of the model, shaping it into what is essentially a new composition; (2) the building block is a motive or phrase of the model, usually in the form of a point of imitation; (3) a movement of a parody Mass customarily draws on various sections of the model; and (4) the parody Mass as a whole is constructed by alternately referring to the model and filling intervening sections with new and original music.

EXAMPLE 22-9. (a) Richafort, *Quem dicunt homines*, mm. 76–81; (b) Mouton, *Missa Quem dicunt homines*, Gloria, mm. 29–34.

ORIGINS AND TERMINOLOGY   Where and when did this new type of Mass originate? What appear to be the earliest full-blown parody Masses were written by La Rue, Mouton, Antoine de Févin (c. 1470–1511/12), Antonius Rycke (known as Divitis, c. 1470–after 1515), and possibly Josquin. Composers of the models include Josquin, Compère, Févin, Brumel, Richafort, and possibly Philippe Verdelot (c. 1470/80–before 1552). Now, if there is a common thread among this group—excepting La Rue and Verdelot—it is their ties to Paris; and there can be little doubt that it was at the French royal court, probably around 1510, to judge from its earliest appearances in manuscripts and prints, that the parody Mass first came to be cultivated. For the composers of the Josquin generation, the parody Mass was still very much a fledgling. Only with the next generation would it truly come to the fore, to remain the dominant Mass type until the sixteenth-century style of pervading imitation itself petered out (see Chapter 26).

The term "parody Mass" has been a musicological commonplace since the mid-nineteenth century. But where does it come from? During the sixteenth century, there were three standard types of Mass titles. The simplest was the most popular and long-lasting: *Missa . . .* , followed by the name of the model on which it was based. From about mid-century on, Italian sources were sometimes more specific, as in *Missa super [on] . . .* , again followed by the name of the model. At the same time, the French coined the designation *Missa ad imitationem* . . . , a form that was soon copied in German publications. Then in 1587, a little-known German composer-organist name Jacob Paix (1556–after 1623) published a Mass based on a motet by Thomas Crecquillon with the title *Missa: Parodia mottetæ Domine da nobis auxilium* . . . And it is from this single appearance of the Greek term *parodia*, which Paix seems to have simply substituted for the Latin *ad imitationem*, that the genre has taken its name.

MASSES BUILT ON MULTIPLE CANTUS FIRMI

The overwhelming majority of Masses by composers of the Josquin generation, whether cantus-firmus, paraphrase, or parody, belonged to what we have called the heart of the tradition: they were cyclic settings of the Ordinary, all the movements of which were based on the same model, be it a monophonic melody (liturgical or secular), a voice part from a polyphonic chanson, or a motet filled with points of imitation. Occasionally, composers broke with the single-model standard. Obrecht, for instance, based his *Sub tuum praesidium* and *De sancto Martino* Masses on seven and eight plainsong melodies, respectively, while La Rue also tried his hand at this procedure. (The champion must surely be the somewhat shadowy Matthaeus Pipelare, who strung together no fewer than twenty chant melodies in his Mass in honor of St. Livinus.) Of the various Mass types that eschewed the idea of a single model—they are often lumped together under the modern generic term "plainsong Masses"—two became full-fledged members of the Franco-Flemish mainstream: the *Missa de Beata Virgine* and the Requiem Mass.

The *Missa de Beata Virgine*

The polyphonic Mass for the Blessed Virgin began to take on a standardized format around 1500 and boldly contradicts the advice offered in Chapter 9's make-believe composition manual of 1450: it draws its cantus firmi from the chants of the Mass Ordinary,[4] and uses a different chant as the basis for each movement. Thus the polyphonic Kyrie is based on a Kyrie chant, the Gloria on a Gloria chant, and so on. Moreover, the choice was limited to chants for the Ordinary that were themselves associated with Masses for the Blessed Virgin: Kyrie IX (occasionally IV), Gloria IX, Credo I, Sanctus XVII (occasionally IX or IV), and Agnus Dei XVII (occasionally IX or IV; the Roman numerals are those assigned to the Ordinary cycles in the *Liber usualis*).

Another feature of the *Missa de Beata Virgine*, at least until the reforms of the Council of Trent later in the sixteenth century, was the addition of six Marian tropes—textual and musical—to the Gloria IX plainsong, which composers then incorporated into their polyphonic settings. Example 22-10, which picks up the chant for Gloria IX at the words "Domine Fili unigenite," shows how the tropes (their words appear in italic) were fit into the plainsong:

4. Composers had done this in the early fifteenth century, but only when setting single movements of the Ordinary. The Masses with multiple cantus firmi by Obrecht, La Rue, and Pipelare use cantus-firmus melodies from Office chants.

EXAMPLE 22-10. Gloria IX with its six Marian tropes.[5]

Example 22-11 demonstrates how Josquin embedded the first of these tropes into the Gloria of his *Missa de Beata Virgine*. The polyphonic *Missa de Beata Virgine* began to enjoy something of a vogue with composers of the Josquin generation. Besides Josquin's, there are settings by Brumel, La Rue, Isaac (four), and the Spaniard Juan de Anchieta (1462–1523). And as with the *L'homme armé* tradition, some of the *Beata Virgine* Masses may have been written in the spirit of (friendly?) competition. In fact, Glarean tells us in his *Dodecachordon* that the

5. After Reese, "The Polyphonic *Missa de Beata Virgine*," 592; the entire chant, without the tropes, is in *Liber usualis*, 40–42.

EXAMPLE 22-11. Josquin, *Missa de Beata Virgine*, Gloria, mm. 80–95 (the plainsong words are in italic).

Masses by Josquin and Brumel were composed under precisely those circumstances: "Josquin excelled by far in my opinion—and so acquitted himself in this contest that it seems to me . . . that finer music cannot be created."[6]

The Requiem Mass

It is hard to say why polyphonic settings of the Requiem Mass—the *Missa pro defunctis*—were so slow in catching on. We know that Du Fay wrote such a Mass, intended for his own funeral and for its anniversaries, and recorded as "newly composed" when it was copied into the choirbooks of the Cathedral of Cambrai in 1470–71. The Mass, however, is lost; the first extant polyphonic Requiem is Ockeghem's. From the Josquin generation, there are Requiem Masses by Brumel, Févin, Prioris, and La Rue.

More than other Mass type with which we have dealt, the Requiem was subject to local practices. Not until Pius V issued a new Missal in 1570 (reflecting the reforms of the Council of Trent) did the items that were to be included in the Mass become standardized. We can see this lack of standardization by

6. Quoted after Reese, "The Polyphonic *Missa de Beata Virgine*," 598.

comparing Pius V's prescriptions with the settings by Ockeghem, Brumel, and La Rue (Table 22-4):

Table 22-4.   Items of the Requiem Mass as prescribed by Pius V in 1570 and as set by Ockeghem, Brumel, and La Rue.

	Pius V	Ockeghem	Brumel	La Rue
Introit				
"Requiem aeternam"		set	set	set
Kyrie		set	set	set
Gradual				
"Requiem aeternam"		"Si ambulem"	not set	not set
Tract				
"Absolve Domine"		"Sicut cervus"	not set	"Sicut cervus"
Sequence				
"Dies irae"		not set	set	not set
Offertory				
"Domine Jesu Christe"		set	not set	set
Sanctus		not set	set	set
Agnus Dei		not set	set	set

(with "Dona eis requiem" and "Dona eis sempiternam" replacing "Miserere nobis" and "Dona nobis pacem")

	Pius V	Ockeghem	Brumel	La Rue
Communion				
"Lux aeterna"		not set	set	set
Absolution Responsory				
"Libera me Domine"		not set	not set	not set

(sung not at the Mass but at the burial service)

Thus none of the three settings from the late fifteenth and early sixteenth centuries agree either with one another from beginning to end or with the scheme that eventually became standard.

LA RUE'S REQUIEM   By far the best-known of the early Requiem Masses is Pierre de la Rue's, possibly written to commemorate the death of Philip the Fair in 1506. Characteristic of the seven movements is the introit (*Anthology* 43): with its descent to the low B_1-flat, it justifies the Mass's reputation for exploring the lowest registers; it also sets an antiphonal chant from the Proper of the Mass with alternation between plainsong and polyphony.

Why did La Rue apportion plainsong and polyphony as he did? The answer lies in the nature of the plainsong introit itself (Ex. 22-12):

EXAMPLE 22-12. The introit *Requiem aeternam.*[7]

7. *Liber usualis,* 1807.

The introit consists of two main sections: an antiphon and, in the case of the Requiem, the first two verses from Psalm 64 (followed by a return to the antiphon). Further, the introit is an example of *antiphonal psalmody*; that is, it is characterized by the alternation of two choirs, the point at which they alternate being indicated in modern chant books by an asterisk (see Ex. 22-12).

As it turns out, then, La Rue's decision as to where plainsong should give way to polyphony was determined by the points at which one choir responded to the other in the plainsong itself. This is clear enough in the antiphon (mm. 1–19), where the articulation between plainsong and polyphony agrees with the placement of the asterisk in modern chant books. The psalm (mm. 20–34), however, appears to contradict that criterion. Yet since all the early settings of the Requiem agree on starting the polyphony at the words "Et tibi," we can be certain that it was there—rather than at "Exaudi," as in the *Liber usualis*—that the alternation of choirs took place in La Rue's time. (Thus we see once again the dangers inherent in drawing conclusions about liturgical practices of the period on the basis of modern chant books.)

THE *DIES IRAE*   Though Antoine Brumel's Requiem Mass surely pales in comparison with La Rue's, it is one of the earliest to set the Requiem's sequence, the *Dies irae*. This chant, perhaps the most famous ever written, would eventually inspire some of the most powerful moments in the Requiems of Mozart, Berlioz, and Verdi. Indeed, beginning in the nineteenth century, composers often used the *Dies irae* melody to stir up images of fear, death, oppression, and the supernatural; a list of works in which it appears includes Berlioz's *Symphonie fantastique*, Liszt's *Totentanz*, Saint-Saëns's *Danse macabre*, and Dallapiccola's *Canti di prigionia*. Example 22-13 shows the first verse of the plainsong, together with Brumel's setting:

EXAMPLE 22-13. The sequence *Dies irae*: (a) first verse of the plainsong;
(b) Brumel's setting, mm. 1–23.

THREE LOCAL MASS TYPES

As noted above, the *Missa de Beata Virgine* and the Requiem Mass belong to the central Franco-Flemish tradition. Certain Mass types, however, cultivated locally, stood outside that tradition. Three of these types attracted the attention of some of the greatest Franco-Flemish masters: the so-called *motetti missales* of Milan, the *alternatim* settings of the Ordinary that were cultivated in the German-speaking areas of central Europe, and cycles of Propers from there as well.

Milan

The *motetti missales* flourished at Milan during the final three decades of the fifteenth century, their birth coinciding with the years in which Galeazzo Maria Sforza stocked his chapel with rising young stars of the Josquin generation. Briefly, the *motetti missales* are cycles of up to eight motets, each of which takes the place of a specific item of the Ordinary or Proper, which was identified by a rubric such as "loco Gloria" (in the place of the Gloria) and presumably recited quietly while the motet was sung. Table 22-5 shows the plan of Loyset Compère's *Missa Galeazescha*, the title of which alludes to Duke Galeazzo Maria, though the Mass was written, as were many of the *motetti missales*, in honor of the Virgin Mary:

Table 22-5. The motets of Compère's *Missa Galeazescha* and the items of the Mass for which they substitute.

Ave virgo gloriosa	loco Introitus
Ave salus infirmorum	loco Gloria
Ave decus Virginale	loco Credo
Ave sponsa verbi summa	loco Offertorii
O Maria! In supremo sita poli	loco Sanctus
Adoramus te, Christe	ad elevationem
	(at the Elevation of the Host)
Salve mater salvatoris	loco Agnus Dei
Virginis Mariae laudes	loco Deo gratias

That Compère conceived the motets as a cycle is evident from their shared Dorian mode and constant dependence upon Marian sequences for their texts, while other cycles even provide hints of melodic unity.

Two German Mass Types and Isaac

When Heinrich Isaac joined the chapel of Emperor Maximilian I at the end of the fifteenth century, he raised certain local Mass types to an aesthetic level they had never before known. It is, then, time to turn toward central Europe. We begin by placing Isaac's imperial sojourn into the context of his life and career as a whole.

Though Isaac was born in Flanders around 1450, we know little about him until June 1485, when, after having spent some time at Innsbruck the previous fall, he arrived in Florence at the invitation of Lorenzo the Magnificent himself. In July, he was listed among the singers at the cathedral, the Baptistry of San Giovanni, and the church of the Santissima Annunziata.

Isaac no doubt felt at home in Florence, where he married Bartolomea Bello (daughter of a local butcher) and enjoyed particularly close ties with the Medici: he set Lorenzo's poetry, probably taught music to his children—one of whom, the future Pope Leo X, dabbled in composition—and, as we have seen, eulogized his patron in the motet *Quis dabit capiti meo aquam?* (Chapter 19). Decades later, in 1514, the Medici showed their appreciation of Isaac's service by granting him a pension when he eventually chose to retire in his adopted city.

When the Medici were exiled in late 1494, Florence obviously became uncomfortable, and in November 1496 Isaac joined the imperial chapel of the Emperor Maximilian I (1469–1519). Apparently the terms of the Habsburg appointment gave the composer liberty to travel, and for the next decade and a half he was often on the move: in 1497 and 1499 at the Saxon court of Frederick the Wise, occasionally back in Florence, and in 1502 applying for the post of chapel master at Ferrara (but losing out to Josquin). Isaac's years with the imperial chapel were productive, the most notable achievement being a monumental cycle of Propers known as the *Choralis Constantinus*. It was also while he served Maximilian that Isaac gave composition lessons to a young Swiss choirboy, Ludwig Senfl, who would go on to become the greatest "German" composer of the period.

The restoration of the Medici in 1512 made it possible for Isaac to return to Florence. The letter in which the Medici provided Isaac with a pension, written by Giuliano de' Medici (Pope Leo's younger brother) on May 10, 1514, shows their appreciation and real fondness for him:

> I understand that Maestro Henrico Isaac, a musician and old servant of our House, is back there [in Florence] again, and because he is old and has a wife and children he would like to settle down and stay if some provision were to be made for him. And since I wish to gratify him as much as possible, out of consideration for his faithful service of many years—dating from the time of our father—and no less for his worthy talents, I pray Your Magnificent Lordship for these reasons and for your love of me to be kind to him and do everything possible so that a provision can be made for him. He had [such a provision] at one time as a singer of San Giovanni, and it could now be drawn from the same source. Any favor and benefit you do him will be worthily placed in a deserving person. You could not do anything that I would appreciate more.[8]

Isaac soon added another pension from Maximilian. He died in March 1517.

MISSA DE APOSTOLIS As its name implies, an *alternatim* Mass consists of sections that alternate between polyphony and plainsong. The genre was most widely cultivated in central Europe.

Like most *alternatim* Masses, Isaac's *Missa de apostolis* is a "plainsong Mass,"

---

8. Quoted after Picker, *Henricus Isaac,* 12–13.

Figure 22-2. *The Emperor Maximilian Hears Mass at Augsburg,* woodcut, c. 1518.

each of the four movements (there is no Credo) based on a chant from the Ordinary of the Mass. The *alternatim* procedure is seen in its most expansive form in the Kyrie (*Anthology* 44), where the nine exclamations (three each) of "Kyrie eleison," "Christe eleison," and "Kyrie eleison" are presented alternately in plainsong and polyphony, with the polyphonic sections assigning the plainsong now to one voice, now to another, sometimes literally in long note values, sometimes paraphrased.

Isaac's Mass could have been performed by voices alone, but it is also possible that the sections Isaac did not set polyphonically were played, with improvisations, on the organ. That the imperial chapel cultivated what might be called an *alternatim*-organ Mass is shown in a woodcut from around 1518, in which we see the famous court organist Paul Hofhaimer seated at the positive across from the choir (Fig. 22-2).[9]

We can get some idea of what Hofhaimer's improvisations may have sounded like from his keyboard setting of the verse "O clemens" from the antiphon *Salve regina* (Ex. 22-14):

9. Note that the woodcut has the organ pipes grow longer in the wrong direction; likewise the large prayer book is on the wrong side of the altar. Evidently the artist who cut the block forgot to account for the mirror-image result inherent in the process.

EXAMPLE 22-14. Hofhaimer, "O clemens," from a setting of the *Salve regina*; the notes of the plainsong are marked with asterisks.[10]

The plainsong rolls out in slow, even note values beneath a blaze of embellishment in the right hand. The contrast with Isaac's lush five-part polyphony could hardly be more stark.

To speak of the "imperial chapel" is difficult, since the emperor's chapels were—to exaggerate in "Kaiser Max's" grandiose fashion—as numerous as the Holy Roman Empire was vast, and sometimes as *ad hoc* as the empire was loosely organized. But the chapel most closely associated with Maximilian was his Vienna Hofkapelle, which counted Isaac and Senfl as members and which in 1520 included six tenors, six basses, seven altos (including Senfl), and twenty-one boys. Figure 22-3 shows the chapel as depicted in one of a series of woodcuts entitled *The Triumph of Maximilian I*, commissioned by the emperor from the artist Hans Burgkmair the Elder in 1512 in order to glorify his court. An accompanying poem (by Maximilian) reads:

> With voices high and low conjoint,
> With harmony and counterpoint,
> By all the laws of music moved,
> My choir constantly improved.
> By not alone through my intent—
> Give thanks to royal encouragement!
>
> The cornett and trombones we placed
> So that the choral song they graced,
> For His Imperial Majesty
> Has often in such harmony
> Taken great pleasure, and rightly so,
> As we have had good cause to know.[11]

What this may tell us about performance practice will be discussed below.

CHORALIS CONSTANTINUS   Although the premier Mass type of the period was the cyclic setting of the Ordinary, settings of the Proper never disappeared.

10. After Reese, *Music in the Renaissance*, 662.

11. Translation quoted after Appelbaum, *The Triumph of Maximilian I*, 4–6.

Figure 22-3. Hans Burgkmair the Elder, *The Triumph of Maximilian I*, woodcut showing the carriage with Maximilian's chapel, 1512.

As we saw in Chapter 9, Du Fay himself might have written a number of such cycles. It was, however, in the German-speaking lands of central Europe that the genre was most enthusiastically cultivated, even if in a sometimes barebones style (Ex. 22-15):

EXAMPLE 22-15. Anonymous, *Congaudent angelorum chori*, MS Trent 93.[12]

During the first decade of the sixteenth century, Isaac must have riveted his attention on the Proper of the Mass. The result was the monumental collection known as the *Choralis Constantinus*, a series of ninety-nine cycles (there are a few Ordinaries and a small number of sections not by Isaac) for Sundays and

12. After Strohm, *The Rise of European Music*, 525.

major feasts throughout the liturgical year. As such, the *Choralis Constantinus* stands together with other efforts to provide music for the entire liturgical year: Leonin's twelfth-century *Magnus liber organi*, William Byrd's late-sixteenth-century *Gradualia*, and Bach's cycles of cantatas for the churches of Leipzig.

The *Choralis Constantinus* was printed posthumously by the Nuremberg publisher Hieronymous Formschneider in three volumes: volume 1 appeared in 1550, volumes 2 and 3 in 1555. And though the title of the work alludes to the city of Constance, only volume 2 was composed for the cathedral of that city (in 1508–9); the cycles in volumes 1 and 3 were written for Maximilian's court chapel. As Isaac did not live to complete the project, his former student Ludwig Senfl added the finishing touches.

PERFORMANCE PRACTICE

Problems about the way in which liturgical music was performed during our two-hundred-year period never go away.

The *a cappella* Tradition

As noted in Chapter 9, there is a strong consensus that during the fifteenth century, music for the liturgy was generally performed *a cappella*. On the other hand, in 1586, the Spanish composer Francisco Guerrero asked that three verses of his *Salve regina* be accompanied with shawms, cornetts, and recorders, successively, "because always hearing the same instrument annoys the listener."[13] Thus from the mid-fifteenth century to the end of the sixteenth, we have gone from one mode of performance to another.

The liturgical music of the Josquin generation seems to represent a period of transition, and it is probably safe to say that after 1500 or so, performances of liturgical music in which instruments supplemented voices became more frequent. There is, for instance, the evidence of Burgkmair's woodcut (Fig. 22-3), in which Maximilian's chapel singers are shown together with trombone and cornetto. To be sure, the musicians are gathered on a float—not in a church—and the artist's aim is to impress; but the scene is unlikely to be one of pure fantasy.

The iconographic evidence for mixed forces finds ever greater documentary support as the fifteenth century gives way to the sixteenth. Thus in 1503, when the chapels of Maximilian and Philip the Fair—father and son—came together at Innsbruck, "The sackbuts of the King [of the Romans: Maximilian] began the Gradual and played the Deo gratias and Ite missa est, and the singers of *monseigneur* [Philip] sang the Offertory."[14]

Grand occasions of state were not the only ones in which singers and instrumentalists joined forces in celebrating the Mass. Erasmus condemned what we

13. Stevenson, *Spanish Cathedral Music in the Golden Age*, 167.
14. Quoted after Picker, "The Habsburg Courts," 224.

may suppose was the everyday music that he heard in English churches and monasteries:

> We have brought into sacred edifices a certain elaborate and theatrical music, a confused interplay of diverse sounds, such as I do not believe was ever heard in Greek or Roman theaters. Straight trumpets, curved trumpets, pipes, and sambucas resound everywhere, and vie with human voices. . . . People flock to church as to a theater for aural delight.[15]

Nor was the situation any different in Italy, as Biagio Rosetti complained in his *Libellus de rudimentes musices*, published at Verona in 1529: "The abusive flutes, trumpets, trombones, and horns . . . have begun to creep into some sacred places. . . . The lascivious congregations gather here to be entertained by these instruments."[16] In short, the liturgical soundscape was changing.

Tempo Relationships

The Kyrie of Josquin's *Missa Pange lingua*, and that of many other Masses of the period, is divided into three large sections with the mensuration signs O, $\mathsf{C}\!\!\!|$, and $\mathsf{O}\!\!\!|$, but without the doubling up of values (in the cut sections) that often accompanies a 2:1 relationship between cut and uncut signs. How, then, did the tempos of the three sections relate to one another? If the semibreve of the "Christe" and Kyrie II really moved at twice the speed that it did in the opening Kyrie, the result would be musical gibberish. Equally unlikely is that the opening Kyrie was performed slowly enough to allow for just such a doubling up of the tempo.

Rather, it seems that when the proportion $\mathsf{C}\!\!\!|$ followed O, the relationship was 4:3—that is, four semibreves of $\mathsf{C}\!\!\!|$ were sung in the time that three semibreves had received in O. And when the proportion $\mathsf{O}\!\!\!|$ took over, it signaled a return to triple meter but with the tempo that had prevailed in $\mathsf{C}\!\!\!|$ so that Kyrie II moved along at a slightly faster clip than Kyrie I.

Pronouncing Latin

In 1608, Joseph Justus Scaliger (1540–1609), one of the most erudite scholars of his time, apologized for having understood little of a Latin speech delivered by an Englishman. The reason: Scaliger's poor command of English, and thus the implication that he had problems with the Englishman's pronunciation of Latin. A French speaker of Latin might have pronounced "per sanctam crucem redemisti mundum" as if it were "per santan crusan redemisti mondon."[17]

The pronunciation of Latin was thus anything but standardized, and there is no reason to assume that sixteenth-century singers in the Low Countries, for example, pronounced the Latin of a Josquin or Obrecht Mass with the Italian

15. Quoted after Miller, "Erasmus on Music," 338–40.

16. Quoted after Reynolds, "Sacred Polyphony," 193.

17. Both examples are cited in James Haar, "Monophony and the Unwritten Traditions," in *Performance Practice*, 262, n. 11.

pronunciation that we refer to today as Church Latin. Whose pronunciation should we use, then? Should the words of Josquin's *Missa Hercules dux ferrariae* be pronounced according to Franco-Flemish traditions on the grounds that that is the sound that presumably buzzed around in Josquin's head? Or should we pronounce them Italian style on the grounds that the work was written for the court of Ferrara? And how did Franco-Flemish singers pronounce Latin anyway once they crossed the Alps? Though these questions are not easily answered, they call on present-day performers to stretch their imagination and try out different solutions. And though decisions must invariably be made, next week's might differ from today's.

BIBLIOGRAPHICAL NOTE

Editions of the Music

To the complete-works editions of Josquin, Brumel, La Rue, and Mouton cited in Chapters 18 and 20 should be added the following. **Compère**: *Opera omnia*, CMM 15, ed. Ludwig Finscher (American Institute of Musicology, 1958–72). **Isaac**: *Opera omnia*, CMM 65, ed. Edward R. Lerner (American Institute of Musicology, 1974–). The *Choralis Constantinus* must be pieced together as follows: vols. 1 and 2 in *DTÖ* 10 and 32, respectively, the latter edited by Anton von Webern (Vienna: Artaria, 1898, 1909; reprint, 1959); vol. 3 in *Heinrich Isaac's Choralis Constantinus Book III*, ed. Louise Cuyler (Ann Arbor: University of Michigan Press, 1950). **Obrecht**: there are three Obrecht editions. The most recent and authoritative is the 17-volume *New Obrecht Edition*, currently in progress under the general editorship of Chris Maas (Utrecht: Vereniging voor Nederlandse Muziekgeschiednis, 1983–); *Opera omnia*, ed. Albert Smijers and Marcus van Crevel, 9 vols. (never completed), contains two controversial editions by Van Crevel (Amsterdam: Vereniging voor Nederlandse Muziekgeschiednis, 1954–64); *Werken van Jacob Obrecht*, ed. Johannes Wolf (Amsterdam and Leipzig: Vereniging voor Noord–Nederlandse Muziekgeschiednis, 1908–21; reprint, 1968). **Divitis**: *Collected Works*, RRMR 94, ed. G. A. Nugent (Madison: A-R Editions, 1993). **Pipelare**: *Opera omnia*, CMM 34, ed. Ronald Cross (American Institute of Musicology, 1966–67).

Cantus-Firmus and Paraphrase Techniques

The most comprehensive study remains Edgar H. Sparks, *Cantus Firmus in Mass and Motet, 1420–1520* (Berkeley and Los Angeles: University of California Press, 1963).

The Parody Mass

Two essays by Lewis Lockwood are required reading: "On 'Parody' as Term and Concept in 16th-Century Music," in *Aspects of Medieval and Renaissance Music: A Birthday Offering to Gustave Reese*, ed. Jan LaRue (New York: Norton, 1966), 560–75, and "A View of the Early Sixteenth-Century Parody Mass," in *Queens College: Twenty-Fifth Anniversary Festschrift*, ed. Albert Mell (New York: Queens College, 1964), 53–77. For an attempt to develop a method of analyzing parody Masses of a slightly later period, see Quentin W. Quereau, "Sixteenth-Century Parody: An Approach to Analysis," *JAMS* 31 (1978): 407–41; see also René B. Lenaerts, "The 16th-Century Parody Mass in the Netherlands," *MQ* 36 (1950): 410–21; Murray Steib, "A Composer Looks at His Model: Polyphonic Borrowing from the Late Fifteenth Century," *TVNM* 46 (1996): 5–41.

Plainsong Masses and Local Mass Types

Masses for the Blessed Virgin: Gustave Reese, "The Polyphonic *Missa de Beata Virgine* as a Genre: The Background of Josquin's Lady Mass," in *Josquin des Prez: Proceedings of the*

International Josquin Festival-Conference, ed. Edward E. Lowinsky (London: Oxford University Press, 1976), 589–98. **Requiem Mass**: Alec Robertson, *Requiem: Music of Mourning and Consolation* (New York: Praeger, 1968). **The Milanese Mass**: Thomas L. Noblitt, "The Ambrosian *Motetti Missales* Repertory," *MD* 22 (1968): 77–103; Lynn Halpern Ward, "The *Motetti Missales* Repertory Reconsidered," *JAMS* 39 (1986): 491–523; Patrick Macey, "Galeazzo Maria Sforza and Musical Patronage in Milan: Compère, Weerbeke, and Josquin," *EMH* 15 (1996): 147–212. **The organ Mass**: Leo Schrade, "The Organ in the Mass of the 15th-Century," *MQ* 28 (1942): 329–36, 467–87.

Individual Composers

Josquin: a starting point is the overview in Gustave Reese and Jeremy Noble, "Josquin Desprez," in *The New Grove High Renaissance Masters*, ed. Stanley Sadie (New York: Norton, 1984); the most detailed discussion appears in vol. 1 of Helmuth Osthoff, *Josquin Desprez*, 2 vols. (Tutzing: Schneider, 1962); a number of articles in *Josquin des Prez: Proceedings of the International Josquin Festival-Conference* deal with the Masses; an essay of particular interest is Michael Long's "Symbol and Ritual in Josquin's *Missa di Dadi*," *JAMS* 42 (1989): 1–22; finally, see the chapter on the Masses in the forthcoming *The Josquin Companion*, ed. Richard Sherr (Oxford University Press). **Obrecht**: the fundamental study is Rob C. Wegman's splendid *Born for the Muses: The Life and Masses of Jacob Obrecht* (Oxford: Clarendon Press, 1994), which also contains the most penetrating biography; two other essays worthy of note are R. Larry Todd, "Retrograde, Inversion, Retrograde Inversion, and Related Techniques in the Masses of Obrecht," *MQ* 54 (1978): 50–78, and Arnold Salop, "Jacob Obrecht and the Early Development of Harmonic Polyphony," *JAMS* 17 (1964): 255–86. **Isaac**: the outstanding study is Martin Staehelin, *Die Messen Heinrich Isaacs*, 3 vols., Publikationen der schweizerischen musikforschenden Gesellschaft, II/28 (Bern and Stuttgart: Paul Haupt, 1977); for bibliographical background, see Martin Picker, *Henricus Isaac: A Guide to Research*, Garland Composer Resource Manuals 35 (New York: Garland, 1991); both Staehelin and Picker have good biographical coverage, for which one should also see Frank D'Accone, "Heinrich Isaac in Florence: New and Unpublished Documents," *MQ* 49 (1963): 464–83. **Compère**: the most comprehensive discussion appears in Ludwig Finscher, *Loyset Compère (c. 1450–1518): Life and Works*, MSD 12 (American Institute of Musicology, 1964).

Maximilian I and Music

Louise Cuyler, *The Emperor Maximilian I and Music* (London: Oxford University Press, 1973); Martin Picker, "The Habsburg Courts in the Netherlands and Austria, 1477–1530," in *The Renaissance: From the 1470s to the End of the 16th Century*, Music and Man 2, ed. Iain Fenlon (London: Macmillian, 1989); there is a fine survey of music in central Europe in Reinhard Strohm's *Rise of European Music, 1380–1500* (Cambridge: Cambridge University Press, 1993).

Performance Practice

There is a good introduction to the basic issues in Christopher A. Reynolds, "Sacred Polyphony," in *Performance Practice: Music Before 1600*, ed. Howard Mayer Brown and Stanley Sadie (New York: Norton, 1989); also helpful is the panoramic series of essays in Jeffery T. Kite-Powell, ed., *A Performer's Guide to Renaissance Music* (New York: Schirmer, 1994); on the particularly knotty problem of how plainsong might have been performed, see Richard Sherr, "The Performance of Chant in the Renaissance and Its Interactions with Polyphony," in *Plainsong in the Age of Polyphony*, Cambridge Studies in Performance Practice 2, ed. Thomas Forrest Kelly (Cambridge: Cambridge University Press, 1992), 178–209.

Also Cited

The Triumph of Maximilian I, ed. Stanley Appelbaum (New York: Dover, 1964); Robert M. Stevenson, *Spanish Cathedral Music in the Golden Age* (Berkeley and Los Angeles: University of California Press, 1961); Clement Miller, "Erasmus on Music," *MQ* 52 (1966): 332–49; James Haar, "Monophony and the Unwritten Traditions," in *Performance Practice: Music before 1600*, ed. Howard Mayer Brown and Stanley Sadie (New York: Norton, 1989), 240–66; Myroslaw Antonowytsch, "Renaissance-Tendenzen in den Fortuna-desperata-Messen von Josquin und Obrecht," *Mf* 9 (1956): 1–26.

CHAPTER 23

Intermedio: 1513–1521

In April 1517, Erasmus wrote to Pope Leo X:

> I congratulate this age of ours, which promises to be an age of gold if ever there was one. . . . Three of the chief blessings of humanity are about to be restored to her; I mean first that truly Christian piety which has in many ways fallen into decay, second, learning of the best sort hitherto partly neglected and partly corrupted, and third, the public and lasting concord of Christendom, the source and parent of piety and erudition.[1]

It is hard to account for Erasmus's optimism, for the decade in which he was writing (the 1513–21 boundaries refer specifically to the reign of Leo X) was marked by tensions on a scale and magnitude hardly known before: tensions between state and state, state and church, and most cataclysmic of all, an established church and its renegade offshoot. And if Europe entered the decade still wearing some of its late medieval garb, it emerged dressed rather more in that of the early modern. Indeed, some of the political fallout lingers with us today.

THE LEADING PLAYERS

Before looking at some of the tensions that wracked the decade, we should meet a few of the leading players.

France: Louis XII and Francis I

When Charles VIII died without heirs in 1498, he was succeeded by the Duke of Orléans, Louis XII (1482–1515). Authoritarian in manner, Louis was obsessed with laying claim to portions of Italy and spent most of his adult life waging war there, in the end with little to show for it.

By the time Francis I (1494–1547; see Fig. 23-1) assumed the throne in January 1515, French involvement in Italy was a habit in which Francis was only too eager to partake. Though motivated primarily by the quest for territorial expansion, Francis truly enjoyed Italian culture and turned its importation into policy. He welcomed Italian artists—Leonardo da Vinci (who died in France in 1519) and the sculptor Benvenuto Cellini among them—and in 1531 arranged for the marriage of his son (the future Henry II [1547–59]) to Catherine de' Medici (great-granddaughter of Lorenzo), whose chefs, as legend exaggeratedly had it, taught the French how to cook.

1. Quoted after Gilmore, *The World of Humanism*, 261.

Figure 23-1. Jean Clouet, portrait of Francis I, c. 1525 (Louvre, Paris).

Figure 23-2. Hans Holbein the Younger, portrait of Henry VIII, 1536 (Museo Thyssen–Bornemisza, Madrid).

Figure 23-3. Titian (Tiziano Vecellio), equestrian portrait of Charles V, 1548 (Prado, Madrid).

England: Henry VIII

Henry VIII (1491–1547; see Fig. 23-2) became king in 1509. His desire to annul his marriage with the first of his six wives—Catherine of Aragon (1485–1536), daughter of Ferdinand and Isabella and widow of his older brother Arthur, Prince of Wales—led him, in the 1530s, to separate England from the Roman church and establish the autonomous Church of England with himself as its head (see Chapters 28 and 34).

The Empire: Charles V

When Maximilian I died in 1519, his grandson Charles V (1500–1558; see Fig. 23-3) outbid two rivals, Francis I and Henry VIII, for the title of Holy Roman Emperor. (The title—there was nothing holy or Roman about it—was neither hereditary nor absolute in its sovereignty; the emperor was elected by a committee of seven members of the nobility and high-placed church officials.) The map in Figure 23-4 shows the extent of Charles's empire, which included (in order of acquisition): the Netherlands and Flanders (from his father, Philip the Fair, Habsburg Duke of Burgundy), where he constantly faced aspirations of political independence fostered by thriving economic self-sufficiency; Spain (from his mother, Juana, another of Ferdinand and Isabella's daughters), where, as a "foreigner," he was hated; the Habsburg domains in Austria and Germany (from his grandfather, Maximilian), where the Protestants despised his Catholicism; Milan (which he himself won by conquest); Bohemia and Hungary (through marriages); the kingdom of Naples; and Spain's territories in the

Figure 23-4. Map showing the extent of Charles V's empire.

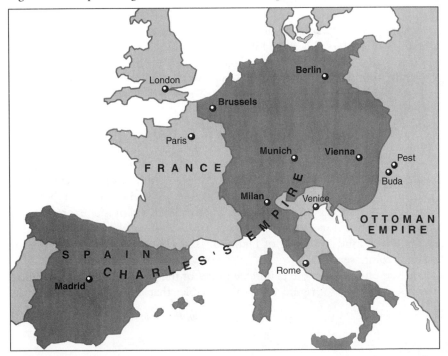

Figure 23-5. Raphael, portrait of Pope Leo X (seated) with Cardinals Giulio de' Medici and Luigi de' Rossi, c. 1517 (Uffizi Gallery, Florence).

Americas. As his chief minister said to him: "God has set you on the path toward world monarchy."[2]

In 1556, a tired Charles abdicated and spent the last two years of his life in a Spanish monastery; his son Philip II inherited Spain, the Netherlands, and the possessions in northern Italy, while Charles's brother Ferdinand received the lands of central Europe, much of which would remain subject to the House of Habsburg until its collapse after World War I.

Two Churches: Leo X and Martin Luther

Giovanni de' Medici, the second of Lorenzo the Magnificent's three sons, was born in 1475 and raised for a career in the church: minor orders at age eight, a cardinal's hat at thirteen, and election to the throne of St. Peter in 1513 (Fig. 23–5). An extremely cultivated man, Pope Leo spent lavishly on both the *belles-lettres* and the visual arts. But his great passion was music, expressed not only by his expansion of the papal chapel to more than thirty singers and his exceptionally kind treatment of Heinrich Isaac, but by his own efforts as an amateur composer.

Leo was one of the more admirable popes of the period, but his great failing was his inability to imagine the unimaginable: that an obscure Augustinian

2. Quoted in Hale, *A Concise Encyclopedia of the Italian Renaissance*, 78.

monk named Martin Luther (1483–1546) could convince almost half of Christianity that there was another way besides Rome's to communicate with God. It was Leo's inaction that let the Protestant Reformation get under way.

TENSIONS BETWEEN STATES

When Charles VIII invaded Italy in 1494 in order to secure his claims to Naples, he initiated the so-called Wars of Italy, which reached their peaks of violence during the 1510s and 1520s and ended only in 1529, when Charles V and Francis I agreed to call it quits. Though Italy had known skirmishes even after the 1454 Peace of Lodi, it had never experienced anything quite like this. The causes were many: conflicting Spanish and French claims to the kingdom of Naples; Louis XII's claim to Milan and Genoa on the grounds that his grandfather had been married to a member of the once-ducal Milanese Visconti family; Maximilian I's designs on portions of northern Italy; the same on the part of the Swiss; and, as always, the shortsighted self-interest of the Italian powers—including the papacy—all of whom looked out only for themselves.

The issue of who would rule Naples was decided by 1504: Spain defeated France, and Naples would remain a Spanish vice-royalty until the eighteenth century. The fight for Milan, however, devastated the northern Italian countryside for thirty years. And though Francis I initially won the battle—at Marignano in 1515—he eventually lost the war at Pavia in 1525. Like Naples, then, Milan would come under Spanish/imperial rule for more than three centuries. Thus what set the Wars of Italy apart from the many conflicts that preceded them is that their outcome froze the political map of Italy and forced upon it centuries of foreign domination.

TENSIONS BETWEEN STATE AND CHURCH

The issue of who had administrative control of the church within national boundaries, Rome or the secular monarchs, was a centuries-old bone of contention. Yet the end of the fifteenth and beginning of the sixteenth centuries witnessed two agreements between church and monarchs that shifted the balance of power decidedly and permanently in favor of the secular rulers and their states.

In 1478, Pope Sixtus IV granted Ferdinand and Isabella the authority to establish the Inquisition in Castile in order to deal with Jews who had converted but "relapsed." Though acting in the name of Rome, the Inquisition was entirely an instrument of the state, and in effect freed the Spanish church to govern itself.

What Sixtus gave to Spain, Leo gave to France. In 1516, with Francis I at the height of his power in Italy, king and pontiff signed the Concordat of Bologna, in which Leo conceded to Francis the right to fill the most important church positions in France with his own nominees and without intervention from Rome. In France, then, the church would be run by the French.

But nowhere, perhaps, was the sentiment against Rome's heavy-handedness as strong as it was in Germany, where there was resentment over everything from what was perceived as foreign taxation to the church's habit of having local lawsuits decided in Rome. In 1509, Maximilian went so far as to consider breaking with Rome (he was aggrieved about having been denied a proper coronation). In 1516, one of Leo's ablest advisers, the Venetian humanist Girolamo Aleandro, warned the pope that a rebellion was brewing in Germany. It came within the year.

TENSIONS BETWEEN CHURCHES

On October 31, 1517, Martin Luther, professor of theology at the University of Wittenberg in Saxony, posted on the door of the city's Castle Church his famous ninety-five theses: *Disputation for the Clarification of the Power of Indulgences*. The immediate provocation for the protest—hence the name "Protestants" (coined in 1529) for his followers—was Leo's authorization of the sale of indulgences (absolution for one's sins for a price) to raise funds for the ongoing rebuilding of St. Peter's in Rome. Yet however much Luther and his allies might have despised the corruption and lack of religiosity that was rampant in Rome—"The faithful city is become a harlot," said John Colet, dean of St. Paul's Cathedral in London—that alone is unlikely to have split the church apart. Rather, Luther found himself in disagreement with some of Christianity's most basic tenets.

Luther did not believe that, as the church taught, a person could buy God's favor and thus salvation through a combination of prayer and good works (the purchase of indulgences among them). For Luther, it was exactly the other way around: people were "justified" through God's kindness to them; faith in God's grace led to salvation. Moreover, one needed neither intermediaries in the form of a clerical hierarchy to communicate with God nor papal pronouncements to augment the Scriptures. In effect, Luther turned the relationship between people and God upside down. And though it was not his intention to be the founder of a new church, the appeal of his ideas made him just that (see Chapter 33).

THREE AUTHORS

Two of the most widely read books of the sixteenth century were *The Prince*, by Machiavelli, and *The Courtier*, by Castiglione.

Machiavelli

Niccolò Machiavelli (1469–1527) wrote *The Prince* (*Il principe*) in 1513 (though it was not printed until 1532). Today, to call someone Machiavellian is to level charges of ruthlessness, even immorality (or amorality). Yet Machiavelli's political thinking was complex; and the most famous phrase attributed to him, "The end justifies the means," appears nowhere in *The Prince*. What

Machiavelli did write was: "In the actions of all men, and especially of princes, where there is no impartial arbiter, one must consider the final result" ("si guarda al fine," chapter 18).

To be sure, Machiavelli gave his prince more than a little moral room in which to maneuver, but he was neither glorifying nor advocating government by tyrant. In fact, Machiavelli himself was an ardent republican, as his involvement in the anti-Medicean Florentine Republic and his later and more carefully considered *Discourses* make clear. Furthermore, we must understand his motives. With the Medici restored in Florence and with a Medici pope, Leo X, at the helm in Rome, Machiavelli hoped that Tuscany and the papal states would come together and form a core around which the other Italian states could rally in the face of foreign domination. He hoped in vain.

Castiglione

With *The Courtier* (*Il libro del cortegiano*, first drafted in 1506 and constantly revised until it was published in 1528), Baldassare Castiglione (1478–1529) produced what may well be the most famous book of manners ever written. Set as a conversation at the court of Urbino, *The Courtier* describes the attributes and attainments of the ideal courtier—the trademarks, so to speak, of the accomplished gentleman. Most important among the attributes of courtly etiquette was the idea of *sprezzatura*, which called for the courtier to display his accomplishments with smooth, graceful ease, to be superior without the crassness of overt professionalism.

Among other things, the courtier was to be well-versed in music:

> I am not satisfied with our courtier unless he is also a musician and unless as well as understanding and being able to read music he can play several instruments. For, when we think of it, during our leisure time we can find nothing more worthy or commendable to help our bodies relax and our spirits recuperate, especially at Court, where, besides the way in which music helps everyone to forget his troubles, many things are done to please the ladies, whose tender and gentle souls are very susceptible to harmony and sweetness.

Castiglione thought that women too should be able to sing and play a musical instrument (as well as dance), though they should be careful to take certain precautions:

> When she is dancing, I should not wish to see her use movements that are too forceful and energetic, nor, when she is singing or playing a musical instrument, to use those abrupt and frequent [diminutions] that are ingenious but not beautiful. And I suggest that she should choose instruments suited to her purpose. Imagine what an ungainly sight it would be to have a woman playing drums, fifes, trumpets, or other instruments of that sort; and this is simply because their stridency buries and destroys the sweet gentleness which embellishes everything a woman does. So when she is about to dance or make music of any kind, she should first have to be coaxed a little, and should begin with a certain shyness, suggesting the dignified modesty that brazen women cannot understand.[3]

3. *The Book of the Courtier*, 94, 215.

Though there were those among Castiglione's contemporaries who thought that any music making was an unseemly activity for a woman, sixteenth-century high society found Castiglione's prescriptions by and large irresistible.

Erasmus

Desiderius Erasmus of Rotterdam (1466?–1536), a towering intellectual, is best-known today through such works as the *Adages* (1500, enlarged in 1508), a collection of thousands of proverbs drawn from ancient authors with commentary that related them to contemporary problems, and the *Praise of Folly* (1511), a biting satire on the abuses of the church (though he remained loyal to Catholicism). But his great scholarly work was a 1516 edition of the New Testament with facing pages of original Greek and Latin translation, and with exegetical notes that helped open the door to modern biblical scholarship.

A GERMAN ARTIST

Albrecht Dürer (1471–1528; Fig. 23-6) is undoubtedly the greatest artist that Renaissance Germany produced. He is just as certainly the supreme master of engraving, whether on woodblock or copper plate, regardless of nationality. Dürer's genius lay in his ability to combine the essentially northern art of en-

Figure 23-6. Albrecht Dürer, *Self Portrait*, 1500 (Bayerische Staatsgemäldesammlungen, Munich).

Figure 23-7. Albrecht Dürer, *Knight, Death, and the Devil*, woodcut, 1513.

graving with the techniques of late-fifteenth-century Italian painting, which he studied closely during two trips to Venice. Moreover, he possessed a mind that was as inquiring in the field of philosophy as it was in mathematics and the laws of perspective.

One of Dürer's most famous engravings is the copper plate entitled *Knight, Death, and the Devil* of 1513 (Fig. 23-7). The knight's attitude here is fascinating. Though he must certainly be aware of his impending death, he pays it no heed. Is Dürer expressing the fatalism of predestination, which would play so powerful a role in the coming Reformation, especially as fashioned by John Calvin? Is the city in the background the heavenly Jerusalem? Is it possible that the letter "S" before the date "1513" and the ubiquitous "AD" monogram (in the lower left corner) is a reference to Savonarola? Savonarolan symbolism could be present in the dog and salamander, which often represented a holy man burned at the stake. Or was the artist merely paying tribute to the reckless bravery of medieval chivalry? Dürer was, after all, fascinated by military hardware, and spent his last years designing both artillery and impregnable fortresses. Or did he have nothing more in mind than to contribute—in the medium he had made his own—to the line of great equestrian statues that stretches back to ancient Rome? As in all great works of art, the meaning of *Knight, Death, and the Devil* is elusive. As for Dürer's skill as an engraver, we can hardly improve Erasmus's simple, nontechnical evaluation: "What does he not express in monochromes—that is, in black lines? Light, shade, splendor, eminences, depressions. . . . These things he places before the eye in the most pertinent lines—black ones, yet so that if you should spread on pigments, you would injure the work."[4]

DELIVERING THE MAIL

For thirty-seven years, 1496–1533, the Venetian aristocrat Marin Sanudo filled his *Diarii* with notes about the dates on which letters to the republic's governing body were sent and received. Thanks to his diligence, we can gain an idea of the speed with which letters reached Venice from various locations (the distances that follow are as the crow flies). From Rome (280 miles), it took less than one week; from Paris (525 miles), less than two weeks; from London (700 miles), more than three weeks; from Lisbon (1,180 miles), over a month and a half. "Special delivery" was possible; for the right price, the normal three-week Nuremberg-Venice route could be cut to four days. In general, the rule of thumb was that under the best of conditions—flat terrain, good roads, and decent weather—people and goods could move about 60 miles a day. It is shocking to realize that Napoleon's armies moved no faster than Julius Caesar's.

BIBLIOGRAPHICAL NOTE

Chapter references indicate where an individual's musical role is taken up in this book. **Francis I**: Desmond Seward, *Prince of the Renaissance: The Life of François I* (London: Constable, 1973); see Chapter 27. **Henry VIII**: two recent biographies, the first scholarly, the second more popular, are J. J. Scarisbrick, *Henry VIII* (Berkeley and Los Angeles: University of California Press, 1968), and Jasper Ridley, *Henry VIII* (New York: Viking, 1985); among early 1990s best-sellers was Alison Weir, *The Six Wives of Henry VIII* (New York: Ballantine, 1991); see Chapter 34. **Charles V**: the standard biography is Karl Brandi, *The Emperor Charles V*, trans. C. V. Wedgewood (London: J. Cape, 1939). **Leo X**: the best study is still Ludwig Pastor, *The History of the Popes*, vols. 7–8, ed. and trans. R. F. Kerr (St. Louis: Herder, 1923); on Leo's musical talents, see André Pirro, "Leo X and Music," *MQ* 21 (1935): 1–16; see also Bonnie J. Blackburn, "Music and Festivities at the Court of Leo X: A Venetian View," *EMH* 11 (1992): 1–37. **Martin Luther**: a classic study is Roland H. Bainton, *Here I Stand: The*

4. Quoted after Stechow, *Northern Renaissance Art*, 123.

Life of Martin Luther (New York: Abingdon-Cokesbury Press, 1950); for an especially vivid account, see William Manchester, *A World Lit Only by Fire: The Medieval Mind and the Renaissance, Portrait of an Age* (Boston: Little, Brown, 1992); see Chapter 33. **Machiavelli**: there is a fine introduction to his work in Peter Bondanella and Mark Musa's *Portable Machiavelli* (Harmondsworth: Penguin, 1979), which contains *The Prince* in its entirety. **Castiglione**: *The Book of the Courtier*, trans. G. Bull (Harmondsworth: Penguin, 1967); on music in *The Courtier*, see James Haar, "The Courtier as Musician: Castiglione's View of the Science and Art of Music," in Robert Hanning and David Rosand, eds., *The Ideal and the Real in Renaissance Culture* (New Haven: Yale University Press, 1983), 165–89; and Walter H. Kemp, "Some Notes on Music in Castiglione's *Il Libro del Cortegiano*," in Cecil H. Clough, ed., *Cultural Aspects of the Italian Renaissance: Essays in Honour of Paul Oskar Kristeller* (New York: A.F. Zambelli, 1976), 354–69. **Erasmus**: one should probably start with Roland H. Bainton, *Erasmus of Christendom* (New York: Scribner, 1969). **Dürer**: there is a fine survey of his works in Peter Strieder, *Albrecht Dürer: Paintings, Prints, Drawings* (New York: Abaris Books, 1982); for those who would dig somewhat deeper, Erwin Panofsky, *The Life and Art of Albrecht Dürer*, 4th ed. (Princeton: Princeton University Press, 1955).

Also Cited

Myron P. Gilmore, *The World of Humanism, 1453–1517* (New York: Harper Torchbooks, 1952); John R. Hale, ed., *A Concise Encyclopedia of the Italian Renaissance* (New York: Oxford University Press, 1981); Wolfgang Stechow, *Northern Renaissance Art, 1400–1600: Sources and Documents* (Englewood Cliffs, N.J.: Prentice-Hall, 1966).

CHAPTER 24

Old Ends and New Beginnings in Song

As noted earlier, both motet and Mass underwent change at the hands of the Josquin generation. Above all else, both genres took up the new style of pervading imitation. But there were changes in the conventions of the individual genres themselves. The Mass saw the emergence of parody technique, as well as the wider cultivation of such Mass types as the polyphonic Requiem and the *Missa de Beata Virgine*. In the motet, a new relationship between music and words brought about what we sense as a greater degree of expressivity. Yet in neither genre were the innovations truly shocking. Some of the changes could already be heard coming in the third quarter of the fifteenth century, and the most basic premises of each genre remained in place: a Kyrie was still a Kyrie, and a motet was still a through-composed setting of a Latin text.

There were shocks, however, in the field of secular song: by the time the Josquin generation had run its course, the *formes fixes*, alive and well in the Du Fay–Binchois and Busnoys-Ockeghem generations, were scarcely to be heard. And if they were snuffed out by a new approach in both poetry and music, one that was more popular, more naturalistic in tone, they gave way just as decidedly in serious, courtly poetry. Thus it is the tale of one tradition's demise and the beginning of another that we will look at in this chapter.

At the same time, there were major developments outside the Franco-Flemish tradition. National styles that had just begun to emerge in the years 1450–75 now began to crystallize and adopt conventions and expectations of their own. The most notable, perhaps, took root at the courts of northern Italy, where the frottola tradition blossomed as no native Italian polyphony had for nearly a century. Likewise, polyphonic song poured out of Spain and Germany. More than any other genre, secular song responded to the quickening pace of a changing world.

THE END OF THE *FORMES FIXES*

To be sure, the *formes fixes* were not abandoned either suddenly or completely, and a few composers—namely Compère, Agricola, and La Rue—still devoted a substantial part of their secular output to them.

A Rondeau by Compère

As noted in Chapter 15, among the most popular of late-fifteenth-century songs were two by Hayne van Ghizeghem: *De tous biens plaine* (*Anthology* 29) and *Allez, regrets*. Example 24-1 provides Hayne's setting of the first line of poetry in the latter:

EXAMPLE 24-1. Hayne van Ghizeghem, *Allez regrets*, mm. 1–11.

One of the many composers who drew on Hayne's song was Compère. In fact, he did so with a vengeance, writing three songs that belong to a miniature subgenre: *chansons à regrets*, songs that deal with the conceit of regret. *Anthology 45* gives us Compère's *Venes, regretz*, which is not a typical cantus-firmus arrangement but rather a parody of Hayne's rondeau, extracting from it new contrapuntal possibilities and adding a healthy dose of freely composed music. One of its nicest touches occurs at the beginning. Quoting Hayne's tenor in his own tenor (imitated in the superius), Compère places Hayne's superius in his own bassus, thus realizing the invertible counterpoint that was inherent in the original. Moreover, the contrapuntal flip-flop seems to mirror the semantics: whereas Hayne commands the regrets to "go," Compère invites them to "come." There was at least some life left in the old rondeau.

An "Anti"-Rondeau by Agricola

For the most part, the *formes fixes* died of benign neglect. If Compère, Agricola, and La Rue continued to cultivate them, other composers—Obrecht, Isaac, Mouton, Brumel, Févin, and Josquin—hardly touched them. No less indicative of the changing attitudes is a chanson by Agricola that actually subverts the customary rondeau form. Example 24-2 shows the entire superius of his *Gardez vous bien de ce fauveau*:

EXAMPLE 24-2. The superius of Agricola's *Gardez vous bien de ce fauveau*.[1]

1. After Brown, *A Florentine Chansonnier*, 1:59–60.

Although the poem is a perfectly normal rondeau quatrain, Agricola sets it in a most unusual fashion. Quite aside from the lack of tonal closure at the end of the refrain (m. 21) and the use of abridged refrains equivalent to the first verse only (mm. 29–35 and 57–63), Agricola writes completely new music for both the short and long strophes, that is, for the expected **a** and **a b** sections (mm. 22–28 and 36–57). In effect, Agricola has written a through-composed rondeau: a nail in the coffin of the *formes fixes*.

THE COURTLY TRADITION CONTINUED

Though the *formes fixes* were on the wane, composers continued to set serious, courtly lyrics. Yet with the old built-in repetition schemes out of fashion, they began to treat the poems much as they would the text of a motet. We can see this in two songs associated with the Habsburg-Netherlands court of Margaret of Austria.

Josquin's *Plus nulz regrets*

In a letter of 1513, Jean Lemaire de Belges, poet and secretary at the court of Margaret of Austria, wrote, "Rhétorique et Musique sont une mesme chose" (rhetoric and music are the same thing).[2] We can hear this union of poetry and music in one of Josquin's masterpieces, his setting of Lemaire's *Plus nulz regretz* (*Anthology* 46), a poem written at the end of 1507 to celebrate both a peace treaty between the Habsburg-Burgundian dynasty and Tudor England and the engagement of the future Charles V to Mary Tudor.

The poem, which follows no conventional scheme and thus exemplifies the break with the *formes fixes* tradition, is a long one (twenty verses):

1. Plus nulz regretz grans moyens ne menuz

 No more discontent, neither large, medium, nor small,

2. De joye nulz ne soyent ditz n'escriptz.

 Of such joy nothing can be spoken or written,

3. Ores revient le bon temps Saturnus

 Now has arrived the happy age of Saturn,

4. Ou peu congnuz furent plaintifs et cris.

 Where complaints and cries are little known.

5. Long temps nous ont tous malheurs infiniz

 For so long we have had unlimited sadness

6. Batuz, pugniz et fais povres maigretz,

 From battles, strife, plundering, and famine,

7. Mais maintenant d'espoir sommes garniz

 But now we are strengthened with hope,

8. Joinctz et unis n'ayons plus nulz regretz.

 Joined and united we have no more discontent.

9. Sur noz preaux et jardinetz herbus

 On our fields and green gardens

10. Luyra Phebus de ses rais ennobliz.

 The lyre of Apollo will shine with its noble rays.

11. Ainsy croistront noz boutoneaux barbus

 And so will grow to maturity the shoots of our beards

12. Sans nulz abus et dangereux troubliz.

 Without any abuse or troublesome perils.

13. Regretz plus nulz ne nous viennent apres

 Discontent no more will come to us afterward.

14. Nostre eure est pres, venant des cieulx beniz.

 Our time is near, coming from celestial blessings.

15. Voisent ailleurs regretz plus durs que gretz,

 Let it go elsewhere, this discontent harder than stone,

16. Fiers et aigretz, et charchent autres nidz.

 Haughty and harsh, and seek out other nests.

17. Se Mars nous tolt la blanche fleur de lis

 If Mars takes from us the white fleur-de-lis,

18. Sans nulz delictz sy nous donne Venus

 Without any offense, and if Venus gives to us

19. Rose vermeille, amoureuse, de pris,

 The amorous vermilion rose of great price,

20. Dont noz espritz n'auront regretz plus nulz.

 With which our spirits will have discontent no more.

2. Quoted after Reynolds, "Compositional Planning in the Renaissance," 70–71, from which article both translation of poem and discussion are drawn.

The most notable aspect of the poem's structure is its insistence on mirror images: the rhyme scheme, which runs a b a b/b c b c for the first eight verses, becomes c b c b/b a b a for the last eight; and while verses 1 and 8 begin and end respectively with "Plus nulz regretz," verses 13 and 20 do the same with "Regretz plus nulz." An obvious result of this mirroring is the division of the poem into three sections, verses 1–8, 9–12, and 13–20, which produces yet another mirror image (8 + 4 + 8). Finally, within his broader rhyme scheme, Lemaire tucks the so-called *rime batelée*: the last syllable of each odd-numbered verse rhymes with the fourth syllable of the next even-numbered verse: for instance, the final syllable of verse 5, "niz" ("infiniz"), rhymes with the fourth syllable of verse 6, "niz" ("pugniz").

How does Josquin, who complicated his task by setting only the first eight verses, reflect all of this in his music? To begin with, he expresses the poetic mirroring in four different ways and at four different structural levels. First, verses 1–2 and 7–8 are set as double canons (with varying degrees of strictness), while the middle verses, 3–6, all involve canons built on a single motive. Table 24-1 summarizes Josquin's use of canons:

Table 24-1.   Canons in Josquin's *Plus nulz regretz*.

Verse	Measures (with overlaps)	Canons
1	1–9	Double canon, one between bass and tenor, the other between contratenor and superius.
2	8–18	Double canon, one between bass and superius with inversion, the other between contratenor and tenor with inversion.
3	16–24	Single canon at the 5th involving all four voices (but with bass/tenor and contratenor/superius paired).
4	22–32	Single canon between bass and tenor, first at the 5th, then at the 4th.
5	32–39	Single canon at the 5th and 8^{ve} involving all four voices.
6	39–53	Single canon at the 5th and 8^{ve} involving all four voices.
7	53–61	Double canon, one between bass and tenor, the other between contratenor and superius (but starting only at m. 57 in the contratenor).
8	60–73	Double canon, one between bass and tenor, the other between superius and contratenor.

Second, two pairs of motives appear in one order during the first part of the piece (mm. 1–32) and then return in reverse order (altered to one degree or another) during the second part (mm. 32–73). Example 24-3 provides a map of sorts:

EXAMPLE 24-3. Mirror-image motives in *Plus nulz regretz*: motives a and b (mm. 1–6) and a′ and b′ (mm. 53–57); motives x and y (mm. 22–26) and x′ and y′ (mm. 43–48).

Third, although we hear *Plus nulz regretz* most immediately in two large sections—**A** and **B**—with the division coming at the end of verse 4 (m. 32), if we listen in such a way that we combine the cadences at the end of each verse with the appearance and reappearance of the mirror-image motives, we can hear the piece just as well divided as shown in Table 24-2. *Plus nulz regretz* can therefore be said to fall into five sections whose lengths relate to one another as 22 + 11 + 12 + 11 + 22.

Table 24-2.   Structural proportions in *Plus nulz regretz* as
determined by cadences and mirror-image motives.

Section	Measures	Length	Signpost
1	1–22	22	Motives a and b
2	22–32	11	Motives x and y/ends at corona
3	32–43	12	No mirror-image motives
4	43–53	11	Motives x' and y'
5	53–73	22^a	Motives a' and b'

^{a}The final long is counted as two breves (= two measures).

Fourth, the song is customarily performed in such a way as to produce an overall shape of **A B A A B**; that is, after verses 1–8 take us through the entire piece (**A B**), verses 9–12 are sung to measures 1–32 (**A**), and verses 13–20 return to the beginning and sweep through the two sections as a whole (**A B**). But since all the verses are the same length—ten syllables—and since measure 32 provides just as great a sense of tonal closure as measure 73, it is equally possible to perform the piece according to the plan **A B A B A**, that is, to build another mirror.

Finally, Josquin puts the finishing touches on the music-text relationship by underscoring Lemaire's use of the *rime batelée*. Just as the poet rhymed the final syllable and fourth syllable, respectively, of the odd- and even-numbered verses, so Josquin sets all but the final pair of those rhymes with matching sonorities: in verses 1–2, the triads on F in measures 9 and 11; in verses 3–4, the triads on E in measures 24 and 26; and in verses 5–6, the triads on D in measures 39 and 43. In its skill at matching the structure of the poem with parallel gestures in the music, *Plus nulz regretz* is an amazing little work. It is difficult to imagine such flexibility in the *formes fixes*.

La Rue's *Pourquoy non*

With its very low range—down to B_1- flat (some sources transmit the piece a fifth higher)—and flatward motion around the circle of fifths to D-flat, *Pourquoy non* (*Anthology* 47) holds a significant place in La Rue's output; it is one of the stylistic yardsticks against which the motet *Absalon, fili mi* is measured and attributed to La Rue (see Chapter 20). The music and text of *Pourquoy non* parallel one another in a number of ways. First, there is the near-literal repeat (mm. 1–9 and 16–24) followed by varied repetition (mm. 10–15 and 25–33) that underscore the first two lines of the poem: "Pourquoy non, ne veuil je morir? / Pourquoy non, ne doy je querir." Second, the introduction of the D-flat at the line "La fin de ma doulente vie" (m. 34) is an obvious attempt to reflect the somber quality of those words. And third, when in the overall a a b b a rhyme scheme the "a" rhyme—"rir"—returns at the end of line 5 (m. 60–61), there is a faint recollection of the gesture with which it was set at the end of line 2 (m. 28–29): the repetition of a short, concise motive that leads to a cadence. The idea of setting rhymes with similar, even identical, music would become a standard ploy in the songs of both the Josquin generation and the one that followed.

In all, the demise of the *formes fixes* did not spell the end either of courtly poetry or of its attraction for composers. But the ways in which such poetry was set clearly underwent change. Gone were the stereotyped repetition schemes, the long, arching melodies, and the rhythmically nervous, melismatic extensions that drove the music to the cadence. Gone also was the three-voice texture with its backbone of superius-tenor duet. Instead, we find a mosaic of sharply etched motives, the rhythms of which seem to grow more naturally out of the declamation of the text. Moreover, the addition of a fourth voice became standard, and the texture encompassed everything from pervading imitation to declamatory chordal writing. In a way, secular song became motet-like, both in its purely musical characteristics and in its relationship between music and text.

LIFE OF LA RUE   Pierre de la Rue was born around 1450–55, probably at Tournai. After stints as a singer at churches in Brussels (1469–70), Ghent (1471–72), and Nieuwpoort (1472–before 1477), where he is consistently identified as a tenor (which means that he sang the tenor part of the polyphonic fabric, not that he had a voice like Caruso's), La Rue drops out of sight until 1489, when he joined the Church of Our Lady at 's-Hertogenbosch.

The turning point in La Rue's career occurred in 1492, when he moved to the Habsburg-Burgundian chapel that Maximilian I was rebuilding for his son Philip the Fair. And it was in the service of the Habsburgs that he would spend the remainder of his career: Maximilian I (1492–93); Philip the Fair (1493–1506), with whom he twice traveled to Spain; Philip's widow, Juana (1506–8), with whom he remained in Spain for two years after Philip died there; Margaret of Austria (Philip's sister, 1508–14); and the future Charles V (1514–15, Philip's son), before he went off to rule the Spanish part of his domain. Having spent a quarter century with the Habsburgs, La Rue retired to Courtrai early in 1516 and died there in November 1518.

What is striking about La Rue's career is his loyalty to the Habsburgs in an age when many composers seem to have spent a good deal of time plotting their next move. The loyalty, moreover, went in both directions. Thus in 1509, Margaret wrote to Maximilian to ask that La Rue be granted a benefice, taking note of the "good service he has performed, and one hopes he will continue to perform, for my late brother and myself during the last fifteen or sixteen years."[3]

Among the Josquin-Obrecht-Isaac-La Rue quartet—and they were the four leading composers of their generation—La Rue is perhaps the most difficult to characterize. Not drawn to Obrecht's brand of extreme constructivism, neither did he don and shed national styles as did Isaac (he had no reason to); and even the most ardent La Rue fans must admit that he did not match the inexhaustible imagination of Josquin. Indeed, he has been credited with influencing such composers as Jean Richafort and Pierre de Manchicourt, solid if unexciting members of what we will only half-jokingly call a "no-name" generation (see Chapter 26).

---

3. Quoted after Picker, *The Chanson Albums of Marguerite of Austria*, 37.

Figure 24-1. Bernard Van Orley,
portrait of Margaret of Austria, 1518
(Musée d'Art Ancien, Brussels).

MARGARET OF AUSTRIA   The Habsburg patron with whom La Rue had the warmest relationship was Margaret of Austria (1480–1530; Fig. 24-1), daughter of Maximilian and Mary of Burgundy. Named Regent of the Netherlands soon after the death of her brother Philip the Fair, Margaret established her court at Malines, where, despite a certain somberness owing to a series of personal misfortunes—and La Rue often captured this mood in his works—she fostered an incredibly rich cultural life. In addition to La Rue, her musicians included the composer Marbriano de Orto and the well-known scribe Pierre Alamire. Among the surviving treasures of her court's musical life are two chanson manuscripts,[4] one a particularly important source of La Rue's secular works, and the beautiful basse danse manuscript mentioned in Chapter 16. In addition, Margaret seems to have been a model ruler; as Castiglione put it in *The Courtier*: "[She] has governed and still governs her state with the greatest prudence and justice."[5]

THE POPULAR TRADITION

As we saw in Chapter 15, songs of a popular nature—*chansons rustiques*—were already playing a role in polyphonic song during the third quarter of the fifteenth century, especially in the combinative chanson, where a pop tune and its poem generally appeared in the tenor as a foil to a courtly song in the superius. It was, however, with the Josquin generation that polyphonic settings of such tunes came into their own, so much so that Josquin based almost half of his secular output on melodies that were probably sung, hummed, and whis-

---

4. Brussels, Bibliothèque Royale, MSS 11239 and 228.

5. *The Book of the Courtier*, trans. George Bull (Harmondsworth: Penguin, 1976), 238.

Figure 24-2. A page from the Bayeux manuscript showing the melody *Baisés moy*.

tled everywhere, from working-class taverns to upper-middle-class homes to music rooms of the nobility.

A Tune, a Poem, a Manuscript

The lyrics of popular songs were customarily disseminated in printed anthologies without their music. There are, however, two large monophonic chansonniers that preserve a generous number of melodies as well. One of these, the elegantly decorated Bayeux Chansonnier (Fig. 24-2),[6] was written for Charles de Bourbon, one of the *grands seigneurs* at the court of Louis XII, and thus shows the extent to which the songs permeated the very highest echelons of courtly society.

One of the many songs in the Bayeux manuscript that were set polyphonically is *Baisés moy* (Ex. 24-4):

6. Paris, Bibliothèque Nationale, fonds française, MS 9346; the other manuscript is MS 12744 in the same collection.

EXAMPLE 24-4. *Baisés moy*, Paris, MS 9346, No. 102.[7]

This song, like *Marchez là dureau*, the *chanson rustique* at which we looked in Chapter 15, contrasts sharply with the courtly tradition. The language of the poem is anything but highfalutin, and the boy-girl pair could easily come from the rural peasant class. As for the kisses, they are modesty itself, and represent the least of what was often at stake in these songs. The music is equally direct: syllabic, square-cut, and repetitive. Finally, like so many of the songs that found their way into polyphonic settings, *Baisés moy* is a *chanson à refrain*: here, two two-line stanzas—lines 2–3 (mm. 4–7) and 5–6 (mm. 12–15)—are preceded, separated, and followed by a refrain (in this instance, one in which the words vary).

Three- and Four-Part Arrangements

It did not take long for polyphonic settings in the popular tradition to develop their own stylistic conventions and expectations. And by 1500 or so, we can distinguish between three- and four-part popular arrangements, the differences between them going well beyond the number of voices.

Example 24-5 shows the opening of *J'ay veu la beaulté*, both in its monophonic guise and in its three-part arrangement as set by Antoine de Févin, who worked at the French court of Louis XII and made a specialty of such arrangements:

EXAMPLE 24-5. *J'ay veu la beaulté*: (a) anonymous monophonic version (Paris 9346); (b) three-part arrangement by Févin, mm. 1–14.

(a)

7. After Gerold, *Le Manuscrit de Bayeux*, with modifications.

(b)

Févin quotes the popular tune in rather literal, phrase-by-phrase fashion in the tenor (here, the middle voice), around which the two others set off points of imitation. The tenor, then, serves as a cantus firmus of sorts, anchoring and controlling the motion of the other voices.

There were occasionally variations. In *Adieu solas*, Févin places what is almost certainly a preexistent tune in the superius (Ex. 24-6):

EXAMPLE 24-6. Févin, *Adieu solas*.

With its simple, syllabic yet lyrical superius, light imitative touches, harmonic bass, opening dactylic rhythm ($\quad$), pause on the fourth syllable of the decasyllabic line, and repetition of both music and poetry at the end, *Adieu solas* is a harbinger of a style that would burst forth in the 1520s and announce the full-blown arrival of a new aesthetic sensibility.

Though four-part arrangements can behave more unpredictably than those in three parts, we can still reconstruct the presumed pop tune on which Ninot le Petit's *Et la la la* (*Anthology* 48) is based (Ex. 24-7):

EXAMPLE 24-7. A reconstruction of the presumed popular tune *Et la la la*.

Assuming that the reconstruction is close, Ninot's setting shows the variety of styles that four-part arrangements admit, even within a single piece: straightforward presentation of the preexistent tune in a single voice (here in the superius, but just as possibly in the tenor); imitative presentations of a snippet of the tune, whether in single voices or in pairs; and outright homophony. Composers thus took the simplest of tunes and achieved variety by running them through the full array of Josquin-generation textures. Equally typical of the four-part arrangements is the bouncy rhythm of *Et la la la*, characterized by the patter of its repeated notes. About the only thing missing in Ninot's setting is the often-used device of shifting between duple and triple meters. The piece, finally, is fun, and it too looks forward to a style that would coalesce in the 1520s.

There is one more difference between the three- and four-part arrangements: the milieu in which they were cultivated. The three-part song developed at the hands of composers working at the court of Louis XII in the early sixteenth century, was transmitted mainly in manuscripts of French provenance, and drew heavily on the tunes included in the two monophonic chansonniers cited above. The four-part arrangement is more problematic: the majority of the tunes on which they are presumed to be based do not survive in the monophonic chansonniers; the arrangements are transmitted mainly in sources copied or printed in Italy; and most of the Franco-Flemish composers who cultivated the style had Italian connections. The four-part arrangement, then, seems to have developed in Italy during the last two decades of the fifteenth century.

JOSQUIN AND THE POPULAR TRADITION

Old stories bear retelling (or else they would not be old stories): whatever Josquin did, he did better than anyone else. This is no less true of his many forays into the popular tradition. Ever the virtuoso, Josquin delighted in treating popular tunes with various kinds of canon, thus highlighting—even amusingly exaggerating—the difference between the simplicity of the melody and its "learned" treatment.

In *Baisés moy* (*Anthology* 49; the monophonic melody appears in Ex. 24-4), Josquin places the pop tune in the bassus and has the tenor answer it in canon at the fourth; above this canon, altus and superius spin out a canon of their own, which sometimes echoes the lower one and therefore seems to turn the two contrasting two-voice canons into a single four-part canon. Although the canon at the fourth between the lower voices was dictated by the time interval chosen, it sets up an occasional who's-leading-whom situation: for example, when the bassus, which is the lead voice, sings its second "baisés moy," it momentarily sounds as though it is answering the tenor at the unison.

The five-part chanson *Faulte d'argent* (*Anthology* 50) affords us another chance to see Josquin interpret his text in the structure of his music, this time in a work that has the quality of a lighthearted romp. Josquin sets only the opening quatrain of a longer poem:

Faulte d'argent, c'est douleur non pareille.	Lack of money is sorrow unequaled.
Se je le dis, las, je sçay bien pourquoy.	If I say this, alas, I well know why.
Sans de quibus il se fault tenir quoy.	Without money, one must remain silent.
Femme qui dort pour argent se resveille.	A woman who sleeps will awake for money.[8]

The last line comes as something of a surprise; its moral is more serious than we thought

The popular melody, in the *quinta pars* (next-to-lowest voice), is clearly in the Hypodorian mode transposed to G (its range is d to c'), and each phrase defines its own clear-cut section, the overall form of the piece being **A B C A'** (mm. 1–24, upbeat/24–36, upbeat/35–44, 44–72). How does the structure of the music mirror the meaning of the text? The answer lies in Josquin's purposeful exploitation of tonal-modal ambiguity. Although the original tune has a strong feeling of tonal closure in G-Hypodorian (respected by all other composers who set the melody), Josquin ends the piece on D, thus providing the unexpected turn in the final line of the poem with an equally surprising tonal twist. Yet he sets us up for this surprise ending from the very beginning. In the **A** section, the popular melody spins out as a strict canon between the tenor on D and the *quinta pars* on G; and though it is the *quinta pars* that has the "real" melody, it is the tenor that leads and thus seems to direct the tonal flow, especially since the *quinta pars*'s cadences on G are constantly undercut. And when the opening section returns at measure 44, the tonal ambiguity between G and D begins again, clearing up—or permanently fogging up—only with the surprise ending on D. In the end, *Faulte d'argent*, barely two minutes long, is a

8. After Bernstein, "A Canonic Chanson," 60, on which the discussion is entirely based.

microcosm of what constantly amazes us about Josquin: his ability to realize the full potential of his materials, both musical and poetic, and to do so in piece after piece, no matter what the genre.

ITALY

In the 1490s, native Italian polyphony awoke from a somnolent three-quarters of a century, primarily at the northern Italian courts of Mantua, Ferrara, and Urbino, and with a type of secular song known as the *frottola*.

The Frottola

The term "frottola" had two meanings for musicians and audiences during the period 1480–1520: it was used in a generic sense to refer to polyphonic settings of secular Italian verse cast in various musical-poetic "fixed forms"; and it was sometimes used to designate one of those forms in particular, the *barzelletta*. While the term also carried certain popular, even rustic, connotations, the frottola was very much a courtly art and, with its emphasis on melancholy love, observed a host of formal conventions. In fact, there is a certain irony in its formality, since the frottola was launched just when composers of French secular song were abandoning the stilted themes and language of their own *formes fixes* for a less formalistic, popular tone.

MANTUA: CARA AND TROMBONCINO   The center of frottola composition was the court of Mantua, where, under the enlightened patronage of the Marchesa Isabella d'Este, two composers took the lead in developing the genre: Marchetto Cara (c. 1465–1525), who served as composer, chapel master, singer, and lutenist from 1494 until his death, and Bartolomeo Tromboncino (c. 1470–after 1535), who arrived at Mantua by 1489, left by 1506 at the latest, and murdered his wife, Antonia, along the way. A letter that the Marchesa Isabella wrote to her husband describing the circumstances of the murder (July 21, 1499) says much about the social-legal outlook of the time as it weighed against women:

> Today around five o'clock in the afternoon, Alfonso Spagnolo came to notify me that Tromboncino had killed his wife with great cruelty for having found her at home alone in a room with Zoanmaria de Triomfo, who was seen by Alfonso at the window asking him [Alfonso] to find a ladder; but, hearing noise in the house, [Alfonso] did not wait and went inside. He found Tromboncino, who had attacked his wife with weapons, climbing the stairs accompanied by [his] father and a boy. Although he [Alfonso] reprimanded him, Tromboncino replied that he had the right to punish his wife [if he] found her in error, and, not having arms, he [Alfonso] was unable to stop him, so that when he returned home for arms, she was already dead. Zoanmaria, in the middle of this, jumped from the window. Tromboncino then retreated to [the church of] S. Barnaba with the father and the boy.
> For myself, I wanted to tell the story to Your Excellency and to beg you that, having had legitimate cause to kill his wife, and being of such goodwill and virtue as you are, to have mercy on them, and also on the father and the

boy, who, as far as Alfonso could tell, did not help Tromboncino in any way except to escape, for he alone wounded and killed her.[9]

Cara's favorite poetic form was the barzelletta. We can see one way in which he treated it in *Ala absentia* (*Anthology* 51), for which he wrote the poem as well as the music. The poem begins:

	Rhyme	Poetic structure	
Ala absentia che me acora,	a	*ripresa*	
Io non trovo altro conforto;	b		
Sol la fe che mia signora	a		
M'ha promesso o vivo o morto.	b		
Lei promisse, et io iurai;	c	*mutazione 1*	
Altri più mai non amare,	d		
Sì che donna al mondo mai	c	*mutazione 2*	
Potrà lei farme lasciare	d		stanza 1
Che fa el spirto vivo ogn'hora	a	*volta*	
Hor cussì lontan a torto.	b		
Sol la fe che mia signora	a	refrain	
M'ha promesso o vivo o morto.	b		

The two-line refrain is then followed by stanzas 2 and 3, with a statement of the refrain at the end of each. Cara's poem departs from the typical barzelletta form in two respects: its *ripresa* rhymes a b a b instead of the more customary a b b a; and the *volta* does not begin with the d rhyme with which the *mutazioni* ended, and so does not so much "turn" as jump directly from stanza to refrain.

In setting a barzelletta, Cara and his fellow frottolists had to make a basic decision: write music only for the *ripresa* (possibly with a variant added for the part that would serve as the refrain), or set both the *ripresa* and the *mutazioni*? In either case, a small number of melodic elements are used in a fixed pattern of repetition. As he usually did, Cara chose the second option in *Ala absentia*: measures 1–18 set the four lines of the *ripresa*, 19–34 set the *mutazioni*, 35–40 (= 1–6) then serve for the *volta*, and 41–51 (= 7–18) provide for the refrain.

Cara's setting of the poem is simple and direct. While there are short bursts of activity in the lower voices, including a brief point of imitation on "Sol la fe"—sung, probably not accidentally, to the solmization syllables *sol, la, fa* in the superius and tenor—*Ala absentia* generally consists of short, clearly declaimed, text-generated melodic phrases in the superius supported by what is essentially a chordal-sounding accompaniment. The rhythm seems lilting—in part a result of the frequent weak (or "feminine") cadences—and the phrases themselves follow one another with almost symmetrical regularity.

Clearly, we are a long way from the complicated polyphony of the Franco-Flemish chanson, but that was not what the frottola aspired to. Composed primarily for the culture-hungry aristocrats of the northern Italian courts, the frottola provided them with music to which they could do more than just

9. Quoted after Prizer, *Courtly Pastimes*, 57.

listen: especially when performed as a piece for solo voice with lute accompaniment, this song form invited participation by well-bred amateurs. And it
was their appetite for such music that led Petrucci and other printers to turn
out frottola publications in droves. In a way, the frottola was the first musical
genre in which art and commerce learned how to accommodate one another.

PERFORMANCE PRACTICE   We wrestle once more with the question of performance practice by comparing two versions of another barzelletta by Cara,
Oimè il cor, oimè la testa: the presumed four-part, polyphonic original as printed
in Petrucci's first book of frottole of 1504, and the arrangement for voice and
lute by Franciscus Bossinensis (from Bosnia?), which appears in his *Tenori e
contrabassi intabulati col soprano in canto figurato per cantar e sonar col lauto, libro primo*,
printed by Petrucci in 1509 (Ex. 24-8):

EXAMPLE 24-8. Cara, *Oimè il cor, oimè la testa*, mm. 1–6: (a) Petrucci, *Libro
primo* (1504); (b) Franciscus Bossinensis, *Tenori e contrabassi* (1509).

The frottola, then, could presumably be performed as a four-part, *a cappella*
vocal piece (though Petrucci usually supplied text only for the superius, and it
is often difficult to fit the words to the lower voices) or as a song for solo voice
with lute accompaniment, in which the solo voice took the superius part, the
lutenist played the tenor and bass parts, and the alto part was omitted altogether.
    We should not assume, however, that all frottole necessarily began life as
four-part polyphonic songs that were only later arranged for voice and lute.

Figure 24-3. Frontispiece to Andrea Antico's *Canzoni nove*, 1510.

Some seem to have been conceived for the duo combination from the outset, as witness a letter that Tromboncino wrote to the music theorist Giovanni del Lago on April 2, 1535: "You ask of me a transcript of *Se la mia morte brami*, and I send it to you with much pleasure, noting that I have written it only to an accompaniment by the lute, that is, in three parts and without alto. For this reason, if it were to be sung a cappella, an alto would have to be added."[10]

In fact, the voice-lute combination seems so compelling a medium for the frottola that one might wonder if it was not the primary means of performance. Yet the frontispiece of Andrea Antico's frottola collection *Canzoni nove* (Rome, 1510) depicts four affluent-looking gentlemen gathered around a tiny songbook, singing *a cappella* (Fig. 24-3), and Antico was no doubt reflecting public taste, not trying to change it.

There must have been still other possibilities: voice and keyboard, for instance, with the keyboard taking over the three lower voices, or solo voice accompanied by a consort of either viols or recorders. What seems clear is that the frottola was essentially a solo song, prized by its literary-minded performers and audiences both for its clear projection of the poetry and for its emotional directness. As such, it betrays its origins in the soloistic, unwritten tradition that the *improvvisatori* had cultivated throughout the fifteenth century.

THE LATER FROTTOLA Cara's *Ala absentia* and *Oimè il cor, oimè la testa* illustrate the rather lightweight nature of the frottola. With time, however, the genre gained some weight. Tromboncino, in particular, turned to poetry of a more serious tone, and by 1514, almost one-third of Petrucci's eleventh and final book of frottole was devoted to settings of works by the poet who would be the main source of inspiration for two generations of sixteenth-century Italian

10. Quoted after Einstein, *The Italian Madrigal*, 1: 48.

poets: Francesco Petrarch (1304–1374). Music quickly followed poetry in this pursuit of seriousness. Thus with its points of imitation, all-vocal conception, shifting textures, and generally careful declamation even in the inner voices, a piece such as the setting of Petrarch's sonnet *Si è debile il filo* by Bernardo Pisano (1490–1548; Ex. 24-9), published in 1520, stands on the threshold of the early madrigal.

EXAMPLE 24-9. Pisano, *Si è debile il filo*, mm. 1–12.

But only on the threshold. What is still entirely frottolistic about Pisano's approach is the fixed formal relationship of one phrase of music for one line of poetry. Thus the music comes to a dead stop at the end of line 1 (m. 9), even though the semantic sense runs directly into the next line: "How frail is the thread to which clings/My weighty life." We must wait for the madrigal to find music that sings the way poetry is read.

ISABELLA D'ESTE   It was not entirely by chance that the frottola came to flourish at Mantua: Isabella d'Este willed it. Born in 1474, the daughter of Duke Ercole I of Ferrara, Isabella came to Mantua in 1490, when she wed the Marchese Francesco Gonzaga. She remained there until her death in 1539, developing a reputation as an avid patron of the arts, a fine performer in her own right, and, like Margaret of Austria in the Low Countries, an exceptionally able administrator.

There are good reasons for Isabella's almost single-minded devotion to the frottola. First, like many a noblewoman, Isabella maintained her own household, quite apart from the larger one that served her husband; yet to keep up a large-scale chapel of her own on her annual "allowance" of eight thousand ducats would have been impossible. Second, Isabella's own musical talents consisted of singing and playing both lute and keyboard instruments; she could, therefore, perform the small-scale songs herself. Finally, Isabella's other great love was Italian poetry, and she was constantly in touch with the leading Italian poets of the day. It was therefore in the frottola that her two great artistic passions came together. As strongly as any other patron of the period, she impressed her own tastes and talents on the music she supported.

Florentine Carnival Songs

Few days of the year were celebrated in Italy with greater revelry than Shrove Tuesday (Mardi Gras), which marked the culmination of the festive carnival season that preceded Lent. And with the support of the Medici, who had an unfailing sense of when to provide their fellow citizens with a touch of bread-and-circus fun, the Florentines made an art of the celebrations.

The musical highlight of the festivities was the performance of *canti carnascialeschi* (carnival songs). The generic term refers not only to the carnival songs proper but also to those written for the *calendimaggio* (first of May) celebrations that marked the return of spring. Sung by masked serenaders who wended their way through torchlit streets, the songs had texts, some by Lorenzo the Magnificent himself, that extolled the virtues of artisans, merchants, and other social groups, often with some obscene *double entendres* aimed at the women to whom the songs were addressed. These double meanings are particularly evident in the songs about the so-called *lanzi*, the German-Swiss mercenaries who waged war across the Italian countryside. The anonymous *Canto di lanzi tamburini*, in which the soldier-drummers sing their own praises in a thick German accent, is good example:

Lanzi maine tamburine,	Lanzi drummers we are,
d'Alte Magne eran fenute	come from Germany
per sonar tambure e flute	to play drums and flutes
dove star guerre e buon vine. . . .	where there is war and good wine. . . .
Noi afer le flute nostre	We have flutes that are large,
grosse, lunghe, e ben bucate;	long, and well bored;
belle donne, ve le mostre,	beautiful ladies, we can show them to you,
tutte dolze far sonate,	they all play sweetly,
buon dinanzi e buon per lato,	good in front as well as on the side,
nel principio, e nelle fine. . . .	at the beginning and at the end. . . .
E se pur voi donne belle,	And if you too, beauteous ladies,
impanar sonar volete,	should wish to learn how to play,
noi loggiar Piazze Padelle,	we are quartered in Piazza Padella

alle stufe là di drete,	opposite the hot baths,
dove scuole consuete	where the school in customary use
far placere a Florentine. . . .	affords pleasure to Florentines. . . .[11]

The music of the carnival songs is as unpretentious as the poems. The setting of the *Canto di zingane* (*Anthology* 52) by the Florentine musician Alessandro Coppini (c. 1465–1527) is typical in its simple homophony, short passage for reduced voices (mm. 21–27), and energetic *sesquialtera* (a 3:2 relationship) at the end. It all adds up to a wonderful marriage of style and function.

Italian Pieces by Franco-Flemish Composers

Some of the best settings of Italian poetry were fashioned by the Franco-Flemish masters, who brought to their work a compositional virtuosity that the new generation of Italian polyphonists had yet to acquire. At times, they drew on popular Italian melodies. Thus when Josquin and Compère were chapel-mates at Milan in the 1470s, they both set a well-known tune about Scaramella going off to war in a style reminiscent of the French four-part popular arrangement (Ex. 24-10):

EXAMPLE 24-10. *Scaramella va alla guerra*: (a) Josquin, mm. 1–10; (b) Compère, mm. 1–8.

11. Text and translation after McGee, "Instruments in Florentine Carnival Songs," 457–58.

(b)

As we might expect, Isaac wrote a slew of Italian pieces during his many years at Florence. In *Donna, di dentro della tua casa,* he strung together a number of popular tunes in the manner of a quodlibet, including two favorites of the period, *Fortuna d'un gran tempo* and *Dammene un pocho di quella mazacrocha* (Ex. 24-11).[12]

At other times, the poem alone served as inspiration, as when Josquin realized the onomatopoetic possibilities offered by the cricket in *El grillo* (*Anthology* 53),

12. *Mazacroche* are deep-fried rice croquettes, usually stuffed with chopped meat, chicken livers, ham, onions, and mozzarella cheese, and coated with breadcrumbs. They are known today as *supplì* and can often be found in Italian neighborhoods of our own cities.

EXAMPLE 24-11. Isaac, *Donna, di dentro della tua casa*, mm. 1–14.

which, whether it meant to poke fun at the Milanese singer Carlo Grillo or not, must be one of the most exuberant and humorous frottole ever written.

SPAIN

Considering that the roots of Spanish secular polyphony reach back only a generation or so to the works of Joan Cornago, the rich repertory of Spanish polyphonic song that emerged during the period of Ferdinand and Isabella (1469–1516) is nothing short of astounding. Like the Italian frottolists, Spanish composers cultivated certain musical-poetic forms, the two most important of which were the *villancico* and the *romance*.

The Villancico

The villancico was by far the most popular form: of the 458 songs in the voluminous Cancionero Musical de Palacio (Palace Songbook), written during the years 1500–1520,[13] more than 300 are villancicos. Though the structure of the villancico was flexible, its broad formal outlines and stylistic characteristics can be seen in Pedro Escobar's *Passame por Dios barquero* (*Anthology* 54). Below is the musical-poetic structure of the opening refrain and first stanza:

13. Madrid, Palacio Real, Biblioteca, MS 1335 (formerly 2-I-5).

	Rhyme	Section of poem	Music
Passame por Dios barquero,	a	*estribillo*	**a**
Daquella parte del rio,	b		
Duelete del amor mio,	b		
Que si pones dilacion	c	*mudanza*	**b**
En venir a socorrerme	d		
No podrás despues valerme	d		**b**
Segun crece mi passion.	c	*copla*	
No quieras mi perdicion	c	*vuelta*	**a**
Pues en tu bondad confio	b		
Duelete del amor mio.	b		

Thus the villancico is closely related to the canción, differing from it primarily in two ways: its *estribillo* (refrain) usually has two or three lines instead of the customary four of the canción; and its *vuelta* always begins with the final rhyme of the *mudanza*, instead of replicating the rhyme scheme of the *estribillo*. In fact, sixteenth-century terminology was rather loose, and the term "villancico" was often applied to any poem with an introductory refrain.

Like the Italian frottola, Spanish polyphonic song displays a sense of melodic directness, simple homophony, clear phrase structure, and a modern-sounding sense of tonal focus. If there is a notable element that distinguishes between them, it is the tendency for the rhythm of Spanish song to fall into less predictable patterns. There are even some villancicos that can be successfully transcribed only in quintuple meter.

The Romance: Juan del Encina

The Spanish *romance*—or ballad—has no precise counterpart in French or Italian song, at least not as those repertories are transmitted in written form. Briefly, the romance, which grew out of a centuries-long tradition of oral dissemination, is a strophic poem (without refrain) that tells a story based on or a historical event or a fictional epic.

Among the forty-some romances in the Palace Songbook are six that tell of the *reconquista*, Ferdinand's campaigns and eventual victory in 1492 over the Muslim kingdom of Granada. One of these is the haunting *Una sañosa porfía*, by Juan del Encina (*Anthology* 55). What is fascinating about the piece—and Encina must also have written the poem—is that it sympathizes with the defeated Moorish king, Boabdil (died c. 1533); indeed, it is Boabdil's voice that we hear, as he laments the loss of his kingdom.[14] Perhaps Encina's somber approach reflects something of Queen Isabella's attitude toward the conquests; after each new advance by the Spanish armies, she is known to have prayed for the Muslims' conversion to Christianity.

Born the son of a shoemaker at Salamanca in 1468, Encina was the most renowned Spanish composer, poet, and playwright of the period. After singing

---

14. For a particularly touching account of Boabdil's defeat, see the chapter entitled "Mementos of Boabdil" in Washington Irving's *Alhambra*, Bibliophile edition, 178–83.

in the choir of the Salamanca Cathedral (from 1484), he entered the service of Don Fadrique Álvarez de Toledo, Duke of Alba, in 1492, where he produced nearly his entire musical and literary output; this included a series of *églogas* (short plays) on religious or pastoral themes, in which Encina himself acted and for which he composed some of his villancicos. Encina left the duke's employ in 1498 and spent most of his remaining years shuttling between Spain and Rome. His final publication, the *Tribagia o via sagrada de Hierusalem* (Rome, 1521), is a two-hundred-stanza narrative of his pilgrimage to the Holy Land, where, as a recently ordained priest, he celebrated his first Mass in August 1519 at the Church of the Holy Sepulchre. Encina died at Léon in 1529.

PERFORMANCE PRACTICE   The Spanish variant on the seemingly eternal question: was Spanish song generally performed by voices only or by a solo voice accompanied by lute or *vihuela* (the Spanish version of the lute)? Like the frottola, it was no doubt performed both ways, as the following evidence shows.

The final play of Encina's 1496 *Cancionero de las obras de Juan del Enzina* concludes with a polyphonic song performed by the play's four characters: the shepherd Mingo (played by Encina himself); his wife, Menga; the courtier Gil; and his wife, Pascuala. Below is the play's ending:

> So that all four [characters] together, dressed in finery, end the play by singing the final villancico.

> MINGO: Come on, Gil, for such an initiation into the courtly way of existence, let's sing with great persistence some pretty composition, and that without further consultation.
> GIL: I think that's just the thing to do.
> MINGO: And you, Pascuala?
> PASCUALA: I agree with you.
> GIL: What about you, Menga?
> MENGA: Without hesitation.

> *Villancico. Ninguno cierre las puertas.*

The four characters then sing Encina's four-part *Ninguno cierre las puertas* (Ex. 24-12), one of the villancicos included in the Palace Songbook; since there are no indications that they or anyone else have instruments, they appear to have sung *a cappella*, one voice to a part.

EXAMPLE 24-12. Encina, *Ninguno cierre las puertas*, mm. 1-9.

Another Spanish literary work, Fernando de Rojas's *La Celestina*, contains the following passage, a dialogue between the courtier Calixto and his servant Sempronio:

CALIXTO: Sempronio!
SEMPRONIO: Sir!
CALIXTO: Bring me the lute.
SEMPRONIO: Sir, here it is.
CALIXTO: What pain could ever equal mine?
SEMPRONIO: This lute's out of tune.
CALIXTO: How can the out-of-tune be tuned? How can he who is so discordant in himself appreciate harmony? . . . But play and sing the saddest song you know.
SEMPRONIO: "Nero looked from Tarpeya at how Rome was burning: young and old were screaming, but he cared nothing."[15]

The song that Sempronio sings was a well-known romance, *Mira Nero de Tarpeya*. And that it could very well have been performed as Sempronio did it—by solo voice and lute/vihuela—is confirmed by an anonymous arrangement for precisely that combination in Juan Bermudo's *Declaración de instrumentos* of 1555 (Ex. 24-13):

EXAMPLE 24-13. Bermudo, arrangement of *Mira Nero de Tarpeya*, mm. 1–5.

Are we taking the literary references too literally? Perhaps. The best course is to keep an open mind.

15. Both excerpts are quoted after Knighton, "The *a cappella* Heresy in Spain," 569–70, 576–77.

GERMANY

In some respects, the development of polyphonic song in Germany (more properly, German-speaking lands) parallels that in Spain. From a trickle that began around the middle of the fifteenth century, the German *Tenorlied*—or *Gesellschaftslied* (social song), as it was called in sixteenth-century publications—reached its first stage of maturity during the years 1500–1520.

Heinrich Finck

One of the more prolific native-German composers was Heinrich Finck (c. 1445–1527), who spent much of his career before 1510 in Poland. Finck's setting of *Ich stund an einem morgen* (*Anthology* 56) shows the direction in which German song was heading in the early sixteenth century. Though the popular tune appears in the tenor in customary cantus-firmus-like fashion, the texture features anticipatory imitation (most pronounced at the beginning of the piece) and seamless cadences. This motet-like texture is even more pronounced in *Ade mit leid*, a song by Maximilian's court organist, Paul Hofhaimer (Ex. 24-14):

EXAMPLE 24-14. Hofhaimer, *Ade mit leid*, mm. 1-7.

Here, even the traces of the tenor's sustained-note, cantus-firmus-like quality have disappeared. Pervading imitation has won out.

In effect, German polyphonic song had its cake and ate it too. On the one hand, it retained its sense of national identity by drawing on popular German tunes, retaining their customary *bar* form and disposing them in the tenor in cantus-firmus fashion; on the other hand, it was beginning to emulate the style and techniques of Franco-Flemish polyphony. Thus after decades of a certain polyphonic provincialism, German song was entering the Franco-Flemish mainstream. With Ludwig Senfl, it would soon reach its high point.

German Song and the Marketplace

German polyphonic song was quick to hit the presses. During the 1510s, three printers—Erhard Oeglin of Augsburg, Peter Schöffer the Younger of

Mainz (whose father had worked with Gutenberg), and Arnt von Aich of Cologne—issued four collections containing a total of 223 songs. To put this in perspective: during the same period, France, the Low Countries, and Spain printed nothing, as music there continued to circulate only by means of manuscripts, while Petrucci alone, in his ten extant frottola collections (1504–14), published no fewer than 641 pieces. German polyphonic song thus quickly spread beyond the courtly society for which much of it was composed and seeped down to a growing, ever more musically literate middle class. In fact, perhaps nowhere else at the time did secular art music become as deeply ingrained in the national conscience as it did in the lands where German was spoken—even, as we will see, to the extent of becoming part of the religious expression of the people.

Isaac's Farewell to Innsbruck

Perhaps no art song from the years around 1500 came to permeate the fabric of everyday life as deeply as Isaac's chorale-like *Innsbruck, ich muss dich lassen* (*Anthology* 57), a heartfelt farewell to the Tyrolean city at the foot of the Alps. Outfitted with various religious texts that replaced the one about Innsbruck, Isaac's melody (or did Isaac himself draw on a popular tune?) became part of the Lutheran chorale literature and the basis of a number of chorale settings by J. S. Bach, as well as the starting point for two of Brahms's *Choralvorspiele* for organ. Even today, one can stop at virtually any souvenir stand in Innsbruck and find picture postcards on which the opening phrase of the melody is written out against a backdrop of snow-capped mountains. At Innsbruck, *Innsbruck* is a cultural treasure.

A chapter that has skipped across the map in survey-like fashion deserves a summary. For French secular song at the beginning of the sixteenth century, the single most notable development was the abandonment of the two-hundred-year-old tradition of the *formes fixes*. And even when composers continued to write in a serious, courtly vein, they turned to poetry that was less stereotypically organized, and they reflected this new flexibility in the poetry with an equally freer, more plastic approach to musical form. At the same time, composers of the Josquin generation cultivated a more popular style, as they arranged tuneful, often bouncy melodies whose appeal must have cut across lines that ordinarily divided aristocracy and bourgeoisie. We might even say that French polyphonic song was becoming democratized, a process that was aided by the printing press, which now made music by Josquin, Isaac, Compère, Mouton, and their contemporaries available to a public whose size and geographic extent could not have been imagined by earlier composers. It was an exciting time for composers and consumers alike.

But the excitement was not limited to the French-speaking world. Italy witnessed the rebirth of native polyphony in the guise of the frottola, while Spain and Germany saw the flowering of polyphonic song traditions that had taken root only a few decades earlier. Thus, while the central Franco-Flemish style continued to dominate in Mass and motet, secular song saw the emergence of national styles, a development that would become even more pronounced starting in the 1520s, when French song itself split into two stylistic camps along national boundaries.

BIBLIOGRAPHICAL NOTE

Editions of the Music

Many of the complete-works editions of the major composers have been cited in Chapters 18–22; to these should be added *Heinrich Isaac: Weltliche Werke*, ed. Johannes Wolf, *DTÖ*, vols. 28 and 32 (Vienna: Artaria, 1907–9; reprint 1959), which must suffice for Isaac's secular music until the *Opera omnia* reaches the secular works. **French song**: to the editions of Florence 229 (see below) and Petrucci's *Odhecaton* (cited in Chapter 18) should be added Martin Picker's *Chanson Albums of Marguerite of Austria* (Berkeley and Los Angeles: University of California Press, 1965) and Helen Hewitt's *Canti B numero cinquanta*, *MRM* 2 (Chicago: Chicago University Press, 1967), which emphasize courtly and popular chansons, respectively; the monophonic chansonniers are edited in Gaston Paris, *Chansons du XVᵉ siècle* (Paris: Firmin-Didot, 1875; Johnson Reprint, 1965), and Théodore Gérold, *Le Manuscrit de Bayeux* (Strasbourg: Palais de l'Université, 1921; reprint, Minkoff, 1971). **Italian frottole and carnival songs**: Prizer's *Courtly Pastimes* (cited below) contains a large selection of Cara's frottole; for Petrucci's frottola books I and IV, see Rudolph Schwartz, *Ottaviano Petrucci: Frottole, Buch I und IV*, *PäM* 8 (Leipzig: Breitkopf & Härtel, 1935); Petrucci's books I, II, and III appear in Raffaello Monterosso, *Le frottole nell'edizione principe di Ottaviano Petrucci*, IMa, ser. I, vol. 1 (Cremona: Athenaeum cremonense, 1954); Petrucci's publications of frottole arranged for voice and lute appear in Benvenuto Disertori, *Le frottole per canto e liuto intabulate da Franciscus Bossinensis* (Milan: G. Ricordi, 1964); there is a collection of late frottola settings in William F. Prizer's edition of the 1526 print entitled *Canzoni frottole et capitoli . . . Libro primo. De la Croce*, Collegium Musicum, Yale University, ser. II, vol. 8 (Madison: A-R Editions, 1978); for a collection of Florentine carnival songs, see Joseph J. Gallucci Jr., *Florentine Festival Music, 1480–1520*, RRMR 40 (Madison: A-R Editions, 1981). **Spanish villancicos and romances**: the Cancionero Musical de Palacio is edited in Higinio Anglés and José Romeu Figueras, *La Música en la Corte de los Reyes Católicos: Polifonía profana— Cancionero musical de Palacio*, 3 vols, MME 5, 10, 14 (Barcelona: Consejo Superior de Investigaciones Cientificas, 1947, 1951, 1965); the slightly earlier Colombina Cancionero is edited in both the same series, vol. 33 (1971), and Gertraut Haberkamp, *Die weltliche Vokalmusik in Spanien um 1500* (Tutzing: Schneider, 1968); still a third, slightly later *cancionero* appears in Gil Miranda, *The Elvas Songbook*, CMM 98 (American Institute of Musicology, 1987); see also Thomas Binkley and Margit Frenk, *Spanish Romances of the Sixteenth Century*, PEMI (Bloomington: Indiana University Press, 1995). **German Lieder**: the songs of Isaac, Hofhaimer, and Finck appear in the Isaac *Weltliche Werke*; Hans Joachim Moser, *Paul Hofhaimer* (Stuttgart and Berlin: J.G. Cotta, 1929; reprint, 1966); and Lothar Hoffman-Erbrecht, *Heinrich Finck: Ausgewählte Werke*, 2 vols., *EDM* 57, 70 (Frankfurt: C.F. Peters, 1962, 1981).

France and the Low Countries

A number of studies by Howard Mayer Brown are musts: "The *Chanson rustique*: Popular Elements in the 15th- and 16th-Century Chanson," *JAMS* 12 (1959): 16–26; *Music in the French Secular Theater* (Cambridge: Harvard University Press, 1963); "The Genesis of a Style: The Parisian Chanson, 1500–1530," in *Chanson and Madrigal, 1480–1530*, ed. James Haar

(Cambridge: Harvard University Press, 1964), 1–50; "The Transformation of the Chanson at the End of the Fifteenth Century," in *International Musicological Society: Report of the Tenth Congress, Ljubljana, 1967,* ed. Dragotin Cvetko (Kassel: Bärenreiter, 1970), 78–96; *A Florentine Chansonnier from the Time of Lorenzo the Magnificent: Florence, Biblioteca Nazionale Centrale, MS Banco Rari 229, MRM* VII (Chicago: Chicago University Press, 1983). See also Lawrence F. Bernstein, "Notes on the Origin of the Parisian Chanson," *JM* 1 (1982): 275–326 ,"Josquin's Chansons as Generic Paradigms," in *Music in Renaissance Cities and Courts: Studies in Honor of Lewis Lockwood,* ed. Jessie Ann Owens and Anthony M. Cummings (Warren, Mich.: Harmonie Park Press, 1997), 35–55, and for an exemplary study of an important manuscript of the period, "A Florentine Chansonnier of the Early Sixteenth Century: Florence, Biblioteca Nazionale Centrale, MS Magliabechi XIX.117," *EMH* 6 (1986): 1–107; also Peter Woetmann Christoffersen, *French Music in the Early Sixteenth Century,* 3 vols. (Copenhagen: Museum Tusculanum Press, 1994), especially vol. 1. On Pierre de la Rue, see Honey Meconi's "Free from the Crime of Venus: The Biography of Pierre de la Rue," *Revista de Musicologia* 162 (1993): 673–83 (which provides the most up-to-date biography), "French Print Chansons and Pierre de la Rue: A Case Study in Authenticity," in *Music in Renaissance Cities and Courts,* and her forthcoming study *Pierre de la Rue.* See also Picker's *Chanson Albums.*

Italy

Indispensable to any serious study of the frottola is the magnificent catalogue of the entire repertory by Knud Jeppesen, *La frottola,* 3 vols, Acta Jutlandica XLI/1 (Aarhus: Universitets Forlaget, 1968–70); on the literary background, see Walter Rubsamen, *Literary Sources of Secular Music in Italy (c. 1500)* (Berkeley and Los Angeles: University of California Press, 1943). There are a number of major studies by William F. Prizer: *Courtly Pastimes: The Frottole of Marchetto Cara* (Ann Arbor: UMI Research Press, 1980), which contains editions of forty-nine of Cara's pieces; "The Frottola and the Unwritten Tradition," *StudM* 15 (1986): 3–37; "Performance Practices in the Frottola," *EM* 3 (1975): 227–35; "Isabella d'Este and Lorenzo da Pavia, 'Master Instrument-Maker,'" *EMH* 2 (1982): 87–127; "Isabella d'Este and Lucrezia Borgia as Patrons of Music: The Frottola at Mantua and Ferrara," *JAMS* 38 (1985): 1–33; "Renaissance Women as Patrons of Music: The North-Italian Courts," in *Rediscovering the Muses: Women's Musical Traditions,* ed. Kimberly Marshall (Boston: Northeastern University Press, 1993), 186–205. On Josquin's frottole in particular, see Claudio Gallico, "Josquin's Compositions on Italian Texts and the Frottola," in *Josquin des Prez: Proceedings of the International Josquin Festival-Conference,* ed. Edward E. Lowinsky and Bonnie J. Blackburn (London: Oxford University Press, 1976), 446–54; on the Florentine carnival songs, see Bonnie J. Blackburn,"Two 'Carnival Songs' Unmasked: A Commentary on MS Florence Magl. XIX.121," *MD* 35 (1981): 121–78.

Spain

There is a comprehensive survey in Robert Stevenson, *Spanish Music in the Age of Columbus* (The Hague: Nijhoff, 1960); on the problem of performance practice, see Tess Knighton, "The *a cappella* Heresy in Spain: An Inquisition into the Performance of the *Cancionero* Repertory," *EM* 20 (1992): 560–81; see also Isabel Pope, "Musical and Metrical Form of the Villancico," *AnnM* 2 (1954): 189–214. Though they extend beyond the chronological limits (on both sides) of the Josquin generation, two entire issues of *Early Music* are devoted to "Iberian Discoveries," vols. 20/4 (1992) and 22/2 (1994).

Germany

English-language literature on German secular song of this period is nearly nonexistent; one way to approach the subject is through Stephen Keyl, "*Tenorlied, Discantlied,* Polyphonic

Lied: Voices and Instruments in German Secular Polyphony of the Renaissance,"*EM* 20 (1992): 434–45.

Also Cited

Christopher A. Reynolds, "Musical Evidence of Compositional Planning in the Renaissance: Josquin's *Plus nulz regrets*," *JAMS* 40 (1987): 57–81; Lawrence F. Bernstein, "A Canonic Chanson in a German Manuscript: *Faulte d'argent* and Josquin's Approach to the Chanson for Five Voices," in *Von Isaac bis Bach—Studien zur älteren deutschen Musikgeschichte: Festschrift Martin Just zum 60. Geburtstag* (Kassel: Bärenreiter, 1991), 53–71; Alfred Einstein, *The Italian Madrigal*, 3 vols., trans. Alexander H. Kruppe, Roger H. Sessions, and Oliver Strunk (Princeton: Princeton University Press, 1949; reprint, 1971); Timothy McGee and Sylvia E. Mittler, "Information on Instruments in Florentine Carnival Songs," *EM* 10 (1982): 452–61.

CHAPTER 25

Instrumental Music

We tend to think of the sixteenth century as a golden age of vocal polyphony: from the mature works of the Josquin generation through the often thick-as-knots counterpoint of Gombert, Ludford, Morales, and Willaert to the achievements of Byrd, Lassus, Palestrina, and Victoria. Yet by century's end, this music was being left behind by the stylistic innovations of the Baroque. It is somewhat ironic, then, that if we wish to find a sixteenth-century repertory that left a more permanent mark on future centuries, we must turn to a more aesthetically modest body of music: instrumental music.

Among the most notable phenomena of the sixteenth century was the maturing of a truly independent tradition of instrumental music, one that began to shed its past dependence on vocal polyphony and the dance (though these continued to leave a mark) and developed according to its own stylistic norms. The sixteenth century saw the development of instrumental chamber music and virtuoso solo repertories for both keyboard instruments and lute truly come into their own; and it produced a number of new compositional types, including the ricercar, fantasia, canzona, and toccata, all of which either continued to thrive in succeeding centuries or served as recognizable springboards for still newer types. Further, the sixteenth century witnessed the development of new instruments and the technological improvement and standardization of older ones. And finally, the ever-increasing activity of the printing press made this music available to professionals and amateurs, aristocrats and merchants, from one end of Europe to the other. It even fostered a new musical-literary genre: the tutor (instruction book), which taught a music-hungry public how to play.

To be sure, musicians of the Josquin generation stand near the beginning of this development. But to musicians of the two succeeding generations, the accomplishments of the first quarter of the sixteenth century in terms of music for ensembles, keyboard, and lute provided solid foundations on which to build.

ENSEMBLE MUSIC

The contribution of the Josquin generation to music for instrumental ensembles followed two tracks: composers wrote arrangements of polyphonic songs, especially the top hits of the day, but they also cultivated a tradition of freely composed pieces in which they broke decisively with both vocal models and dance types and began to develop an idiomatic ensemble style. It was these freely composed instrumental pieces, often referred to as *tricinia* when written for three voices, that pointed to the future.

Ghiselin's *La Alfonsina*

In some respects, Johannes Ghiselin's three-part *La Alfonsina* (*Anthology* 58) can stand as the quintessential ensemble piece of the late fifteenth century, even down to its name within the title. In fact, a number of instrumental works of the period appear to be named after individuals: Isaac's *La mora* may refer to Ludovico il Moro, Duke of Milan; Gaspar van Weerbeke's *La Stangetta* probably honors Marchesino Stanga of Cremona, Ludovico's secretary; and perhaps Josquin's *La Bernardina* pays tribute to the popular poet-improviser Bernardo Accolti (1458–1535), better-known as Unico Aretino, who was a constant presence at the Italian courts. The most likely connection for *La Alfonsina* is with Alfonso d'Este, son and successor (in 1505) of Duke Ercole I and an ardent viol player.

Ghiselin loaded *La Alfonsina* with many of the style characteristics that became clichés in ensemble pieces composed around 1500: comfortably spaced imitation at the opening, as well as a passage or two of imitation at the short time interval of a minim (see mm. 37–39); rapid scale passages, often played in thirds, sixths, or tenths between two of the voices; and syncopated sequences in two voices against sustained notes in a third (here, the rhythm is further complicated by the proportional foreshortening of the sustained notes at mm. 37–40).

There is much of the same in two pieces by Josquin, *La Bernardina* and *Ile fantazies de Joskin*, while Isaac's *La mora* and Weerbeke's *La Stangetta* verge on overkill (Ex. 25-1):

EXAMPLE 25-1. (a) Josquin, *La Bernardina*, mm. 29–37, and (b) *Ile fantazies de Joskin*, mm. 1–12; (c) Isaac, *La mora*, mm. 36–44; (d) Weerbeke, *La Stangetta*, mm. 44–50.

(a)

(b)

(c)

(d)

Unlike the phrase structure of Martini's *La martinella* (*Anthology* 35, discussed in Chapter 17), which was similar to a rondeau setting, *La Alfonsina*'s phrase structure is utterly un-song-like: 9 + 10 + 22 + 15 (or 16) + 7 (or 6). Nor is there the predictable rondeau-style rhythmic pacing within a phrase: the slow start and acceleration approaching the cadence. In truth, *La Alfonsina* seems to ramble a bit, as though Ghiselin missed the line-by-line/phrase-by-phrase foundation normally provided by a text.

What all of these pieces tell us is that by 1500 or so, composers were well on their way toward developing a distinctive style for instrumental ensembles that was no longer dependent on either vocal models or dance patterns but had found its own melodic, rhythmic, and structural voice. Music for instrumental ensembles now stood firmly as an independent genre.

THE ENSEMBLES

Composers would not begin to specify the instruments for which their ensemble music was intended with any regularity until around 1600. Yet by the first decade of the sixteenth century, certain types of ensembles had firmly established themselves. These groups generally consisted of different sizes of the same instrument, and, at least in sixteenth-century England, came to be called *consorts*. Besides the *alta cappella*, or shawm band (with or without added sackbut), two other consorts came to the fore: viol and recorder.

Before taking up these two groups, however, we need to look more broadly at the late-fifteenth- and early-sixteenth-century *instrumentarium*—that is, at instruments that would have been available to musicians of the period.

The Partial *Instrumentarium*

Our starting point is Hans Burgkmair's woodcut entitled "Maximilian with His Musicians," engraved for the emperor's autobiographical *Weisskunig* in 1514–16 (Fig. 25-1). In the left forefront is a positive organ (showing the artist's initials and depicting the organist's assistant pumping the bellows) and in the center a harp, which by now had faded from the limelight. Toward the rear, in front of the four singers, a musician plays a *cornetto diritto*, or straight cornett (as opposed to the curved variety, which superseded it later in the century), using the often-depicted side embouchure. The cornett was made out of wood covered with leather (the circumference was carved into an octagonal shape), fitted with six finger holes and another for the thumb, and supplied with a trumpet-like mouthpiece. It was, therefore, a brass-woodwind hybrid, capable of brilliance but with the agility of a woodwind instrument. And with its piercing clarino register—its normal range was $g–a''$—the cornett enjoyed its heyday first in the brassy music of late-sixteenth- and early-seventeenth-century Venice and then in the German "tower music" of such composers as Johann Pezel and Johann Schein, who knew the instrument as the *Zinck*.

At the right, another musician plays an oblong keyboard instrument that rests

Figure 25-1. Hans Burgkmair the Elder, *Maximilian I Surrounded by His Court Musicians and Instruments*, woodcut for *Weisskunig*, c. 1514.

on a table; it is either a harpsichord—also called virginal, whose strings were plucked—or clavichord, whose strings were struck. The instrument at the far end of the table is a viol, while closer to us lie a bunch of flutes and recorders, another cornett (hanging over the end of the table), and a crumhorn (curved horn). The crumhorn, which was probably developed in Germany toward the end of the fifteenth century, was a double-reed instrument whose player blew not directly on the reed but into a slotted reed-cap in which the reed was enclosed. As did most woodwinds, the crumhorn, which had a range of only a ninth, came in a variety of sizes. Thus Sebastian Virdung's *Musica getutscht* of 1511, a gold mine of information on instruments and how to play them (and our earliest printed music tutor), contains a woodcut with four crumhorns (Fig. 25-2), though his commentary accounts for only three: bass (*F–g*), alto-tenor *c–d'*), and discant (*g–a'*).

Finally, piled up on the floor to the right in Figure 25-1 are (from front to

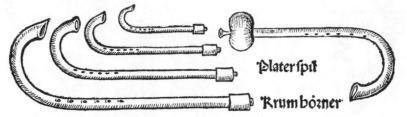

Figure 25-2. Crumhorns as depicted in Virdung's *Musica getutscht*, 1511.

back) a kettledrum (normally used in pairs together with the ceremonial trumpeters) with a sackbut on top, a type of drum called a tabor (with two sticks), a lute case, and the oddly named *tromba marina* (marine trumpet), normally a one-string instrument—the two additional strings here might be a reference to the sympathetic strings that were sometimes enclosed within the body of the instrument.

The Viol Consort

Contrary to popular perception, the history of the viol—or *viola da gamba*, since it was held upright and supported between the legs (*gamba*)—does not extend back to the Middle Ages; nor can it really be called the ancestor of the violin, since viol and violin originated within about seventy-five years of one another and then coexisted comfortably throughout the sixteenth and seventeenth centuries.

The viol (Fig. 25-3) seems to have been developed in the Valencia region of eastern Spain around the middle of the fifteenth century, apparently as a bowed, drone-type instrument since it initially lacked the arched bridge that permits the player to play on only one string at a time. During the final quarter of the century, the instrument came to Italy—where, if it had not already done so, it acquired its arched bridge—and from there quickly crossed the Alps, as witness its inclusion in Virdung's *Musica getutscht* (1511).

Figure 25-3. Viola da gamba as shown on the title page of Ganassi's *Regola rubertina*, 1542.

At first, viols varied widely in shape (standardization came about only around 1600). Yet certain features were fixed early on: the neck, wider than the violin's, was fitted with frets; the instrument came in three sizes, treble, tenor, and bass; there were normally six strings (occasionally five), tuned in fourths with a third in the middle, so that the tenor, for example, was tuned G-c-f-a-d'-g' (bass and treble started upward from D and d); the sound holes were C-shaped (the violin's are F-shaped); and the bow was held underhand.

That consorts of viols quickly became a fixture is evident from descriptions such as Castiglione's in *The Courtier*: "No less delightful [than keyboard instruments] is the playing of a quartet, with the viols producing music of great skill and suavity."[1] Thus Castiglione put his high-society seal of approval on it: the viol was an acceptable instrument for men and women of good breeding. The violin, which was in the early course of its own development at the time, was another matter:

> The violin is very different from the viol. . . . The form of the body is smaller, flatter, and in sound it is much harsher. . . . We call viols those with which gentlemen, merchants, and other virtuous people pass their time. . . . The other type is called the violin; it is commonly used for dancing. . . . It is also easier to carry, a very necessary thing while leading wedding processions or mummeries.[2]

Further evidence that the viol consort already enjoyed a certain prestige as early as the turn of the sixteenth century appears in the Venetian Marin Sanudo's diary, which notes a performance by a six-viol consort at the wedding of Alfonso I d'Este (soon to be Duke of Ferrara and himself one of the players) and Lucrezia Borgia in 1502. In fact, Ferrara became an important center of viol playing in Italy; and a 1520 inventory of instruments owned by Cardinal Ippolito d'Este (Alfonso's brother) shows that he owned as many as nine viols, though this pales in comparison with the twenty-five later owned by the music-loving Henry VIII.

The Recorder Consort

There was nothing new about consorts of recorders in 1500. In 1468, a quartet of recorders (the players dressed as wolves) played at the marriage of Charles the Bold and Margaret of York: "And there appeared four wolves with flutes in their paws, and they began to play a chanson."[3] This notice, however, raises a terminological question: just what were these flutes? After all, the term "flute" was often used on the Continent to mean all flute-like instruments, while the term "recorder" was limited to England. Yet Continental musicians did distinguish between flute and recorder. The instrument we now call the flute was sometimes referred to as the *transverse* flute or *fleuste d'Allemande* (German flute, in recognition of its popularity in Germany). The recorder could be

1. *The Book of the Courtier*, trans. George Bull (Harmondsworth: Penguin, 1967), 120–21.

2. Philibert Jambe de Fer, *Epitome musical* (1556), quoted after Douglass, "The Violin," 126.

3. Translated after Marix, *Histoire de la musique et des musiciens de la cour de Bourgogne*, 106.

called *flûte d'Angleterre* (English flute), *flûte à neuf trous* (flute with nine finger holes), *flûte douce* (sweet flute), or in Italy, *flauto dritto* (straight flute).

For information about the members of the recorder consort around 1500 we turn again to Virdung, who, though he refers in *Musica getutscht* to the instruments with the German word *Flöten* (flutes), illustrates his discussion with a woodcut that clearly shows recorders. These are of three different sizes: bass, with a low note of "written" *F*; tenor, which descended to *c*; and discant (called "alto" today in America, "treble" in Britain), which began on *g*. Each had a range of an octave plus a sixth or seventh, and each would sound an octave higher than Virdung's written indications. Ghiselin's *La Alfonsina*, then, falls nicely within the range of Virdung's consort. Though Virdung describes three recorders, the standard consort consisted of four: a bass, two tenors, and a discant.

We should not assume, however, that the pitches to which Virdung's recorders were tuned—*F*, *c*, and *g*—were absolute and fixed or that all recorders of a given type were exactly the same size and similarly tuned. Pitches and tuning were relative; and to the extent that there was standardization, it extended only to the recorders within an individual consort, which were constructed together and tuned a fifth apart. Beyond that, we can assume little.

Viols weren't the only instrument Henry VIII collected. The 1547 inventory of his instruments accounts for seventy-two flutes and seventy-six recorders; eighteen recorders were made of ivory, and some were decorated with silver or gold. Obviously, Henry prized them.

KEYBOARD MUSIC

There were three main types of keyboard music: pieces that served a liturgical function, that is, settings of monophonic sacred melodies; arrangements of polyphonic vocal works, becoming ever more elaborate in their decoration of the model; and freely composed compositions, which begin to show a new sense of expansiveness. Cutting across these genres were two particularly important centers of activity: southern Germany-Austria and Italy.

Germany-Austria

To judge from the music that comes down to us, the epicenter of the production of organ music was southern Germany and Austria, partly because of the presence there of the most famous organist of the time, Maximilian's court musician, Paul Hofhaimer (1459–1537). So powerful was Hofhaimer's influence that during his lifetime his students were dubbed Paulomines, and they consistently landed many of the most prestigious organist's positions—at Constance, Vienna, Venice, and the court of Henry VIII, among other places.

LITURGICAL ORGAN MUSIC In 1511, Arnolt Schlick (c. 1460–after 1531) published the first printed book on organ building, the *Spiegel der Orgelmacher und Organisten*. He followed it a year later with *Tabulaturen etlicher Lobgesang*, a collection of pieces for solo keyboard, solo lute, and solo voice with lute ac-companiment. Here, Schlick broke new stylistic ground by adapting to the keyboard the full-blown imitative style of the Josquin generation. We can see this development in his setting of the German devotional song *Maria zart von edler art* (*Anthology* 59). The thirteen short phrases of the preexistent melody unfold in the top voice, while the lower voices imitate or anticipate each phrase.

In another liturgical work (not included in the 1512 publication), Schlick set the antiphon *Ascendo ad patrem meum* in a way that exploited the organ to its fullest capacity and pushed the idea of keyboard virtuosity beyond anything previously known (Ex. 25-2):

EXAMPLE 25-2. Schlick, *Ascendo ad patrem meum*, mm. 1–7.

As Schlick himself described it: "I have succeeded in setting the chant *Ascendo ad patrem meum* for ten voices, which one may play on the organ, four parts on the pedals and six on the manual, as I can illustrate for the eyes and ears of an audience."[4] Among composer-organists who worked in the decades around 1500, Schlick must be regarded as the most talented.

ARRANGEMENTS OF VOCAL COMPOSITIONS   Although Leonhard Kleber (c. 1495–1556) can hardly be considered a member of the Josquin generation, he compiled his large collection of 112 organ works while still a young man, between 1515 and 1524,[5] and its contents are representative of the early six-

4. Quoted after Apel, *The History of Keyboard Music*, 91.

5. The manuscript is at Berlin, Staatsbibliothek, MS 40026.

teenth century. Example 25-3 presents two excerpts from what is likely Kleber's own arrangement of Josquin's *Ave Maria . . . virgo serena* (*Anthology* 37):

EXAMPLE 25-3. Kleber (?), *Ave Maria . . . virgo serena*: (a) mm. 1–12, (b) mm. 133–141.

(a)

(b)

While both excerpts stay close to their model, the decoration and embellishment are lavish. And therein lies the arranger's art, one that would reach a highpoint in melodic embroidery with the arrangements of the so-called colorists later in the century.

Whatever the aesthetic merits of sixteenth-century German keyboard music—and the mordents, trills, and turns can get tiresome—the repertory provided the groundwork for a tradition that would last two and a half centuries, culminating in the works of Buxtehude and Bach and still retaining meaning enough for the likes of Brahms a hundred years later.

Figure 25-4. Title page of Andrea Antico's *Frottole intabulate*, 1517 (Dobrovský Library, Prague).

Italy

Before turning to examples of Italian keyboard music, we might consider two items that stand as the first of their kind.

THE EARLIEST PRINT   In December 1516, Pope Leo X transferred to Andrea Antico da Montona the privilege for printing keyboard music that had formerly been held by Petrucci, who had in fact failed to publish any such volumes. Within a month, Antico issued his *Frottole intabulate da sonare organi, libro primo* (there was no follow-up), the earliest print of Italian keyboard music.

The title page of Andrea's collection is particularly interesting (Fig. 25-4). Although it states that the frottole are arranged for organ, the woodcut shows a young man seated at the harpsichord. That music for one keyboard instrument was often played on other keyboard instruments is clear from the little pages of other keyboard collections as well. For example, the title of the French publisher Pierre Attaingnant's first keyboard publication (1531) reads, "Nineteen chansons reduced in tablature for organs, spinets [harpsichords], clavichords, and such similar musical instruments."[6]

Antico's woodcut is also notable for its allusion to the competition among printers that was already beginning to take shape. There can be little doubt that the monkey holding a lute represents Antico's rival, Petrucci. Both the monkey and the young woman have rather pained expressions on their faces, while the woman seems also to be casting aside her music book. The message is clear: it was time for Petrucci's publications of frottole for solo voice and lute to step aside and make room for what Antico hoped would be the new vogue of keyboard arrangements.

One of these arrangements can be seen in Example 25-4, underneath its model, Marchetto Cara's *Cantai mentre nel core*:

6. Quoted after Brown, *Instrumental Music Printed Before 1600*, 35.

EXAMPLE 25-4. (a) Cara, *Cantai mentre nel core*, mm. 1–7; (b) Antico's arrangement.

THE OLDEST EXTANT HARPSICHORD?   Although the earliest known reference to a "clavicembalum" dates from 1397 and the earliest artistic representation of such an instrument is from 1425, the first important wave of harpsichord construction took place in early-sixteenth-century Italy. And not until the last quarter of the century, when a Flemish school of harpsichord builders came to the fore, was Italian supremacy in the field challenged.

One early Italian harpsichord, built by Hieronymous of Bologna in 1521 and now preserved at the Victoria and Albert Museum in London (Fig. 25-5), is generally thought to be the oldest extant, securely datable harpsichord. Looking at Hieronymous's keyboard, we get the impression that its forty-seven keys cover a range of three octaves plus a seventh, *E* to *d'''*. Yet owing to a device

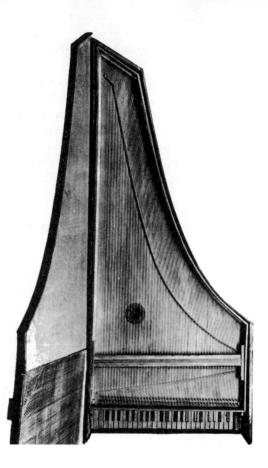

Figure 25-5. Harpsichord by Hieronymous of Bologna, 1521 (Victoria and Albert Museum, London).

known as the "short octave" (also used on organs), the instrument has a slightly wider range of just over four octaves—the lowest note is really a *C* (Fig. 25-6). Thus the notes C-sharp, D-sharp/E-flat, F-sharp, and G-sharp/A-flat were sacrificed in the lowest octave, since in practice they were rarely needed.

There was another way of expanding the range without increasing the number of keys, and that was through the use of "split keys": certain black keys were literally split in two horizontally, the front of the key giving one pitch, the back portion giving another. This device was often used with D-sharp/E-flat and G-sharp/A-flat, pitches that, in the meantone tuning of the period, were not enharmonic equivalents. And though it means digressing, we should address the problem of tuning.

TUNING SYSTEMS In his *Discourse on Ancient Music and Good Singing*, addressed to Giulio Caccini around 1580, Count Giovanni de' Bardi, a member of the

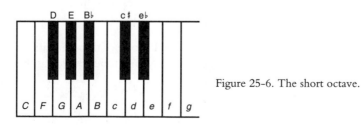

Figure 25-6. The short octave.

famed Florentine Camerata, described a difficulty that keyboard players experienced: "More than once I have felt like laughing when I saw musicians struggling to put a lute or viol into proper tune with a keyboard instrument."[7] The problem was that fretted string instruments and keyboard instruments did not necessarily use the same tuning systems.

Today we are accustomed to what we call equal temperament: (1) we can start on any note, go completely through the circle of fifths (all of which are the same size), and end up on a note that forms a perfect unison with the one on which we started; (2) we can ascend through any three successive major thirds—C–E, E–G-sharp, and G-sharp/A-flat–C, say—and land a perfect octave higher than where we began; and (3) we can play a chromatic scale in which all the semitones are equidistant from one another. We achieve all of this by "tempering" (narrowing) each acoustically pure fifth by approximately 1/50 of a semitone. Otherwise, a complete circle of pure fifths (with their 3:2 ratios) would land us on a note that was about a quarter semitone sharper than the one on which we started, while a series of three pure major thirds would result in an octave that was almost half a semitone flat.

As noted in Chapter 1, however, the prevailing tuning system for vocal music of our period was the Pythagorean, which had two different-size semitones and was based on maintaining the integrity of the pure fifths downward to E-flat and upward to G-sharp, the result being that there was a so-called "wolf" fifth between the out-of-tune G-sharp and E-flat. The pure fifths were not maintained without another sacrifice: major and minor thirds in the Pythagorean system were respectively wider and narrower than they are in their own pure states. The Pythagorean system seems to have worked well enough in keyboard music through about the mid-fifteenth century. Yet by the time Ramos de Pareja wrote his *Musica practica* in 1482, a reaction had set in. Ramos implies (and later theorists confirm) that keyboard instruments were now being tuned in a way that favored the purity of the thirds (a 5:4 ratio for major thirds) and sacrificed that of the fifths. In fact, the fifths were narrowed almost three times as much as they are in equal temperament to come up with a system known as meantone tuning, which had its own set of different-size semitones and out-of-tune "wolf" fifth.

As for the fretted string instruments, players seem to have favored a system of tuning that approximated equal temperament from about the middle of the sixteenth century. Thus in the revised edition of his *Musica instrumentalis deudsch* (1545), Martin Agricola states that viol players and lutenists generally set their frets equally and thereby used only one kind of semitone. Perhaps when they played with keyboard accompaniment, then, viol and lute players shaded their intonation somewhat, and perhaps Count Bardi sometimes only smiled. In the end, the problem of tuning remains a thorny one.

FREELY COMPOSED PIECES   As we saw in Chapter 17, one of the innovations of the Buxheim and related mid-fifteenth-century German repertories was the

---

7. Quoted after Strunk, *Source Readings* (1965), 297.

development of short, freely composed works called preambulums or preludes. Such compositions continued to be cultivated in the early sixteenth century. And though they tended to remain relatively small-scale, as befits a work that was intended as a prelude to another one, they grew to almost monstrous proportions at the hands of Marco Antonio Cavazzoni (c. 1490–c. 1560), who included two such works—called *ricercars* (the earliest use of this term in connection with keyboard music)—in his *Recerchari, canzoni, motetti . . . libro primo* of 1523. Example 25-5 shows the opening of Cavazzoni's *Recercare secondo* together with a few appearances of what might be called one of its "themes":

EXAMPLE 25-5. Cavazzoni, *Recercare secondo*, mm. 1–13, 40–42, 112–116, 134–136, 142–146.

In order to appreciate what Cavazzoni has done, we should place his ricercar in the context of the genre to which it belongs. The term *ricercare* (to search out, to seek out) seems to have been used for the first time in Francesco Spinacino's landmark *Intabulatura de lauto, libro primo*, the first printed source of lute music, published by Petrucci in 1507. The pieces called "ricercars" there are usually short, improvisatory-like compositions that were apparently intended to serve as preludes (and postludes) to Spinacino's arrangements of secular vocal pieces. Thus the first two ricercars are called *Recercare de tous biens* and *Recercare a Juli amours* and functioned as preludes to his arrangements of Hayne's famous *De tous biens plaine* and Johannes Ghiselin's *Je loe amours*, respectively, both of which appear earlier in the collection.

In another Petrucci lute publication, Joan Ambrosio Dalza's *Intabolatura de lauto* (1508), some of the ricercars are themselves preceded by a type of piece labeled *tastar de corde* (try out the strings). It seems, then, that the term "ricercar" could also be applied to an independent composition. In either instance, the pieces were texturally freewheeling, alternating between chordal textures and rapid scale passages.

Cavazzoni's ricercar stands squarely in this tradition: it is rhapsodic in its rapid, seemingly unpredictable changes from one texture to another; and it serves a prelude-like function in that it introduces a keyboard arrangement of a motet, *O stella maris*, to which it is related by a common final on G. Where it begins to strike out from the tradition is in its approach to theme and insistence on what can almost be called a sense of thematic development.

Two final notes about the ricercar: by 1540, the term would be used to describe a very different type of piece, one that was thoroughly imitative in style; and the old, rhapsodic kind of ricercar of the early sixteenth century came to be called a toccata (see Chapter 31).

FINGERING   Among the earliest keyboard tutors to deal with fingering is the *Fundamentum* written around 1520 by Hans Buchner (1483–1538), who was one of Hofhaimer's pupils. Example 25-6 shows some of the contortions Buchner frequently called for:

EXAMPLE 25-6. Buchner, *Quem terra pontus*, mm. 15–18.

How one sustains the bass in measures 15 and 16–17 is anyone's guess. In fact, fingering in the sixteenth century generally did lean toward the awkward (from our point of view), as one more example from the late sixteenth century shows (Ex. 25-7):

EXAMPLE 25-7. Elias Ammerbach, an exercise from the *Orgel oder Instrument Tabulatur* (1581).

Evidently, scale passages were often a two-finger affair, as the young woman on the famous title page of *Parthenia, or The Maydenhead of the first musicke that ever was composed for the Virginalls* demonstrates in 1612 or 1613 (Fig. 25-7). It is possible that the information about fingering that reaches us in tutors, annotated manuscripts, and prints was intended primarily for beginners. Perhaps the pros played quite differently.

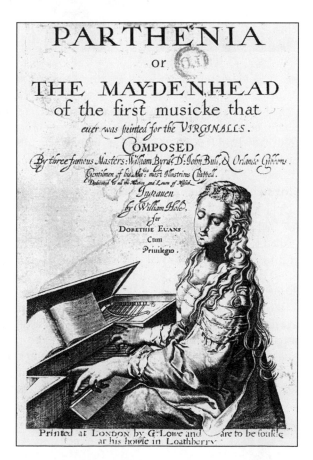

Figure 25-7. Title page of *Parthenia*, c. 1612–13.

Figure 25-8. *Young Girl Playing the Lute*, by an unknown Flemish artist, second quarter of sixteenth century (?) (private collection, Brussels).

LUTE MUSIC

If there is a single instrument that most characteristically represents the sixteenth century, it may well be the lute. As the great English lutenist-composer John Dowland (1563–1626) put it: the lute was the instrument that "ever hath been most in request."[8]

Construction, Shape, and Tuning

The lute is distinctively shaped (Fig. 25-8): the almost paper-thin soundboard (or belly) is flat and often adorned with an exquisitely executed sound hole (called a "rose") carved directly into the soundboard itself; the back is vaulted and made out of individual ribs (there can be as many as thirty to forty thin ones) bent and glued together; and the pegbox is bent back at an angle of about 80 degrees to the neck.

From around 1500 on, the lute normally had six sets of gut strings, called *courses*. The highest-sounding course (the lowest on the instrument itself) consisted of a single string called the *chanterelle*; the next two courses down (in pitch) each had two strings tuned in unison; and the final three courses each had a pair of strings tuned in octaves. From bottom to top (in terms of pitch), the tenor lute—the most popular size—was customarily tuned as shown in Example 25-8 (the entire tuning was sometimes raised a whole step):

8. Quoted after O'Dette, "Plucked Instruments," 139.

EXAMPLE 25-8. Standard tuning for the lute.

The Repertory

The third quarter of the fifteenth century witnessed a major transformation in lute playing. Whereas lutenists had formerly played with a plectrum, so that the instrument was limited to single-line melodies and thus relegated to ensembles, players now began to pluck the strings with their fingers, thereby making it possible to play the most intricate polyphony and turning the instrument into a self-sufficient solo vehicle. And with the new polyphonic technique came a new form of notation and, in the years around 1500, manuscript and printed sources that began to transmit one of the richest instrumental repertories of the sixteenth century.

The lute repertory consisted largely of arrangements of vocal polyphony (songs, motets, and even Mass movements) and freely composed, quasi-improvisatory ricercars. We can get a taste of the latter from one of the ricercars in the manuscript compiled at Venice around 1517 for the nobleman and lutenist Vincenzo Capirola (1474–1548; *Anthology* 60). Typically, the contrapuntal texture is treated freely, as voice parts seem to come and go at will.

Still another type of piece, one that would give rise to an especially brilliant tradition first in late-sixteenth-century England and then in the Baroque period, was the fledgling dance suite. Fifteenth-century ballroom music customarily paired slow and fast dances built on the same tenor melody. Thus the stately basse dance was followed by a quick, sprightly saltarello. Still another tradition stated a basse dance melody four times, each time in a different mensuration. And it was no doubt this latter practice that led lutenists to group together pieces in which they subjected similar melodic and harmonic material to a succession of rhythmically differentiated, stylized dance patterns. Joan Ambrosio Dalza called attention to this procedure in the preface to his lute publication of 1508: "All the pavanes have their saltarello and piva."[9] (The *piva* was an especially fast dance, marked by jumps and turns.) Thus the three movements of his second set of dances *alla venetiana* begin as follows (Ex. 25-9):

EXAMPLE 25-9. Dalza, *Pavana-saltarello-piva alla venetiana*, No. 2, mm. 1–10 (pavane), 1–8 (saltarello), 1–11 (piva).

9. Quoted after *New Grove*, 18:336.

Saltarello

Piva

Lute Tablature

With the lute now transformed into a self-contained polyphonic instrument, it was necessary to find a way to notate its music. The answer was the shorthand system called *tablature*, of which there were three national types: German (which Sebastian Virdung claims was invented by the organist Conrad Paumann), Italian (which was also used in Spain), and French.

The Italian system is the most logical and clear-cut. Figure 25-9 reproduces the third ricercar from Francesco Spinacino's *Intabolatura de lauto, libro primo* of 1507. What looks like a six-line staff represents the six courses of the lute as

Figure 25-9. A ricercar from Francesco Spinacino's *Intabulatura de Lauto, libro primo*, 1507.

we would see them if a lutenist were playing the instrument in front of us. The top line is the lowest-sounding string; the staff gives us the six open strings *G, c, f, a, d', g'* (reading from top to bottom and assuming a tuning in G).

The numerals represent the frets as they go from the end of the fingerboard toward the belly of the instrument: 0 = open string, 1 = first fret, 2 = second fret, and so on through fret 9; frets 10–12 are indicated with the letter "x," above which there are one, two, or three dots, respectively. (This avoids potential confusion between, say, 11 [eleven] and 1 1 [two ones]). Figure 25-10 shows what fret produces what pitch on each course:

Figure 25-10. A diagram of the courses, frets, and notes on a lute tuned to G.

Frets:	12	11	10	9	8	7	6	5	4	3	2	1	Open string
	g	f♯	f	e	e♭	d	c♯	c	B	B♭	A	G♯	G
	c′	b	b♭	a	g♯	g	f♯	f	e	e♭	d	c♯	c
	f′	e′	e♭′	d	c♯′	c′	b	b♭	a	g♯	g	f♯	f
	a′	g♯′	g′	f♯′	f′	e′	e♭′	d′	c♯′	c′	b	b♭	a
	d″	c♯″	c″	b′	b♭′	a′	g♯′	g′	f♯′	f′	e′	e♭′	d′
	g″	f♯″	f″	e″	e♭″	d″	c♯″	c″	b′	b♭′	a′	g♯′	g′

Rhythm is indicated by means of stems/flags above the fret numbers. As Spinacino puts it in his prefatory *Regula*:

> These are the (metrical) signs: ❘ ⌐ ⌐ ⌐. The first signifies the measure (beat) to be observed, which has to be taken slowly enough so as to allow for the beats of the smaller values; because the second sign is the half of the first, the third the half of the second.[10]

The dot beneath a numeral told the lutenist to pluck with the index finger.

Armed with this information, we can transcribe measures 1–4 in either of the ways shown in Example 25-10:

EXAMPLE 25-10. Two transcriptions of Spinacino, *Recercare* from *Intabolatura de lauto, libro primo*, No. 24, mm. 1–4: (a) strict transcription, (b) transcription with sustained tones and voice leading realized.

Although the rhythmic signs indicate the point at which each note enters, they fail to prescribe the precise duration of the notes; nor do they measure the difference in duration between two or more notes that enter simultaneously. Thus it is up to the editor—who presumably understands the acoustical qualities of the lute (a note can neither be sustained forever, nor continue to sound after another fret on the same string is stopped)—to decide which of two basic transcription philosophies to follow: a strict transcription, which shows only the point at which a note enters; or a transcription in which sustained tones and voice leading are indicated. There is no right or wrong. The decision depends in part on the function of the transcription, playing or study; and good editions of lute music will generally superimpose a facsimile of the original notation above the transcription.

A TRUMPET MANUFACTURER

The explosion of instrumental music in the sixteenth century was accompanied by a burst of activity in the manufacturing of instruments. Indeed, the century witnessed the founding of a number of family dynasties of instrument

10. Quoted after Apel, *The Notation of Polyphonic Music*, 62.

makers. And some of the family names are still meaningful to us today. Thus the Amati family, founders of the famous Cremona school of violin makers (to which Stradivarius eventually belonged), was active in that city by mid-century, while the 1580s saw the emergence of the Ruckers family and their famous keyboard instruments at Antwerp.

Less well-known is the Neuschel (or Meuschel) family of Nuremberg, which was a major center for the manufacturing of brass instruments. In his *General History of the Science and Practice of Music* (1776), music historian Sir John Hawkins offers this little biography of Hans Neuschel the Younger (d. 1533):

> The trumpet is said by Vincentio Galilei . . . to have been invented at Nuremberg; and there is extant a memoir which shews that trumpets were made to great perfection by an artist in that city, who was also an admired performer on that instrument; it is as follows: "Hans Meuschel of Nuremberg, for his accuracy in making trumpets, as also for his skill in playing on the same alone, and in the accompanyment with the voice, was of so great renown, that he was frequently sent for to the palaces of princes the distance of several hundred miles. Pope Leo X, for whom he had made sundry trumpets of silver, sent for him to Rome, and after having been delighted with his exquisite performance, dismissed him with a munificent reward.[11]

Today Nuremberg honors the trumpet maker with a street named after him: Meuschelstrasse.

BIBLIOGRAPHICAL NOTE

Editions of the Music

Ensemble music: many of the pieces in Petrucci's *Odhecaton* were presumably intended for instrumental ensembles (see the edition cited in the Bibliographical Note in Chapter 18; see also the complete works editions listed in Chapters 18, 20, 22, 24). **Keyboard music**: the works of the early-sixteenth-century German organists have been edited in large number: two editions that cut across composers are Hans Joachim Moser and Fritz Heitmann, *Frühmeister der deutschen Orgelkunst* (Leipzig: Breitkopf & Härtel, 1930), and Hans Joachim Marx, *Tabulaturen des XVI. Jahrhunderts*, vol. 1: *Die Tabulaturen aus dem Besitz des Basler Humanisten Bonifacius Amerbach*, SMd 6 (Kassel and Basel: Bärenreiter, 1967) **Schlick**: *Tabulaturen etlicher Lobgesang und Lidlein*, ed. Gottfried Harms (Hamburg: Ugrino, 1924); Macario Santiago Kastner, *Arnolt Schlick: Hommage à l'empereur Charles-Quint* (Barcelona: Boileau, 1954). **Buchner**: *Sämtliche Orgelwerk*, EDM 54–55, ed. J. H. Schmidt (Frankfurt: H. Litolff, 1974). **Hofhaimer**: Hans Joachim Moser, *Paul Hofhaimer* (Stuttgart: J.G. Cotta, 1929; reprint, 1969). **Kotter**: *Die Tabulaturen des Organisten Hans Kotter*, ed. Wilhelm Merian (Leipzig: Breitkopf & Härtel, 1916). For the Italian repertory, see Knud Jeppesen's *Die italienische Orgelmusik am Anfang des Cinquecento* (Copenhagen: Munksgaard, 1943), which contains a selection of pieces from both Antico's *Frottole intabulate* (1517) and Cavazzoni's *Recerchari, motetti, canzoni* (1523); there is an interesting edition of keyboard arrangements of Josquin compositions in Thomas Warburton, *Keyboard Intabulations of Music by Josquin Des Prez*, RRMR 34 (Madison: A-R Editions, 1980). **Lute music**: One can get a good idea of the lute music of the first two decades of the century in Otto Gombosi, *Capirola Lute Book: Compositione di Meser Vincenzo Capirola* (Neuilly-sur-Seine: Société de Musique d'Autre-

11. Quoted after the Dover reprint, 2: 612.

fois, 1955); Benvenuto Disertori, *20 ricercari di Franciscus Bossinensis* (Milan: Suvini Zerboni, 1954); Helmut Mönkemeyer's edition of Dalza's *Intabolatura de Lauto, Petrucci, 1508* (Hofhein-am-Taunus: Hofmeister, 1967); and Harms's edition of Schlick's *Tabulaturen* cited above.

Specialized Journals

There are a number of outstanding organological journals: *The Galpin Society Journal* and *Journal of the American Musical Instrument Society* cover the field as a whole, as does the wide-ranging *Early Music*; among journals that specialize in one particular instrument are *Historic Brass Society Journal, Journal of the Viola da Gamba Society of America, Journal of the Lute Society of America, The Lute: The Journal of the Lute Society* (Britain), and *The Organ Yearbook*.

The Instrumentarium

There is no better introduction to the instruments of the fifteenth and sixteenth centuries than David Munrow, *Instruments of the Middle Ages and Renaissance* (London: Oxford University Press, 1976); see also Elizabeth V. Phillips and John-Paul Christopher Jackson, *Performing Medieval and Renaissance Music: An Introductory Guide* (New York: Schirmer, 1986); also worth consulting are the informative articles on instruments in Jeffery T. Kite-Powell, *A Performer's Guide to Renaissance Music* (New York: Schirmer, 1994); there are articles on all the instruments in *The New Grove Dictionary of Musical Instruments*, ed. Stanley Sadie (London: Macmillan, 1984); Howard Mayer Brown's "Instruments," in *Performance Practice: Music Before 1600*, ed. Howard Mayer Brown and Stanley Sadie (New York: Norton, 1989), 167–84, contains a gold mine of bibliographical information in the footnotes.

Viol: Ian Woodfield, *The Early History of the Viol* (Cambridge: Cambridge University Press, 1984); Alison Crum and Sonia Jackson, *Play the Viol: The Complete Guide to Playing the Treble, Tenor, and Bass Viol*, Early Music Series 10 (Oxford: Oxford University Press, 1989); Keith Polk, "Vedel und Geige—Fiddle and Viol: German String Traditions in the Fifteenth Century," *JAMS* 42 (1989): 504–46. **Crumhorn**: Kenton Terry Meyer, *The Crumhorn: Its History, Design, Repertory, and Technique*, Studies in Musicology 66 (Ann Arbor: UMI Research Press, 1983). **Recorder and flute**: a good overview is Edgar Hunt, *The Recorder and Its Music* (New York: Norton, 1962); John Solum's *Early Flute*, Early Music Series 15 (Oxford: Clarendon Press, 1992), contains a chapter on the Renaissance flute by Anne Smith. **Harpsichord**: Frank Hubbard, *Three Centuries of Harpsichord Making* (Cambridge: Harvard University Press, 1965). **Lute**: for those who can manage the French, there is a wide range of essays in Jean Jaquot, *Le Luth et sa musique*, Colloques Internationaux du Centre National de la Recherche 511 (Paris: CNRS, 1976); both Friedemann Hellwig in "Lute Construction in the Renaissance and Baroque," *GSJ* 27 (1974): 21–30, and Gerhard Söhne in "On the Geometry of the Lute," *JLSA* 13 (1980): 35–54, deal with the physical aspects of the instrument.

Repertory and Performance

The reference tool that opens the door to the repertory of instrumental music of the sixteenth century is Brown, *Instrumental Music Printed Before 1600: A Bibliography* (Cambridge: Harvard University Press, 1965). **Ensemble music**: there is no comprehensive study in English; those who read German might consult Dietrich Kämper, *Studien zur Instrumentalen Ensemblemusik des 16. Jahrhunderts in Italien* (*Analecta musicologica* 10) (Cologne: Böhlau, 1970). On one aspect of viol playing, see Brown, "Notes (and Transposing Notes) on the Viol in the Early Sixteenth Century," in *Music in Medieval and Early Modern Europe: Patronage, Sources and Texts*, ed. Iain Fenlon (Cambridge: Cambridge University Press, 1981), 61–78, while the same author's "Notes (and Transposing Notes) on the Transverse Flute in the Early Sixteenth Century," *JAMS* 12 (1986): 5–39, deals with flute and recorder; on the cornetto, see Polk, "Agustein Schubinger and the Zinck: Innovation in Performance Practice," *HBSJ*

1 (1989): 83–92; see also the essays by Warwick Edwards and Louise Litterick cited in the Bibliographical Note in Chapter 17. **Keyboard music**: the most comprehensive survey is still Willi Apel, *The History of Keyboard Music to 1700*, rev. ed. (Bloomington: Indiana University Press, 1972); for another survey, see Alexander Silbiger, ed., *Keyboard Music before 1700* (New York: Schirmer, 1995); on fingering, see Mark Lindley, "Renaissance Keyboard Fingering," in *A Performer's Guide to Renaissance Music*, ed. Jeffrey T. Kite-Powell (New York: Schirmer, 1994), 189–99; Calvert Johnson, "Early Italian Keyboard Fingering," *EKJ* 10 (1992): 7–88; on the use of the organ in church, see Otto Gombosi, "About Organ Playing in the Divine Service, circa 1500," in *Essays on Music in Honor of Archibald Thompson Davison* (Cambridge: Harvard University Press, 1957), 51–68. **Lute music**: on the earliest tablatures and their repertory, see David Fallows, "15th-Century Tablatures for Plucked Instruments: A Summary, a Revision, and a Suggestion," *LSJ* 19 (1977): 7–31; Diana Poulton, *Lute Playing Technique* (London: The Lute Society of the United Kingdom, 1981).

Tuning Systems

Ross W. Duffin, "Tuning and Temperament," in *A Performer's Guide to Renaissance Music*, 238–47.

Three Tutors in Translation

Virdung's *Musica getutscht* (1511) is edited and translated in Beth Bullard, *Musica getutscht: A Treatise on Musical Instruments by Sebastian Virdung* (Cambridge: Cambridge University Press, 1993); Martin Agricola's *Musica instrumentalis deudsch*, first published in 1529 and revised in 1545, is edited and translated in William Hettrick, *Musica instrumentalis deudsch: A Treatise on Musical Instruments (1529 and 1545) by Martin Agricola* (Cambridge: Cambridge University Press, 1994); Schlick's treatise on organ building, *Spiegel der Orgelmacher und Organisten*, is available in a facsimile edition and English translation by Elizabeth Barber in the series *Bibliotheca organologica*, 113 (Buren: Fritz Knuf, 1980).

Also Cited

David Douglass, "The Violin," and Paul O'Dette, "Plucked Instruments," in *A Performer's Guide to Renaissance Music*, ed. Jeffery T. Kite-Powell (New York: Schirmer, 1994); Jeanne Marix, *Histoire de la musique et des musiciens de la cour de Bourgogne sous la règne de Philippe le Bon (1420–1467)* (Strasbourg: Heitz, 1939); Willi Apel, *The Notation of Polyphonic Music, 900–1600*, 5th ed. (Cambridge, Mass.: Mediaeval Academy of America, 1961).

PART FIVE

THE 1520s TO THE 1550s

INCLUDED: ARCADELT • ATTAINGNANT • BERCHEM • BROWNE •
BUUS • CABEZÓN • G. CAVAZZONI • CLAUDIN DE SERMISY •
CLEMENS NON PAPA • CORNYSH • CRECQUILLON • FAYRFAX •
FESTA • FRANCESCO DA MILANO • A. GABRIELI • GERO • GERVAISE •
GOMBERT • GOUDIMEL • JACHET OF MANTUA • JANEQUIN • JULIO
SEGNI • LUDFORD • MERULO • MILÁN • MORALES • NARVÁEZ •
NOLA • PASSEREAU • PELLEGRINI • REDFORD • SACHS • SENFL •
TAVERNER • TYE • VERDELOT • WALTER • WILLAERT

CHAPTER 26

The Catholic Church and Its Music

The generation of composers that reached its full maturity during the second quarter of the sixteenth century—among the bigger names are Nicolas Gombert, Adrian Willaert, Jacobus Clemens non Papa, Cristóbal de Morales, Clément Janequin, and Claudin de Sermisy—has often been treated somewhat casually. Some call it the "post-Josquin" generation. Yet this disparaging designation implies that the composers were little more than followers of Josquin or afterthoughts to the earlier era. Perhaps we might dub them a "no-name" generation, though that is no less disrespectful. We should in any case be clear about who considers these composers as standing on the edge of anonymity.

Certainly not their contemporaries. If there is a constant in fifteenth- and sixteenth-century literary, art, and music criticism, it is the notion of progress: that each succeeding generation rescued the arts from a state of imperfection (if not downright squalor) and lifted them to new and glorious heights. Giorgio Vasari (1511–1574) spoke for the period when he wrote about his contemporaries in his *Lives of the Artists* (1568):

> The distinguished artists described in the second part of these *Lives* made an important contribution . . . adding to what had been achieved by those of the first period. . . . Their work was in many ways imperfect, but they showed the way to the artists of the third period . . . and made it possible for them, by following and improving on their example, to reach the perfection evident in the finest and most celebrated modern works.[1]

The idea of progress was just as pervasive in discussions of music. It certainly lies at the base of what Tinctoris wrote in the preface to *The Art of Counterpoint* in 1476: "There is no composition written over forty years ago that is thought by the learned as worthy of performance." And it is just as clearly what Gioseffo Zarlino had in mind when he praised Willaert in the preface to *Le istitutioni harmoniche* (1558):

> God has shown us the favor of causing Adriano Willaert to be born in our day, in truth one of the rarest masters who has ever practiced music and who, a new Pythagoras as it were, after examining thoroughly all music's possibilities and finding a vast number of errors, set to work to eliminate them and to restore [music] to that honor and dignity that were once its own and that should be its own by right.[2]

---

1. Revised edition, trans. George Bull (Harmondsworth: Penguin, 1976), 249.
2. Quoted after Weiss and Taruskin, *Music in the Western World*, 114.

For whom, then, does this generation consist of no names? For us. It is we who have tended to neglect them, especially their sacred music, which may be the most forgotten repertory in the two hundred years that interest us. Yet no music of 1520–50 displays a greater sense of continuity with the immediate past than does the sacred music composed for the Catholic Church. Its style and genres grew directly out of those cultivated by the preceding generation. The parody (or imitation) Mass became the overwhelming favorite; and in both Mass and motet, the driving stylist force was pervading imitation, which grew ever thicker and more seamless. We will look at the motet first.

THE MOTET

The second quarter of the sixteenth century produced three great Flemish motet composers: Nicolas Gombert, Adrian Willaert, and Jacobus Clemens non Papa. We should consider the lives of the three composers, for there is a lesson to be learned from them.

Gombert

After a period in his late teens during which he is said to have studied with Josquin, Gombert (c. 1495–c. 1560) joined the chapel of Charles V in 1526, serving as singer, *maître des enfants* (master of the boys), and unofficial court composer, traveling with it across the vast expanse of Charles's empire. As much as anyone, Gombert was influential in transplanting the central tradition to Spain (where Charles customarily held court). In 1540, his name suddenly disappears from chapel records. The mathematician Jerome Cardan (1501–1576) tells us why: "The musician, Gombert, was condemned to the triremes [a warship with three tiers of oars] for violation of a boy in the service of the emperor."[3] Gombert, then, had sexually abused one of the choirboys in his charge and was sentenced to the galleys. Just how long he spent at sea—where he apparently continued to compose—is not known, but he was residing at Tournai in 1547 and, according to Cardan, spent his final years in peace.

Willaert

Born around 1490, Willaert (Fig. 26-1) was probably the most influential musician of his generation. According to Zarlino, who formulated his rules of counterpoint and composition in his *Istitutione* "according to the way and manner of Adrian Willaert," the composer went to Paris to pursue a law degree but ended up studying music with Jean Mouton. By July 1515 at the latest, he was in Italy, in the service of Cardinal Ippolito I d'Este, with whose family he subsequently enjoyed more than a decade-long association.

In December 1527, Willaert became *maestro di cappella* at St. Mark's in Venice, where he remained for the rest of his life, shaping its musical establishment into one of the most prestigious of the period. The roster of those who studied

3. Quoted after Miller, "Jerome Cardan on Gombert," 413.

Figure 26-1. Portrait of
Willaert from *Musica
nova*, 1559.

with Willaert reads like a who's who of mid-century musicians: the theorists
Zarlino and Nicola Vicentino; the madrigalist Cipriano de Rore, who succeeded him at St. Mark's in 1563; and the well-known organist-composer
Andrea Gabrieli, uncle of the even more famous Giovanni. In effect, Willaert
was the founder of the Venetian School, which flourished so brilliantly
throughout the second half of the sixteenth century.

Willaert held a very special place in the view of his contemporaries. When,
in 1607, Giulio Cesare Monteverdi wrote a now-famous defense of his brother
Claudio's music, he divided the recent past into two phases; the earlier one,
which he called the *prima prattica*, extended from Ockeghem through Josquin,
La Rue, and Mouton and then on to Gombert and Clemens, and was "finally
perfected by Messer Adriano with actual composition and by the most excellent
Zarlino with most judicious rules."[4] By the time he died, on December 17,
1562, Willaert had achieved the status of a classic.

Clemens non Papa

The final member of this prolific trio is Jacobus Clemens (or Jacob Clement)
non Papa (c. 1510/15–c. 1555), the suffix "non Papa" probably having been

4. Quoted after Strunk, *Source Readings*, vol. 4, *The Baroque Era*, ed. Margaret Murata (New
York: Norton, 1997), 34.

added to his name as a joke (in order to distinguish him from either Pope Clement VII or a local poet named Jacobus Papa?). Clemens held church positions at Bruges, 's-Hertogenbosch, Ypres, and Leiden (all in modern-day Belgium or Holland) and may have had connections with the private chapel of Philippe de Croy, one of Charles V's leading generals, as well as with Charles himself.

Now, although the three composers followed different paths—Gombert in the private chapel of Charles V, Willaert at St. Mark's in Venice, and Clemens at various churches in the Low Countries—their careers share one important feature: none of them was associated with the royal court of France or its satellite institutions in and around Paris. It is a common thread of no small importance. The geography of music was changing. The homogeneous, century-old Franco-Flemish tradition, born in the early fifteenth century in the Burgundian-controlled Low Countries and subsequently infused with the artistic genius of both the Flemish and the French, was showing stylistic fissures. And if the sacred music of the second quarter of the century only hints at the split, the secular music—the chanson—drives the point home clearly. We can no longer conveniently connect "Franco" and "Flemish" with a hyphen.

A Motet by Gombert

In his *Practica musica* of 1556, Hermann Finck wrote that Gombert "shows all musicians the path, nay more, the exact way to refinement and the requisite imitative style. He composes music altogether different from what went before. For he avoids pauses, and his work is rich with full harmonies and imitative counterpoint."[5] We can hear Gombert's "rich" style in his *Quem dicunt homines* (*Anthology* 61), the text of which we have already encountered in the motet by Jean Richafort that served as the basis for Mouton's parody Mass (see Chapter 22).

Gombert set the biblical text for six voices, which, together with five-part writing, was becoming ever more popular. The six voices, moreover, are almost constantly busy, as Gombert generally avoids the textural contrasts between different combinations of voices that was a hallmark of the Josquin generation. Nor are there contrasts between imitative and homophonic sections or passages in duple and triple meter. Still another aspect of Gombert's "richness" is the seamlessness of the music. There is not a clear-cut cadence followed by silence until the end of each *pars*; even when the superius, say, cadences emphatically, one or more of the other voices continue to spin along. And three further features of Gombert's imitative style keep us guessing and thus add to the complex swirl of sound: (1) the imitation may be strict or almost variation-like in its freedom; (2) even when strict, imitative answers may be real or tonal; and (3) the number and order of the entries may vary from point to point. The contrapuntal variety is infinite.

We can appreciate the complexity of Gombert's counterpoint by comparing

5. Quoted after *New Grove*, 7: 512.

one moment in his setting of the biblical text with the analogous spot in Richafort's, the point near the beginning where Peter addresses Christ: "Respondens Petrus dixit (ei): Tu es Christus, filius Dei" (And Simon Peter answered and said: "Thou art the Christ, the Son of the living God"; Ex. 26-1):

EXAMPLE 26-1. *Quem dicunt homines*: (a) Richafort, mm. 12–20; (b) Gombert, mm. 18–24.

Whereas Richafort sets up Peter's speech with a clear cadence and change in texture, Gombert plows right through the change of speaker; there is no real musical equivalent of colon and quotation marks. There is also no sense of drama. Instead, there is a kind of sameness that downplays highlights and does not, therefore, invite relaxed listening. And though Gombert pushed this style of dense, seamless counterpoint to the extreme, it was symptomatic of other Flemish (or Netherlandish, as they are often called) composers as well, and stands in contrast to the somewhat "airier" approach of composers more closely associated with the royal court of France.

Expanding the Tonal Space

It is this very sense of drama that seems to be missing from much of the sacred music of this period, and not only because of the tendency toward a continuous, unrelieved texture. The melodic style is often just as uniform— motives tend to lack sharply etched, memorable profiles, so that melodies tend almost to meander. Rhythm too leans toward homogeneity. And the harmonic language seems tame. Or is it?

At times, it might actually have been less tame than the notation would indicate. In one of the most controversial hypotheses ever proposed about music of the fifteenth and sixteenth centuries, Edward Lowinsky argued in 1946 that a number of Flemish composers sometimes practiced a "secret chromatic art," with bursts of highly charged, "modulatory" harmonies that expressed equally emotional texts, some of which bordered on subversiveness and heresy (hence the secrecy).[6] As an example, he pointed to Clemens non Papa's setting of *Fremuit spiritu Jesu*, the poignant text of which, from the Gospel of St. John, describes the resurrection of Lazarus. Example 26-2 shows the first thirteen measures, setting the words "and Jesus groaned in His spirit," with two different versions of the accidentals:

6. Lowinsky, *Secret Chromatic Art*, and the follow-up essay, "*Secret Chromatic Art* Re-examined."

EXAMPLE 26-2. Clemens non Papa, *Fremuit spiritu Jesu*, mm. 5–13: (a) *CMM* 4/14; (b) Lowinsky, "*Secret Chromatic Art* Re-examined," 104–5.

Did singers of the period perform version b, which traverses the circle of fifths to G-flat? We cannot know.[7] But it was precisely during this period that tonal space was expanding at the hands of both theorists and composers. And

7. The idea of a "secret chromatic art" has met with both praise and scorn, and in connection with both its musical basis and its political-social-religious background. For the most recent expression of skepticism (applied to this motet in particular), see Van Benthem, "Lazarus versus Absalon."

the piece that did more than any other to set that expansion in motion was Willaert's famous *Quid non ebrietas* (probably composed in 1519), which gave theorists something to talk about for two centuries. Example 26-3 shows why:

EXAMPLE 26-3. Willaert, *Quid non ebrietas*, superius and tenor, mm. 11–39.[8]

8. Lowinsky, "*Secret Chromatic Art* Re-examined," 115.

Though superius and tenor end on what appears to be a seventh—*e–d′*—a few strategically placed, notated flats in the tenor (mm. 13, 15, 19, and 21), combined with the rule that leaps of fourths and fifths must be perfect, push the tenor first to *f*-flat (m. 21) and then into the realm of double flats. Thus the final note in the tenor, which appears to be an *e*, was in fact an *e*-double-flat and sounded as a *d*; the two voices thus end happily on an octave.

Willaert's piece was revolutionary on three counts: (1) it extended the gamut until it was bent into a circle; (2) it raised questions concerning tuning and temperament, for as the theorist Giovanni Spataro quickly recognized, the use of enharmonic equivalents was incompatible with Pythagorean tuning; and (3) it called into question the meaning of accidental signs, which no longer functioned only as signals for the solmization syllables *mi* and *fa* but were beginning to be used as they are in our own system, as indications to raise or lower a note's pitch. Indeed, not only did Willaert's piece defeat the singers of Pope Leo X, who found it impossible to perform, but it sparked a heated and protracted exchange among music theorists of the period. Finally, assuming that *Quid non ebrietas* dates from 1519, we can hardly fail to note that as Willaert was circling the domain of tonal space, Magellan was setting out to circumnavigate the globe. The spirit of exploration was alive on all fronts.

Motets and Politics

In earlier chapters, we encountered sacred works that seem to deliver a political message: Ciconia's Gloria, with its cry of "pax, pax, pax" calling for an end to the Great Schism (Chapter 3); the crusading militarism of the mid-fifteenth-century *L'homme armé* Masses (Chapter 11); and Josquin's veiled sympathy for Savonarola in his *Miserere* for Ercole I d'Este (Chapter 20). During the years 1520–50, one event in particular sparked the composition of a number of motets: the fall of the Republic of Florence in August 1530, intensified by the memory of the martyrdom of Savonarola in May 1498.

With the overthrow of the Medici in 1494, Florence, led by Savonarola, established republican rule. This lasted until 1512, when Cardinal Giovanni de' Medici (soon to be Pope Leo X) restored his family to power. The tables turned once again in 1527: following the Sack of Rome (by the troops of Charles V) and the consequent humiliation of the Medici Pope Clement VII, Florence again rebelled against Medicean rule and established another republic. The anti-republicans reacted, and in October 1529 Charles V, at Clement's invitation, layed siege to Florence, which held out against all odds until August 1530. A new Medici regime assumed official titles of nobility (eventually, grand dukes of Tuscany) and remained in power for two centuries. For the pro-republican Florentines who were driven into exile, memories of Savonarola and the fallen republics burned for decades.

VERDELOT'S *LETAMINI IN DOMINO*   Philippe Verdelot (1470/80–before 1552) proclaims his politics loudly in *Letamini in Domino*, which appears in a motet collection whose political contents make it something of a sixteenth-century musical op-ed page.[9] Example 26-4 begins just after the opening measures. Underpinning the polyphony is an ostinato-like canon in the tenor (third lowest) and quintus (third highest) parts, which sing the text "Ecce quam bonum et quam iocundum habitare fratres in unum" (Behold how good and how lovely it is for brothers to dwell in unity). This line, drawn from the opening of Psalm 132, was the rallying cry of Savonarola's followers; and perhaps the simple, popularistic tune with which Verdelot set the words recalls the melody of the now-lost *lauda*, or penitential song, that Savonarola is known to have written on the text. In any event, politically conscious listeners would have immediately identified "Ecce quam bonum," and thus the motet, with both Savonarola and pro-republican sentiments.

EXAMPLE 26-4. Verdelot, *Letamini in Domino*, mm. 6–21.

9. Rome, Biblioteca Vallicelliana, MS Vall. Borr. E.II.55–60.

WILLAERT'S *RECORDARE DOMINE* Willaert expressed his political leanings more subtly. Example 26-5 gives the final twenty-one measures of his *Recordare Domine*:

EXAMPLE 26-5. Willaert, *Recordare Domine*, mm. 178–198.

There are three possible references to Savonarola and the republicans. First, at measures 183–185, the bassus clearly alludes to a version of a plainsong melody (known in Tuscany) that sets the words "Ecce quam bonum" when they serve in their liturgical capacity as a Vespers antiphon (Ex. 26-6):

EXAMPLE 26-6. The antiphon *Ecce quam bonum*, as transmitted in Tuscany, transposed down a fifth.[10]

Second, the reiterated *f–e* half steps that shoot through the three lower voices at measures 191–197 may refer to Josquin's Savonarola-related *Miserere*, in which the half step plays a crucial role in expressing the anguish of the text. And though some might argue that the shared use of a half step is slim evidence on which to relate one work to another, there can be no doubt that Willaert knew Josquin's setting of Psalm 50 and its Savonarola associations. Finally, the line of text beginning at measure 178, "et ne in aeternum obliviscaris nostri" (and for eternity do not forget us), can be understood as invoking the memory of Savonarola.

MUSICA NOVA   Recordare Domine is the fourth motet in one of the most famous music prints of the sixteenth century: Willaert's collection of motets and madrigals entitled *Musica nova* (Fig. 26-2), a volume that has left an otherwise unheard-of paper trail of almost one hundred documents. Published by the French-born, Venetian-based music printer Antonio Gardano in 1559 (though some of the pieces were composed during the 1540s), the collection is rife with pro-republican sentiments, and it may have been intended primarily for the colony of Florentine exiles residing in Venice. In fact, a pre-publication manuscript version of the collection belonged to Polissena Pecorina, singer, patron, friend of Willaert, and herself an exiled Florentine patrician. And while the *Musica nova* was greeted warmly at Venice, Mantua, and Ferrara (the guiding spirit behind its publication was Duke Alfonso II d'Este), it was received un-

10. Fromson, "Willaert's *Musica Nova*," 455.

Figure 26-2. Title page
of *Musica nova*, 1559.

favorably at Florence and ran into censorship problems with the Inquisition at both Rome and Venice. At least in certain circles, then, motets could pack a political punch!

MUSIC FOR THE MASS

As we saw in Chapter 22, the Josquin generation developed new Mass types and cultivated older ones with renewed vigor. To review, two types proved to be especially important: (1) the parody Mass (we will settle on that term), which took for its preexistent model the entire polyphonic texture of a piece—sacred or secular—that was itself based on the new style of pervading imitation and therefore lacked a structural cantus firmus of its own; and (2) the paraphrase Mass, in which a monophonic model—again, sacred or secular— wound its way imitatively through all voices in such a way that it blended into the prevailing polyphony, sometimes to the extent of almost losing its own identity.

In addition, there were Masses for special liturgical occasions, such as the *Missa de Beata Virgine*, in which each movement of the Ordinary was based on a chant of its own kind (polyphonic Kyrie on a Kyrie chant, and so on), and the Requiem Mass, which, however, did not become standardized with respect to its chants until the second half of the sixteenth century. Finally, there were Masses that used strict cantus-firmus technique, were built on a newly invented *soggetto*, disposed a monophonic model in canon, or were freely composed from start to finish.

To this array of Mass types our no-name generation added nothing. Nor, for that matter, did the generation that followed it. In short, polyphonic settings of the Ordinary of the Mass lived out the remainder of the sixteenth century in conservative splendor. And musically splendid many of them were.

Morales

Perhaps the outstanding Mass composer of this generation was the Spaniard Cristóbal de Morales. Born (c. 1500) and raised in Seville, Morales first held positions at Ávila and Plasencia (1526–31) and then went to Italy, where in 1535 he became a member of the papal chapel, which, thanks in part to earlier Spanish popes of the Borja family, had a long tradition of employing Spanish singers. Morales spent a decade at Rome. But though often honored and widely published, his final years in the chapel were marked by illness and frustration at being passed over for lucrative benefices. In May 1545, he returned to Spain permanently, putting in unhappy stints at the cathedrals of Toledo and Málaga. He died in 1553.

The testimonials to Morales's fame are numerous: in his *Declaración de instrumentos* (1555), the Spanish theorist Juan Bermudo declared him "the light of Spain in music," while in 1559, a Mexican choir—Spanish polyphony in particular was quick to reach the New World—sang his music at a service commemorating the death of Charles V. Morales was still revered in certain circles as late as the early eighteenth century, when Andrea Adami da Bolsena, biographer of many papal musicians, praised him as the papal chapel's most important composer between Josquin and Palestrina.

A PARODY MASS BY MORALES   To give us an idea of the prominence that the parody Mass enjoyed, Table 26-1 shows the total number of complete Masses by six composers, the number of parody Masses among those works, and the split between sacred and secular models:

Table 26-1.   The prominence of the parody type among the Masses of six composers.

	Masses	Parody type	Sacred model	Secular model
Clemens	15	13	7	6
Gombert	12	8	6	2
Morales	22	8	6	2
Lassus	74	52	26	26
Palestrina	104	54	45	9
Victoria	20	16	15	1

Sources: New Grove 4: 477–78, 7: 514, 12: 557; New Grove High Renaissance Masters, 134–35, 202–3, 313.

Only for Morales did the parody Mass not constitute a majority, though even he wrote more of this type than of any other. What is also clear is the overall preference for sacred models, that is, motets. (We will consider the models for the parody Masses in Chapter 37.)

To see how composers went about transforming their polyphonic models into Masses, we may consider the Kyrie of Morales's *Missa Quaeramus cum pastoribus* (*Anthology* 62), published at Rome in 1544. Morales based his five-voice Mass (it expands to six voices in the final Agnus Dei) on a similarly named four-part motet by Mouton. Example 26-7 shows the five motives from the motet on which Morales based his Kyrie:

EXAMPLE 26-7. Mouton, *Quaeramus cum pastoribus*: (a) mm. 1–14, motive A; (b) mm. 27–34, recurring refrain; (c) mm. 35–39, motive B; (d) mm. 75–84, motive C; (e) mm. 115–117, motive D.

In Mouton's motet, motive A constitutes the beginning of the *prima pars*; the refrain motive appears four times, at the middle and end of each of the two *partes*, and provides a real sense of closure on three of its four appearances;

motive B follows directly after the first statement of the refrain and serves as a clear starting point for the second half of the *prima pars*; motive C opens the *secunda pars*; and motive D occurs in passing toward the end of the *secunda pars*. Thus all of the motives except for D play an important structural role in Mouton's motet.

We can understand the transformation of Mouton's motet into Morales's Mass in three stages, each showing increased attention to detail:

(1) To begin with, Morales expanded the four voices of the motet into five, not unusual for a composer who belonged to a generation for which five- and six-part writing was becoming popular. And since the added voice is a second bassus, the mass has a thicker, darker sound than did Mouton's work.

(2) As noted above, Morales drew on motives that had functioned as structural pillars in the motet and assigned them a similar role in each movement of his Mass. Thus Kyrie I opens with motive A and ends with the closure-producing refrain. The "Christe" begins with motive B and also ends with the refrain. And Kyrie II begins with motive C, ends with the now-expected quotation of the refrain, and in between fleetingly refers to motive D. Thus Morales preserved Mouton's sense of function, assigning motives that had opened sections of the motet to similar duty in the Mass, using Mouton's closure-producing refrain to bring each of the three sections of the Kyrie to an end, and filling the spaces between quotations with freely composed polyphony. Table 26-2 provides the measure numbers at which the motives appear in the two works:

Table 26-2.   Location of motives A, B, C, and D and the recurring refrain in Mouton's motet and Morales's Kyrie.

Morales		*Mouton*	
1–22: opening of Kyrie I	=	1–14:	opening of motet
30–37: end of Kyrie I	=	27–34:	first statement of refrain
38–47: opening of Christe	–	35–39:	opening of second half of *prima pars*
61–67: end of Christe	=	68–74:	second statement of refrain/end of *prima pars*
68–85: opening of Kyrie II	=	75–91:	opening of *secunda pars*
86–87: motive d	=	116–117:	"passing" motive
96–106: end of Kyrie II	=	128–134:	final statement of refrain/end of motet

(3) The art of parody technique resides in the composer's ability to rework the polyphonic fabric of the model, to transform something old into something new. Kyrie I, for example, begins with Mouton's opening point of imitation. There are, however, five significant differences: Morales has added a driving countermelody—derived from the refrain?—to the main motive, dismantled the symmetrical sense of paired imitation, altered the time intervals between entrances, further avoided the neat symmetry of strict tonic-dominant alternation of entrances, and added a fifth entrance on an unexpected subdominant. Mouton's graceful, almost predictable sense of balance and hear-right-through-

it transparency thus gives way to Morales's more refractory approach, as the asymmetry affects texture, rhythm, and harmonic motion. In the end, Morales's transformation of Mouton's motet reflects the stylistic differences between the two generations.

Today, we may wonder about the popularity of—and the honor accorded to—a technique in which originality took something of a back seat to the skill of rearranging and transforming. It was, however, an idea that was deeply embedded in sixteenth-century aesthetics. In discussing the drawings that Pierino del Vago based on works by Raphael and Michelangelo, Giovan Battista Armenini put it this way:

> In drawing them, he went about changing now one thing, now another . . . adding, deleting, and enriching them, and in sum reproducing them in such a way . . . that it was difficult for experts to recognize from whence he had derived them. . . . In the end, one concludes that . . . one can with facility use someone else's ideas and with little effort treat them as one's own, and do oneself credit without attracting censure from anyone.[11]

If in Chapter 11 we were somewhat hesitant to accept the notion that Franco-Flemish composers of the third quarter of the fifteenth century were influenced by Italian humanist-literary ideas of imitation and emulation when they first began to quote the entire fabric of their polyphonic models in their Masses, we must reconsider that position in connection with mid-sixteenth-century composers, who were drenched in humanist modes of thinking. No doubt, the borrowing and transformation of the full-blown parody Mass reflects an aesthetic position that had come to saturate all the arts.

Prescriptions for Writing a Parody Mass

Though the great composers handled parody technique in an infinite variety of ways, certain broad approaches to the genre settled in as the sixteenth century wore on. And eventually there were attempts at codification. In 1613, the Italian theorist Pietro Cerone (1566–1625) published his massive *El melopeo y maestro*, which he wrote in Spanish in order to gain favor with the Spanish rulers of Naples. Following is an excerpt from the chapter entitled "The Manner to Be Observed in Composing a Mass," based "lovingly" on the practice of Palestrina:

> 1. The inventions [motives] at the beginnings of the first Kyrie, the Gloria, the Credo, the Sanctus, and the Agnus Dei should be one and the same; one and the same in invention, that is, but not in consonances and accompaniments. . . . For example, if the treble began the imitation in the first Kyrie, let another voice . . . begin it in the Gloria, another in the Credo. . . . And should it happen that the treble or some other part begins two or three times, take care that the other parts enter each time with consonances other than those with which they entered before.
> 2. When the first Kyrie is finished, the Christe may be written upon some subsidiary motive . . . the composer may here use some invention of his own.

11. Quoted after Carter, *Music in Late Renaissance and Early Baroque Italy*, 71.

3. The beginnings of the last Kyrie and of the second and third Agnus Dei are in every respect at the composer's pleasure. . . . there is nothing to forbid his borrowing some other subsidiary motive.

4. The endings of the last Kyrie, the Gloria, the Credo, the Sanctus, the Osanna . . . and the third Agnus Dei should perforce be in imitation, following the invention of the motet or madrigal upon which the Mass is composed.

6. In the course of the Mass, the more use one makes . . . of motives from the middle or inside of the composition upon which the Mass is written, the better and the more praiseworthy the work will be.

12. As a rule, the Mass is usually composed upon some motet, madrigal, or chanson . . . even though by another author.[12]

What is striking about Cerone's advice is that it is devoted entirely to the parody Mass. The sixteenth century was, in terms of Mass composition, very much the century of the parody Mass.

VESPERS PSALMS FOR *CORI SPEZZATI*

In 1550, Antonio Gardano, the publisher of Willaert's *Musica nova*, issued a volume whose long title reads: *Di Adriano et di Jachet. I salmi appertinenti alli vesperi per tutte le feste dell'anno, parte a versi, et parte spezzadi accomodati da cantare a uno et a duoi chori* . . . Adriano, of course, is Willaert. Jachet is the French-born composer Jacques Colebault (1483–1559), a prolific composer of Masses and motets who was better known as Jacquet of Mantua, since he spent more than thirty years as that city's leading composer. Vespers, we will recall, is one of the eight Offices celebrated each day, specifically the evening Office, and consists largely of psalms, hymns, and the Magnificat. And *parte spezzadi*—or *cori spezzati*, as they are more commonly called—are double, or split, choirs (the Italian *spezzare* means "to break" or "to split").

Music for double choirs was not new in the mid-sixteenth century. Among early examples of such writing are psalms that Johannes Martini and Johannes Brebis wrote for the court of Ferrara in the 1470s. The favoring of psalms for double-chorus treatment grows naturally out of the antiphonal manner in which they are sung as chants: part of the choir, situated on one side of the altar, sings one verse, and the other part, on the other side, the next verse.

What is new in the settings by Willaert is the manner in which he treats the double choirs. During the first half of the sixteenth century, the rich tradition of northern-Italian double-choir music had the choirs alternate in the simplest fashion: each sang a self-contained verse in turn. With Willaert, the choirs begin to interact more closely. Though the choirs still sing individually most of the time, one verse now runs directly into the next with only the briefest of cadences, the articulations between the choirs are sometimes blurred (Ex. 26-8a), and the two choirs sing together at the end (Ex. 26-8b). Willaert's eight large-scale *salmi spezzati* must be seen as the first highpoint—perhaps the real starting point—of the double-choir tradition at St. Mark's in Venice, a tradition

12. Quoted after Strunk, *Source Readings* (1965), 265–68.

that reached its brilliant peak in the music of Giovanni Gabrieli at the end of the century.

Around that tradition there have developed some myths. First, there is not a shred of evidence to show that, as is often thought, the choirs were dispersed stereo-like in the organ lofts. Rather, they were either situated at floor level next to the altar or squeezed into one of the two pulpits that stood in front of

EXAMPLE 26-8. Willaert, *Credidi, propter quod locutus est*, Psalm 115 (Catholic numbering): (a) articulation between verses 7 and 8, mm. 73–82; (b) conclusion of doxology, mm. 123–135.

(b)

a partition separating altar from nave. The latter deployment is described in a mid-century account of ceremonies at St. Mark's:

> On the Vigil of Ascension the singers . . . sing alternatim, divided in two choirs. His Serenity mounts the great pulpit and there hears Vespers. . . . The singers sing in the new pulpit of the lessons, although they are tight in it. Whenever Our Most Serene Lord the Doge sits in the choir, the singers are situated in the great pulpit.

Second, the two choirs did not sing antiphonally, that is, with equal numbers in each group. The same book of ceremonies describes each choir's forces: "the psalms they sing divided into two choirs, namely four singers in one choir and all the rest in the other."[13] Since "all the rest" could mean up to nine singers, the psalms were, in effect, sung responsorially: a choir of four "soloists" against a larger choral force. And this soloist-versus-chorus arrangement explains Willaert's disposition of the voice parts. Instead of pitting a high choir against a low one, which would make sense for choirs of equal numbers, Willaert assigns choir I both the high and low extremes, while he bunches the four voice parts of choir II compactly in the middle. In effect, Willaert was staking out one of the style traits that would come to characterize the end-of-the-century Venetian tradition: *concertino* versus *ripieno*, a trademark of the early Baroque.

THE USE OF SCORES

A long-overdue question: how did composers of the fifteenth and sixteenth centuries control and keep track of their complex polyphonic textures without

13. Bryant, "The *cori spezzati* of St. Mark's," 172, 168.

the aid of a score, without a constant visual map of the time/space interrelationships between voices? How, in other words, did they compose? Did scores
exist, and if so, for what were they used?

Scores were not new to musicians of the period. After all, the practice of
superimposing one voice of a polyphonic composition above the other and
aligning the voices in time (even if only roughly) reaches back to the earliest
notation of polyphony and extends through the late-twelfth-century *organa* of
Leonin and Perotin. And though scores for the preservation of polyphonic
music for ensembles fell into disuse in the thirteenth century, as the development of the motet gave rise to individually written parts in choirbook format,
keyboard sources from the fourteenth century on customarily aligned the
voices—or the hands—one above the other, even going so far as to use bar
lines.

In his *Compendium musices* of 1537, the German theorist Lampadius (c. 1500–
1559) presented a carefully aligned score, bar lines and all—he called it a *tabula*—of the opening of a four-voice motet by Verdelot (Fig. 26-3). Moreover,
he seems to say in his text (his meaning is not clear) that Josquin and Isaac used
such scores to compose, while beginners used a single ten-line staff with bar
lines drawn every two semibreves. There are also a number of references from
later in the century that attest to the use of scores, not as an aid for the composer
but to make it easier to study a piece or to facilitate its performance at the
keyboard. For example, in 1570, Palestrina wrote to the Duke of Mantua, an
amateur composer, that he had "scored" one of the duke's motets so that he
(Palestrina) could more easily analyze it; and the title page of Antonio Gardano's

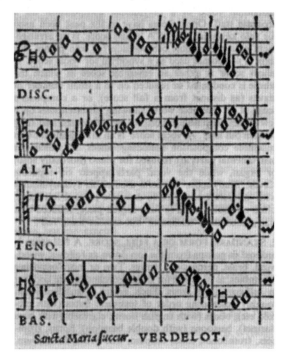

Figure 26-3. A score (*tabula
compositoria*) of the beginning of
Verdelot's *Sancta Maria, succurre
nobis* in Lampadius's
Compendium musices, 1537.

1577 publication of four-part madrigals by Cipriano de Rore reads: "Scored and arranged for performance on any keyboard instrument and for any student of counterpoint."

But does this indicate that composers customarily used scores to compose? No. There is, for instance, a mid-century set of partbooks that shows Rore composing without the aid of a score; he makes corrections in and recomposes parts of a motet voice part by voice part. The nature of the errors in the parts is such that it is hard to imagine them having been made had Rore worked with a score.

Still another question: if composers worked with scores, where have they all gone? The answer is probably that composers employed a kind of reusable material that allowed a composition to be erased after it was completed and copied out part by part; the substance could then be used again. Thus among the items mentioned in the will of Francesco Corteccia (1502–1571), a prominent Florentine composer, was a "tablet of stone for composing music." But to just what purpose Corteccia or other composers put their tablets of stone, slate, or wood is hard to say.

To sum up: scores were certainly known in the sixteenth century; they were definitely used for didactic purposes; some composers might have used them in the process of composition itself. Much more than that we cannot say. In the end, it is important that we avoid falling into the trap of imposing our own notions of what is and is not possible on musicians of the fifteenth and sixteenth centuries. Because we, perhaps, cannot imagine writing the *Missa Prolationum* or the *Miserere mei, Deus* or the *Missa Quaeramus cum pastoribus* without keeping visual track of things with a score does not mean that Ockeghem, Josquin, and Morales were incapable of doing so. Ours, after all, is a culture dependent on writing. We can hardly remember a phone number if we fail to jot it down. Men and women of the fifteenth and sixteenth centuries were not quite as handicapped. And composers in particular—with their still-living legacy of orality, with their specific musical training, and with a short-term compositional process that probably took one point of imitation and one semantic-syntactical division of text at a time—may well have done the unimaginable every day.

BIBLIOGRAPHICAL NOTE

Editions of the Music
  Clemens non Papa: *Opera omnia*, CMM 4, ed. K. P. Bernet Kempers (American Institute of Musicology, 1951–76). **Gombert**: *Opera omnia*, CMM 6, ed. Joseph Schmidt-Görg (American Institute of Musicology, 1951–75). **Morales**: *Opera omnia*, MME 11, 13, 15, 17, 20, 21, 24, 34, ed. Higini Anglès (Madrid: Consejo Superior di Investigaciones Cientificas, 1952–). **Verdelot**: *Opera omnia*, CMM 28, ed. Anne-Marie Bragard (American Institute of Musicology, 1966–). **Willaert**: *Opera omnia*, CMM 3, ed. Heinrich Zenck and Walter Gerstenberg (American Institute of Musicology, 1950–77). See also H. Colin Slim, *A Gift of Madrigals and Motets*, 2 vols. (Chicago: Chicago University Press, 1972), and the appendix entitled *The Altus Parts at Oscott College, Sutton Coldfield*; and *The Sixteenth-Century Motet*, ed. Richard Sherr (New York: Garland, 1991–).

A Short Survey

Although there is no single, in-depth survey of the sacred music of this generation, a fine complement to this chapter is chapter 5, "Sacred Polyphony in the Mid Sixteenth Century," in Tim Carter, *Music in Late Renaissance and Early Baroque Italy* (Portland: Amadeus Press, 1992).

Parody Mass

See the items by Lewis Lockwood, Quentin W. Quereau, and René B. Lenaerts cited in the Bibliographical Note in Chapter 22; on the parody Masses of Morales in particular, see Robert M. Stevenson's *Spanish Cathedral Music in the Golden Age* (Berkeley and Los Angeles: University of California Press, 1961), the most extended English-language coverage of the composer; also on Morales, see Jo-Ann Reif's "Music and Grammar: Imitation and Analogy in Morales and the Spanish Humanists," *EM* 6 (1986): 227–43, which deals with the connection between Morales's Masses and the practice of rhetoric.

Motets, Politics, Willaert's Musica nova

Edward E. Lowinsky, "A Newly Discovered Sixteenth-Century Motet Manuscript at the Biblioteca Vallicelliana in Rome," *JAMS* 3 (1950): 173–232; Slim, *A Gift of Madrigals and Motets*; for an essay in which the politics take a decidedly religious turn, see George Nugent, "Anti-Protestant Music for Sixteenth-Century Ferrara," *JAMS* 43 (1990): 228–91. The literature on Willaert's *Musica nova* is extensive: Michelle Fromson, "Themes of Exile in Willaert's *Musica nova*," *JAMS* 47 (1994): 442–87; Anthony A. Newcomb, "Editions of Willaert's *Musica nova*: New Evidence, New Speculations," *JAMS* 26 (1973): 132–45; David S. Butchart, "'La Pecorina' at Mantua, *Musica nova* at Florence," *EM* 13 (1985): 358–66; Armen Carapetyan, "The Musica Nova of Adriano Willaert," *JRBM* (*MD*) 1 (1946): 200–21; and, for those who can manage the Italian, the thorough documentary account in Jessie Ann Owens and Richard Agee, "La stampa della 'Musica Nova' di Willaert," *RIM* 24 (1989): 219–303. *Musica nova* is edited in vols. 5 and 13 of the *Opera omnia*; see also Patrick Macey, "Savonarola and the Sixteenth-Century Motet," *JAMS* 36 (1983): 442–52, and "The Lauda and the Cult of Savonarola," *RQ* 45 (1992): 439–83.

Cori spezzati

The most comprehensive study is Anthony F. Carver, *"Cori spezzati": The Development of Sacred Polychoral Music to the Time of Schütz*, 2 vols. (Cambridge: Cambridge University Press, 1988); see also David Bryant, "The *cori spezzati* of St Mark's: Myth and Reality," *EMH* 1 (1981): 165–86.

The Expansion of Tonal Space and Willaert's Quid non ebrietas

The starting point remains the provocative studies by Edward E. Lowinsky: *Secret Chromatic Art in the Netherlands Motet* (New York: Columbia University Press, 1946; reprint, 1967); *"Secret Chromatic Art* Re-examined," in *Perspectives of Musicology*, ed. Barry S. Brook, Edward O. D. Downes, and Sherman Van Solkema (New York: Norton, 1970), 91–135; "Adrian Willaert's Chromatic 'Duo' Re-examined," *TVMM* 18 (1956): 1–36; "Echoes of of Adrian Willaert's Chromatic 'Duo' in Sixteenth- and Seventeenth-Century Compositions," in *Studies in Music History: Essays for Oliver Strunk*, ed. Harold Powers (Princeton: Princeton University Press, 1968), 183–238; "The Goddess Fortuna in Music," *MQ* 29 (1943): 45–77; and "Matthaeus Greiter's *Fortuna*: An Experiment in Chromaticism and in Musical Iconography," *MQ* 42 (1956): 500–19, 43 (1957): 68–85. Two recent rebuttals of Lowinsky's hypotheses are Jaap van Benthem's "Fortuna in Focus: Concerning 'Conflicting' Progressions in Josquin's *Fortuna d'un gran tempo*," *TVNM* 30 (1980): 1–50, and "Lazarus versus Absalon: About Fiction and Fact in the Netherlands Motet," *TVNM* 39 (1989): 54–82; see also Dorothy Keyser, "The Character of Exploration: Adrian Willaert's 'Quid non ebrietas,'" in *Musical Repercussions of 1492: Encounters in Text and Performance*, ed. Carol E. Robertson (Washington, D.C.: Smithsonian Institution Press, 1992), 185–207; and the works by Karel Berger and Margaret Bent cited in the Bibliographical Note of Chapter 17. On the theoretical debate sparked by Willaert's piece, see Bonnie J. Blackburn, Clement Miller, and Edward E. Lowinsky, *A Correspondence of Renaissance Musicians* (Oxford: Oxford University Press, 1991).

Scores and Compositional Process

Lowinsky, "On the Use of Scores by Sixteenth-Century Musicians," *JAMS* 1 (1948): 17–23, and "Early Scores in Manuscript," *JAMS* 13 (1960): 126–71; Jessie Ann Owens, "The Milan Partbooks: Evidence of Cipriano de Rore's Compositional Process," *JAMS* 37 (1984): 270–98, and *Composers at Work: The Craft of Musical Composition, 1450–1600* (Oxford: Clarendon Press, 1996).

Also Cited

Clement Miller, "Jerome Cardan on Gombert, Phinot, and Carpentras," *MQ* 58 (1972): 412–19.

CHAPTER 27

National Song Styles

If the sacred music of the second quarter of the sixteenth century was essentially conservative in nature, secular song hitched itself to the spirit of innovation already set in motion by the Josquin generation. More specifically, two new genres sprang up and came to dominate the scene: the Italian madrigal (for the remainder of the century) and the rather misleadingly named "Parisian" chanson (for a considerably shorter time).

THE CHANSON

With the second quarter of the century, the once homogeneous Franco-Flemish song style shattered decisively. As we saw in Chapter 24, there was already a stylistic–aesthetic gulf between the settings of serious poetry that Pierre de la Rue composed for the Netherlandish court of Margaret of Austria (see *Anthology* 47) and the lighter, more airy approach of the three-part popular arrangements that found such favor at the French royal court of Louis XII. Likewise, a piece such as Josquin's motet-like *Plus nulz regretz* (*Anthology* 46) inhabits a different world from that of, say, Ninot le Petit's *Et la la la* (*Anthology* 48). And when, during the 1520s, the split finally passed the point of no return, it hardened along geographic lines: there was one style of chanson in the Low Countries and another in France; to these we generally attach the labels "Netherlandish" and "Parisian," respectively.

The Netherlandish Chanson

With its thick, imitative counterpoint, the Netherlandish chanson was a direct offspring of the Franco-Flemish central tradition. Example 27-1 illustrates the style with the opening measures of a chanson by Thomas Crecquillon (c. 1480/1500–1557), a singer in the chapel of Charles V and perhaps the most highly regarded Netherlandish song composer of his time. Though Crecquillon's approach to structure was typical of the Netherlandish chanson in that he favored motet-like, through-composed continuity over self-enclosed sections with various repetition schemes, he often repeated either the music of the opening couplet for the two verses that followed (as he does here beginning at m. 14) or both music and text of the final phrase. And when, as in Gombert's

EXAMPLE 27-1. Crecquillon, *Si mon travail*, mm. 1–19.

setting of the same poem (Ex. 27-2), the repetition comes at the end (m. 71
= m. 64), its effect can be powerful, as it wraps up structurally and provides
rhetorical emphasis.

Like their sacred works, though, the hundreds of chansons by Crecquillon,
Gombert, and Clemens have gotten lost between the songs of Josquin on one
end and those of Lassus on the other. It is a shame, for a great deal of beautiful
music continues to go unheard.

EXAMPLE 27-2. Gombert, *Si mon travail*, mm. 64–79.

The Parisian Chanson

It is not neglect from which the so-called Parisian chanson suffers. Rather, it is an identity crisis.

To begin with, the term "Parisian" does not fix the genre geographically: many of the chansons to which we affix the label were composed outside Paris in the French provinces, and not all chansons that were composed at Paris necessarily wear the "Parisian" stylistic label comfortably. Nor can the label automatically be attached (as it sometimes is) to any chanson that came off the presses of the Parisian music publisher Pierre Attaingnant, who, despite his close association with the genre, printed chansons in a wide variety of styles, including works that belong squarely to the Netherlandish tradition. Finally, the term is applied to chansons written in more than one style, with the problem becoming more acute as we move from the relatively narrow stylistic range of the late 1520s to the greater diversity of mid-century. Perhaps we should drop "Parisian" altogether and replace it with "French" (though the poetry of the Netherlandish chanson is equally French).

Here we consider the three basic styles of the Parisian chanson in the late 1520s and early 1530s: the lyrical, the narrative, and the programmatic. But first we should meet a poet who was one of the driving forces behind the genre.

CLÉMENT MAROT   Marot (1496?–1544) was the most famous and widely imitated French poet of his time and a special favorite of Claudin de Sermisy, Clément Janequin, and other chanson composers (both French and Netherlandish). Breaking with the formality of the *formes fixes*, and magically reconciling the opposing courtly and popular traditions, he infused French poetry with a sense of wit and elegance, simplicity and spontaneity. From his pen flowed some of the earliest French sonnets and *épigrammes*. Having turned to Protestantism in the 1520s, Marot undertook the task of translating the psalms into French verse and thus laid the groundwork for the later Calvinist psalters. He paid for his religious sympaties by spending the last years of his life in exile.

A LYRICAL CHANSON BY CLAUDIN   Born around 1490, Claudin de Sermisy spent the major part of his career at two of the most musically prestigious institutions in Paris: the French royal chapel and the Sainte Chapelle, one of the churches frequented by members of the court. Though he wrote a significant amount of sacred music, Claudin is best-known to us today as a chanson composer (approximately 175 songs). For some, Claudin's name is virtually synonymous with the Parisian chanson. He died in October 1562.

There is hardly a more textbook example of the lyrical chanson than Claudin's *Je n'ay point plus d'affection* (*Anthology* 63). The poem runs as follows:

	Rhyme	Music	Cadences
Je n'ay point plus d'affection,	a	**A**	
Que ce qu'il me plaist d'en avoir.	b		i
Et si ne porte passion,	a	**A**	
S'il ne me plaist la recepvoir.	b		i
J'ay gaigné sur moy tel pouvoir,	b	**B**	III
Tel credit et auctorité,	c		v
Que je commande a mon vouloir,	b	**A**	
Rein n'y peult la fragilité,	c		i
Que je commande a mon vouloir,	b	**A**	
Rien n'y peult la fragilité.[1]	c		i

From the music, we can see the characteristic features of the style: (1) a texture that is decidedly homophonic-homorhythmic; (2) a lyrical melody confined entirely to the superius; (3) all voices fully texted; (4) syllabic declamation at the level of the semibreve and minim (half note and quarter note in the transcription); (5) clear-cut, balanced phrases; (6) a tightly knit "tonal" scheme, here progressing i–i–III–v–i–i; (7) clearly discernible sections, with repetition

---

1. Quoted after *CMM*, 52/3: 121–22.

at the beginning and/or the end; (8) an opening rhythmic motive that is virtually always dactylic (♩ ♪ ♪); and (9) a full triad at the final cadence, something that was becoming increasingly popular in the second quarter of the century. (Though Claudin settles for a G–B-flat third, there is a full triad at the end of Gombert's *Si mon travail* in Ex. 27-2.)

Finally, Claudin was concise! In *Je n'ay point plus d'affection*, the ten octosyllabic lines of the poem are set from beginning to end with only thirty-seven breves (including the repeat of the opening section and counting the final long as two). In Gombert's *Si mon travail*, on the other hand, the expansive points of imitation and presumed repetition of short snippets of text require the same number of breves just to get us barely through four decasyllabic lines. Thus Claudin set syllables at about twice the real-time rate of speed.

Claudin's song breathes equally of clarity, grace, expression, and simplicity. Its tone is neither entirely courtly nor entirely popular. Rather, it brings those worlds together and strikes a balance between the two, much as Marot's poetry did. In short, both Claudin and Marot embodied the spirit of the court of Francis I: "the most radiant, the most creative in French history, a reign in which two brilliant cultures came together, those of Gothic France and Renaissance Italy."[2]

A NARRATIVE CHANSON BY PASSEREAU   Pierre Passereau seems to have spent his career mainly in the provinces from 1509 to 1547. Though he turned out a few chansons of the lyrical type, he was far more at home with the narrative chanson, with poems that told stories that were either rustic or dirty (or both).

The witty *Il est bel et bon* (*Anthology* 64), printed by Attaingnant in 1534, is Passereau's best-known piece. The rather freely constructed poem, which has a recurring refrain, reads as follows (the "x" indicates that the line is set imitatively and/or begins after a clear-cut cadence):

	Imitation	Clear cadence
Il est bel et bon, commère, mon mari	x	
Il estoit deux femmes toutes d'ung pays	x	x
Disans l'une à l'autre: avez bon mari?	x	x
Il est bel et bon, commère, mon mary.	x	
Il ne me courouce, ne me bat aussi	x	x
Il faict le mesnage, il donne aux poulailles	x	
Et je prens mes plaisirs		
—Commère, c'est pour rire—	x	x
Quant les poulailles crient	x	x
Co, co, dac; petite coquette, qu'esse cy?	x	x
Il est bel et bon, commère, mon mary.[3]	x	x

Though almost every line begins with a point of imitation, we are a long way from the typical Netherlandish chanson: (1) most points begin only after

2. Seward, *Prince of the Renaissance*, 13.

3. Quoted after *CMM*, 45: xiv.

the preceding material has cadenced; (2) imitation notwithstanding, the texture is often chordal; and (3) the combination of clear-cut cadences and the recurring refrain imparts a sense of distinct sections, even if the seams between them are not quite as blatant as they were in Claudin's chanson.

Il est bel et bon illustrates yet another characteristic of the narrative chanson. The declamation is rapid-fire from beginning to end, with syllables spit out at the level of the minim and semiminim (quarter note and eighth note in the transcription). The chanson is thus an excellent example of a Renaissance "patter" song. And we can hardly miss the humorous realism with which Passereau depicts the clucking of the hens—"Co, co, dac"—in the altus and bassus at measures 43–47. It is a stylistic touch that, as we will now see, Janequin handled with genius.

A PROGRAM CHANSON BY JANEQUIN Clément Janequin's career is almost singular among the careers of the great composers of the period, for he never held a regular position at either a major church or important court. Born around 1485, Janequin spent most of his life in the provinces, first at Bordeaux, then at Angers. Only in 1549 did he move to Paris, where, after receiving the honorary titles of *chantre* and *compositeur du roi*, he died in 1558. For some, Janequin's 250-plus chansons make *his* name synonymous with the Parisian chanson.

What Passereau did when he imitated the clucking of the hens, Janequin turned into an industry of sorts, in which he was the undisputed master. As the sixteenth-century poet Jean-Antoine de Baïf wrote:

> If he with heavy chords motets compose
> Or dare to reproduce alarms of battle,
> Or if in song he mimic women's prattle,
> Or imitate birds' voices in design,
> Good Janequin in all his music shows
> No mortal spirit—he is all divine.[4]

Baïf knew what he was talking about. The reference to birds alludes to *Le chant des oiseaux*, the prattling women to *Le caquet des femmes*, and the alarms of battle to the most famous of Janequin's pieces, *La guerre*, which supposedly depicts Francis I's victory at the Battle of Marignano in 1515.

If *La guerre* is the most famous of Janequin's program chansons, *Les cris de Paris* must be the most riotously funny (*Anthology* 65). After opening with a question addressed directly to us, "Do you want to hear the cries of Paris?" Janequin drops us on the streets of sixteenth-century Paris, where we are bombarded by the cries of vendors selling everything from wine (altus, mm. 42–44) to sweet turnips (three upper voices, mm. 130–133). Performed by singers who have a sense of humor, some of the characters are almost huggable: the mustard man (bassus, mm. 51–58), the pine seed hawkers (all voices, mm. 106–109), and the seller of not-so-sweet turnips (altus, mm. 121–123), while the sweet-talking duo that sells pears, spinach, and sorrel is difficult to resist (superius and altus, mm. 96–102). The piece ends by addressing us once more: if

4. Quoted after Reese, *Music in the Renaissance*, 297.

we wish to hear some other vendors, we should go and fetch them. Would that Janequin had done it for us.

In sum, what we call the Parisian chanson was composed both in and outside Paris, and both its music and its poetry embraced multiple styles. The one constant that runs through and unifies this rich and wonderful repertory is its stylistic differentiation from the Netherlandish chanson.

ORIGINS   Early attempts to find the stylistic roots of the Parisian chanson located them squarely in the Italian frottola, since the two repertories shared a chordal style, lyrical melody in the superius, clear-cut phrases, and a terse, lucid approach to structure. Simply put, the conclusion will not stand. First, the criteria are too general, and they can just as well describe the style of the Spanish villancico. Second, not all Parisian chansons fit the description; it works fairly well for the lyrical chanson, somewhat less well for the more imitative narrative chanson, and perhaps not at all for the kaleidoscopic texture of Janequin's program chansons. Third, the poetry of the two genres is miles apart; while Claudin and his fellow chanson composers were setting the likes of Marot, the frottolists had been content with little more than doggerel. And fourth, there is no strong evidence to show that Claudin, Janequin, Passereau, and their French contemporaries were even acquainted with the works of Cara and Tromboncino.

Eventually this view was corrected: (1) French composers had no reason to look to Italy for inspiration; (2) they drew on their own tradition of popular polyphonic song; and (3) the lyrical Parisian chanson grew out of the three-part popular arrangement, while its narrative counterpart flowed from the four-part popular arrangement. To be sure, we can hear the stylistic affinity between such pairs of pieces as Claudin's *Je n'ay point plus d'affection* and Févin's *Adieu solas* (Ex. 24-6) on the one hand, and Passereau's *Il est bel et bon* and Ninot's *Et la la la* (*Anthology* 48) on the other.

Yet even this seemingly powerful argument has its loose ends. For example, although the composers of the four-part popular arrangement were solidly Franco-Flemish, surviving sources seem to indicate that they cultivated the genre mainly on Italian soil. And perhaps in the end we are looking for phantom roots. Perhaps the pin has more than one point.

THE MADRIGAL

Among the musical genres of the sixteenth century, none is more closely associated with Italy than the madrigal, the first genre in which Italian composers truly found a voice that resonated on the international scene. Given this "Italianness," it is ironic that the early madrigal developed mainly at the hands of French and Flemish composers. For aside from Costanzo Festa (c. 1490–1545), the leading madrigalists during the second quarter of the century were the Frenchmen Philippe Verdelot and Jacques Arcadelt and the Flemish Adrian Willaert. And it is with their madrigals, written over the course of three decades (1520s–1540s), that we are concerned here.

1520s: Verdelot

Verdelot was at Florence by 1522–23 at the latest, and it was there and then that the madrigal was born. His *Madonna, per voi ardo* (*Anthology* 66) exemplifies its earliest stage. Here is the poem:

1. Madonna, per voi ardo,	My lady, I burn with love for you,
2. Et voi non lo credete,	And you do not believe it,
3. Perchè non pia quanto bella sete.	For you are not as kind as you are beautiful.
4. Ogn' hora io miro et guardo.	I look at you and admire you constantly.
5. Se tanta crudeltà cangiar' volete,	If you wish to change this great cruelty,
6. Donna, non v' accorgete	Lady, are you unaware
7. Che per voi moro et ardo?	That for you I die and burn?
8. Et per mirar vostra beltà infinita	And in order to admire your infinite beauty
9. Et voi sola servir bramo la vita.	And to serve you alone, I desire life.[5]

One of the myths about the madrigal is that it quickly began to set poetry that was highly literate, emotionally charged, and drew on Petrarch for inspiration. While this is an accurate enough description for the madrigal of the 1540s and beyond, Verdelot's *Madonna* shows why it must be qualified for the beginnings of the genre. True, *Madonna* leaves behind the jangle of the frottolists, and its rhyme scheme and structure are no longer tied to the old Italian fixed forms. Further, there are a few loaded words, such as "moro" and "ardo" (I die, I burn), and even an attempt at a Petrarchan play with antithesis: the lover dies for his beloved in line 7, but desires life in line 9. Yet in the end, the poem is rather tame, and even the opening plea to "My lady" is commonplace.

Verdelot's setting is equally tame. The chordal texture is largely unvaried, with relief provided only by the contrasting pairs of voices at line 7 (mm. 26–29) and the short-lived imitation in the lower voices at line 9 (mm. 35–36 and 40–41). There is, however, a real difference between Verdelot's chordal writing and that of the earlier frottolists. Although the superius has the melody (or what there is of one), the texture is full-throated and vocally conceived from top to bottom. Unlike the frottola, then, which was probably most often performed by solo voice and lute, the madrigal was an all-vocal affair.[6] Nor is there anything daring about the relationship between music and text. Verdelot sets the poetry syllabically, with the only flourishes coming on "bramo" (I desire) at measures 34–36 (repeated at mm. 39–41) and at the lightly decorated cadences. In addition, each phrase of music fits neatly with one line of verse, just as it had in the frottola. And though the music is through composed—and

---

5. After Slim, *A Gift of Madrigals*, 2:443.

6. Occasionally, however, madrigals were performed by a singer on the top part with instrumental accompaniment. Thus Willaert arranged a number of Verdelot madrigals, including *Madonna,* for voice and lute in his *Intavolatura de li madrigali di Verdelotto* of 1536.

therefore as far removed from the repetition schemes of the fixed forms as the poetry—Verdelot repeats line 3/phrase 3 in almost sequence-like fashion in order to emphasize it rhetorically, and then does the same for the final line, now with the music repeated exactly.

There are some understated attempts to underscore the meaning of the text: certainly, the large-scale syncopated effect on the opening word, "Madonna"—and the similar gambit on "Donna" (mm. 22–23)—lends some urgency to the lover's plea, while the E-flat chord on "crudeltà" (m. 18) places that crucial word in relief. On the other hand, the emotionalism of "ardo" and "moro" receive no special attention. Verdelot seems to have had a single aim: to project the text as simply and as clearly as possible. And he does so in such a way that, as one critic perceptively put it, it is as if four readers are reciting the same poem at the same time, with each one reading it with a slightly different twist.[7] This attitude will characterize the madrigal, and in ever more dramatic ways, for the remainder of the century.

1530s: Arcadelt

Jacques Arcadelt (c. 1505–1568), who may have enjoyed a close association with Verdelot, probably spent time at Florence in the early 1530s (at the ducal court of the recently restored Medici) and then moved to Venice later in the decade. He was definitely at Rome in the 1540s, and passed the last dozen or so years of his life in his native (?) France.

In late 1538 or early 1539, the Venetian printer Antonio Gardano issued the *Primo libro di madrigali d'Archadelt . . .* Its commercial success was spectacular, and it was reissued more than fifty times. The book's main selling point was no doubt the madrigal with which it opened, *Il bianco e dolce cigno* (*Anthology* 67), on a text by the Marquis Alfonso d'Avalos:

1. Il bianco e dolce cigno	The white and gentle swan
2. cantando more, et io	dies singing, and I,
3. piangendo giung' al fin del viver mio.	weeping, approach the end of my life.
4. Stran' e diversa sorte	Strange and diverse fates,
5. ch'ei more sconsolato	that he dies disconsolate
6. et io moro beato.	and I die happy.
7. Morte che nel morire	Death, that in the [act of] dying
8. m'empie di gioia tutt' e di desire.	fills me wholly with joy and desire.
9. Se nel morir' altro dolor non sento	If in dying I feel no other pain,
10. di mille mort' il dì sarei contento.	I would be content to die a thousand times a day.[8]

Arcadelt's setting is gorgeous. It also moves the madrigal somewhat closer to maturity in two respects: in the way it treats the occasional conflict between meaning and structure in the poem, and in its obvious attempts at word painting.

---

7. Haar, *Essays on Italian Music*, 72 (on which this discussion is based).

8. After Fuller, *The European Musical Heritage*, 265.

Meaning and formal division rub against one another in the first three lines. This is a technique known as *enjambment*, in which semantic meaning cuts across both lineation and rhyme scheme. There can be no doubt about how Arcadelt read the poem: phrase 1 (mm. 1–5), which sets "The white and gentle swan/ dies singing," runs right through the end of line 1 to the middle of line 2, while phrase 2, "and I,/weeping, approach the end of my life" (mm. 6–10), picks up from there and continues to the end of line 3. What is significant is this: whereas Verdelot's *Madonna*, with its one-to-one relationship between musical phrase and line of poetry, respected the formal structure of its poem (as had earlier settings of poetry in any of the fixed forms, whether French or Italian), Arcadelt emphasizes the semantic meaning. And with that shift in emphasis, both Arcadelt and the madrigal took an important step toward meeting both the sense and the emotion of high-quality, sophisticated poetry on their own terms.

Arcadelt also expresses the meaning of the poem by calling attention to certain words or phrases. For example, (1) there is an unexpected, almost brooding, flat seventh on "piangendo" (weeping, mm. 6–7); (2) there are affective half steps, always in the superius and always on $a–b$-flat, on "more," "sconsolato," and "morire" (dies, disconsolate, dying, mm. 4–5, 18–19, and 25–26, respectively); (3) there is a short melismatic flourish, the only one in the piece, followed by a sense of repose—a V–i cadence—on "beato" (happy, mm. 21–24); and (4) there is a broad, contrasting point of imitation to underscore the words "di mille mort' il dì sarei contento" (I would be content to die a thousand times a day, m. 34 to the end), which, to any well-versed reader of the period, meant a day's worth of sex.

Thus Arcadelt brought the madrigal to a new level of expressivity within about a decade of its birth. The next level would come in the 1540s. But before moving on, we would do well to consider various hypotheses concerning the origins of the madrigal.

Origins

In his classic study *The Italian Madrigal*, Alfred Einstein (Albert's cousin) outlined the origins of the madrigal: "The transformation of the frottola, from an accompanied song with a supporting bass and two inner voices serving as 'fillers' into a motet-like polyphonic construction with four parts of equal importance, can be followed as easily as the transformation of a chrysalis into a butterfly" (1:121). Einstein attributed the transformation to the influence of the Netherlandish motet and the growing vogue for the serious poetry of Petrarch. But his hypothesis has lately been called into question. First, as we saw in connection with Verdelot's *Madonna, per voi ardo*, the poetry of the early madrigal was not always superior to that of the frottola. Nor was Petrarch completely unknown to the frottolists, especially during the frottola's final years. In fact, much of the poetry of the early madrigal is just as much *poesia per musica*—that is, poetry without great pretense, expressly written to be set to music—as that of the frottola.

As for the assertion that the early madrigal donned a "motet-like polyphonic construction," we can test this by comparing Verdelot's *Madonna* and Arcadelt's *Il bianco e dolce cigno* with the dense, imitative polyphony of a motet such as Gombert's six-voice *Quem dicunt homines (Anthology* 61). We may as well compare apples and bananas. As with the appropriation of serious poetry, it was only in the 1540s that the madrigal began to appropriate the thick, contrapuntal texture of the motet.

There is another point to consider: though frottola and madrigal coexisted for a while during the 1520s, and though a piece such as Bernardo Pisano's *Si è debile il filo* (Ex. 24-9) stands on the stylistic threshold of the early madrigal, the two genres seem to have traveled in very different geographical circles. Whereas the frottola was primarily a northern Italian phenomenon, based at such courts as Mantua and Ferrara, the madrigal took shape mainly at Florence. Simply put, the paths of the fading frottola and the nascent madrigal were not very closely intertwined.

Where, then, should we look for the origins of the madrigal? One place may be the French chanson, more specifically to whatever fed the lyrical style of Claudin. After all, both Verdelot and Arcadelt were Frenchmen, and Arcadelt, especially, turned out a rich body of lyrical chansons written in a sentimental, early-madrigal vein.

In the end, there is probably no single seed from which the madrigal grew. On the one hand, we might think of the madrigals of Verdelot and Arcadelt as the Italian counterpart of the Claudin-style, lyrical French chanson. On the other hand, the madrigal displays some sense of stylistic continuity with the late frottola. What can certainly be said is that only in the 1540s does Einstein's version of the butterfly—his motet-like construction that sets Petrarchan poetry—come into sight, and we see it for the first time in the madrigals of Willaert.

1540s: Willaert

As noted in Chapter 26, 1559 saw the publication of Willaert's *Musica nova*, his landmark collection of motets and madrigals. And among its twenty-five madrigals, many of which were composed in the 1540s, all but one are based on poems by Petrarch, who now deserves our attention.

PETRARCHISM AND PIETRO BEMBO   Poet, historian, essayist, classicist, textual critic, and never-tiring letter writer (all but the first endeavor carried on in Latin), Francesco Petrarca (1304–1374; Fig. 27-1) was, together with Dante and Boccaccio, one of the three great literary figures of late-thirteenth- and fourteenth-century Italy. His chief contribution to Italian poetry resides in the 366 poems that make up his *Canzoniere*. There Petrarch developed his thoughts about spirituality, earthly values, and ideal beauty by means of deeply contemplative sonnets addressed to his beloved and mythical (?) Laura.

Petrarch's poetry was overlooked by his contemporaries (the composers of the trecento, for example, favored a more manageable *poesia per musica*), and

Figure 27-1. Portrait of Petrarch by a Venetian artist (Galleria Borghese, Rome).

the first phase of his influence becomes apparent only in the works of certain late-fifteenth-century poets. In music, we must wait even longer for him to emerge. Though his poems began to attract the last wave of frottolists, it was only in the madrigals of Willaert and his Venetian protégés—written in the 1540s and 1550s—that Petrarch became something of the rage, and this largely as a reaction to the work of Italy's most influential literary figure of the time: Pietro Bembo.

Bembo (1470–1547), who served as secretary to Pope Leo X and who became a cardinal himself in 1539, was both a poet and a literary theorist. In his most important work, *Prose della volgar lingua*, completed by 1512 and published at Venice in 1525, Bembo set out to defend Italian as a literary language and place it on a par with Latin. For Bembo, "Italian" was the Tuscan Italian of Dante, Boccaccio, and especially Petrarch, whose poetry he analyzed in close detail and held up as a model of perfection. He also developed a theory according to which words could convey feelings of *gravità* (dignity) or *piacevolezza* (charm or sweetness) depending on their vowels, consonants, rhythm, rhyme, and context in long or short lines: words could have a visceral effect.

Bembo's ideas were especially rife in the Venetian intellectual circles frequented by Willaert. And while Bembo and music theorists seem to have paid little attention to one another, perhaps the new style that Willaert developed in his *Musica nova* madrigals represents an attempt to transfer Bembo's theories into the musical language of the madrigal.

WILLAERT'S *ASPRO CORE*   Though we will look only at snippets of *Aspro core*, we should read through Petrarch's sonnet in its entirety.

1. Aspro core e selvaggio, e cruda voglia	Bitter and savage heart, and cruel will
2. In dolce, humile, angelica figura,	In sweet, humble, angelic figure,
3. Se l'impreso rigor gran tempo dura	If the hardness you have set upon lasts for long,
4. Avran di me poco honorata spoglia,	There will be little honor for my remains;
5. Che, quando nasce e mor fior, herba, e foglia,	For when flowers, grass, and leaves are born and die,
6. Quando è 'l dì chiaro e quando è notte oscura,	When the day is bright and when the night is dark,
7. Piango ad ogni or. Ben ho di mia ventura,	I weep at all times, because of my fate,
8. Di madonna e d'Amore onde mi doglia.	Of my lady and love, for which I mourn.
9. Vivo sol di speranza, rimenbrando	I live only from hope, remembering
10. Che poco umor già per continua prova	That a little water, with continuous trying,
11. Consumar vidi marmi e pietre salde.	I have seen consume marble solid rocks.
12. Non è sì duro cor che, lagrimando,	There is no heart so hard that, with weeping,
13. Pregando, amando, talhor non si smova,	Pleading, and loving, will not someday be moved,
14. Né freddo voler, che non si scalde.	Nor a will so cold that it will not be warmed.

We have not seen poetry—whether French, Italian, Spanish, or German—of this quality before. It is both beautiful and complicated. Petrarch plays with antithetical images, and our emotions ride a seesaw: "Bitter . . . savage . . . cruel/sweet, humble, angelic" (lines 1–2); "day is bright . . . night is dark" (line 6). And the syntax can be dizzying, not only within lines, but across them: "That a little water, with continuous trying, I have seen consume" (lines 10–11). Little wonder, then, that composers shied away for so long.

The fourteen-line Petrarchan sonnet divides into two parts: octave and sestet. Willaert divided his setting accordingly (there are two *partes*), and so initiated the tradition of the large-scale, multipartite madrigal that would become standard in the second half of the sixteenth century. But this is perhaps the least of Willaert's new ideas about the madrigal. Example 27-3 presents three excerpts from *Aspro core*.

Here, finally, is Einstein's "butterfly": Petrarch's poetry set in a dense, complicated, motet-like texture. And if Verdelot's *Madonna, per voi ardo* could be characterized as four readers reciting the poem at the same time, Willaert's *Aspro core* is a heated, six-way debate on how to read the poem, as the texture varies from the full six voices to various combinations of trios and quartets, from polyphony both imitative and nonimitative to chordal declamation. Even the counterpoint of words is dense, as voices rarely initiate—or even pronounce—the same syllable at the same time.

Yet despite the counterpoint of syllables, Willaert manages to express the meaning of the text in almost graphic terms:

(1) Measures 1–21 set lines 1–2, in which Petrarch contrasts the bitter, savage, and cruel with the sweet, humble, and angelic. Willaert interprets the

EXAMPLE 27-3. Willaert, *Aspro core*: (a) mm. 1–21; (b) mm. 42–49; (c) mm. 103–115.

(a)

harshness of line 1 with unsettled first-inversion triads and parallel major thirds that form biting tritone cross-relationships (the two lowest-sounding voices at mm. 2–3 and the two middle ones at 7–8), and then virtually melts down the same melody with root-position triads and a touch of implied triple meter to express the sweetness of line 2 (m. 11). It is subtle, understated—Willaert generally shuns high drama—and extremely effective.

(2) Willaert is more obvious with line 6 (mm. 42–49), which juxtaposes the bright day with the dark night: the top voice plummets an octave and then continues down another third as it falls from day to night, with the unexpected flatted seventh on "scura" (dark) leaving no doubt about the matter.

(3) Willaert's treatment of lines 12–13 is brilliant (mm. 103–115). With an enjambment that cuts across the lines, Petrarch develops the image of the hard heart that can, however, still be moved by weeping, pleading, and loving. And here Willaert plays with the antithesis on two different levels. For the listener without the music, the top voice makes the point clearly enough: the whole step (on a'–b'-natural) that continues to ascend (mm. 103–105, 106–108) contrasts with the half step (on a'–b'-flat) that immediately turns back down (mm. 109–111 and 112–114). For the sixteenth-century singer who performed that part, however, Willaert's musical oxymoron is even more pointed: the word "duro" (hard) is sung to a b-natural, that is, the "hard" b that must be solmized as *mi*; "lagrimando" (weeping) and "amando" (loving), on the other hand, are sung to b-flat, the "soft" b called *fa*. Undetectable to the listener, it is nevertheless a wonderful touch.

Willaert extends the musical sensitivity to the poem to yet another level: the syntactical unit. Example 27-4 shows the setting of line 5. Willaert read and set the line as follows: "For when [are] born and die/flowers, grass, and leaves," with each syntactical unit spawning a miniature "fantasia" of its own. And with his tendency to repeat the individual unit and his skill at setting one

EXAMPLE 27-4. Willaert, *Aspro core*, mm. 35–43.

unit off from the other, Willaert creates a rich interplay of prosody, semantic meaning, and syntax that matches the complexity of Petrarch's thought. In fact, we could say that in *Aspro core*, each of the six readers is reading the poem silently, now mulling over a word or phrase, now speeding up on another, now stopping to reconsider things altogether. The composer has done nothing less here than devise a new way of interpreting vernacular poetry through music.

Whether Willaert consciously attempted to apply Bembo's theories about poetry to music or not, he certainly followed Bembo's ideas in one respect. Just as Bembo set out to place the Italian language on a par with Latin, so Willaert placed the madrigal on a stylistic par with the motet. *Aspro core* is not

a ditty; it goes beyond "song." Willaert and his fellow Venetians developed a
new kind of madrigal, one in which serious poetry called forth equally serious
music. In effect, they reinvented the genre by striking a delicate balance between poetry and music, in which neither is fully subservient to the other.

The beauty of this new invention was not lost on Willaert's audience. As
Antonfrancesco Doni put it in the dedication of his *Dialogo della musica* (1544):

> If you could hear the heavenly things which with the ears of understanding I
> have enjoyed here in Venice, you would be amazed. . . . One evening I heard
> a concert of *violoni* and voices . . . the perfect master of this music was Adriano
> Willaert; [it was] in that diligent style of his . . . so well wrought, so sweet,
> so appropriate, so marvelously adapted to the text that I own to having never
> known what harmony is until that evening.[9]

Though Doni does not specify that he heard madrigals, it is hard to imagine
that the music that so moved him could have been anything else.

The Lighter Forms

Unlike the French chanson, which could move unself-consciously between
brows both high and low, the madrigal viewed "genre" in more box-like terms:
it voted yes to Petrarch and poetry like his, no to tales about country folk and
urban poor; it voted yes to the motet, no to the patter song. In effect, the
madrigal turned its back on lightweight entertainment and anything that
smacked of the popular. The void, however, was quickly filled by a variety of
types often referred to as the "lighter forms" (a term coined by Einstein), the
most widespread of which was the *canzone villanesca alla napolitana*, also known
as the *villanella*.

The villanella (the term was derived from the Italian *vile*, "vile" or "base")
had its roots in the pop culture of Naples, and its texts—often with local dia-
lect—dealt with stereotyped characters and situations of everyday life: whining
lovers, scolding lovers, derisive lovers (old hags were a favorite target), and
lovers with nothing but sex on their minds. The music was just as unpretentious, as witness Example 27-5, *Cingari simo venit'a giocare*, by one of the early
masters of the genre, Gian Domenico da Nola (c. 1510/20–1597):

EXAMPLE 27-5. Gian Domenico da Nola, *Cingari simo venit'a giocare*.

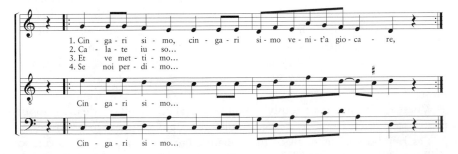

9. Quoted after Carter, *Music in Late Renaissance and Early Baroque Italy*, 39.

A translation of the poem in its entirety, which is nothing more than a strambotto with a refrain after each couplet, would read:

> We are gypsies come to play
> the game called Queen of hearts.
>
> This one's in—that one's out,
> it's more fun when round about.
>
> Come on down and have some fun
> as we gamble a little for your love.
>
> This one's in . . .
>
> To keep you happy, we'll make sure
> you have this club in your hands all the time.
>
> This one's in . . .
>
> If we lose, we'll pay a carlino,
> and if you lose, you'll buy the wine.
>
> This one's in . . . [10]

10. After Cardamone, *Adrian Willaert and His Circle*, xxxiv.

The poem, with which no self-respecting madrigal would be caught dead, is typical of the genre, especially with its crude *double entendre* about the "club": one of four suits in a deck of cards and, of course, the male sex organ. The music is also typical: three parts (tightly packed), homophonic and declamatory, strophic, and with its share of intentional parallel fifths strewn about in order to drive home the villanella's down-to-earth character.

Though the villanella was Neapolitan and popular in origin, it quickly became a favorite of refined audiences all over Italy. Nola, in fact, had two collections of villanelle published at Venice, and Willaert and his followers thought enough of them to arrange some for four voices and to write some of their own. Indeed, the villanella became so popular that it soon drew the wrath of moralists. One, Thomaso Garzoni da Bagnacavallo, complained specifically about hot-tempered, often drunk musicians who showed a "preference for singing lascivious madrigals and empty, ridiculous Neapolitan *villanelle*."[11]

As a whole, the second quarter of the sixteenth century was an exciting period for secular music in France and Italy. New genres sprang up, national styles emerged, courtly and popular elements mingled amicably in the Parisian chanson, as did Petrarch's poetry and the complicated polyphony of the motet in the madrigal. And with the coming of age of music printing (see Chapter 29), the chansons and madrigals of Claudin, Janequin, Arcadelt, and Willaert reached a wider audience, and more quickly, than ever before.

THE LIED

German secular song was more conservative. For the most part, it was content to continue the tradition of the Tenorlied as it had developed at the hands of Isaac and Heinrich Finck. By far its greatest exponent, in terms of both quantity (more than 250 songs) and quality, was the Swiss-born Ludwig Senfl.

Ludwig Senfl

Born in or near Basel around 1486, Senfl spent most of his career in the service of two great courts. He entered the service of Maximilian I as a choirboy in 1496 and remained there until the emperor died in 1519. For a while, he was both a pupil and chapelmate of Isaac, whose *Choralis Constantinus* he eventually completed and saw through the press. In 1523, Senfl joined the Munich court of Duke Wilhelm IV of Bavaria, where, with the title *Komponist*, he reorganized the chapel along imperial lines. Senfl remained at Munich for the remainder of his life, and died there in 1542 or 1543.

With Senfl, we have our first composer who might have felt squeezed by the religious tensions that were beginning to wrack sixteenth-century Europe. Though Senfl remained loyal to the Catholic Church throughout his life, he enjoyed a long and warm relationship with the Lutheran Duke Albrecht of Prussia and eventually came to have contacts with Martin Luther himself. There can be little doubt, then, that Senfl sympathized with the Reformation, enough

---

11. Cardamone, *Adrian Willaert and His Circle*, xi.

so that in 1529 he renounced his clerical position and married. But while the Catholic court at Munich caused Senfl little grief in connection with his religious outlook, it was less kind to one of his successors, the Protestant Ludwig Daser (c. 1525–1587), who was dragged before the Inquisition and eventually relieved of his post. As we will see in ensuing chapters, other composers would also be "inconvenienced" by the religious tensions of the period.

The Tenorlied

The Tenorlied of 1520–50 continued its adherence to cantus-firmus style. The texts, however, covered a wide range of subject matter. Two of Senfl's songs illustrate the point.

Example 27-6 shows the opening measures of *Ich stuend an einem Morgen*, a sentimental—and often-set—song about lovers on the verge of separation:

EXAMPLE 27-6. Senfl, *Ich stuend an einem Morgen*, mm. 1–11.

Against the ornamental backdrop of superius, altus, and bassus, the tenor sings the popular tune in cantus-firmus fashion. From a stylistic point of view, the piece, which was published in 1534, could just as well have been written by Isaac or Finck twenty years earlier.

In *Gottes Gewalt, Kraft und auch Macht*, on the other hand, Senfl set a religious text—probably for the Protestant court of Duke Albrecht—expanded the number of voices to five, and disposed the main tune in canon at the unison in the first and second tenors (Ex. 27-7):

EXAMPLE 27-7. Senfl, *Gottes Gewalt, Kraft und auch Macht*, mm. 1–14.

With the surrounding voices anticipating the tune in a full-blown point of imitation, the setting shows that the German Lied continued to be receptive to the Netherlandish motet style.

Eventually, the cantus-firmus-style Tenorlied paid a price for its conservatism: it died shortly after 1550. Already subject to steady infiltration by the Netherlandish motet and the French chanson throughout the second quarter of the century, the Tenorlied could not withstand a third, even more powerful outside influence: the madrigal, which invaded Germany around mid-century.

In fact, what may well be Senfl's best-known song, *Das G'läut zu Speyer* (*Anthology* 68), published (together with *Ich stuend* and *Gottes Gewalt*) in Johannes Ott's *Hundert und ainundzweintzig newe Lieder . . . lustig zu singen* of 1534, already points in new directions. *Das G'läut* is, as the title of Ott's collection boasts, "lustig zu singen" (fun to sing). With its constant "ding dong"s (the Germans said "gling glang"), which represent the pealing bells of the Cathedral of Speyer, and its incessant repetition of three chords—C major, F major, and A minor—it is German beer hall music *par excellence*.

The Meistergesang

If sixteenth-century German music has a sentimental hero, it must be Hans Sachs (1494–1576; Fig. 27-2), who still comes to life today in performances of Wagner's *Die Meistersinger von Nürnberg*.

Figure 27-2. Jost Amman, engraving of Hans Sachs, 1576.

A shoemaker by profession, Sachs was the leading figure among the *Meistersinger* (master singers) of Nuremberg. A cross between a musical society and an artisans' guild, the Meistersinger, who stood at the end of a centuries-long tradition of German monophonic song, held monthly competitions at which the contestants had to sing a previously assigned song. Both song (including its poem) and performance were subject to rules, and each singer was meticulously graded by a panel of judges who sat hidden behind drapes (recall Beckmesser in Wagner's opera). The winner received a chain of medallions called the David (patron of the Meistersinger), which he kept until the next competition.

Sachs wrote about 4,300 poems and thirteen melodies; his *Klingende Ton* illustrates the Meistersinger's art (Ex. 27-8):

EXAMPLE 27-8. Sachs, *Klingende Ton.*

What strikes us immediately is the lack of precise rhythm, as befits a genre that belonged to a long tradition of secular monophony—Provençal troubadors, French trouvères, and German Minnesinger—that was customarily notated without precise note values. The songs were probably sung in a kind of free-flowing, rhapsodic declamation.

Sachs's song is cast in the Meistersinger's customary *Barform*: **a a b (a)**, in which the **a** sections were called *Stollen* (the two *Stollen* together formed the *Aufgesang*), and the **b** section was the *Abgesang*; the final **a** section (part of the *Abgesang*) was optional, and could recall the opening section either in whole or in part. (For other examples of *Barform*, see *Anthology* 31 and 57.) Equally typical is the opening flourish, called a *Blume* (flower). As for the text, Sachs's song paraphrases the biblical story of the conflict between Saul and David. It is thus part of the trend that placed the art of the Meistersinger at the service of the Reformation.

Although the Meistersinger tradition spread beyond Nuremberg to other German centers and continued into the seventeenth century, it reached its high point with Hans Sachs and his contemporaries. With their passing, its creative energy waned.

BIBLIOGRAPHICAL NOTE

Editions of the Music

Chanson. **Claudin de Sermisy**: *Opera omnia*, CMM 52, ed. Gaston Allaire and Isabelle Caseaux (American Institute of Musicology, 1970–86). **Janequin**: *C. Janequin (c. 1485–1558): Chansons polyphoniques*, ed. A. Tilman Merritt and François Lesure (Monaco: L'Oiseaux-lyre, 1965–71). **Passereau**: *Opera omnia*, CMM 45, ed. Georges Dottin (American Institute of Musicology, 1967). Four valuable editions that cut across composers are Lawrence F. Bernstein's *La Couronne et fleur des chansons a troys*, 2 vols., MMR 3 (New York: The Broude Trust, 1984), which presents in its entirety a publication of 1536 that is rich in the music of the young Willaert; Leta E. Miller, *Thirty-Six Chansons by French Provincial Composers (1529–1550)*, RRMR 38 (Madison: A-R Editions, 1981); Frank Dobbins, *The Oxford Book of French Chansons* (Oxford: Oxford University Press, 1988); and the 30-volume collection edited by Jane A. Bernstein, *The Sixteenth-Century Chanson* (New York: Garland, 1987–), which takes the genre through the 1570s.

Madrigal. **Arcadelt**: *Opera omnia*, CMM 31, ed. Albert Seay (American Institute of Musicology, 1965–70). **Willaert**: see the *Opera omnia* cited in the Bibliographical Note in Chapter 26. **Verdelot**: though the *Opera omnia* does not yet include the madrigals, a number of them are edited in H. Colin Slim, *A Gift of Madrigals and Motets*, 2 vols. (Chicago: Chicago University Press, 1972); still more of his madrigals will appear in volumes 29–30 of *The Italian Madrigal in the Sixteenth Century* (see below). For the villanella, see Donna G. Cardamone's *Adrian Willaert and His Circle: Canzone villanesche alla napolitana and villotte*, RRMR 30 (Madison: A-R Editions, 1978), which contains a number of villanelle by Nola, together with Willaert's arrangements of them. Parallel with the Garland 30-volume chanson series is Jessie Ann Owens's *Italian Madrigal in the Sixteenth Century* (New York: Garland, 1987–), which in addition to the selection of Verdelot madrigals contains three volumes devoted to madrigalists of Willaert's circle: Giachet de Berchem (vol. 1), Perissone Cambio (vols. 2–3), and Baldassare Donato (vol. 10).

Tenorlied and Meistergesang. **Senfl**: *Sämtliche Werke*, ed. Walter Gerstenberg et al. (Wolfenbüttel: Möseler, 1937–74); there is a nice selection of German polyphonic Lieder in Helmuth Osthoff, *German Part Song from the 16th Century to the Present Day*, Anthology of Music (Cologne: Arno Volk, 1955); **Hans Sachs's** thirteen melodies appear in G. Münzer, *Das Singebuch des Adam Puschman* (Leipzig: Breitkopf & Härtel, 1906).

The Chanson

Three works should be considered required reading: Howard Mayer Brown, "The Genesis of a Style: The Parisian Chanson, 1500–1530," in *Chanson and Madrigal, 1480–1530*, Isham Library Papers 2, ed. James Haar (Cambridge: Harvard University Press, 1964), 1–50; and important articles by Lawrence F. Bernstein, "The 'Parisian Chanson': Problems of Style and Terminology," *JAMS* 31 (1978): 193–240, and "Notes on the Origin of the Parisian Chanson," *JM* 1 (1982): 275–326. See also Daniel Heartz, "The Chanson in the Humanist Era," in *Current Thought in Musicology*, ed. J. W. Grubb (Austin: University of Texas Press, 1976), 193–230. Musical life at the court of Francis I and the city of Lyons is discussed in John T. Brobeck, "Musical Patronage in the Royal Chapel of France under Francis I (r. 1515–1547)," *JAMS* 48 (1995): 187–239; Richard Freedman, "Paris and French Court under François I," in *The Renaissance*, ed. Iain Fenlon (London: Macmillan, 1989), 174–96 and 197–215; Frank Dobbins, *Music in Renaissance Lyons* (Oxford: Oxford University Press, 1992); Isabelle Cazeaux, *French Music in the Fifteenth and Sixteenth Centuries* (Oxford: Blackwell, 1975).

The Madrigal

The literature on the madrigal is enormous; two good points of entry to the early madrigal are James Haar, *Essays on Italian Poetry and Music in the Renaissance, 1350–1600* (Berkeley and Los Angeles: University of California Press, 1986), chapter 3, and Tim Carter, *Music in Late Renaissance and Early Baroque Italy* (Portland: Amadeus Press, 1992), chapter 6. The classic study of the madrigal is Alfred Einstein, *The Italian Madrigal*, 3 vols., trans. Alexander H. Krappe, Roger H. Sessions, and Oliver Strunk (Princeton: Princeton University Press, 1949); for a more modest introduction to the subject, see Jerome Roche, *The Madrigal*, 2nd ed. (New York: Scribner, 1990). On the early sources and dissemination, see Iain Fenlon and James Haar, *The Italian Madrigal in the Early Sixteenth Century: Sources and Interpretation* (Cambridge: Cambridge University Press, 1988). On the literary background, Dean T. Mace, "Pietro Bembo and the Literary Origins of the Italian Madrigal," *MQ* 55 (1969): 65–86; Don Harrán, "Verse Types in the Early Madrigal," *JAMS* 22 (1969): 27–53. On Florentine patronage, Richard J. Agee, "Ruberto Strozzi and the Early Madrigal," *JAMS* 36 (1983): 1–17, and "Filippo Strozzi and the Early Madrigal," *JAMS* 38 (1985): 227–37. On the musical interpretation of Petrarch, Martha Feldman, "The Composer as Exegete: Interpretations of Petrarchan Syntax in the Venetian Madrigal," *StudM* 18 (1989): 203–38. On the madrigal and rhetoric, Feldman, *City Culture and the Madrigal at Venice* (Berkeley and Los Angeles: University of California Press, 1995). The lighter forms, especially the villanella, are discussed in Donna G. Cardamone, *The Canzone villanesca alla napolitana and Related Forms, 1537–1570*, 2 vols. (Ann Arbor: UMI Research Press, 1981); Margaret Mabbett, "Some Thoughts on Italian Secular Vocal Music of the Sixteenth Century," in *Companion to Medieval and Renaissance Music*, ed. Tess Knighton and David Fallows (New York: Schirmer, 1992), 127–30.

The Lied and the Meistersinger

There is a comprehensive catalogue of the entire Tenorlied repertory in Norbert Böker-Heil, Harald Heckman, and Ilse Kindermann, *Das Tenorlied: Mehrstimmige Lieder in deutschen Quellen, 1450–1580*, 3 vols. (Kassel: Bärenreiter, 1979–86); on the demise of the Tenorlied, see Ludwig Finscher, "Lied and Madrigal, 1580–1600," in *Music in the German*

Renaissance: Sources, Styles, and Contexts, ed. John Kmetz (Cambridge: Cambridge University Press, 1994), 182–92. The literature on the Meistersinger is virtually all in German; Bert Nagel, *Meistergesang*, 2nd ed. (Stuttgart: Metzler, 1971), stands as a general introduction; on the poetry, see Archer Taylor, *The Literary History of Meistergesang* (New York: Modern Language Association of America, 1937); there is a fine essay on musical life in Nuremberg, including the Meistersinger, in Susan Gattuso, "16-Century Nuremberg," in *The Renaissance*, ed. Iain Fenlon (London: Macmillan, 1989), 286–303.

Petrarch and Marot

A classic study of Petrarch is Ernest Hatch Wilkins, *Life of Petrarch* (Chicago: Chicago University Press, 1961); the *Canzoniere* is translated in R. M. Durling, *Petrarch's Lyric Poems: The "Rime sparse" and Other Lyrics* (Cambridge: Harvard University Press, 1971); for the poetry of Marot, see C. A. Mayer, *Clément Marot: Oeuvres lyriques* (London: Athlone Press, 1964).

Also Cited:

Desmond Seward, *Prince of the Renaissance: The Golden Life of François I* (London: Constable, 1973); Sarah Fuller, *The European Musical Heritage: 800–1750* (New York: Knopf, 1987).

CHAPTER 28

Intermedio: 1533–1536

HENRY VIII AND ANNE BOLEYN

For Englishmen and -women who kept tabs on religion and politics during the 1520s and 1530s, the year 1533 began with an act of either brave defiance or blasphemy. Which way one leaned depended on one's stance on such issues as papal authority, church-state relationships, and the divine supremacy of kings. As we saw in Chapter 23, Europe was split over all three issues.

The act of defiance/blasphemy occurred on January 25: in a secret, predawn ceremony, Henry VIII married the already pregnant Anne Boleyn (Thomas Cranmer, recently nominated by Henry to be Archbishop of Canterbury, officiated). It was not Anne's being with child that caused the stir. Rather, in the eyes of the Roman church, Henry was still married to his first wife, Catherine of Aragon. The consequences of this marriage were as shattering for the political-religious map of Europe as were the actions of Martin Luther.

The story begins in 1509, when Henry married Catherine, daughter of Ferdinand and Isabella of Spain, after a betrothal of eight years. The marriage was problematic from the outset, as Catherine had previously been married to Henry's older brother Arthur (Prince of Wales), who left her a widow when he died in 1501, just five months after their marriage. In order for Henry to marry his brother's widow, his father, Henry VII (who arranged both matches), requested and received a special dispensation from Pope Julius II.

Henry hoped for a male heir. But the only one of his and Catherine's five offspring to survive infancy was a daughter, the future Queen Mary I (1553–58). To make matters worse, Henry fell in love with one of Catherine's young ladies-in-waiting, Anne Boleyn (1507–1536). And in the summer of 1527, having decided to marry Anne, he began his campaign to divorce Catherine.

Henry first appealed to Pope Clement VII for an annulment. Though annulments were not unheard of, Clement refused to issue one. He did not wish to anger Charles V (Catherine's nephew), and further, Henry's appeal had been couched in language that clearly challenged papal authority—the king argued that Julius II had himself violated both divine and natural law by permitting him to marry his brother's widow in the first place, and that Julius had therefore overstepped his authority.

With support from the growing anti-Rome, reform-minded circles that were taking shape in England at the time, Henry ordered Archbishop Cranmer to proclaim his marriage to Catherine null and void. Clement responded by excommunicating Henry. Thus in 1534, Henry had Parliament declare the Act of Supremacy, which affirmed that the pope had no authority in England and established the Church of England as an independent institution with the king at its head. There were now two Reformations: Luther's on the Continent, which was based on differences in religious doctrine (and to which Henry, by the way, was adamantly opposed), and Henry's in England, which, at least initially, was grounded in personal and political affairs.

Anne Boleyn's own tenure as queen was short-lived. After she and Henry had another daughter, the future Elizabeth I (the Protestant half-sister of the Catholic Mary), she was charged with infidelity and beheaded in 1536.

MICHELANGELO'S *LAST JUDGMENT*

Terribilità (terribleness, in the sense of terrifying) is one word Giorgio Vasari used to describe Michelangelo's *Last Judgment* in his *Lives of the Artists* (1561), along with "awesome," "grandeur," "amazing," and "sublime."[1] As any tourist who has ever visited the Sistine Chapel will attest, Vasari's descriptions are on the mark.

Sculptor, architect, painter, and poet, Michelangelo Buonarotti (1475–1564) first began to work in the Sistine Chapel in 1508, when Pope Julius II commissioned him to paint the ceiling (it was finished in 1512). There, 80 feet above the polychrome pavement (the ceiling itself measures 133 by 43 feet) and high above the frescoes that had already been painted along the walls, Michelangelo executed nine rectangular panels that depict the history of the world, from God separating the light from the dark through Adam and Eve to the Flood (Fig. 28-1) and the Drunkenness of Noah. And to express a view of humankind that embodied both Christian and classical worlds, he surrounded

Figure 28-1. Michelangelo, *Flood*, Sistine Chapel ceiling, 1508–12.

1. Penguin edition, 380–83.

the panels with prophets, biblical heroes, ancestors of Christ, sibyls (mythological prophetesses), and the great, almost sculptured *ignudi* (nudes).

Michelangelo's work in the Sistine Chapel did not end with the ceiling. More than two decades later, in April 1535, now at the insistence of Pope Paul III, he undertook the fresco on the wall behind the altar. And with that work— the *Last Judgment* (Fig. 28-2)—Michelangelo contributed profoundly to a change in style that left its mark on the remainder of the century. The grace, poise, and equilibrium of Raphael's classicism (Fig. 28-3), for many the very essence of the High Renaissance, were left behind and forgotten. Here all is motion, contortion, turmoil, and even violence, conceived with a virtuosity

Figure 28-2. Michelangelo, *The Last Judgment*, Sistine Chapel, 1535–41.

Figure 28-3. Raphael, *School of Athens*, fresco, 1510 (Stanza della Segnatura, Vatican).

that sometimes appears to be there simply for its own sake. For some, then, the *Last Judgment* stands among the works that ushered in the movement known as Mannerism.

Among the cast of about four hundred figures in the *Last Judgment*, Christ and the Virgin are clearly central. But perhaps the most eye-catching figure is the menacing-looking St. Bartholomew (just below and to the right of Christ), shown with his traditional attributes: an oddly-shaped knife and a loose, sack-like human skin, echoes of the legend about the saint having been skinned alive before he was crucified. But as with so much of the fresco, both saint and attributes are personalized. The face on the skin is almost certainly a self-portrait of Michelangelo, while the reassembly of the saint's hide might point toward the possibility of salvation. It is a theme that Michelangelo had expressed in his *Rime*: "Passing like an old serpent through a narrow place, leaving my old armour, I may be renewed, taken up into life, abandoning my old ways and every human thing; covered by a surer shield, I know that, faced with death, the world is less than nothing."[2]

Reactions to the *Last Judgment* were mixed, and the fresco was greeted with anything but the "stunned silence" that had welcomed the ceiling. Vasari tells us that the papal master of ceremonies, Biagio da Cesena, a very "high-minded"

2. Quoted after Giacometti, *The Sistine Chapel*, 206.

person, found the fresco obscene: "It was most disgraceful that in so sacred a place there should have been depicted all those nude figures, exposing themselves so shamefully, and that it was no work for a papal chapel but rather for the public baths and taverns."[3] In fact, some years later, the painter Daniele da Volterra clothed some of the figures in drapery. The criticism went beyond charges of obscenity, however. There were those who saw the *Last Judgment* as heretical, not only in terms of doctrine, but aesthetically as well. Thus a mid-century Venetian critic complained that there was a "lack of a certain measured proportion and a certain well-considered decorum, without which nothing can be graceful or look well."[4]

Fortunately, late-sixteenth-century ideas about destroying the *Last Judgment* were never carried out. And recently, both this work and the ceiling have been painstakingly cleaned and restored. We can now see one of the most monumental works of art ever conceived and executed by a single artist almost as the artist himself saw it on the day the paint dried.

CARTIER EXPLORERS NORTH AMERICA

During the 1530s, the French navigator Jacques Cartier (1491?–1557) made two trips to Canada: one in 1534, another in 1535–36. (He returned a third time in 1541.) The aim of the first voyage was to find both a northern passage to the Orient and precious metals. Cartier found neither, but he did explore the Gulf of St. Lawrence, claiming Terre-Neuve (Newfoundland) and the Gaspé Peninsula for France. And when he returned to France in the fall of 1534, he carried with him what were probably the first bushels of corn ever seen in northern Europe.

Thanks to Cartier's own *Brief recit*, printed at Paris in 1545, we are better informed about his second voyage, on which he set out on Whitsunday, May 16, 1535. His commission, dated October 1534, read in part: "by royal command, to conduct, lead and employ three ships equipped and victualed for fifteen months, for the perfection of the navigation of lands by you already begun, to discover beyond *les Terres Neufves*."[5] Cartier's crew numbered 112, of whom a dozen were his own relatives. And in addition to seven carpenters, a barber-surgeon, and an apothecary, there was the ubiquitous trumpeter, a mainstay on oceangoing ships for two centuries: his signals hailed passing ships, recalled lifeboats, told the crew to assemble, and marked the changing of the watch.

Charged with exploring lands beyond those that he had discovered on the first voyage, Cartier sailed up the "chemyn de Canada," the St. Lawrence River. On September 10, he reached the Indian village called Stadaconé, where in 1608 Samuel de Champlain would establish the city of Quebec, the first per-

3. *Lives of the Artists*, 379.

4. Ludovico Dolce, *Dialogo della pittura* (1557); quoted after Giacometti, *The Sistine Chapel*, 195.

5. Quoted after Morison, *The European Discovery of America*, 388–89.

manent French settlement in the New World. Pushing farther up the river, Cartier three weeks later reached the Iroquois settlement called Hochelaga, the site of modern Montreal. And though the Indians told him of precious metals and pointed him in the direction of Ottawa and Lake Superior, he did not continue. After spending the winter of 1535–36 at Quebec, he returned to France in July.

Cartier's second voyage eventually resulted in a notable medical advance. With most of his crew suffering from scurvy—rotting gums, swollen joints— Cartier adopted the Indians' remedy: a potion derived from the needles and bark of a local evergreen tree. The cure worked; but though Cartier transplanted some of the trees to France and described their magical effect, it was only two centuries later that a Scottish surgeon, James Lind, discovered the benefits of the juice of citrus fruits and the scourge of seafarers was eradicated.

CALVIN'S *CHRISTIANAE RELIGIONIS INSTITUTO*

In 1536, Jean Calvin (1509–1564), one of the great theologians of the Reformation, published his *Institutes of the Christian Religion*. Revised and expanded a number of times, and issued in a French edition in 1545, the *Institutes* lays out Calvin's ideas about religion, society, and humanity in general, and became one of the bedrocks of Reformation literature.

Three passages from the *Institutes* will give us a glimpse into Calvin's thinking. First, he was not quite the ascetic that popular imagination sometimes holds him to be. The world should be enjoyed:

> Has the Lord clothed the flowers with the great beauty that greets our eyes and the sweetness of smell that is wafted upon our nostrils, and yet it is not permissible for our eyes to be pleased by that beauty, or our sense of smell by the sweetness of that odor? Did the Lord not distinguish colors, making some more lovely than others? Did he not endow gold and silver, ivory and marble, with a loveliness that renders them more precious than other metals or stones? Did he not, in short, render many things attractive to us, apart from their utility?

On the need for perseverance:

> Let each of us proceed according to the measure of his puny capacity and set out upon the journey. No one shall start so inauspiciously as not daily to make some headway, though it be but slight. Therefore let us not cease so to act that we may make unceasing progress in the way of the Lord. And let us not despair at the slightness of our success; for even though attainment may not correspond to desire, when today outstrips yesterday, the effort is not lost. Only let us look toward our mark with sincere simplicity and aspire to our goal, not fondly flattering ourselves nor excusing our own evil deeds, but with continuous effort striving toward this end: that we may surpass ourselves in goodness until we attain to goodness itself.

Though he appreciated differences, Calvin recognized that the church required a sense of discipline and organization:

> Some form of organization is necessary in all human society to foster the common peace and maintain concord . . . [it] ought especially to be observed in churches, which are best sustained when all things are under a well-ordered constitution and which, without concord, become no churches at all.[6]

We will return to Calvin's views on the place of music in the church in Chapter 33.

BIBLIOGRAPHICAL NOTE

Henry and Anne

Henry's divorce is treated at length in chapter 7–8 of J. J. Scarisbrick, *Henry VIII* (Berkeley and Los Angeles: University of California Press, 1968); see also Jasper Ridley, *Henry VIII: The Politics of Tyranny* (New York: Viking, 1985); and John Guy, *Tudor England* (Oxford: Oxford University Press, 1988).

Michelangelo

Two good general studies are by Frederick Hartt, *Michelangelo* (New York: Abrams, 1964), and Howard Hibbard, *Michelangelo* (New York: Harper & Row, 1974); the standard life and works is Charles de Tolnay, *Michelangelo*, 5 vols. (Princeton: Princeton University Press, 1943–60); for an interesting psychoanalytic biography, see Robert S. Liebert, *Michelangelo: A Psychoanalytic Study of His Life and Images* (New Haven: Yale University Press, 1983); on the Sistine Chapel, see the comprehensive collection of essays edited by Massimo Giacometti, *The Sistine Chapel: The Art, the History, and the Restoration* (New York: Harmony, 1986), which contains a rich supply of photographic reproductions.

Cartier

Cartier's Canadian voyages can be followed in Samuel Eliot Morison, *The European Discovery of America: The Northern Voyages, A.D. 500–1600* (New York: Oxford University Press, 1971); and in less detail in Francis Jennings, *The Founders of America* (New York: Norton, 1993).

Calvin

The obvious place to start is with William Bouwsma, *John Calvin: A Sixteenth-Century Portrait* (Oxford: Oxford University Press, 1988); the *Institutes* has been translated more than once, most recently by Ford Lewis Battles in the Library of Christian Classics (London, 1961).

Also Cited

Giorgio Vasari, *Lives of the Artists*, rev. ed., trans. George Bull (Harmondsworth: Penguin, 1976).

6. Quoted after Bouwsma, *John Calvin*, 135, 186, 217.

CHAPTER 29

The Growth of Music Printing

The chansons of Claudin and Janequin, the madrigals of Verdelot and Arcadelt, the motets of Gombert, Clemens, and Willaert, and perhaps even the Masses of Morales (with their prescribed function as part of the liturgy) all reached an audience that, in terms of size, geographic spread, and socioeconomic diversity, lay beyond anything that Du Fay, Busnoys, and Ockeghem could have imagined or that Josquin and Isaac could have dimly begun to perceive. The reason is clear enough: during the second quarter of the sixteenth century, music printing truly came of age. And as it did, it created—and reacted to—new markets, played a role in dictating musical tastes, changed the economic basis of music, began to alter the composer-patron relationship, and took the first steps in establishing a "canon." Simply put, music printing changed both the artistic and social nature of musical life.

PRINTERS

What started as a trickle with Ottaviano Petrucci and his *Harmonice musices odhecaton A* in 1501 turned into a torrent during the second quarter of the century. For example, whereas the first quarter saw the publication of sixty-five multicomposer anthologies of polyphonic music, the second quarter produced upward of five hundred. But there is more to the story than just the numbers of publications produced. Until the late 1520s, the printing and publishing of polyphony was largely an Italian affair, with a smattering of contributions from Germany. As improvements in technology and marketing made printing and publishing music ever more practical, new entrepreneurs took to the presses, new firms came into existence, and the business of printing music spread out geographically.

The picture began to change in 1528. On April 4, the Parisian printer, publisher, and bookseller Pierre Attaingnant, using a new technology, issued his *Chansons nouvelles en musique*, and with it launched an almost quarter-century-long career that made him one of the most influential music publishers of his time. Within four years, he had a rival at Lyons in the person of Jacques Moderne. And for two decades, Attaingnant and Moderne dominated French music publishing, turning out hundreds of publications, from Masses to lute tablatures to dance music, and putting the Parisian chanson in particular at the top of the charts. Their domination ended only in 1551, when the lutenist Adrian Le Roy and his cousin Robert Ballard succeeded Attaingnant as "music printers to the king." This new and powerful publishing dynasty, which was carried on by Ballard's heirs, would last for more than two centuries.

In 1543, music printing moved to the Low Countries, as Tylman Susato—composer, civic trumpeter, instrument dealer, and calligrapher—obtained a privilege to print polyphonic music at Antwerp. Within a decade, he was joined by the firms of Pierre Phalèse (earlier at Louvain) and Christopher Plantin, who, with his business acumen and ties to King Philip II of Spain (who ruled the Low Countries), soon became the largest and most prolific printer in the region. As we might expect, all three publishers featured music of Netherlandish composers.

As music printing spread through France and the Low Countries, Italy kept pace, thanks in part to the great demand for madrigals. The center of the Italian industry was Venice, where by the late 1530s the two firms of Girolamo Scotto and the French émigré Antoine Gardane (he changed the spelling to "Antonio Gardano" in 1555) were in full gear. Gardano devoted more than half of his almost 450 publications to the madrigal and came to be the primary Italian publisher for Arcadelt, Cipriano de Rore, and eventually Orlande de Lassus. As for Scotto, who was highly regarded for publishing translations of and commentaries on Aristotle, his notable publications include two books of four-voice madrigals (1568–70) by Maddalena Casulana, the earliest extant publications devoted to a woman composer. Scotto capped his career in 1571, when he was elected the first prior of the Venetian Guild of Printers and Booksellers. Together, Scotto and Gardano, both of whom also dabbled at composition, dominated the Italian music-printing scene for about thirty years.

In Germany, music printing flourished particularly at Nuremberg. There Heironymous Formschneider (who issued Luther's German translation of the psalms and executed woodcuts for Dürer), Johann Petreius, and the partners Johann Berg and Ulrich Neuber published numerous volumes of music by German composers.

By the mid-sixteenth century, then, printing was an essential part of the musical landscape. Indeed, in 1549 alone, ten publishers in seven cities—Attaingnant and Nicolas du Chemin at Paris, Moderne at Lyons, Susato at Antwerp, Phalèse (still at Louvain), Scotto and Gardano at Venice, Berg and Neuber and Johann Fabritius at Nuremberg, and Philipp Ulhart at Augsburg—turned out forty-three multicomposer volumes with about 1,500 pieces by almost 200 composers, who now seemed to spring up from everywhere. If the average press run was about 500–1,000 copies per anthology, the publishing industry would have dumped tens of thousands of sets of partbooks (even more for single-composer collections) on the market, or about one set of partbooks for every five or six persons in Venice, which by 1540 had a population of about 170,000. And when we consider that much of the European population was illiterate and that probably only a small portion of those who could read could also read music, the productivity of the music publishers at mid-century is mind-boggling.

Pierre Attaingnant

If there is a single sixteenth-century music printer after Petrucci who deserves our attention, it is Pierre Attaingnant, who was born in northern France, probably in the mid-1490s. In January 1514, he is recorded as a bookseller in Paris; he had been apprenticed there to the printer-engraver Philippe Pigouchet, whose daughter he married and to whose business he thus became heir. Attaingnant's first extant publication is a breviary dating from 1525 for the diocese of Noyon. But his career really took off in 1528 with the *Chansons nouvelles en musique*, in which he introduced both the Claudin-style Parisian chanson and a new technique of printing (to which we will turn presently). By October 1529, Attaingnant had obtained the first of the royal privileges that ostensibly prevented others from copying the contents and technology of his publications (it was renewed in 1531 and then at six-year intervals thereafter), and in 1537 he could style himself "imprimeur & libraire du Roy en musique." He had, in effect, "made it," and his career continued to flourish until he died in 1551 or 1552.

THE ROYAL PRIVILEGE OF 1531   Though the privilege of 1531 (Attaingnant printed it in the *Primus liber viginti missarum* of 1532) is a long document, it is worth reproducing, not only for the insights it provides into Attaingnant's concerns as a businessman, but for what it tells us about the attempts to regulate the new industry:

> Having received the humble supplication of our well-loved Pierre Attaingnant, printer-bookseller . . . stating that heretofore no person in this our realm had undertaken to cut, found, and fashion notes and characters for the printing of figural music . . . or tablatures for the playing of lutes, flutes, and organs, because of the intricate conception, long consumption of time, and very great expenses and labors necessary to that purpose, the said suppliant by protracted excogitation and mental effort and with very great expense, labor, and genius, has invented and brought to light the method and industry of cutting, founding, and printing the said notes and characters both of the said music . . . as of the said tablatures . . . of which he has printed, has had printed, and hopes in the future to print, many books and quires of Massess, motets, hymns, chansons, as well as for the said playing of lutes, flutes, and organs, in large volumes and small, in order to serve the churches, their ministers, and generally all people, and for the very great good, utility, and recreation of the general public. Nevertheless, he fears that after having brought to light his said invention and opened to other printers and booksellers the method and industry of printing the said notes and tablatures, these printers and booksellers will similarly wish to attempt printing the said music. . . . And by this means the said suppliant would totally lose the merit of his labors and the recovery of expenses and investments which he has made and contracted for the invention and composition of the above said characters, unless he is patented and succored by us, having humbly sought our grace. Thus we, having con-

sidered these things, do not wish that the said suppliant's labors, applications, expenses, and investments in the said affair go unrewarded. May he succeed in it and experience the benefit. For such causes and others stirring us to this we have willed and ordained: we will and ordain that for the time and term of six years to follow, starting with the date of this present day, other than the said suppliant or those having charge from him, may not print nor put up for sale the said books and quires of music . . . declared above. We charge and command therefore by these present orders that every person look to the said suppliant's enjoying and fully tranquilly exercising the ordinance entreated from our grace. Making strictures and prohibitions to all booksellers and other persons generally, whatever they may be, to print or put up for sale the said books and quires of music and tablature for the said time of six years without the express power and consent of the said suppliant. And this on great penalty to be levied by us and loss and confiscation of the said books and quires.[1]

King or no king, the privilege had no teeth. In 1532, after Attaingnant had printed the privilege as a warning for all to see, Jacques Moderne issued the first of his *Motetti del fiore* volumes; Attaingnant's "method and industry of cutting, founding, and printing" had become common property.

SINGLE-IMPRESSION PRINTING   When Ottaviano Petrucci and his contemporaries printed music from movable type, they did so in distinct stages: with one impression they printed the blank staves, and with another they impressed upon those staves the notes and other musical symbols. But though the results could be both accurate and beautiful in the masterful hands of a Petrucci or Peter Schöffer, the technology had two major drawbacks. First, there was the problem of achieving the proper registration of the notes on the staves (printers constantly ran the risk of printing an entire line of music a bit too high or too low); and second, the method was slow and costly, as each page of music had to go through the press more than once.

Attaingnant overcame these problems in the *Chansons nouvelles*: he combined each note or symbol with its own short segment of staff on a single piece of type.[2] From the business end of things, it was a brilliant solution. Both the time and the cost of printing were substantially reduced. From the aesthetic viewpoint, however, Attaingnant paid a price. As we can see in Figure 29-1, which reproduces a page from Book III of his *Viginti missarum* of 1532, the staves are rather bumpy, and the blank spaces left between the segments of type are clearly visible. But since music printing was a business, printers decided that they could live with the bumps and spaces. Attaingnant's technological innovation was universally adopted and remained the industry standard until Johann Gottlob Immanuel Breitkopf (of what eventually became the venerable firm of Breitkopf and Härtel) introduced innovations of his own in the mid-eighteenth century.

1. The translation is from Heartz, "A New Attaingnant Book," 22–23; the original French appears in Heartz, *Pierre Attaingnant*, 174–75 (with a facsimile in plate X).

2. Though Attaingnant claimed to have developed the new technique, and though he was the first to use single-impression technology successfully on a large scale, the process was in fact anticipated a few years earlier by the English printer John Rastell, who seems to have limited his production to a few broadsides.

Figure 29-1. A page from Attaingnant, *Viginti missarum*, Book III, 1533, showing an excerpt from Mouton's *Missa d'allemaigne*.

The Business of Music Publishing

We now look briefly at five aspects of the music-printing-publishing trade: the organization of the shop, strategies of financing, the size of editions, marketing and distribution procedures, and ways in which printers cultivated and reacted to the public's tastes.

THE SHOP   Figure 29-2 shows us a French printing shop around 1530. At the center of the operation was the printing press itself, operated by the "puller," who worked in conjunction with an "inker" (he stands behind the puller in the illustration). At the middle right is the compositor, who arranged the type from which (after it was inked) the pages were printed. Since most printers probably did not have enough type to set a large volume in its entirety, the compositor was kept busy throughout the printing process, dismantling type from pages already printed and setting it up anew. The two other, elegantly dressed gentlemen to the right are reading proof. At the most prestigious presses—those run, for example, by master printer-scholars—this task often fell to the owner. At presses located near a university, students sometimes served as proofreaders in exchange for room and board. Thus in 1551, the composer Claude Goudimel, probably near the end of his student days at the University of Paris, served as a proofreader in the shop of Nicolas du Chemin, with whom he soon became a partner.

Figure 29-2. View of a printing shop (c. 1530) as depicted in a manuscript minature (Bibliothèque National, Paris).

One job in the printers' shop has gone unmentioned: the editor, the person who decided on repertory, selected and determined the order of pieces for a volume, and made sure that the music was correct before it went to press. Printers who were themselves musicians probably performed this task themselves. Otherwise, they brought in hired hands. Thus the "house music editor" at Jacques Moderne's shop during the 1530s was the well-known composer-organist Francesco de Layolle, while Nicolas du Chemin employed the composer Nicolas Regnes, from whom he took singing lessons. Attaingnant's publications are silent on the matter until 1550, when the title pages of three books tell us that they were prepared under the direction of the "scavant musicien" Claude Gervaise.

The shop in our figure probably had more presses than we see. The influential printer Robert Estienne (not of music) had three in 1531; Claude Chevallon, printer for the University of Paris, had six in 1538. And in 1565, the Plantin firm of Antwerp, by then the largest in northern Europe, employed twenty-one printers, eighteen compositors, three apprentices, two type-founders, a shopboy, and five proofreaders.

FINANCING   Finances were a never-ending problem for printers and publishers of music: paper, for example, was extraordinarily expensive. One strategy printers used to stay out of the red was to honor a person of means with a dedication. Thus Gardano dedicated two of his early volumes, including the best-selling first volume of Arcadelt's four-part madrigals (with *Il bianco e dolce cigno*), to Bishop Leone Orsini, from whose name Gardano derived his company logo of a lion (*leone*) and bear (*orso*) holding a rose (Fig. 29-3). The hope was that the dedicatee would subsidize the publication.

Sometimes composers secured a donor's subsidy. In 1599, for example, Ruggiero Giovanelli received 100 *scudi* from his patron, Cardinal Pietro Aldobrandini, for the express purpose of financing the publication of Giovanelli's third book of five-part madrigals. At other times, the composers themselves underwrote the cost of publication: in 1600, no less a figure than Tomás Luis de Victoria, the greatest Spanish composer of the century, paid for the printing of his *Missae, Magnificat, motecta, psalmi*. Still another strategy saw members of the trade band together in order to spread out the financial risk. For example, the colophon (a verbal statement at the end of a volume) in Verdelot's first book of madrigals (1533) describes the publication as a cooperative venture in which the Scotto firm published the collection, the Da Sabio brothers printed it, and Andrea Antico engraved the woodblocks.

One printer, Christopher Plantin, often forced composers whose music he published to purchase as many copies of their own works as he needed to reach the break-even point. Here is a contract to which the composer George de la Hèle (1547–1586) had to submit in 1578 in order to get Plantin to publish his *Octo missae* for five, six, and seven voices:

> I, the undersigned, recognize and confess having made an agreement with Christopher Plantin, printer to the King [Philip II of Spain] to wit: I promise that, once the work is printed, I will buy forty copies at the price charged

Figure 29-3. Antonio Gardano's logo.

booksellers, with whatever additional rebate Plantin may be gracious enough to give me. The copies will be delivered by the half-dozen and paid for immediately, before dispatch of the other obligatory copies, all copies to be received and paid for within the term of a year.[3]

SIZE OF PRESS RUNS   The customary press run for a music print was about 500–1,000 copies. To give three examples: in 1552, the lutenist Guillaume Morlaye contracted with the printer Michel Fezandat to issue the works of Morlaye's teacher, Albert de Rippe, in a run of 1,200 copies; in 1578, Hernando de Cabezón printed 1,200 copies of his father's (Antonio's) *Obras de música para tecla, harpa y vihuela*; and in 1600, John Dowland's *Second Book of Ayres* was printed in an edition of 1,023. To be sure, these publications consisted of single volumes and were no doubt issued in larger runs than most multi-partbook publications.

MARKETING AND DISTRIBUTION   With publishers turning out music books in numbers that surely exceeded what their own local market could possibly absorb, it was necessary for them to reach out to as wide an audience as possible. For this, they had a number of means at their disposal.

First, there were the great book fairs, particularly those held at Lyons and Frankfurt each fall and spring, drawing publishers and book dealers from all over Europe. Beyond the fairs, dealers could advertise their publications through catalogues. In 1564, the organizers of the Frankfurt fair issued a comprehensive catalogue of the books displayed by all participating dealers. Would-be music buyers with a scholarly bent could consult such bibliographies as Conrad Gesner's *Pandectae* of 1548 or Antonfrancesco Doni's *Libraria* of 1550. These contain extensive lists of music books in print, including some that no longer survive and for which Gesner and Doni therefore provide the sole testimony to their onetime existence. By century's end, the music publishers themselves were issuing catalogues of their own.

In such ways, sixteenth-century publishers, printers, and book dealers formed international networks of communication and commerce. And if these worked a bit slowly from our point of view, they nevertheless made the likes of Attaingnant's chanson series available in Italy, Gardano's collections of madrigals available in Germany, and Susato's books of dances available in France. Music circulated more quickly and freely than it ever had before.

CULTIVATING TASTES   As the best publishers have always done, sixteenth-century music publishers performed a balancing act between influencing public taste and catering to it. Clearly, what they chose to make available was what most music lovers were stuck with. Yet they could not afford to take many chances on music that would not sell. In general, new was safer than old. Thus Attaingnant published nothing of the Busnoys/Ockeghem generation, only about 75 pieces by 9 composers of Josquin's generation, but almost 3,500 works by over 160 composers of his own. Even Josquin was becoming a hard sell (except in Germany).

---

3. Quoted after Heartz, *Pierre Attaingnant*, 94.

Once the contents of a print cleared the generation gap, it did not become old overnight. As we have seen, some prints were reprinted time and again. An inventory drawn up in the late 1580s for the small Florentine bookshop of Piero di Giuliano Morosi shows that Morosi still had in stock at least one print from the 1530s (thus a half century old) and a larger number from the 1540s, while the bulk of his shelf space was occupied by publications from the 1550s–1570s. In fact, nothing in the store was less than a few years old.

On occasion, publishers would commission or even compose themselves simplified arrangements of well-known pieces for amateur music makers. Susato lays out the rationale in his *Premier livre des chansons a deux ou a troix parties* of 1544:

> In that nowadays an ever growing multitude of noble souls is induced and moved to learn and practice the notable science of music—singing and playing divers instruments—instead of other useless pastimes . . . I have set forth to compose these love songs, which may be sung in two ways . . . *à deux* and *à troix*—*à deux*, [by] omitting the bass, as the rubrics added above [the chansons] indicate. Another reason induced me to compose and print these [chansons] for the benefit of the amateurs of said science: namely, that a novice or pupil lacks the assurance to sing with a large ensemble. But by means of these chansons, he will limit himself to practicing with a small group until he becomes more skilled and more confident—for more difficult things.[4]

In fact, the combination of wanting to provide music for the amateur, teach the rudiments of composition, and sell music books gave rise to one of the most popular genres of the sixteenth century: the duo. One of the most popular collection of duos was Ihan Gero's *Il primo libro de' madrigali italiani et canzoni francese a due voce*, issued by Gardano in 1541 and subsequently reprinted at least twenty-four times down to 1687. Though the madrigals seem to be original two-part compositions, the chansons are two-part arrangements of preexisting songs. *Anthology* 69 presents Gero's arrangement (b) of Claudin's popular *Tant que vivray* (a), which is itself based on a preexistent tune. Here Gero paraphrases Claudin's superius and accompanies it with an imitative counterpoint that sometimes develops into straightforward canon.

What did the amateur learn from such pieces? Certainly, the duos provided a clear model of how to write a point of imitation, construct a canon, form a cadence, and paraphrase a preexistent melody, and they did so in a more immediately comprehensible way than could a piece for four or more voices. As another composer of duos, Agostino Licino, put it in his *Duo cromatici* of 1546: duos were not only better than card games, they served as a "musical alphabet."[5]

We must admire this second generation of music printer-publishers. They took a fledgling industry and set it firmly on its feet. By the middle of the sixteenth century, musicians—professionals and amateurs alike—must have wondered how their predecessors had ever done without it.

4. Quoted after Bernstein, "Claude Gervaise as Chanson Composer," 365.
5. Cited after Bernstein and Haar, *Ihan Gero: Il primo libro*, xviii.

COMPOSERS

Composers reacted to the growing music-publishing industry in a number of ways: some saw it as an opportunity to make money or achieve fame, while others understood that it presented a means of controlling the dissemination and substance of their music. Further, composers now realized that they were no longer writing only for a local patron and audience.

Money

On September 5, 1536, Costanzo Festa wrote to his patron, Filippo Strozzi:

> Magnificent Sir, Godfather [to his child] . . . I would like a service of Your Lordship that would make me most grateful: that one of your [agents] search in Venice for someone who prints music (although I have been asked, I do not know the name). Have him [the printer] understand that if he wants my works, that is, the hymns [and] the Magnificats, that I do not want less than one hundred fifty scudi and, if he wants the *basse*, two hundred in all. If he wants to print them, he can place the hymns and Magnificats in a large book [choirbook format] like that of the 15 Masses [Antico's *Quindecim missarum* of 1516], so that all choirs would be able to make use of them. The *basse* are good for learning to sing, [to write] counterpoint, to compose, and to play all instruments.[6]

Festa, then, hoped to sell an extensive collection of his compositions to an unnamed Venetian printer for a flat fee. It seems, though, that his plans came to naught. And given the financial caution that music printers normally exercised, it is unlikely that other composers were any more successful. Rather, the flow of money normally went in the opposite direction, from composer to printer, as composers either paid their own way or sought subsidies from a third party.

Fame

Though there may have been little quick money to be made in publishing one's music, there was fame to be gained. A slew of minor composers, even rank amateurs, jumped at the opportunity to get their names in print. In fact, by the middle of the century, the glut of less-than-greats who were getting published had begun to annoy the theorist Hermann Finck:

> Many of those, whom I have mentioned, even dare to claim for themselves the title of composer. In the span of half a year, [they] manage with great toil to produce a little song of whatever quality, with scarcely three consonances in it, and immediately take care to have it printed, so that their great and glorious name can be known to the whole world.[7]

Now, there had long been composers who are known today only by a piece or two. But as Finck noted, by his time there were many. We can see this

---

6. Quoted after Agee, "Filippo Strozzi and the Early Madrigal," 232–34. The *basse* may have been some some kind of pedagogical pieces.

7. In his *Practica musica* of 1556; quoted after Bernstein, "Financial Arrangements," 48.

clearly enough just in Attaingnant's publications, which include 41 composers who are represented by one piece only. This is a substantial percentage of the 175 composers whose works Attaingnant printed.

Control

Composers also looked to the printing industry as a way of maintaining control over their works. If, as was often the case, they were able to watch over the publication of their compositions, they could check the pieces' attribution as well as the musical substance (this note here, that note there). It was the former motive in particular that led the Flemish-born madrigalist Jacquet de Berchem (c. 1505–c. 1565) to go to press with his five-part madrigals in 1546. In the dedication, Berchem complains about "crows who dress themselves in the feathers of the swan": that is, either outright plagiarists or those under whose name appeared (intentionally or not) the occasional misattributed piece that he himself had written. His *Madrigali a cinque voci* would "set the record straight."

The Collective Patron

One of the most interesting notions about the relationship between composers and music printing comes from the pen of the composer-theorist Adriano Banchieri (1568–1634). In his *Cartella musicale*, originally published in 1601, Banchieri describes composers who were guilty of what we might call "compositional miscalculations":

> [They] find themselves with sopranos and altos who can ascend to the stars, and tenors and basses who descend to the antipodes and who [the composers], because their compositions succeed for them, believe that they will produce the same effect in the hands of others. I conclude that given that those compositions which are sent to the press have to serve universally, all the parts should be convenient, otherwise they will for the most part give poor satisfaction.[8]

In other words, a style that was suitable and effective for the composer's own patron and performing forces could spell disaster elsewhere. It is an interesting idea, and we might wonder about the degree to which sixteenth-century composers anticipated Banchieri's idea when composing music intended for the press.

CONSUMERS

Publishers would not have turned out music books by the hundreds of thousands had there not been a market for them. Nor would dealers have cluttered their shelves with volumes that were likely to gather dust. Clearly, the market existed. Moreover, those who bought music books came from a broad spectrum of socioeconomic backgrounds.

8. Quoted after Carter, *Music in Late Renaissance and Early Baroque Italy*, 43.

An Elite Musical Institution

From about the 1530s on, the Vatican maintained two prestigious choirs: the Cappella Sistina and the Cappella Giulia, the latter directed by Palestrina, first in 1551–55 and then from 1571 until his death in 1594. We can identify some of the polyphonic prints owned by the Cappella Giulia thanks to an inventory drawn up by one of its singers between 1559 and 1566. As we might expect, they are publications of Masses and motets: the *Liber quindecim missarum*, engraved by Antico in 1516; two books of Morales Masses (including the *Missa Quaeramus cum pastoribus*), issued by the firm of Dorico at Rome in 1544; and Masses by Claudin, Goudimel, and Jean Maillard (c. 1538–1570), issued by Le Roy and Ballard in 1558. In all, the publications contain a cross-section of contemporary Masses, with a slight bias in favor of French publications.

An Adviser to a King

Jean de Badonvilliers was from a wealthy Parisian family and served as an adviser to Francis I. When he died in 1544, the inventory of his library included two books on music theory (both in Latin), a volume of Masses (publisher and date not indicated), and four of Attaingnant's publications: two collections of chansons (both bound and valued at twenty sous each), a volume of Claudin motets (unbound and valued at twelve sous), and a book of motets by the Flemish composer Johannes Lupi (also unbound and worth eight sous).

That the chanson volumes were considered more valuable than the motet books is explained by their being bound, since bindings had to be custom-ordered by the purchaser. (Books were normally sold unbound, the sixteenth-century equivalent of our paperback.) That the Claudin motets were valued at a higher price than those of Lupi, on the other hand, is more difficult to explain, since both volumes were published in the same year (1542), printed in the same format, and had the same number of folios. Perhaps Claudin's name had a certain magic in Paris.

A Banking Family

To say that the Fugger family of Augsburg was rich is like saying that Michael Jordan is a good basketball player. From about the mid-fifteenth century until the Thirty Years' War (1618–48), the Fuggers' international banking and mining interests (including claims in Latin America) probably made them the wealthiest family of the period. It was to the Fuggers, especially Jacob II (called "the Rich"), that emperors, kings, and popes went for loans to feed their extravagant ways of life.

We can tell just how extensive the family's collection of music prints must have been from two facts. First, one of the greatest present-day collections of sixteenth-century music prints is housed at the Bayerische Staatsbibliothek at Munich; the core of this collection came from the library of the ducal court of Bavaria, which in turn owed its origins to the private collection of Johann Hans Jacob Fugger (1516–1575). Second, during the period 1560–1624, the Fuggers were the dedicatees of no fewer than forty-two music publications. Had the family collection, which also included numerous manuscripts that they had commissioned earlier in the century, consisted of nothing more than the volumes dedicated to them, it would have been judged impressive.

A Professional Musician and Some Middle-Class Folks

One of the many musicians who enjoyed the Fuggers' beneficence was the German composer-organist Gregor Aichinger (1564/65–1628). Among the sixteenth-century music prints at the present-day Staats- und Stadtbibliothek of Augsburg is a series of a dozen prints whose title pages contain the inscription "Ex libris Gregorij Aichinger." The prints include madrigal books of Cipriano de Rore, Orlande de Lassus, and Giaches de Wert, as well as volumes of Gardano and Scotto anthologies. There can be no doubt that professional musicians constituted an important segment of the music-buying public.

And so did members of the middle class. We know about three who purchased music books at the decidedly middlebrow bookshop of Piero di Giuliano Morosi. In October 1592, a customs inspector named Pietro Concini purchased a book by Matteo Rampollini (1497–c. 1553), probably the *Primo libro della musica*, a collection of four-part madrigals on poems by Petrarch, published by Moderne at Lyons around 1544. In July 1596, one Giovanni d'Ippolito Libanori, a local leather worker, bought a second-hand copy of unspecified music, together with a dictionary (of music?). And in July 1600, a cleric from the Florentine church of the Badia treated himself to a bound set of fifteen-year-old *madrigali spirituali* by Felice Anerio (c. 1560–1614). The information is fascinating: music that today forms the stuff of slickly packaged early-music concerts was purchased, performed, and no doubt enjoyed by a leather worker, a customs inspector, and a cleric who was probably closer to the bottom of the ecclesiatical hierarchy than to the top.

That those far removed from the upper echelons of the socioeconomic scale could afford to buy such items speaks eloquently about the intelligence of the printing industry's pricing strategies. There was one range of prices for folio-size, leather-bound collections of sacred music with elaborately decorated title pages and dedications; there was quite another—at Venice, about one lira, or the equivalent of a day's pay for a working man—for octavo-size collections of madrigals, villanelle, and lute music that did without the fancy decorations and binding.[9]

The Music Academies

One of the music dealers' most cherished sources of customers must surely have been the academies that sprang up during the fifteenth and sixteenth

9. The terms customarily used to describe the format of books were "folio," "quarto," and "octavo" (we still use them today). In a folio, each large sheet of paper is folded once, giving two leaves, or four pages; in a quarto, the same paper is folded twice and produces four leaves, or eight pages; in an octavo, the paper is folded three times, making eight leaves, or sixteen pages.

centuries from one end of Italy to the other. These first developed as informal gatherings of aristocratic intellectuals who would discuss matters ranging from classical studies to contemporary philosophy, literature, drama, and music. The most famous was the Accademia Platonica, founded at Florence in 1470 and led by Marsilio Ficino with the financial and moral support of Lorenzo de' Medici.

By the mid-sixteenth century, Italy could boast a couple of hundred such academies, including some that specialized in music. Among the latter, the best-known was certainly the Accademia Filarmonica of Verona. Founded in 1543, it hired its first music director in 1547, the Flemish composer Jan Nasco (c. 1510–1561), whose duties were clearly spelled out: for a yearly salary of thirty ducats, he was to be at the academy each evening in order to give music lessons to its members; he was required to set to music any poems that the members might give to him (the membership paid for the music paper); and his compositions remained the property of the academy. Rigorous though the approach might have been, Verona's academy also produced results, and within a few years its public concerts made it the envy of other such organizations. (The academy, which played host to Mozart in 1770, still thrives today.)

In all, the growth of the music-printing business in the second quarter of the sixteenth century was a matter of the proverbial right idea being in the right place at the right time. The entrepreneurial and artistic vision of the likes of Attaingnant, Gardano, Susato, and others meshed neatly with the energetic spirit of capitalism, the growth of literacy, and the demand for "culture" that these entailed. And so well did all the parts of the publisher-composer-consumer triangle come together that it would remain essentially unchanged until the revolution brought about by the recording industry at the beginning of our own century.

BIBLIOGRAPHICAL NOTE

General Studies

There are interesting studies of the sixteenth-century printing industry in Elizabeth L. Eisenstein, *The Printing Revolution in Early Modern Europe* (Cambridge: Cambridge University Press, 1983), and H. S. Bennett, *English Books and Readers, 1475–1557*, 2nd ed. (Cambridge: Cambridge University Press, 1969); on music printing in particular, see Donald W. Krummel and Stanley Sadie's *Music Printing and Publishing* (New York: Norton, 1990), which has a useful "Dictionary of Music Printers and Publishers," an extremely informative Glossary by Stanley Boorman, and a well-organized Bibliography by Krummel; for a concise statement of many of the issues raised by sixteenth-century music prints, see Mary S. Lewis, "The Printed Music Book in Context: Observations on Some Sixteenth-Century Editions," *Notes* 46 (1990): 899–918.

Studies of Individual Printers

Attaingnant: Daniel Heartz, *Pierre Attaingnant, Royal Printer of Music* (Berkeley and Los Angeles: University of California Press, 1969). **Dorico**: Suzanne G. Cusick, *Valerio Dorico: Music Printer in Sixteenth-Century Rome* (Ann Arbor: UMI Research Press, 1981). **Du Chemin**: François Lesure and Geneviève Thibault, "Bibliographie des éditions musicales publiées par Nicolas du Chemin (1549–1576)," *AnnM* 1 (1953): 269–373; 4 (1956): 251–

53; 6 (1958–63): 403–6. **Gardano**: Mary S. Lewis, *Antonio Gardano, Venetian Music Printer, 1538–1569: A Descriptive Bibliography and Historical Study* (New York: Garland, 1988). **Le Roy** and **Ballard**: Lesure and Thibault, *Bibliographie des éditions d'Adrian Le Roy et Robert Ballard (1551–1598)* (Paris: Heugel, 1955), with supplement in *RdM* 40 (1957): 166–72. **Moderne**: Samuel Pogue, *Jacques Moderne* (Lyons: Droz, 1969). **Scotto**: Jane A. Bernstein, *Music Printing in Renaissance Venice: The Scotto Press (1539–1572)* (New York: Oxford University Press, 1998). **Susato**: Ute Meissner, *Der Antwerpener Notendrucker Tylman Susato* (Berlin: Merseberger, 1967); Kristine Forney, "New Documents of the Life of Tielman Susato, Sixteenth-Century Music Printer and Musician," *RBM* 35–38 (1982–84): 18-57.

Typographical Studies

James Haar, "The *Libro Primo* of Costanzo Festa," *AcM* 52 (1980): 147–55; Donna G. Cardamone, "*Madrigali a tre et arie napolitane:* A Typographical and Repertorial Study," *JAMS* 35 (1982): 436–81; Kristine Forney, "Orlando di Lasso's 'Opus 1': The Making and Marketing of a Renaissance Music Book," *RBM* 39–40 (1985–86): 33–60; Donna G. Cardamone and David L. Jackson, "Multiple Formes and Vertical Setting in Susato's First Edition of Lassus's 'Opus 1,'" *Notes* 46 (1989): 7–24; Stanley Boorman, "Some Non-Conflicting Attributions, and Some Newly Anonymous Compositions, from the Early Sixteenth Century," *EMH* 6 (1986): 109–57.

The Social-Commercial Context of Music Printing

Daniel Heartz, "*Au pres de vous*—Claudin's Chanson and the Commerce of Publishers' Arrangements," *JAMS* 24 (1971): 193–225; Richard J. Agee, "The Venetian Privilege and Music-Printing in the Sixteenth Century," *EMH* 3 (1983): 1–42, and "A Venetian Music Printing Contract and Edition Size in the Sixteenth Century," *StudM* 15 (1986): 59–65; Jane A. Bernstein, "The Burning Salamander: Assigning a Printer to Some Sixteenth-Century Music Prints," *Notes* 42 (1986): 483–501, and "Financial Arrangements and the Role of Printer and Composer in Sixteenth-Century Italian Music Printing," *AcM* 63 (1991): 39–56; Bonnie J. Blackburn, "The Printing Contract for the *Libro primo de musica de la salamandra* (Rome, 1526)," *JM* 12 (1994): 345–56; Stanley Boorman, "Early Music Printing: Working for a Specialized Market," in *Print and Culture in the Renaissance: Essays on the Advent of Printing in Europe*, ed. G. P. Tyson and S. S. Wagonheim (Newark: University of Delaware Press, 1986), *222–45*; Tim Carter, "Music-Selling in Late Sixteenth-Century Florence: The Bookshop of Piero di Giuliano Morosi," *ML* 70 (1989): 483–504; "Music Printing in Late Sixteenth- and Early Seventeenth-Century Florence: Giorgio Marescotti, Cristofano Marescotti, and Zanobi Pignoni," *EMH* 10 (1990): 27–72; Nicoletta Guidobaldi, "Music Publishing in Sixteenth- and Seventeenth-Century Umbria," *EMH* 9 (1989): 1–36; Giulio Ongaro, "The Library of a Sixteenth-Century Music Teacher," *JM* 12 (1994): 357–75.

Indices to Printed Repertories

All instrumental prints of the period are catalogued in Howard Mayer Brown, *Instrumental Music Printed Before 1600: A Bibliography* (Cambridge: Harvard University Press, 1965); printed anthologies of the sixteenth century are listed in François Lesure, *Recueils imprimés: XVIᵉ–XVIIᵉ siècles*, RISM B/I/1 (Munich-Duisberg: G. Henle, 1960); madrigal prints devoted to a single composer are indexed in *Il nuovo Vogel: Bibliografia della musica italiana vocale profana pubblicata dal 1500 al 1700*, ed. François Lesure and Claudio Sartori (Pomezia: Minkoff, 1977).

Academies

Two standard works on the academies of Italy and France are Michele Maylender, *Storia delle accademie d'Italia*, 5 vols. (Bologna: L. Cappelli, 1926–30), and Francis Yates, *The French*

Academies in the Sixteenth Century (London: The Warburg Institute, 1947); the Accademia Filarmonica of Verona is covered in Giuseppe Turrini, *L'Accademia Filarmonica di Verona dalla fondazione (maggio 1543) al 1600 e il suo patrimonio musicale* (Verona, 1941); on the musical activities of a less famous academy, see Allan W. Atlas, "The Accademia degli Unisoni: A Music Academy in Renaissance Perugia," in *A Musical Offering: Essays in Honor of Martin Bernstein*, ed. Edward H. Clinckscale and Claire Brook (New York: Pendragon Press, 1977), 5–23.

Also Cited

Daniel Heartz, "A New Attaingnant Book and the Beginnings of French Music Printing," *JAMS* 14 (1961): 9–23; Lawrence F. Bernstein, "Claude Gervaise as Chanson Composer," *JAMS* 18 (1965): 359–81; Lawrence F. Bernstein and James Haar, *Ihan Gero: Il primo libro de' madrigali italiani et cantoni francese a due voci* (New York: Broude Bros., 1980); Richard J. Agee, "Filippo Strozzi and the Early Madrigal," *JAMS* 38 (1985): 227–37; Tim Carter, *Music in Late Renaissance and Early Baroque Italy* (Portland: Amadeus Press, 1992).

CHAPTER 30

Editing a Chanson:
Barring, Sources, Critical Report

By now, we have transcribed the Dijon 517 version of Busnoys's song into modern notation, added the necessary editorial accidentals, and placed the words beneath the music of at least the superius. With the most frustrating parts of the project thus behind us, we are ready to head down the home stretch.

Four tasks remain: we must decide what kind of barring we wish to use; collate the sources—that is, compare the readings of the music in Dijon 517 and Mellon in order to see if there are variants (if we were doing this for publication, we would also need to collate the two poetry sources); make a final decision about which manuscript should be our principal source and possibly emend it in light of the collation; and draw up a "critical report."

BARRING

Editors of fifteenth- and sixteenth-century music do not necessarily agree about the use of bar lines. Example 30-1 illustrates four different methods of barring:

EXAMPLE 30-1. Busnoys, *A vous sans autre*, mm. 1–8: (a) conventional bar lines; (b) *Mensurstriche*; (c) according to the sense of the rhythm; (d) no bar lines.

(a)

(a) Regularly recurring bar lines that go through the staves: that is, the conventional bar lines we are accustomed to today.

(b) The type of bar lines known in German as *Mensurstriche* (measuring lines), which are placed between the staves instead of through them; they were first introduced by Heinrich Besseler (editor of the complete works of Du Fay) in the 1920s.

(c) Bar lines that go through the staves but at irregular intervals according to the sense of the rhythm; championed by Otto Gombosi, the system appears in *Anthology* 60.

(d) No bar lines at all, the wedges simply marking the end of one breve and the beginning of another.

Friends and enemies of these systems might express their advantages and disadvantages as follows:

(a) The chief advantage to conventional bar lines is familiarity; moreover, the concept of barring was certainly known in the fifteenth and sixteenth centuries, as witness its consistent use in music for solo lute and keyboard. Opponents argue that they were not used for polyphonic ensemble music; they result in the use of ties, which are foreign to the notation of the period; they imply unstylistic, accented downbeats, which impede and even falsify the flow of the rhythm; and they may cause the same music to appear in different parts of the measure (the other half) when a section is repeated.

(b) Proponents of *Mensurstriche* claim that placing the bar lines between the staves allows the rhythm of each voice part to flow freely, without the implication of an accented downbeat; in addition, the system eliminates the need for ties. Opponents argue that one can too easily lose one's metrical bearings, especially in passages involving long-range syncopations (over the nonexistent bar lines). To this, adherents might reply that the typical vocal music of the period had no syncopation to begin with, since there was no regularly recurring "oomph" against which it was felt.

(c) The chief argument of the few who favor barring according to the sense of the music is that it shows the often complex rhythmic counterpoint, both between the individual voices and between any given voice and the prevailing metrical scheme. Two arguments against the system are that it does little more than freeze in print a particular editor's subjective analysis of rhythm and meter (to which adherents might reply that there is nothing wrong with an edition that is in effect a personal interpretation, or a performance on paper); and it can produce a score that looks more like Stravinsky than Josquin.

(d) Advocates of doing away with bar lines completely claim that doing so permits us to get as close as possible to the original notation. Opponents might say: why bother transcribing into modern notation in the first place?

In the end, each system can emphasize one aspect or another of the music; each in its own way is a compromise with the original notation; but none need necessarily obliterate the original entirely. And while each system might have its preferred audience, no system automatically precludes any audience. We are not dealing with a moral issue.

COLLATING THE SOURCES

Why should we compare the readings that Dijon 517 and Mellon offer for *A vous sans autre*? Above all, it is because neither version of the piece is, so far as we know, a Busnoys autograph, and we therefore have no right to assume that the version in either manuscript necessarily presents the piece as Busnoys conceived it. What the collation helps us do is to evaluate the relative worth of the versions in each manuscript.

Since the readings for *A vous sans autre* in Dijon 517 and Mellon are not identical, we can conclude that neither version of the song was copied from the other and that the two versions were not copied directly from a common parent source. In other words, the readings in the two manuscripts are to some degree independent of one another. This leads to an important principle: where Dijon 517 and Mellon agree with one another, we can reasonably suppose that they transmit "original Busnoys" (or something as close as we can get to it). When Dijon 517 and Mellon fail to agree at a given spot, we must evaluate the differences—and this can be a formidable task.

Measures 36–44

As we saw in Chapter 4, Dijon 517 places a ₵ in all voices at the beginning of measure 36. Now, in the mid-fifteenth century, when the sign ₵ followed a prevailing C successively and simultaneously in all voices (thus without any overlap between the old C and the new ₵), it had two possible meanings:

(1) The ₵ could function as a sign (synonymous with C 2) for *proportio dupla*, in which case it instructed the singer to shift the *tactus* (basic beat) from the semibreve to the breve (the origin of our term *alla breve*) and sing two of each note value to the time previously accorded to one; in effect, it doubles the tempo. Yet if this is what the sign meant here, we would expect the values that followed it to be written at the next-highest level, otherwise the last phrase of the song would literally go twice as fast as the music that preceded it, something that makes no musical sense. Example 30-2 shows how the movement from C to ₵ normally works:

EXAMPLE 30-2. Change in note values accompanying the shift from C to ₵.

C ◊ ◊ ♩ ♩ ♩· ♦ ♮ = ₵ ♮ ♮ ◊ ◊ ◊· ♩ ♮

(2) The ₵ could function according to Tinctoris's dictum: "It is proper to the stroke [drawn through a mensuration sign] to signify the acceleration of the measure."[1]

Here, rather than doubling the tempo, the sign merely speeds it up by an unstated amount; but while we may regard a slight *accelerando* as unexceptional, especially toward the end of a piece, fifteenth-century chansons did not generally behave that way.

---

1. Quoted after Wegman, "What Is 'Acceleratio mensurae'?" 515.

Puzzled by the notation of Dijon 517, we may then turn to Mellon in the hopes of clarifying the situation. And there we find that there is no ₵ at all. Clearly, this seems to solve the problem. Or does it? For if we decide that Mellon is correct and that the three ₵ signs in Dijon 517 are superfluous, we are left with the problem of explaining how the scribe of Dijon could have created such glaring errors of commission.

Measures 11 and 42

Far more typical of the variants found in manuscripts are two that appear in the tenor at measures 11 and 42 (Ex. 30-3):

EXAMPLE 30-3. Measures 10–11 and 41–42: (a) tenor of Dijon 517, (b) tenor of Mellon.

Which manuscript is more likely to offer the note that Busnoys had in mind? In both instances, either version will work.

THE PRINCIPAL SOURCE

The decision to transcribe from Dijon 517 was made somewhat arbitrarily. Yet we now see that its reading does not go entirely uncontested. What should we do? There are three basic ways to go about editing music that appears in more than one source.

Conflation

The conflation method hops about among the sources without rhyme or reason. It subjectively settles on manuscript X's reading at one point, on manuscript Y's at another. Thus it does not give priority to the reading in any one manuscript. And while this may make the editor's life simple, it results in something of an uncritical hodgepodge, as the final result is often a version that cannot be shown ever to have existed at one place at any one time.

Reconstructing the Original

We can make an attempt to reconstruct Busnoys's original by using the technique known as stemmatics (originally developed for literary texts): we compare errors and variants among the sources, study the interrelationships, eliminate as witnesses those manuscripts that are clearly derived from earlier ones, and try thereby to work our way back to the author's lost original, the "archetype."

Consider these excerpts from manuscripts X, Y, and Z:

> Manuscript X: Twinkle, twinkle, little star,
> I wonder what you are.
>
> Manuscript Y: Twinkle, shminkle, little star,
> How I wonder what you are.
>
> Manuscript Z: Twinkle, shminkle, little star,
> How I wonder what U R.

The interrelationships might be shown as follows, with o standing for the archetype and a for a hypothetical lost intermediary:

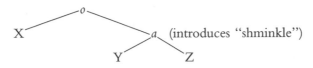

That Y and Z are related is evident from their both transmitting the word "shminkle," perhaps some scribe's joking attempt to jazz up the second "twinkle." In the language of textual criticism, "shminkle" is a conjunctive error (or variant): that is, it indicates that the manuscripts that transmit it must have been copied either from one another or from a common parent, since two or more scribes are unlikely to have made the same error or come up with the same variant independently. Thus we may speculate that Y and Z derived their readings from the now-lost a, which can be reconstructed from the points at which Y and Z agree with one another. Playing off X against a, we work our way back to the archetype o and the presumed original, in which we favor the second "twinkle" in X (there is no such word as "shminkle") and adopt the "How" of a (necessary in order to preserve the meter of the poem).

As with conflation, we end up with a reconstruction that does not exist in any extant manuscript. Here, though, we have gone about the task in a systematic, commonsense way. Yet inviting though the technique is, stemmatics will not always work. It requires that certain conditions be met that do not always obtain in the transmission of fifteenth-century music.

The Best-Source Method

This method settles on one source as the best and uses it as the principal source. But how do we define "best"? Is it the source with the reading that gives the editor the most aesthetic pleasure, the one with the fewest errors, or the one that is most neatly written?

For most editors, the best source stands closest to the composer chronologically and geographically: it presents the shortest line of transmission and thus the fewest opportunities for corruption to have crept in. And if the chronological-geographical match between manuscript and composer is close enough, perhaps the composer even stood over the scribe's shoulder. Using this criterion, we should go with Dijon 517 as the principal source. It was probably compiled in the region of the Loire Valley during the 1460s and therefore stands close to Busnoys's own whereabouts during the same period.

What do we do, though, if we firmly believe that at a certain spot Mellon has the better (more "authentic") reading? We can adopt it, possibly even enclosing it in parentheses. In fact, we might even decide that a particular note is wrong in both Dijon 517 and Mellon; once again, we should emend the error, now placing the emendation in square brackets (in order to show that it lacks manuscript authority). In the end, we hitch our edition to Dijon 517 and adopt its reading except where it clearly seems to be corrupt.

THE CRITICAL REPORT

The critical report is the bridge between the editor and those who use the edition. It tells scholar and performer alike what the editor has done. Moreover, an intelligent report will provide the "why" for each decision made.

There are almost as many ways to organize the critical report as there are editors who draw them up. Some reports contain more detail than others. Some are truly critical; others resemble telephone books. Some pretend to be for the scholar; others wrongheadedly justify a bare-bones approach by claiming to serve "only" performers. If the critical report is to be useful, it should list the principal source (with an explanation of why that source was chosen); all concordant sources, both musical and literary; all available facsimile editions of the sources; all useful modern editions; emendations made to the principal source, with an explanation, preferably with comparative music examples, of why each emendation was made; and variants (both musical and poetic) in the concordant sources. (One never knows what use someone might make of a seemingly trivial piece of information.)

The bottom line is that the critical report should try to answer every question that the user of the edition could possibly ask, not only about the finished edition itself, but about the editorial decisions that were made to arrive at it; it should give the user confidence that the editor has thought about every note on the page; and it should allow the user to go back and reconstruct every source that the editor consulted.

There is one thing left to do: look at the critical reports listed in the Bibliographical Note. They provide a cross-section of approaches from the critical to the uncritical, from the exhaustive to the skimpy, from the composition-oriented to the source-oriented. Each has its advantages and disadvantages. And with the critical report, we really are dealing with a moral issue: the editor owes the rest of us an honest account.

BIBLIOGRAPHICAL NOTE

Barring

There is a concise introduction in Bernard Thomas, "Renaissance Music in Modern Notation," *EM* 5 (1977): 4–11; see also John Caldwell, *Editing Early Music* (Oxford: Clarendon Press, 1985); for a hard, anti-*Mensurstriche* view, see Edward E. Lowinsky, "Early Scores in Manuscript," *JAMS* 13 (1960): 126–73; Otto Gombosi discusses barring according to the sense of the rhythm in *The Capirola Lutebook: Compositione di Meser Vincenzo Capirola* (Neuilly-sur-Seine: Société de Musique d'Autrefois, 1955).

Textual Criticism

Literary: among the classic introductions to the subject are A. E. Housman, "The Application of Thought of Textual Criticism," *Proceedings of the Classical Association* 18 (1921): 67–84, reprinted in *Art and Error: Modern Textual Editing*, ed. Ronald Gottesman and Scott Bennett (Bloomington: Indiana University Press, 1970), 1–16; Paul Maas, *Textual Criticism*, trans. Barbara Flower (Oxford: Clarendon Press, 1957); L. D. Reynolds and N. G. Wilson, *Scribes and Scholars: A Guide to the Transmission of Greek and Latin Literature* (Oxford: Oxford University Press, 1968); James Thorpe, *Principles of Textual Criticism* (San Marino, Calif.: Huntington Library, 1972); Martin West, *Textual Criticism and Editorial Technique Applied to Greek and Latin Texts* (Stuttgart: Teubner, 1973); George Kane and E. Talbot Donaldson, *Piers Plowman: The Three Versions*, rev. ed. (London, 1988); the journal *Text*, published by the Society for Textual Scholarship (1984–), contains a gold mine of interesting articles on problems of editing.

Musical: a good starting point is James Grier, *The Critical Editing of Music: History, Method, and Practice* (Cambridge: Cambridge University Press, 1996). From there, one might proceed to two volumes (many of the essays in which are in English) that grew out of conferences held in the early 1980s: Ludwig Finscher, ed., *Quellenstudien zur Musik der Renaissance*, vol. 1: *Formen und Probleme der Überlieferung mehrstimmige Musik im Zeitalter Josquins Desprez*, Wolfenbüttler Forschungen 6 (Munich: Kraus, 1981), vol. 2: *Datierung and Filiation von Musikhandschriften der Josquin-Zeit*, Wolfenbüttler Forschungen 26 (Wiesbaden: Otto Harrassowitz, 1983); see also Margaret Bent, "Some Criteria for Establishing Relationships between Sources of Late-Medieval Polyphony," and Stanley Boorman, "Limitations and Extensions of Filiation Technique" (with an extremely useful bibliography), both in *Music in Medieval and Early Modern Europe: Patronage, Sources, and Text*, ed. Iain Fenlon (Cambridge: Cambridge University Press, 1981), 295–317 and 319–46; Boorman, "The Uses of Filiation in Early Music," *Text* 1 (1984): 167–84.

Critical Reports

The following critical reports illustrate a number of different approaches. **Editions of composers**: Cornago, *Complete Works*, RRMMAER 15, ed. Rebecca L. Gerber (Madison: A-R Editions, 1984); Du Fay, *Opera Omnia*, CMM 1, ed. Heinrich Besseler (American Institute of Musicology, 1951–66); Dunstable, *Complete Works*, MB 8, ed. Manfred F. Bukofzer, rev. Margaret Bent, Ian Bent, and Brian Trowell (London: Stainer & Bell, 1970); Morton, *The Collected Works*, RMR 2, ed. Allan Atlas (New York: Broude Bros., 1981); Obrecht, *New Obrecht Edition*, ed. Barton Hudson, Chris Maas, and Thomas Noblitt (Utrecht: Vereniging voor Nederlandse Muziekgeschiedenis, 1983–). **Editions of individual manuscripts**: Howard Mayer Brown, *A Florentine Chansonnier from the Time of Lorenzo the Magnificent: Florence, Biblioteca Nazionale Centrale, MS Banco Rari 229*, MRM 7 (Chicago: Chicago University Press, 1983); Leeman Perkins and Howard Garey, *The Mellon Chansonnier*, 2 vols. (New Haven: Yale University Press, 1979); Martin Picker, *The Chanson Albums of Marguerite of Austria* (Berkeley and Los Angeles: University of California Press, 1965).

Also Cited

Rob C. Wegman, "What Is 'Acceleratio mensurae'?" *ML* 73 (1992): 515–24.

CHAPTER 31

Instrumental Music to the End of the Century

If there is a single word that characterizes the spirit of instrumental music during the final three quarters of the sixteenth century (we will track its course up to about 1600), it is "innovation." And if there is one place where that spirit took hold most strongly, it is Italy. To be sure, some old practices continued to thrive: keyboard players and lutenists continued to adapt vocal pieces, and church organists kept on setting chant melodies. Yet new genres and styles sprouted everywhere, and they seemed to point in the same direction: instrumental music loosened its old ties with vocal models and increasingly developed according to abstract, non-word-related principles of its own. To the sixteenth century we owe the creation of such modern instrumental genres as the imitative ricercar (precursor of the fugue), the virtuoso keyboard toccata, and the idea of theme and variations.

This chapter looks at seven types of instrumental music: (1) transcriptions based directly on vocal models; (2) settings of chant melodies for use in the liturgy; (3) sets of variations; (4) ricercars; (5) canzonas; (6) preludes and toccatas; and (7) dance music. Occasionally we pause to consider some aspects of instrumental music that cut across these types, including ornamentation and improvisation.

TRANSCRIPTIONS BASED ON VOCAL MODELS

By the second quarter of the sixteenth century, the practice of arranging preexistent vocal pieces—songs, motets, and even Mass movements—for solo keyboard or lute was old hat. In fact, we have already seen three such arrangements, all for keyboard, in such diverse collections as the Buxheim Organ Book of 1470 and Antico's *Frottole intabulate* of 1517. Two final examples complete the survey.

Two Keyboard Arrangements of French Chansons

Example 31-1 presents the opening of a keyboard arrangement of Claudin's *Jatens secours* (together with the original), published in Attaingnant's *Vingt et cinq chansons* of 1531. Typically, the anonymous arranger retained virtually all of Claudin's polyphony, filling it out with the customary runs and ornamental embellishments. In fact, the art of arranging vocal music for solo keyboard or lute remained largely unchanged during the course of the sixteenth century; and this 1531 arrangement does not differ markedly in spirit or technique from the mid–fifteenth–century arrangement of Robert Morton's *Le souvenir* (see *Anthology* 34).

EXAMPLE 31-1. Claudin, *Jatens secours*, mm. 1–8: (a) the keyboard arrangement; (b) the original chanson.

What did change was the amount of embellishment that arrangers added, and this increased in avalanche-like proportions. Example 31-2 shows the opening of an arrangement by Claudio Merulo (published posthumously in 1611) of Orlande de Lassus's *Susanne un jour*, a chanson that gained such popularity with keyboard players, lutenists, and authors of improvisation manuals that there are at least thirty-five different arrangements.

EXAMPLE 31-2. *Susanne un jour*, mm. 1–5: (a) Merulo's keyboard arrangement, (b) Lassus's chanson.

The dizzying embellishment is not at all exceptional for end-of-the-century
keyboard arrangements. Moreover, it is entirely in keeping with the style of
improvised embellishment recommended by a dozen sixteenth-century tutors.

Problems in Printing Keyboard Music

In 1531, Pierre Attaingnant issued seven volumes of keyboard music—three volumes of chanson arrangements, another of motets, two collections of liturgical settings, and one book of dances—but never published another keyboard work in the remaining twenty years of his career. And he was not alone: while the period from 1531 to the end of the century saw the publication of more than two hundred printed volumes of music for solo lute, it produced only about eighty such volumes for keyboard instruments.

There are several reasons for this discrepancy. First, the lute was the most popular instrument of the time, at home across a broad socioeconomic spectrum. At best, keyboard instruments, which were expensive and considered by some more difficult to learn, held second place, perhaps even trailed recorders and viols. Second, though we might imagine that there was a ready-made market for printed keyboard music among the countless church organists alone, most of them probably had little need for such books: as we will see, the art of the church organist was largely the art of improvisation.

Finally, it may be that the printing of keyboard music was stymied by typographical problems. Figure 31-1 reproduces the page from Attaingnant's *Vingt et cinq chansons* on which the arrangement of Claudin's *Jatens secours* begins. As we can see, the typography is less than elegant, as the stems of more than a few notes get scrunched, while others are missing altogether. In general, music printers had difficulty placing two or more closely spaced notes vertically on the same staff.

No doubt this last problem must have been one of the factors that led mu-

Figure 31-1. Keyboard arrangement of Claudin's *Jaten secours* in Attaingnant's *Vingt et cinq chansons*, 1531.

sicians to devise new shorthand systems of keyboard tablature and to further develop old ones. As we saw in connection with the fifteenth-century Buxheim Organ Book (see Chapter 16), German keyboard players had long used a system in which only the melody line (the right hand) was written in musical notation, while the other "voices" were spelled out with letter names and rhythmic indications. By the final quarter of the sixteenth century, the shorthand became still shorter: now even the melody was written with letter names.

Given the printing problems, keyboard players were content to circulate their music in manuscripts, many of which were copied by amateurs for their own personal use. And it was not only keyboard music that circulated largely in manuscripts. Printers seemed to be reluctant to invest in instrumental music in general. Although Italy led the way in publishing instrumental music, rarely did Italian printers of the sixteenth century devote more than about 10 percent of their annual production to instrumental music; of the 430 music volumes listed in a Gardano catalogue of 1591, only 18 are instrumental collections.

Vocal Music Played by Instrumental Ensembles

Much of the vocal music published in the sixteenth century was clearly intended to reach instrumentalists as well. The point is made on the title page of a 1543 Susato publication that features the chansons of Gombert, Crecquillon, Clemens non Papa, and others: "Premier livre des chansons a quatre partes auquel sont contenues trente et une nouvelles chansons, convenables tant a la voix comme aux instruments."

"Suitable for voices as well as instruments": this refrain was repeated on many a title page of the period. And players in viol or recorder consorts must have spent countless evenings reading through the latest chansons, madrigals, and motets without their words.

SETTINGS OF CHANT MELODIES

A large portion of the sixteenth-century keyboard repertory consists of organ music for both Mass and Office, most of which was based on appropriate plainchant melodies and intended to be performed in *alternatim* fashion with music—either chant or polyphony—sung by the choir.

A Hymn Setting by Girolamo Cavazzoni

Perhaps the greatest composer of liturgical organ music in Italy during the years 1520–80 was Girolamo Cavazzoni (c. 1525–after 1577), the son of Marco Antonio Cavazzoni, one of whose ricercars we considered in Chapter 25. We can see Girolamo's approach to treating a chant melody in his setting of the hymn *Christe redemptor omnium* (*Anthology* 70), intended for first Vespers on Christmas Day and published in his *Intavolatura . . . recercari canzoni himni magnificati libro primo* (Venice, 1543). Example 31-3 gives the plainchant hymn, which since the Council of Trent has begun with the name "Jesu" in place of "Christe."

EXAMPLE 31-3. The hymn *Jesu redemptor omnium*, first stanza.[1]

Cavazzoni assigns the first phrase of the melody to the lowest voice (mm. 5–11), anticipating it with a point of imitation. After a two-measure interlude, the same voice picks up the second phrase in measure 13; but after having its first seven notes quoted clearly enough, the chant melody seems to vanish, not to appear again until the third beat of measure 20, where the third phrase now enters in the bass. The fourth and final phrase (in musical terms, a repeat of the first) gets under way at measure 25: after the lower voices hint at the melody in imitative fashion, the chant finally rings out clearly in the top voice.

Cavazzoni's hymn can stand as a model for the various ways organists treated plainsong melodies: cantus-firmus-like statements alternate with paraphrase technique, which at times seems to melt into passages so free that there is little more than a hint of the chant melody; likewise, points of imitation alternate with free, toccata-like passages; and always, voices duck in and out with a sense of freedom that became one of the chief characteristics of keyboard music in general. Cavazzoni's setting takes us a step closer to a truly idiomatic keyboard style, characterized not only by the long tradition of rapid passage work and ornamentation, but by a textural freedom that has broken away from the strict part-writing of music conceived for voices.

VARIATIONS

The idea of variation technique was not new to the sixteenth century. Recall, for instance, the melodic relationships that unify the upper voices from one talea to the next in Du Fay's *Nuper rosarum flores* (Chapter 7). What was new—and it was a corollary of the growing independence of instrumental music—was the formalizing of variation technique: the idea of variation as a form- or structure-defining compositional principle. And though the variation principle may have produced its first true masterpieces only in the works of the English virginalists around 1600, it got off the ground in Spain and Italy during the century's second quarter.

Two Sets of Spanish Variations

Sixteenth-century variations followed one of two procedures: either each variation was a self-enclosed entity, or the variations ran on continuously. We can see both types in works for vihuela and keyboard by Luys de Narváez and Antonio de Cabezón, respectively.

1. *Liber usualis*, 365.

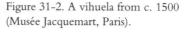

Figure 31-2. A vihuela from c. 1500
(Musée Jacquemart, Paris).

The vihuela was the Spanish counterpart to the lute. Like the lute, it had six courses, tuned at intervals of 4th-4th-3rd-4th-4th, and its music was notated in a tablature system. Where it differed from the lute was in its shape (Fig. 31-2), most significantly in its flat back, slightly indented waist, and pegbox that angled back only slightly. It actually looked more like a guitar.

Beginning in 1536 with Luis de Milán's *Libro de música de vihuela de mano. Intitulado El maestro* (Valencia, 1536), Spanish vihuelists turned out six great collections of music for the instrument. Among their special features are some of the earliest examples of tempo indications: "apriessa" (hurried), "espacio" (slowly). The vihuela was for many decades the favorite instrument of Spanish courtly culture, but its popularity began to wane around the end of the century, as it came to be overshadowed by the guitar. Its demise was lamented by the Spanish lexicographer Sebastian Covarrubias:

> This instrument has been highly esteemed until the present time, and it has had excellent players; but since the invention of the guitar, only very few people give themselves to the study of the vihuela. It has been a great loss, because on it one could put all kinds of notated music, and now, the guitar is nothing more than a harness bell, so easy to play, especially in the strummed style, that there isn't a stable boy who isn't a guitarist.[2]

SELF-ENCLOSED VARIATIONS BY NARVÁEZ Variations—or *diferencias*, as the Spanish called them—make what is perhaps their first full-fledged appearance

2. In his *Tesoro de la lengua Castellana o Española* (Madrid, 1611); quoted after Griffiths, "At Court and at Home with the *Vihuela de mano*," 26.

in Luys de Narváez's *Los seys libros del Delphin de musica* of 1538. One well-known set of variations in the collection is based on the *ground* that was known in Spain as *Guárdame las vacas* or, as it came to be called (both in Spain and elsewhere), the *romanesca* (*Anthology* 71). Example 31-4 illustrates the *romanesca*.

EXAMPLE 31-4. The *romanesca* pattern.

| III | VII | i | V | III | VII | i | V | i |

In *Guárdame*, Narváez wrote four self-enclosed variations on the "theme," the underlying *romanesca* pattern itself. Though the self-enclosed character of each variation imposes a certain static quality on the work, the intensity mounts with each successive variation: the rhythmic activity increases; the range expands; the texture becomes more complicated; the third and fourth variations are double variations, as they vary each half of the ground; and the coda of the final variation packs a bit of a punch.

CONTINUOUS VARIATIONS BY CABEZÓN   Antonio de Cabezón (1510–1566) was sixteenth-century Spain's most famous composer for the keyboard. He too was drawn to *Guárdame*, and his posthumous *Obras de música para tecla, arpa y vihuela de Antonio de Cabezón*, published by his son Hernando in 1578, includes three sets of *Diferencias sobre las vacas*. The last of these (*Anthology* 72) can serve as an example of the technique of continuous variations.

Cabezón stretches out the *romanesca* chord progression over a twenty-four-measure period, clearly divided into two parts, and states it without interruption four times: measures 1, 25, 49, and 73. The seams between the variations are covered skillfully, as the end of one variation—the final eleven beats—functions as an upbeat to the next. But the upbeats serve more than a rhythmic purpose: they also introduce a melodic motive that will figure prominently in the first half of the following variation. The clearest instance of this occurs at the juncture of variations 3 and 4; here the ascending scales that constitute the main melodic material of the first half of variation 4 (beginning at m. 73) already get under way above the final tonic of variation 3 (m. 70).

It is not only with his imaginative inter-variation bridges that Cabezón impresses us. Each statement of the *Guárdame* ground is varied in a dazzling way; there is not a single unvaried statement of even the bass pattern. And the consistency with which short motives are thrown back and forth between the voices, often in *stretto*, makes that as much what the piece is all about as the variation technique itself.

Finally, as in Narváez's variations, there is a gradual buildup of intensity as one variation follows the other. Thus even in the formative stages of the variation tradition, composers sought to balance the inherent stasis of the genre (constant repetition) with a sense of overall dynamic growth. And therein, no doubt, lies the great appeal of variation sets: they offer the listener a structure that is at once both dynamic and relatively uncomplicated.

PERFORMANCE PRACTICE

We live in a period in which the printed note rules, at least in the realm of "classical" music. Sixteenth-century musicians, on the other hand, were less uptight. Whether instrumentalists or singers, soloists or members of ensembles, they embellished the written music in front of them. The evidence is overwhelming.

The Tutors

The decades between the mid-1530s and the end of the century produced more than a dozen tutors/treatises that provide instruction on how to improvise ornamentation. Some were written by and intended for instrumentalists, others by and for singers; they all make it clear that ornamentation was commonplace and that there was a stock of ornamental clichés common to both singers and instrumentalists.

We will look at ornamentation as it is discussed in four tutors. In 1535, Silvestro di Ganassi (1492–c. 1550), a viol and recorder player in the employ of the Republic of Venice, published his *Opera intitulata Fontegara*. The title page makes explicit that while the volume was intended primarily for flute players, the tables of ornaments could be used by all instrumentalists as well as singers:

Opera intitulate Fontegara / La quale insegna a sonare il flauto chon tutta l'arte opportuna a esso instrumento / massime il diminuire il quale sara utile ad ogni instrumento di fiato et chorde: et anchora a / chi si dileta di canto.	Work entitled Fontegara, which teaches how to play the flute, with all the art available to this instrument, especially the [art of] diminution, which will be useful on any wind or string instrument, as well as for those who delight in singing.

"Diminution" was one of the terms—another was "division"—that would mean ornamentation and embellishment for the next two hundred years.

In 1553, the Spanish viol player Diego Ortiz (c. 1510–c. 1570), then *maestro de capilla* of the Spanish Viceroy of Naples, published his *Tratado de glosas sobre clausulas . . .* (at Rome). In addition to the Ganassi-style tables of ornaments, Ortiz gave copious music examples in which he embellished well-known compositions of the day.

The same broad coverage described on the title page of Ganassi's tutor is also advertised on that of *Il vero modo di diminuir, con tutte le sorti di stromenti, di fiato, & corda, & di voce humana* (Venice, 1583) by Girolamo Dalla Casa (d. 1601), who, with his two brothers, was a member of the first permanent instrumental ensemble at St. Mark's in Venice, formed in 1568. Our fourth tutor, *Il transil-*

vano (1594), for organists and other keyboard players, was written by Girolamo Diruta (c. 1554–after 1610), organist at the Cathedral of Chioggia, a small town across the lagoon from Venice.

The Style of Ornamentation

The tutors provide three different categories of ornaments: (1) embellishments for single notes, (2) decorations that fill in intervals between notes, and (3) ornamented versions of the top voice part of entire compositions.

Example 31-5, taken from Diruta, illustrates the two most common manners of ornamenting a single note. The *tremolo* (or *mordant*, as the Germans called it) is nothing more than a trill between the main note and an upper or lower note, whether a half step, whole step, or even a third. The *groppo* is a cadential ornament on the leading tone.

EXAMPLE 31-5. Diruta, *Il transilvano*: (a) *tremoli* and (b) *groppi*.

Though ornaments on a single note may have been the type of embellishment most frequently employed (they required the least amount of skill), the tutors pay far greater attention to the so-called *passagi*: melodic formulas that broke up sustained notes into rapid shorter ones and that connected one note to the next. Example 31-6 shows some of the ways in which Ortiz and Ganassi suggest ornamenting two semibreves a whole tone apart:

EXAMPLE 31-6. *Passagi* on semibreves a whole tone apart: (a) Ortiz and
(b) Ganassi.

Some tutors applied ornaments to real pieces of music. Thus Dalla Casa
shows how the superius of a madrigal by Alessandro Striggio, *Anchor ch'io possa
dire* (1566), can be turned into a virtuoso showstopper (Ex. 31-7):

EXAMPLE 31-7. *Anchor ch'io possa dire*, superius, mm. 1–8: (a) Striggio's
original; (b) Dalla Casa's ornamented version.

Presumably, the addition of such ornamentation meant that the madrigal was performed by a solo voice with a keyboard accompaniment. In effect, it turns a piece conceived for an all-vocal ensemble into an accompanied song.

It is out of this tradition of improvised ornamentation that the profusely decorated keyboard arrangements of vocal models no doubt grew. While the tutors are certainly handy, we can probably learn the lesson just as well from a piece such as Merulo's arrangement of Lassus's *Susanne un jour* (Ex. 31-2). The line between "improvisation" and "composition" has always been difficult to draw.

The Church Organist and Improvisation

If the art of embellishment and improvisation was part and parcel of every good musician's bag of tricks, it formed the very lifeblood of the church organist's art. Just how important a skill improvisation was can be appreciated from the audition requirements for the post of second organist at St. Mark's in 1541:

1. Opening a choirbook and finding at random the beginning of a Kyrie or a motet, one copies this and gives it to the competing organist. The latter must, at the organ, improvise a piece in a regular fashion, without mixing up the parts, just as if four singers were performing.
2. Opening a book of plainchant equally at random, one copies a cantus firmus from an introit or another chant, and sends it to the said organist. He must improvise on it, deriving the three other parts [from it]; he must put the cantus firmus now in the bass, now in the tenor, now in the alto and soprano, deriving imitative counterpoint from it, not simple accompaniments.[3]

What is striking is the sophisticated level of improvisation that was required: a full, four-part, imitative piece known by the 1540s as a ricercar. Further, the piece was to be improvised in two ways: by keeping a chant melody going as a cantus firmus in one or another voice from beginning to end, and by essentially completing a composition begun by someone else. In other words, the successful candidate—in this instance, the Flemish composer-organist Jacques Buus—had to be able to do more than just doodle.

THE RICERCAR

In broad terms, the development of the ricercar (also called *fantasia* and, in Spain, *tiento*) went through three phases. As we saw in Chapter 25, the ricercar

3. Quoted after Haar, "The *Fantasie et recerchari* of Giuliano Tiburtino," 235.

first emerged in the lute books published by Petrucci during the first decade of the sixteenth century. Example 31-8 gives one of the ricercars in its entirety from the 1509 collection by Franciscus Bossinensis:

EXAMPLE 31-8. Franciscus Bossinensis, *Ricercar* No. 6, from *Tenori e contrabassi . . . libro I* (1508).

The early ricercar, then, was a rather slight, improvisatory-sounding piece that consisted largely of passage work punctuated by chords. Even its function was without pretense, as it often did nothing more than set up (in which case it established the mode) or follow a more substantial composition. This tradition continued into the 1520s.

Francesco Canova da Milano

The ricercar began to change during the 1530s. And most prominent among those who effected the change was Francesco Canova da Milano (1497–1543), the most famous and prolific lutenist of the first half of the sixteenth century and one of the first native-Italian musicians to enjoy a truly international reputation. Born in Monza (near Milan) and trained at the Mantuan court of Isabella d'Este, Francesco spent the greater part of his career at Rome, where he was employed by the highest dignitaries of the church.

We can see the change in style in a posthumously published (1548) *Fantasia* by Francesco (*Anthology* 73). What are striking here are the sharply defined motives that are worked out imitatively (mm. 1–3, 9–10, 12, 13–15, and 16–17). To be sure, the imitation is neither systematic nor structural. But it has laid its claim to being one of the ricercar's defining style characteristics.

The Imitative Ricercar

The ricercar became a thoroughly imitative piece—and thus the first instrumental genre to be based on the systematic use of imitation—with the ricercars intended for instrumental ensemble and published in the collection entitled *Musica nova* in 1540 (not to be confused with Willaert's *Musica nova* of 1559). *Anthology* 74 presents one of thirteen ricercars by the best-represented composer in the collection, Julio Segni da Modena (1498–1561). Here, imitation is the underlying principle; it forms the essence of the piece and defines its shape. It is as persistent as the imitation in the motets of Gombert, Clemens, and Willaert, and there can be little doubt that the impetus for the imitative ricercar came from an attempt to transfer the contrapuntal style of the motet to an instrumental idiom.

There are, however, important differences in the ways in which the ricercar and motet treat their imitation. In a motet, each point of imitation is based on a new motive and generally has about as many entries as there are voice parts; nonimitative writing usually follows and leads to a cadence, at which spot a new point of imitation gets under way. In Segni's ricercar, the points of imitation are worked over far more insistently; for example, the motive that opens the four-voice piece is stated fourteen times through the downbeat of measure 18. The imitative instrumental ricercar thus operates according to its own independent, non-word-related procedures.

Though the ricercars in *Musica nova* were conceived for an instrumental ensemble, and though the collection is printed in partbooks (one for each player), the full title of the volume reminds us that instruments and voices, ensembles and soloists, social gatherings and liturgical services could all share the same repertory: "Musica nova accommodata per cantar et sonar sopra organi; et altri strumenti." The ricercars, then, were considered suitable for singers, who undoubtedly sang the music either with solmization syllables or with something akin to "la, la, la." Likewise, the ricercars were appropriate for organists, who would have scored them up (or written them out in tablature, read from the four partbooks simultaneously, or played them by ear) and used them in church as an accompaniment to the liturgy.

With the *Musica nova*, the imitative ricercar became the genre's standard, and the use of imitation quickly spilled over to ricercars composed for keyboard and lute. A good example of a ricercar for lute can be found in *Intabulatura . . . transilvani coronensis*, by the Romanian lutenist Valentin Bakfark (1507–1576), printed by Jacques Moderne in 1553 (Ex. 31–9):

EXAMPLE 31-9. Bakfark, *Ricercar*, mm. 1–27.

It is some of the most elegant lute music of the time.

A Note on Terminology

The Italian verb *ricercare* means "to seek out" or "to search out." What was the ricercar looking for? We usually associate the search with the working out of the imitative possibilities inherent in the subject or, keeping in mind the ricercar's often-preludial function, the modal or thematic links with the piece it introduced. But sixteenth-century musicians might have answered the question in terms of rhetorical devices. For instance, when Felice Figliucci translated Aristotle's *Rhetoric* (c. 336 B.C.) into Italian in 1548, he rendered the passage dealing with the *proem*—the beginning of the speech—as follows:

> The proem is the beginning of the oration . . . like that first touching of the strings in lyre playing. And especially the proems of epideictic orations are similar to the ricercars of the instrumentalists before they begin to play, since they, when they must play some good dance, first run over the frets of the strings which prevail in the dance they intend to play.[4]

The ricercar was thus like a *proem* (or *exordium*, as Cicero called the device in 90 B.C.): it set up the proper tonality of the piece that followed. For the sixteenth-century ear, there was more to analyzing music—even wordless music—than keeping track of dissonance treatment, cadential formulas, and the like. For some listeners, music—even a ricercar—was nothing less than a manner of speech.

THE CANZONA

Like the ricercar, the *canzona* went through three phases of development. But whereas each stylistic phase of the ricercar supplanted the one before it,

---

4. Kirkendale, "Ciceronians versus Aristotelians," on which the discussion is based.

the various phases of the canzona piled up on one another and coexisted. Thus by the final quarter of the century, the term "canzona" could be applied to three different kinds of pieces.

Faithful Transcription

Had the keyboard version of Claudin's *Jatens secours* (Ex. 31-1) been published in Italy, it would probably have been called a canzona (as was Merulo's arrangement of Lassus's chanson) or, specifically, since the model was a French chanson, a *canzone alla francese*. In its most elemental guise, then, the canzona was simply an arrangement of a secular song, usually a French chanson, and most often for keyboard (but eventually for ensemble as well). And such canzonas continued to be written right up to the last years of the century.

A Transitional Phase

In 1543, Girolamo Cavazzoni took the first step in loosening the ties between vocal chanson and instrumental canzona in his *Intavolatura . . . recercari canzoni himni magnificati*. Included in the collection were keyboard arrangements of Josquin's *Faulte d'argent (Anthology* 50) and Passereau's *Il est bel et bon (Anthology* 64). But these were no faithful transcriptions. Rather, Cavazzoni reworked his models to the extent that model and arrangement hardly share a measure in common. In effect, Cavazzoni treated his model as would a composer who was using it as the basis of a parody Mass.

Independent Compositions

During the final quarter of the century, the canzona began to cast off its vocal models altogether. Whether composed for ensemble (in which case it might be called a *canzone da sonar*) or for keyboard, the canzona became an independent piece.

For an example of the genre, we may turn to the little-known composer Vincenzo Pellegrini (c. 1560–c. 1631/32), whose *Canzon detta la Serpentina (Anthology* 75) was published in his *Canzoni de intavolatura d'organo fatte alla francese* (Venice, 1599). Though freely composed, *La Serpentina* still betrays the canzona's origins in the French chanson with its lively rhythm (including the characteristic dactylic motive at the beginning) and the contrasting sections, here **A B C A′ B′ C.** In fact, the canzona's sections are clearly differentiated not only thematically but by changes in both meter and texture. *La Serpentina* also contains a good deal of imitation, a trait that sometimes blurred the distinction between canzona and ricercar.

PRELUDES AND TOCCATAS

Standing at the other end of the stylistic spectrum from the imitative ricercar and the bouncy canzona were two genres that grew out of the quasi-rhapsodic improvisatory practices of keyboard players: the *intonazione* and the toccata.

The *Intonazione*

Intended for use in the liturgy, the *intonazione* (intonation) developed out of a long-standing tradition in which church organists improvised a short prelude in order to establish for the choir singers both the pitch and the mode of the chant they were to sing. One of the most famous collections of such pieces is the 1593 *Intonationi d'organo di Andrea Gabrieli et di Gio[vanni] suo nepote . . .* , which includes intonations for each mode by both Andrea Gabrieli and his nephew Giovanni. Example 31-10 provides the whole of Andrea's intonation *del secondo tono* (second tone, on D), which he transposed to G. Giovanni's contributions are even shorter, usually running between five and eight measures.

EXAMPLE 31-10. Andrea Gabrieli, *Intonatione del secondo tono.*

ANDREA GABRIELI   Though he is overshadowed today by his brilliant, innovative nephew Giovanni (c. 1553/56–1612), who was to play a vital role in the development of the early Baroque style, Andrea Gabrieli (c. 1510–1586) was an important musician in his own right. Organist at St. Mark's from 1566 until his death, and a close friend of Lassus, whom he met while in Germany during the early 1560s and whose dramatic motet style had a direct influence on his own sacred compositions, Andrea was one of the musicians who made Venice a hotbed of progressivism, in both vocal and instrumental music. But perhaps it was as a teacher that he was most important. Aside from his nephew, his students included the Italian theorist Ludovico Zacconi (1555–1627), as well as the important German composer-organists Gregor Aichinger and Hans Leo Hassler (1562–1612). Gabrieli's contact with students from Germany is particularly significant, as it spawned a number of associations between musicians from Venice (and northern Italy in general) and Germany/Austria, none more telling for the eventual spread of the Venetian brand of early Baroque style in Germany than that between Giovanni Gabrieli and Heinrich Schütz during the years 1609–12.

The Toccata

In Book III of his *Syntagma musicum* (1619), Michael Praetorius likened the toccata to

> a praeambulum or praeludium, which an organist, starting to play . . . improvises out of his head before he commences a motet or fugue, consisting of simple single chords and coloratura passages. . . . They are named "toccata" by the Italians because . . . [they] say "Toccate un poco" which means: "Strike the instrument" or "Touch the clavichord a little." Thus a toccata may be named a touching or handling of the clavichord.[5]

The toccata, then, at least when played as part of the church service, served a prelude-like function and grew out of a tradition of improvisation.

Although the term "tochata" occurs for the first time in a lute tablature of 1536, it was only toward the end of the century that the genre came into its own, and then mainly at the hands of organists active at St. Mark's, of whom the most brilliant was Claudio Merulo (1533–1604). Merulo's two volumes of toccatas (published in 1598 and 1604) brought the genre to the peak of its late-sixteenth-century development. *Anthology* 76 is one of the pieces from his 1604 collection. As one would expect, there is the usual dazzling passage work over sustained chords, here spiced up with dissonances both prepared (as suspensions) and unprepared. But Merulo broke new ground by expanding the toccata into a broad, multisectional piece, in this instance an **A B A'**-like form: **A** is in an improvisatory toccata style (mm. 1–33), **B** switches to an imitative ricercar style on three different subjects (mm. 33–89), and **A'** returns to the improvisatory toccata style with a reaffirmation of the tonic and a slowing down of the harmonic rhythm, leading to a brilliant, coda-like climax (mm. 90–125).

5. Quoted after Valentin, *The Toccata*, 3.

DANCE MUSIC

The years from 1530 and the publication of Attaingnant's *Dixhuit basses dances* . . . (for solo lute) to 1599 and the second edition of Valentin Haussmann's *Neue artige und liebliche Täntze* (for four-part ensemble) witnessed the publication of a voluminous amount of dance music, though we can only wonder how much of it was actually used for dancing. Certainly, the myriad dance pieces issued for lute and keyboard were stylized arrangements that never saw the inside of a ballroom. On the other hand, the many collections of dance music published in partbook format and thus presumably intended for ensembles probably do record repertory played by sixteenth-century dance bands.

A Pavan-Galliard Pair by Claude Gervaise

We can probably catch a glimpse of real dance music in Claude Gervaise's five-part *Pavane d'Angleterre* and the *galliard* that followed it in the paired, thematically related slow dance–fast dance fashion of the time (*Anthology* 77).[6] The piece, published by Attaingnant in 1555, raises many questions for which there are no certain answers.

(1) Is this an original composition by Gervaise, or did he merely arrange what might have been a popular dance tune of the day?

(2) What instruments would have played the piece? The contratenor (middle voice) partbook of the copy of Attaingnant's print preserved at the Bibliothèque National in Paris has the following sixteenth-century, handwritten inscription at the beginning of the preceding piece: "Qui est fait bonne pour les violons."[7] Did members of the violin family, which had particularly close associations with dance music, therefore take part?

(3) Even with all the repeats, and with the stately pavan at the stateliest of tempos, the pair as a whole takes no more than about two minutes to perform. What happened after that: was the music played over and over, or were two minutes an eternity on the dance floor?

(4) And finally, how far down the social ladder would a Gervaise pavan-galliard have gone? As we can see from Pieter Brueghel's famous *Peasants' Dance* (on the cover), those on the lower socioeconomic rungs probably made do without the courtly pavan in general and without Claude Gervaise in particular.

The Choreography

Thanks to the survival of a number of dance manuals from the final twenty years of the century, we have a rather good idea of the dance steps themselves and how they worked in conjunction with the music.

The most useful of the manuals is Thoinot Arbeau's *Orchésographie*, written in the form of a dialogue and published in 1588. Arbeau describes a wide range

---

6. The English spelling is generally "pavan" and "galliard"; the French is "pavane" and "gaillarde."

7. Heartz, *Pierre Attaingnant*, 373.

of social dances, and, by means of diagrams and illustrations, shows how the steps and the music go together. He also gives such weighty advice as "Spit and blow your nose sparingly" and "Kiss [your] mistresses . . . to ascertain if they . . . emit an unpleasant odour as of bad meat."

About the pavan, Arbeau says that it "is easy to dance, consisting merely of two single steps and one double step forward, [followed by] two single steps and one double step backward. It is played in duple time; note that the forward steps begin on the left foot and the backward steps begin on the right foot."[8] He goes on to suggest that the pavan could be played on "viols, spinets, transverse flutes, and flutes with nine holes [recorders], haut boys," and that it could be used as a wedding march or "when musicians head a procession of . . . some notable guild." He also mentions that dance music could be sung.

In his *Plaine and Easie Introduction* (1597), Thomas Morley notes that the pavan is

> a kind of staid music ordained for grave dancing and most commonly made of three strains, whereof every strain is played . . . twice; a strain they make to contain eight, twelve, or sixteen semibreves . . . fewer than eight I have not seen in any Pavan. In this you may not so much insist in following the point as in a Fantasy. . . . Also in this you must cast your music by four, so that if you keep that rule it is no matter how many fours you put in your strain for it will fall out well enough in the end.

Gervaise's pavan fits the descriptions perfectly: duple meter, three strains of 8 + 8 + 16 semibreves (including the final breve of each strain), and homophonic texture (no "points" of imitation).

The galliard was more demanding; in fact, it provided a good aerobic workout (Fig. 31-3). The dance was done to a variation of the so-called *cinque pas* (five steps) spread out over six beats (one beat = one half note in the edition): on beats 1–4, dancers took four steps (one to a beat, each called a *grue* and consisting of jumping onto the ball of one foot while kicking the other forward in the air); on beat 5, they took one big leap (the *saut majeur*, with legs flailing in midair), resting on the leg on which they landed for beat 6 (the *posture*).

Morley adds:

> After every Pavan we usually set a Galliard (that is a kind of music made out of the other), causing it to go by a measure which the learned call "trochaicam rationem" [triple meter], consisting of a long and short stroke successively . . . the first being in time of a semibreve and the latter of a minim. This is a lighter and more stirring kind of dancing than the Pavan, consisting of the same number of strains; and look how many fours of semibreves you put in the strain of your Pavan, so many times six minims you must put in the strain of your Galliard.

And again, Gervaise's galliard is on the mark: triple meter, thematically related to ("made out of") the pavan, the same number of strains, and with the number of semibreves per strain standing in a 3:2 relationship to that of the pavan.

8. *New Grove*, 14:311.

Figure 31-3. Hans Hofer,
woodcut showing a couple
dancing a galliard, c. 1540.

Dancing and dance music were everywhere. And if Brueghel's peasants did
not take their dancing quite as seriously as did the members of courtly society
(for whom it counted, along with such activities as fencing practice, as part of
the daily routine) and their middle-class imitators, they might still have sub-
scribed to the sentiments expressed in John Davies's *Orchestra, a Poem of Dancing*
(c. 1594):

> Dancing, bright lady, then began to be
> When the first seeds whereof the world did spring,
>   The fire air earth and water, did agree
> By Love's persuasion, nature's mighty king
> To leave their first disorder'd combatting
> And in a dance such measure to observe
> As all the world their motion should preserve.

The instrumental music of the period 1525–1600 set out boldly in new
directions. To see how boldly, consider this: Mozart and Ciconia stand approximately equidistant from Merulo's toccatas; Mozart would have taken
Merulo in stride; Ciconia might not have believed his ears. Whether we think
in terms of genres, formal patterns, or compositional processes, our idea of what
constitutes instrumental music first becomes recognizable in the sixteenth cen-

tury. And as it would continue to do for at least another century, Italy led the way.

BIBLIOGRAPHICAL NOTE

There is a good complement to this chapter in Tim Carter, *Music in Late Renaissance and Early Baroque Italy* (Portland: Amadeus Press, 1992), chapter 10.

Individual Instruments

Keyboard: there is still no more comprehensive study than Willi Apel's *History of Keyboard Music to 1700*, trans. and rev. Hans Tischler (Bloomington: Indiana University Press, 1972); see also Alexander Silbiger, *Keyboard Music before 1700* (New York: Schirmer, 1995); the dozens of volumes in the series *CEKM*, which contain editions of composers great and not so great, are indispensable. **Lute**: no single study wraps up the lute music of the period tidily; yet one can pretend to take period lute lessons with Julia Sutton, "The Lute Instructions of Jean-Baptiste Besard," *MQ* 51 (1965): 345–63; for three representative editions of lutenists, see Arthur J. Ness, *The Lute Music of Francesco Canova da Milan (1497–1593)*, Harvard Publications in Music 3–4 (Cambridge: Harvard University Press, 1970), Jean-Michel Vaccaro, *Albert de Rippe: Oeuvres* (Paris: Centre Nationale de la Recherche Scientifique, 1972–75), and Istvan Homolya and Daniel Benkö, *Bálint Bakfark: Opera omnia* (Budapest: Editio Musica, 1976). **Vihuela**: a wonderful introduction to the instrument is John Griffiths, "At Court and at Home with the *Vihuela da mano*: Current Perspectives on the Instrument, Its Music, and Its World," *JLSA* 22 (1989): 1–26; *Luis de Milán: El Maestro*, ed. Charles Jacobs (University Park: Penn State University Press 1971); *Luys de Narváez: Los seys libros del Delphin*, *MME* III, ed. Emilio Pujol (Barcelona: Consejo Superior de Investigaciones Científicas, 1945); *Miguel de Fuenllana: Orphenica Lyra*, ed. Charles Jacobs (Oxford: Oxford University Press, 1978). **Guitar**: James Tyler, *The Early Guitar* (London: Oxford University Press, 1976). **Instrumental ensembles**: for those who can manage the German, Dietrich Kämper's *Studien zur instrumentalen Ensemblemusik des 16. Jahrhunderts in Italien*, *AnMc* 10 (Cologne and Vienna: Böhlau, 1970), provides a comprehensive survey (there is an Italian translation by Lorenzo Bianconi, *La musica strumentale nel Rinascimento* [Turin: ERI, 1976]); of major importance are the thirty volumes of *Italian Instrumental Music of the Sixteenth and Early Seventeenth Centuries*, ed. James Ladewig (New York: Garland, 1987–).

Transcriptions Based on Vocal Models

There is a fine introduction on the general practice of basing instrumental music (regardless of genre) on vocal models in John Ward, "The Use of Borrowed Material in 16th-Century Instrumental Music," *JAMS* 5 (1952): 88–98; for a selection of the keyboard arrangements published by Attaingnant, see Albert Seay, *Pierre Attaingnant: Transcriptions of Chansons for Keyboard*, *CMM* 20 (American Institute of Musicology, 1961), and Yvonne Rokseth, *Treize Motets et un Prélude pour orgue parus chez Pierre Attaingnant en 1531* (Paris: Société Française de Musicologie, 1930).

Settings of Chant Melodies

Apel's *History of Keyboard Music* (see above) is a good starting place; the role of the organ in the liturgy is discussed in Benjamin Van Wye, "Ritual Use of the Organ in France," *JAMS* 33 (1980): 287–325; for an edition of Girolamo Cavazzoni, see Oscar Mischiati, ed., *G. Cavazzoni: Orgelwerke* (Mainz: B. Schott, 1959–61).

Variations

Imogene Horsley, "The 16th-Century Variation: A New Historical Survey," *JAMS* 12 (1959): 118–32; Robert U. Nelson, *The Technique of Variation: A Study of the Instrumental*

Variation from Antonio de Cabezón to Max Reger (Berkeley and Los Angeles: University of California Press, 1948); Cabezón's *diferencias* are included in *The Collected Works of Antonio de Cabezón*, ed. Charles Jacobs (Brooklyn: Institute of Mediaeval Music, 1967–86).

Ricercar and Canzona

There is a succinct summary of the ricercar's development in H. Colin Slim's *Musica Nova, MRM* I (Chicago: Chicago University Press, 1964), which contains a complete edition and historical study of the 1540 print; see also Warren Kirkendale, "Ciceronians versus Aristotelians on the Ricercar as Exordium," *JAMS* 32 (1979): 1–44; the entire issue of *JLSA* 22 (1990) is devoted to the "fantasia," especially as it was cultivated for the lute.

The studies by Apel and Kämper cited above provide the best introductions to the keyboard and ensemble canzonas, respectively; there is an interesting article by Robert Judd, "Repeat Problems in Keyboard Settings of *Canzoni alla francese*," *EM* 17 (1989): 198–214. **A. Gabrieli**: *Ricercari für Orgel, Canzoni alla francese*, and *Canzonen und ricercari ariosi*, ed. Pierre Pidoux (Kassel: Bärenreiter, 1952, 1953, 1961); a new edition of Gabrieli's works is now in progress, published by G. Ricordi; in addition, there is an entire volume of essays, a number of which are in English: Francesco Degrada, *Andrea Gabrieli e il suo tempo: Atti del convegno internazionale (Venezia 16–18 settembre 1985)* (Florence: Olschki, 1987). **Merulo**: *Canzonen (1592)*, ed. Pierre Pidoux (Kassel: Bärenreiter, 1941); *Canzoni d'intavolatura d'organo, PRMR* 90–91, ed. Walker Cunningham and Charles McDermott (Madison: A-R Editions, 1992); the *Collected Keyboard Compositions*, ed. Robert Judd, is now in preparation for inclusion in the *CEKM* series (American Institute of Musicology).

Preludes and Toccatas

Murray C. Bradshaw, *The Origin of the Toccata*, MSD 28 (American Institute of Musicology, 1972), and "Andrea Gabrieli and the Early History of the Toccata," in *Andrea Gabrieli e il suo tempo* (see above); for editions, Erich Valentin's *The Toccata* (Cologne: Arno Volk, 1958) contains a nice selection of sixteenth-century toccatas. **A. Gabrieli**: the intonations are edited in *Intonazionen für Orgel*, ed. Pierre Pidoux (Kassel: Bärenreiter, 1971). **Merulo**: *Toccate per organo*, ed. S. Dalla Libera (Milan: Ricordi, 1959).

Dance Music

Though dated in some respects, Curt Sachs's *World History of the Dance* (New York: Norton, 1937) presents a readable overview; on the problem of reconstructing dances from the contemporary manuals, see Yvonne Kendall, "Rhythm, Meter, and *Tactus* in 16th-Century Italian Court Dance: Reconstruction from a Theoretical Base," *DR* 8 (1990): 3–27. Two editions of dance music: Daniel Heartz, *Keyboard Dances from the Earlier Sixteenth Century*, CEKM 8 (American Institute of Musicology, 1965), and Henry Expert, *Claude Gervaise, Estienne du Tertre, et anonymes: Danceries*, MMRF 23 (Paris: Leduc, 1908); Arbeau's *Orchésographie* is available in an English translation by Mary Stewart Evans (New York: Dover, 1967). Two videotapes are useful: *Il ballarino (The Dancing Master): The Art of Renaissance Dance*, dir. Julia Sutton and Johannes Holub (Pennington, N.J.: Princeton Book, 1991), and *Le gratie d'amore (The Graces of Love): European Dance of the Late Renaissance*, Court Dance Company of New York (New York: Historical Dance Foundation, 1992).

Improvisation and Ornamentation

The best starting point is Howard Mayer Brown, *Embellishing Sixteenth-Century Music* (London: Oxford University Press, 1976); see also Timothy J. McGee, *Medieval and Renaissance Music: A Performer's Guide* (Toronto: Toronto University Press, 1985); Carol Mac-Clintock, *Readings in the History of Music in Performance* (Bloomington: Indiana University Press, 1979); Ernst T. Ferand, "Improvised Vocal Counterpoint in the Late Renaissance and Early Baroque," *AnnM* 4 (1956): 129–74, and "Didactic Embellishment Literature in the

Late Renaissance: A Survey of Sources," in *Aspects of Medieval and Renaissance Music: A Birthday Offering to Gustave Reese*, ed. Jan LaRue (New York: Norton, 1966), 154–72, which presents a complete list of ornamentation manuals for the period 1535–1688; Imogene Horsley, "Improvised Embellishment in the Performance of Renaissance Polyphonic Music," *JAMS* 4 (1951): 3–19; for an anthology of music with contemporary, written-out embellishments, see Ferand's *Improvisation* (Cologne: Arno Volk, 1956). A number of the important tutors are available in English translation or in facsimile: Dalla Casa—*Il vero modo di diminuir* (Bologna: Forni, 1970); Diruta—*Il transilvano* (Bologna: Forni, 1969); Ganassi—tr. Dorothy Swainson (Berlin: Leinav, 1959); Ortiz—*Trattado de Glosas* (Kassel: Bärenreiter, 1967); Thomas de Sancta Maria—Almonte C. Howell and Warren E. Hultberg, *The Art of Playing the Fantasia* (Pittsburgh: Latin American Literary Review Press, 1991).

Bibliographical Tools

Howard Mayer Brown's *Instrumental Music Printed Before 1600: A Bibliography* (Cambridge: Harvard University Press, 1965) catalogues all printed instrumental collections in detail; Wolfgang Boetticher's *Katalog der Handschriften in Lauten- und Gitarren-tabulatur des 16.–18. Jahrhunderts*, *RISM* B VII (Munich: G. Henle, 1978), catalogues manuscripts of lute and guitar music.

Also Cited

James Haar, "The *Fantasie et recerchari* of Giuliano Tiburtino," *MQ* 59 (1973): 223–38; Daniel Heartz, *Pierre Attaingnant, Royal Printer of Music: A Historical Study and Bibliographical Catalogue* (Berkeley and Los Angeles: University of California Press, 1969).

CHAPTER 32

Intermedio: 1543–1547

ADVANCES IN SCIENCE

It seems safe to say that the origins of modern science fall roughly into the period between the death of Leonardo da Vinci (himself no mean observer of the natural world) in 1519 and the maturity of Galileo Galilei (1564–1642) around the beginning of the seventeenth century. New ideas about humankind, nature, and the relationship between the two seemed to spring up everywhere. And whether they dealt with anatomy or zoology, with how people caught a cold or how the universe worked, people were, as the physician Jean Fernel put it in 1548, "witness to the triumph of [a] New Age."[1]

The year 1543 was especially productive, as it witnessed the publication of epoch-making works in both the physical and biological sciences: Copernicus's on the solar system and Vesalius's on human anatomy, both of which, in one of those quirks of history, overturned theories first developed in second-century Alexandria.

Copernicus

It was only as he lay on his deathbed in 1543 that the Polish astronomer and priest Nicolaus Copernicus (1473–1543) saw a copy of his newly published *De revolutionibus orbium celestium* (Concerning the Revolution of the Celestial Spheres). Here Copernicus took issue with the Aristotelian-Ptolemaic idea that the earth stood still at the center of the universe (geocentrism). Rather, Copernicus theorized (he himself did little observation), it was the sun that stood at the center of things, while the earth and the other planets revolved around both it (heliocentrism) and their own axes. Though Copernicus's views did not go unchallenged, they were upheld once and for all by Johannes Kepler (1571–1630), who, with the aid of the newly invented telescope (developed in Holland during the first decade of the seventeenth century), fine-tuned Copernicus's theories and demonstrated that the planets' revolutions were elliptical.

Within theological circles, the opposition to Copernicus's implied heresy was most immediate among Protestants. Luther, for example, was outraged: "People give ear to an upstart astronomer who strove to show that the Earth revolves, not the heavens or the firmament, the sun and the moon . . . the fool wishes to reverse the entire science of astronomy." Rome's position, at least initially, was almost nonchalant. A Dutch spokesman, Gemma Frisius, wrote in 1541: "It hardly matters to me whether he claims that the Earth moves or

---

1. Quoted after Sherrington, *The Endeavour of Jean Fernel*, 136.

that it is immobile, so long as we get an absolutely exact knowledge of the movements of the stars and the periods of their movements, and so long as both are reduced to altogether exact calculations."[2]

In fact, with some creative use of allegory, it was even possible to find justification for Copernicus's theories in the Scriptures: "who shaketh the earth out of her place, and the pillars thereof tremble" (Job 9:6). But when, toward the end of the century, the church came to realize the dangers inherent in Copernicus's theories, it changed its tune: in 1616, *De revolutionibus* was placed on the Inquisition's *Index librorum prohibitorum*, with the condition that it remain there "until corrected" (that is, until statements of reality were qualified as hypotheses); the church lifted the ban only in 1828.

Vesalius

Born and educated in the Low Countries, Andreas Vesalius (1514–1564) made his mark in science as a professor at the University of Padua. Often dubbed the "father" of modern anatomy, he published his *De humani corporis fabrica* (Concerning the Fabric of the Human Body) in 1543. What distinguished the work was its emphasis on both the structure and the function of the organs, its observations based on dissections of human corpses carried out by Vesalius himself, and its large, brilliant illustrations (Fig. 32-1). The *Fabrica* quickly became the standard anatomy text of its time.

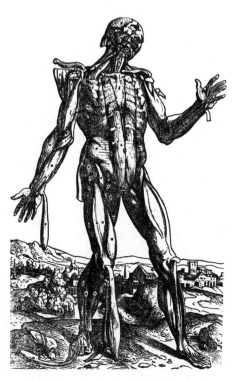

Figure 32-1. Andreas Vesalius, *De humani corporis fabrica*, 1543, engraving showing musculature.

2. Burke, *The Day the Universe Changed*, 136.

Here is Vesalius on the fibers of the veins:

> Nature gave straight fibres to the vein: by means of these it draws blood into
> its cavity. Then since it has to propel the blood into the next part of the vein,
> as through a water-course, she gave it transverse fibres. Lest the whole blood
> should be taken at once into the next part of the vein from the first without
> any pause, and be propelled, she also wrapped the body of the vein with
> oblique fibres. . . . The Creator of all things instituted the veins for the prime
> reason that they may carry the blood to the individual parts of the body, and
> be just like canals or channels, from which all parts take their food.[3]

In the end, there was nothing revolutionary about Vesalius or his work,
certainly not as there was about Copernicus's theories. Yet with its systematic
thoroughness and superb illustrations, the *Fabrica* rendered its greatest prede-
cessor, the second-century observations of Claudius Galen, obsolete and paved
the way for the great discoveries about the circulatory system that William
Harvey would make in 1628.

THE COUNCIL OF TRENT

Musicians tend to have a somewhat limited view of the objectives and accomplishments of the Council of Trent: it rid the liturgy of all but a few
sequences; it standardized the Mass; it called for a revision of Gregorian chant
in keeping with contemporary aesthetic ideas; it gave rise to polyphonic Masses
in which the text could be understood. To be sure, the musical fallout and the
revisions of the liturgy had their effect on composers who remained loyal to
Catholicism. But in truth, the council devoted very little time to music, and
even then, only as the delegates were nearly out the door.

The Council of Trent was convened by Pope Paul III in 1545, in part at the
urging of Charles V, who hoped that it might provide a solution to the religious
turmoil that was tearing his empire apart. The council's three rounds of sessions
stretched out over eighteen years: December 1545–January 1548, May 1551–
April 1552 (now under Pope Julius III), and January–December 1563 (under
Pope Pius IV). Its objectives were threefold: to consider matters of church
doctrine, especially in the face of the theological challenges from the Protestant
Reformation; to clean up ecclesiastical abuses; and to discuss yet again the possibility of a crusade against the world of Islam.

In terms of doctrine, conservatism won the day. Any hopes for compromise
with the Protestants were squelched. With respect to "justification," the issue
that Luther saw as the key to the Protestant-Catholic split, the council re-
affirmed that faith alone did not justify a person; charity and good works were
equally necessary. In addition, it upheld the validity of the sacraments, the
sacrificial nature of the Mass, and the traditional view of transubstantiation. Nor
was there any loosening in the structure of the church: the council supported
papal supremacy, the special status of the priesthood, and the nonparticipatory
role of the laity in the administration of the church.

3. Quoted after Hall, *The Scientific Renaissance*, 147–48.

The delegates took a more progressive stance in correcting abuses, especially within the episcopate. Henceforth, bishops had to live in their dioceses, visit their parishes, maintain standards in ordaining priests, enforce the rules against concubinage, and generally set a good example with their own behavior. The council also abolished the sale of indulgences.

As a result of the council's work, there emanated a new spirituality shaped by a new breed of churchmen: Ignatius of Loyola (1491/95–1556), who had already founded the Jesuit order at Paris in 1534; Carlo Borromeo (1538–1584), the ascetic Cardinal-Bishop of Milan, who took the lead in putting into practice the Tridentine "poor relief" reforms; and Francis de Sales (1567–1622), who, as Bishop of Geneva, won back a portion of the French Protestant population to Catholicism. More than any other single factor, it was the Council of Trent that set the stage for the century of reinvigorated Catholicism—from the mid-sixteenth to the mid-seventeenth—known as the Counter-Reformation.

BIBLIOGRAPHICAL NOTE

Advances in Science

Three eminently readable introductions are George Sarton, "The Quest for Truth: Scientific Progress during the Renaissance," in *The Renaissance: Six Essays* (New York: Harper & Row, 1962), 55–76; Marie Boas Hall, *The Scientific Renaissance, 1450–1630* (New York: Harper, 1962); and, covering a wider chronological span, I. Bernard Cohen, *Revolution in Science* (Cambridge, Mass.: Belknap Press, 1985). On Copernicus, see Fred Hoyle, *Nicolaus Copernicus: An Essay on His Life and Work* (New York: Harper & Row, 1973); there is a facsimile edition of *De revolutionibus* published by Macmillan (1972), translated in *Great Books of the Western World*, vol. 16, ed. Robert Maynard Hutchins (Chicago: William Benton, 1952).

The Council of Trent

For a particularly clear account of the objectives and accomplishments of the council, see Thomas Bokenkotter, *A Concise History of the Catholic Church* (New York: Doubleday, 1977), chapter 19; see also Henri Daniel-Rops, *The Catholic Reformation*, trans. John Warrington (London: J. M. Dent, 1962); Arthur Geoffrey Dickens, *The Counter Reformation* (London: Thames & Hudson, 1968).

Also Cited

Charles Scott Sherrington, *The Endeavor of Jean Fernel* (Folkestone, Eng.: Dawson, 1974); James Burke, *The Day the Universe Changed* (Boston: Little, Brown, 1985).

CHAPTER 33

The Protestant Reformation

Though we generally speak of the Reformation in the singular, the religious revolution that swept across Europe starting about 1520 had a number of faces. Its pluralism, moreover, went beyond the obvious realms of theology, liturgy, and ceremony. It also colored attitudes toward music. If some strains of the Reformation honored music and placed it at the very center of worship, others rejected it entirely, while still others took a stance somewhere between the two extremes. Here we will deal with music as it was incorporated into the liturgies developed by the three men who spearheaded the Reformation on the Continent: Martin Luther, Huldreich Zwingli, and Jean Calvin (on the English Reformation, see Chapter 34).

The map in Figure 33-1 shows the religious divisions of Europe around 1560.

Figure 33-1. Map showing religious divisions in Europe, c. 1560.

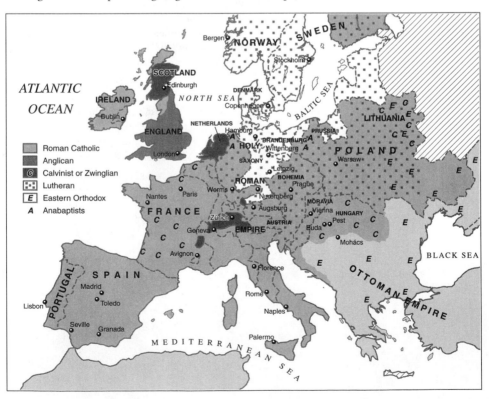

A few things catch the eye immediately: (1) the Reformation was mainly a northern-European phenomenon; though Italy, Spain, and Portugal felt its sting, they launched a Counter-Reformation of their own and remained solidly in the Catholic fold; (2) France and Poland, both of which ultimately remained loyal to Rome, either were moving toward Protestantism (France) or even adopted it for a while (Poland); and (3) while Luther's influence extended through northern Germany and points north and northeast, Calvin's ideas fanned out from Geneva mainly to points west and northwest.

There are, however, things that the map does not tell us. (1) By around 1570, about 40 percent of the population was Protestant; this would fall to 20 percent by the mid-seventeenth century, as Protestantism was beaten back in such countries as France, Poland, and Austria. (2) At the same time, approximately 70 percent of the subjects of the Holy Roman Emperor were Protestants. (3) From 1559 to 1562, the explosion of Calvinism was so powerful that the number of its churches in France expanded from about one hundred to seven hundred. And (4) the bloodiest rifts over religion were experienced in the central-European territories of the Holy Roman Empire, where, after more than a century of religious wars, peace was achieved only in 1648, with the signing of the Peace of Westphalia. For most Europeans, whose horizons did not extend beyond their own continent, it must have seemed as though "World War I" was fought between the middle of the sixteenth and seventeenth centuries.

LUTHER

On October 4, 1530, Martin Luther (1483–1546; Fig. 33-2) wrote to the Swiss-German composer Ludwig Senfl: "Next to theology there is no art that is the equal of music, for she alone, after theology, can do what otherwise only

Figure 33-2. Lucas Cranach, woodcut of Martin Luther, 1546.

theology can accomplish, namely, quiet and cheer up the soul of man."[1] Even more passionate in its praise of music is the preface that Luther wrote to the *Symphoniae iucundae*, a collection of fifty-two Latin motets (composed mainly for the pre-Reformation Catholic Church) issued by his friend the Wittenberg publisher Georg Rhau in 1538:

> Here it must suffice to discuss the uses of this great thing called music. But even that transcends the greatest eloquence of the most eloquent, because of the infinite variety of its forms and benefits. We can mention only one point . . . namely, that next to the Word of God, music deserves the highest praise. She is mistress and governess of those human emotions . . . which as masters govern men or more often overwhelm them. No greater commendation can be found. . . . For whether you wish to comfort the sad, to terrify the happy, to encourage the despairing, to humble the proud, to calm the passionate, or appease those full of hate . . . what more effective means of music could you find? . . . Thus it was not without reason that the fathers and prophets wanted nothing else to be associated with the Word of God as music.[2]

Indeed, Luther assigned music a vital role in his theological reforms. He was, after all, a musician himself, capable of singing, playing both flute and lute, adapting old melodies to new words, and harmonizing a melody in four parts.

But before we take up the music of Luther's Reformation, we should consider the context of which it was a part.

Theological and Liturgical Reforms

When Luther and his followers set out to fill what they saw as the spiritual void of their time, they started by asking an age-old question: how could men and women gain salvation? Not, they believed, through sacrifice and good works, as Rome taught; salvation could not be bought by commissioning a fresco or, for that matter, a polyphonic Mass. Nor was it to be gained through obedience to the theological interpretations and edicts of popes and church councils. Rather, argued Luther, salvation was to be found through faith in Christ, through God's forgiving grace, which itself justified people and made them righteous. Nor did men and women need to be represented by a hierarchy of pope, priest, and councils. They stood directly before God themselves; and the only guide they needed was the Word as it appeared in the Scriptures.

Though the seeds of the Reformation had been sown more than a century earlier, its crucial years of development extended from 1517 to 1530. Below are among the most significant events of those years.

The 95 theses: The Reformation got its unofficial start on October 31, 1517. Provoked by Pope Leo X's sale of indulgences, Luther, then an Augustinian monk and professor of theology at the University of Wittenberg, posted his ninety-five theses on the bulletin board of Wittenberg's Castle Church. Thanks to the power of the printing press, the theses circulated quickly throughout

---

1. Quoted after Buszin, "Luther on Music," 84.

2. The entire preface appears in Weiss and Taruskin, *Music in the Western World*, 101–3.

Germany and Europe and drew him into direct conflict with the Church of Rome.

Excommunication and the Diet of Worms: In June 1520, Leo X excommunicated Luther, who had continued to deny both the supremacy of the pope and the infallibility of the councils of the church, first in a confrontation with the theologian Johannes Eck and then in a series of published pamphlets. In April 1521, Charles V ordered Luther, whose following was growing, to appear before the Diet of Worms (a parliamentary meeting of nobles and high-placed clergy of the empire) in order to recant. Luther refused, and paid for his convictions with a year in exile.

The Latin Mass revised: Having returned to Wittenberg in 1522, where he taught, preached, and wrote under the sympathetic protection of Duke Frederick the Wise, Luther issued his *Formula missae et communionis pro Ecclesia Wittembergensis* in 1523. This revised version of the Latin Mass, intended specifically for use in the churches of Wittenberg, exemplified Luther's evangelical dualism. While it retained Latin and the basic order of the Mass, it was nevertheless radical from a theological point of view: Luther interpreted the Mass not as a sacrifice offered to God by the priest on behalf of the congregation, but rather as a gift of grace and forgiveness from God to the people. He thus turned the meaning of the Mass on its head. It was also in the *Formula missae* that Luther began to alter the role of music in the Mass. Though Luther's revisions were far-reaching, they failed to satisfy the more radical reformers, who, at the very least, were clamoring for a Mass in the vernacular.

The German Mass: By 1524, reformers in Strasbourg were celebrating the Mass in German. Luther quickly followed suit, and in 1526 he published his *Deutsche Messe und Ordnung Gottesdiensts* (German Mass and Order of God's Service). After noting that he had no wish to abolish Latin entirely, he stated in the preface that "the German Mass and Order of Service . . . should be introduced for the sake of the simple laymen. These two Orders of Service [Latin and German] must be used publicly, in the churches, for all the people."[3] Thus Luther intended the German Mass mainly for congregations unfamiliar with Latin, which, however, would continue to be used in the cathedrals and churches of cities in which there were universities and Latin schools. (In fact, Luther strongly believed that the Latin Mass had an important educational function.) Yet even in these latter churches, parts of the German Mass were adopted, and Lutheran Germany quickly developed a tradition of worship that was bilingual.

The Augsburg Confession: In 1530, Charles V convened the Diet of Augsburg in an attempt to quell the religious tensions that were dividing his empire. Needless to say, the representatives of the Roman church leveled their attacks. Luther's chief associate, the German humanist Philipp Melanchthon (1497–1560), answered them with the so-called *Augsburg Confession*, the definitive doctrinal statement of the Lutheran faith. And though it would take another

---

3. Quoted after Thompson, *Liturgies of the Western Church*, 124–25.

quarter century before the emperor would officially recognize its legitimacy, the Lutheran Church was, in effect, established.

Finally, though the Reformation, whether Luther's or Zwingli's or Calvin's, was primarily theological in nature, it left its mark on politics, economics, and other aspects of everyday life: (1) it promoted the dualism of nationalism (state churches) and democratic individualism; (2) with its emphasis on the responsibility for one's self, it was a boon for capitalism, as well as for the notion of thrift and industriousness (we speak, after all, of the "Protestant work ethic"); and (3) it promulgated science and education with such vitality that within about a century, the Protestant North stood at the forefront of science and technology.

Music for the Lutheran Service

Luther loved and appreciated music, both for its sheer beauty and for its power to move the listener spiritually (recall his special admiration for the music of Josquin, as noted in Chapter 18). And as the *Formula missae* of 1523 makes clear, Luther assigned music a central role in his reformed liturgy:

> I also wish that we had as many songs as possible in the vernacular, which the people could sing during Mass, immediately after the Gradual and also after the Sanctus and Agnus Dei. For who doubts that originally all the people sang these that now only the choir sings or responds to while the bishop is consecrating the Host? The bishops may have these congregational hymns sung either after the Latin chants, or use the Latin on one Sunday and the vernacular on the next, until the time comes that the whole Mass is sung in the vernacular. But poets are wanting among us, or not yet known, who could compose evangelical and spiritual songs, as Paul calls them, worthy to be used in the church of God. In the meantime, one may sing after communion, "Let God be blest, be praised, and thanked, Who to us himself hath granted." Another good hymn is "Now Let Us Pray to the Holy Ghost" and also "A Child So Worthy." For few are found that are written in a proper devotional style. I mention this to encourage any German poets to compose evangelical hymns for us.[4]

In the *Deutsche Messe*, Luther went still further, proposing that spiritual songs in the vernacular be sung at other places in the Mass. Within short order, then, the *chorale* became the central musical item of the Lutheran service.

Quite aside from the use of the vernacular, what is striking about Luther's ideas concerning music is the notion that the congregation as a whole should participate. No longer would the act of praising God in song be reserved solely for the *Kantorei* (choir). And this coincided with Luther's belief that the congregation as a whole should participate fully in praising God. To some extent, Luther was drawing on an old German tradition, in which congregations sometimes sang German folk hymns—called *Leisen*—as extra-liturgical ornaments to the Mass during Christmas, Lent, Easter, and Pentecost. But whereas the

4. Quoted after Weiss and Taruskin, *Music in the Western World*, 103–4.

pre-Reformation liturgy relegated the *Leisen* to a purely occasional, extra-liturgical function, Luther placed the congregational singing of chorales at the very heart of his service.

SOME CHORALES AND THEIR SOURCES   Luther's revised role for music pre-sented a problem. He needed an instant repertory that the congregation could sing: chorale melodies with German texts. Ever the pragmatist, and knowing a good tune when he heard one, Luther turned to two repertories with which his followers were already familiar: some of the more tuneful chants of the Roman church, the texts of which he translated or paraphrased; and the pre-Reformation *Leisen*, some of which were themselves derived from chants.

Thus two chants for Pentecost, the Vespers hymn *Veni creator spiritus* and the sequence *Veni sanctus spiritus* (recall the brilliant isorhythmic motet Dunstable fashioned from these chants, *Anthology* 4) were transformed into the Lutheran chorales *Komm, Gott Schöpfer, heiliger Geist* and *Komm heiliger Geist, Herre Gott*, respectively. At times, Roman chant and *Leise* repertories came together. Ex-ample 33-1 shows the transformation of the Gregorian sequence for the Easter Mass, *Victimae paschali laudes*, through a six-part setting (thus for the choir) of the *Leise Christ ist erstanden* to the chorale *Christ lag in Todesbanden*, as it appears in Bach's great Cantata No. 4.

EXAMPLE 33-1. The opening phrase of (a) *Victimae paschali laudes*;
(b) Anonymous, *Christ ist erstanden*; (c) Bach, *Christ lag in Todesbanden*.

(a)

(b)

Occasionally, Luther composed some chorale melodies himself. The most famous of those traditionally attributed to him is *Ein feste Burg ist unser Gott*, the text of which is a translation of Psalm 46 (Ex. 33-2):[5]

5. It is Psalm 45 in the Catholic system. Following are the discrepancies between the Jewish-Protestant and Catholic numbering systems:

Jewish-Protestant		Catholic
1–8	=	1–8
9–10	=	9
11–113	=	10–112
114–115	=	113
116/verses 1–9	=	114
116/verses 10–19	=	115
117–146	=	116–145
147/verses 1–11	=	146
147/verses 12–29	=	147
148–150	=	148–150

From now on, psalms are numbered according to the tradition that is under discussion, with the other tradition cited in parentheses.

EXAMPLE 33-2. *Ein feste Burg.*[6]

Ein fe - ste Burg ist un - - - ser
Er hilft uns frei aus al - - - ler

Gott, ein gu - te Wehr und Waf - - - fen.   Der
Not, die uns jetzt hat be - trof - - - fen.

alt___ bö - se Feind, mit Ernst ers jetzt meint;   gross

Macht und viel List sein grau - sam Rü - stung ist;   auf Erd ist

nicht seins Glei - - - chen.

About three hundred years later, Felix Mendelssohn would incorporate *Ein feste Burg* as the theme for the fourth-movement variations of his *Reformation Symphony*, a work conceived to celebrate the tricentenary of the Augsburg Confession. Likewise, Giacomo Meyerbeer used the melody to represent the Protestant cause in his operatic chronicle of Catholic-Protestant tensions in late-sixteenth-century France, *Les Huguenots*. As much as any other chorale tune, *Ein feste Burg* became a symbol of the Reformation.

Some chorales were derived from secular songs. Finding Isaac's popular *Innsbruck, ich muss dich lassen* irresistible (see Chapter 24 and *Anthology* 57), one of Luther's associates refashioned it as *O Welt, ich muss dich lassen*:

Innsbruck	*O Welt*
Innsbruck, I now must leave thee,	O world, I now must leave thee,
My way takes me far from here	My way takes me far from here,
From here to distant lands.	To the eternal Fatherland.
My joy is taken from me,	My soul I'll render up,
I don't know how I'll regain it	Likewise my body and life
Where I am made to suffer so.	Will I place in God's gracious hands.[7]

By the mid-1520s, Luther had collected more than three dozen chorale tunes, which were circulated among his followers by means of printed broadsheets.

WALTER'S HYMNAL   What Luther needed now were polyphonic settings for choirs; and for these he called on Johann Walter (1496–1570), a bass in the

6. After Joseph Klug's *Geistliche Lieder* (1533).

7. After Weiss and Taruskin, *Music in the Western World*, 105–6.

Hofkapelle of Duke Frederick. Walter responded with the *Geystliches gesangk Buchleyn* (1524), which, with its thirty-eight chorale settings and five Latin motets, is the first monument of Protestant church music.

Though Walter's collection must certainly have been used by church choirs at Wittenberg and elsewhere, Luther's primary aim was pedagogical, as his preface makes clear:

> These songs were arranged in four parts [some are in three, others in five] to give the young—who should at any rate be trained in music and other fine arts—something to wean them away from love ballads and carnal songs and to teach them something of value in their place, thus combining the good with the pleasing, as is proper for youth . . . I would like to see all the arts, especially music, used in the service of him who has given and created them.[8]

Walter set the chorale melodies in two styles: one leaned toward homophony, while the other was somewhat more florid; in both styles, the chorale melody sounded clearly and unadorned mostly in the tenor. *Anthology* 78 presents the more florid setting of *Ein feste Burg* (from a later edition of the hymnal). When all four stanzas of the chorale were sung as part of the Lutheran service, stanzas of Walter's polyphonic setting sung by the choir presumably alternated with the melody sung in unison by the congregation.

AFTER WALTER   Walter and his *Chorgesangbuch*, as it is sometimes called, stand at the beginning of a long tradition of Lutheran cantors and chorale books. And if the tradition is marked by a certain everyday, business-like approach, it nevertheless produced some solid compositions and interesting hymnals.

Among the latter is Georg Rhau's *Newe deudsche geistliche Gesenge CXXIII . . . für die gemeinen Schulen* of 1544. Though he intended the collection of 123 pieces for use in schools, Rhau (1488–1548), one of the most important of the Reformation printers (and also a composer), freely mixed music by both Protestant and Catholic composers, as well as pieces in both the "cantional" (homophonic) and Netherlandish-polyphonic styles. In fact, as the sixteenth century wore on, Catholic composers frequently set religious music in the vernacular, while Protestant composers did not completely forsake Latin texts.

We see a more full-blown polyphonic-imitative style in a five-part setting of one of the favorites of the *Leise* repertory, *Nun bitten wir den heiligen Geist*, by Johannes Rasch (1542–?1612), a Benedictine monk and an expert on the cultivation of wine (Ex. 33-3):

EXAMPLE 33-3. (a) Opening of the monophonic *Leise Nun bitten wir den heiligen Geist;* (b) the setting by Rasch, mm. 1–10.

(a)

Nun bit-ten wir den hei - li - gen Geist   um den rech - ten glau - ben al - ler— meist,

8. Quoted after Leaver, "The Lutheran Reformation," 269.

Rasch placed the *Leise* melody in the bass, anticipating it with and incorporating it into the opening point of imitation.

Though the music of the sixteenth-century Lutheran cantors may fail to overwhelm us, we should remember that it was this very tradition that eventually produced the glory of J. S. Bach.

ZWINGLI

If Walter's music for Luther's Wittenberg congregation is meager in comparison with that produced by Morales or Willaert, say, for the great churches of Rome and Venice, it is downright luxurious in comparison with the music for the Swiss-German Reformation led by Huldreich (Ulrich) Zwingli (1484–1531).

Ordained a Catholic priest in 1506, and by one account an extremely talented musician and something of a composer, Zwingli first came under the influence of Erasmus and others who wished to reform the Roman church from within.

He soon sought a more radical approach, however, and in the summer of 1524, with his own ideas on reform taking ever-clearer shape—he had already officially broken with Rome in 1520, the first reformer to do so—Zwingli and his followers literally began to clean house in the churches of Zurich: they whitewashed the frescoes, carted away sculpture, relics, vestments, and service books, and began to dismantle the organs.

Zwingli's liturgy, entitled *Action or Use of the Lord's Supper*, published in 1525, was absolutely clear about the place of music: it was excluded altogether. For Zwingli, music was a secular activity that distracted the worshipper from the Word and thus had no place in the service. And for those parts of northern Switzerland that adopted Zwingli's liturgy, the effect on sacred music was devastating. The situation in Constance was described movingly by the Netherlands-influenced composer Sixt Dietrich (c. 1493–1548), one of the most important Protestant composers of the early Reformation: "I have no one in Konstanz who sings with me. Music is destroyed, lies in ashes, and the more it is destroyed, the more I love it."[9]

Zwingli, whose reforms took hold in the northern cantons of Switzerland, lost his life fighting the Catholics of the southern cantons in the second of the so-called Kappel wars (1531). For the first of these wars, fought in 1529, he had composed a song and arranged it for four voices!

CALVIN

In terms of music and its role in the liturgy, Jean Calvin (Fig. 33-3), whose *Institutes of the Christian Religion* (1536) were discussed briefly in Chapter 28, stood closer to Zwingli than to Luther. In the liturgy that he developed at Geneva, where he settled permanently in 1541, Calvin permitted only the narrowest range of music: psalms sung monophonically by the congregation in French translations. Polyphony, which would too easily distract worshippers from the meaning of the Word, was relegated to the home, though even there it was limited to music of a religious nature.

Drawing on Plato and St. Augustine, Calvin expressed his views about music most succinctly in the 1543 edition of the so-called Geneva Psalter:

> There is hardly anything in the world that has greater power to bend the morals of men this way or that, as Plato wisely observed. And in fact we find from experience that [music] has an insidious and well-nigh incredible power to move us whither it will. And for this reason we must be all the more diligent to control music in such a way that it will serve us for good and in no way harm us. . . . Now in treating music I recognize two parts, to wit, the word, that is the subject and text, and the song, or melody. It is true, as St. Paul says, that all evil words will pervert good morals. But when the melody goes with them, they will pierce the heart much more strongly and enter within. Just as wine is funneled into a barrel, so are venom and corruption distilled to the very depths of the heart by melody. So what are we to do? We should have songs that are not only upright but holy, that will spur us to

9. Quoted after *New Grove*, 10: 725.

Figure 33-3. Woodcut of Jean Calvin, 1559.

pray to God and praise Him, to meditate on His works so as to love Him, to fear Him, to honor Him and glorify Him.[10]

Calvin here expresses the deep mistrust—even fear—of music that was shared by many of the more radical Protestants.

The Geneva Psalter

For the development of music among French-speaking Protestants who followed Calvin, no publication was more influential than the so-called Geneva Psalter. Published and constantly enlarged and revised under Calvin's watchful eye over the course of two decades, the psalter became the official songbook of Calvin's Reformed Church.

THE MONOPHONIC PSALTER   The genesis of the Geneva Psalter is drawn-out and complicated; in fact, there is no single publication that bears that title. Suffice it to say that in its "definitive" version of 1562 (a series of partial editions dated back to 1539), *Les Pseaumes mis en rime française, par Clément Marot et Théodore de Bèze* consisted of rhymed, metrical, French translations of all 150 Psalms of David (plus two canticles—lyrical passages from the Bible other than the psalms) and monophonic melodies to which they were sung. As the title implies, Marot and Bèze (1519–1609), a Protestant theologian, supplied the translations, while slightly more than half of the 125 monophonic melodies are the work of a local Geneva musician, Loys Bourgeois (c. 1510/15–1560 or after).

The most famous melody in the Geneva Psalter is that for Psalm 134 (133), *Or sus, serviteurs du Seigneur* (Ex. 33-4):

10. Quoted after Weiss and Taruskin, *Music in the Western World*, 107–9.

EXAMPLE 33-4. Bourgeois(?), *Or sus, serviteurs du Seigneur.*

Having made its debut in the 1551 edition of the Geneva Psalter, the melody of *Or sus* was picked up by English reformers then living in exile on the Continent. And after 1563, it appeared in the Anglican psalter compiled by Sternhold and Hopkins (see Chapter 34), sung to the words of Psalm 100: "All people that on earth do dwell," from which association it came to be known in the late seventeenth century as "Old Hundredth."

In the Geneva Psalter, Marot and De Bèze rendered the psalms in rhymed, metrical verse, and divided them into stanzas of equal length. We can see what this does to the structure of a psalm by looking at the opening of three versions of Psalm 130 (129): the Latin, as used in the Catholic liturgy; the English translation in the King James version of the Bible; and the French translation by Marot:

1. De profundis clamavi ad te Domine: Domine exaudi vocem meam.
2. Fiant aures tuae intendentes in vocem deprecationis meae.
3. Si iniquitatis observaveris Domine: Domine quis sustinebit?
4. Quia apud te propitiato est: et propter legem tuam sustinui te Domine.

1. Out of the depths have I cried unto thee, O Lord.
2. Lord, hear my voice: let thine ears be attentive to the voice of my supplications.
3. If thou, Lord, shouldest mark iniquities, O Lord, who shall stand?
4. But there is forgiveness with thee, that thou mayest be feared.

> Du fond de ma pensée
> Au fond de tous ennuis,
> Dieu, je t'ay addresse
> M'a clameur jours et nuictz.
>
> Entés ma voix plantive,
> Seigneur, il est saison.
> Ton aureille en tentive,
> Soit à mon oraison.
>
> Si ta rigueur expresse,
> En noz pechez tu tiens:
> Seigneur, Seigneur, qui est-ce,
> Qui demourra des tiens?
>
> Si n'es-tu point severe:
> Mais, propice à mercy.
> C'est pourquoy on revere,
> Toy et ta loy aussi.

Thus the nonmetrical, unrhymed, nonstanzaic psalm has been turned into verse that has meter, rhyme, and stanzas of equal length; furthermore, each pair of stanzas is sung to the same melody, in the manner of a strophic song. Thus the psalm has, in effect, been turned into a hymn, and the centuries-old distinction between psalm and hymn obliterated.

POLYPHONIC SETTINGS OF THE GENEVA MELODIES   Though Calvin banned polyphony from the services of his Reformed Church, he permitted its use at social gatherings in the home. Among the composers (both Protestant and Catholic) who set the melodies of the Geneva Psalter, the most substantial contribution to the repertory belongs to Claude Goudimel (c. 1514/20–1572).

A convert to Protestantism, Goudimel lost his life during the infamous St. Bartholomew's Day Massacre, the bloodiest and most treacherous event of the four decades of Catholic-Protestant tensions in France. The massacre was apparently unleashed by Catherine de' Medici, mother of the twenty-two-year-old king, Charles IX, on the eve of St. Bartholomew's Day (August 24), 1572, and wiped out an estimated 50,000 French Huguenots in a little more than three weeks. Goudimel fell victim when the killing swept through heavily Protestant Lyons (where he resided) during the final days of August.

During the 1560s, Goudimel set the entire stock of Geneva Psalter melodies twice: once in a strict, four-voice, note-against-note style in which all voices sang the syllables of the text together, and once in a more embellished style (also for four voices). He also set a selection of tunes in the style of full-blown, imitative motets for up to six voices. Undoubtedly it was the simpler settings that were most popular. We can see his approach in his two versions of *Or sus, serviteurs du Seigneur* (Ex. 33-5). Polyphonic settings of the Geneva Psalter melodies enjoyed spectacular popularity, both among Protestants and, until Rome prohibited them, among Catholics. France and Switzerland alone witnessed the publication of some two thousand such settings; and to these one could easily add another thousand pieces that drew on melodies from other psalters, belonged to the repertory of *chansons spirituelles* (secular songs in which the original text was replaced by a new religious or moralizing one), or arranged the psalms for solo voice with lute accompaniment.

EXAMPLE 33-5. Goudimel, two settings of *Or sus, serviteurs du Seigneur:*
(a) note–against–note style, with psalm tune in tenor (1564); (b) embellished style, with psalm tune in superius (1568).

(a)

De - dans sa mai- son le ser - vez, Lou - ez le, et son nom es - le - vez.

De - dans sa mai- son le ser - vez, Lou - ez le, et son nom es - le - vez.

De - dans sa mai- son le ser - vez, Lou - ez le, et son nom es - le - vez.

(b)

Or sus, ser - vi - teurs du sei - gneur, Vous

Or sus, ser - vi - teurs du Sei - gneur, Vous qui de

Or sus, ser - vi - teurs du___ Sei - gneur, Vous qui de nuit___

Or sus, ser - vi - teurs du sei - gneur, Vous qui de nuit en

qui de nuit en son hon - neur De - dans sa mai- son le

nuit en son___ hon- neur De - dans sa mai - son___ le ser -

___ en son hon - neur De- dans sa mai - - son le ser- vez, de-

son___ hon - neur De - dans sa mai - son, de- dans sa mai- son

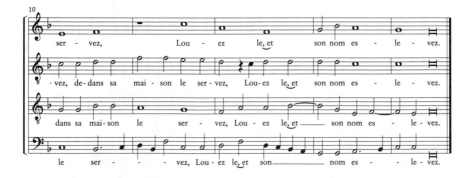

ser - vez, Lou - ez le, et son nom es - le - vez.

- vez, de- dans sa mai - son le ser- vez, Lou- ez le, et son nom es - le - vez.

dans sa mai- son le ser - vez, Lou- ez le, et___ son nom es - le - vez.

le ser - - vez, Lou- ez le, et son___ nom es - le - vez.

In the end, music turned out to be a good propaganda tool for the Reformed Church. One onlooker at Lyons reported that the Protestants attracted converts from the lower classes with "the melody of their songs of Marot and Bèze. . . . Satan always used the voices of men and women, singing together melodiously and in musical harmony as bait to attract women and ignorant people to his cause."[11] Thus music, which Calvin looked upon with such suspicion, ended up helping his cause.

THE DUTCH *SOUTERLIEDEKENS*

The spread of the Reformation to the Low Countries was accompanied by the usual political-religious tensions: while the northern provinces (present-day northern Netherlands) embraced Protestantism, those in the south (modern-day southern Netherlands and Belgium) remained largely Catholic. Moreover, the tensions were exacerbated by a Catholic absentee ruler, the Habsburg Emperor Charles V, who resided in Spain, considered himself a Spaniard, and saw it as his duty to persecute the religious opposition. When Charles was succeeded by his son Philip II, King of Spain, feelings boiled over, and the years from 1568 on were marked by open Dutch rebellion against Spanish-Catholic rule. Only in 1648 did Spain finally recognize Dutch independence.

The Monophonic Psalter

Dutch Protestants had an entire psalter in their own language, complete with monophonic melodies, even before their French-speaking counterparts: it was entitled *Souterliedekens* (Little Psalter Songs), published by Symon Cock at Antwerp in 1540, and consisted of rhymed, metrical translations of the psalms into Dutch. For the melodies, the compilers drew primarily on popular and folk tunes: love songs, drinking songs, dance tunes, and religious songs, with an occasional chant or French chanson melody thrown in. The *Souterliedekens* was an instructional tool; the unsigned preface, which claims its purpose was "to give the young cause for liking to sing, in place of foolish fleshly songs, something good, by means of which God may be honored and they edified,"[12] anticipates the lengthy statement with which Calvin prefaced the 1543 edition of the Geneva Psalter. Yet despite their similar concern with morale edification, there are two significant differences between the two psalters: while the monophonic version of the Geneva Psalter was meant to be used in church, the *Souterliedekens* was intended for use in the home; and while most of the translations of the Geneva Psalter preceded the melodies to which they were sung, those in the *Souterliedekens* were made to fit a preexistent repertory of well-known tunes.

The *Souterliedekens* must have sold like hotcakes. Cock ran through nine

11. Quoted after Dobbins, "Lyons," 210.
12. Quoted after Reese, *Music in the Renaissance*, 357.

printings in 1540 alone, while about twenty other editions by printers scattered throughout the Low Countries followed on their heels.

Polyphonic Settings

Three composers set the entire cycle of *Souterliedeken* psalms polyphonically. Two of them are minor figures: Gherardus Mes and Cornelis Buscop. The third, however, is one of the giants of the period: Clemens non Papa (see Chapter 26), whose settings were published by Susato in 1556–57.

Two of Clemens's settings illustrate his approach: Psalm 36 (35), "Die boose sprack in zyn ghedacht," and Psalm 66 (65), "Vrolick enhly loeft god ghi aertsche scaren" (*Anthology* 79). These are no mere harmonizations. They are intimate, lyrical gems (especially Psalm 36) that betray the hand of one of the period's finest chanson composers. In both instances, Clemens assigned the popular melody of the monophonic psalter to the tenor: "Rosina waer was u ghestalt" (Rosina, where were you?) in Psalm 36, "Ick seg adieu" (I say good-bye) in Psalm 66. (Other times, the monophonic model appears in the superius.) And though Clemens set the melodies for three voices throughout, he used a wide array of voice combinations. Thus while Psalm 36 calls for the customary superius-tenor-bass combination, Psalm 66 is for three low voices. In all, there are no fewer than twenty-six different combinations of voices. Of all the strictly congregational music of the early Reformation, Clemens's settings of the *Souterliedekens* are by far the most rewarding.

BIBLIOGRAPHICAL NOTE

Editions of the Music

Johann Walter: *Sämtliche Werke*, ed. Otto Schröder (Kassel: Bärenreiter, 1953–73). A number of **Rhau's** publications are edited in *Musikdrucke aus den Jahren 1538 bis 1545 in praktischer Neuausgabe* (Kassel: Bärenreiter, 1955–80). **Claude Goudimel**: *Oeuvres complètes*, ed. Pierre Pidoux et al. (Brooklyn: Institute of Mediaeval Music, 1967–83). **Clemens non Papa**: the *Souterliedekens* appear in vol. 2 of the *Opera omnia* (see the Bibliographical Note in Chapter 26). **Geneva Psalter**: the monophonic version appears in the study by Pidoux cited below; there is a representative collection of polyphonic settings of *Leisen* in Johannes Riedel, *Leise Settings of the Renaissance and Reformation Era*, RRMR 35 (Madison: A-R Editions, 1980).

General Studies on the Reformation

Three excellent introductions to the Reformation are Arthur Geoffrey Dickens, *Reformation and Society in Sixteenth-Century Europe* (New York: Harcourt, Brace & World, 1966); H. J. Grimm, *The Reformation Era*, 2nd ed. (New York: Macmillan, 1973); and Bob Scribner, Roy Parker, and Mikuláš Teich, *The Reformation in National Context* (Cambridge: Cambridge University Press, 1994). See also Hans Joachim Hillerbrand, *The World of the Reformation* (New York: Scribner, 1973), and *The Protestant Reformation* (New York: Walker, 1968), the latter a collection of important documents; Lewis William Spitz, *The Protestant Reformation, 1517–1559* (New York: Harper & Row, 1985).

General Studies on Protestant Church Music

Friedrich Blume, *Protestant Church Music: A History* (New York: Norton, 1974); Robert M. Stevenson, *Patterns of Protestant Church Music* (Durham: Duke University Press, 1953).

Luther

An accessible introduction to Luther's life and thought is Roland H. Bainton's *Here I Stand: The Life of Martin Luther* (New York: Abingdon-Cokesbury Press, 1950); see also Heiko A. Oberman, *Luther: Man between God and the Devil*, trans. Eileen Walliser-Schwarzbart (New Haven: Yale University Press, 1989), and for a more popular account, William Manchester, *A World Lit Only by Fire: The Medieval Mind and the Renaissance, Portrait of an Age* (Boston: Little, Brown, 1992).

Luther and Music

Three basic studies are Walter E. Buszin, "Luther on Music," *MQ* 32 (1946): 80–97; Paul Nettl, *Luther and Music* (Philadelphia: Muhlenberg Press, 1948); and Carl Schalk, *Luther on Music: Paradigms of Praise* (St. Louis: Concordia, 1988). For expanded perspectives, see Robin A. Leaver, "The Lutheran Reformation," in *The Renaissance*, ed. Iain Fenlon (London: Macmillan, 1989), 263–85, and "Christian Liturgical Music in the Wake of the Protestant Reformation," in *Sacred Sound and Social Change: Liturgical Music in Jewish and Christian Experience*, ed. Lawrence A. Hoffman and Janet R. Walton (Notre Dame, Ind.: Notre Dame University Press, 1992), 124–44; John W. Barker, "Sociological Influences upon the Emergence of the Lutheran Chorale," *MMA* 4 (1969): 157–98; Johannes Riedel, *The Lutheran Chorale: Its Basic Traditions* (Minneapolis: Augsburg Publishing, 1967).

Zwingli and Calvin

George R. Potter, *Zwingli* (Cambridge: Cambridge University Press, 1976); William J. Bouwsma, *John Calvin: A Sixteenth-Century Portrait* (Oxford: Oxford University Press, 1988); John W. Bratt, *The Heritage of John Calvin* (Grand Rapids, Mich.: Eerdmans, 1973).

The Geneva Psalter

Pierre Pidoux, *Le Psautier huguenot* (Basle: Bärenreiter, 1962); Ulrich Teuber, "Notes sur la redaction musicale du psautier genevois (1542–1562)," *AnnM* 4 (1956): 113–28; Waldo Selden Pratt, *The Music of the French Psalter of 1562* (New York: Columbia University Press, 1939).

Also Cited

Bard Thompson, *Liturgies of the Western Church* (Philadelphia: Fortress Press, 1961; reprint, 1980); Frank Dobbins, "Lyons: Commercial and Cultural Metropolis," in *The Renaissance*, ed. Iain Fenlon (London: Macmillan, 1989), 197–215.

CHAPTER 34

Early Tudor England

England has been out of the spotlight since Chapters 1 and 9. There we observed English musicians playing a pathbreaking role during the first forty years of the fifteenth century: led by John Dunstable and Leonel Power, they forged a new sound based on the triad, showed how to paraphrase a cantus-firmus melody and shoot it from one voice to another, developed the cyclic cantus-firmus Mass, and, with the *Missa Caput*, established the four-part texture that became the standard for that genre. The English did not keep these innovations to themselves but exported them to the Continent, where they were absorbed by Du Fay, Binchois, their contemporaries, and succeeding generations.

Then something happened. By the 1470s (if not before), it had certainly caught Tinctoris's ear: "The French contrive music in the newest manner for the new times, while the English continue to use one and the same style of composition, which shows a wretched poverty of invention."[1] Though "wretched poverty of invention" seems a bit unfair, the fact is that English music had turned in on itself, had cut itself off from the central Franco-Flemish tradition.

To be sure, English-Continental contacts did not dry up entirely in the second half of the fifteenth century. Robert Morton, for instance, served in the Burgundian chapels of both Philip the Good and Charles the Bold, and his *Le souvenir* is one of the gems of the Franco-Flemish chanson repertory (see Chapter 13 and *Anthology* 34). Likewise, the Oxford-educated theorist John Hothby (c. 1410–1487) was active at Florence and Lucca from the 1450s until shortly before his death, and left his mark on the next generation of Italian theorists (see Chapter 16). And even though there is no evidence that either John Bedyngham or Walter Frye ever left England, their music circulated widely on the Continent, with Bedyngham's *O rosa bella* (*Anthology* 10) and Frye's *Ave regina caelorum* ranking high on the hit parade list. Moreover, the early sixteenth century saw a trickle of Continental musicians emigrating to England. Thus in 1516, organists from Venice and the Low Countries—Dionisio Memmo and Benedictus de Opitis (fl. c. 1500–25), respectively—entered the ranks of instrumentalists at the court of Henry VIII, to be joined within a few years by the Flemish lutenist-composer Philip van Wilder (c. 1500–1553). Yet while musicians continued to cross the channel from about 1450 to 1520, they did so in numbers that are trifling compared with the heavy north-south traffic that criss-crossed the Alps.

---

1. From the *Proportionale musices* (c. 1473–74); quoted after Strunk, *Source Readings*, 15.

England was immune to another activity that blossomed on the Continent: music printing. In fact, the entire first half of the sixteenth century produced only a single substantial collection of printed polyphony in England: an anthology of songs entitled *In this boke ar conteynd .XX. songes .ix. of iiii. partes, and xi. of thre partes . . .* , published in partbook format at London in 1530. We will meet three of the composers represented there: William Cornysh, Robert Fayrfax, and John Taverner.

Beginning around the mid-fifteenth century, then, music in England and music on the Continent went their separate ways. The profound influence that the English had exerted on Continental composers during the first half of the century came to an end, and we can only wonder about the English reception of, say, Ockeghem and Josquin during the final decades of the century. The England of Henry VII and Henry VIII cultivated a distinctive style of its own, most brilliantly in the sacred music written for a still-Catholic England prior to the English Reformation.

We will consider three aspects of this English style: secular music in the early part of Henry VIII's reign, Latin sacred music during the reigns of Henry VII and Henry VIII, and music for the English Reformation under Henry VIII and Edward VI. But first we should see how the Tudor dynasty established itself in the first place.

THE TUDOR DYNASTY

When England withdrew from the Continent at the end of the Hundred Years' War in 1453, it was ruled by Henry VI of the House of Lancaster, who had occupied the throne since 1422. His ineffectual rule was undermined both by a faction-ridden nobility and by popular rebellions. In 1455, the rival House of York challenged Henry's rule and so set off the thirty-year period of the Wars of the Roses, so dubbed because each house sported a rose as an emblem (red for Lancaster, white for York).

Fortunes swung back and forth: in 1461, Edward IV of York gained the throne; in 1470, Lancaster's Henry VI won it back; in 1471, York's Edward was victorious again and imprisoned Henry in the Tower of London, where he soon died. When Edward himself died in 1483, his brother Richard, Duke of Gloucester, imprisoned Edward's young sons (they were never seen again), went on a killing spree among Edward's chief supporters, and declared himself Richard III. The stage was then set for Henry Tudor.

HENRY VII The House of Tudor was related to that of Lancaster through marriage; and it was Henry (1457–1509) who took up the Lancastrian cause. The decisive battle was fought at Bosworth in 1485: Richard III was killed (but not before exclaiming, "A horse! A horse! My kingdom for a horse!," at least according to Shakespeare), and Henry became king. Five months later, in one of his typically shrewd moves, Henry married Elizabeth of York and thus united the kingdom's rival parties. As much as anything else, Henry brought stability and sobriety—both political and financial—to England. It was a healthy beginning for a dynasty that would remain in power until 1603.

HENRY VIII   The most significant event during the reign of Henry VIII (b. 1491, r. 1509–47) was the separation from Rome and the establishment of the Church of England with the king at its head. Yet Henry accomplished much in other areas as well. With his lord chancellors—first Thomas Wolsey and then Thomas Cromwell—he left his mark on everything from extending the powers of central government to revamping the navy and thereby setting England on the road to prominence on the seas. On the other hand, Henry repeatedly dipped into the nation's coffers to support useless campaigns against the French and a lifestyle that required sixteen royal residences.

EDWARD VI   Edward (born in 1537) was the son of Henry VIII and his third wife, Jane Seymour. Together with his regents, the teenaged king continued his father's religious reforms; and it was during his short reign (1547–53) that Parliament passed the two Acts of Uniformity, which effectively made Protestantism the offical state religion.

With Edward's death, the first phase of Tudor rule comes to an end. We will consider the final two Tudor monarchs—Mary I ("Bloody Mary") and Elizabeth I—in Chapter 40.

SECULAR SONG AT THE COURT OF HENRY VIII

The major source of both secular song and instrumental ensemble music at Henry's court, nicknamed "Henry VIII's Songbook," was compiled in or around London shortly before 1520.[2] Its contents are overwhelmingly English, with the best-represented composer being King Henry himself.

As we have already seen, Henry loved music and had impressive collections of viols and recorders (see Chapter 25). Further, he himself sang and played both lute and keyboard instruments. In 1517, a Venetian visitor to the court remarked that Henry made everyone listen "to a lad who played upon the lute . . . his Majesty . . . never wearies of him";[3] a few months later, the same visitor noted that Henry sat for four hours listening to his recently arrived organist, Dionisio Memmo, play.

That Henry dabbled at composition should not surprise us. After all, both Charles the Bold and Leo X did the same. And like them, Henry was every bit the amateur. Many of the pieces in the Songbook ascribed to "the Kynge H. viij" are little more than reworkings of preexistent pieces. Thus *Gentyl prince de renom* simply adds a fourth voice—somewhat clumsily—to an anonymous piece that had appeared in Petrucci's *Odhecaton* in 1501 (Ex. 34-1):

2. London, British Library, MS Additional 31922.

3. *New Grove*, 8: 486.

EXAMPLE 34-1. Henry VIII, *Gentyl prince de renom*, mm. 1–6.

William Cornysh

The leading song composer at Henry's court was William Cornysh (d. 1523). Singer, composer, actor, playwright, and stage director, Cornysh must have been a driving force behind the court's rich tradition of secular entertainment. In addition, he was a "Gentleman" (as each member was called) of the royal chapel from 1501, and became its master of the children in 1509.

Cornysh's *Ah Robin, gentle Robin* (*Anthology* 80) is one of a dozen songs in the manuscript that contain a canon. Yet no one would confuse the use of canon in *Robin* with the canonic virtuosity of the Franco-Flemish composers. Rather, the canon is a simple, popularistic round like *Three Blind Mice*: what the thirteenth and fourteenth centuries called a *rota*, a compositional technique well-liked in England and best-known to us through the famous thirteenth-century *Sumer is icumen in*. Cornysh's setting of the poem, which consists of a three-line refrain and two four-line stanzas, is both simple and subtle:

	Measures	Motives
A Robyn, gentyl Robyn, Tel me how thy lemman doth, And thow shal know of myne.	1–12	A + A/B + A/B/C
My lady is unkinde I wis. Alac, why is she so? She lovyth another better than me And yet she will say no.	13–16	d + A/B
A Robyn . . .	17–20	A/B/C
I cannot thynk such doubylnes For I fynd women trew; In faith my lady lovith me well; She will change for no new.	21–24	e (= d') + A/B
A Robyn . . . [4]	25–28	A/B/C

4. Quoted after J. Stevens, *Music and Poetry in the Early Tudor Court*, 405; "lemman" in line two means "sweetheart."

Robin combines two popular traditions that permeated English court circles: the round and songs about Robin, which were just as popular in England as they were in France. And when we consider that *Robyn* is contemporary with such chansons as La Rue's courtly *Pourquoy non* (*Anthology* 47) and Josquin's more popular *Faulte d'argent* (*Anthology* 50), we see just how distinctive the English approach to secular song could be. There is nothing quite like Cornysh's song on the Continent.

PRE-REFORMATION SACRED MUSIC: THE ETON CHOIRBOOK

Nor, around 1500, did the Continent have anything quite like the sacred music of the Eton Choirbook. When Henry VI founded Eton College in 1440, its statutes made ample provision for music. There was to be a sixteen-voice choir and organist, as well as instruction in the singing of polyphony. And in addition to the daily observation of Masses and Offices, which were apparently sung in chant, the statutes prescribed that an antiphon be sung to the Virgin each evening:

> Every day at a suitable time in the evening . . . all sixteen choristers of our Royal College if they be present, and in place of those who are absent we desire that some of the scholars shall be added so that there may always be sixteen, walking two by two in surplices shall reverently go into chapel, accompanied by the master of the choristers. . . . They shall kneel before the crucifix and say *Pater noster*, then they shall rise and sing before the image of the Blessed Virgin in the time of Lent the antiphon *Salve regina* with its verses [tropes]; outside of Lent and also on feast days during Lent the sixteen choristers shall likewise sing in the best manner of which they have knowledge some other antiphon of the Blessed Virgin.[5]

The manuscript known as the Eton Choirbook is the most significant extant collection of English sacred music between the Old Hall manuscript of the early fifteenth century and the Reformation.[6] Compiled specifically for use at Eton College during the period 1490–1502, it is in effect a national collection, with music by composers who were active at a number of English institutions. In its original state (it is now missing ninety-eight folios), the manuscript included ninety-three pieces by twenty-five composers, most of whom are roughly contemporary with the Josquin generation. The repertory is devoted almost entirely to the veneration of Mary—Marian antiphons and Magnificats, with fifteen settings of *Salve regina* alone—which fits nicely with the choir's responsibility to sing antiphons in Mary's honor every evening. Three of these pieces show typically English characteristics of the Eton repertory.

The Eton Style

About John Browne, whose *O Maria salvatoris mater* opens the Eton manuscript, we know only that he enjoyed some kind of association with Oxford

5. Quoted after Harrison, *The Eton Choirbook*, 1: xv.
6. Eton College Library, MS 178.

and that he probably flourished in the 1480s–1490s. Except for its size (eight voices), *O Maria*, which is built on an unidentified cantus firmus that sounds in the tenor, can stand as representative of the Eton repertory. Example 34-2 offers an excerpt from this lengthy work (231 measures):

EXAMPLE 34-2. Browne, *O Maria salvatoris mater*, mm. 1–31.

The eight-voice texture is exceptional: Browne added to the typical five or six voices an additional bass, contratenor, and "quatreble," permitting some dramatic contrasts in sonority, as when the full choir gives way to a duet for the two highest voices at measure 15. Indeed, Browne plays with sonorities (number of voices and register) the way an architect might juxtapose materials that are alternately massive and light, dense and transparent.

What is representative of the repertory? Perhaps most notable is the extremely florid, melismatic writing, which, when combined with the often fussy, almost herky-jerky rhythms, seems to leave music and words on separate planes. Surely, the music-word relationship is driven by an entirely different aesthetic from the one already beginning to operate in, say, Josquin's roughly contemporary *Ave Maria . . . virgo serena* or the later *Miserere mei, Deus*. Humanist notions about the relationship between music and words had not yet infected English music, even indirectly.

No less notable, in light of what Continental composers of the late fifteenth century were doing, is the scarcity of imitation. It is not entirely absent (witness the rough imitation between quatreble and mean beginning at mm. 24–25); but it does not play a vital structural role. Imitation is the exception, not the rule.

Another feature of the Eton repertory is its tendency toward bold, biting dissonances. Example 34-3 shows instances from antiphon settings by Cornysh and Edmund Turges (born c. 1450). Cornysh both exposes an augmented fifth (b'-flat–f''-sharp) between the upper voices and has the voice just beneath them (on g') also join the clash (m. 68), while Turges puts his upper voices in an oblique cross-relationship.[7] In both pieces, the manuscript is absolutely explicit about the accidentals; the dissonances should not be edited away.

In all, the Eton repertory overflows with music that bursts with energy. And yet it still awaits recognition among many early-music fans. Some gossip would be welcome.

7. For an example of a simultaneous cross-relationship, see the Sanctus (m. 163) of Taverner's *Western Wind* Mass in *Anthology* 81, where the dissonance is compounded by one voice leaping a diminished octave.

EXAMPLE 34-3. (a) Cornysh, *Salve regina*, mm. 68–69; (b) Turges, *Gaude flore virginali*, mm. 90–91.

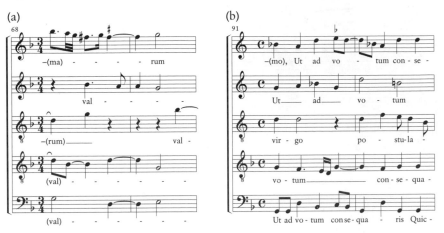

THE MASS BETWEEN ETON AND THE REFORMATION

Though the Eton Choirbook contains no Mass settings, English composers of the late fifteenth and early sixteenth centuries continued to cultivate the cyclic cantus-firmus Mass (it was, after all, the English who "invented" it), at least until the Reformation took firm hold and made such pieces liturgically irrelevant. Two of the leading Mass composers during the reign of Henry VIII were Robert Fayrfax and John Taverner.

Fayrfax and Taverner

With twenty-nine pieces securely attributed to him, Robert Fayrfax (born 1464) has left us more music than any other English composer of his generation. His life was full of honors: Gentleman of the Royal Chapel by 1497; doctorates in music from both Cambridge (1504) and Oxford (1511); leader of the "lay clerks" (members of the chapel who were not clerics) at such state occasions as Henry VII's funeral and Henry VIII's coronation; an annuity and other financial rewards from the crown; and possibly some kind of honorary association with the Abbey of St. Albans, for which he wrote a number of ceremonial pieces, including the *Missa Albanus*. Fayrfax died in October 1521, about two months after Josquin.

John Taverner is without question the towering figure among English composers between Dunstable and the soon-to-arrive William Byrd. Probably born in the early 1490s, Taverner belonged to the generation that followed the Eton composers and was a contemporary of Willaert, Gombert, and Janequin on the Continent. What is surprising about Taverner's career is that he was never a member of Henry's chapel. Instead, he held positions at the collegiate church of Tattershall in 1524–25, the newly founded Cardinal College (today Christ Church) at Oxford in 1526–30, and, from about 1530 to 1537, a small parish church at Boston in his native Lincolnshire, which, thanks to its wealthy St. Mary's Guild, supported a musical establishment of cathedral-like proportions. Though Taverner became personally involved in a case having to do with Protestant-sympathizer singers whom he had recruited for Oxford in 1528, there is no evidence that he ever abandoned his Catholic faith. Taverner died in October 1545, a wealthy and respected Boston alderman.

The Masses by Fayrfax and Taverner that we will look at have a number of things in common, both with one another and with other English Masses of the period: (1) they are cantus-firmus Masses based on monophonic melodies; (2) they omit the Kyrie, which customarily contained a textual trope and was sung to plainsong; (3) they truncate the text of the Credo; and (4) the four movements that are set polyphonically—Gloria, Credo, Sanctus, and Agnus Dei—are often nearly equal in length.

Fayrfax's *Missa Albanus*

Fayrfax drew the cantus firmus for this Mass from the opening of an antiphon in St. Albans's honor (Ex. 34-4a). Throughout most of the Mass, Fayrfax relegates the cantus firmus to the tenor (next-to-lowest voice), in inversion, retrograde motion, and retrograde inversion as well as in its normal guise. But in the section that sets the words "dona nobis pacem" (Ex. 34-4b), five statements of the nine-note ostinato pattern dart from voice to voice, starting on either *c*

EXAMPLE 34-4. (a) Opening of the antiphon *Albanus domini laudans mirabile nomen*; (b) Fayrfax, *Missa Albanus*, Agnus Dei, mm. 102–124.

(a)

(b)

or *f* (mm. 102–113); Fayrfax keeps us guessing by toying with the motive's metrical placement (or displacement). Finally, the tenor alone captures the ostinato (starting in the middle of m. 113) and states it five times on descending notes of the scale. In his manipulation of the cantus firmus, Fayrfax's approach in the *Missa Albanus* is not unlike some of Obrecht's forays into serial-like constructivism.

Taverner's *Western Wind* Mass

Just as Continental composers had their great tradition of *L'homme armé* Masses, sixteenth-century English composers developed a miniature tradition of their own around a beautiful song called *Western Wind* (or *Westron wynde*). Three composers based Masses on it: Taverner, Christopher Tye (c. 1505–?1572), and John Sheppard (c. 1515–1558/59), with Taverner's Mass presumably serving as inspiration and structural prototype for the other two.

Nothing definite is known about the origins of the *Western Wind* song. Perhaps it began life as a popular monophonic song or was incorporated into a polyphonic setting. In any event, two different melodies came to be associated with the title: a short one that survives in an early-sixteenth-century manuscript with a four-line poem, and a slightly longer one, without text and known to us only through its appearance as the cantus firmus of the three Masses (Ex. 34-5):

EXAMPLE 34-5. *Western Wind*: (a) short version, (b) long version.

(a)

(b)

Taverner uses the long version of the melody as his cantus firmus. In the Sanctus (*Anthology* 81), the melody is heard nine times altogether. Table 34-1 summarizes their appearances:

Table 34-1.   The nine statements of the *Western Wind* melody in the
             Sanctus of Taverner's Mass.

Statement	Measures	Voice with cantus firmus	Number of voices
1	1–23	treble	4
2 (lacks phrase 3)	24–38	treble	2
3	39–61	treble	4
4	62–84	contratenor	3
5	85–107	bass	3
6	108–132	treble	4
7	133–155	treble	2/3
8	156–179	contratenor	3
9	180–202	contratenor	4

Since the *Western Wind* tune is by and large unvaried, Taverner achieves contrast through the varied placement of the tune and what goes on around it. Thus he assigns the melody to three different voice parts (never to the mean, whose range would have required a transposition up to D) and constantly varies the number and makeup of the voices that accompany it: no two successive statements are identical in these respects. In effect, the Sanctus—and the Mass as a whole, as the other movements are similar in structure—is a giant set of variations on the *Western Wind* tune.

Taverner's overall style differs from that of the composers in the Eton Choir-book. Most striking, he has smoothed out and simplified the rhythm; it breathes easily instead of hyperventilating. And as a corollary, the melodic writing has begun to take on a more lyrical, song-like quality. If there is an English composer who clearly deserves more of our attention, it is Taverner.

The Masses of Fayrfax and Taverner (and Nicholas Ludford) bring to an end a hundred years of English cantus-firmus Masses. Viewed especially from the perspective of the early sixteenth century (the generations of Josquin and Morales on the Continent), the English tradition is clearly distinct from that on the Continent. Whereas Continental composers had begun to concentrate on the parody Mass, Fayrfax and Taverner, almost without exception, remained loyal to the cantus-firmus tradition. Whereas Continental composers drew freely on secular models, the English favored sacred ones. And though the middle and late years of Henry VIII's reign saw a resumption of English-Continental musical contacts, any subsequent opportunities for English and Continental Mass traditions to come together were snuffed out by the English Reformation. Indeed, the Reformation would soon make polyphonic settings of the Ordinary not only liturgically irrelevant but politically incorrect.

FABURDENS AND SQUARES

When browsing through sixteenth-century manuscripts of English music, we are likely to find pieces described as written "upon the faburden" or "upon the square." These distinctly English compositional processes merit a brief description.

Upon the Faburden

We have already seen how improvised faburden in England of the late fourteenth and early fifteenth centuries permitted a group of three singers to fashion a simple polyphonic setting from a chant. This practice continued right into the sixteenth century, as Erasmus testifies: "Those who are more doltish than really learned in music are not content on feast days unless they use a certain distorted kind of music called *Fauburdum*."[8] Indeed, faburden-like singing was still heard around 1560.

But the sixteenth century knew another type of faburden. Now a composer chose a plainsong, wrote a counterpoint beneath it, discarded the original plainsong altogether, and used the newly composed counterpoint as the cantus firmus of a piece. Thus it was the new counterpoint—the "faburden"—upon which the piece was written (recall that the term "faburden" could refer both to the improvisatory process as a whole and to the specific voice part beneath the plainsong). Although the practice was used in the composition of some sacred vocal music, it was particularly favored by organists in their settings of hymns.

The leading English organist of 1520–50 was John Redford (d. ?1547), singer, almoner, and organist at St. Paul's Cathedral in London. Example 34-6 gives the first two phrases of the Sarum hymn *Salvator mundi domine (Veni creator spiritus* in the Roman rite; see *Anthology* 4), the faburden that Redford wrote beneath it, and his *Salvator withe a meane*, based on that counterpoint, which appears in the lowest voice. Both Redford and this particular hymn are significant for several reasons. (1) With Redford and his contemporaries, English keyboard music for the liturgy took a new turn; while church organists certainly continued their improvisatory practices of the past, they now began to "compose" and notate music of greater complexity. (2) *Salvator withe a meane* contains

8. Quoted after Miller, "Erasmus on Music," 339.

EXAMPLE 34-6. (a) Sarum hymn *Salvator mundi Domine*; (b) Redford's faburden; (c) Redford's *Salvator withe a meane.*

imitation, and thus testifies to its absorption into English music by the latter part of Henry VIII's reign. And (3) *Salvator* is the opening piece in the so-called Mulliner Book, an important source of English keyboard music compiled by Thomas Mulliner during the quarter century after Redford's death.[9]

Upon the Square

Squares are rather more mysterious. They seem to have been monophonic melodies that were notated in mensural fashion, copied into collections of such melodies (or into liturgical books), and then drawn upon as cantus firmi for liturgical works, often in votive Masses for the Virgin Mary. They may therefore be thought of as ready-made cantus-firmus melodies that stood outside the plainsong repertory. Some of the melodies have even been identified as voice parts extracted from polyphonic compositions.

9. London, British Library, Add. MS 30513.

One composer who used squares as cantus firmi was Nicholas Ludford (c. 1485–?1557), who spent the major portion of his career at St. Stephen's, Westminster, Henry VIII's private chapel. Among Ludford's fourteen extant Masses (these make him England's most prolific Mass composer of the period) is a series of seven *alternatim* Lady Masses, one for each of the daily votive Masses in honor of Mary. For each, Ludford set the five movements of the Ordinary (including a polyphonic Kyrie), as well as the alleluia and sequence from the Proper. The movements of the Ordinary are based on squares, those of the Proper on their own plainsongs.

We can see a square in action in the Kyrie of the *Missa Feria iii* (the Tuesday Mass). Example 34-7 gives (a) the beginning of the square, drawn from the tenor of an anonymous song, *Or me veult bien Esperance mentir* in the Mellon Chansonnier; (b) its appearance as the opening invocation of the Kyrie, sung monophonically; and (c) Ludford's setting of the same:

EXAMPLE 34-7. (a) The tenor of *Or me veult*, mm. 1–9 (at its original pitch); (b) the opening invocation of the Kyrie; (c) Ludford's polyphonic Kyrie, mm. 10–18.

Ludford places the square in the lowest voice and decorates it freely. In the following "Christe," he picks up the square at the point at which he left off in the Kyrie (in other words, at m. 10 of the chanson tenor). Each movement of the Ordinary would then have used the same square as its cantus firmus.

THE ENGLISH REFORMATION

In some respects, the Reformation in England followed the pattern established earlier on the Continent. Rome's lack of spiritual leadership was as apparent to Englishmen as to anyone else: "a harlot," the dean of St. Paul's called Rome. Further, papal corruption and monetary greed were seen as a drain on national finances. In fact, England's realization that it was suffering from a balance-of-trade deficit with Rome sparked the first real attack on papal supremacy in England: in 1532, Parliament drafted the Bill of Annates, the preamble of which noted that since 1486, English clergymen had lined the pockets of the pope with about 160,000 pounds in annate taxes (paid by clergymen upon receiving new benefices). Nor did the English ecclesiastical establishment escape criticism, not when the Bishop of Westminster enjoyed an annual income of more than 4,000 pounds while unbeneficed rural priests were virtually destitute.

But there was an important difference between the English and Continental Reformations: reform in England was driven less by the doctrinal-theological beliefs that shaped the movements led by Luther and Calvin than by personal politics pure and simple. In fact, in October 1521, more than a year after he had excommunicated Luther, Pope Leo X dubbed King Henry "defender of the [Catholic] faith" in recognition of his virulent anti-Lutheranism. And when copies of William Tyndale's English translation of the New Testament—printed in Germany—reached England in 1526, they had to be sold black-market style. Only gradually, after Henry had broken with Rome on political and personal grounds, did doctrinal changes come to the fore. And even then, England's theological reforms were conservative in comparison with the Lutherans', and must have seemed like no reforms at all to the Calvinists.

We can track the major stages in the development of the new church as follows: Henry defied Rome by marrying Anne Boleyn (January 1533); two months later, the Act of Appeals removed England from Rome's authority, and Thomas Cranmer became the first Protestant Archbishop of Canterbury; the Act of Supremacy (November 1534) recognized Henry as the "supreme head" of the Church of England; the First and Second Acts of Uniformity (January 1549, March 1552) established and revised a single service in English for the entire church and mandated the use of the *Book of Common Prayer*.

With the Second Act of Uniformity, the religious transformation of England was essentially complete. The liturgy had been cleansed of things popish. And though Edward VI's half-sister and successor, Mary I (daughter of Henry and Catherine of Aragon), was a devout Catholic and returned England to Catholicism during her reign of 1553–58, she was succeeded by another half-sister, the Protestant Elizabeth I (daughter of Henry and Anne Boleyn), who reinstituted Protestantism, which remained unchallenged for the duration of Tudor rule (to 1603).

MUSIC FOR THE ANGLICAN CHURCH

The Reformation drastically curtailed the use of music. The new Anglican Church simply needed less of it. Moreover, what music there was would be sung to English texts. An injunction dated April 15, 1548, from Lincoln Cathedral states that

> the choir shall henceforth sing or say no anthems of our Lady or other Saints, but only of our Lord, and them not in Latin; but choosing out the best and most sounding to Christian religion they shall turn the same into English, setting thereunto a plain and distinct note for every syllable one: they shall sing them and none other.[10]

The likes of Taverner's Masses or the Eton Choirbook's florid Marian antiphons would now give way to simpler settings of English texts.

From 1536 to 1540, as part of the Reformation's progress, eight hundred monasteries were dissolved (followed by the collegiate churches in 1548). This caused the demise of many skilled choirs and shifted the center of liturgical music making to the cathedrals, parish churches (witness Taverner's situation), other institutions that found royal favor—including the royal chapel—and even private households. Thus the great sixteenth-century composer Thomas Tallis left the Abbey of Waltham Holy Cross when it was dissolved in 1540, went to Canterbury Cathedral, and then moved on to the royal chapel. This shifting center of musical gravity also affected the makeup of the choirs: though lay singers had been included in the past, their presence would now become standard practice.

Liturgical settings of Latin texts, however, were never entirely abolished. There was, after all, a Catholic minority among the aristocracy; and those who remained loyal to Rome were usually permitted to practice their faith and perform the music that went with it in the privacy of their homes. As we will see in Chapter 40, William Byrd wrote some of his greatest works for precisely that purpose.

Monophony

Two collections of monophonic music for the Anglican Church stand out, for their historical interest and for the influence they exerted on church music in their own time and beyond.

JOHN MERBECKE'S *COMMON PRAIER NOTED*   Thomas Cranmer's *Book of Common Prayer*, the official prayer book of the new liturgy, included rubrics

---

10. Quoted after Le Huray, *Music and the Reformation in England*, 9.

that indicated where and when music was to be sung but did not provide the music itself. This need was met by John Merbecke (c. 1505/10–c. 1585), who published his *Booke of Common Praier Noted* in 1550.

Merbecke, who was arrested in 1543 because of his sympathies with Calvinism (Henry VIII issued a reprieve), intended his book for use in parish churches, and supplied music for the new liturgy's three daily services: Matins, Communion, and Evensong. Some of the music he drew from the repertory of Sarum chants; some melodies he wrote himself. In both instances, the music was simple, and the strictly syllabic settings fully complied with Cranmer's utilitarian ideas about music. In addition, he used a kind of "shape-note" notation to express the four necessary note lengths (Fig. 34-1). Merbecke's collection enjoyed a short life; the 1552 revisions to the liturgy called for by the Second Act of Uniformity rendered it obsolete.

THE STERNHOLD AND HOPKINS PSALTER As noted in Chapter 33, metrical translations of the psalms, along with melodies with which to sing them, played an important role in the agenda of the Continental reformers. They were also a mainstay of Protestant worship in England.

The earliest psalter for the New Anglican Church was Miles Coverdale's *Goostly psalms and spirituall songes*, published by around 1535 and burned within a year of publication because of its heavily Lutheran leanings. Fate was kinder to the Sternhold and Hopkins Psalter (Fig. 34-2), which, like its Geneva counterpart, had a long and complicated genesis. In 1548 or 1549, Thomas Sternhold, "grome of the kynge's Majesties roobes," issued a collection of nineteen psalms without music. After Sternhold's death in 1549, John Hopkins enlarged the publication (still without music), which continued to grow during the course of a number of reprintings. The first edition with music (the composer

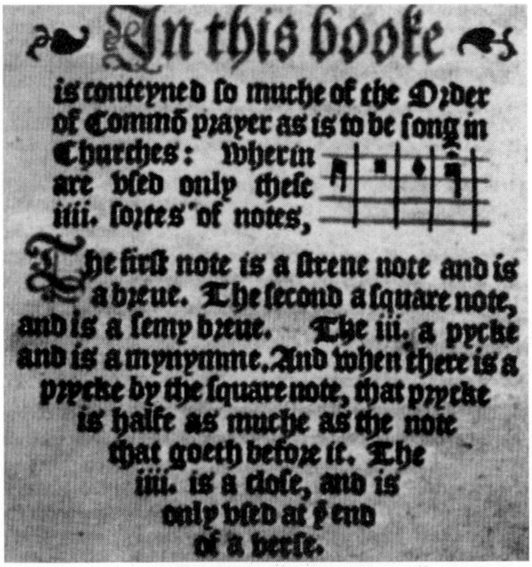
In this booke is conteyned so muche of the Order of Commō prayer as is to be song in Churches: wherin are vsed only these iiii. sortes of notes, The first note is a strene note and is a breue. The second a square note, and is a semy breue. The iii. a pycke and is a mynymme. And when there is a prycke by the square note, that prycke is halfe as muche as the note that goeth before it. The iiii. is a close, and is only vsed at ye end of a verse.

Figure 34-1. Shape-note notation in Merbecke's *Book of Common Praier Noted*, 1550.

Figure 34-2. A page from the Sternhold-Hopkins Psalter (1569) showing *sol-fa* letters next to the notes.

is unknown) was published in 1556 at Geneva, where many of the leading English Protestants went into exile during the reign of the Catholic Queen Mary. And the completed edition, with music for forty-eight psalms and eighteen hymns, was finally published in once-again Protestant London by John Day in 1562: *One and fiftie psalmes of David in Englishe metre.*

The Sternhold and Hopkins Psalter gained tremendous authority, and during the next century close to five hundred editions rolled off the presses. It was Sternhold and Hopkins from which the Pilgrims sang when they landed in America in 1620.

Polyphony

Late Henrician and Edwardian polyphony for the new Anglican liturgy was varied in style, ranging from the simplest note-against-note harmonizations to settings that approach the more elaborate, contrapuntal style of Continental motets. Examples of each appear in the so-called Wanley partbooks, a set of four manuscripts (the tenor partbook is missing) that was probably compiled for a London parish church during the short reign of Edward VI, and the most important source of early-Reformation polyphony.[11]

A SIMPLE SETTING BY JOHN HEATH   In response to the music he heard at Westminster Abbey on November 4, 1547, the diarist Charles Wriothesley wrote: "Afore the masse of the Holie Ghost there was a sermon made before the King [Edward VI] by Doctor Ridley, Bishopp of Rochester; and after that the masse beganne, Gloria in excelsis, the Creede, Sanctus, Benedictus, and the Agnus were all songen in Englishe."[12] Though we cannot identify the specific setting of this Communion (as the Mass of the Anglican liturgy was called), it was probably similar in style to a setting by John Heath (fl. c. 1550) that is preserved in the Wanley partbooks. Example 34-8 gives Heath's "Agnus Dei"—now sung in English as "O Lamb of God" (after the translation in the *Book of Common Prayer*)—in its entirety:

EXAMPLE 34-8. Heath, "O Lamb of God."[13]

11. Oxford, Bodleian Library, MSS Mus. Sch.e.420–22.

12. Quoted after Wrightson, *The Wanley Manuscripts*, 1: xi.

13. The tenor (in small notes) as reconstructed in Wrightson, *The Wanley Manuscripts*, 1: 15.

Here, then, is an approximate English answer to Walter's harmonizations of the Lutheran chorale melodies or Goudimel's simple settings of the tunes in the Geneva Psalter. Heath's setting, however, neither places a preexistent melody in any of the voices nor invites congregational participation, whether in the church or in the home.

A MOTET-LIKE SETTING BY TYE There is a wonderful anecdote about Christopher Tye told by the seventeenth-century antiquarian and musical amateur Anthony Wood:

> Dr. Tye was a peevish and humoursome man, especially in his latter dayes, and sometimes playing on ye organ in ye chap. [el] of qu. [een] Elizab. wh[ich] contained much musick but little delight to the ear, she would send ye verger to tell him yt he play'd out of tune: whereupon he sent word yt her eares were out of Tune.[14]

The text of *Lord, let thy servant now depart in peace* (*Anthology* 82) is a translation of the New Testament's *Nunc dimittis*, known as the Canticle of Simeon (Luke 2:29–32). In the Catholic Church, it is sung as part of Compline; in the new Anglican liturgy, it is part of Evensong. Since the translation does not square precisely with that in the *Book of Common Prayer*, Tye's piece must date from before its publication in 1549.

What is noteworthy about Tye's setting is its liberal use of imitation. Indeed, almost every phrase begins with a point of imitation involving all four voices; and there is even one example (mm. 25–29) of paired imitation. Tye's composition thus illustrates the change in style that gradually took place in English liturgical polyphony during the second third of the sixteenth century. The nonimitative, luxuriously florid style of the Eton Choirbook was now becoming a thing of the past; the imitative, Netherlandish motet style was making its influence felt. Yet Tye's piece still stops short of the full-blown Gombert-Willaert style: each phrase comes to a cadential full stop, without the elided cadences and interlocking phrases of the Netherlanders; and in keeping with the preferences of the religious reformers, Tye's setting is predominantly syllabic. Thus a sense of Englishness, of standing aside from developments on the Continent, is still apparent. We must wait until Chapter 40 and the Latin motets of William Byrd and Thomas Tallis to see the reconciliation.

BIBLIOGRAPHICAL NOTE

Editions of the Music
   Fayrfax: *Collected Works, CMM* 17, ed. Edwin B. Warren (American Institute of Musicology, 1959–66); Margaret Lyon, *Sacred Music from the Lambeth Choirbook: Robert Fayrfax, RRMR* 69 (Madison: A-R Editions, 1985). **Carver**: *Collected Works, Musica Scotica* 1, ed. Kenneth Elliott (Glasgow: University of Glasgow Press, 1996). **Ludford**: *Collected Works, CMM* 27, ed. John Bergsagel (American Institute of Musicology, 1963–77). **Taverner**: *J. Taverner, c. 1495–1545, TCM* 1, 3, ed. Percy Buck et al. (London: Oxford University Press, 1923–24); *J. Taverner: The Six-Part Masses* (vol 1), *The Votive Antiphons* (vol. 2), *Four- and Five-Part Masses* (vol. 3), *EECM* 20, 25, (London: Stainer & Bell, 1978–89).

14. Quoted after *New Grove*, 19: 298.

Manuscripts: four volumes of Musica Britannica (all published in London by Stainer & Bell) are devoted to manuscripts of the period: vol. 1—*The Mulliner Book*, 3rd ed., ed. Denis Stevens (1962); vols. 10–12—*The Eton Choirbook*, 2nd ed., ed. Frank Ll. Harrison (1969–73); vol 18—*Music at the Court of Henry VIII*, rev. ed., ed. John Stevens (1969); vol. 38—*Early Tudor Songs and Carols*, ed. John Stevens (1975). See also James Wrightson, *The Wanley Manuscripts*, RRMR 99 (Madison: A-R Editions, 1995); Judith Blezzard, *The Tudor Church Music of the Lumley Books*, RRMR 55 (Madison: A-R Editions, 1985).

General Studies

There is a comprehensive survey of early Tudor music in chapters 4–5 of John Caldwell's *Oxford History of English Music*, vol. 1: *From the Beginnings to c. 1715* (Oxford: Clarendon Press, 1991), which has an extensive bibliography; Frank Ll. Harrison's *Music in Medieval Britain*, 4th ed. (Buren: Knuf, 1980), remains a classic; a study of major importance is Andrew Ashbee's *Records of English Court Music*, 8 vols. (Aldershot, Eng.: Scolar Press, 1991–95), which presents a "calendar" of musical materials drawn from the records of the English royal court for the period 1485–1714; Richard Turbet's *Tudor Music: A Research and Information Guide* (New York: Garland, 1994), is a valuable guide to the literature; the entire issue of *EM* 25/2 (1997), called "Music in and around London," is devoted to the subject.

Liturgical Music

Denis Stevens, *Tudor Church Music* (New York: Merlin, 1955; reprint, Norton, 1966); Hugh Benham, *Latin Church Music in England, c. 1460–1575* (London: Barrie & Barrie, 1975); Peter Le Huray's *Music and the Reformation in England: 1549–1660* is indispensable; see also Peter Phillips, *English Sacred Music: 1549–1649* (Oxford: Gimell, 1991); David Flanagan, "Some Aspects of the Sixteenth-Century Parody Mass in England," *MR* 49 (1988): 1–11; Nick Sandon, "The Henrician Partbooks at Peterhouse, Cambridge," *PRMA* 103 (1976–77): 106–40.

Secular Music

John Stevens, *Music and Poetry in the Early Tudor Court* (London: Methuen, 1961); Warwick Edwards, "The Instrumental Music of Henry VIII's Manuscript," *The Consort* 34 (1978): 274–82.

Four Composers

Cornysh: Nan C. Carpenter, "Skelton's Hand in William Cornish's Parable," *Comparative Literature* 22 (1970): 157–72; David Skinner, "William Cornysh: Clerk or Courtier?" *MT* 138 (May 1997): 5–17. **Fayrfax**: Edwin B. Warren, *Life and Works of Robert Fayrfax, 1464–1521*, MSD 22 (American Institute of Musicology, 1969). **Taverner**: David S. Josephson, *John Taverner: Tudor Composer* (Ann Arbor: UMI Research Press, 1979); Hugh Benham, "The Formal Design and Construction of Taverner's Works," *MD* 26 (1972): 239–59; "The Music of Taverner: A Liturgical Study," *MR* 33 (1972): 251–74; Nigel S. Davison, "The *Western Wind* Masses," *MQ* 57 (1971): 429–43; Denis Stevens, "John Taverner," in *Essays in Musicology in Honor of Dragan Plamenac on His 70th Birthday*, ed. Gustave Reese and Robert J. Snow (Pittsburgh: University of Pittsburgh Press, 1969). **Ludford**: Hugh Baillie, "Nicholas Ludford (c. 1485–c. 1557)," *MQ* 44 (1958): 196–208; John Bergsagel, "An Introduction to Ludford," *MD* 14 (1960): 105–30; "On the Performance of Ludford's *alternatim* Masses," *MD* 16 (1962): 35–55; David Skinner, " 'At the mynde of Nycholas Ludford': New Light on Ludford from the Churchwardens' Accounts of St Margaret's, Westminster," *EM* 22 (1994): 393–413.

The Tudor Dynasty

Two fine studies are Geoffrey R. Elton, *Reform and Reformation: England, 1509–1558* (Cambridge: Harvard University Press, 1977); John Guy, *Tudor England* (Oxford: Oxford

University Press, 1988); see also Charles Ross, *The Wars of the Roses: A Concise History* (London: Thames & Hudson, 1976); on Henry VIII in particular, see the Bibliographical Note in Chapter 23.

Also Cited

Clement Miller, "Erasmus on Music," *MQ* 52 (1966): 332–49.

PART SIX

THE 1550s TO c. 1600

INCLUDED: BULL • BYRD • CASULANA • DOWLAND • FARNABY • FERRABOSCO • G. GABRIELI • GALILEI • GASTOLDI • GESUALDO • GLAREAN • KERLE • LASSUS • LE JEUNE • LUZZASCHI • MARENZIO • MONTEVERDI • MORLEY • MUNDY • PALESTRINA • RORE • RUFFO • TALLIS • VECCHI • VICENTINO • VICTORIA • WEELKES • WERT • WILBYE • ZARLINO

CHAPTER 35

Music Theory

The mid-sixteenth century was an exciting time for music theory. New ideas were cropping up, especially in Italy and other places where humanist thought held sway. In this chapter, we concentrate on three theorists and the ideas for which they are best-known: Glarean and the modal system, Vicentino and chromaticism, and Zarlino and counterpoint. Glarean and Vicentino will serve as springboards for a discussion of some present-day analytical concerns and the music of Don Carlo Gesualdo.

GLAREAN AND THE MODES

Heinrich Glarean (Fig. 35-1) was born in the Swiss canton of Glarus in June 1488. Erudite and deeply involved in the humanist tide that swept across northern Europe during the early sixteenth century, Glarean defended Gregorian

Figure 35-1. Hans Holbein the Younger, drawing of Glarean (Kupferstichkabinett, Offentlichen Kunstsammlung, Basle).

chant against Protestant reformers who wished to replace it with music in the vernacular (1520s), edited Boethius's famed *De musica* (1546), and played a role in reorganizing the school curricula in Switzerland (1558). He died in 1563.

The *Dodecachordon*

Glarean's great contribution to music theory is the *Dodecachordon* (Twelve Strings), published at Basel in 1547, in which he promulgated new ideas about the modal system. To the eight traditional church modes with their finals on *d, e, f,* and *g* Glarean added four more: the Aeolian and Hypoaeolian with finals on *a* (modes 9 and 10), and the Ionian and Hypoionian with finals on *c* (11 and 12). (Recall that in the eight-mode system, a melody that ended on *c* would have been classified as a transposed Lydian mode; a final on *a* would have belonged to either the transposed Dorian [if the *b* was natural] or transposed Phrygian [if the *b* was flat].)

As Glarean himself pointed out, he was not the first to advance a twelve-mode system. In fact, he thought of his theoretical system as a reconstruction of sorts, which synthesized ideas derived from the humanist-inspired study of antiquity with certain largely forgotten ideas of the Middle Ages. His contribution, then, lay in his ability to bring together ideas from diverse intellectual worlds, build a logical theoretical system from them, and apply that theoretical system to the practical music making of his own day.

Glarean's twelve-mode system received mixed reviews. On the one hand, Zarlino adopted it in his *Dimostrationi harmoniche* (1571), though he failed even to mention Glarean's name and reshuffled his numbering system. In addition, a number of keyboard composers, especially in Italy, wrote *intonazioni* and ricercars in sets of twelve, one in each of Glarean's twelve modes, while the French composer Claude le Jeune composed two sets of similarly ordered vocal works. On the other hand, both Lassus and Palestrina preferred to retain the old eight-mode system in their own modally ordered collections. In effect, musicians in the second half of the sixteenth century knew two modal systems, one traditional and with centuries of ecclesiastical sanction, the other new and humanist-oriented.

The *Dodecachordon* is valuable for other, nonmodal reasons as well. Glarean offers a wealth of biographical information on composers of the period and includes an anthology of more than 120 pieces by such composers as Josquin, Obrecht, Isaac, and—reaching back—even Ockeghem. His work is the first true monument in the series of predominantly humanist-informed treatises on music theory that began to appear around the mid-sixteenth century.

The Problem of Mode and Polyphony

"Is mode real?" What this question, the title of a recent article on the relationship between mode and polyphony, really asks is, did composers think in terms of this or that mode when they sat down to write a piece? In other words, did Claudin de Sermisy think, "I'll write *Je n'ay point plus d'affection* [*Anthology*

63] in the Hypodorian mode transposed to G," in the same way that Beethoven must certainly have thought, "I'm going to write my first symphony in C major"? Did mode have the same meaning and define the same compositional conditions for composers of the fifteenth and sixteenth centuries that major and minor keys did for composers of the so-called common-practice period?

THE THEORISTS' VIEW   The idea of analyzing polyphonic compositions in terms of mode did not take hold until the late fifteenth century. It seems that Tinctoris, writing in the mid-1470s, was the first theorist to confront the matter head-on. Using Du Fay's(?) three-part *Le serviteur* as a test case, he claimed that the mode of the tenor voice, which for him formed the structural backbone of the piece, was the mode of the chanson as a whole (see Chapter 7). Clearly, such reasoning is a little arbitrary. And we saw how aurally irrelevant it could be in connection with a piece such as Du Fay's *Nuper rosarum flores*.

A half century would pass before another theorist addressed the problem in depth: Pietro Aaron, in his *Trattato della natura et cognitione di tutti gli tuoni di canto figurato*, published at Venice in 1525. Indeed, Aaron went hog-wild. Combing the publications of Petrucci and Andrea Antico, and also equating the tenor's mode with the composition's mode (unless there was a preexisting plainsong in another voice), Aaron instructed singers on how they "ought to judge the tone" of more than seventy compositions. At times, Aaron's judgment puzzles us. For instance, he dug down into the fine points of medieval modal theory, which permitted a mode to have a "pseudo-final" called a *differentia*, and assigned the tenor of Josquin's *Comment peult avoir joye* (Ex. 35-1) to mode 7 (Mixolydian) instead of to the seemingly more probable mode 6 (Hypolydian transposed to C).

EXAMPLE 35-1. Josquin, tenor of *Comment peult avoir joye.*

Glarean picked up the analytical torch and brought to it his new system of twelve modes. With the final on *c* now having its own pair of authentic-plagal modes, Glarean assigned the same Josquin piece, which he included in the *Dodecachordon* with the text *O Jesu fili David*, to mode 12 (Hypoionian).

There are two things we must keep in mind here. First, the theorists were analyzing pieces and assigning them to modes only after the compositional fact, which is not the same as saying that the composers consciously composed those pieces in a particular mode (nor do any of the three theorists ever claim that). And second, the theorists' opinions did not necessarily reflect widely held views. Indeed, there is no reason to believe that Tinctoris, Aaron, and Glarean were any more on the same analytical wavelength with the everyday musician than set theorists are with the everyday musician of today.

THE COMPOSERS' VIEW   Whatever the situation may have been before the middle of the sixteenth century, there can be no doubt that the second half of the century began to see a conscious correlation between mode and composition. The evidence lies in the growing number of single-composer, multipiece collections in which mode and the progression through the entire modal system (whether eight or twelve modes) serve as the underlying principle around which the collection is organized. The earliest of these seems to have been Cipriano de Rore's first book of five-voice madrigals of 1542. But perhaps the most telling example is Lassus's *Psalmi Davidis poenitentialis*, which, though not published until 1584, was probably composed before 1560. Here Lassus set each of the seven Penitential Psalms in a different mode (1–7), and then, having run out of psalms, added another as a pretext for completing the eight-mode cycle. Indeed, the very subtitle of the collection—"modis musicis reddit" (ordered according to the musical modes)—calls attention to the plan.

Once chosen, a mode suggested certain melodic and harmonic characteristics for a piece, since its final, tenor, ambitus, and species of fifth and fourth conditioned such things as the contour of melodic subjects and the degrees on which cadences fell. Example 35-2 provides the opening point of imitation of motets 1–4, all in untransposed Dorian, of Palestrina's *Offertoria totius anni* (1593). The similarities are striking: for the most part, the motives carve out mode 1's species of fifth (*re–la*) and often top it with its upper-neighbor B-flat (*fa super la*). The cadences are consistent: they emphasize D and A, final and tenor. In fact, we need not wait until the second half of the sixteenth century to find mode so influencing motivic contour and scale degree of cadences. The melodies of Du Fay's secular songs and the cadential patterns of Josquin's Masses are equally suggestive of modal influence.

EXAMPLE 35-2. Palestrina, *Offertoria totius anni*, Nos. 1–4.[1]

1. After Powers, "Modal Representation in Polyphonic Offertories," 79.

The Ethos of the Modes

The idea that each mode possessed a certain affective quality goes back to the ancient Greeks. And though that idea never quite died during the Middle Ages, it was taken up with renewed interest toward the end of the fifteenth century, as music theorists earnestly began their humanistic love affair with antiquity.

Thus Zarlino described the expressive quality of the Dorian mode as follows in his *Istitutioni harmoniche*: "The first mode has a certain effect midway between sad and cheerful. . . . By nature this mode is religious and devout and somewhat sad; hence we can best use it with words that are full of gravity and that deal with lofty and edifying things."[2]

There was, however, no unanimity about expressive qualities. Indeed, four different theorists described the Dorian mode as constant and severe (Gaffurius, 1518); happy and joyful (Aron, 1525); grave, prudent, dignified, and modest (Glarean, 1547); and a mode that roused the somnolent and relieved cares and mourning (Finck, 1556). On the other hand, there was at least a near consensus on the Phrygian mode: it incited anger, and was therefore suitable for war. Eventually, the idea that each mode had its own expressive quality would be transferred to the various major and minor keys and would live on right into the early nineteenth century.

VICENTINO AND CHROMATICISM

To mid-century listeners accustomed to the modal purity of, say, Gombert or Morales, the 1550s might have seemed like the beginning of the end of music as they had known it. Among the compositions that would have fueled their dismay were two by Cipriano de Rore and the young Orlande de Lassus.

Chromatic Works by Rore and Lassus

Example 35-3 gives the opening chromaticism-filled (in the modern sense) measures of Rore's *Calami sonum ferentes*, a kind of madrigalian motet published by Susato at Antwerp in 1555:

EXAMPLE 35-3. Rore, *Calami sonum ferentes*, mm. 1–16.

2. Quoted after Cohen, *On the Modes*, 58.

Lassus's contribution to the rumblings was the *Prophetiae sibyllarum*, a twelve-motet cycle probably composed shortly before 1560. (Each motet represents one of the Sibylline Prophets, mythological figures whom Michelangelo depicted in his Sistine Chapel ceiling.) *Anthology* 83 gives the entire Prologue to the work.

The chromaticism here is intense; and the text itself, possibly by Lassus, calls our attention to it: "Polyphonic songs which you hear with a chromatic tenor, these are they, in which our twice-six sibyls once sang with fearless mouth the secrets of salvation."[3] In the first nine measures alone, Lassus uses all twelve tones and includes triads on ten different roots, six of which stand entirely outside the Mixolydian mode, to which a musician tied to traditional modal categorization might have tried to assign the piece. In fact, there are passages where our loss of tonal orientation is complete.

What led to this sudden spurt of chromaticism? Two trends fed it, both of them driven by the spirit of humanist inquiry. First, as we saw in Chapter 26, the second quarter of the sixteenth century had witnessed a general expansion of the gamut, a development sparked by Willaert's enharmonic jaunt through the circle of fifths in *Quid non ebrietas*. Second, the fascination with Greek music theory led a few musicians to experiment with the ancient *genera*, one of the systems of classification through which the Greeks ordered their tonal world. The genders, as we may call them, consisted of three tetrachords, each with a different combination of whole, half, and quarter tones (Ex. 35-4):

3. Quoted after Bergquist, "The Poems of Lasso's *Prophetiae Sibyllarum*," 533.

EXAMPLE 35-4. The Greek genders: (a) diatonic, (b) chromatic, and (c) enharmonic.

And it was in the work of the brilliant theorist Nicola Vicentino that the expanded gamut and the Greek genders most notably came together.

Vicentino's *L'antica musica*

Vicentino (1511–c. 1576; Fig. 35-2) spent the most productive years of his career shuttling between Ferrara (fast becoming a center of the musical avant-garde) and Rome in the retinue of his patron, Cardinal Ippolito II d'Este. The most notable musical event in his life occurred at Rome in 1551, when he engaged the Portuguese musician Vicente Lusitano in a debate about the Greek genders. Vicentino argued for the validity and independence of the three genders, while Lusitano held that the diatonic gender alone was sufficient to explain most contemporary music. The judges, members of the papal chapel, declared Vicentino the loser. Yet the experience may have spurred Vicentino to develop his ideas into his theoretical masterpiece, *L'antica musica ridotta alla musica moderna* (1555; 2nd ed. 1557).

Among the highlights of the treatise is a discussion of the Greek genders,

Figure 35-2. Portrait of Vicentino, woodcut from *L'antica musica*, 1555.

which Vicentino illustrated with his own compositions. Example 35-5 shows the opening of the piece that, with its half-step inflections of a single pitch class (B-flat/B-natural and E-flat/E-natural), represents the chromatic gender:

EXAMPLE 35-5. Vicentino, *Essempio del genere cromatico*, mm. 1–13.

Even more radical—and really the main focus of the treatise—is the discussion of the *arcicembalo*, a harpsichord that Vicentino constructed in order to demonstrate the viability of writing music in the three genders (Fig. 35-3). According to Vicentino's description, the instrument had 132 keys, used a mean-tone tuning, and divided the octave into thirty-one parts. There were two keyboards, each with three ranks of keys (the top two on each keyboard consisting of split keys). The six ranks (from bottom to top) consisted of (1) the normal white notes with their diatonic scale; (2) the black notes customarily used in the sixteenth century; (3) the less frequently used black notes (in the context of a mean-tone tuning); (4) notes parallel to those in the first rank but tuned a *diesis* (fifth of a tone) higher (indicated by the dot); (5) notes parallel to those in the second and third ranks but also tuned a *diesis* higher;

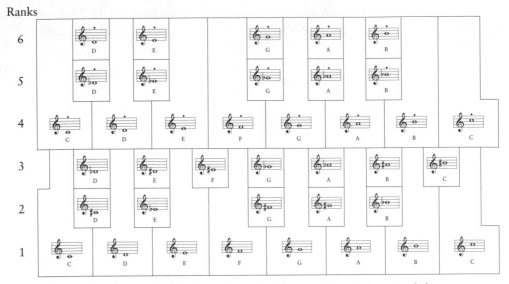

Figure 35-3. The two keyboards and six ranks of keys on Vicentino's arcicembalo (adapted from *New Grove*, 19: 700).

and (6) notes parallel to those of the first and fourth ranks but tuned halfway between them (indicated by the comma).

Vicentino's keyboard was far too complicated to be of practical use, but this was not important. For his aim was as much aesthetic as anything else; he urged composers to go beyond the strictures of the modal system and obey one law: "breathe life into the text, and . . . demonstrate with the harmonies chosen its passions, now harsh, now sweet, now gay, now sad."[4] In the end, Vicentino was a visionary!

Gesualdo

Chromaticism found its warmest welcome in Italy, especially in the madrigals of Carlo Gesualdo (c. 1561–1613), Prince of Venosa, who made it a hallmark of his style. Gesualdo came from a noble family of southern Italy. Among the most notable of his relatives was Cardinal Carlo Borromeo of Milan, who was canonized in 1610. The day that stands out in Gesualdo's life is October 16, 1590: having caught his wife, Maria d'Avalos (daughter of the Marquis of Pescara), and her aristocratic lover in a compromising act, he murdered both of them. The excitement that the double murder occasioned has colored the literature about the composer right down to the present day.

Gesualdo's fame rests mainly on his six books of madrigals (he also wrote sacred music), with Books V and VI (both published in 1611) containing his most stylistically distinctive works. Here we consider the most famous of them, *Moro, lasso, al mio duolo* (*Anthology* 84), an example of both his mature style and the culmination of sixteenth-century chromaticism.

4. Quoted after Lowinsky, *Tonality and Atonality in Sixteenth-Century Music*, 43.

Here is the poem:

1. Moro, lasso, al mio duolo	I die, wearily, in my suffering,
2. E chi mi può dar vita	And she who could give me life,
3. Ahi, che m'ancide e non vuol darmi aita!	Alas, is she who kills me and will not help me!
4. O dolorosa sorte,	O painful fortune,
5. Chi dar vita mi può, ahi, mi dà morte!	She who could give me life, alas, gives me death.

The poem is typical of much late-sixteenth-century madrigalian poetry in two respects: it is dark and brooding, and it plays with the idea of antithesis—here, the paradox of the lover who can offer both life and death. Gesualdo underscores these attributes of the poem with his own display of musical antitheses: harmonic, rhythmic, and textural. The music for the first three lines makes the point.

1. Gesualdo sets the dark opening line, which dwells on death and suffering, with a low-lying passage (omitting the top voice) that bristles with chromaticism, moves homophonically, and lacks any sense of rhythmic pulse.

2. With the poetic turn to "life," the top voice chimes in, melody and harmony become diatonic, the texture turns imitative, the rhythm gains a pulse, and there is even a little melisma on "vita."

3. The poem need only say "alas," and the music takes the hint.

Thus Gesualdo does not use chromaticism merely for its own sake. He employs it for expressive purposes, and at the same time uses it in alternation with diatonicism to build a structure defined by short bursts of antithetical musical ideas that echo those of the poem. First and foremost, Gesualdo places chromaticism at the service of the text.

Today, *Moro, lasso, al mio duolo* is a favorite. It was not always so, however. In volume 2 of his *General History of Music* (1782), Charles Burney wrote that the piece

> is presented to the musical reader as a specimen of [Gesualdo's] style, and harsh, crude, and licentious modulation; in which, the beginning a composition in A minor, with the chord of C-sharp, with a sharp third, is neither consonant to the present laws of *modulation*, nor settled and determined on the fixed principles of major and minor . . . but a more offensive license is taken in the second chord of this madrigal than in the first; for it is not only repugnant to every rule of transition at present established, but extremely shocking and disgusting to the ear, to go from one chord to another in which there is no *relation*, real or imaginary; and which is composed of sounds wholly extraneous and foreign to any key to which the first chord belongs.[5]

It never fails to amaze how one age—including our own—can misconstrue the intentions of another.

Gesualdo was, by all accounts, a deeply disturbed personality, and during the final decade of his life he more or less withdrew from society. He also began to act out certain masochistic tendencies, maintaining a group of young men

5. Excerpted from Watkins, *Gesualdo*, 302–5.

Figure 35-4. Portrait of Zarlino by an unknown artist (Civico Museo Bibliografico Musicale, Bologna).

whose job it was to flagellate him daily; the philosopher–natural scientist Tommaso Campanella (1568–1639) wrote that Gesualdo "was unable to move his bowels without having been previously flogged by a valet kept expressly for the purpose."[6]

It is tempting to draw a connection between the neurotic personality and the daring, even startling, use of chromaticism. Yet Gesualdo's use of chromaticism reflects influences he encountered at both Naples (in effect, his hometown) and Ferrara, where he spent two very productive years in 1594–96, after taking Leonora d'Este as his second wife. At Ferrara, for example Gesualdo openly admired the works of Luzzasco Luzzaschi (c. 1545–1607), a brilliant member of the Ferrarese avant-garde who introduced him to Vicentino's chromatic *arcicembalo*. In short, chromaticism was very much in the late-sixteenth-century air and ear.

ZARLINO AND COUNTERPOINT

Gioseffo Zarlino (Fig. 35-4) is the central theorist of the sixteenth century. More than anyone else, he synthesized the traditions of the mathematical *musica theorica* with the everyday problems of *musica pratica*. As he put it in his *Istitutioni harmoniche* (1558; 2nd ed. 1573): "Music considered in its ultimate perfection contains these two parts so closely joined that one cannot be separated from the other."[7]

Born in the small town of Chioggia in 1517(?), across the lagoon from Venice, Zarlino served as singer and organist in the town's cathedral between 1536 and 1540. In 1541, he went to Venice, where he studied with Willaert. On July 5, 1565, he succeeded Rore as *maestro di cappella* at St. Mark's and held this

6. Watkins, *Gesualdo*, 83.

7. Quoted after Marco and Palisca, *The Art of Counterpoint*, xvi. All examples in this section are drawn from Marco and Palisca's translation.

prestigious position until his death in 1590. Zarlino's influence was enormous: he taught some of the finest composers and organists of the period; and parts of his *Istitutioni* were still being used well into the eighteenth century. In a way, he summed up the musical practice of his time and passed it on to future generations.

The centerpiece of the *Istitutioni* is a textbook on counterpoint, which Zarlino codified after the style and teaching of Willaert. Here we look briefly at three aspects of counterpoint as taught by Zarlino.

INVERTIBLE COUNTERPOINT   Zarlino seems to be the first theorist to discuss *invertible counterpoint* (in which the voices of a polyphonic complex change positions, the higher one becoming the lower one and vice versa) in a thorough way. Moreover, he discusses two different types: in one, the two voices retain their original melodic identities when changing places; in the other, the melodies themselves are inverted as they change places.

Example 35-6 shows the two voices retaining their original contours on changing places, while Example 35-7 inverts both the position of the voices and the individual melodies:

EXAMPLE 35-6. Invertible counterpoint with melodic contours retained, mm. 1–9: (a) principal version, (b) inversion.

EXAMPLE 35-7. Invertible counterpoint with the melody itself inverted, mm. 1–9: (a) principal version, (b) inversion.

Zarlino's discussion of invertible counterpoint was taken up and further developed by seventeenth-century theorists.

EVADED CADENCES   Zarlino defines an *evaded cadence* as one in which "the voices give the impression of leading to a perfect cadence, and turn instead in a different direction." In effect, Zarlino is describing the often seamless counterpoint of the Willaert generation. Example 35-8 is from Zarlino's one example:

EXAMPLE 35-8. How to avoid a cadence.

How many cadences has he avoided?

FUGA AND *IMITATIONE*   Zarlino gives two explanations for the difference between these types of counterpoint:

> Fugue is the copy or repetition by one or more parts . . . using the same intervals . . . Imitation . . . is like what I have already described for the Fugue, except that it does not proceed by the same but by quite different intervals.

> Fugue, whether strict or free, occurs in many voice-parts of a piece, and these contain . . . the same intervals as does the Guide—whether in similar or contrary motion. . . . On the other hand, imitation, whether free or strict . . . does not show in its course the identical intervals in the consequent voices as are formed in the Guide.[8]

As always, Zarlino provides music examples:

EXAMPLE 35-9. Fugue and imitation: (a) strict fugue, (b) strict imitation.

(a)

(b)

The difference, then, is akin to the one that we make between "real" and "tonal" answers: in Zarlino's fugue, the answer is exact, each interval being answered precisely; in imitation, the intervals may be modified, so that a minor third is answered by a major third (as in Ex. 35-9b).

8. From Haar, "Zarlino's Definition of Fugue and Imitation," 228–30.

Had knowledgeable musicians of the late 1500s been asked to choose the music theorist-encyclopedist of the century, there can be little doubt that Zarlino would have won hands down. To be sure, he came to his task with the predispositions then current: the best music was of his own time, and he accepted many things uncritically. Yet we can surely close an eye to that. To read through even the driest portions of the *Istitutioni* is to sense that Zarlino lived, breathed, and ate music and simply wanted to tell anyone who would listen everything he knew about it.

BIBLIOGRAPHICAL NOTE

Editions and Translations of the Theorists

Glarean: the treatise is translated by Clement Miller, *Dodecachordon*, 2 vols., MSD 6 (American Institute of Musicology, 1965). **Vicentino**: there is a facsimile edition of *L'antica musica*, with an introduction by Edward E. Lowinsky, in the series Documenta musicologica, series I, vol. 17 (Kassel: Bärenreiter, 1959); a translation under the title *Ancient Music Adapted to Modern Practice* by Maria Rika Maniates appears in the Music Theory Translation Series published by Yale University Press under the general editorship of Claude V. Palisca; another treatise by Vicentino, *Descrizione dell'arciorgano* (1561), is translated in Henry W. Kaufmann, "Vicentino's Arciorgano: An Annotated Translation," *JMT* 5 (1961): 32. Kaufmann also edited Vicentino's compositions: *Opera omnia*, CMM 26 (American Institute of Musicology, 1961); and one should certainly consult Kaufmann's *Life and Works of Nicola Vicentino*, MSD 11 (American Institute of Musicology, 1966). **Zarlino**: Part III of *Le Istitutioni harmoniche* is translated by Guy A. Marco and Claude V. Palisca as *The Art of Counterpoint*, Music Theory Translation Series 2 (New Haven: Yale University Press, 1968), Part IV by Vered Cohen, *On the Modes*, Music Theory Translation Series 7 (New Haven: Yale University Press, 1983). There are two facsimile editions: the original edition of 1558 by Broude Brothers (New York, 1965), that of 1573 by Gregg Press (Ridgewood, N.J., 1966); in addition, there are facsimile editions of Zarlino's *Dimostrationi harmoniche* (1571) and *Sopplimenti musicali* (1588) by Broude Brothers (New York, 1965, 1979).

Mode

Two scholars in particular have made major contributions to the subject—Bernhard Meier, *The Modes of Classical Vocal Polyphony*, trans. Ellen Beebe (New York: Broude Bros, 1988; original German, 1974); and Harold S. Powers, "Is Mode Real? Pietro Aron, the Octenary System, and Polyphony," *BJfHM* 16 (1992): 9–52, "Modal Representation in Polyphonic Offertories," *EMH* 2 (1982): 43–86, "Tonal Types and Modal Categories," *JAMS* 34 (1981): 428–70. See also the important article by Cristle Collins Judd, "Modal Types and *Ut, Re, Mi* Tonalities: Tonal Coherence in Sacred Vocal Polyphony from about 1500," *JAMS* 45 (1992): 428–67; Sarah Fuller, "Defending the *Dodecachordon*: Ideological Currents in Glarean's Modal Theory," *JAMS* 49 (1996): 191–224; Peter N. Schubert, "Mode and Counterpoint," in *Music Theory and the Exploration of the Past*, ed. Christopher Hatch and David W. Bernstein (Chicago: Chicago University Press, 1993), 103–36; Jeffrey G. Kurtzman, "Tones, Modes, Clefs, and Pitch in Roman Cyclic Magnificats of the 16th Century," *EM* 22 (1994): 641–64. On the expressive qualities of the modes, see Meier, "Rhetorical Aspects of the Renaissance Modes," *JRMA* 115 (1990): 182–90; Palisca, "Mode Ethos in the Renaissance," in *Essays in Musicology: A Tribute to Alvin Johnson*, ed. Lewis Lockwood and Edward H. Roesner (Philadelphia: American Musicological Society, 1990), 126–39.

Chromaticism

For an overview (a subjective one), see Edward E. Lowinsky, *Tonality and Atonality in Sixteenth-Century Music* (Berkeley and Los Angeles: University of California Press, 1962); another entry point is the literature on Lassus's *Prophetiae sibyllarum*: William J. Mitchell, "The Prologue to Orlando di Lasso's *Prophetiae Sibyllarum*," *MF* 2 (1970): 264–73; Karol Berger, *Theories of Chromatic and Enharmonic Music in Late Sixteenth-Century Italy*, Studies in Musicology 10 (Ann Arbor: UMI Research Press, 1980), "Tonality and Atonality in the Prologue to Orlando di Lasso's *Prophetiae Sibyllarum*: Some Methodological Problems in Analysis of Sixteenth-Century Music," *MQ* 65 (1980): 484–504, and "The Common and the Unusual Steps of *Musica Ficta*: A Background for the Gamut of Orlando di Lasso's *Prophetiae Sibyllarum*," *RBM* 39/40 (1985/1988): 61–73; see also Kenneth J. Levy, "Costeley's Chromatic Chanson," *AnnM* 3 (1955): 213–63.

Gesualdo

His works are edited in *Carlo Gesualdo: Sämtliche Werke*, 9 vols., ed. Wilhelm Weismann and Glenn Watkins (Hamburg: Ugrino, 1957–67); the standard monograph is Watkins, *Gesualdo: The Man and His Music* (Chapel Hill: North Carolina University Press, 1973).

Humanism

Any research on humanism's influence on music theory must begin with Claude V. Palisca, *Humanism in Italian Renaissance Musical Thought* (New Haven: Yale University Press, 1985).

Also Cited

Peter Bergquist, "The Poems of Orlando di Lasso's *Prophetiae Sibyllarum* and Their Sources," *JAMS* 32 (1979): 516–38; James Haar, "Zarlino's Definition of Fugue and Imitation," *JAMS* 24 (1971): 226–54.

CHAPTER 36

Intermedio: 1560–1562

A COOKBOOK

Domenico Romoli may not have been much better-known in the sixteenth century than he is in ours. But in 1560, he published *La singolar dottrina dello scalco* (The Whole Doctrine of the Office of the Chef), one of many cookbooks that were published throughout the century. In fact, small, often pamphlet-sized cookbooks became a mainstay of the printer's trade, especially in Elizabethan England, where the tradition was initiated in 1545 with *A Proper Newe Booke of Cookerye*, the first cookbook to be printed in English.

The sixteenth century was a time of changing tastes in food, at least among the upper classes and particularly in Italy, which, as it did in so many cultural areas, led the way. The trend was away from the heavily spiced, hacked-up hashes and gruels and toward a cooking in which the various ingredients, aided by a sauce, retained their natural taste and appearance. The high point of this shift occurred in the middle of the seventeenth century, when François Pierre de la Varenne published his two great classics: *Le vray cuisinier* and *Le patissier françois*, which ushered in the art of French *haute cuisine*.

In addition, new foods were imported from the New World: turkeys were introduced by Spanish conquistadors in the 1530s; in the 1550s, the Portuguese returned from Brazil with the pineapple; the 1560s saw the Spaniards bring back potatoes from Peru, and from Spain potatoes made their way to the Low Countries and Italy, reaching Ireland in the 1580s. Also new to some extent was the orange, which, though known to medieval tables, was only cultivated on a large scale beginning in the sixteenth century. Coffee, consumed by European travelers to the Islamic world, reached Venice around 1615.

There was another trend: starting around the middle of the century, the consumption of meat declined dramatically, as the production of livestock plummeted and prices rose sharply. As a Swabian gentleman named Heinrich Müller wrote in 1550:

> In the past they ate differently at the peasant's house. Then, there was meat and food in profusion every day; tables at village fairs and feasts sank under their load. Today, everything has truly changed. Indeed, for some years now, what a calamitous time, what high prices! And the food of the most comfortably-off peasants is almost worse than that of day-labourers and valets in the old days.[1]

1. Quoted after Braudel, *The Structures of Everyday Life*, 194–95.

Müller's lament was echoed many times. As noted in Chapter 19, the sixteenth century was one in which a decline in the standard of living for the working class was the general rule.

Finally, there were new developments in the way the table was set. Each guest was now provided with a goblet; no longer was a single glass passed from mouth to mouth. Guests were also supplied with their own knives; they no longer had to bring their own. And by the end of the century, an idea that first sprang up at Venice would soon spill over to other parts of Europe: the fork. This new utensil was remarked on by the English traveler Thomas Coryat in the first decade of the seventeenth century:

> I observed a custome in all those Italian Cities and towns through which I passed, that is not used in any other country that I saw in my travels. . . . The Italian and also most strangers that are commorant in Italy, doe alwaies at their meales use a little forke when they cut their meat. For while with their knife which they hold in one hand they cut the meate out of the dish, they fasten their forke which they hold in their other hand upon the same dish, so that whatsoever he be that sitting in the company of any others at meale, shoulde unadvisedly touch the dishe of meate with his fingers from which all at table doe cut, he will give occasion of offence unto the company. . . . This forme of feeding I understand is generally used in all places of Italy, their forkes being for the most part made of yron or steele, and some of silver. . . . The reason of this their curiosity is, because the Italian cannot by any means indure to have his dish touched with fingers, seeing all men's fingers are not alike cleane.[2]

Here is Domenico Romoli's recipe for "friars' fritters" (modernized for our kitchens):

2 tsp. rosemary	¼ tsp. cinnamon
1 tsp. taragon	¼ tsp. pepper
1 tsp. thyme	¼ pint sweet white wine
2 oz. butter	3 oz. white breadcrumbs
3 eggs	2 tsp. grated Parmesan

Fry herbs lightly in butter, without browning. If fresh herbs are used, increase quantities to about 1 tbs. each. Allow to cool, beat lightly with the eggs, and add cinnamon, pepper, wine, and breadcrumbs. Allow to stand for 1 hour. Add Parmesan. Fry in fresh butter, making fritters about 1 inch thick.[3]

A COUNTRY VILLA

In 1561, the Venetian-based painter Paolo Veronese (1528–1588) finished decorating the interior of the Villa Barbaro, which had recently been completed by the architect Andrea Palladio. (His real name was Andrea di Pietro della Gondola; "Palladio," referring to Pallas Athene, goddess of wisdom, was a nickname given him by an early patron.) Located at Maser (about thirty miles northwest of Venice, pretty much in the middle of nowhere), the Villa Barbaro

2. Quoted after Barber, *Cooking and Recipes,* 110.

3. Barber, *Cooking and Recipes,* 119.

(Fig. 36-1) was commissioned as a principal residence by the brothers Daniele and Marcantonio Barbaro, members of one of Venice's great patrician families and landowners in the area. In effect, the villa was a working farm; the arcades that fan out from each side of the main dwelling housed animals, grain, and supplies.

Daniele Barbaro (1513–1570) was a cleric and delegate to the Council of Trent, a mathematician and philosopher, superintendent of the botanical gardens at Padua (considered by some contemporaries as the best in Europe), Venetian ambassador to England (1548–50), coeditor (with Palladio) of Vitruvius's famous *De architectura* (1556), and author of a book on perspective (1569). Barbaro and others like him made Venice the great intellectual and artistic center that it was.

Palladio

Except for expeditions to central and southern Italy in order to study Roman ruins firsthand, Palladio (1508–1580), a stone cutter by training, spent virtually his entire career in the Veneto, where he designed country villas, urban palaces, and churches. Even a fleeting glance at the Villa Barbaro is enough to tell us the source of Palladio's inspiration: classical antiquity (Roman in particular), with its emphasis on symmetry, grandeur, and stillness. Yet his nineteen country villas, sixteen urban palaces and public buildings, and nine churches are anything but look-alikes. For example, Palladio based the symmetry of the design

Figure 36-1. Palladio, Villa Barbaro, at Maser, c. 1555–59.

Figure 36-2. Palladio, Villa Rotonda, at Vicenza, c. 550–51.

of his most famous villa, *La Rotonda* (Fig. 36-2), built in 1550–51 at Vicenza, on a dome-capped cylinder rising through the center of a Greek cross (one with arms of equal length).

What did remain constant throughout Palladio's work was an insistence on what might be called "harmonic proportion": the proportions of the various parts of a villa (or palace or church) stood in a logical and aesthetically pleasing relationship with one another. And as he explained in his *Quattro libri dell'architectura* (1570), the ultimate source of this relationship was "nature": the cosmic numbers that imparted reason and beauty to the universe (and, for that matter, to music, according to theorists from Pythagoras to Zarlino). For Palladio, this translated into three guiding principles: (1) a sense of hierarchy in which the various parts were built up systematically to a central focal point; (2) the proportional integration of the parts to one another and to the whole; and (3) the coordination of exterior and interior.

There is hardly a better example of such proportional design than the ground plan of the Villa Chiericati, built just outside Vicenza in the mid-1550s (Fig. 36-3).[4] There is more at work here than the customary mirror-image of the two sides that flank the see-through central axis. The rooms that run along either side from back to front (the measurements are in *piedi*, or feet) are 18 wide × 12 deep, 18 wide × 18 deep, and 30 wide × 18 deep. Thus as we go from one room to the next, one dimension remains the same while the second one changes; and all dimensions are factors of six. In musical terms, the rooms sound a perfect fifth (18 × 12 = 3:2), unison (18 × 18 = 1:1), and major sixth (30 × 18 = 5:3). Thus the villa forms a silent major triad! And if the central hall is only 16 *piedi* deep instead of the expected 18, the narrowing was necessary for structural reasons.

Thanks in large part to the accessibility of his *Quattro libri*, which nicely

4. Derived from Palladio's *Quattro libri*, reproduced in Ackerman, *Palladio*, 166.

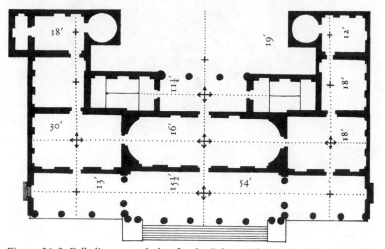

Figure 36-3. Palladio, ground plan for the Palazzo Chiericati at Vancimuglio, 554–57 (after Ackerman, *Palladio*, 166).

translated the essence of his style in line-cut illustrations, Palladio's influence was nothing short of spectacular, especially in the English-speaking world. In the seventeenth century, Inigo Jones transferred the style of the Palladian villa to England, while our own Southern plantation owners—Washington and Jefferson, among them—dotted the American landscape with it in the eighteenth. One estimate puts Palladio's architectural offspring in the hundreds of thousands.

TERESA OF ÁVILA AND EL GRECO

In 1562, Teresa of Ávila (1515–1582) left the Carmelite convent of La Encarnación, where she had lived as a nun since the mid-1530s. Unlike the young nun whose complaints we heard in the popular fifteenth-century song *Ora may, que fflora·n ço* (Chapter 6), Teresa did not leave in order to gain her freedom. Rather, she was distressed with the convent's lack of discipline and spirituality. In fact, for those, like Teresa, who were daughters of aristocratic families—and class distinctions were rigidly enforced—La Encarnación, like Carmelite convents in general, was not unlike a five-star hotel.

In the mid-1540s, Teresa had begun to have visions, which she interpreted as rebuking her easy convent life. Gradually the visions became more intense, until by the mid-1550s they had become trance-like. The most famous of these occurred around 1560:

> In his [an angel's] hands I saw a long golden spear and at the end of the iron tip I seemed to see a point of fire. With this he seemed to pierce my heart several times so that it reached to my entrails. When he drew it out, I thought he was drawing them out with it, and he left me completely afire with a great love of God.[5]

5. Quoted after Rabb, *Renaissance Lives*, 103.

Her experience, which marked the completion of Teresa's "conversion," eventually inspired one of the greatest monuments of seventeenth-century sculpture: Gian Lorenzo Bernini's *Ecstasy of St. Teresa* (1544–52; Fig. 36-4).

Having left La Encarnación, Teresa and four companions founded a new, reformed order: the "Discalced" (barefoot, though they wore sandals) Carmelites. Teresa's intention was to restore the Carmelite nuns to their original monastic way of life: worldly goods were renounced; class distinctions within the convent were abolished; contact with the outside world was kept to a minimum; and obedience to authority was paramount.

Befriended by a like-minded Carmelite monk who took the name Juan de la Cruz, Teresa set out to transform the Carmelite order throughout Spain. The resistance from both church and civil authorities, neither of which took kindly to having the status quo upset, was fierce: nuns were excommunicated, Teresa was charged with being possessed by demons, and both she and Juan were arrested. Yet Teresa's persistence finally led to success. During the last twenty years of her life, she founded sixteen convents and fourteen monasteries. And in 1581, the Discalced Carmelites gained official recognition from both king (Philip II) and church (Gregory XIII). Teresa was canonized in 1622.

In a way, Teresa represents the essence of the Counter-Reformation: the answer to those who questioned the church was not to doubt, but to believe ever more passionately, even mystically. Among Teresa's contemporaries in Spain was a painter with mystical visions of his own.

Figure 36-4. Bernini, *The Ecstasy of St. Teresa*, 1644–52 (S. Maria della Vittoria, Rome).

El Greco

Born on the island of Crete, Domenikos Theotokopoulos (?1541–1614) emigrated to Italy around 1560 and then went on to Spain in 1577, where he settled at Toledo and was known as El Greco. There is hardly a better artistic counterpart to the visions of Teresa and Juan de la Cruz than El Greco's *Resurrection of Christ* (1600–5; Fig. 36-5). The elongated and contorted bodies, which seem to float in space, both repel and beckon invitingly. The contrasts in light both disturb and soothe. The message, though, is singular: believe! And that same message would resound clearly in the works of the greatest Spanish composer of the period, Tomás Luis de Victoria.

Figure 36-5. El Greco,
Resurrection of Christ,
c. 1600–5 (Prado, Madrid).

BIBLIOGRAPHICAL NOTE

Eating Habits

There is a concise survey, with illustrations and recipes, in Richard Barber, *Cooking and Recipes from Rome to the Renaissance* (London: Allen Lane, 1973); see also chapter 3 in Fernand Braudel, *The Structures of Everyday Life: The Limits of the Possible*, vol. 1: *Civilization and Capitalism, 15th–18th Century*, trans. Siân Reynolds (Berkeley and Los Angeles: University of California Press, 1992).

Palladio

James S. Ackerman's two studies are a good starting point: *Palladio* (Harmondsworth: Penguin, 1966), and *Palladio's Villas* (Locust Valley, N.Y.: J.J. Augustin, 1967); on the artist-patron relationship between Palladio and Barbaro, see Douglas Lewis, "Patterns of Preference: Patronage of Sixteenth-Century Architects by the Venetian Patriciate," in *Patronage in the Renaissance*, ed. Guy Fitch Lytle and Stephen Orgel (Princeton: Princeton University Press, 1981), 354–80.

Teresa of Avila and El Greco

The English title of Teresa's autobiography is *The Life of Saint Teresa of Avila by Herself*, trans. J. M. Cohen (Harmondsworth: Penguin, 1957); there is a wonderfully concise and informative outline of Teresa's life and accomplishments in Theodore K. Rabb, *Renaissance Lives: Portraits of an Age* (New York: Pantheon, 1993); on Teresa's mysticism, see Catherine Swietlicke, *Spanish Christian Cabala: The Works of Luis de León, Santa Teresa de Jesus, and San Juan de la Cruz* (Columbia: University of Missouri Press 1986). The standard study and catalogue of El Greco's works is Harold E. Wethey, *El Greco and His School*, 2 vols. (Princeton: Princeton University Press, 1962); see also Jonathan Brown et al., *El Greco of Toledo* (Boston: Little, Brown, 1982).

CHAPTER 37

The Counter-Reformation
in Italy and Spain

The second half of the sixteenth century produced four great composers of
sacred music: Palestrina, Lassus, Byrd, and Victoria. Yet how different they
were with respect to background, artistic personality, and career track. Palestrina and Victoria were essentially church musicians, products of the Counter-
Reformation fervor that enveloped both Italy and Spain. Victoria wrote nothing
but sacred music, while a mature Palestrina saw fit to apologize for the madrigals
that he had written in his youth. Both composers figure prominently in this
chapter. Lassus was mainly a court composer, and spent the greater part of his
career in the service of the dukes of Bavaria, first Albrecht IV and then his son
Wilhelm V. A composer of mercurial genius, he was equally at home in genres
both sacred and secular, but it is primarily as a motet composer that he will
figure in Chapter 38 (though he sneaks in briefly below). Byrd was just as
versatile: a Catholic in a Protestant country, he composed music for both
churches, some of it behind closed doors; he was also productive as a composer
of instrumental music, writing for both consorts and keyboard. Byrd will take
center stage when we survey music in Elizabethan England in Chapter 40.

To begin, we look at the musical reforms called for at the Council of Trent.

THE COUNCIL OF TRENT I

When the Council of Trent convened for its third and final round of sessions
in 1562, it took up a number of matters pertaining to church music. The noisiest
debate centered on the nature of sacred polyphony. Simply stated, the council
put polyphony—specifically, the contrapuntal style of the Netherlanders—on
trial. The charges: such music obscured the words and too often infused sacred
music with secular elements, as in parody Masses based on chansons or madrigals. None of this was new. Calvin had already found such polyphony guilty
about a quarter century earlier; and we can trace anti-polyphony sentiments all
the way back to the fourteenth century, when Pope John XXIII railed against
the complexities of the *Ars nova*.

In September, a group of deputies issued a statement in which they emphasized that secular elements should be eliminated from church music, and music
should not obscure the words:

All things should indeed be so ordered that the Masses, whether they be celebrated with or without singing, may reach tranquilly into the ears and hearts of those who hear them, when everything is executed clearly and at the right speed. In the case of those Masses which are celebrated with singing and with organ, let nothing profane be intermingled, but only hymns and divine praises. The whole plan of singing in musical modes should be constituted not to give empty pleasure to the ear, but in such a way that the words be clearly understood by all, and thus the hearts of the listeners be drawn to desire of heavenly harmonies, in the contemplation of the joys of the blessed. . . . They shall also banish from church all music that contains, whether in the singing or in the organ playing, things that are lascivious or impure.[1]

Clearly, this is a far cry from Calvin's total ban on polyphony. Indeed, all attempts at such a ban were defeated, thanks, it seems, to a series of pieces by the Netherlander Jacob de Kerle (1531/32–1591) in which he demonstrated to the delegates that polyphony was capable of projecting the words in an intelligible manner. Kerle, then—and not Palestrina, as legend has it—may have been the first "savior" of polyphony.

In August 1564, a committee headed by Cardinals Carlo Borromeo and Vitellozzo Vitelli was charged with carrying out the council's decrees on music. In the next months, Cardinal Borromeo, Archbishop of Milan and papal secretary of state (and thus residing at Rome), wrote three letters concerning music to his vicar at the Cathedral of Milan:

> January 20, 1565
> Speak to the master of the chapel [Vincenzo Ruffo] . . . and tell him to reform the singing so that the words may be as intelligible as possible, as ordered by the council. You might have him compose some motets and see how matters go.

> March 10
> I desire above all that the matter of the intelligible music succeed according to the hope you have given me. Therefore I would like you to order Ruffo, in my name, to compose a Mass that should be as clear as possible and send it to me here.

> March 31
> I shall await Ruffo's Mass; and if Don Nicola [Vicentino], who favors chromatic music, should be in Milan, you can also ask him to compose one. Thus by the comparison of the work of many excellent musicians we will be better able to judge this intelligible music.[2]

Though we do not know if Vicentino ever complied, Ruffo did; and we therefore turn to him now.

Vincenzo Ruffo

Between 1551 and 1572, Vincenzo Ruffo (c. 1508–1587) held two of the most prestigious musical posts in northern Italy: *maestro di musica* at the Acca-

1. Quoted after Reese, *Music in the Renaissance*, 449.
2. Quoted after Lockwood, *Palestrina: Pope Marcellus Mass*, 20–22.

demia Filarmonica of Verona and, from 1563, chapel master at the Duomo of
Milan. This latter post marked a turning point in his career; having been a
prolific composer of madrigals, he turned his back on the genre and devoted
himself entirely to sacred music in the spirit of the Tridentine reforms.

In 1570, Ruffo published a collection of Masses entitled *Missae quatuor con-
cinate ad Ritum concilii Mediolani*. As the title makes clear, the Masses were composed in "accordance with Conciliar decree"; moreover, the preface makes it
equally clear that he composed the Masses as part of a special project

> which Cardinal Borromeo had formerly imposed on me, that in accordance
> with the decrees of the Most Holy Council of Trent I was to compose some
> Masses that should avoid everything of a profane and idle manner in wor-
> ship. . . . Accordingly . . . I composed one Mass in this way; so that the num-
> bers of the syllables and the voices and tones together should be clearly and
> distinctly understood by the pious listeners. . . . Later, imitating that example,
> I more readily and easily composed other Masses of the same type.[3]

In Example 37-1, from the *Missa Quarti toni*, the homophonic texture projects
the words in a way that fits Ruffo's description and the council's decree:

EXAMPLE 37-1. Ruffo, *Missa Quarti toni*, Gloria, mm. 1–17.

3. Quoted after Lockwood, *Vincenzo Ruffo: Seven Masses*, 1: viii.

Needless to say, Ruffo would not have published the collection with that title and preface had the Masses not pleased Cardinal Borromeo and convinced him and his committee that polyphony and the desires of the council were perfectly compatible. Perhaps, then, Ruffo may be called the second "savior" of polyphony.

In truth, the whole affair is rather disappointing. For the end result after all the debate, commissions, test pieces, trials, and so on was simply syllabic homophony. Any Protestant reformer could have saved them the trouble. And though even Palestrina and Lassus occasionally wrote Masses and other liturgical works in a rigorously syllabic style, there can be no doubt that they found the council's solutions artistically impoverished. They continued to write in a rich contrapuntal style (tempered by homophony), and they continued to draw on secular models without looking over their shoulder. They would find other ways to express the heightened religiosity of the Counter-Reformation.

Yet the council did bring about some changes: it inspired the development of the *Missa brevis* and the "spiritual madrigal"; it reawakened interest in the *lauda*; and it undertook major revisions in both the liturgy and the plainsong repertory that served it. We will consider these below. First, however, it is time to turn to the composer with whom history has most closely associated the Counter-Reformation in general and the council in particular.

PALESTRINA

When musicians of the seventeenth and eighteenth centuries looked back to music from before 1600, they looked mainly to music of one composer: Giovanni Pierluigi da Palestrina (Fig. 37-1, p. 589). For when the music of Palestrina's contemporaries was gathering dust, his remained alive and was even raised to the status of a pedagogical model. As one critic has put it: "Palestrina's historical reputation resembles that of no other composer in musical history."[4] In large part, his reputation rests on two myths.

Myth 1: The Savior of Polyphony

In 1607, the theorist Agostino Agazzari published a treatise on figured bass in which he voiced his pleasure that imitative polyphony was no longer in fashion, for it obscured the words to the point that they were unintelligible. He then noted:

> And on this account music would have come very near to being banished from the Holy Church by a sovereign pontiff had not Giovanni Palestrina found the remedy, showing that the fault and error lay, not with music, but with the composers, and composing in confirmation of this the Mass entitled *Missa Papae Marcelli*.[5]

4. Lockwood, "Palestrina," 130–31.

5. Quoted after Lockwood, *Palestrina: Pope Marcellus Mass*, 28–29.

So began the story that Palestrina and his *Pope Marcellus* Mass saved polyphonic church music from the clutches of the Tridentine censors.

The title of the Mass, which was published in 1567 as part of Palestrina's second book of Masses, refers to Pope Marcellus II, who reigned for a grand total of twenty days in 1555. It is one of Palestrina's "free" Masses, not based on preexistent material; its Gloria, in particular, is written in an almost severe homophonic-syllabic style (Ex. 37-2):

EXAMPLE 37-2. Palestrina, *Pope Marcellus* Mass, Gloria, mm. 1–16.

Other movements, however, are more contrapuntal, with the Agnus Dei culminating in a grand seven-voice complex built on a three-part canon (Ex. 37-3).

From Agazzari's treatise, the story about Palestrina and his Mass spread throughout the seventeenth and eighteenth centuries. It reached its most highly

EXAMPLE 37-3. Palestrina, *Pope Marcellus* Mass, Agnus Dei II, mm. 1–13.

embroidered point in 1828, when Giuseppe Baini published his pathbreaking biography of Palestrina. Baini now told the story in soap-opera fashion:

> It was finally resolved, to the mutual satisfaction of Cardinal[s] Vitellozzi . . . and . . . Borromeo . . . that Palestrina should be given a commission to write a Mass that should be serious, ecclesiastical, free of every admixture of the

secular in its subject, melodies, and measure. . . . If Palestrina succeeded, the cardinals promised to make no changes in the state of church music; if not, they let it be known that the steps that would be taken would be decided by them and the other six members of the congregation on the enforcement of the decrees of the Council of Trent.

Cardinal Borromeo took on this commission himself. Summoning Palestrina before him, he told him face to face to compose a Mass in the desired manner, enjoining on him all possible effort to prevent the possibility that the pope and the Congregation of Cardinals might be encouraged to ban music from the apostolic chapel and from the church. . . .

Poor Pierluigi! He was placed in the hardest straits of his career. The fate of church music hung from his pen, and so did his own career, at the height of his fame.[6]

And though "poor Pierluigi" has yet to hit the wide screen, the episode described by Baini did become the subject of an opera, Hans Pfitzner's *Palestrina* (1917).

In fact, there is not a shred of evidence to show that Palestrina composed the *Marcellus* Mass for the "auditions" at Cardinal Vitelli's home in April 1565. In fact, the Mass may date from as early as 1562–63. On the other hand, the Mass could well have been composed in response to the signals already coming out of the Council of Trent. Beyond this, nothing can be said.

Myth 2: The Pedagogical Model

In the early seventeenth century, Palestrina was held up as the model of the so-called *stile antico*, the strict style of *a cappella* diatonic counterpoint that, though out of fashion by then, was still cultivated from time to time as a way of giving sacred music an aura of nostalgic religiosity. This was a tradition that would live on well into the nineteenth century, so that even Beethoven studied Palestrina-style counterpoint (as well as Zarlino's *Istitutioni harmoniche*) in preparation for writing his own *Missa solemnis*.

This pedestal-like image of Palestrina—or what is often called the "Palestrina style"—as a pedagogical model for teaching counterpoint reached high gear in 1725, when Johann Joseph Fux published his famous *Gradus ad parnassum*. For Fux, who wrote his treatise in the form of a dialogue between himself as student and Palestrina as master, Palestrina was "the celebrated light of music . . . to whom I owe everything that I know of this art and whose memory I shall never cease to cherish." In other words, Fux turned Palestrina's style into the pedagogical norm.

The first problem here is one of overstatement: the myth too casually makes Palestrina the representative of sixteenth-century—or "modal"—counterpoint as a whole, something he decidedly was not. The second problem is that the myth is based on too limited a view of Palestrina's style. That Palestrina was a great contrapuntist is undeniable, but he was also a great "homophonicist"; how else, after all, could he have "saved" polyphonic church music?

It is time to turn from the myth to the man.

6. Quoted after Lockwood, *Palestrina: Pope Marcellus Mass*, 35.

A Biographical Sketch

Once we get past the period of Palestrina's youth, we know a great deal about his life. He traveled little and spent virtually his entire career in the service of three Roman churches whose records are well preserved.

Thanks to a eulogy that states that Palestrina was sixty-eight years old when he died on February 2, 1594, we know that he was born between February 3, 1525, and February 2, 1526, probably in the small town of Palestrina (in the hills just outside Rome), from which his name is derived. His training was gained at Rome, at the church of Santa Maria Maggiore, where he was a choir-boy by October 1537 and where he studied with two well-respected French musicians, Robin Mallapert and Firmin Le Bel. By October 1544, he is recorded as organist and *maestro di canto* in his native town. And there he met two people who would play important roles in his life: Lucrezia Gori, who became his wife in June 1547 (and with whom he had three sons), and Cardinal Giovanni Maria del Monte, Bishop of Palestrina, who was elected pope as Julius III in 1550 and soon thereafter brought Palestrina back to Rome.

The remainder of Palestrina's career is laid out in Table 37-1:

Table 37-1.   Palestrina's career, 1551–94.

Date	Employment and other events	Comments
9/1551	Appointed maestro of the Cappella Giulia at St. Peter's.	Recruited by Julius III, former Bishop of Palestrina; succeeded his former teacher, Mallapert.
1554	Published Book I of Masses.	Dedicated to Julius III; first record of Palestrina as a composer, and only the second published collection of Masses by an Italian composer.
1/1555	Appointed singer in the papal chapel.	Julius III pulled strings: no audition, no consent of the other singers, and in violation of the prohibition of married singers.
9/1555	Dismissed from papal chapel by Paul IV.	Dismissed together with two other married singers; received a pension worth $\frac{2}{3}$ his salary.
10/1555	Appointed maestro at church of San Giovanni in Laterano.	Position formerly held by Lassus; retained until 7/1560.
3/1561	Returned to Santa Maria Maggiore.	Stayed until 1566.
1564	Entered service of Cardinal Ippolito II d'Este on part-time basis.	Directed summer music at Villa d'Este.
1566	Began teaching music at the Seminario Romano.	This provided free schooling for two sons; retained post until 3/1571.

Date	Employment and other events	Comments
8/1567	Entered full-time service with Cardinal Ippolito II d'Este.	Kept position until 3/1571, thus holding two posts.
1567	Published Book II of Masses.	Contains *Marcellus* Mass.
1568	Declined position of imperial choirmaster at court of Emperor Maximilian II.	Post went to Philippe de Monte.
	Began two-decade correspondence with Duke Guglielmo Gonzaga of Mantua.	12 letters survive; Palestrina's only known correspondence.
4/1571	Returned to Cappella Giulia as maestro.	Succeeded Giovanni Animuccia; held post until his death.
1572–80	Death of brother (1573), two sons (1572, 1575), and wife (1580).	A third son survived him; after his wife died, he considered the priesthood.
1581	Married a well-off widow, Virginia Dormoli.	
1583	Declined post of chapel master at Mantua.	
1583–84	Published *Song of Songs*.	Contains apology for early secular music.
1592	Honored as dedicatee of collection of Vespers psalms.	
2/1594	Palestrina dies.	

Figure 37-1. Palestrina presenting his work to Pope Julius III, from title page of *Missarum liber primus*, 1554.

In addition, Palestrina occasionally free-lanced at various Roman churches and was one of the founding members of the *Compagnia dei musici di Roma*, the musicians' "union" founded at Rome in 1584.

That Palestrina was the most highly respected musician in Rome and probably in all of Italy can hardly be doubted. But the stuff of myth he was not. For despite the accolades and prestigious positions, he was very much a workaday church musician, often struggling to make ends meet and always saddled with musical and administrative responsibilities, which, for the head of the Cappella Giulia, were laid out in the following way: "As for the *maestro di cappella*, it were better not to lay down definite rules for his service, since he needs to be occupied much of the time in writing compositions and in continuing to teach the young boy singers, as well as the other young clerics."[7] And it was no doubt the requirement to compose, as much as inspiration, that resulted in Palestrina's enormous output.

The Masses

Palestrina composed about 700 works. Of these, 94 are secular madrigals; the rest are either for the liturgy itself or fall into the functionally slippery category of the motet. Of these sacred works, it is the 104 Masses—no other composer has equaled that number—for which he is most famous. They exemplify every Mass type known in the sixteenth century: parody (51), paraphrase (34), cantus firmus (8), free (6), and canonic (7), the last overlapping with some of the others.

Palestrina's favorite models for his parody Masses were his own works, especially his motets: twenty-four times he "parodied" himself. The other twenty-seven models were mainly motets by French, Netherlandish, and Spanish (Morales) composers of the preceding generation, particularly those with ties to Rome. What is striking, though, is the absence among the models of works by that generation's three greatest motet composers: Gombert, Clemens, and Willaert. Only once did he look as far back as the Josquin generation, and then to draw on a motet by Josquin himself. And though Palestrina presumably composed parody Masses until the end of his career, there is only one instance in which the model was a work published after 1563. In his choice of models, then, Palestrina tended to look backward.

MISSA DUM COMPLERENTUR The *Missa Dum complerentur*, which appeared in the posthumous eighth book of Masses (1599), is based on Palestrina's own motet on that text, published in 1569 but already circulating in manuscript during the early 1560s.

The motet (*Anthology* 85a) draws its text from a Matins responsory for Pentecost. And though Palestrina does not use the plainsong (*Liber usualis*, 873–74), he respects its customary two-part structure in which each part ends with the same music and text. Thus the motet has two *partes* (these correspond to

---

7. Quoted after O'Regan, "Palestrina, a Musician and Composer in the Market Place," 556.

the "respond" and "verse" of the chant), with the final thirty-one measures of each *pars* being identical: **a** (mm. 1–52), **B** (mm. 52–84), **c** (mm. 85–118), **B** (mm. 118–150).

The motet illustrates three of Palestrina's style characteristics. First, no single texture predominates, as imitation and homophony alternate freely and without fuss. Thus while the *prima pars* opens homophonically, the *secunda pars* begins with invertible, paired imitation. The style of the preceding generation, in which virtually every line of text began with a point of imitation, had become a thing of the past. Second, with as many as six voices with which to play, Palestrina often uses a polychoral-like approach, though the makeup of the split choirs at any moment is unpredictable; this was one of his favorite techniques. And third, there are light touches of word painting: after splitting the six voices antiphonally for the opening line, Palestrina brings them all together at "erant omnes pariter dicentes" (they were all in accord, saying); and after the imitative opening of the *secunda pars*, the texture turns homophonic at "in unum discipuli congregati" (the disciples congregated as one).

Anthology 85b offers the entire Gloria of the Mass. As we might expect, Palestrina's parody technique agrees closely with the process we saw described by Pietro Cerone (Chapter 26), who based his prescriptions on Palestrina's practice. Thus the opening of the Gloria reworks the opening of the motet; the "Qui tollis" begins with the *secunda pars*; and the movement closes with reference to the end of the motet. Table 37-2 provides a road map:

Table 37-2. *Missa Dum complerentur*, Gloria: points of correspondence with the motet.

Mass			Motet	
Measure	Text	Pars	Measure	Text
1	Et in terra pax	I	1	Dum complerentur
16	Gratias agimus		12	erant omnes
21	propter magnam		17	Alleluia (I)
28	Domine Deus Rex		17	Alleluia (I)
36	Domine Fili		17	Alleluia (I)
43	Domine Deus		55	tamquam spiritus
58	Qui tollis	II	85	Dum ergo essent
82	ad dexteram	I	41	Alleluia (II)
96	tu solus sanctus	II	102	sonus repente
110	Jesu Christe		115	venit super eos
114	cum sancto Spiritu		121	tamquam spiritus
119	in gloria Dei Patris		131	Alleluia (II)

Source: Roche, *Palestrina*, 25.

There is no immediate explanation for why, after drawing on the *secunda pars* at the beginning of the "Qui tollis," Palestrina backtracks to the *prima pars* at "ad dexteram." But we might speculate about why he returned to the *secunda pars* when he did: perhaps he wished to match the music for *solus sanctus* in the Mass with that of *sonus* in the motet. Such musical-verbal matching seems to have been one of the criteria that Palestrina sometimes used to decide what to quote from the model.

One must marvel at Palestrina the Mass composer. The sheer quantity and endless invention are overwhelming. And yet! For all their brilliance and splendor, the Masses often seem abstract, emotionally disengaged. For a more intense Palestrina, we must look to the motets.

Motets

Palestrina's motets constitute the single largest chunk of his output. They come in a myriad of sizes and shapes: long and short, with preexistent cantus firmus and without, and with every kind of mood.

In 1584, Palestrina published his *Motettorum liber quartus ex Canticis canticorum*, which contains twenty-nine modally ordered motets based on the biblical Song of Songs. It also includes Palestrina's famous apology to Pope Gregory XIII for having composed secular music in earlier years:

> Exceedingly many songs of the poets are on no theme other than that of loves alien to the name and profession of Christians. These very songs, by men carried away with passion and corrupters of youth, the majority of musicians have chosen as material for their art and industry. . . . I blush and grieve to have been among their number. But since the past can never be changed, nor things already done rendered undone, I have changed my views. And therefore I have before this worked on those songs which had been written in praise of Our Lord Jesus Christ and his most holy mother the Virgin Mary. And at this time I have chosen the Songs of Solomon, which unquestionably contain the divine love of Christ and his spouse, the [human] soul.[8]

Did Palestrina really mean it? All we know is that after 1584, Palestrina published only a single collection of secular music, a volume of madrigals in 1586 (which, however, he may have written years before).

NIGRA SUM   The third motet in the cycle is *Nigra sum (Anthology* 86), which can stand as a compact microcosm of Palestrina's technique. Like all the motets in the cycle, it is freely composed. Palestrina begins with a typically impressive point of imitation, built around two different—but unpaired—motives. Yet after the quintus (next-to-lowest part) enters with what we might call the "b" motive on the final beat of measure 4, tenor and superius (at mm. 7 and 9, respectively) show us that this can just as well function as a continuation of "a" as a counterpoint against it. Though imitation is one of the bedrocks of Palestrina's style, it is less transparent than that of the Josquin generation and less insistent than that of Gombert and his fellow Netherlanders.

There is one other lesson to be learned from the opening point of imitation. When the altus enters with the "theme" on *g'* at measure 5, the voices that had preceded it land on (from top to bottom) *b'*-flat, *d'*, and *g*; in other words, a G-minor triad, the tonic of the piece. Indeed, Palestrina will often have one

---

8. Quoted after Powers, "Modal Representation in Polyphonic Offertories," 44–45, note 2.

of the opening voices in a point of imitation go out of its way to set up a triad at the point at which a later voice enters; and as often as not, that triad is the tonic. Thus even when he is at his most rigorously contrapuntal, Palestrina has both the immediate vertical and long-range harmonic plan in mind.

The end of the work is particularly interesting. The tonic of *Nigra sum* is G. And starting at measure 54, Palestrina hammers it home with a vengeance. Three times—always on the same unit of text—he travels the same taut harmonic route: a quick spin through a short circle of fifths, twice emphasizing the dominant by approaching it via its "Neapolitan" on E-flat (mm. 57 and 61). To help us understand the reason for these repetitions, Table 37-3 provides an outline of the textual-tonal relationships in the piece:

Table 37-3.   The relationship between units of text and tonal-cadential degrees in *Nigra sum.*

Song of Songs	Unit	Text	Cadence	Measure
Chapter 1, Verse 5:	I	Nigra sum, sed formosa, I am black but comely,	G	13
	II	filiae Jerusalem, O ye daughters of Jerusalem,	B♭ (elided)	18
	III	sicut tabernacula Cedar, as the tents of Kedar,	E♭	26
	IV	sicut pelles Salomonis. as the curtains of Solomon.	D	36
Verse 6:	V	Nolite me considerare, Look not upon me,	B♭	39
	VI	quod fusca sim, because I am black,	D	42
	VII	quia decoloravit me sol! because the sun has looked upon me:	C	45
	VIII	Filii matris meae pugnaverunt contra me, my mother's children were angry with me;	C	53
	IX	posuerunt me custodem in vineis. they made me the keeper of the vineyards.	G G G	58 63 68

Definitive though the musical closure is, with the three cadences on G, the text yields a surprise: Palestrina stopped one text unit before the end of verse 6—"vinum meam non custodivi" (but mine own vineyards have I not kept)—which is needed to bring the verse to a logical semantic conclusion, and used that unit as the opening line of the following motet. On purely musical grounds, perhaps the threefold reiteration of the tonic compensates for its not having been used as a cadential degree since the end of the opening unit (m. 13). But perhaps also, Palestrina wanted to compensate for the lack of semantic closure by exaggerating its musical counterpart.

In any event, *Nigra sum* and the motets in general represent a less abstract

Palestrina, a composer who was not insensitive to the humanist view of the relationship between music and text. Humanism and the church were not, after all, necessarily at odds with one another.

Other Liturgical Types

In addition to the Masses and motets, Palestrina produced music for specific sections of the liturgy: Magnificats, lamentations, litanies, psalms, and cycles of hymns and offertories for the entire liturgical year. Example 37-4 shows the wide stylistic range of such pieces. Whereas the offertory setting is imitative and motet-like, the litany (a prayer intoned by a soloist that consists of a series of parallel petitions and invocations, to which the congregation responds with "Kyrie eleison" or "Ora pro nobis" [Pray for us]) is in the fifteenth and sixteenth centuries' best let's-get-through-the-long-text-quickly tradition. A combination of liturgical function, the nature of the text, and, by Palestrina's time, about a century and a half of tradition determined the musical style.

EXAMPLE 37-4. Palestrina: (a) The offertory *De profundis*, mm. 1–17; (b) a litany in honor of the Virgin Mary, mm. 1–22.

(a)

The "Palestrina Style"

No other composers of our two-hundred-year period have had their me-
lodic-contrapuntal style dissected with the microscopic intensity bestowed on
Palestrina's. That style, after all, became the pedagogical model for teaching
counterpoint. Following are some of its "rules":

All augmented and diminished intervals are prohibited; so too are leaps of
the seventh, major sixth, and intervals greater than an octave. The minor sixth
is permitted only when it ascends. In balancing the up-and-down arch of a
melody, the ascent should be slightly steeper, the descent more leisurely and
always by step.

No dissonance should be longer than a minim, and each should be preceded
by a consonance equally long. Notes longer than a minim must be consonant,
even if they cause a motive to be melodically altered in a point of imitation.
In duple meter, the first and third beats should be consonant, unless the dissonance is prepared as a suspension; the suspension must be prepared as a consonant note on the preceding weak beat. Anticipations may appear only in
descending motion.

As noted above, Palestrina's feeling for tonality is often apparent in a work's
opening point of imitation, where the voices pile up in such a way as to form
a complete triad at one of the later entries; in addition, the motives themselves
are often arpeggio-like. Finally, Palestrina customarily paid scrupulous attention
to the proper accentuation of the Latin.

Palestrina is generally seen as a conservative composer. Yet we must be wary
of oversimplifying. To be sure, Palestrina did not belong to the avant-garde:
he did not indulge in Gesualdo-like chromaticism or fill his music with the
vivid, pictorial word painting that became the stock-in-trade of contemporary
madrigalists; nor did he pack his motets with the overt dramatic punch of a
Lassus or Giovanni Gabrieli. On the other hand, Palestrina did not stand still.

One could easily write a history of fifteenth- and sixteenth-century music
from the point of view of the gradual systematization of dissonance: the way it
was prepared, its duration, and its location within the measure. In a history of
this sort, Palestrina becomes a progressive: he fine-tuned and limited the use

of dissonance as no one had before him. Nor did he take a back seat to any of his contemporaries in developing what can only be called a sense of tonal thinking.

In the end, it is true that Palestrina was not a bold innovator. Rather, he pulled things together and summed things up. He is the point at which a fairly straight line of development from the mature Du Fay through the "classicizing" Josquin reached a still-viable and even vibrant end of the road. Only in the seventeenth century, when his imitators froze his style in its tracks, did his music come to be archaic.

THE COUNCIL OF TRENT II

The influence of the Council of Trent and the spirit of the Counter-Reformation made themselves felt in other musical areas besides the nature of polyphony. New or reawakened genres came to the fore, most of them characterized by a simplicity of style, and all of them intended to instill the listener with piety. Further, the council left the church with the task of revising both the liturgy and its chant.

The *Missa brevis*

If Vincenzo Ruffo's homophonic-syllabic approach to the Mass had the effect of reducing its overall length, the *Missa brevis* made that its main goal. In effect, the *Missa brevis* is a setting of the entire Ordinary in which the overall proportions and sense of pomp are greatly reduced. Though the genre gained some popularity at Milan, Ferrara, and Mantua, it produced no body of masterpieces.

The Lauda

The *lauda* was a small-scale, nonliturgical piece intended for religious-devotional purposes. The genre extends back to the thirteenth century, when Franciscans and various lay orders cultivated a monophonic variety. The fifteenth century saw the development of the polyphonic lauda, which, around 1500, enjoyed a spate of popularity through the publications of Petrucci.

The Counter-Reformation sparked new interest in the genre; and in 1563, influential lauda collections by Serafino Razzi and Giovanni Animuccia came off the presses. Razzi (1531–1611), who included pieces for one to four voices and who often derived his devotional texts from secular poems, noted that the lauda was sung "not only in monasteries and convents . . . but also at social gatherings and in private homes."[9] Animuccia's laude, for example, were sung at the Congregazione dell'Oratorio, an academy with a religious bent founded by St. Philip Neri (1515–1595) in 1575. The lauda, then, was the Counter-Reformation's answer to the simple psalm settings cultivated by the Protestants. Like the *Missa brevis*, the lauda produced no musical monuments.

9. *Libro primo delle laude spirituali*; quoted after Reese, *Music in the Renaissance*, 453.

Madrigali spirituali

There were definitely masterpieces among the *madrigali spirituali*, which were no different musically from their nonspiritual counterparts. Their poetry, on the other hand, *was* different. A favorite ploy was to transform the poet-beloved relationship into one between poet and Mary, poet and Christ, or Christ and his flock. For the first of these, there was a model: Petrarch's powerful *Stanzas to the Virgin*, which brings his *Canzoniere* to a close. More than a century after Du Fay had set the opening stanza only, first Cipriano de Rore (1548) and then Palestrina (1581) turned Petrarch's stanzas into multimadrigal cycles.

For sheer, sustained beauty, though, perhaps no cycle of spiritual madrigals measures up to that with which Lassus brought his career to a close, the *Lagrime di San Pietro*. Lassus based his cycle of twenty madrigals plus concluding motet on the first twenty stanzas of a very long poem—1,277 eight-line stanzas—by Luigi Tansillo (1510–1568). Tansillo, a soldier-poet who hailed from Gesualdo's hometown of Venosa, began to write the poem, which deals with Peter's penance for his denial of Christ, in 1559, probably as his own act of penance for an earlier book that had been placed on the Inquisition's Index. He was still tampering with the work when he died. For Lassus too, the *Lagrime* was a testament of sorts. It was written at the very end of his life, in 1594, when he suffered from bouts of "melancolia hypocondriaca," as it was diagnosed. Example 37-5 contains three short excerpts from the cycle, each of which shows the various ways in which Lassus transformed Tansillo's poetic images into sound.

The poetry of the three excerpts may be translated as follows:

No. 5, lines 1–4: A young woman never saw her beautiful face in a shining crystal mirror as clearly as, at that moment, the miserable old man [Peter] saw his sin in the eyes of the Lord.

No. 15, lines 1–2: "Go away, life, depart," he said, weeping, "to where there is no one who hates or despises you."

No. 20, lines 3–4: . . . a calm life that does not fear or hope; nor can its course ever reach its bank.

In No. 5, Lassus expresses the contrast between the beautiful young woman and the miserable old man by means of range; in No. 15, he turns the change of voice from Peter to the narrator and back to Peter into a moment of drama; and in No. 20, the life that can never reach its destination quite literally gets stuck on a *redictum*, a repeated motive. As we will see in Chapter 38, Lassus was a master of musical rhetoric.

Finally, Lassus imbues the cycle with a sense of symbolism based on the number seven: the work's twenty-one movements are divided into three groups of seven and set for seven voices throughout. Lassus's contemporaries, for whom the symbolism of numbers was part of everyday life, would have been mindful that seven was the number of mortal sins, Sorrows of Mary, and Penitential Psalms. It was also Peter's number of forgiveness: "Lord, how oft shall my brother sin against me, and I forgive him? up to seven times?" (Matthew 16:21).

EXAMPLE 37-5. Lassus, *Lagrime di San Pietro:* (a) No. 5, mm. 1–17; (b) No. 15, mm. 1–10; (c) No. 20, mm. 8–17.

(a)

(c)

Revisions of Liturgy and Chant

As we have seen, one of the goals of the Council of Trent was to reform the liturgy of the church. And in 1568 and 1570, respectively, Rome issued new versions of the Breviary and Missal, the adoption of which was obligatory for churches throughout the Roman Catholic world unless they could show that their own local customs had been in place for more than two hundred years. Clearly, the intent was to standardize the liturgy; and music was not exempt.

On October 25, 1577, Pope Gregory XIII extended the spirit of reform to the church's chant books,[10] in the form of a brief addressed specifically to Palestrina and the Roman musician Annibale Zoilo (c. 1537–1592):

> It having come to our notice that the books of Office chants, Mass chants, and psalters which contain the music for the plainsong used in all divine services are full of barbarisms, obscurities, inconsistencies, and superfluities as a result of the ineptitude, the negligence, even the malice of composers, scribes, and printers alike, and so that these books may be made to conform with the Breviary and Missal recently published in accordance with the order of the Council of Trent, and so that the superfluities we have mentioned may be pruned away and the barbarisms and obscurities corrected (so that God's

10. Gregory's most far-reaching reform had to do with the calendar. The standard system for more than 1,500 years, the so-called Julian calendar (put into effect by Julius Caesar in 46 B.C.), had accounted for a calendar year that was approximately eleven minutes longer than the solar year. Slowly but surely, calendar and sun got out of sync; and in 1580, the spring equinox fell on March 11, ten days too early. In October 1582, on the advice of his astronomers, Gregory ordered that ten days be struck from the year: October 5 simply became October 15. The next spring equinox was thereby back on track. He further decreed that the month of February should have an extra day in some century years. Under this system, the difference between calendar year and solar year is about twenty-six seconds.

name may be the more easily praised with reverence, distinctness, and devotion), . . . thus we give you the responsibility of revising, purging, correcting, and reforming these books of chants, and any others that may be used in
the churches according to the rite of the Holy Roman Church.[11]

At first, Palestrina and Zoilo accepted the task. But their enthusiasm apparently
waned, and they soon gave up the project. In 1611, it was entrusted to Felice
Anerio (c. 1560–1614) and Francesco Soriano (1548/49–1621), who published
the authorized version of the chants in the so-called *Editio medicea* in 1614.

We should take note of two liturgical-musical reforms in particular. First,
the liturgy of the Requiem Mass was standardized; no longer would some chants
be sung in one place and others someplace else. Second, of the thousands of
sequences that had accrued to the liturgy during the course of the Middle Ages,
only four escaped the council's censure: *Victimae paschali laudes* for Easter, *Veni
sancte spiritus* for Pentacost, *Lauda Sion* for the Feast of Corpus Christ, and the
Dies irae for the Requiem Mass. And to these the *Stabat mater*, sung at the Feast
of the Seven Sorrows of the Virgin, was restored in 1727.

Both the council's decrees and Gregory's brief are splendid testimony to the
sixteenth century's high opinion of itself. After all, the plainsong repertory,
which, as legend had it, had been created by Pope Gregory I, had been regarded
as virtually sacrosanct by centuries of musicians and church officials alike. Now
it was to be brought into accord with modern tastes. And not until the monks
of Solesmes undertook their chant research in the nineteenth century, which
led to the publication of the "Vatican edition" (authorized by Pius V in 1904),
was the work of the sixteenth century undone.

To assess the influence that the Counter-Reformation in general and the
Council of Trent in particular had on music in the late sixteenth century is a
tricky business. On the one hand, the church sought to stifle and bring about
conformity; on the other, it clearly meant to inspire. For even the decrees that
seemed on the surface to limit artistic expression were intended to bring music
and the faithful closer to one another. And in the end, that goal produced such
masterpieces as Lassus's *Lagrime*, Palestrina's *Song of Songs*, and Victoria's *Officium defunctorum*, some of the most beautiful and sensual music ever written.

VENICE

It was no doubt the prodding of a conformist Rome as much as his own
personality that shaped Palestrina's surface conservatism. Things were different
at Venice, which owed its fame, fortune, and fierce sense of independence to
its position as a mercantile center. Here, religious and civic life and ceremony
were inextricably intertwined. One can even speak of a "civic liturgy,"[12] as
when the Venetians joined the annual celebration of their "marriage to the
sea" to the Feast of the Ascension (forty days after Easter). Even the highest
state office, that of doge, was invested with a religious function.

11. Quoted after Weiss and Taruskin, *Music in the Western World*, 139.
12. Carter, *Music in Late Renaissance and Early Baroque Italy*, 114.

Figure 37-2. Gentile Bellini, *Procession in Piazza San Marco*, St. Mark's Cathedral in the background, 1496 (Gallerie dell'Accademia, Venice).

At Rome, sacred music sought to instill piety in accordance with the decrees of the Council of Trent. Though it may have tried to do the same at Venice, there it had to express the splendor of the state as well, and this new role resulted in a very different style.

St. Mark's

The focal point of Venetian sacred music was the Basilica of St. Mark's (Fig. 37-2), which, beginning with the appointment of Willaert as *maestro di cappella* in 1527, boasted one of the premier musical establishments of the time. Table 37-4 lists the succession of chapel masters and famous organists:

Table 37-4.   Chapel masters and organists at St. Mark's during the sixteenth and early seventeenth centuries.

Chapel masters		Organists	
Willaert	1527–62	Jacques Buus II[a]	1541–50
Rore	1563–64	Girolamo Parabosco I	1551–57
Zarlino	1565–90	Annibale Padovano II	1552–65
Baldassare Donato	1590–1603	Claudio Merulo I	1557–84
Giovanni Croce	1603–9	Andrea Gabrieli II	1566–84
G. C. Martinengo	1609–13	I	1584–85
Monteverdi	1613–43	Giovanni Gabrieli II	1585–1612

Source: Carter, *Music in Late Renaissance and Early Baroque Italy*, 116.
[a]Roman numerals indicate first or second organist.

Moreover, in 1568, a permanent ensemble of instrumentalists was established under the direction of Girolamo dalla Casa, whose treatise on ornamentation we considered in Chapter 31. By the early seventeenth century, the musical establishment of St. Mark's included a chapel master and an assistant, twenty-four singers, two organists, two *maestri di concerti* (leaders of the instrumental ensembles), and sixteen instrumentalists. And though it was smaller during the final decades of the sixteenth century, it was sufficient even then to give free reign to the fertile imagination of Giovanni Gabrieli.

Giovanni Gabrieli

In 1597, Giovanni Gabrieli (1533/36–1612) published a collection of motets entitled *Sacrae symphoniae*. The contents consisted mainly of large-scale, ceremonial, polychoral motets; but they were different from any motets that, say, Willaert or Palestrina had written. Example 37-6 provides an excerpt from one of the grander pieces, *Plaudite, psallite, jubilate Deo omnis terra:*

EXAMPLE 37-6. Giovanni Gabrieli, *Plaudite, psallite, jubilate Deo omnis terra,* mm. 1–17.

EXAMPLE 37-6 (continued)

We need not listen beyond the opening two measures, with their rhetorical cries of "Plaudite, psallite" (Applaud, play [an instrument]), probably sung by soloists, to realize that Gabrieli has taken leave of mainstream Netherlandish polyphony. Subsequently, the three choirs, each consisting of a different combination of voices, bombard us with a dialogue of short, rhythmically animated bursts of declamation. Here, contrast is the key: contrasts of register and probably solo versus choir to differentiate the choirs; and contrasts of motive, meter, and eventually tonal center to set off the recurring "alleluia" refrain, a favorite device of Gabrieli's that makes the piece behave as if it were a rondo. In short, *Plaudite* is sheer theater.

Although the 1597 collection sometimes labels the choirs "voce" (soloist) and "cappella" (choir), it does not do so for *Plaudite*; nor are there any indi-

EXAMPLE 37-6 (continued)

cations of instrumental participation. Yet instrumentalists must certainly have taken part. Perhaps they doubled certain voice parts; perhaps they took some over in their entirety. What is clear, though, is that the tradition of *a cappella* singing that continued to be maintained by the papal singers of the Sistine Chapel had become an anomaly; and instruments were heard on a regular basis in late-sixteenth-century churches.

Gabrieli carried his innovations further in his second book of *Sacrae symphoniae*, published posthumously in 1615. Example 37-7 gives the opening of the well-known *In ecclesiis*. Most of us would no longer call this "Renaissance" music. Here Gabrieli has turned issues that had formerly belonged to the domain of decorative color—for instance, solo versus choir, instruments versus voices, or the keyboard accompaniment—into compositional issues that de-

EXAMPLE 37-7. Gabrieli, *In ecclesiis*, mm. 1–12.

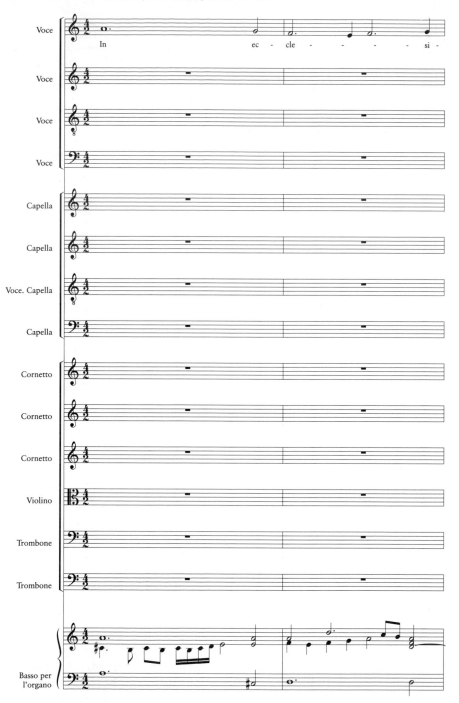

termine and define the very structure of the piece. In other words, Gabrieli's concerns in *In ecclesiis* have breached the boundaries of the issues—melody, rhythm, counterpoint, and so on—that concerned composers from Du Fay to Palestrina.

SPAIN

Under Philip II (r. 1556–98), who made it his mission to defend the Roman Catholic faith, Spain was intensely religious. It was also intensely musical. Evidence of its zest for religion can be seen in a 1591 census and description of Toledo, the adopted city of El Greco, who depicted it in one of the most haunting paintings of the period (Fig. 37-3). In a city of approximately 50,000 inhabitants, there were twenty-six churches, thirty-six monasteries and convents, eighteen shrines (each devoted to a different saint), twelve oratories, and four religious colleges. The two-thousand-plus clergy constituted about 5 percent of the population. And as its population dwindled during the years that followed, nine new religious houses were added.

Figure 37-3. El Greco, *View of Toledo*, c. 1610 (Metropolitan Museum of Art, New York).

Spain's musical intensity was expressed by Francisco Guerrero (1528–1599), who enjoyed a tremendous wave of posthumous success in Spain's American colonies, and Tomás Luis de Victoria, the greatest Spanish composer of the sixteenth century.

Victoria

Born in St. Teresa's hometown of Ávila in 1548, Victoria spent about twenty years at Rome starting in the mid-1560s. Upon returning to Spain, he was rewarded with the post of chaplain to Philip's sister, the Dowager Empress Maria (widow of Emperor Maximilian II), who in 1581 had retired to the luxurious royal convent of the Barefoot Nuns of St. Claire (Madrid). There Victoria served her—both as personal chaplain and as chapel master—from 1587 at the latest until her death in 1603. He remained with the convent's musical forces as organist until his death in August 1611.

Victoria is perhaps the Counter-Reformation's composer *par excellence*. Unlike Palestrina, he never had to apologize for early compositional indiscretions: he composed no secular music at all.

TWO MOTETS Victoria's two most frequently performed works are undoubtedly the motets *O magnum mysterium* and *O vos omnes* (Ex. 37-8):

EXAMPLE 37-8. Victoria: (a) *O magnum mysterium*, mm. 1–14; (b) *O vos omnes*, mm. 52–68.

(a)

(b)

Both motets possess a dark quality that permeates many of Victoria's best-known works. For the most part, this is achieved by conventional means: half-step motion, especially "Neapolitan" relationships, both melodic and harmonic; and suspensions, which tend to pile up and resolve at their leisure. At times, though, Victoria takes that extra step, as when he underscores the final statement of "sicut dolor meus" at the end of *O vos omnes* with the chromatic twist of successive minor triads on F-sharp (first inversion) and G (m. 66). For a moment, Victoria seems to have heard the world as El Greco saw it.

THE *OFFICIUM DEFUNCTORUM*   If the two motets just cited are Victoria's best-known compositions, the *Officium defunctorum* is his greatest. Published in 1605, the work was written to commemorate the death of the Empress Maria in 1603. In addition to setting the chants of the Requiem Mass itself, now standardized by the Council of Trent and Pius V's Missal of 1570, Victoria appended three other pieces: a motet; the prayer for absolution, "Libera me," which is sung after the Mass; and one of the lessons from the Book of Job, which are recited at Matins of the Office of the Dead.

Anthology 87 presents two movements from the work: the Agnus Dei and the extra-liturgical motet, *Versa est in luctum*. As was customary in the Requiem Mass, the Agnus Dei is based on its plainsong, which rolls out, after the monophonic intonation, in the next-to-highest voice. Agnus II is sung in chant from beginning to end.

Versa est in luctum is a different story. It draws its text from two passages in the Book of Job, 30:31 and 7:16; there is no plainsong. What there is, though, is poignancy, extending over an arch whose three-part dynamic Victoria controls in breathtaking fashion: from the hushed, almost mysterious, paired imitation at the opening, through the agony at "nihil enim sunt dies mei" (for my days are nothing), with its riveting high *e″*s and piled-up suspensions, to the sense of quiet acceptance at the end. It is as heartbreaking a piece of music as the sixteenth or any other century has ever produced.

PERFORMANCE PRACTICE

That instruments regularly participated in the performance of late-sixteenth-century sacred music seems beyond question. Descriptions of combined vocal and instrumental forces abound. In one, Gregory Martin, an English Jesuit, describes music in Roman churches in 1576–78:

> A man may goe to so many Churches in one day, chose where he wil, so heavenly served, with such musicke, such voices, such instrumentes, al ful of gravitie and majestie, al moving to devotion and ravishing a mans hart to the meditation of melodie of Angels and Saintes in heaven. With the Organs a childes voice shriller and louder than the instrument, tuneable with every pipe: Among the quyre, Cornet or Sagbut, or such like above the voices.

Another notice, by the Venetian architect Jacopo Sansovino, describes the music that was performed at St. Mark's to honor the visit of a delegation of Japanese princes to the city in 1585:

> The Church of St. Mark . . . was so full of people that one could not move a step, and a new platform was built for the singers, adjoining which there was a portative organ, so that together with the two famous [organs] of the church and other musical instruments the music could be made more splendid, in which the best singers and players that can be found in this region took part. . . . and so the mass began.[13]

Just what, however, did the instrumentalists play at a time when "concerted" music was still more a matter of decorative color than a compositional factor (as it is in Gabrieli's *In ecclesiis*)? An answer begins to take shape in a fascinating document of 1586 (bearing the heading "Order that must be observed by the instrumentalists in playing") from the Cathedral of Seville, where Francisco Guerrero was chapel master:

> First, Rojas and Lopez shall always play the treble parts; ordinarily on shawms. They must carefully observe some order when they improvise passages both as to places and to times. When the one player adds passages to his part, the other must yield to him and play simply the written notes; for when both together embellish at the same time, they produce absurdities that stop one's ears. Second, the same Rojas and Lopez when they at appropriate moments play on cornetts must again observe the same moderation in embellishing: the one deferring to the other; because, as has been previously said, for both simultaneously to add improvised passages creates insufferable dissonance. As for Juan de Medina, he shall ordinarily play the contralto part, not obscuring the trebles nor disturbing them by exceeding the passages that belong to a contralto. When on the other hand his part becomes the top above the sackbuts, then he is left an open field in which to glory and is free to add all the passages that he desires and knows so well how to execute on his instrument. As for Alvanchez, he shall play tenors and the bassoon. At greater feasts there shall always be a verse played on recorders. At Salves one of the three verses that are played shall be on shawms, one on cornetts and the other on recorders; because always hearing the same instruments always wearies the listener.[14]

This document is particularly valuable because, unlike the descriptions by awestruck tourists and architects, it is obviously the work of a practicing musician (Guerrero?) for other practicing musicians. It further tells us that instrumental doubling was taken for granted, instrumentalists embellished the vocal lines, at times the instrumentalists might have alternated with the singers, and at times they might have taken over altogether.

The document also raise some questions: Does it refer to music for the Mass, to ceremonial motets, or to sacred music in general? Was the Seville practice commonplace elsewhere? How far back can we push such practices? The "Orders" keep us thinking.

---

13. Both descriptions quoted after Carter, *Music in Late Renaissance and Early Baroque Italy*, 102, 114.

14. The document is given in Stevenson, *Spanish Cathedral Music*, 167; Weiss and Taruskin, *Music in the Western World*, 160–61.

BIBLIOGRAPHICAL NOTE

Editions of the Music

Palestrina: there are two complete editions—*Werke*, 32 vols., ed. F. X. Haberl (Leipzig: Breitkopf & Härtel, 1862–1907), the first complete critical edition devoted to a composer of our period; and *Opere complete*, 35 vols., ed. Raffaele Casimiri et al. (Rome: Istituto Italiano per la Storia della Musica, 1939–). **Giovanni Gabrieli**: the state of the *Opera omnia*, CMM 12 (American Institute of Musicology), is this: vols. 1–6 were edited by Denis Arnold (1956–74), vols. 7–12 are being edited by Richard Charteris (1991–), who will also reedit vols. 1–6. **Victoria**: there are two complete editions—*Opera omnia*, 7 vols., ed. Felipe Pedrell (Leipzig: Breitkopf & Härtel, 1902–13); and *Opera omnia*, 4 vols., MME 15–16, 30–31, ed. Higini Anglès (Barcelona: Consejo Superior de Investigaciones Científicas, 1965–68). **Ruffo**: *Seven Masses*, RRMR 32 (in two parts), ed. Lewis Lockwood (Madison: A-R Editions, 1979).

General Studies

A good complement to this chapter is Tim Carter, *Music in Late Renaissance and Early Baroque Italy* (Portland: Amadeus Press, 1992), chapter 7, which has a perceptive discussion of the differences between Roman and Venetian style.

Council of Trent

Lewis Lockwood, "Vincenzo Ruffo and Musical Reform after the Council of Trent,"*MQ* 43 (1957): 342–71; *The Counter Reformation and the Masses of Vincenzo Ruffo* (Vienna: Universal Edition, 1970); and the edition of Ruffo's Masses cited above. See also Richard Sherr, "A Letter from Paolo Animuccia: A Composer's Response to the Council of Trent," *EM* 12 (1984): 75–78; Karl Gustav Fellerer, "Church Music and the Council of Trent," *MQ* 39 (1953): 576–94.

Palestrina

The literature on Palestrina is vast; for surveys, see Lockwood, "Giovanni Pierluigi da Palestrina," in *The New Grove High Renaissance Masters*, ed. Stanley Sadie (New York: Norton, 1984), 93–153 (work list by Jessie Ann Owens); and with greater detail, Jerome Roche, *Palestrina*, Oxford Studies of Composers 7 (Oxford: Oxford University Press, 1971). On the myth about Palestrina as the "savior" of music, see Lockwood, *Palestrina: Pope Marcellus Mass* (New York: Norton, 1975), with an edition of the Mass. For detailed studies on the contrapuntal style, see the two classics by Knud Jeppesen, *The Style of Palestrina and the Dissonance*, 2nd ed. (Copenhagen: Munksgaard, 1946), and *Counterpoint: The Polyphonic Vocal Style of the Sixteenth Century*, trans. Glen Haydon (New York: Prentice-Hall, 1939; reprint, Dover, 1992); see also Malcom Boyd's *Palestrina's Style: A Practical Introduction* (Oxford: Oxford University Press, 1973), which contains compositional exercises. On Palestrina's parody technique, see Quentin Quereau, "Aspects of Palestrina's Parody Procedures," *JM* 1 (1982): 198–216; a lavish iconographical study of Palestrina and his time is Lino Bianchi and Giancarlo Rostirolla, *Iconografia Palestriniana: Giovanni Pierluigi da Palestrina, il suo tempo e la sua fortuna nelle immagini* (Lucca: Libreria Musicale Italiana, 1994); for an idea of current trends in Palestrina research, see the "Palestrina Quartercentenary" issue of *EM* 22/4 (1994), which is devoted entirely to the composer.

Venice and Giovanni Gabrieli

On the role of music at Venice, see Ellen Rosand, "Music in the Myth of Venice," *RQ* 30 (1977): 511–37; on Gabrieli, see Denis Arnold, *Giovanni Gabrieli*, Oxford Studies of Composers 12 (Oxford: Oxford University Press, 1974), and *Giovanni Gabrieli and the Music of the Venetian High Renaissance* (Oxford: Oxford University Press, 1979); for a catalogue of his works, see Richard Charteris, *Giovanni Gabrieli: A Thematic Catalogue of His Music*, Thematic Catalogue Series 20 (Stuyvesant, N.Y.: Pendragon Press, 1996). See also on Venice, Jonathan Glixon, "A Musicians' Union in Sixteenth-Century Venice," *JAMS* 36 (1983): 392–421; and the article by David Bryant cited in the Bibliographical Note in Chapter 26.

Spain and Victoria

The starting point is still Robert M. Stevenson, *Spanish Cathedral Music in the Golden Age* (Berkeley and Los Angeles: University of California Press, 1961), and "Tomás Luis de Victoria," in *The New Grove High Renaissance Masters*, 291–319; the issues of *EM*, vol. 22, no. 2 (1994), and vol. 23, no. 3 (1995), entitled "Iberian Discoveries II–III," are devoted mainly to music in sixteenth-century Spain; see also Eugene C. Cramer, *Tomás Luis de Victoria: A Guide to Research*, Composer Resource Manuals 43 (New York: Garland, 1998).

Also Cited

Noel O'Regan, "Palestrina, a Musician and Composer in the Marketplace," *EM* 22 (1994): 551–72; Harold S. Powers, "Modal Representation in Polyphonic Offertories," *EMH* 2 (1982): 43–86.

CHAPTER 38

Music in the Service of Words

In 1607, Giulio Cesare Monteverdi issued one of the most famous manifestos in the history of Western music. It took the form of a "Declaration," appended to the end of his brother Claudio's *Scherzi musicali* and written in response to criticism leveled by the theorist Giovanni Maria Artusi at Claudio's madrigal *Cruda Amarilli*:

> My brother says that his works are not composed at random, for, in this kind of music, it is his goal to make the words the mistress of the harmony and not its servant, and it is from this point of view that his work should be judged. But in the event Artusi takes a few details, or, as he calls them, "passages" from my brothers's madrigals without any regard to the words, which he ignores as if they had nothing to do with the music. By judging these passages without their words, my brother's opponent implies that all merit and beauty lie in following exactly the rules of the First Practice, in which the harmony is the mistress of the words.
>
> "First Practice" refers to that style which is chiefly concerned with the perfection of the harmony; that is, in which harmony is not ruled, but rules, is not the servant but the mistress of the words. Its founders were the first to write down music for more than one voice, later followed and improved upon by Ockeghem, Josquin des Prez, Pierre de la Rue, Jean Mouton, Crequillon, Clemens non Papa, Gombert, and others of those times. It reached its ultimate perfection with Messer Adriano [Willaert] in composition itself, and with the extremely well-thought-out rules of the excellent Zarlino.
>
> "Second Practice"—which was originated by Cipriano de Rore, later followed and improved upon by Ingegneri, Marenzio, Giaches de Wert, Luzzasco, still more by Jacopo Peri, Giulio Caccini, and finally by yet more exalted spirits who understand even better what true art is—is that style which is chiefly concerned with the perfection of the setting; that is, in which harmony does not rule but is ruled, and where the words are the mistress of the harmony. This is why my brother calls it "second" rather than "new," and "practice" rather than "theory," for its understanding is to be sought in the process of actual composition. Thus, it is my brother's aim to follow the principles taught by Plato and practiced by the divine Cipriano and those who have followed him in modern times, which are different from the principles taught and laid down by the Reverend Zarlino and practiced by Messer Adriano.[1]

---

1. Quoted after the slightly telescoped translation in Weiss and Taruskin, *Music in the Western World*, 172–73. To see how Giulio Cesare's "Declaration" interfaces with Claudio's earlier defense of his music (in the preface to his Fifth Book of Madrigals, 1605), see the translation in Strunk, *Source Readings in Music History*, rev. ed., ed. Leo Treitler, *The Baroque Era,* ed. Margaret Murata (New York: Norton, 1997), where the "Declaration" is given in its entirety.

Here, then, is the landmark distinction between the *prima prattica*, in which the harmony—that is, the counterpoint—was the mistress (the boss) of the words, and the more modern *seconda prattica*, in which the words were the mistress and the harmony the servant. And though the *seconda prattica* is often equated with the birth of the Baroque period around 1600, Giulio Cesare is quite explicit in extending it back to the middle of the sixteenth century and the madrigals of Cipriano de Rore.

The brothers Monteverdi were hardly the first musicians of the period to call for a change in the hierarchical relationship between words and music. Already in 1569, the little-known madrigalist Marc'Antonio Mazzone had this to say in the dedication of his First Book of Madrigals:

> The notes are the body of music, while the text is the soul and, just as the soul, being nobler than the body, must be followed and imitated by it, so the notes must follow the text and imitate it, and the composer must pay due attention to it, expressing its sense with sad, gay, or austere music, as the text demands, and he must even sometimes disregard the rules.[2]

Even Zarlino, who codified the contrapuntal rules of the *prima prattica*, joined the chorus: "Plato places the words before [harmony and rhythm] as the principal thing, and considers the other two components to be subservient to [them]. . . . He says that harmony and rhythm should follow the words."[3]

Three points should be clear: (1) the idea that music should serve the words (rather than rule them) became a rallying cry in the late sixteenth century, and a loudly proclaimed one at that; (2) the *seconda prattica* did not so much succeed the *prima prattica* at the beginning of the seventeenth century as run concurrently alongside it during the second half of the sixteenth; and (3) even musicians whom Monteverdi associated with the first practice—Zarlino, for example—were not adverse to the idea of music as servant to the text (some musicians simply went less far with it than others).

There was another way in which music had to respect the words: it had to preserve their accentuation and syntax. As Zarlino put it in his *Istitutioni harmoniche*:

> We should . . . take care to accommodate the words of the text to the written notes in such a manner and with such rhythm that no barbarism is heard, as when in a vocal piece a syllable that should be short is made long, or vice versa . . . something heard every day in innumerable compositions and really a shameful thing. . . . Care should also be taken not to separate any parts of the text by rests while a clause, or any of its parts, remains unfinished. . . . One should not make a cadence . . . nor put in rests larger than a minim, unless the sentence or the full sense of the word is completed.[4]

In all, the second half of the sixteenth century saw something of a tug-of-war between the two practices, though one in which the dividing line between proponents became fixed only gradually. And as we will see, some composers—Lassus, for example—had no trouble formulating a style and aesthetic that reconciled the two.

2. Quoted after Weiss and Taruskin, *Music in the Western World*, 143.
3. *L'Istitutioni harmoniche*, part IV, ch. 32; quoted after Cohen, *On the Modes*, 94–95.
4. Quoted after Cohen, *On the Modes*, 96.

We will observe the ways in which music served words from three vantage points: (1) a strain of radical humanism that fostered a kind of overt antiquarianism; (2) the motets of Orlande de Lassus and the ever-thorny problem of the meaning of the term *musica reservata*; and (3) a survey of trends in the late-sixteenth-century madrigal.

ANTIQUARIANISM

Zarlino's remarks about proper accentuation notwithstanding, most sixteenth-century composers adopted a casual approach to the matter. There was, however, a strain of humanism—first in Germany, later in France—that recognized that the meters of ancient Latin poetry were not qualitative (made up of accented and unaccented syllables), but "quantitative": that is, the syllables were arranged in various patterns of long and short, with the duration of a syllable determined both by phonetic quality and position in the verse.

We can see how this works by looking at the opening stanza of an ode by the Roman poet Horace (65–8 B.C.). The meter is known as Sapphic, named after the Greek poetess Sappho of Lesbos (born c. 600 B.C.); the signs - and ˘ indicate long and short syllables, respectively:

Iām sătīs tērrīs nĭvĭs ātquĕ dīrǣ grāndĭnīs mīsīt pătĕr ēt rŭbēntī dēxtĕrā sācrās iăcŭlātŭs ārcēs tērrŭĭt ūrbĕm.	More than enough, the omens of snow and sleet sent by the Father to earth: his right hand glowed as he hurled his bolts at our sacred hills: the city trembled with fear.[5]

At the urging of certain humanists, some musicians sought to replicate the quantitative meters of Latin poetry in their music, though they did so under two very different banners: one "pedagogic," the other "artistic."

"Pedagogy": Settings of Horatian Odes

In 1507, the musician and Latin teacher Petrus Tritonius, encouraged by the German humanist Conrad Celtis, issued a collection of four-part settings of nineteen of Horace's odes, to be used as an aid in teaching Latin metrics. Example 38-1 illustrates Tritonius's setting of Horace's *Iam satis terris.*

EXAMPLE 38-1. Tritonius, *Iam satis terris.*

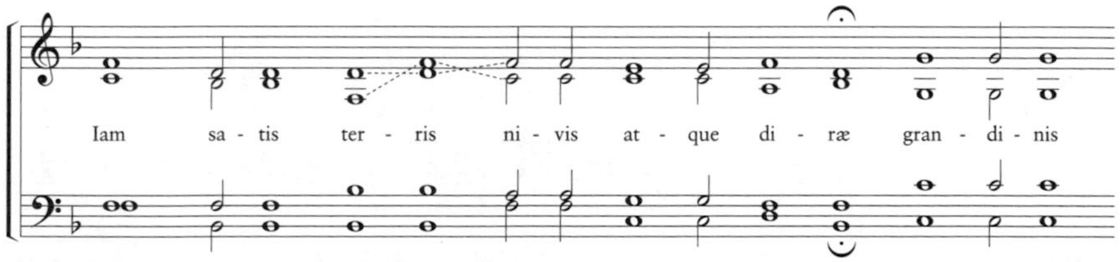

5. Translation from Clancy, *The Odes and Epodes of Horace*, 25. This stanza is from Ode 2 in the first of Horace's four books of odes.

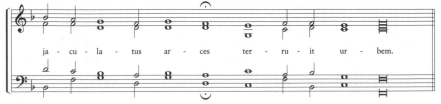

Thus Tritonius reproduces Horace's Sapphic meter faithfully, setting the long syllables with long notes, the short ones with short notes (except for the final note, which had to be long for the cadence).

Though Tritonius's settings are devoid of artistic pretense, they must have succeeded admirably as a pedagogical tool, for the collection was reprinted and spawned imitations and arrangements by Paul Hofhaimer and Ludwig Senfl. Tritonius's combination of long-short rhythms and strict homophony seems to have exerted some influence as well on later settings of classical Latin poetry that *were* artistically ambitious. Thus pieces such as Lassus's *Prophetiae sibyllarum* (*Anthology* 83) and Rore's setting of lines from Virgil's *Aeneid* (Ex. 38-2) strike a similar, if more sophisticated, pose. Andrea Gabrieli also used the technique in 1585 when he provided music for a performance of the first Italian translation of an ancient Greek tragedy, Sophocles's *Oedipus rex*. No doubt, the audience at Vicenza's Teatro Olimpico must have thought the music quite "authentic."

EXAMPLE 38-2. Rore, *Dissimulare etiam sperasti*, mm. 1–14.

"Artistry"—*Musique mesurée à l'antique*

Antiquarianism followed a different path in France, where, in the final decades of the sixteenth century, the poets of the Académie de Poésie et de Musique and the composer Claude le Jeune collaborated to produce music that was simply enchanting.

In 1549, the poet and classicist Joachim Du Bellay (1522–1560) published his *Deffense et illustration de la langue françoise*, which constituted a manifesto for a group of poets known as the Pléiade. Du Bellay turned his back on the French medieval tradition and even Marot, and urged his colleagues to imitate the forms and meters of classical antiquity: "Sing to me those odes, yet unknown to the French music, on a lute well tuned to the sound of the Greek and Roman lyre."[6] Du Bellay here expresses one of the humanists' most deeply held convictions: that ancient poetry was sung, that there was a tight-knit union between poetry and music. And it is precisely the rebirth of this union that Pierre de Ronsard (1524–1585), the greatest of the Pléiade poets, called for in his *Abrégé de l'art poétique françoys* (1565)—"poetry without instruments, or without the charm of a single or several voices, is just as little delightful as are instruments lacking the expressiveness of melody produced by a pleasant voice"—and that the poet-humanist-mathematician-diplomat Jean-Antoine de Baïf (1532–1589) echoed in a poem addressed to the composer Guillaume Costeley:

> In olden times, musicians, poets, and the learned
> Were authors all, but in the course of age
> Through time, that changes all, the three were separated;
>
> O, if we boldly could partake of that
> Golden Era and reestablish its abolished custom
> So that the three were re-united by good will of Kings.[7]

THE ACADÉMIE   In 1570, Baïf and Joachim Thibault de Courville, a lyre player at the French royal court, founded the Académie de Poésie et de Musique (Charles IX added his royal support the following year). With its strictly

6. Quoted after Reese, *Music in the Renaissance*, 382.

7. Quoted after Lesure, *Musicians and Poets of the French Renaissance*, 57 and [7].

secret meetings at Baïf's home and a membership made up of *musiciens* (poets, composers, singers, and instrumentalists) and dues-paying *auditeurs*, the Académie set out, as its charter put it, to restore the "measure and regulations of the music used by the old Greeks and Romans. . . . measured verse set to music, with music itself being measured according to the laws, approximately, of the music masters of the good old age."[8] In effect, Baïf and his fellow academicians sought to (1) impose on French verse the quantitative meters of classical Greek and Latin, producing a poetic style known as *vers mesurés à l'antique*; and (2) set the verse to music in a style known as *musique mesurée à l'antique*, in which the long and short syllables of the verse were matched by long and short notes in the music. That Baïf insisted on the union of poetry and music was fortunate, for the rather lackluster verse was brought to life by the music of Claude Le Jeune.

LE JEUNE AND *MUSIQUE MESURÉE*   Le Jeune (1528/30–1600) was the leading composer of the Académie and a mainstay on the Parisian musical scene from the 1560s until his Protestant activism forced him to flee the city in 1590. (Eventually he returned, and even reentered the service of Henry IV.) Le Jeune's *La bel' aronde (Anthology 88)*, published for the first time in his 1603 collection entitled *Le Printemps*, illustrates the fruits of his collaboration with Baïf. The technique with which Tritonius could do no more than plod along sparkles in Le Jeune's hands. The meter—if one can speak of it—is extraordinarily fluid, the ambiguity being further underscored harmonically by long notes on the mediant when we might have expected a simple tonic. Moreover, Le Jeune is anything but pedantic: he embellishes the basic long-shorts of the meter with occasional melismas and throws meter to the wind altogether with the patter-like "Elle vole moucherettes." Finally, *La bel' aronde* is typical of Le Jeune's strophic structures with refrain. Here, five four-line strophes, set for four voices and called the *chant*, are introduced by and then alternate with a six-voice, recurring refrain called the *rechant*.

Tritonius's ode and Le Jeune's chanson are worlds apart: one is a didactic exercise, the other the epitome of Gallic wit and grace. Yet they share a common starting point: they both pay homage to classical antiquity. No other music of the century did so with such determination.

LASSUS

Of the great composers of the second half of the sixteenth century, Orlande de Lassus (Fig. 38-1) was the most universal, equally at home in the Mass and the villanella. Lassus was born at Mons, in the province of Hainault (present-day Belgium), most likely in 1532. In 1544, he entered the service of the Mantuan Gonzaga family and then went on to Sicily (1545) and Milan (1546–49). From there, Lassus moved to Naples and Rome, where in 1553 and though still relatively unknown as a composer, he became *maestro di cappella* at

8. Quoted after Lesure, *Musicians and Poets of the French Renaissance*, 95–96.

Figure 38-1. Portrait of Lassus, woodcut from *Livre de chansons nouvelles*, 1571.

the church of St. John Lateran, the position to which Palestrina would succeed two years later. By 1555, Lassus had returned north and settled at Antwerp, where he broke into print with the printer Tylman Susato in 1555–56.

In 1557, Lassus's career took a decisive turn when he joined the Bavarian court chapel of Duke Albrecht V. Though engaged as just another singer (a *tenor secundus*), Lassus took over the post of chapel master in 1563 and presided over the chapel until his death on June 14, 1594 (just a few months after the death of Palestrina). Lassus led a rich and active life during his almost forty years at Munich. He traveled often on behalf of the ducal family, and his fame spread quickly and widely. Both Andrea and Giovanni Gabrieli came under his influence, and it was to the musical establishment at Munich, with its mixed vocal and instrumental forces, that the Venetian style no doubt owed some of its splendor. In 1604, Lassus's sons Ferdinand and Rudolph published the *Magnum opus musicum*, a collection of 516 of their father's motets, including some that had never been printed before. It was a fitting tribute to the man whom some consider to be the greatest composer of the late sixteenth century.

The *Penitential Psalms*

It was in his motets that Lassus most clearly and convincingly exemplified the late sixteenth century's concern with music expressing the meaning of the text. The cycle of seven *Penitential Psalms* plus one "free" motet (to complete the cycle of eight modes) was composed around 1559, at the express wish of Duke Albrecht. And just how much the duke valued them is evident from the small fortune he spent to have them copied into a two-volume manuscript, lavishly illuminated by the court artist Simon Mielich.[9]

Lassus expresses the text in two ways that must be clearly distinguished. On the one hand, he conveys the emotional content of the text; thus he captures the somber quality of the psalms with music that is generally dark and restrained.

9. Munich, Bayerische Staatsbibliothek, Mus. MS A I–II

We can hear this in Example 38-3, which gives the first verse of the opening psalm of the cycle—"O Lord, rebuke me not in thy indignation, nor chastise me in thy wrath":

EXAMPLE 38-3. Lassus, *Penitential Psalms*, Psalm I, verse 1.

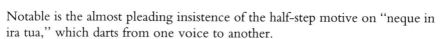

Notable is the almost pleading insistence of the half-step motive on "neque in ira tua," which darts from one voice to another.

On the other hand, Lassus also latches on to a specific word or phrase and depicts it "iconically": that is, he sets it with a musical figure that represents its physical imagery. Three examples will illustrate the technique (Ex. 38-4). Lassus uses every trick in the book: (a) the fall from heaven to earth ("de caelo in terram") is expressed spatially and emphasized with the dramatic descent of an eleventh in the superius (mm. 12–13); (b) after the single word "velociter" (speedily) sets off a chain of galloping semiminims, the phrase "my spirit hath fainted away" (mm. 5–8) ends in a rhythmic swoon followed by silence; (c) the idea of looking the other way in the plea "Turn not away thy face from me" is suggested by two–part writing in which straightforward imitation alternates with contrary motion. Thus musical space, rhythm, and counterpoint are all placed in the service of the text.

EXAMPLE 38-4. Lassus, *Penitential Psalms*: (a) Psalm V, verse 20, mm. 10–14;
(b) Psalm VII, verse 7 (complete); (c) Psalm V, verse 2, mm. 1–8.

MUSICA RESERVATA   In his commentary on the *Penitential Psalms* of around 1560, Lassus's contemporary biographer, Samuel Quickelberg (an official at the Bavarian court), wrote:

> Lassus expressed these psalms so appropriately in accommodating, according to necessity, thoughts and words with lamenting and plaintive tones, in expressing the force of the individual affections, and in placing the object almost alive before the eyes, that one is at a loss to say whether the sweetness of the affections enhanced the lamenting tones more greatly, or whether the lamenting tones brought greater ornament to the sweetness of the affections. This genre of music they call *musica reservata*.[10]

Although there are more than a dozen references to *musica reservata* during the period 1552–1625, not all of them fall directly into line with Quickelberg's explanation as music that vividly expresses the emotions and images of the text. Thus Vicentino, in his *L'antica musica* of 1555, suggests that it was music for "trained ears at entertainments of lords and princes," while the musician-astrologer-mathematician Jean Taisnier associated it with chromaticism (1559); still other references seem to equate the term with music that is new.

There is probably no single, simple definition of *musica reservata*. But we can generally understand the term as referring to late-sixteenth-century music that expressed the meaning, emotion, and imagery of the text with an intensity (at least to contemporary ears) unknown to previous generations; it was, moreover, music intended for an elite, cultivated audience.

Cum essem parvulus

We can appreciate Lassus's power of expression over the course of an entire motet in *Cum essem parvulus* (*Anthology* 89), which was copied into one of the Bavarian court manuscripts in 1579. The text, drawn from the Epistle of St. Paul, 1 Corinthians 13:11, reads:

Cum essem parvulus,	When I was a child,
loquebar ut parvulus,	I spoke as a child,

10. Quoted after *New Grove*, 12: 825.

sapiebam ut parvulus,	I understood as a child,
cogitabam ut parvulus;	I thought as a child;
quando autem factus sum vir,	but when I became a man,
evacuavi quae erant parvuli.	I put away childish things.
Videmus nunc per speculum	Now we see through a mirror
in aenigmate, tunc autem	in riddles, but then
facie ad faciem.	face to face.[11]

Lassus sets the first line (mm. 1–4) for high voices, with quick, "little" notes; it is the child's voice we hear. The next three lines are structurally and rhetorically parallel: "I spoke . . . I understood . . . I thought . . . " The music maintains this parallelism (mm. 4–16): each line begins with a varied statement of a progression from G to B-flat in the four lower voices, which represent the adult St. Paul, while the motive for "as a child" that follows functions as a flashback to Paul's childhood (a modern film director could not improve on Lassus, who was in fact an amateur actor). Then at measure 20, St. Paul's growth to manhood brings the number of voices to six for the first time.

If to this point Lassus has painted a musical picture of the contrast between St. Paul as child and as man, he now contrasts enigma and clarity, dark and light. At measure 28, he represents the mirror and its riddles by darkening the harmony and thickening the counterpoint, all of which give way to the "face to face," note-against-note, homophonic lightness at measure 39.

In *Cum essem parvulus*, then, Lassus builds an entire motet whose structure and musical-rhetorical strategies are dependent on the text: textual parallelism prompts musical parallelism; textual contrast occasions musical contrast. What the word could do, music could do. Lassus was the period's supreme musical rhetorician.

In me transierunt

We should not underestimate the late sixteenth century's tendency to view music as rhetoric, to understand a musical composition as being analogous to a well-made speech. In his *Musica poetica* of 1606, the German theorist Joachim Burmeister in fact analyzes Lassus's *In me transierunt* (the first full-scale, published analysis of a polyphonic piece) according to its use of rhetorical figures:

> This harmonic piece can be divided very appropriately into nine periods. The first comprises the *exordium*, which is adorned by two figures: *fuga realis* and *hypallage*. Seven inner periods comprise the body of the piece, similar to the confirmation of a speech (if one may thus compare one cognate art with another). The first of these is adorned with *hypotyposis*, *climax*, and *anadiplosis*; the second is likewise, and to those figures may be added *anaphora*.[12]

Example 38-5 provides as much of the motet as corresponds to Burmeister's first three "periods":

11. After *NAWM*, vol. 1, no. 33.

12. Quoted after Rivera's translation in *Musical Poetics: Joachim Burmeister*, 207.

EXAMPLE 38-5. Lassus, *In me transierunt*, mm. 1–32.

The first period (mm.1–20, "In me passed over your wrath") is the *exordium*, the introduction to the speech. The *fuga realis* (imitation with identical or similar intervals) describes the cantus-tenor I-tenor II and altus-bassus relationships, respectively; *hypallage* (contrary motion/inversion) describes the relationship of one imitative unit to the other, as altus and bassus rise a third (instead of a sixth) and then momentarily proceed in contrary motion. The second period (mm. 20–26, "and your terrors") is the first "inner" period and stands at the head of the body, or *confirmatio*, of the speech. *Hypotyposis* (the depiction of the text in such a way that an inanimate object is brought to life) refers to the setting of "et terrores" in the cantus on a single repeated note with a touch of syncopation, as if the cantus had been reduced to stuttering in dumbstruck fashion; *climax* (melodic sequence) occurs in the bassus at measures 21–25; *anadiplosis* (double imitation) must refer to the repeated imitation in the four upper voices throughout the period. The third period (mm. 26–32, "upset me") contains the three rhetorical figures in period 2 plus *anaphora* (motivic imitation) involving some but not all of the voices.

What sense would Lassus have made of Burmeister's analysis? Did he, for example, know that he was using a rhetorical figure called *hypallage* when he began *In me transierunt* with paired imitation, a standard opening gesture since the time of Josquin (did Josquin know it)? Had Lassus read Cicero and Quintilian on the art of oration? We cannot say. Yet even if Lassus never dreamed of composing in Burmeister's terms, his music nevertheless captures the essence of the words. He made his music "speak."

A Chanson

Lassus's concern with expressing the text spilled over into his secular works. A wonderful example is his setting of Du Bellay's *La nuict froide et sombre (Anthology* 90). Here, Lassus paints an evocative naturescape, his palette filled with contrasting hues of musical space, texture, and harmony. Among the broad brushstrokes that his audience could hardly have missed: (1) the contrast not only between high and low on "La terre et les cieux" (the earth and the heavens, mm. 7–10) but, together with a shift in harmonic color, between the somber night and the light of the following day (mm. 18–19); (2) the cantus dipping beneath the altus for a moment on "Courant d'obscure," so that the melody is covered and obscured (mm. 4–6); and (3) the descending motive on "Fait couleur" in order to evoke the image of sleep falling from the heavens (mm. 13–14). What Lassus did in a chanson such as *La nuict froid et sombre* was to transfer to the French chanson, which had been rather neutral in its emotionalism and use of musical imagery, the more text-conscious aesthetic of the late-sixteenth-century Italian madrigal. And therein lies his contribution to the development of the chanson.

With the exception of some of the more radical madrigalists and humanists, no composer of the period was more sensitive to the idea that music should serve the text than Lassus. And whereas some of the express-the-text zealots tipped the scales heavily in favor of the "mistress" text, Lassus never lost sight of the need to balance "her" claims with those of the "servant" music. His solution to the relationship between music and text may well be the most satisfying of the period.

THE ITALIAN MADRIGAL

More than any other genre of the period, the madrigal became intoxicated with the idea that music should be placed in the service of words. It was, after all, in connection with the madrigal that the brothers Monteverdi formulated the notion of a second practice in which "the words are the mistress of the harmony."

When we last considered the madrigal, in Chapter 27, we left it in the hands of Adrian Willaert, who brought to both music and words a heightened sense of seriousness and thus set the stage for the genre's future development. Here we pick up the story at about the mid-sixteenth century and follow it through to the turn of the seventeenth, with the focus mainly on the relationship between music and text.

Rore and the Beginning of the Second Practice

Born in the Low Countries in 1515 or 1516, Rore (Fig. 38-2) probably arrived at Venice in the early 1540s, where he was associated with Willaert's circle. (For those keeping count: with Rore, we have our sixth generation of

Figure 38-2. Portrait of Rore by an unknown artist (Kunsthistorisches Museum, Vienna).

northern composers who flocked to Italy since Johannes Ciconia began the trend in the late fourteenth century.) After stints at Ferrara (as head of the chapel for more than a decade beginning in 1547) and Parma, he succeeded Willaert as chapel master of St. Mark's in 1563, where, however, things did not go well. The following year he was back at Parma, where he died in September 1565.

Among the madrigals that Giulio Cesare Monteverdi praises in his "Declaration" is Rore's *Da le belle contrade d'oriente (Anthology* 91), published in his Fifth Book of Madrigals of 1566, and possibly his best-known work. The anonymous poem is an Italian sonnet, with the typical structure of octave (subdivided 4 + 4) plus sestet (3 + 3):

1. Da le belle contrade d'oriente	From the beautiful regions of the East
2. Chiara e lieta s'ergea Ciprigna, et io	Clear and joyful rose the morning star, and I
3. Fruiva in braccio al divin idol mio	Was enjoying, in the arms of my divine idol,
4. Quel piacer che non cape humana mente	That pleasure that transcends human understanding,
5. Quando sentii dopo un sospir ardente:	When I heard, after a passionate sigh:
6. "Speranza del mio cor, dolce desio,	"Hope of my heart, sweet desire,
7. T'en vai, haime, sola mi lasci, adio.	You go, alas, you leave me alone, farewell!
8. Che sarà qui di me scura e dolente?	What will happen to me here, gloomy and sad?
9. Ahi crudo Amor, ben son dubbose e corte	Alas, cruel Love, how uncertain and short-lived
10. Le tue dolcezze, poi ch'ancor ti godi	Are your pleasures, for it even pleases you
11. Che l'estremo piacer finisca in pianto."	That the greatest pleasure should end in tears."
12. Nè potendo dir più, cinseme forte	Unable to say more, she held me tightly,
13. Iterando gl'amplessi in tanti nodi,	Repeating her embraces in more entwinings
14. Che giamai ne fer più l'edra o l'acanto.	Than ivy or acantus ever made.

Rore expresses the text on two different levels: the imagery of individual words or short phrases, and the larger, emotion-laden drama as a whole. At the short-term level, we may single out the sob-like, fragmented texture at "T'en vai, haime," underscored by the falling seventh in the bassus (mm. 30–33), the solo cantus on "sola mi lasci" (mm. 33–34), and the almost serpentine melodic line with which the cantus sings "nodi" (mm. 66–67). They are instances of the type of iconic representation, or word painting, that became the stock-in-trade of the late-sixteenth-century madrigal.

But it is in the task of capturing the overall emotion of the poem that Rore's imagination truly shines. He pays no attention to the sonnet form, but rather takes his cue from the quotation marks that enclose lines 6–11 and that signal a change of voice from male storyteller to female lover and back to storyteller. Rore sets this little three-part drama with a matching **A B A** form in which the **B** section (mm. 25–56) cuts across the articulation between the sonnet's octave and sestet.

And how he distinguishes between the lovers! Whereas the harmonic language of the male narrator is conventional, that of the woman is anything but. After two chromatic gestures at measures 33–36, the second following the fateful "adio," Rore turns the harmony loose: his triads move simply enough at first, from E major to a A major (mm. 36–40); he then wrenches our ears on "Ahi" by plopping onto C minor (and thus pays some attention to the beginning of the sestet), which in turn sets off a chain that lands on D-flat major seven measures later (mm. 41–48). From E major to D-flat major in thirteen measures: it is *Tristan* boiled down to about forty seconds. No less remarkable is the manner in which Rore sets the stage for the woman's words of passion. The cantus is silent from the middle of measure 21 to the upbeat of measure 26. When, therefore, it reenters with the woman's opening line, "Speranza del mio cor," it is as if "she" is a soloist, speaking to us directly in the first person. The effect is nothing less than operatic.

Yet despite the shifting voices, emotions, and harmonic worlds, Rore maintains a sense of overall musical homogeneity; though the music serves the text, the two elements seem in perfect balance. It was a feat that not all later madrigalists, upon whom Rore had a tremendous influence, could match.

Marenzio and Wert

Madrigalists after Rore faced a crucial question: how, within a musical language that was essentially homogeneous, could they express the ever-changing imagery and shifting emotions of the poetry without having the music seem to fall apart? How, in other words, could the music serve the text but still retain a sense of musical cohesiveness? There was no single solution. And even within the works of a single composer, the approach could vary from one madrigal to another. Two madrigals, by Claudio Marenzio and Giaches de Wert, illustrate the spectrum.

MARENZIO'S SCALDAVA IL SOL   When the composer-theorist Adriano Banchieri offered his views on the recent history of music in 1614, he named Claudio Marenzio as the successor to Rore, praising him for his new ideas in the realm of word painting. Born near Brescia (in northern Italy) in 1553 or 1554, Marenzio was probably the most stylistically wide-ranging of the end-of-the-century madrigalists. Certainly, he was the greatest of the native Italians. He spent most of his career at Rome, most notably in the employ (1578–86) of the high-living Cardinal Luigi d'Este, and published more than four hundred madrigals (in twenty-two books) between 1580 and his death in 1599.

A good illustration of Marenzio's mastery of word painting is *Scaldava il sol* (1582; *Anthology* 92). The poem (by Luigi Alamanni) is given with a literal translation that matches word for word; words or phrases that Marenzio singles out for special treatment appear in italics:

1. Scaldava il   sol di mezo giorno *l'arco*
    Burned the sun of mid- day   *the arch*
2. Nel dorso   del   Leon suo albergo caro.
    on the back of the lion, its lodging dear.
3. Sotto'l   boschetto *più di   frondi* carco
    Under the bush   *more with leaves* laden
4. *Dormia'l pastor*   con le sue greggi *a paro.*
    Slept the shepherd with his   flock *beside* (him).
5. *Giaceva*   il   *villanel* de   l'opra scarco
    Stretched out, the *peasant,* from work freed,
6. Vie più   di posa che di spighe avaro.
    Far more for rest than for food   greedy.
7. Gl'augei, le fere,   ogn'huom *s'asconde e   tace.*
    The birds, the beasts, all men   *hide   and keep still.*
8. *Sol*   la   *Cicala* non   si sente in pace.
    Alone/Only the *cicada* does not feel   at peace.

As Table 38-1 shows, Marenzio's word painting ranges from the obvious to the subtle:

Table 38-1.   Word painting in Marenzio's *Scaldava il sol.*

Verse	Measures	English words	Musical description
1	8–11	"arch"	The melodic contour forms the curved outline of an arch.
3	19–20	"more with leaves"	Quick, patter-like figure for light, numerous leaves.
4	22–26	"Slept the shepherd"	Sustained notes for repose.
	27–28	"beside"	The homophonic texture has the notes beside one another.
5	29–31	"Stretched out"	Sustained notes.
	31–34	"peasant"	Lively, dance-like rhythm.
7	46–50	"hide"	With their downward leaps of an octave, the voices seemingly hide beneath one another.
	50–53	"and keep still"	The voices drop out one by one.
8	53–54	"Alone/Only"	A double play on the word: one voice alone is left to sing it; and when the other voices enter, they do so on pitches that can be solmized as *sol.*
	55–57	"cicada"	The dotted rhythms and patter of short notes imitate the insect's chirping.

Here, it is not changing voices or shifting emotional states that threaten to disrupt the cohesiveness of the music, but rather the piling up of musical pictographs in almost box-like, comic-strip fashion. Nevertheless, one must admire Marenzio's virtuosic wit and ingenuity. As we will see, these were attributes much admired by late-sixteenth-century Italian audiences, whether in music, literature, or the visual arts.

TASSO AND GUARINI   It is safe to say that the two favorite poets of the end-of-the-century madrigalists were Torquato Tasso (1544–1595) and Giambattista Guarini (1538–1612), both of whom enjoyed close ties with the Ferrarese court of Alfonso II d'Este, one of the hotbeds of avant-garde madrigal composition. Tasso's great work was his epic poem *Gerusalemme liberata* (completed in the mid-1570s), which was still being used as a vehicle for opera librettos in the eighteenth century. Guarini rode to fame on the strength of *Il pastor fido* (1589), a pastoral drama with elements of both tragedy and comedy that became spectacularly popular with madrigal composers: more than a hundred composers produced over five hundred settings of its verses.

Two excerpts from the *Pastor fido*, which has one of the most complicated plots imaginable, illustrate the intricacy, ingenuity, gloominess, and even violent juxtapositions of style (the translations are crudely literal):

Act III: Mirtillo, who is spurned by Amarilli, says:

E sento nel partire	And I feel in parting
Un vivace morire	A lively death
Che dà vita al dolore	That gives life to a grief
Per far che mora immortalmente core.	That will make die without end my heart.

Act V: Carino observes the following about Mirtillo:

Di quel che fa morendo	Of him [Mirtillo] who makes, in dying,
Viver chi gli dà morte	To live who [Amarilli] gives him death,
Morir chi gli diè vita.	[And] to die, him [Montano] who gave him life.

To set such stanzas is to take on the challenge of dealing with the idea of a lively death, or an unending act of dying, or death causing life (all with sexual connotations). Among those who felt up to it was Giaches de Wert.

WERT'S *GIUNTO A LA TOMBA*   Giaches de Wert (1536–1596) was yet another Fleming who came to Italy and became a prolific composer of madrigals. In 1565, he became chapel master at the Gonzaga court of Mantua, which, thanks to its close ties with Ferrara, permitted him to associate with Tasso and Guarini and placed him near the center of the most musically progressive thinking. Though Wert, like Marenzio, cultivated a wide stylistic range, he is best-known for his settings of the new dramatic poetry of Tasso and Guarini.

Example 38-6 gives Wert's setting of the first five lines of *Giunto a la tomba* (1581), the scene from Tasso's *Gerusalemme liberata* in which Tancredi visits the tomb of Clorinda:

EXAMPLE 38-6. Wert, *Giunto a la tomba*, mm. 1–24.

The text and translation:

1. Giunto a la tomba ove al suo spirto vivo	Arrived at the tomb where, for his living spirit
2. Dolorosa prigion' il ciel prescrisse;	A sorrowful prison heaven prescribed;
3. Di color, di calor, di moto privo	Of color, of warmth, of motion deprived,
4. Già marmo in vista al marmo il viso affise.	Already marble his visage, to the marble he affixed his face.
5. Al fin sgorgando un lagrimoso rivo.	At last gushing forth a river of tears.

Wert sets the first four gloomy and emotion-filled lines as a homophonic, recitative-like dirge, the rhythm of the music wedded closely to that of the natural declamation of the text. The overall sense of despair is heightened by such harmonic twists as the move to the flatted seventh (m. 4), the fleeting $\frac{6}{4}$ chord over G (m. 5), the cross relationship between major triads on C and A (mm. 7–8), and the subsequent return to A minor (m. 11). Along the way, there is also the light touch of iconic representation on "il ciel" (m. 6), as the two lower voices both leap up an octave. The setting of these four lines is like an *exordium* to the speech that follows.

What follows is music that seems to go berserk. The word "sgorgando" sets off a sudden and torrential downpour of rapid descending scales, only to hit the brakes hard on "lagrimoso rivo." It is as if Wert has gone from the beginning of one madrigal to the rousing coda of another. In addition, the twelve measures of line five are only one less than the thirteen needed to set all of the first four lines.

Overall, music may do more than serve the text in *Giunto a la tomba*. Perhaps it sacrifices some inner coherence and, as some of Wert's contemporaries might have said, begins to subvert the text altogether.

Criticism and Reception

The madrigal was the darling of the smart set. It was prized in the households of the worldly cardinals at Rome, at the aristocratic courts of northern Italy, at the literary salons and academies of Venice and Verona. Nor was its success limited to the aristocratic elite. That madrigal collections came off the presses in droves must surely indicate that the genre made deep inroads among the middle classes as well, though the vocal virtuosity demanded may have placed madrigals such as *Giunto a la tomba* beyond the abilities of amateur, Saturday-night singers. Indeed, we will soon see that a new professionalism, featuring virtuoso singers, was clearly on the rise. The madrigal was also popular in Germany, and it set off something of a craze in England, which developed an English-language counterpart of its own (see Chapter 40).

And yet the nature of the music-text relationship provoked some criticism. In 1587, Tasso completed a treatise entitled *La cavaletta*, in which he complained that the madrigal, with its fixation on representing individual words and phrases, was losing sight of the overall structure of the poetry. No less vocal—and certainly more influential in the long run—was the attack launched by a group of Florentine literati and musicians known as the Camerata. It was this group, meeting at the home of Count Giovanni de' Bardi during the 1570s and 1580s, that "invented" monody and, with a little stretching, opera itself. One member, the theorist Vincenzo Galilei, attacked the madrigal in his *Dialogo della musica antica e della moderna* of 1581:

> [The madrigalists] will say they have imitated the words when among the ideas in the text are some that have the meaning "to flee," or "to fly." These will be declaimed with such speed and so little grace as can hardly be imagined. As for words like "to vanish," "to swoon," "to die," they will make the parts fall silent so abruptly that far from inducing any such effect, they will move their listeners to laughter . . . setting this particular line from one of Petrarch's sestinas: "And with the lame ox he will go in pursuit of Laura," will have it declaimed with such jerkiness, wavering, and syncopations that it will sound like nothing so much as a case of hiccups. . . . Another time they will have a verse like this: "He descended into Hell, into the lap of Pluto," and they will make one of the parts descend so that the singer sounds to the listener more like someone moaning . . . than like someone singing. . . . And where they find the opposite: "He doth aspire to the stars"—they will have it declaimed in such a high register that no one screaming in pain has ever equaled it. Unhappy men, they do not realize that if any of the famous orators of old had ever once declaimed words in such a fashion they would have moved their hearers to laughter and contempt at once, and would have been ridiculed and despised by them as stupid, abject, and worthless men.[13]

Thus according to Tasso and Galilei, the madrigal, rather than placing music in the service of the text, was making a mockery of it. No less ironic is this: when at the turn of the seventeenth century the polyphonic madrigal began to give way to accompanied monody, both loser (madrigal) and victor (monody)

---

13. Quoted after Weiss and Taruskin, *Music in the Western World*, 167.

could claim to have fought under the same banner—"music in the service of words."

Beyond the Problem: Monteverdi

Although Rore, Marenzio, and Wert each expressed the poetry of their madrigals in a different way, they nevertheless stayed within the accepted boundaries and language of sixteenth-century polyphony. Monteverdi, on the other hand, looked beyond them.

Born at Cremona (hometown of the Stradivarius family) in 1567, Claudio Monteverdi (Fig. 38-3) entered the service of the court of Mantua in the early 1590s, where he raised a family and established his reputation as a composer: five books of madrigals, the operas *L'Orfeo* and *L'Arianna*, one of the last examples of a parody Mass (on a motet by Gombert), and the *Vespro della Beata Virgine*, to cite just a few of his outstanding achievements. Nevertheless, it was on bitter terms that he left Mantua in 1612 to take the post of chapel master of St. Mark's at Venice, where he remained for the rest of his career, his style then taking him far beyond the scope of our study. Monteverdi died in 1643.

With his Fourth (1603) and Fifth (1605) Books of Madrigals, Monteverdi began to stretch the accepted musical language of the sixteenth century. The "rules" could simply no longer contain the power of his expression. Two madrigals from these books will illustrate the point.

CRUDA AMARILLI As noted at the beginning of the chapter, Monteverdi's treatment of dissonance in *Cruda Amarilli* drew the criticism of the theorist

Figure 38-3. Bernardo Strozzi, portrait of Monteverdi, c. 1635 (Tiroler Landesmuseum Ferdinandeum, Innsbruck).

Giovanni Maria Artusi (c. 1540–1613), who was a generation older than Monteverdi, a student of Zarlino, and a staunch advocate of first-practice rules of counterpoint. Among the passages that irked Artusi was the setting of "ahi lasso" (alas; Ex. 38-7):

EXAMPLE 38-7. Monteverdi, *Cruda Amarilli*, mm. 12–14.

Artusi's criticism: the *a″* in the cantus (m. 13) enters as an unprepared dissonance against the *g* in the bass; it then moves directly to the equally unprepared dissonance *f″*. Monteverdi's counter-criticism: Artusi "pays no attention to the words." The generation gap was not easily bridged.

SFOGAVA CON LE STELLE   There is hardly a more famous opening in all of Monteverdi's madrigals than that of *Sfogava con le stelle* (Ex. 38-8):

EXAMPLE 38-8. Monteverdi, *Sfogava con le stelle*, mm. 1–20.

The madrigal opens with a technique known as *falsobordone*: a kind of declamatory, chordal recitative on a repeated triad, with the singers declaiming the text as if they were speaking naturally. Now, there was nothing new about the technique; during the second half of the sixteenth century, it was used frequently in psalm settings as a quick and easy way to set the many repeated notes of psalm tones. Here, though, Monteverdi employs *falsobordone* to express the stark, emotionally neutral voice of the narrator, who says: "A lovesick man poured forth his grief to the stars under the nighttime sky, and said, [his eyes] fixed on them . . . " Only when that lovesick man enters at measure 15 does the "music" get under way. It is as if the mensural system could no longer accommodate Monteverdi's sense of drama, just as the rules of counterpoint were unable to allow for the expression of sobbing in *Cruda Amarilli*.

With Monteverdi, the sixteenth century was giving way to the seventeenth: one musical language was giving way to another. Music still had to be placed in the service of words. But if in the process music broke the rules, then the rules simply had to be rewritten. If music violated conventions of style, then the conventions had to change.

THE LIGHTER FORMS

Just as the serious madrigal of the second quarter of the century had a light-hearted counterpart in the villanella, so the later madrigal enjoyed the company of the *canzonetta*, *balletto*, and the madrigal comedy.

CANZONETTA   The canzonetta originated at the hands of Orazio Vecchi (1550–1604). The four-voice *Caro dolce mio bene (Anthology* 93), published in Vecchi's *Canzonette . . . libro terzo* of 1585, is typical of the genre: the poem treats love in a less-than-heated fashion; and the music is homophonic (with a touch of imitation between tenor and bass at mm. 4–7), bouncy, and cast in the customary **A A B B** repetition scheme.

Vecchi's canzonettas took the marketplace by storm: they were outfitted with new texts in four languages (including Thomas Morley's in English), arranged for various combinations of instruments, and still being reprinted into the 1620s. Vecchi's success spilled over onto the genre as a whole; and it was with a book of three-voice canzonettas that the seventeen-year-old Monteverdi broke into print in 1584.

BALLETTO   What Vecchi was to the canzonetta, the Mantuan composer Giovanni Giacomo Gastoldi (?1550s–?1622) was to the balletto. To the already fluffy canzonetta, the balletto added a "fa la la" (or other nonsense syllables) between couplets (Ex. 38-9). Gastoldi introduced the balletto in his *Balletti a cinque voci* of 1591, with titles that invoked a character type: *Lo schernito* means "The Rejected One." The songs may well have been performed as part of costumed entertainments at theater-happy Mantua, though there is no suggestion of a plot. Like the canzonetta, the balletto enjoyed tremendous success beyond Italy, especially in England.

EXAMPLE 38-9. Gastoldi, *Lo schernito*, mm. 1–10.

MADRIGAL COMEDY   From the unrelated "character pieces" of Gastoldi's collection of balletti, it was but a short step to the idea of the "madrigal comedy" (a modern term), which consisted of a cycle of madrigals strung together around a discernible plot. Vecchi took the step with his *L'Amfiparnaso* (sub-titled "comedia musicale") of 1597.

The cycle takes its title from the two slopes of Parnassus—comedy and tragedy—and consists of a prologue and thirteen scenes divided into three acts. Vecchi drew his characters both from the tradition of improvised theater known as the *commedia dell'arte* and from his own imagination. And though *L'Amfiparnaso* was published with woodcuts that illustrate each scene (Fig. 38-4), it was not meant to be staged. The madrigal comedy, then, is not quite a *Gesamtkunstwerk*.

Figure 38-4. A "scene" from Vecchi's *L'Amfiparnaso*, 1597.

THE LADIES OF FERRARA

During the final quarter of the century, Venice slipped in its position as the epicenter of madrigal composition. That distinction was now shared by Rome, where Marenzio held forth, and the Ferrarese court of Duke Alfonso II d'Este (r. 1559–97), which in addition to its own lineup of Luzzasco Luzzaschi, Vicentino, the visiting Gesualdo, and the poets Tasso and Guarini also had access to the madrigals of Wert at the nearby court of Mantua, to which it was related by marriage.

Ferrara in particular gained a reputation as the home of what might be called the virtuoso madrigal, given the technical demands made on the singers. We get a glimpse of these in the collection by Luzzaschi (?1545–1607) entitled *Madrigali . . . per cantare, et sonare a uno, e doi, e tre soprani*, first published in 1601 but probably composed during the 1580s. As the title makes clear, the madrigals were for one, two, or three sopranos over a keyboard accompaniment that reduced the customary voices-only forces (Ex. 38-10):

EXAMPLE 38-10. Luzzaschi, *O dolcezza amarissime d'Amore*, mm. 10–20.

Luzzaschi wrote the madrigals for a specific group of singers: the court's *Concerto delle donne*, established in 1580 and made up of the three sopranos Laura Peverara (daughter of a well-to-do Mantuan merchant), Anna Guarini (the poet's daughter), and Livia d'Arco (daughter of a minor Mantuan nobleman); in 1583, they were joined by Tarquinia Molza, an accomplished poet. Though listed on the Ferrarese payroll as "ladies in waiting" to the duchess, there was no doubt that their position at the court was that of professional musician. The singers formed part of the duke's *musica secreta*: their duties consisted of singing for the duke and his guests every evening, for which they received the handsome salary of three hundred scudi (more than twice what Luzzaschi earned) plus rooms in the ducal palace for them and their families (Luzzaschi had the same plus a farm in the country). There were also fringe benefits: Duke Alfonso provided Laura Peverara with a dowry of ten thousand scudi upon her marriage in 1583. The women's singing was, by all accounts, nothing short of ravishing.

There is an important point to all this: the final quarter of the sixteenth century saw a thorough transformation in the status of women musicians. From their earlier position as ladies of the court who also happened to sing (that is, Castiglione's ideal of the well-bred amateur, as he expressed it in *The Courtier*), they were transformed into singers who also happened to be ladies of the court. And by 1600, they had made even further progress: women now had the opportunity to embark on full-time careers as professional musicians, something that had already been anticipated in the theater a half century earlier. It is, then, to the end of the sixteenth century that we may trace the birth of the diva.

Women also began to make their presence more strongly felt as composers. The most notable of the period was Maddalena Casulana (fl. 1566–83), a well-known singer who, with her two books of madrigals (1568 and 1570), was the first woman composer to gain publication. Her *Ahi possanza d'amor (Anthology 94)* shows why Lassus thought enough of her music to perform one of her pieces—together with a madrigal by Caterina Willaert, surely a relative of her famous namesake—at the Munich celebrations for the marriage of Wilhelm IV and Renée of Lorraine. Other women composers were Paola Massarenghi, Cesarina Ricci de' Tingoli, and Vittoria (Raphaela?) Aleotti, whose *Ghirlanda de madrigali* was published at Venice in 1593. No doubt, the activities of all five women helped ease the way for two especially talented composers of the early seventeenth century: Francesca Caccini (daughter of the famous monodist) and Barbara Strozzi.

TALKING ABOUT MUSIC

We close this chapter by considering how musicians of the late sixteenth century might have perceived and talked about music. Were there alternatives to Zarlino's technical discussion about counterpoint, on the one hand, and Burmeister's somewhat esoteric rhetorical figures, on the other? Perhaps the answer lies in Ludovico Zacconi's discussion of Lassus and Palestrina in Book II of his *Prattica di musica*, which, though not published until 1622, recalls a conversation that took place in the 1580s:

> *Musica armoniale* is distinguished by seven particular aspects . . . *arte, modulatione, diletto, tessitura, contraponto, inventione*, and *buone dispositione*. . . . Lasso possessed *modulatione, arte*, and *bonissima inventione*. . . . Palestrina had *arte, contraponto, ottima dispositione*, and a flowing *modulatione*.[14]

Only *contraponto* among these terms is a musical one; the others are drawn from rhetoric and oratory, though their flavor is very different from Burmeister's terminology. *Modulatione*, for instance, may refer to nothing more than good melody, which, for Zacconi, flowed in Palestrina. *Inventione* is an imaginative idea, a good point of imitation, for example; Lassus was "very good" at such things. *Dispositione* is the way certain musical elements are disposed:

14. Quoted after Haar, "A Sixteenth-Century Attempt at Music Criticism," 193–94.

melodies should be graceful and remain true to their mode; counterpoint should make good harmonic sense—in all of which Palestrina "excelled."

What might surprise us is just how modern Zacconi's description sounds. It is a subtle blend of lightly worn technical analysis and aesthetic appreciation, both of which are closely attuned to clearly audible features of the music. It shows a solid feel for the music. And it might well have been the language of music criticism at its enlightened best.

BIBLIOGRAPHICAL NOTE

Editions of the Music

Aleotti: *Ghirlanda de madrigali a quatro voci*, ed. C. Ann Carruthers, Music at the Courts of Italy 1 (New York: The Broude Trust, 1994). **Casulana**: *I madrigali di Maddalena Casulana*, ed. Beatrice Pescerelli (Florence: Olschki, 1979). **Lassus**: there are two editions—the old one is *Sämtliche Werke*, ed. F. X. Haberl and Adolph Sandberger (Leipzig: Breitkopf & Härtel, 1894–1926); the new one is still in progress, *Sämtliche Werke: Neue Reihe*, ed. Horst Leuchtmann et al. (Kassel: Bärenreiter, 1956–). **Le Jeune**: one can piece together many of the secular works by using *Anthologie de la chanson Parisienne au XVIᵉ siècle*, ed. François Lesure (Monaco: L'Oiseaux-lyre, 1953), and *Claude Le Jeune: Le Printemps*, MMRF 12–14, ed. Henry Expert (Paris: Leduc, 1900–1). **Marenzio**: one should approach him from two in-progress angles—*Opera omnia*, CMM 72, ed. Bernhard Meier and Roland Jackson (American Institute of Musicology, 1976–), and *L. Marenzio: The Secular Works*, ed. Steven Ledbetter and Patricia Myers (New York: Broude Bros., 1977–). **Monteverdi**: *Tutte le opere*, 17 vols., ed. G. Francesco Malipiero (Asola: G.F. Malipiero 1926–42; Vienna: Universal Edition, 1966). **Rore**: *Opera omnia*, CMM 14, ed. Bernhard Meier (American Institute of Musicology, 1959–). **Vecchi**: *The Four-Voice Canzonettas*, RRMR 92–93, ed. Ruth DeFord (Madison: A-R Editions, 1993). **Wert**: *Collected Works*, CMM 24, ed. Carol MacClintock and Melvin Bernstein (American Institute of Musicology, 1961).

French Secular Song

There is a concise introduction in François Lesure, *Musicians and Poets of the French Renaissance*, trans. Elia Gianturco and Hans Rosenwald (New York: Merlin Press, 1955); the entire issue of *Early Music History* 13 (1994) is devoted to the topic. On the background of French humanism, see the classic study by F. A. Yates, *The French Academies of the Sixteenth Century* (London: The Warburg Institute, 1947); on *musique mesurée*, see the series of articles by D. P. Walker, "The Aims of Baïf's Académie de Poésie et de Musique," *JRBM* 1 (1946): 91–100; (with Lesure) "Claude Le Jeune and Musique Mesurée," *MD* 3 (1949): 151–70; "The Rhythm and Notation of Musique Mesurée," *MD* 4 (1950): 163–86.

Lassus

The two central studies are both in German: Wolfgang Bötticher, *Orlando di Lasso und seine Zeit, 1532–1594* (Kassel: Bärenreiter, 1958), and Horst Leuchtman, *Orlando di Lasso*, 2 vols. (Wiesbaden: Breitkopf & Härtel, 1976–77); in English, the best starting points are two essays by James Haar, "Orlande de Lassus," in *The New Grove High Renaissance Masters*, ed. Stanley Sadie (New York: Norton, 1984), 157–227, and "Munich at the Time of Orlande de Lassus," in *The Renaissance*, ed. Stanley Sadie and Iain Fenlon (London: Macmillan, 1989), 243–62; see also Jerome Roche, *Lassus*, Oxford Studies of Composers 19 (London: Oxford University Press, 1982); Clive Wearing, "Orlandus Lassus (1932–1594) and the Munich Kapelle," *EM* 10 (1982): 147–53.

The Italian Madrigal

In addition to the general studies by Haar, Einstein, Carter, and Roche cited in the Bibliographical Note in Chapter 27, one should consult the following on individual composers. **Marenzio**: Denis Arnold, *Marenzio*, Oxford Studies of Composers 2 (London: Oxford University Press, 1965). **Wert**: Carol MacClintock, *Giaches de Wert (1535–1596): Life and Works*, MSD 17 (American Institute of Musicology, 1966). **Monteverdi**: a good general survey is Silke Leopold, *Monteverdi: Music in Transition*, trans. Anne Smith (Oxford: Oxford University Press, 1991); Leo Schrade's *Monteverdi: Creator of Modern Music* (New York: Norton, 1950), though dated, is a classic; there is an edition of the composer's letters edited and translated by Denis Stevens, *The Letters of Claudio Monteverdi* (New York: Columbia University Press, 1980), and a fine collection of essays in *The New Monteverdi Companion*, ed. Denis Arnold and Nigel Fortune (Oxford: Clarendon Press, 1985); on the madrigals, see Denis Arnold's little *Monteverdi Madrigals* (London: British Broadcasting Corporation, 1967); Gary Tomlinson's penetrating *Monteverdi and the End of the Renaissance* (Berkeley and Los Angeles: University of California Press, 1987) has excellent opening and closing chapters on the intellectual background; two entire volumes of *Early Music*, 21/4 (1993) and 22/1 (1994), are devoted to Monteverdi.

Ferrara and Mantua

Anthony Newcomb, *The Madrigal at Ferrara, 1579–1597*, 2 vols. (Princeton: Princeton University Press, 1980); Iain Fenlon, *Music and Patronage in Sixteenth-Century Mantua*, 2 vols. (Cambridge: Cambridge University Press, 1980–82).

Women Musicians

Karin Pendle, *Women and Music: A History* (Bloomington: Indiana University Press, 1991); Anthony Newcomb, "Courtesans, Muses, or Musicians? Professional Women Musicians in Sixteenth-Century Italy," in *Women Making Music: The Western Art Tradition, 1150–1950*, ed. Jane Bowers and Judith Tick (Urbana: University of Illinois Press, 1986), 90–115; Martha F. Schleifer and Sylvia Glickman, eds. *Women Composers: Music Through the Ages*, vol. 1: *Composers Born Before 1599* (New York: G. K. Hall, 1996), which includes music by Aleotti, Casulana, Massarenghi, and the mother-daughter pair Isabella de'Medici and Leonora Orsini.

Also Cited

Vered Cohen, *On the Modes* (New Haven: Yale University Press, 19??); Joseph P. Clancy, trans., *The Odes and Epodes of Horace* (Chicago: University of Chicago Press, 1960); *Musical Poetics: Joachim Burmeister*, ed. Claude Palisca, trans. Benito Rivera (New Haven: Yale University Press, 1993); James Haar, "A Sixteenth-Century Attempt at Music Criticism," *JAMS* 36 (1983): 191–209.

CHAPTER 39

Intermedio: 1588–1590

THE DEFEAT OF THE SPANISH ARMADA

To single out one particular event as having altered the relationship between two nations and shaped their destinies for centuries to come may seem simplistic. Yet some events do nudge things along more than others. And in Anglo-Spanish relations and the subsequent history of each country, one event does stand out: the English victory over the Spanish Armada in 1588.

During the reign of Elizabeth I (1558–1603), relations between England and Spain went from bad to worse. The antagonism was fueled by King Philip II's insatiable appetite for imperial expansion, English economic interests in the Spanish-ruled Netherlands, conflict between England and Spanish-ruled Portugal (gobbled up by Spain in 1580) in the African–West Indies slave trade, and general rivalry on the high seas, where Sir Francis Drake (?1540–1596) and other English "sea dogs" practiced piracy along the Spanish Main. And behind everything, as usual, was that perpetual tinderbox of sixteenth-century politics: religion. Under Elizabeth, Protestant England lived in constant fear of invasion by a Spanish-led Catholic coalition. It was against the backdrop of this simmering hostility that two events finally pushed things over the edge.

THE REVOLT OF THE NETHERLANDS   The Netherlands began its rebellion against Spanish rule in 1567–68. And though the Catholic south (mainly present-day Belgium) eventually withdrew from the fray, the Protestant north formed the United Provinces (present-day Netherlands), declared its independence in 1581, and continued to fight. In 1585, after almost two decades of covert aid, England intervened openly on behalf of the Dutch. For Philip II, the intervention was an act of war.

THE EXECUTION OF MARY, QUEEN OF SCOTS   Mary led a life that was filled with equal parts adventure and tragedy. Born a Catholic in 1542, she inherited the throne of Scotland when she was one week old. Having married the French dauphin at age fifteen, she became a widow at eighteen (1560). She then returned to Scotland (1561), married a cousin, Henry Stuart (she is also called Mary Stuart), known as Lord Darnley (1565), and promptly subdued a Protestant rebellion. In 1566, Mary was present when her private secretary—and, according to the gossip mill, lover—the Italian musician David Rizzio, was stabbed to death. Within the year (early 1567), her husband's house was blown up with him in it. Popular opinion held that the latter crime had been planned by the Earl of Bothwell, whom Mary married three months later.

In 1567, Mary abdicated in favor of her son and was soon jailed. She escaped in 1568, failed in an attempt to retake Scotland, and fled to England. There she became implicated in plots to overthrow and kill Elizabeth and return England to Catholicism. Elizabeth gained the upper hand, and once again Mary was jailed. And though she insisted on her innocence, she was beheaded on February 18, 1587. Catholic Europe was outraged.

THE "ENTERPRISE OF ENGLAND"   For Philip II, who had long been thinking about invading England and restoring it to Catholicism, the events of 1585 and 1587 were the final provocation. He now undertook the "Enterprise of England." Confident that he possessed a navy whose power was unmatched, Philip planned to attack the English fleet in their home waters, gain control of the English Channel, and then ferry a large Spanish army that was fighting in the Netherlands across the channel for a full-scale land invasion.

Philip's "invincible Armada," under the command of the Duke of Medina Sidonia, consisted of 130 ships, stretching out for some seven miles in a crescent-shaped formation. They were outfitted with about 2,500 guns, more than 120,000 cannonballs, and 30,000 men, 19,000 of them soldiers. (About 180 priests and friars looked after their spiritual needs.) Provisions included bacon, fish, cheese, rice, beans, biscuits, oil, vinegar, wine, and water.

Spain must have thought England's fleet puny. Under the command of Lord High Admiral Charles Howard (Drake was one of his lieutenants), its core consisted of 34 ships with about 6,000 men. In addition, the fleet mustered up a number of privately owned ships, many of which, however, were either too small or too poorly equipped to be of much use. Yet what the English lacked in numbers, they would make up in grit and strategy.

The Battle

The Spanish and English staked out very different strategies. Coming off their great victory at the Battle of Lepanto in 1571, at which they led the Christian fleets against the forces of the Turks, the Spanish chose to stick to the tried and true: an oars-driven, close-in battle, the aim being to board and overrun the opposition. The English, on the other hand, hoped to fight at a distance, making use of their long-range culverins (the largest cannons of the day).

The fate of the Armada played out in just over four months: the Spanish set sail from Lisbon on May 29 and began to limp back to Santander (on Spain's northern coast) at the end of September (see the map in Fig. 39-1). The face-to-face skirmishes themselves, however, went on for just twelve days:

July 29: The English sighted the Spanish south of the Scilly Isles; Howard and Drake sailed from Plymouth.

July 30: The English battered one of the Spanish ships for an hour from

Figure 39-1. The route of the Spanish Armada, with overall route and engagements in the English Channel.

about three hundred yards; the damage was slight, and the ship was rescued by its squadron.

July 30–31: After a short exchange of gunfire, two Spanish ships surrendered off Plymouth; with the waters still wide enough, Lord Howard worked his way around and behind the Spanish.

August 2: A Spanish attempt to isolate and corner one of the English squadrons off Portland Bill failed; the gunfire went on till sunset.

August 4: The Armada sailed past the Isle of Wight; though two ships were lost in the process, the Armada was still achieving its objective—to make its way through the channel in order to rendezvous with Spanish land forces on the coast of Flanders and ferry them to England.

August 6: The Armada anchored at Calais.

August 7–8: During the night, the English launched eight "fireboats" (sixteenth-century equivalents of the torpedo) into the anchored, tightly packed Spanish fleet; the Spanish cut their lines and sailed out of Calais in confusion. In the ensuing battle off Gravelines, the English attacked individual ships, driving some of them ashore.

August 8–9: A gale separated the two fleets, blowing the Armada into the North Sea. Medina Sidonia decided to call it quits and turn north, giving up any hope of uniting with Spanish ground troops.

Though the English had not inflicted heavy combat casualties, the Armada had lost. It failed to destroy the English fleet or mount the intended invasion of ground troops. And what the English had not done themselves, storms, heavy seas, and shortages of provisions did for them as the Armada wended its way back to Spain up and around the northern coast of Scotland and down the coast of western Ireland. (Many shipwrecked Spaniards straggled ashore, settled down, and intermarried with the native Irish, giving rise to the dark-haired, dark-eyed progeny known as the "black Irish.") In the end, only about half the fleet and one-third of the men returned.

Though the defeat of the Armada can fairly be called decisive, it was so more in the long term than in the short (the war continued until 1604), and it was decisive for each side in a different way. For England, it was as much a moral and psychological victory as anything else, confirming what had already become evident in decades leading up to the battle: England had become a dominant sea power. Indeed, for the better part of the next four centuries, it was England that had the invincible armada. For Spain, which was already in economic decline since about the middle of the century (its population was heading in the same direction), the defeat added the first chink in its military armor, the shedding of which would continue steadily for more than three centuries, until the nation was stripped bare in the Spanish-American War of 1898.

Finally, the defeat of the Armada was decisive for those in the two religious camps who watched from the sidelines. For Protestants, it was cause for hope and rejoicing: the military champion of Catholicism had been defeated. At the same time, perhaps there was a quiet sense of hope and joy among Catholics in France, Italy, and elsewhere who had themselves felt the heavy hand of Spain's military might; we might even wonder for whom some of Catholic Europe really rooted.

LEON MODENA AND THE VENETIAN GHETTO

In July 1590, the noted rabbi Leon (of) Modena (1571–1648; Fig. 39-2), who was also a musician and poet (and compulsive gambler), married his cousin Rachel Simḥah. In his autobiography, *The Life of Judah* (begun in 1617), he looked back on the event:

Figure 39-2. Portrait of Rabbi Leon Modena.

In order to please my mother . . . I agreed to marry the aforementioned Rachel. Immediately we wrote up the agreement and were married on Friday the [4th] of Tammuz 5350 [July 6, 1590], under a favorable star. On that Sabbath, Rabbi Solomon Sforno gave a beautiful sermon on the Torah portion Korah [Numbers 16–18] in the Italian synagogue [one of five synagogues in the two Venetian ghettos]. By the authority of the three gaons [leading rabbinic authorities], Rabbi [Judah] Katzenellenbogen [1521–1597; one of the sixteenth century's most influential rabbis] of blessed memory, Rabbi Jacob Cohen, and Rabbi Avigdor Cividal of blessed memory, who were present there along with all the gaons of the city, including the Levantine Jews [Jewish merchants from the eastern Mediterranean], who at that time abounded in important persons, he [Rabbi Sforno] decreed that I should be granted the title of ḥaver [honorific title given to rabbinical students before their ordination]. I responded with "ten words" of explanation of the mishnaic dictum, "Find yourself a teacher . . . " which pleased the hearers very much. Then we returned home to Montagnana.[1]

The Ghetto

When Modena, Rachel, and their one-year-old son Mordekhai moved to Venice permanently in 1592, they settled into an all-Jewish community. They had no choice. Though Italian Jews (there were about 35,000 in 1600), like their counterparts elsewhere in Europe, had long chosen to live in their own communities, segregation was now the law.

In 1509, the armies of the League of Cambrai (whose members were France, the Habsburg Empire, Mantua, Ferrara, and the pope) rolled over Venetian territories on the Italian mainland. The Jews of the overrun areas flooded into Venice, swelling the city's Jewish population to never-before-seen levels. Initially, the Venetian government tolerated their presence; after all, Jewish moneylenders were not only favorable to the economy (as Jewish doctors were to the state of health), but they helped Christians heed the biblical strictures

---

1. Quoted after Cohen, *The Autobiography of a Seventeenth-Century Venetian Rabbi*, 92.

against interest-bearing loans to fellow Christians. The Catholic clergy, on the other hand, was not at all tolerant, and whipped up anti-Semitic sentiment to a fever pitch.

In 1516, state and church reached an accord of sorts. The Jews could stay in Venice, but would henceforth live on the island known as the Ghetto Nuovo, so named after the onetime presence of foundries at which artillery was man-ufactured (*ghetto*, or *getto*, comes from the verb *gettare*, "to pour" or "to cast"). Gates put up at the two footbridges leading on and off the island were locked at sunset and reopened at sunrise. Thus segregation was reinforced by a curfew. And to sweeten the deal for the Christian landlords who might object to renting to Jews, rents were raised by one-third, with that extra third being tax-free. In 1541, in the face of a swelling population and nowhere to build but up, a second ghetto, the Ghetto Vecchio, was established across the canal from the first one.

Inside the ghettos, Jews were free to follow their customs. And by the latter part of the sixteenth century, there were five synagogues, each with its own school and each catering to its own ethnic congregation: specifically the Ash-kenazim who had come from German-speaking lands and the Sephardim who had come from Iberia after the expulsion of 1492. Culture also thrived. Thus in 1628, Rabbi Modena became director of the Accademia degl' Impediti, a music academy made up entirely of Jewish musicians. That the performances at its annual Simḥat Torah concert must have been good is attested by the need for the police to intervene in order to control the Christian crowds who flocked to the ghetto to attend.

Outside the ghetto, the story was rather different. Jews had to wear a badge of identification or hats of a certain color; and beginning in 1548, Venetian Jews were barred from printing books. The situation was harsher at Rome, where, under the Counter-Reformation Popes Paul IV and Pius V, anti-Semitism sometimes turned vicious. There the Talmud and other Jewish books were burned in 1553. Still other cities refused to deal with their Jewish pop-ulation at all: both Genoa and Lucca simply expelled them. In all, late-sixteenth-century Italy saw its Jewish population become increasingly isolated, a situation that did not begin to change until 1797, when Napoleon gained control of Venice and abolished the ghettos.

BIBLIOGRAPHICAL NOTE

The Armada

Garrett Mattingly's *Armada* (Boston: Houghton Mifflin, 1959) is a classic study; see also Colin Martin and Geoffrey Parker, *The Spanish Armada* (New York: Norton, 1988); on Spain's rise and fall as an imperial power, see John H. Elliott, *Imperial Spain: 1469–1716* (London: Penguin, 1970).

Leon Modena and the Venetian Ghetto

A translation and exceptionally fine historical-bibliographical context is in Mark Cohen, trans. and ed., *The Autobiography of a Seventeenth-Century Venetian Rabbi: Leon Modena's Life of Judah* (Princeton: Princeton University Press, 1988); see also Brian Pullan, *The Jews of*

Europe and the Inquisition of Venice, 1550–1670 (Totowa, N.J.: Barnes and Noble, 1983); for general introductions on Jews in sixteenth-century Italy, see Cecil Roth, *The Jews in the Renaissance* (Philadelphia: Jewish Publication Society of America, 1959), and M.A. Shulvass, *The Jews in the World of the Renaissance*, trans. E. Koss (Leiden: Brill, 1973; originally in Hebrew, 1955); there is a fascinating account of fifteenth-century anti-Semitism in R. Po-Chia Hsia, *Trent, 1475: Stories of a Ritual Murder* (New Haven: Yale University Press, 1982).

CHAPTER 40

Elizabethan England

Having begun our survey in England in the early fifteenth century, we end it there in the late sixteenth. In general, music in Elizabethan England exhibits an interesting mixture of independence from and movement toward music on the Continent. Thus while music for the Anglican liturgy continued along rather independent lines—the very nature of the liturgy virtually guaranteed such independence—music for the Catholic rite (practiced behind closed doors once the Catholic Mary Tudor was out of the way) finally fell comfortably into line with the Netherlandish, imitative style. Some genres were Janus-faced. For example, if the English madrigal looked to Italy for inspiration, it filtered what it found through English sensibilities. Composers of solo keyboard music learned what they would from their Continental counterparts and then simply outdid them at their own game. Finally, "high-class" music in England differed from Continental music in its high degree of centralization. More than elsewhere, music was centered at the royal court and was therefore subject to the whims and tastes of the dynamic woman who presided over it, Elizabeth I.

We will survey Elizabethan music in four broad sections: sacred music for the Catholic liturgy; sacred music for the Anglican Church; secular song, including the consort song, madrigal, and lute song; and instrumental music, both for consort and for solo keyboard. First, though, we pick up the story of the Tudor dynasty from where we left it in Chapter 34, and consider the phenomenon of the centralization of music.

THE LATE TUDORS: MARY AND ELIZABETH

Mary Tudor, or Mary I (1516–1558), daughter of Henry VIII and Catherine of Aragon, came to the throne in 1553. A devout Catholic bent on bringing England back to the papal fold, she repealed Edward VI's religious legislation establishing the Church of England as the official church of the state, and revived charges of heresy against those who disagreed with Catholic doctrine. In fact, Mary persecuted Protestants ruthlessly, and many of the leading voices of Protestantism were either burned at the stake (probably as many as three hundred, among them Thomas Cranmer, first Protestant Archbishop of Canterbury and author of the *Book of Common Prayer*) or sought refuge with Protestant enclaves on the Continent. She also alienated the "silent majority" by marrying the widowed Philip II of archenemy Spain, who convinced her to join him in a futile war against France. She was eventually and unlovingly nicknamed "Bloody Mary."

Figure 40-1. Nicholas Hilliard, portrait of Elizabeth I, with ermine as a symbol of royalty, 1585 (collection of the Marquess of Salisbury).

Elizabeth I (Fig. 40-1), the daughter of Henry VIII and Anne Boleyn, was born in 1533. Upon succeeding her half-sister Mary in 1558, she restored Protestantism as the official state religion. Yet Elizabeth was neither fanatical nor dogmatic, and lay Catholics who could reconcile their religion with loyalty to the crown were generally left alone. For it was not religious doctrine that mattered to Elizabeth, but the well-being of England itself.

Under Elizabeth, and especially after the defeat of the Armada, England enjoyed a self-confidence it had hardly known before. The feeling spilled over into the arts, and English drama and lyric poetry reached new heights: it was, after all, the age of Shakespeare, Christopher Marlowe, and Edmund Spenser, the last of whom described Elizabeth as a "Mirror of grace and Majestie divine" in *The Fairie Queene* (1590).

As a ruler, Elizabeth was temperate and cautious. And though she listened to counsel, none of her Tudor predecessors—her father included—so single-handedly controlled every matter of government. She was also intelligent and talented: she spoke French, Italian, and Spanish, read Latin, played the lute and virginal, and enjoyed both dancing and hunting. Elizabeth was undoubtedly the greatest of the Tudor monarchs. She was also the last, as she died unwed and heirless in 1603.

THE CENTRALIZATION OF MUSIC

In 1599, the German traveler Thomas Platter wrote: "London is not in England, but England is in London."[1] This was certainly true with respect to high-level music making, which was centralized to such an extent that to talk about music in Elizabethan England is to talk about music in Elizabethan London. This high degree of centralization was not new with Elizabeth. It had already begun in the 1530s and 1540s, when the dissolution of the great monasteries and collegiate churches was accompanied by the disbandment of their long-standing musical establishments. And far more than any other institution in the realm, the chapel of the royal household filled the void and came to employ almost every great English musician of the period. (By way of comparison, neither of Spain's greatest composers of the second half of the sixteenth century—Victoria and Guerrero—ever served in Philip II's royal chapel.)

The Chapel Royal

At full strength, the chapel royal comprised thirty-two "Gentlemen" and twelve boy choristers. On special occasions, they were augmented by "Gentlemen extraordinary," honorary members of the chapel who received no pay; on the other hand, normal weekday services called for no more than sixteen singers to be present.

The administrative head of the chapel was the dean, always a church official of high rank and the person who, in consultation with the choirmaster, chose the music for each service. The choirmaster, also a cleric and elected by the Gentlemen, was in charge of day-to-day musical matters. Next in the hierarchy was the master of the choristers, whose job it was to oversee the daily routine, both musical and nonmusical, of the boy singers. In addition to the singers, there were two organists and a group of "servants."

Unlike the great chapels of Italy, Germany, Spain, and even France, all of which imported foreign musicians, Elizabeth's chapel was entirely homegrown, as the politics of religion practically mandated that its members be English. While a native Catholic of the stature of a Thomas Tallis or William Byrd could be tolerated, a foreign "papist" might have been suspect. Conversely, Continental Protestants would have found both the doctrine and ceremony of the Church of England distasteful (as England's own Puritans did). The membership of the chapel was also remarkably stable: Tallis served for forty-five years, Byrd for fifty-four, Robert Stone for sixty. What is impressive about such a feat is not the length of service but the singers' ability to roll with the political-religious punches.

For the musicians, service in the chapel royal was simply the best job in town. Aside from the prestige, the average base salary of thirty pounds per annum was two to three times higher than that of cathedral chapels (the typical income for a blacksmith or butcher in 1590 was about six pounds). And in the

1. Quoted after Monson, "Elizabethan London," 304.

event that prestige, money, and other perks were not enough to secure the services of England's best musicians, the royal chapel enjoyed the power of conscription. Only three other chapels were off limits to its raids: those at the Cathedral of St. Paul's, Westminster Abbey, and St. George's, Windsor, all of which were satellites of the court anyway.

The chapel royal was immune to the Puritans' attempts to impose their preferences in church music: simple congregational singing of metrical psalms. While parish churches and provincial cathedrals often felt their crusading zeal, the chapel royal was beholden to no one except "the supreme head on earth of all things ecclesiastical and temporal": Elizabeth.

Music Printing

Centralization is no less evident in the field of music printing. Unlike such "national" printing centers as Paris, Venice, and Nuremberg, which faced competition from Lyons, Rome, and Augsburg, respectively, London monopolized the English music-printing industry as well. But to Continental music printers, English music printing must have seemed anemic. During the period from 1570, when Thomas Vautrollier published a collection of Lassus chansons with English texts, to the end of the century, English printers turned out about 40 collections of polyphony (not including the ubiquitous metrical psalm settings). The same period saw Venetian presses alone issue more than 370 collections, and that number accounts only for multiauthor anthologies.

Among the more notable items in the English crop was the *Cantiones quae ab argumento sacrae vocantur* of 1575, published jointly by Tallis and Byrd, each of whom contributed seventeen motets (probably in honor of the seventeenth year of Elizabeth's reign). The *Cantiones* was the first publication for either Tallis (then about seventy years old) or Byrd; it was the first publication of Latin church music by anybody in England; and it was the first publication issued under the patent—granted by the crown—that Tallis and Byrd had received earlier that year and that gave them a twenty-one-year monopoly over the publication of polyphony and the printing and selling of ruled music paper. Despite its landmark status, the *Cantiones* was a commercial flop, and Byrd waited thirteen years before venturing into print once again, this time with far greater success. At the very least, that the *Cantiones sacrae* sold so poorly raises a question about the reception of Latin-texted church music in Protestant England, one we will consider presently.

LATIN CHURCH MUSIC

The genre in which Elizabethan music most clearly turned its back on its English past was Latin sacred music. In fact, it was with that repertory that English music came closest to merging with the Netherlandish mainstream of the Continent. Three motets from the Tallis and Byrd *Cantiones sacrae* illustrate the point.

Three Motets from the *Cantiones sacrae*

As we saw in Chapter 34, English sacred music of the pre-Reformation period had a distinctive style of its own: little use of imitation, with that more decorative than structural; florid, melismatic writing; a rather abstract relationship between words and music; and a preponderance of votive texts in honor of Mary.

This changed in the third quarter of the century. First, both Tallis and Byrd fully embraced imitation and related techniques as a structural device. Example 40-1 provides excerpts from motets by both composers. Tallis (c. 1505–1585), who probably entered the royal chapel in the early 1540s, gives us as clear-cut a series of imitative entries as can be found anywhere, while Byrd combines cantus firmus and double canon (in superius–alto I and tenor II–bassus) with as sure a hand as any Netherlander.

EXAMPLE 40-1. (a) Tallis, *Salvator mundi* (I), mm. 1–10; (b) Byrd, *Miserere mihi Domine*, mm. 20–27.

(a)

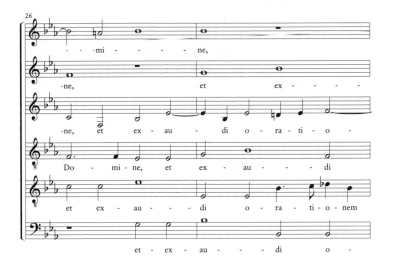

There was also a change in the texts on which Elizabethan composers drew and the way they treated these texts. In Tallis's *In ieiunio et fletu (Anthology* 95), which sets a Matins respond for the first Sunday in Lent, the priests' invocation, "Spare, O Lord, your people, and let not your people fall into perdition," is passionate in its appeal. Tallis's setting is emotionally equal to the task: the opening imitative entries—really *stretti*—melt into affective, quasi-homophonic declamation; the harmonies are dark and brooding; throughout the motet, the tonal worlds of the narrator and priests are kept apart; and the repetition of the same text at different tonal levels intensifies the narrator's gravity and the priests' urgent supplications. It is "music in the service of words"—music turned to rhetoric—such as English sacred music had hardly known before. Perhaps it is also music that offers a hidden prayer for the community of English Catholics.

Who or what pushed the English to absorb the full-blown imitative style of the Continent? Though there is no single answer, we might give some credit to Alfonso Ferrabosco the Elder (1543–1588), the first of three generations of Ferrabosco musicians to make their mark in England. Alfonso arrived at London in 1562 and served Elizabeth's court intermittently until the end of 1578, when he left after being charged with murder. As much as anyone, Ferrabosco was a model for the younger Elizabethan composers, and there can be no doubt that he played an influential role in the formation of Byrd's style. The "master" in Thomas Morley's *Plaine and Easie Introduction* calls him "Master Alfonso, a great musician, famous and admired for his works amongst the best."[2]

We might also wonder where, with Protestantism and an English-language liturgy restored, these Latin motets would have been sung. Since Tallis and Byrd dedicated the *Cantiones sacrae* to Elizabeth, she must have approved of the collection, and we may presume that the motets could have been performed

2. Quoted after the Harman edition, p. 148.

by the chapel royal itself. Elizabeth had a certain fondness for ritual and ceremony, and in 1560 she authorized a Latin translation of the *Book of Common
Prayer*. Thus as long as the texts were unoffensive from a doctrinal point of
view, the motets could well have fulfilled a paraliturgical function in the chapel.
In addition, they were no doubt welcome in the services celebrated by Catholics behind closed doors.

William Byrd

William Byrd (Fig. 40-2) was born in 1542/43(?), possibly at Lincoln, where,
after having apparently studied with Tallis at London, he accepted the post of
cathedral organist and master of the choristers in 1563. During the decade he
spent at Lincoln, Byrd reached his first maturity as a composer and, perhaps
with one eye on London, probably wrote a good deal of his sacred music for
the Anglican Church. In February 1570, Byrd was sworn in as a Gentleman of
the chapel royal, though full-time service may not have begun until December
1572, when he joined Tallis as one of the chapel's two organists. At London,
Byrd quickly climbed the social ladder, mingling with the aristocracy, more
than a few of whom were Catholics.

In the 1580s, religious issues came to a head and forced Byrd to come to
terms with his conscience. In 1581, Father Edmund Campion and two other
Jesuits were executed on charges of sedition. The affair sent shock waves
through England and caused anti-Catholic sentiment to turn into outright per-
secution: the fine for saying Mass, for instance, was 133 pounds and a year in
prison. From this time on, Byrd increased his commitment to the Catholic
community. Indeed, the years that followed saw him and his family cited more
than once for recusancy: that is, for loyalty to Rome and devotion to the old
Sarum rite.

In 1593, Byrd set up house at Stondon Massey, Essex, near the country estate
of Sir John Petrie, one of the composer's patrons and a leader of the Catholic
community. At Petrie's home, local Catholics held their "undercover" services,

Figure 40-2. Portrait of
William Byrd, eighteenth-
century engraving, by
G. Vander Gucht and
N. Haym.

and it was probably for that circle, as well as for that around Edward Paston, a former court poet and amateur musician who had retired to the country in order to practice his religion, that Byrd wrote his music for the Catholic liturgy.

THE ORDINARIES AND THE *GRADUALIA* Byrd's three settings of the Ordinary of the Mass—one each for three, four, and five voices—are his best-known Latin works. Published during the years 1592–95, they were issued without title pages, since publication of the Roman liturgy in any form was illegal.

Continental musicians would have found the Masses curious in some respects: all are freely composed (no parody, paraphrase, or cantus firmus); the three short-text sections—Kyrie, Benedictus, and Agnus Dei—lack the musical expansiveness with which they were generally set in Continental Masses; the main division in the Gloria comes at "Domine Deus" instead of at "Qui tollis"; and the Credo is divided into three large sections (at "Qui propter" and "Et unam sanctam") instead of the usual two (at "Et incarnatus est"). But those same musicians would no doubt also have been deeply moved by certain passages, most of all, perhaps, by the "Dona nobis pacem" with which the *Mass for Four Voices* comes to an end (Ex. 40-2). Here Byrd piles up 4–3 suspensions, all but the last of which resolve to a minor triad. It is as eloquent a musical prayer as we could hope to find.

EXAMPLE 40-2. Byrd, *Mass for Four Voices*, Agnus Dei, mm. 24–33 (transposed down a second).

Byrd poured his final efforts as a composer of Catholic sacred music into the two-volume *Gradualia*, a giant-size cycle of 109 Mass Propers for major feasts of the liturgical year. As with the settings of the Ordinary, publication was marred by politics. Book I was published in 1605 but had to be quickly withdrawn owing to the hostile anti-Catholic atmosphere that followed in the wake of the Gunpowder Plot. This was a plot by a group of English Catholics, headed by Robert Catesby and Guy Fawkes, to blow up Parliament on November 5, 1605, with the new king, James I, in it; the plot was discovered, the schemers were executed, and a Jesuit was even arrested when he was found with a copy of the *Gradualia* in his possession. Book II was published in 1607; and the two books were reissued together under somewhat calmer conditions in 1610. Together with such collections as Leonin's twelfth-century *Magnus liber organi*, Isaac's *Choralis Constantinus*, and Bach's cantatas for eighteenth-century Leipzig, Byrd's *Gradualia* stands as one of the monumental one-composer cycles of music for the liturgical year.

MUSIC FOR THE ANGLICAN CHURCH

Music for the Anglican Church, at least that destined for the chapel royal and similar establishments (as opposed, say, to domestic psalmody or the simple congregational singing of the parish churches), differed from music of any of the Protestant denominations on the Continent. The reason has to do with the nature of the liturgy.

The Liturgy

With Elizabeth's Acts of Supremacy and Uniformity of 1559, the daily round of Anglican services took shape as laid out in Table 40-1:

Table 40-1.   The Anglican liturgy, with major musical items and equivalents in the Catholic liturgy.

Anglican liturgy	Major musical items (all sung in English)	Sarum rite
I. Matins (morning service)	"Venite exultemus" (Psalm 95, "O come let us sing unto the Lord") "Te Deum" ("We praise thee, O God") "Benedictus Dominus Deus Israel" ("Blessed be the Lord, God of Israel")	Matins and Lauds
II. Communion	Basically the Ordinary of the Mass, but without the Agnus Dei; the Gloria came after the Communion and was often recited instead of sung.	Mass
III. Evensong	Magnificat ("My soul doth magnify the Lord") "Nunc dimittis" ("Lord, now lettest thou thy servant depart in peace")	Vespers and Compline

That Elizabeth envisioned a role for music is clear from her Injunctions of 1559, which reinforced the Oath of Supremacy and the *Book of Common Prayer*:

> And that there be a modest distinct song, so used in all parts of the common prayers in the Church, that the same may be as plainly understood, as if it were read without singing, and yet nevertheless, for the comforting of such that delight in music, it may be permitted that in the beginning, or in the end of common prayers, either at morning or evening, there may be sung an Hymn, or such like song, to the praise of Almighty God, in the best sort of melody and music that may be conveniently devised, having respect that the sentence of the Hymn may be understood and perceived.[3]

As we will see, the music was not always "modest."

With this liturgy and the 1559 Injunctions before them, Elizabethan composers cultivated two genres: anthem and service.

Anthem

The anthem was the characteristic genre of the Anglican liturgy. It was the counterpart of the Catholic Church's motet, the paraliturgical "Hymn" at the end of Matins or Evensong to which the 1559 Injunctions refer. The term itself is derived from "antiphon," and can be traced back to the eleventh century. Yet that the Injunctions use the word "hymn" instead probably indicates that "anthem" was still not part of the everyday, mid-sixteenth-century musical

3. Quoted after Phillips, *English Sacred Music*, 7.

vocabulary (it would become so in the early seventeenth century). Anthem texts were wide-ranging. They had to be in English, but they could be drawn from Scriptures or be newly invented, explicitly liturgical or merely moralizing. As for the music, composers developed two types of anthems: "full" and "verse."

The full anthem was simply one for unaccompanied choir (though an organ accompaniment can never be ruled out). William Mundy's (c. 1529–1591) *O Lord, the maker of all things (Anthology* 96) is an example of the genre during its formative years (before 1565). Among the features of *O Lord* that are typical are the **A B B** form, in which the repeat of the **B** section was optional; the use of antiphonal choirs (mm. 16–25), their entrances indicated with the rubrics "Decani" (the dean's side of the altar) and "Cantoris" (the singers' side); and the generally unrelieved, syllabic, note-against-note counterpoint.

The verse anthem was the most significant development in Elizabethan sacred music, with no parallel on the Continent. Although Byrd did not invent the verse anthem—that honor probably goes to Richard Farrant (c. 1525/30–1580), for a while master of the choristers at both the chapel royal and St. George's Chapel, Windsor—he was surely the first to realize its potential. In the verse anthem, a solo voice (indicated by the rubric "verse") supported by an organ or consort of viols alternates with the full choir, whose parts are doubled by the same instruments.

BYRD'S *CHRIST RISING AGAIN*   One of the finest examples of the genre is Byrd's Easter anthem *Christ rising again*, published in his *Songs of Sundrie Natures* of 1589; *Anthology* 97 presents the first of its two parts. Here, after the customary instrumental opening, Byrd expands the solo role into a dialogue-like duet for two high voices (sung by boys), a technique that would become a favorite with composers of the next generation. Two features of the solo writing seem particularly noteworthy: the short, energetic, sharply etched motives (how different from the "floating" melodies of Palestrina), which give the work a sense of dramatic urgency; and the snippets of word painting on "Christ rising again" (mm. 6–12) and "he liveth unto God" (mm. 38–43).

If there was a traditional approach to disposing the text between soloist and chorus, it was to have them split verses or alternate verse-by-verse in psalm-like fashion. In fact, the verse anthem has at least one of its roots in precisely that method of singing metrical psalms. And though Byrd follows that procedure most of the time, thus keeping soloists and chorus relatively independent, he seems to up the dramatic ante at measures 31–32 by having the chorus interrupt the soloists, not only with their own words but with their own melodic motive. The final chorus (mm. 57ff.) goes one step further: it develops the soloists' material on its own terms.

Service

To compose a "service" was to set any or all of the components that made up the three-part complex of daily prayers: Matins, Communion, and Evensong. Thus a composer might set items from all three services on one occasion, set only the two canticles that make up Evensong on another, or choose from the items for Matins on still another.

Cutting across these options were three musical styles: "short," "great," and "verse." The short service was characterized by syllabic homophony; the great service called for a more elaborate and varied texture. Example 40-3 provides excerpts from works in both the short and great styles:

EXAMPLE 40-3. (a) The "Venite" from Tallis's (short) Dorian Service, mm. 1–16; (b) Magnificat from Byrd's Great Service, mm. 68–79 (transposed up a minor third).

(a)

The verse style simply transferred to the service the solo-choir alternation of the verse anthem.

Like the verse anthem, the service too, with its easy cutting across Office and Mass, had no direct counterpart on the Continent. Thus while English music for the Catholic Church finally snuggled up to its Continental counterpart, Anglican Church music retained its English independence.

SECULAR SONG

Elizabethan composers cultivated three chief genres of secular song: the consort song, with solo voice supported by a consort of viols; the part song, in effect the English madrigal and related lighter types; and the lute song, with

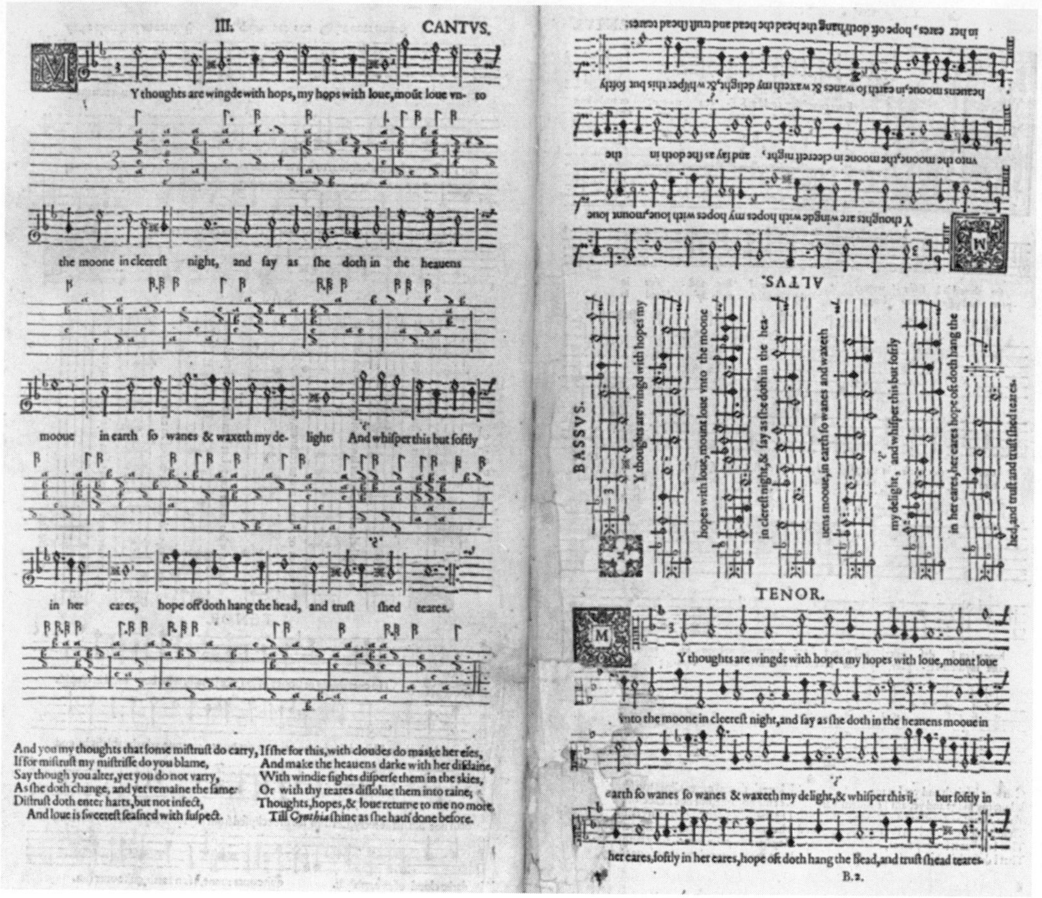

Figure 40-3. An example of "table book" format in Dowland's *First Booke of Songes*, 1597.

solo voice accompanied by lute. Yet the boundaries between them were sometimes more apparent than real. Consider the title of John Dowland's first publication of lute songs (1597): "The First Booke of Songes or Ayres of fowre partes with Tableture for the Lute: So made that all the partes together, or either of them severally may be sung to the Lute, Orpharion or Viol de gambo." And as Figure 40-3 shows, the very layout of the songbook—called "table-book" format—invites various manners of performance: solo voice and lute; voices only, with the singers disposed around the sides of a table; voices with instrumental doubling; or voices on some parts, instruments on others.

One more example should illustrate the ease with which a song could slip from one medium to another. Byrd begins his *Psalms, Sonets, & Songs of Sadness and Pietie* of 1588 with an "Epistle to the Reader": "Heere are divers songs . . . originally made for Instruments to express the harmonie, and one voyce to pronounce the dittie, [the words] . . . now framed in all parts for voyces to sing the same."[4]

Thus consort songs could become all-vocal part songs merely by adding words to the once-instrumental lower parts.

4. Quoted after Reese, *Music in the Renaissance*, 818.

There was, of course, nothing new about this crossover process. We have seen how the Italian frottola of the early sixteenth century was often published both for voices alone and for solo voice and lute (Chapter 24), how Willaert arranged a number of Verdelot's madrigals for solo voice and lute in the middle of the century (Chapter 27), and how music publishers advertised their wares as being suitable for either voices or instruments (Chapter 31). And what crossing over composers and publishers did not make explicit, the music-making public would have done on their own.

The Consort Song

The consort song, which probably grew out of courtly entertainments in which the boy choristers of the chapel royal sang to the accompaniment of viols, was the most "English" of the secular genres. Its master during the final decades of the sixteenth century was Byrd.

Example 40-4 shows the opening stanza of *O that most rare breast*, one of two funeral songs that Byrd wrote on the death of the poet and courtier Sir Philip Sidney (1554–1586) and that he included in the 1588 *Psalms, Sonets, & Songs*. As usual, the solo voice is the highest part (occasionally it was the next-to-highest). But though it is more vocal in character than the other parts, it remains, thanks to the points of imitation (mm. 12ff.) Byrd introduced to the genre, very much part of the ensemble. Particularly notable are the rhetorical exclamations that stand out in a style that generally avoids repeating text: first on "O, O that, O that most rare breast," and then on "O Sidney! prince of fame." The rhetorical strategy of the opening measures still echoes in the "motto" openings of many a Handel aria.

EXAMPLE 40-4. Byrd, *O that most rare breast*, mm. 1–38.

-line sin - cere,　　　　Through which like gold　thy prince-

- -ly heart did shine;　　　　O sprite he- roic,　O va -

- -li-ant wor-thy— knight,　　　O Sid - ney!

O Sid - ney! prince of fame　and men's— good—

The consort song had no real parallel on the Continent. In fact, its English-ness would have seemed even more pronounced in its own day, given the flood of Italian influence to which English musical tastes succumbed during the final two decades of the sixteenth century.

The English Madrigal

Save for its dislike of pope, Jesuits, and Catholicism in general, Elizabethan England had something of a love affair with Italian culture, music—and the madrigal in particular—included. As Thomas Morley put it in 1597: "Such be the new-fangled opinions of our countrymen who will highly esteem what-soever cometh from beyond the seas (and specially from Italy) be it never so simple, condemning that which is done at home though it be never so excellent."[5]

No less indicative of the vogue is the voluminous amount of Italian music that circulated in England, both in print and in manuscript. Moreover, not only did so great a talent as John Dowland feel it necessary to go to Rome in order to study with Marenzio (although his plan never did work out), but the com-poser John Cooper, a violinist at the court of James I, did go to Italy and, on returning to England, styled himself "John Coprario." Italy was fashionable!

The Italian madrigal began to make inroads in England during the 1560s, no doubt helped along by Alfonso Ferrabosco's presence at the court. From there it spread not only to the country homes of such aristocrats as the Earl of Arun-

5. *A Plain and Easy Introduction*, 293.

del, who, when he was in Italy in 1566, commissioned sets of villanelle and madrigals for his own collection, but to the homes of London merchants and other members of the middle class.

MUSICA TRANSALPINA   In 1588, a milestone was reached when Nicholas Yonge (d. 1619), a singer and music editor, published an anthology entitled *Musica transalpina*, the full title of which explains its significance: "Madrigales translated of foure, five and sixe parts, chosen out of divers excellent Authors, with the first and second part of *La Verginella*, made by maister *Byrd*, upon two stanzas of *Ariosto*, and brought to speake English with the rest." This was, then, a collection of Italian madrigals by the likes of Palestrina, Marenzio, Ferrabosco, and others translated into English. Yonge explains his reason for the venture in the dedication of the volume:

> Right honourable, since I first began to keepe house in this Citie, it hath been no small comfort unto mee, that a great number of Gentlemen and Merchants of good accompt (as well of this realme as of forreine nations) have taken in good part such entertainment of pleasure, as my poore abilitie was able to affoord them, both by the exercise of Musicke daily used in my house, and by furnishing them with Bookes of that kinde yeerely sent me out of Italy and other places, which beeing for the most part Italian Songs, are for sweetnes of Aire, very well liked of all, but most in account with them that understand that language. As for the rest, they doe either not sing them at all, or at the least with litle delight.

Thus *Musica transalpina* broke the language barrier and, together with the tireless entrepreneurship and propagandizing of Thomas Morley, paved the way for the development of the English madrigal in the 1590s.

The English madrigal developed along two lines, one "serious," the other "light."

THE SERIOUS MADRIGAL: WEELKES AND WILBYE   Two of the finest English madrigalists were Thomas Weelkes (?1574–1623), who was also a prolific composer of church music, and John Wilbye (1574–1638). Oddly enough, neither one was associated with the royal household. Wilbye spent the greater part of his career in the private service of the wealthy Kytson family, while Weelkes, "noted and famed for a common drunkard and a notorious swearer and blasphemer,"[6] got "stuck" at the provincial Cathedral of Chichester.

Weelkes's best-known madrigal is *As Vesta was from Latmos hill descending* (*Anthology* 98). A few words about the text: Vesta was the Roman goddess of fire and the symbol of the home; the oldest daughter of Saturn and the sister of Jupiter, she never married; Latmos hill was where she lived. The "maiden Queen" is Elizabeth. Diana was the goddess of virginity; her darlings were the Vestal Virgins, who guarded the eternal flame that burned in Vesta's honor. And Oriana was the mythological name for Elizabeth. Table 40-2 provides a guide to Weelkes's obvious word painting:

---

6. Quoted after Philipps, "Patronage in the Career of Thomas Weelkes," 46.

Table 40-2.   Word painting in Weelkes's *As Vesta was from Latmos hill descending.*

Measures	Word(s)	Musical imagery
1–9	"Latmos hill"	"Hill" is always set with the highest note in the phrase.
	"descending"	Descending scales and leaps.
12–22	"ascending"	Ascending scales.
36–46	"running down"	Quickly descending scales.
48–49	"two by two"	Paired voices.
50–51	"three by three"	Trios of voices.
51–52	"together"	The full group of six voices.
56–57	"all alone"	The top voice sings alone.
84–100	"Long live fair Oriana"	After beginning with a "longa," the lowest voice continues with long, sustained notes.

Clearly, the English madrigalists were receptive to the Italian madrigal's bag of word-painting tricks (compare the word painting in *Vesta* with that in Marenzio's *Scaldava il sol, Anthology* 92). Only occasionally, however, were they drawn to its drama—to its sudden contrasts and daring chromaticism (Ex. 40–5). Though Weelkes's combination of chromaticism (mm. 58–59, 61–62), unresolved cadences, and heaped-up suspensions and Wilbye's expressive juxtapositions of major and minor show an awareness of Italy's avant-garde tendencies, the English madrigalists were far more attuned to the lyrical-pastoral elements of the Italian madrigal. For them, the madrigal was primarily a "musical" genre, an attitude as apparent in their style as it was in their choice of poetry. Melancholy and despair were more often left to the lute song.

EXAMPLE 40-5. (a) Weelkes, *O care thou wilt dispatch mee,* mm. 56–69; (b) Wilbye, *Draw on sweet night,* mm. 65–70 and 113–116.

(a)

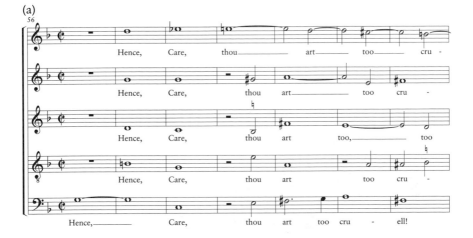

As Vesta was from Latmos hill descending appeared in what is certainly the most famous anthology of English madrigals, *The Triumphs of Oriana*, compiled and published by Thomas Morley in 1601. The anthology, which is modeled closely after a 1592 Venetian publication entitled *Il trionfo di Dori*, consists of twenty-five madrigals by twenty-three composers (including Morley), all of which end with the lines "Then sang the shepherds and nymphs of Diana / Long live fair Oriana!" The *Triumphs*, then, is a madrigalistic tribute to Elizabeth, as it is also to the Italianization of English secular music in general and Morley in particular. In one fell swoop, it unites one of England's chief sources of musical inspiration (Italy), its most vibrant musical spirit (Morley), and its leading patroness (Elizabeth).

BALLETT AND CANZONET: MORLEY   What Weelkes and Wilbye were to the serious madrigal Thomas Morley was to its lighter side. More than that, however, Morley was an important driving force in the world of Elizabethan music. The son of a Norwich (East Anglia) brewer, Morley was born in 1557 or 1558. Though documentation about his early training is lacking, it seems that he studied with Byrd, since Morley refers to him as his "master" in the dedication of his *Plaine and Easie Introduction to Practicall Musicke* (1597). The first definite record of his activity as a musician places him at the Cathedral of Norwich in 1583, where he held the post of organist through July 1587. A year later, Morley received his bachelor's degree from Oxford, and by 1589 he was organist at St. Paul's in London. In 1592, Morley was sworn in as a Gentleman of the chapel royal, and in 1593 he issued the first of the eleven publications that made him a household name in English music circles. He died in 1602.

Morley had his hand in all facets of Elizabethan musical life. As a composer, he cultivated all of its genres, including sacred music, both Catholic (to which religion he leaned) and Anglican; as a printer-publisher, he inherited in 1598 the patent formerly held by Byrd; his *Plaine and Easie Introduction to Practicall Musicke* stands as the major English treatise of the period and provides a wealth of information about English musical life at the time; and as an arbiter of musical tastes, he played a crucial role in spreading Italian influence and guiding the development of the English madrigal.

In his *Plaine and Easie Introduction*, Morley defined the *canzonet* as little more than a lightweight, "counterfeit" madrigal that belonged to the "second degree of gravity." And the *ballett* was even fluffier. It was the English counterpart of the Italian balletto, which, as cultivated by Gastoldi, added a "fa la la" refrain at the end of each stanza. Morley knew Gastoldi's music well and in fact reworked a number of the Italian composer's balletti. *Anthology* 99 offers Gastoldi's *A lieta vita* and the ballett Morley based on it: *Sing we and chant it*, from the composer's *First Booke of Balletts* (1595). Morley's greater invention in the "fa la" section is apparent.

The English madrigal enjoyed a brief, though intense, career. Incredibly, Weelkes and Wilbye together published all the madrigals they ever would during the years 1597–1609; Weelkes called it quits in 1600, at age twenty-six (he lived another twenty-three years), Wilbye in 1609, at age thirty-five (he lived another twenty-nine). The genre then declined slowly at the hands of less talented composers.

The Lute Song

It was in the lute song that English song composers expressed their deepest pathos. Though these songs were typically published in a multimedia, tablebook format (see Fig. 40-3), there can be little doubt that they were generally conceived for solo voice with lute accompaniment. Thus they stand apart from the Continental practice of arranging polyphonic part songs for solo voice and lute. In fact, with its occasional instructions that the lowest voice of the lute part be doubled on a bass viol, the lute song looks forward to the seventeenth-century "continuo" song, in which only the solo voice and bass were notated.

Lute song composers began to turn to a simpler, more direct style of expression than was typical of the madrigal; and this resulted in an equally direct, more declamatory melodic style. Like the madrigal, the lute song enjoyed a brilliant but brief career. Though it may have been cultivated as early as the reign of Henry VIII, its paper trail really gets under way only with Dowland's *First Booke of Songes or Ayres* of 1597. It appeared in print for the last time a mere quarter century later, with John Attey's *First Booke of Ayres* (also his last) in 1622. Even more than the madrigal, then, the lute song belongs primarily to Jacobean England, to the reign of James I.

JOHN DOWLAND   The greatest composer of lute songs was John Dowland (1563–1626; the name rhymes with "Poland"). His career had its share of ups and downs. Only in 1612, after many years abroad, did Dowland, the most famous lutenist of his time, secure a position among the musicians of the royal household. It is hard to say if his earlier rebuffs were a result of his ties to Catholicism, an apparently irascible disposition, or simply an attempt on the part of the court to cut back on its staff and expenses. In any event, he spent some of his most productive years, 1598–1606, at the Danish court of Christian IV.

Dowland was by his own account a melancholy soul. With a pun on his name, he called one of his lute pieces *Semper Dowland semper dolens* (Always Dowland, Always Sorrow), described himself as an "infoelice Inglese" (unhappy Englishman), and set poems that are filled with expressions of despair and references to sin. In his late years, he was bitter about being forgotten by a new generation of musicians. One of his greatest works bears the title *Lachrimae, or Seaven Teares*, and features a sad melody with which his name became most closely associated. As we will see, his melancholy left its mark on both his lute songs and his instrumental music.

In 1610, Dowland's son Robert published an anthology entitled *A Musicall Banquet*, which included his father's *In darkness let me dwell (Anthology* 100). Here Dowland went beyond the customary structural, harmonic, and even emotional boundaries of the lute song. Gone is the strophic form of the early songs. Words such as "sorrow," "despair," and "woe" set off nerve-jangling dissonances in the lute (mm. 8–10 and 23–24), while "hellish jarring sounds" prompts a descending chromatic line (mm. 17). "O, let me, living, die" is set in a style that approaches pure recitative (mm. 27–30). And with their unusual instrumental interlude, repetition of the opening line, and open-ended cadence, the concluding measures are among the most amazing of the period. We can only wonder about the pain with which Dowland had come to view the world.

As noted above, the lute song had a brief career. Yet during the quarter century in which it flourished, such composers as Dowland, John Danyel (1564–c. 1626), Thomas Campion (1567–1620), and Philip Rosseter (1567/ 68–1623) turned out a body of English-language song that, for sheer and consistent beauty, would not be matched until the outpouring of songs by the likes of Jerome Kern, George Gershwin, and Cole Porter in our own century.

INSTRUMENTAL MUSIC

Elizabethan England produced the finest instrumental music of the period. With Dowland, lute music left behind what had been mainly an amateur tradition and reached a level of sophistication and virtuosity on a par with anything produced on the Continent. Byrd's music for viol consort brought instrumental "chamber music" to new heights. And in the field of keyboard music, which now broke away from its former, primarily liturgical function, the English simply had no rivals. It is little wonder, therefore, that whereas the ricercars of Julio Segni and the toccatas of Merulo live on mainly in scholarly editions, early music groups revel in Byrd's consort music, while the repertory of the Fitzwilliam Virginal Book lies in the fingers of many a present-day harpsichordist.

Here we look mainly at works for viol consort and solo keyboard (lute music is dealt with only in passing). But first, we should consider the royal household's roster of instrumentalists, for we will find an interesting sociological phenomenon at work there.

The Queen's Musick and Other Groups

If, as we have seen, the members of the chapel royal were English to the core, the roster of instrumentalists at the court was flamboyantly international (continuing a tradition begun by Henry VIII around 1540): one-half to two-thirds of the thirty or so musicians who made up the "Queen's Musick" were foreigners. Many were from Italy, especially from the rich pool of instrumentalists in and around Venice, and many seem to have been Jewish.

Italian-Jewish instrumentalists began to arrive at the court in the 1530s and 1540s, sometimes as whole families of musicians. And having immigrated, they tended to stay, even to the extent of establishing—as did the families Lupo and Bassano—musical dynasties that spanned generations. That the English court was a magnet for these Venetian Jews is understandable. The royal court was both anti-papal and anti-Lutheran, and thus represented welcome relief from these two sources of sixteenth-century anti-Semitism. The move to England also afforded the possibility of escape from the recently established ghetto (see

Chapter 39). And for the court, unlike foreign Catholics or radical dissenting Protestants, the Jews posed no religious or political threat.

There was one feature of the Queen's Musick that appealed to both English and foreign musicians: the salaries. Though the educational level and social status of the instrumentalists were probably lower than that of their chapel royal counterparts, their pay was generally higher; the average salary was just over forty-six pounds a year, plus an allowance for livery (compared with thirty pounds for a chapel royal singer). And when Elizabeth was really determined to obtain the services of a particular musician, she was willing to pay the price. Thus Alfonso Ferrabosco earned more than sixty-six pounds when he arrived in England in 1562, while five years later he was offered the fabulous sum of one hundred in order to lure him back to England from the Continent.

The Queen's Musick was not the only band in town. The city of London supported its own town band, the Company of Waits: these half-dozen musicians and their apprentices provided instrumental music for official civic occasions. Having begun simply as a band of shawm players, they gradually added sackbuts, viols, recorders, and cornetts, until, in Elizabeth's time, they were as fully equipped as the royal musicians themselves.

Beginning in 1571, one of the duties of the waits was to play from late March through September "upon their instruments upon the turret at the Royal Exchange every Sunday and holiday towards the evening."[7] In effect, the waits were presenting London's first regularly scheduled public concerts. Just how much the city officials valued their services is apparent from their doubling the musicians' salaries from about six pounds in 1568 to almost twelve in 1582. And since the waits, like the members of the Queen's Musick, could also freelance, they seem to have made out quite well.

Still another group of musicians formed the Wardens and Commonality of the Fellowship of Minstrels Freemen of the City of London. To them fell the crumbs left over by the royal musicians and the waits. At the same time, they had to ward off the attempts of the many nonguild members and part-time musicians who were trying to eke out a living. Eventually they took to providing wake-up serenades in the streets, as the visiting Duke of Stettin-Pomerania noted in his diary in 1602.

> This day early we arrived at Rochester . . . where we heard beautiful music of viols and pandoras, for in all England it is the custom, that even in small villages the musicians wait on you for a small fee; in the morning about wakening time, they stand outside the chamber, playing religious songs.[8]

If the duke found the music beautiful, others considered it little more than noise pollution; and early in the seventeenth century, guild members were barred from playing "upon any kind of instrument or instruments, either evening or morning, at or under any nobleman, knight, or gentleman's window or lodging in the street." Even merry olde England had its Dickensian Scrooges.

---

7. Monson, "Elizabethan London," 327.

8. This and the quotation that follows are after Monson, "Elizabethan London," 329.

Figure 40-4. A detail from *The Life of Sir Henry Unton* showing a broken consort (National Portrait Gallery, London).

Consort Music

There were, to use terminology that came into being only in the seventeenth century, two kinds of consorts: "whole" and "broken" (or "mixed"). The whole consort consisted of different-size instruments from the same family; the broken, of instruments from different families.

We can see the standard broken consort in a detail from a famous painting that commemorates the life of Sir Henry Unton (Fig. 40-4): transverse flute (or recorder), treble viol (or violin), cittern (plucked string instrument), lute, bandora (another plucked string instrument), and bass viol. It was for this uniquely English ensemble that such anthologies as Morley's *First Booke of Consort Lessons* (1599) and Rosseter's *Lessons for Consort* (1609) were issued. Example 40-6 gives the opening of one of the pieces from Morley's collection, Richard Alison's (fl. 1592–1606) setting of the popular melody (in the flute/recorder part) *Go from my window*.

Colorful though the broken consort was, it played second fiddle to the whole consort, especially that made up of viols. The viol consort was the preeminent medium for instrumental chamber music, as many an aristocratic and upper-middle-class household had its own chest of viols. Music for this consort was typically for three to six parts and scored for a combination of treble, tenor ("mene"), and bass viols. The repertory was wide-ranging: freely composed fantasias; stylized dances, such as pavan-galliard pairs; cantus-firmus settings, especially the tradition based on *In nomine* (see below); and variations on popular melodies.

EXAMPLE 40-6. *Go from my window*: (a) the popular tune; (b) Alison's setting for broken consort, mm. 1–4.[9]

(a)

9. Reese, *Music in the Renaissance*, 875.

(b)

BYRD'S *BROWNING*   Though the viol consort had become a fixture at the court by the 1540s (when Henry VIII imported an ensemble made up of Italian Sephardic Jews), Byrd raised its repertory to a never-before-heard artistic level. One of his best-known works is *Browning my dear (Anthology* 101), a set of variations on a popular ballad of the period. Example 40-7 shows one of the verses:

EXAMPLE 40-7. The melody of *Browning my dear* ("The leaves bee greene").

Byrd wrote twenty variations on the eight-measure melody, placing it in each of the five voices four times. At the largest structural level, he seems to have thought of the piece as falling into three broad sections: variations 1–10 (mm. 1–81), 11–15 (mm. 81–121), and 16–20 (121–161). For example, the broadly chordal texture of variation 11 slows things down after the ever-increasing imitation that had gotten under way in variation 3 (m. 17); variation 16 introduces a rhythmically biting, three-note motive in the lowest part, which is then developed until it explodes into the triplets of variations 18–19 (mm. 136–137ff.); and though variation 11 serves to calm things down, its statement of the melody in the dominant moves things forward instead of wrapping them up—while variations 16–20, on the other hand, present the melody in nothing but the tonic, the only instance of five successive presentations at that pitch level.

Byrd pays just as much attention to the musical architecture within each section. Variations 1–2 are both for three voices, thus leaving room for the texture to expand to the tutti of variation 3. A number of the variations are paired: 1–2 by invertible counterpoint, 5–6 (mm. 33ff.) by the inversion of a prominent scale motive, 7–8 (mm. 50ff.) by transposition, and 9–10 (mm. 65ff.) by the use of short rhythmic motives that seem to turn on the brakes prior to the simultaneous textural slowing down and harmonic speeding up of variation 11.

Overall, Byrd contributed mightily to the consort repertory in particular and to instrumental music in general. At a time when most composers still seemed more comfortable when they had a text or a sustained-note cantus firmus or even a preexistent polyphonic piece to guide their structural plans, Byrd possessed an intellect that was unparalled in its ability to deal with large-scale, abstract musical architecture. He may well be the first composer—and perhaps the only one before Bach and Handel—who could build dynamic, large-scale structures in music both with and without words.

DOWLAND'S *LACHRIMAE*   Dowland's *Lachrimae, or Seaven Teares*, which adds
a lute to the customary five viols, is the crown jewel of the Elizabethan consort
repertory. When it was published in 1604, listeners must surely have thought
it the saddest instrumental music they had ever heard.

Although the *Lachrimae* consists of twenty-one pieces, its heart is made up
of the first seven, which are closely related to one another and represent the
"seaven teares" in the title. The title of each of the seven pieces begins with
the word "Lachrimae" (tears) and then goes on to describe the tears: old, new,
sighing, sad, forced, lover's, and true. These pieces were not newly composed,
however. Indeed, there is hardly a better demonstration of the ease with which
a work could cross over from one genre to another. The history of the work
seems to begin with one of Dowland's pieces for solo lute, the *Lachrimae pavan*,
composed by the mid-1590s. Example 40-8a provides the first strain of the
pavan's typical **a a' b b c' c'** structure. The *Lachrimae pavan* was wildly successful; it was parodied by other lutenists, arranged for other instruments (Byrd
and others arranged it for keyboard), and quoted in completely new compositions, both in England and on the Continent, both in Dowland's own time
and long thereafter. The piece made Dowland famous virtually everywhere.

Dowland cashed in on its success. He adapted the solo lute piece for performance as a lute song, *Flow, my tears* (Ex. 40-8b), and published it in his *Second
Booke of Songs* of 1600. Dowland now had another hit; the song was still being
printed in the 1680s. He reworked the piece yet again as the first "movement"
in the consort version (Ex. 40-8c), and followed it with six other "teares" that
draw closely on its melodic, harmonic, and rhythmic substance. If the result is,
as some might argue, a sequence of seven closely related pieces that lack contrast, it nevertheless wrings us dry emotionally. Dowland's melancholia knew
no end.

EXAMPLE 40-8. Dowland, *Lachrimae*: (a) *Lachrimae pavan* for solo lute; (b) the
lute song *Flow my tears*; (c) first movement of *Lachrimae, or Seaven Teares*
(opening strain of each).

(a)

(b)

Flow my teares, fall___ from your springs, Ex - iled___ for ev - er
Downe vaine lights, shine___ you no more, No nights___ are dark e -

let me mourne where night's black bird hir sad in - fa-my
nough for those That in dis - paire their lost for - tuns de -

sings, There let mee live___ for - - lorne.___
plore, Light doth but shame___ dis - - close.___

(c)

THE *IN NOMINE* TRADITION   Probably in the late 1520s, Taverner wrote his *Missa Gloria tibi trinitas*, based on a plainsong antiphon sung in the Sarum rite at First Vespers on Trinity Sunday (Ex. 40-9):

EXAMPLE 40-9. The Sarum antiphon *Gloria tibi trinitas*.

One section of the Mass, the part of the Benedictus sung to the words "In nomine Domini" (Ex. 40-10), was so well liked that it broke off from the rest of the Mass and circulated as a textless piece under the title *In nomine*.

EXAMPLE 40-10. Taverner, the "In nomine" section of the Benedictus of the *Missa Gloria tibi trinitas*, mm. 117–128.

In effect, this became the starting point of a tradition of instrumental *In nomine* compositions (mainly for viol consort, but also for keyboard) to which at least fifty-eight other composers contributed more than 150 settings from about the mid-sixteenth century to around the mid-seventeenth. All the settings are based on the cantus firmus (in the mene) of Taverner's Mass, while some of them also allude to his polyphonic complex as a whole.

The champion among *In nomine* composers was the good-humored Christopher Tye (see Chapter 34), who contributed twenty-one settings to the tradition. Example 40-11 provides the opening of his *In nomine Trust* (he or a contemporary supplied his settings with nicknames):

EXAMPLE 40-11. Tye, *In nomine Trust*, mm. 1–16.

Tye's work illustrates a number of the tradition's typical features: the long-note cantus firmus (in the next-to-highest part), the abundance of imitation, the often angular, sharply etched melodic motives, and the English lack of fear in the face of a cross relationship (m. 13). Unique to *Trust*, on the other hand, is the "meter," which results in a modern $\frac{5}{4}$.

Keyboard Music

There is something fitting about ending our survey of Elizabethan music with pieces for solo keyboard, for the sixteenth century produced no finer or fresher-sounding (still) keyboard music than that of the English virginalists. (Although the term "virginal" is used today to describe an instrument with one keyboard and a single set of plucked strings that run at right angles to the keys, as opposed to the parallel strings and keys of the harpsichord, late-sixteenth- and early-seventeenth-century England casually applied the term to all plucked keyboard instruments.) Like the consort repertory, music for solo keyboard included a wide array of genres and styles: preludes; cantus-firmus settings and fantasias designed to display contrapuntal mastery; dance movements, both single and in pairs; "character" and "descriptive" compositions, including an occasional piece of outright program music; and sets of variations on popular melodies, ground basses, and harmonic formulas. We will look at one of the shortest dance pieces and one of the longest sets of variations, both from the so-called Fitzwilliam Virginal Book.

The Fitzwilliam Virginal Book (Fig. 40-5) is the period's largest and most

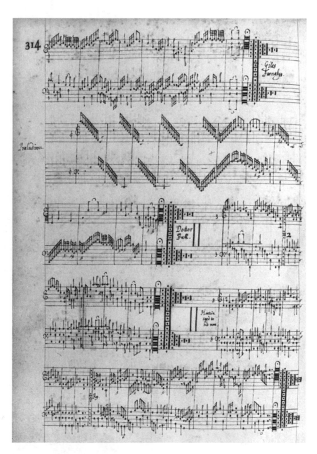

Figure 40-5. A page from the Fitzwilliam Virginal Book, with pieces by Farnaby and Bull.

comprehensive collection of keyboard music:[10] 297 pieces representing about a half century's worth of music. It was copied by Francis Tregian (1574–1619) from 1609, while he languished in London's Fleet Prison, to which he had been sentenced for recusancy. Despite its fame, the manuscript is riddled with faulty readings and questionable attributions. Obviously, Tregian was in no position to check his sources.

A DANCE BY FARNABY   Though Giles Farnaby (c. 1563–1640) wrote his share of contrapuntal fantasias, he was a miniaturist at heart. In *Tower Hill* (Ex. 40-12), Farnaby lays out each of the two phrases of what must have been a popular dance tune of the time (in one manuscript, it bears the title *A Gigge*) and immediately varies each of them with its "reprise." Measures 3–4 vary 1–2 (the first phrase), and measures 9–12 vary 5–8 (the second phrase). Even the stylized dance movements could not escape the virginalists' love of variation technique.

EXAMPLE 40-12. Farnaby, *Tower Hill* (complete).

10. Cambridge, Fitzwilliam Museum, MS 32.g.29.

One of the questions surrounding the English keyboard repertory concerns its ornamentation signs: the single and double strokes that are strewn about Farnaby's piece. Unfortunately, there is no contemporary explanation of their meaning, nor do manuscripts always apply them consistently when they transmit the same piece. Yet we can hazard some guesses. The double stroke probably indicated some kind of mordant or trill, while the single stroke might have signaled a slide, in which that note was approached stepwise from the third below. Another possibility is that both strokes simply indicated that the performer could add any ornament. Finally, at times the strokes might have had an entirely different meaning: to mark off the notes of a cantus firmus.

VARIATIONS BY BULL   An organist in the chapel royal, John Bull (?1562/63–1628) fled England in 1613 in the face of charges of adultery and spent the remainder of his life at Brussels and Antwerp. Bull probably wrote *Walsingham* (*Anthology* 102), which opens the Fitzwilliam collection, in response to Byrd's set of variations on the same popular tune, "As I was going to Walsingham," that is, to the famous Marian shrine about a hundred miles northeast of London. (The notes of the original tune are marked with an asterisk.) In comparing another pair of pieces by Byrd and Bull, the composer Thomas Tomkins (1572–1656) wrote that Byrd's setting was "excellent for matter," Bull's "excellent for the hand."[11] Tomkins could have said the same about their *Walsingham* settings, for Bull's thirty variations raise keyboard music to a new level of virtuosity. But the razzle-dazzle is no longer limited to the old familiar scale passages or finger-twisting ornaments. Rather, Bull creates whole new textures and techniques that are as original as they are acrobatic. At times—variations 12 and 25, for example, or the second half of 14—the texture takes on the wispiness of a nineteenth-century etude. In variation 28, the performer must first cross hands (*à la* Domenico Scarlatti a century later) and then play machine-gun-like repeated notes. The technical demands are notable even today.

The virginalists hold a special place in Elizabethan music. Certainly, theirs is not the greatest music that late-sixteenth-century England produced. That honor must probably go to the sacred music of Byrd and the lute songs of Dowland. Yet Byrd's music for the Catholic liturgy had nowhere to go, since Netherlandish, imitative polyphony was reaching the end of its line, while his music for the Anglican Church was unexportable for liturgical reasons. The lute song too was a dead end, as its exquisite accompanimental filigree soon succumbed to the simpler, outer-parts-only approach of the continuo song.

The virginalists, on the other hand, left a legacy, principally in their attitude toward instrumental music in general and the keyboard in particular. They took the keyboard seriously, imbued the formerly lightweight with a sense of gravity, and, to paraphrase one critic, lit a fire that even gave off sparks on the Continent.[12] For a brief moment, then, another group of English musicians were leading the way, just as they had two centuries earlier.

11. Kerman, "William Byrd," 253.
12. Kerman, "William Byrd," 265.

BIBLIOGRAPHICAL NOTE

Editions of the Music

Madrigal: *English Madrigal School*, 36 vols., ed. Edmund H. Fellowes (London: Stainer & Bell, 1914–24; rev. Thurston Dart et al., 1958–), includes all the madrigals of Weelkes and Wilbye; *English Madrigal Verse, 1588–1632*, 3rd ed., ed. Frederick W. Sternfeld and David Greer (Oxford: Oxford University Press, 1967). **Lute song**: *The English School of Lutenist Song Writers*, 32 vols., ed. Fellowes (London: Stainer & Bell, 1920–32; rev. Dart et al., 1959–), includes the songs of Dowland; *English Lute Songs, 1597–1632: A Collection of Facsimile Reprints*, 9 vols., ed. Frederick W. Sternfeld (Menston: Scolar Press, 1967–69); *Lyrics from English Airs, 1596–1622*, ed. Edward Doughtie (Cambridge: Harvard University Press, 1970). **Keyboard music**: *Tudor Keyboard Music c. 1520–1580*, MB 66, ed. John Caldwell (London: Stainer & Bell, 1995); *Elizabethan Keyboard Music*, MB 55, ed. Alan Brown (London: Stainer & Bell, 1989); *The Fitzwilliam Virginal Book*, 2 vols., ed. J. A. Fuller Maitland and W. Barclay Squire (London and Leipzig: Breitkopf & Härtel, 1894–99; reprint, New York: Dover, 1963). **Consort music**: *Elizabethan Consort Music*, MB 44–45, ed. Paul Doe (London: Stainer & Bell, 1979–88); Morley, *The First Book of Consort Lessons 1599 and 1611*, ed. Sydney Beck (New York: C.F. Peters, 1959).

Bull: *Keyboard Music*, MB 14, 19, ed. John Steele et al. (London: Stainer & Bell, 1960–63; rev. 1967–70). **Byrd**: *The Byrd Edition*, 17 vols., ed. Philip Brett, Craig Monson, Alan Brown, and Kenneth Elliot (London: Stainer & Bell, 1970–), includes everything except the keyboard compositions, which appear in *William Byrd: Keyboard Music*, 2nd ed, MB 27–28, ed. Alan Brown (London: Stainer & Bell, 1976). **Dowland**: *The Collected Lute Music of John Dowland*, ed. Diana Poulton and Basil Lam (London: Faber & Faber, 1978); *Complete Consort Music*, ed. Edgar Hunt (London: Schott, 1985); the lute songs in *English School of Lutenist Song Writers* (see above). **Farnaby** (Giles and Richard): *Keyboard Music*, MB 24, ed. Richard Marlowe (London: Stainer & Bell, 1965). **Morley**: see *English Madrigal School* and *English School of Lutenist Song Writers*; the keyboard music appears in *Keyboard Works*, Stainer and Bell Keyboard Series 12–13, 2nd ed., ed. Thurston Dart (London: Stainer & Bell, 1964). **Tallis**: the Anglican music appears in *English Sacred Music*, vol. 1: *Anthems*, vol. 2: *Service Music*, EECM 12–13, ed. Leonard Ellinwood (London: Stainer & Bell, 1971; rev. Paul Doe, 1974); the Catholic music appears in *TCM* 6, ed. Fellowes et al. (London: Oxford University Press, 1928); for a convenient cross-section of English and Latin sacred music, see *A Tallis Anthology: 17 Anthems and Motets*, ed. John Milsom (Oxford: Oxford University Press, 1992); the keyboard music appears in *Complete Keyboard Works*, ed. Denis Stevens (London: Hinrichsen, 1953). **Tye**: *The Instrumental Music*, RRMR 3, ed. Robert Weidner (New Haven: A-R Editions, 1967). **Weelkes** and **Wilbye**: see *English Madrigal School*, above.

General Studies

As it did for the material in Chapters 1 and 34, John Caldwell's *Oxford History of English Music*, vol. 1: *From the Beginnings to c. 1715* (Oxford: Clarendon Press, 1991), chapters 6–8, presents a comprehensive survey; there is a lively overview of musical life in Craig Monson, "Elizabethan London," in *The Renaissance*, ed. Iain Fenlon (London: Macmillan, 1989), 304–40. Though Thomas Wythorne was a minor composer, *The Autobiography of Thomas Wythorne*, ed. J. M. Osborne (Oxford: Oxford University Press, 1961), offers a vivid and detailed picture of the life of a musician; Walter Woodfill's *Musicians in English Society from Elizabeth to Charles I* (Princeton: Princeton University Press, 1953; rev. 1969) remains a classic study; Andrew Ashbee's *Records of English Court Music*, 8 vols. (Aldershot, Hampshire: Scolar Press, 1991–95), is extremely valuable. On aspects of patronage, see Charles W. Warren, "Music at Nonesuch," *MQ* 54 (1968): 47–57, and Lynn Hulse, "The Musical Patronage of Robert Cecil, First Earl of Salisbury (1563–1612)," *JRMA* 116 (1991): 24–40.

Liturgical Music

To the items by Stevens, Benham, Le Huray, and Phillips cited in the Bibliographical Note in Chapter 34, add Nicholas Temperley, *The Music of the English Parish Church* (Cambridge: Cambridge University Press, 1979); and the relevant items listed below under Byrd and Tallis.

Secular Song

The classic study of the madrigal is Joseph Kerman, *The Elizabethan Madrigal: A Comparative Study* (New York: American Musicological Society, 1962); Philip Brett's "English Consort Song, 1570–1625," *PRMA* 87 (1961–62): 73–88, gives a succinct account of that genre; Ian Spinks's *English Song: Dowland to Purcell* (London: Batsford, 1974; rev. 1986), is a good starting point for the lute song.

Keyboard Music

John Caldwell, *English Keyboard Music before the Nineteenth Century* (New York: Praeger, 1979); Willi Apel, *The History of Keyboard Music to 1750*, trans. Hans Tischler (Bloomington: Indiana University Press, 1972); and Alexander Silbiger, ed., *Keyboard Music before 1700* (New York: Schirmer, 1994), provide good introductions; on the ornamentation, see Desmond Hunter, "The Application of (Ornamental) Strokes in English Virginal Music: A Brief Chronological Survey," *PPR* 9 (1996): 66–77. For an inventory of the entire repertory, see Virginia Brookes, *British Keyboard Music to c. 1660: Sources and Thematic Index* (London: Oxford University Press, 1996).

Byrd

The literature is extensive; the concise account in Joseph Kerman, "William Byrd," in *The New Grove High Renaissance Masters*, ed. Stanley Sadie (New York: Norton, 1984), skillfully weaves life and works into a single narrative; the best large-scale introduction is still Edmund H. Fellowes, *William Byrd* (London: Oxford University Press, 1948); see also Imogen Holst, *Byrd* (London: Faber, 1972). There is a proposed three-author, three-volume study of his works entitled *The Music of William Byrd*, of which two volumes are available: Oliver Neighbour, *The Consort and Keyboard Music of William Byrd*, and Kerman, *The Masses and Motets of William Byrd* (Berkeley and Los Angeles: University of California Press, 1978 and 1981); the third volume will be Philip Brett, *The Songs, Services, and Anthems of William Byrd*. H. K. Andrews's *Technique of Byrd's Vocal Polyphony* (London: Oxford University Press, 1964) is a close-up look at his style; there is a fine collection of essays in Alan Brown and Richard Turbet, eds., *Byrd Studies* (Cambridge: Cambridge University Press, 1992), which commemorates the 450th anniversary of Byrd's birth; for a comprehensive guide to the literature, see Turbet, *William Byrd: A Guide to Research*, Garland Composer Resource Manuals 7 (New York: Garland, 1987), with an update in "Byrd at 450," *Brio* 31 (1994): 96–102.

Other Composers

Bull: Walker Cunningham, *The Keyboard Music of John Bull*, Studies in Musicology 71 (Ann Arbor: UMI Research Press, 1984). **Dowland**: Diana Poulton, *John Dowland: His Life and Works* (Berkeley and Los Angeles: University of California Press, 1972). **Morley**: since there is no comprehensive monograph on Morley, he is best approached through his own treatise: *A Plain and Easy Introduction to Practical Music*, ed. R. Alec Harman (New York: Norton, 1973; originally published 1952). **Tallis**: Paul Doe, *Tallis*, Oxford Studies of Composers 4 (London: Oxford University Press, 1968). **Weelkes**: David Brown, *Thomas Weelkes: A Biographical and Critical Study* (New York: Prager, 1969); G.A. Philipps, "Patronage in the Career of Thomas Weelkes," *MQ* 62 (1976): 46–57. **Wilbye**: Brown, *John Wilbye* (London: Oxford University Press, 1974).

Mary and Elizabeth

   John Guy's *Tudor England* (Oxford: Oxford University Press, 1988) cuts across the reigns of both queens; on Mary, see David Loades, *Mary Tudor: A Life* (Oxford: Blackwell, 1989); on Elizabeth, see D. M. Palliser, *The Age of Elizabeth* (London: Longman, 1983), and the essays in Christopher Haigh, *The Reign of Elizabeth* (London: Macmillan, 1985); for the contemporary eyewitness account of William Harrison, see *The Description of England: The Classic Contemporary Account of Tudor Social Life*, ed. Georges Edelen (Washington, D.C., and New York: Folger Shakespeare Library/Dover, 1968).

Epilogue

The title of our book is *Renaissance Music*. But what exactly do we mean by the term "Renaissance"? Assuming that there was one, how did it manifest itself in music? And when and where did that period begin and end?

THE RENAISSANCE

Neither Du Fay, near the beginning of our period, nor Palestrina, near the end, thought of himself as a Renaissance composer. The idea did not exist. As a term that defines the chronological boundaries and characteristics of a historical period, "Renaissance"—meaning "rebirth"—was first coined in 1855 by the French historian Jules Michelet in volume 7 of his 19-volume *Histoire de France* (1833–67).

Five years later, the term spread far and wide in Jacob Burckhardt's profoundly influential (right down to the present day) *Civilization of the Renaissance in Italy* (1860). For Burckhardt, the Renaissance began in Italy around the turn of the fourteenth century, reached full flower there in the fifteenth, and then spread to the north around 1500. And by the time its spirit and ideas exhausted themselves in the seventeenth century, it had thoroughly transformed virtually all aspects of society.

Rebirth and Recovery

For those who believe in the idea of a Renaissance, it was a period of rebirth, one that repudiated and looked back beyond the immediate past (about a thousand years' worth of "Middle Ages") and sought inspiration from the newly recovered achievements of classical antiquity. This process of rebirth and recovery followed two different lines: one was narrow and specific, even elitist, in scope; the other was as much an attitude as anything else, and trickled down through all strata of society.

In the narrow sense, there was the rebirth of classical studies, which, though never entirely forgotten during the Middle Ages, now became the predominant intellectual movement of the time. Its centerpiece was the pedagogical agenda of humanist education, with grammar, rhetoric, history, moral philosophy, and poetry at its core, and with a flood of classical texts as model and inspiration. This love affair with classicism quickly made itself felt in the visual arts: free-standing sculptures, three-dimensional perspective with the brush, and villas that seemed to have leaped out of the ancient Roman landscape to land on sixteenth-century hillsides.

In the broader sense, the age also recovered what it perceived to be classical antiquity's optimism, its sense of individualism and quest for discovery. Thus the fifteenth and sixteenth centuries saw attempts at republican government and even open rebellion against foreign rule; the remapping of both the world and the universe; the spread of literacy, fanned by the printing press; capitalism and new opportunities for investment; and new ways of communicating with God. For all its kings and dukes, dogmatism and inherited habits, the Renaissance was marked by a strong sense of self-determination and anti-authoritarianism.

Denying the Renaissance

In recent decades, the idea of the Renaissance as an autonomous period has been squeezed from two directions. On the one hand, there are those who see its earlier phase—up to about 1500—as still wearing remnants of the immediate past; for them, much of what took place during the fifteenth century, especially north of the Alps, would be better described as "late medieval." On the other hand, there are those who see the sixteenth century in terms of its ramifications for the future; they speak of the beginning of an "early modern" period, one that extends through the end of the eighteenth century. Those who wish to squeeze the Renaissance into nonexistence argue that the idea of classical antiquity reborn was elitist in nature, touching only a tiny and privileged fraction of the population. They tend to concentrate on such things as economic trends, industry and agriculture, family structure, and popular culture; thus they often look at history from the vantage point of working-class people who did not ordinarily read Quintilian, live in Palladian villas, or listen to Josquin motets. And they foster an interdisciplinary approach in which the study of literature, art, and music tends to lose its autonomy and, perhaps, its ties to the idea of a Renaissance.

Was there a Renaissance? Or are the two hundred years with which we have been concerned more neatly split between late medieval and early modern periods? Are Renaissance and late medieval/early modern mutually exclusive views of history, or are they complementary? Whatever the answers, the differences go beyond mere labels. They can suggest different ways of looking at the same event. For example, those who hold to the idea of the Renaissance would probably interpret the "Age of Discovery" from a Eurocentric/Mediterranean point of view and would no doubt consider the episode as positive, as spreading culture, learning, and technology. Adherents of the early modern idea might look at things from the vantage point of the colonized, and colonialism has a bad name.[1] In the end, the fifteenth and sixteenth centuries were filled with tensions and contradictions. And neither labels nor well-developed points of view can always handle them neatly.

1. Marcus, "Renaissance/Early Modern Studies," 60.

THE RENAISSANCE AND MUSIC

To hold with the traditional view of the Renaissance: how did it rub off on music? What was reborn, what was recovered?

Rebirth and Recovery

With respect to the rebirth of classical ideas, music differs from literature and the visual arts in two ways. First, music rediscovered its affinity with antiquity a good deal later than its sister arts. The idea seems to have taken hold only in the late fifteenth century. Among the first hints is Tinctoris's dedication to his *Proportionale musices* (c. 1474—a hundred years after the death of Petrarch), which looks back to Plato's praise of music as the "mightiest" of the arts:

> How potent, pray, must have been that melody by whose virtue gods, ancestral spirits, unclean demons, animals without reason, and things insensate were said to be moved! This (even if in part fabulous) is not devoid of mystery, for the poets would not have feigned such things of music had they not apprehended its marvelous power with a certain divine vigor of the mind.[2]

Even more important in setting music apart from the other arts was the nature of the classical inspiration. Unlike an Erasmus, say, who could pull manuscripts or printed editions of classical texts off the shelves of his library, or a Palladio, who could walk among the ruins of ancient Rome, Du Fay, Josquin, and Palestrina never heard the music of antiquity. Not until Vincenzo Galilei published some fragments of Greek music in his *Dialogo* of 1581 did anyone have any idea of what such music might have sounded like. For music, then, the rebirth and recovery of classical antiquity played out mainly in the works of theorists, often as antiquarianism, but sometimes as the source of and justification for new ideas: Glarean's revamping of the modal system and Vicentino's explorations of chromaticism.

Yet the intoxication with things classical rubbed off on "real music" as well. Certainly, the chromaticism of the mid- and late sixteenth century is unthinkable without it, as is that all-powerful sixteenth-century idea of the union of music and poetry, which influenced composers in any number of ways. Even performance practice felt antiquity's influence, as witness the humanists' preference for music for solo voice and simple instrumental accompaniment (a practice that anticipates monody by a full century, and thus blurs one of the traditional distinctions between Renaissance and Baroque).

The idea that music was being born anew was also expressed without reference to antiquity: as part of the general self-confidence of the period. Indeed, some writers even took pride in what they saw as contemporary music's lack of classical antecedents and new invention. As Sebald Heyden put it in his *De arte canendi* of 1540: "Although this art is new and was completely unknown to ancient Greeks, it will be no less admired and praised than any of the oldest

---

2. Quoted after Strunk, *Source Readings*, 14.

arts, unless perhaps out of envy we refuse to give some measure of glory to the inventions of our times."[3]

In all, Renaissance writers were secure in the belief that the accomplishments of their own age—musical and otherwise—were unparalleled. No one put it more succinctly than Tinctoris, who, in the prologue of his *Art of Counterpoint* (1476), showed his contempt for even the recent past in a single, sweeping statement (the most famous in all of fifteenth-century music theory): "There is no composition written over forty years ago which is thought by the learned as worthy of performance." The latest music was the best. And as the period wore on, composers were often relegated to the ranks of *antichi* within a generation.

If today our conviction that almost everything is relative causes us to smile at the Renaissance image of itself as better, we can hardly argue with its appreciation of its own ingenuity. Consider this: of the three major genres inherited by Du Fay and his contemporaries in the 1420s—isorhythmic motet, individual or paired Mass movements, and secular song cast in the *formes fixes*—not one managed to outlive the century in good health. At times, it seems that innovation, whether in style (pervading imitation, for example), aesthetic intent (*seconda prattica* concerns with expression of the text), or genre (instrumental music shorn of its vocal models), was so fundamental and permanent that we may question the very idea of a unified musical fabric that stretches across the period. There are some who do.

Denying the Musical Renaissance

We see the late medieval/early modern idea in the titles of two books cited in earlier chapters: Reinhard Strohm's *Music in Late Medieval Bruges*, which deals mainly with the fifteenth century, and the collection of essays edited by Iain Fenlon, *Music in Medieval and Early Modern Europe*, which does not go beyond the end of the sixteenth. Finally, there is Strohm's masterful *Rise of European Music, 1380–1500*, which sets out to "unhook" the fifteenth century from the sixteenth. For them, the idea of a single period covering the fifteenth and sixteenth centuries that might be called the Renaissance does not exist.

CHRONOLOGICAL BOUNDARIES

In general, music historians who believe in the traditional idea of a Renaissance period have been more concerned with determining when it began than when it ended. We will follow suit.

The Traditional View

Since Tinctoris made his famous forty-years-ago pronouncement in the 1470s, he must have believed that a new era in music got under way during the 1430s, with the coming to maturity of the Du Fay generation. It was, after

3. Quoted after Owens, "Music Historiography," 307–8.

all, the decade that saw Continental composers absorb the triadic writing of the English, the hard-driving rhythm of the fourteenth century give way to the more flowing rhythmic style of the fifteenth, and the first examples of the cyclic cantus-firmus Mass.

Four centuries later, Tinctoris's view was shored up by a work that would have a profound influence on music historiography. In volume 3 of his *Geschichte der Musik* (1868), the Austrian music historian August Wilhelm Ambros promulgated a view of a unified period that spanned the fifteenth and sixteenth centuries and ran from Du Fay to Palestrina. Though it has occasionally been challenged, Ambros's view has prevailed. Thus Lewis Lockwood's pithy *New Grove* article on the Renaissance begins:

> In the conventional periodization of Western music history, a term denoting the era from about 1430 to about 1600; this period coincides with the later phases of the broad historical developments in Western culture, society, art and technology (c. 1300–1600) for which the French term "Renaissance" has been in use since Michelet (1855), who coined it for general history.[4]

Another View

An alternate view argues that the Renaissance in music got under way during the fourteenth century, with music of the *Ars nova*. After all, that century saw the development of isorhythm, an interest in polyphonic settings of the movements of the Ordinary, the polyphonic *formes fixes*, triadic writing in England, and the mensuration-prolation system of notation, all of which carried on into the 1430s and beyond. Moreover, supporters of this view might argue:

(1) Why give so much weight to Tinctoris's statement? He was not alone in singling out a moment at which music was "rediscovered"; in the late sixteenth century, the theorists Gaspar Stocker and Zarlino equated that moment with Willaert.

(2) Ambros was not particularly familiar with music of the fourteenth century, especially that of Italy—neither was Tinctoris—the style and fresh spirit of which left its mark on the likes of Ciconia and early Du Fay; had he been so, perhaps he would have moved his starting point back a hundred years.

(3) By moving the musical Renaissance back a century—and with due regard for the role of Italy—we bring music into both chronological and geographical line with developments in literature and the visual arts.

(4) The fourteenth, fifteenth, and sixteenth centuries can form a historically tidy "Age of Mensural Notation."

A CONCLUDING FANTASIA

We end by exercising our historical imagination.

Antoine Busnoys died on November 6, 1492. By then, his everyday musical world (in terms of polyphony) probably consisted of about forty years' worth

4. *New Grove*, 15: 736.

of music: that of late Du Fay through early Josquin, all of which still circulated only in manuscript. Beyond that, he lived in a world of one church, believed that the earth was the center of the universe, knew Italy to be ruled mainly by Italians, and would have to have lived another five months to hear the news about the Americas.

Pretend that in 1592 Busnoys awakes from a century-long sleep and decides to survey the musical scene. He begins at Rome, where he hears the Masses (including one on *L'homme armé*) and motets of Palestrina and Victoria, as well as the madrigals of Marenzio filled with word painting. Heading north, he stops at Ferrara; here he takes in Gesualdo's chromaticism and purchases a copy of Vicentino's treatise, with its description of the microtonal *arcicembalo*. At Venice two days later, St. Mark's is filled with one of Giovanni Gabrieli's ceremonial pieces and Merulo's toccatas. In the evening, there is a local "academy": the musical fare is a virtuoso lutenist and a consort of viols. He cannot leave without stopping at Gardano's shop and buying a few sets of printed partbooks.

Crossing the Alps, Busnoys next visits Munich, where an erudite music lover interprets a Lassus motet for him as though it were a speech. At a Calvinist church in Geneva, he joins the congregation in singing monophonic psalms in French. Glarean's discussion of a twelve-mode system provides the reading matter on the road to Paris, which welcomes him with an evening of *musique mesurée*, followed by a grand ball at which the musicians smile politely when he asks them to play a basse danse. Polyphonic Requiem Masses three days apart set the identical chants (is it coincidence? he wonders).

Finally, he arrives in England. Wanting to attend a Catholic Mass, he must do so at a private home; as Byrd's guest, he hears the singers and instrumentalists of the royal household perform a verse anthem. The visit ends with a conversation with Thomas Morley, who reads to him from his forthcoming *Plaine and Easie Introduction*: "We must also take heed of separating any part of a word from another by a rest, as some dunces have not slacked to do, yea one whose name is Johannes Dunstaple (an ancient English author) hath not only divided the sentence but in the very middle of a word hath made two Long rests."[5] The trip over, Busnoys returns to "early modern" Bruges, where, a hundred years earlier, he had died in "late medieval" times.

What sense would Busnoys have made of the music he heard? Would he have found some of it familiar, some of it astounding? What would he have thought of the treatises he read? Would he have considered the late-sixteenth-century musical world an extension of his own, or had he crossed the line into a new musical age? Conversely, would musicians of the late sixteenth century have felt any affinity with him, especially since he had already been relegated to the *antichi* by Pietro Aaron in 1523, to the "as long ago as" by Heyden in 1540, and to the "infancy of the art" by Glarean in 1547?

The problem of periodization is double-edged. Whatever the time in question contributes is mediated by our interpretive hindsight (always biased, which

5. Quoted after the edition by R. Alec Harman (New York: Norton, 1973), p. 291. What irony: lauded by Martin le Franc and Tinctoris as one of the composers who set the fifteenth century on its musical course, Dunstable is now a stylistic "dunce."

is not necessarily bad); *history* (or *herstory* or *theirstory*) is really *ourstory*. Would it have been better to call our book something like *High-Brow Music in Western Europe, c. 1400–c. 1600?*

BIBLIOGRAPHICAL NOTE

The Idea of the Renaissance
Three good starting points are Paul Oskar Kristeller, *Renaissance Thought* and *Renaissance Thought II* (New York: Harper & Row, 1961/65); Erwin Panofsky, *Renaissance and Renascences in Western Art* (London: Paladin, 1965); and Michael Levey, *Early Renaissance* (Hardmondsworth, Eng.: Penguin, 1967).

Renaissance and Late Medieval/Early Modern
On the differences between Renaissance and early modern from the point of view of literary studies, see Leah S. Marcus, "Renaissance/Early Modern Studies," in *Redrawing the Boundaries: The Transformation of English and American Literary Studies*, ed. Stephen Greenblatt and Giles Gunn (New York: Modern Language Association of America, 1992), 63.

Renaissance and Music
Among recent discussions of the historiographical issues, see Lewis Lockwood, "Renaissance," *New Grove*, 15:736–41; Jessie Ann Owens, "Music Historiography and the Definition of the 'Renaissance,' " *Notes* 47 (1990): 305–30; Reinhard Strohm, *The Rise of European Music, 1380–1500* (Cambridge: Cambridge University Press, 1993); Don Harrán, "Research into Music of the Renaissance: New Perspectives, New Objectives," *ISM* 6 (1996): 81–98, the last three questioning the traditional view. See also Friedrich Blume's *Renaissance and Baroque Music: A Comprehensive Survey*, trans. M. D. Herder Norton (New York: Norton, 1967), which has a useful survey of views from the first half of our own century; Edward E. Lowinsky, "Music in the Culture of the Renaissance," *JHI* 15 (1954): 509–53 (reprint in *Music in the Culture of the Renaissance and Other Essays*, ed. Bonnie J. Blackburn and Lowinsky [Chicago: University of Chicago Press, 1991], 1: 19–39), views music of the Renaissance (beginning in the fifteenth century) not only as autonomous, but as breaking sharply with the past.

INDEX

Illustrations are indicated by italic page numbers.